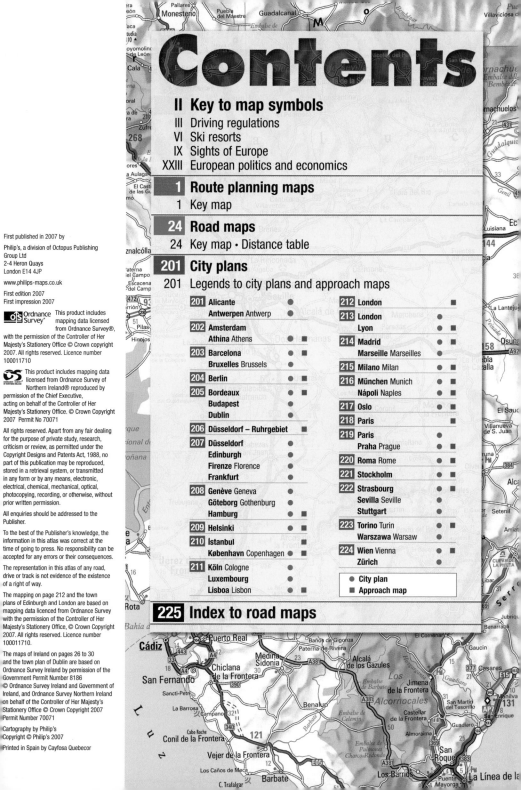

Contents

First published in 2007 by

Philip's, a division of Octopus Publishing Group Ltd
2-4 Heron Quays
London E14 4JP

www.philips-maps.co.uk

First edition 2007
First impression 2007

Ordnance Survey® This product includes mapping data licensed from Ordnance Survey®, with the permission of the Controller of Her Majesty's Stationery Office © Crown copyright 2007. All rights reserved. Licence number 100011710

This product includes mapping data licensed from Ordnance Survey of Northern Ireland® reproduced by permission of the Chief Executive, acting on behalf of the Controller of Her Majesty's Stationery Office. © Crown Copyright 2007 Permit No 70071

Cartography by Philip's
Copyright © Philip's 2007

Printed in Spain by Cayfosa Quebecor

Legend to route planning maps pages 2–23

	Motorway with selected junctions
	tunnel, under construction
	Toll motorway
	Pre-pay motorway
	Main through route
	Other major road
	Other road
25	European road number
56	Motorway number
55	National road number
56	Distances – in kilometres
	International boundary
	National boundary
LE HAVRE	Car ferry and destination
≍	Mountain pass
✈	International airport
1089	Height in metres
	National park

Town – population

MOSKVA ▣	5 million +
BERLIN ▣	2–5 million
MINSK ▣	1–2 million
Oslo ◉	500000–1 million
Århus ◉	200000–500000
Turku ◉	100000–200000
Gävle ◉	50000–100000
Nybro ○	20000–50000
Ikast ○	10000–20000
Skjern ○	5000–10000
Lillesand ○	0–5000

Scale Pages 2–23

1:4525526 1cm = 42.3km 1 inch = 71.4 miles
0 20 40 60 80 miles
0 20 40 60 80 100 120 140 km

Pages 26–181

1:1066044 1cm = 10.66km 1 inch = 16.8 miles
0 5 10 15 20 miles
0 5 10 15 20 25 30 35 km

Pages 182–200

1:2132088 1cm = 21.3km, 1 inch = 33.6miles
0 10 20 30 40 miles
0 10 20 30 40 50 60 70 km

Legend to road maps pages 26–200

⑦ ⑧	Motorway with junctions – full, restricted access
◇	services
	tunnel
	under construction
	Toll Motorway
	Pre-pay motorway – (A)(CH)(CZ)(H)(SK) 'Vignette' must be purchased before travel, see pages III–VI
	Principal trunk highway – single / dual carriageway
	tunnel
	under construction
	Other main highway – single / dual carriageway
	Other important road
	Other road
E25	European road number
A49	Motorway number
135	National road number
Col Bayard 1248	Mountain pass
	Scenic route, gradient – arrow points uphill

Distances – in kilometres

143	major
28	minor
	Principal railway
	tunnel
Nápoli 15:30	Ferry route with journey time – hours : minutes
	Short ferry route
	International boundary
	National boundary
	National park
	Natural park
Sevilla	World Heritage town
Verona	Town of tourist interest

✈	Airport	✿	Park or garden
⚑	Ancient monument	✝	Religious building
≋	Beach	⚐	Ski resort
⌂	Castle or house	悪	Theme park
⌂	Cave	◉	World Heritage site
✦	Other place of interest	1754▲	Spot height

Driving regulations

A national vehicle identification plate is always required when taking a vehicle abroad. It is important for your own safety and that of other drivers to fit headlamp converters or beam deflectors when taking a right-hand drive car to a country where driving is on the right (every country in Europe except the UK and Ireland). When the headlamps are dipped on a right-hand drive car, the lenses of the headlamps cause the beam to shine upwards to the left – and so, when driving on the right, into the eyes of oncoming motorists.

The symbols used are:

🚗 Motorway	△ Warning triangle
⚠ Dual carriageway	✚ First aid kit
⚠ Single carriageway	💡 Spare bulb kit
🚘 Surfaced road	🔥 Fire extinguisher
🚛 Unsurfaced / gravel road	🪖 Motorcycle helmet
🏙 Urban area	⊖ Minimum driving age
🔘 Speed limit in kilometres per hour (kph)	📋 Additional documents required
🔒 Seat belts	📱 Mobile phones
👶 Children	★ Other information
🍷 Blood alcohol level	

All countries require that you carry a driving licence, green card/insurance documentation, registration document or hire certificate, and passport.

The penalties for infringements of regulations vary considerably from one country to another. In many countries the police have the right to impose on-the-spot fines (you should always request a receipt for any fine paid). Penalties can be severe for serious infringements, particularly for drinking when driving which in some countries can lead to immediate imprisonment. Insurance is important, and you may be forced to take out cover at the frontier if you cannot produce acceptable proof that you are insured.

Please note that driving regulations often change.

Andorra (AND)

🚗	⚠	⚠	🏙
n/a	90	90	50

- 🔒 Compulsory in front seats
- 👶 Over 10 only allowed in front seats if over 150cm
- 🍷 0.05%
- △ Compulsory
- ✚ Recommended
- 🔥 Compulsory
- 💡 Recommended
- 🪖 Compulsory for all riders
- ⊖ 18 (16-18 accompanied)
- 📱 Use not permitted whilst driving

Austria (A)

🚗	⚠	⚠	🏙
130	100	100	50

If towing trailer under 750kg

🔘			
100	100	100	50

If towing trailer over 750kg

🔘			
100	100	80	50

- 🔒 Compulsory in front seats and rear seats
- 👶 Under 14 and under 150cm in front seats only in child safety seat; under 14 over 150cm must wear adult seat belt
- 🍷 0.05%
- △ Compulsory
- ✚ Recommended
- 🔥 Recommended
- 🪖 Compulsory for all riders
- ⊖ 18 (16 for mopeds)
- 📋 Third party insurance
- 📱 Use permitted only with hands-free speaker system
- ★ If you intend to drive on motorways or expressways, a motorway vignette must be purchased at the border. These are available for 10 days, 2 months or 1 year.
- ★ Dipped headlights must be used at all times on motorbikes.

Belarus (BY)

🚗	⚠	⚠	🏙
110	90	90	60

If towing trailer under 750kg

🔘			
90	70	70	

Vehicle towing another vehicle 50 kph limit

- 🔒 Compulsory in front seats, and rear seats if fitted
- 👶 Under 12 in front seats only in child safety seat
- 🍷 0.05%
- △ Compulsory

Belgium (B)

🚗	⚠	⚠	🏙
120*	120	90	50

*Minimum speed of 70kph on motorways

If towing trailer

🔘			
90	90	60	50

- 🔒 Compulsory in front and rear seats
- 👶 Under 12 in front seats only in child safety seat
- 🍷 0.05%
- △ Compulsory
- ✚ Compulsory
- 🔥 Recommended
- 🔥 Compulsory
- 🪖 Compulsory for all riders
- ⊖ 18 (16 for mopeds)
- 📋 Third party insurance
- 📱 Use only allowed with hands-free kit

Bulgaria (BG)

🚗	⚠	⚠	🏙
130	90	90	50

If towing trailer

🔘			
100	70	70	50

- 🔒 Compulsory in front and rear seats
- 👶 Under 10 not allowed in front seats
- 🍷 0.05%
- △ Compulsory
- ✚ Compulsory
- 🔥 Recommended
- 🔥 Compulsory
- 🪖 Compulsory for all riders
- ⊖ 18 (16 for mopeds)
- 📋 Driving licence with translation or international driving permit, third party insurance
- 📱 Use only allowed with hands-free kit
- ★ Fee at border
- ★ Vignette system in operation, can be purchased from all border-crossing points and available annually, monthly and weekly.

Croatia (HR)

🚗	⚠	⚠	🏙
130	80	80	50

If towing

🔘			
110	80	80	50

- 🔒 Compulsory if fitted
- 👶 Under 12 not allowed in front seats
- 🍷 0.00%
- △ Compulsory
- ✚ Compulsory
- 🔥 Compulsory
- 🪖 Compulsory for all riders
- ⊖ 18
- 📱 Use only allowed with hands-free kit
- ★ It is compulsory to carry a fluorescent jacket in case of breakdown

Cyprus (CY)

🚗	⚠	⚠	🏙
100	100	80/50	50

If towing

🔘			
100	100	80/50	50

- 🔒 Compulsory for front and rear seat passengers (for vehicles manufactured after 01/01/1988)
- 👶 Children under 12 years old or less than 150cm height must be fastened with special fastening belts
- 🍷 0.05% blood, 0.02% breath
- △ Compulsory
- ✚ Compulsory for public vehicles, recommended for the rest
- 💡 N/A
- 🔥 Compulsory for public vehicles, recommended for the rest
- 🪖 Compulsory for all riders
- ⊖ 18 (17 for mopeds)
- 📱 Use only allowed with hands-free kit
- ★ Speed restriction for trucks: 80 kph on motorways and dual carriageways
- ★ No tolls apply but a circulation license is paid according to engine capacity. Trucks pay the circulation license according to the type of suspension and number of axies.

Czech Republic (CZ)

🚗	⚠	⚠	🏙
130	130	90	50

If towing

🔘			
80	80	80	50

- 🔒 Compulsory in front seats and, if fitted, in rear
- 👶 Under 12 or under 150cm not allowed in front seats
- 🍷 0.00%

IV

△ Compulsory

🔲 Compulsory

☂ Compulsory

© Compulsory for all riders

⊖ 18 (16 for motorcycles under 125 cc)

🪪 International driving permit

📱 Use only allowed with hands-free kit

★ Vignette needed for motorway driving, available for 1 year, 60 days, 15 days. Toll specific to lorries introduced 2006.

Denmark (DK)

🔭	⚠	▲	🚚
110/130	80	80	50

If towing

🔭			
80	70	70	50

🚗 Compulsory in front seats and, if fitted, in rear

🚸 Under 3 not allowed in front seat except in a child safety seat; in rear, 3 to 7 years in a child safety seat or on a booster cushion

☂ 0.05%

△ Compulsory

🔲 Recommended

☂ Recommended

© Recommended

© Compulsory for all riders

⊖ 18

🪪 Third party insurance

📱 Use only allowed with hands-free kit

★ Dipped headlights must be used at all times

Estonia (EST)

🔭	⚠	▲	🚚
n/a	90	70	50

🚗 Compulsory in front seats and if fitted in rear seats

🚸 Under 12 not allowed in front seats; under 7 must have child safety seat in rear

☂ 0.00%

△ Compulsory

🔲 Compulsory

☂ Recommended

© Compulsory

© Compulsory for all riders

⊖ 18 (16 for motorcycles, 14 for mopeds)

🪪 International driving permit recommended

📱 Use only allowed with hands-free kit

Finland (FIN)

🔭	⚠	▲	🚚
120	80*	100/80	30-60

*100 in summer

If towing

🔭			
80	80	80	30-60

If towing a vehicle by rope, cable or rod, max speed limit 60 kph.

Maximum of 80 kph for vans and lorries

Speed limits are often lowered in winter

🚗 Compulsory in front and rear

🚸 Children use a safety belt or special child's seat

☂ 0.05%

△ Compulsory

🔲 Recommended

☂ Recommended

© Recommended

© Compulsory for all riders

⊖ 18

🪪 Third party insurance

📱 Use only allowed with hands-free kit

★ Dipped headlights must be used at all times

France (F)

🔭	⚠	▲	🚚
130	110	90	50

On wet roads

🔭			
110	90	80	50

50kph on all roads if fog reduces visibility to less than 50m. Licence will be lost and driver fined for exceeding speed limit by over 40kph

🚗 Compulsory in front seats and, if fitted, in rear

🚸 Under 10 not allowed in front seats unless in approved safety seat facing backwards; in rear, if 4 or under, must have a child safety seat (rear facing if up to 9 months); if 5 to 10 may use a booster seat with suitable seat belt

☂ 0.05%

△ Compulsory unless hazard warning lights are fitted; compulsory for vehicles over 3,500kgs or towing a trailer

🔲 Recommended

☂ Recommended

© Compulsory for all riders

⊖ 18 (16 for light motorcycles, 14 for mopeds)

📱 Use not permitted whilst driving

★ Tolls on motorways

Germany (D)

🔭	⚠	▲	🚚
*	*	100	50

If towing

🔭			
*	*	80	50

*no limit, 130 kph recommended

🚗 Compulsory

🚸 Children under 12 and under 150cm must have a child safety seat, in front and rear

☂ 0.05%

△ Compulsory

🔲 Compulsory

☂ Recommended

© Recommended

© Compulsory for all riders

⊖ 18 (16 if not more than 125cc and limited to 11 kW)

🪪 Third party insurance

📱 Use permitted only with hands-free kit – also applies to drivers of motorbikes and bicycles

★ Motorcyclists must use dipped headlights at all times.

Greece (GR)

🔭	⚠	▲	🚚
120	110	110	50

If towing

🔭			
90	70	70	40

🚗 Compulsory in front seats and, if fitted, in rear

🚸 Under 12 not allowed in front seats except with suitable safety seat; under 10 not allowed in front seats

☂ 0.025%

△ Compulsory

🔲 Compulsory

☂ Recommended

© Recommended

© Compulsory for all riders

⊖ 18 (16 for low cc motorcycles)

🪪 Third party insurance

📱 Use only allowed with hands-free kit

Hungary (H)

🔭	⚠	▲	🚚
130	110	90	50

If towing

🔭			
80	70	70	50

🚗 Compulsory in front seats and if fitted in rear seats

🚸 Under 12 or under 140cm not allowed in front seats

☂ 0.00%

△ Compulsory

🔲 Compulsory

☂ Compulsory

© Recommended

© Compulsory for all riders

⊖ 18

🪪 Third party insurance

📱 Use only allowed with hands-free kit

★ All motorways are toll and operate the vignette system, tickets are available for 4 days, 10 days, 1 month, 1 year

★ Dipped headlights are compulsory during daylight hours (cars exempted in built-up areas)

Iceland (IS)

🔭	🚗	🚙	🚚
n/a	90	80	50

🚗 Compulsory in front and rear seats

🚸 Under 12 or under 140cm not allowed in front seats

☂ 0.00%

△ Compulsory

🔲 Compulsory

☂ Compulsory

© Compulsory for all riders

⊖ 18

🪪 Third party insurance

📱 Use only allowed with hands-free kit

★ Headlights are compulsory at all times

★ Highland roads are not suitable for ordinary cars

★ Driving off marked roads is forbidden

Ireland (IRL)

🔭	⚠	▲	🚚
120	100	80	50

If towing

🔭			
80	80	80	50

🚗 Compulsory in front seats and if fitted in rear seats. Driver responsible for ensuring passengers under 17 comply.

🚸 Under 4 not allowed in front seats unless in a child safety seat or other suitable restraint

☂ 0.08%

△ Recommended

🔲 Recommended

☂ Recommended

© Recommended

© Compulsory for all riders

⊖ 17 (16 for motorbikes up to 125cc; 18 for over 125cc; 18 for lorries; 21 bus/minibus)

🪪 Third party insurance; international driving permit for non-EU drivers

📱 No specific legislation

★ Driving is on the left

Italy (I)

🔭	⚠	▲	🚚
130	110	90	50

If towing

🔭			
80	70	70	50

🚗 Compulsory in front seats and, if fitted, in rear

🚸 Under 12 not allowed in front seats except in child safety seat; children under 3 must have special seat in the back

☂ 0.08%

△ Compulsory

🔲 Recommended

☂ Compulsory

© Recommended

© Compulsory for all motorcyclists

⊖ 18 (14 for mopeds, 16 for up to 125cc, 20 for up to 350cc)

🪪 International Driving Licence unless you have photocard licence

📱 Use only allowed with hands-free kit

Latvia (LV)

🔭	⚠	▲	🚚
n/a	90	90	50

If towing

🔭			
n/a	80	80	50

In residential areas limit is 20kph

🚗 Compulsory in front seats and if fitted in rear

🚸 If under 150cm must use child restraint in front and rear seats

☂ 0.05%

△ Compulsory

🔲 Compulsory

☂ Recommended

© Compulsory

© Compulsory for all riders

⊖ 18 (14 for mopeds, 16 for up to 125cc, 21 for up to 350cc)

🪪 International driving permit if licence is not in accordance with Vienna Convention

📱 Use only allowed with hands-free kit

★ Dipped headlights must be used at all times all year round

★ Cars and minibuses under 3.5 tonnes must have winter tyres from 1Dec-1Mar

Lithuania (LT)

🔭	⚠	▲	🚚
130	110	90	60

If towing

🔭			
70	70	70	60

🚗 Compulsory in front seats and if fitted in rear seats

- Under 12 not allowed in front seats unless in a child safety seat
- 0.04%
- Compulsory
- Compulsory
- Recommended
- Compulsory
- Compulsory for all riders
- 18 (14 for mopeds)
- Visa
- No legislation
- Dipped headlights must be used day and night from Nov to Mar (all year for motorcyclists) and from 1 to 7 Sept

Luxembourg (L)

🏛	⛰	🚗	🛣
130/110	90	90	50

If towing

🏛	⛰	🚗	🛣
90	75	75	50

- Compulsory
- Under 12 or 150cm not allowed in front seats unless in a child safety seat; under 3 must have child safety seat in rear seats; 3 - 11 must have child safety seat or belt if under 150cm
- 0.08%
- Compulsory
- Compulsory (buses)
- Compulsory
- Compulsory (buses, transport of dangerous goods)
- Compulsory for all riders
- 18 (16 for mopeds)
- Third party insurance
- Use permitted only with hands-free speaker system
- Motorcyclists must use dipped headlights at all times.

Macedonia (MK)

🏛	⛰	🚗	🛣
120	100	60	60

If towing

🏛	⛰	🚗	🛣
80	70	70	50

- Compulsory in front seats; compulsory if fitted in rear seats
- Under 12 not allowed in front seats
- 0.05%
- Compulsory
- Compulsory
- Compulsory
- Recommended
- Compulsory for all riders
- 18 (mopeds 16)
- International driving permit; visa

- Use not permitted whilst driving
- ★ Headlights must be used at all times

Moldova (MD)

🏛	⛰	🚗	🛣
90	90	90	60

If towing or if licence held under 1 year

🏛	⛰	🚗	🛣
70	70	70	60

- Compulsory in front seats and, if fitted, in rear seats
- Under 12 not allowed in front seats
- 0.00%
- Compulsory
- Compulsory
- Recommended
- Compulsory
- Compulsory for all riders
- 18 (mopeds and motorbikes, 16; vehicles with more than eight passenger places, taxis or towing heavy vehicles, 21)
- International driving permit (preferred), third party insurance, vehicle registration papers, visa
- Use only allowed with hands-free kit
- ★ Motorcyclists must use dipped headlights at all times
- ★ Winter tyres recommended from November to February

Montenegro (CG)

🏛	⛰	🚗	🛣
n/a	100	80	60

- Compulsory in front and rear seats
- Under 12 not allowed in front seats
- 0.05%
- Compulsory
- Compulsory
- Recommended
- Compulsory
- Compulsory
- 18 (16 for motorbikes less than 125cc; 14 for mopeds)
- International driving permit; visa
- No legislation
- ★ Tolls on some primary roads
- ★ All types of fuel available at petrol stations
- ★ 80km/h speed limit if towing a caravan

Netherlands (NL)

🏛	⛰	🚗	🛣
120	80	80	50

- Compulsory in front seats and, if fitted, rear

- Under 12 not allowed in front seats except in child restraint; in rear, 0-3 child safety restraint, 4-12 child restraint or seat belt
- 0.05%
- Recommended
- Recommended
- Recommended
- Recommended
- Compulsory for all riders
- 18 (16 for mopeds)
- Third party insurance
- Use only allowed with hands-free kit

Norway (N)

🏛	⛰	🚗	🛣
90	80	80	50

If towing trailer with brakes

🏛	⛰	🚗	🛣
80	80	80	50

If towing trailer without brakes

🏛	⛰	🚗	🛣
60	60	60	50

- Compulsory in front seats and, if fitted, in rear
- Under 4 must have child restraint; over 4 child restraint or seat belt
- 0.02%
- Compulsory
- Recommended
- Recommended
- Recommended
- Compulsory for all riders
- 18 (16 mopeds, heavy vehicles 18/21)
- Use only allowed with hands-free kit
- ★ Dipped headlights must be used at all times
- ★ Tolls apply on some bridges, tunnels and access roads into major cities

Poland (PL)

🏛	⛰	🚗	🛣
130	110	90	*50-60

*50kph 06.00–22.00 60kph 23.00–05.00

If towing

🏛	⛰	🚗	🛣
80*	70	70	30

*40kph minimum; 20kph in residential areas

- Compulsory in front seats and, if fitted, in rear
- Under 12 not allowed in front seats unless in a child safety seat or the child is 150cm tall
- 0.02%
- Compulsory
- Recommended
- Recommended
- Compulsory

- Compulsory for all riders
- 18 (mopeds and motorbikes – 16)
- International permit (recommended)
- Use only allowed with hands-free kit
- ★ Between 1 Nov and 1 Mar dipped headlights must be used day and night

Portugal (P)

🏛	⛰	🚗	🛣
120*	100	90	50

If towing

🏛	⛰	🚗	🛣
100*	90	80	50

*40kph minimum; 90kph maximum if licence held under 1 year

- Compulsory in front seats; compulsory if fitted in rear seats
- Under 3 not allowed in front in a child seat; 3 – 12 not allowed in front seats except in approved restraint system
- 0.05%. Imprisonment for 0.12% or more
- Compulsory
- Recommended
- Recommended
- Recommended
- Compulsory for all riders
- 18 (motorcycles under 50cc 16)
- Use only allowed with hands-free kit
- ★ Tolls on motorways

Romania (RO)

Cars

🏛	⛰	🚗	🛣
120	90	90	50

Vehicles seating eight persons or more

🏛	⛰	🚗	🛣
90	80	80	50

Motorcycles

🏛	⛰	🚗	🛣
100	80	80	50

Jeep-like vehicles: 70kph outside built-up areas but 60kph in all areas if diesel

- Compulsory in front seats and, if fitted, in rear
- Under 12 not allowed in front seats
- 0.00%
- Recommended
- Compulsory
- Recommended
- Recommended
- Compulsory for all riders
- 18 (16 for mopeds)
- Visa (only if stay over 30 days for EU citizens); third party insurance

---

- Use only allowed with hands-free kit
- ★ Tolls on Bucharest to Constanta motorway and bridges over Danube

Russia (RUS)

🏛	⛰	🚗	🛣
130	120	110	60

- Compulsory in front seats
- Under 12 not allowed in front seats
- 0.00%
- Compulsory
- Compulsory
- Recommended
- Compulsory
- Compulsory
- 18
- International driving licence with translation; visa
- No legislation

Serbia (SRB)

🏛	⛰	🚗	🛣
120	100	80	60

- Compulsory in front and rear seats
- Under 12 not allowed in front seats
- 0.05%
- Compulsory
- Compulsory
- Recommended
- Compulsory
- Compulsory
- 18 (16 for motorbikes less than 125cc; 14 for mopeds)
- International driving permit; visa
- No legislation
- ★ Tolls on motorways and some primary roads
- ★ All types of fuel available at petrol stations
- ★ 80km/h speed limit if towing a caravan

Slovak Republic (SK)

🏛	⛰	🚗	🛣
130	90	90	60

- Compulsory in front seats and, if fitted, in rear
- Under 12 not allowed in front seats unless in a child safety seat
- 0.0
- Compulsory
- Compulsory
- Compulsory
- Recommended
- Compulsory for motorcyclists
- 18 (15 for mopeds)
- International driving permit

- Use only allowed with hands-free kit
- Tow rope recommended
- Vignette required for motorways, car valid for 1 year, 30 days, 7 days; lorry vignettes carry a higher charge.

Slovenia (SLO)

🚗	🚙	🛣	🏙
130	100*	90*	50

If towing

🚗	🚙	🛣	🏙
80	80*	80*	50

*70kph in urban areas

- Compulsory in front seats and, if fitted, in rear
- Under 12 only allowed in the front seats with special seat; babies must use child safety seat
- 0.05%
- Compulsory
- Compulsory
- Compulsory
- Recommended
- Compulsory for all riders
- 18 (motorbikes up to 125cc – 16, up to 350cc – 18)
- Use only allowed with hands-free kit
- Dipped headlights must be used at all times

Spain (E)

🚗	🚙	🛣	🏙
120	100	90	50

If towing

🚗	🚙	🛣	🏙
80	80	70	50

- Compulsory in front seats and if fitted in rear seats
- Under 12 not allowed in front seats except in a child safety seat
- 0.05% (0.03% if vehicle over 3,500 kgs or carries more than 9 passengers, and in first two years of driving licence)
- Two compulsory (one for in front, one for behind)
- Recommended
- Compulsory in adverse weather conditions
- Recommended
- Compulsory for all riders
- 18 (18/21 heavy vehicles; 18 for motorbikes over 125cc; 16 for motorbikes up to 125cc; 14 for mopeds up to 75cc)
- Third party insurance
- Use only allowed with hands-free kit
- Tolls on motorways

Sweden (S)

🚗	🚙	🛣	🏙
110	90	70	50

If towing trailer with brakes

🚗	🚙	🛣	🏙
80	80	70	50

- Compulsory in front and rear seats
- Under 7 must have safety seat or other suitable restraint
- 0.02%
- Compulsory
- Recommended
- Recommended
- Recommended
- Compulsory for all riders
- 18
- Third party insurance
- No legislation
- Dipped headlights must be used at all times

Switzerland (CH)

🚗	🚙	🛣	🏙
120	100	80	50/30

If towing up to 1 tonne

🚗	🚙	🛣	🏙
80	80	80	50/30

If towing over 1 tonne

🚗	🚙	🛣	🏙
80	80	60	50/30

- Compulsory in front and, if fitted, in rear
- Under 7 not allowed in front seats unless in child restraint; between 7 and 12 must use child restraint or seatbelt
- 0.05%
- Compulsory
- Recommended
- Recommended
- Recommended
- Compulsory for all riders
- 18 (mopeds up to 50cc – 16)
- Third party insurance compulsory
- Use only allowed with hands-free kit
- Motorways are all toll and a vignette must be purchased at the border. Can also be purchased online at www.swisstravelsystem.com/uk, by phone on 020 7420 4900 or freephone 00800 10020030. The vignette costs £18.50 and is valid for one calendar year.

Turkey (TR)

🚗	🚙	🛣	🏙
120	90	90	50

If towing

🚗	🚙	🛣	🏙
70	70	70	40

- Compulsory in front seats
- Under 10 not allowed in front seats
- 0.05%
- Two compulsory (one in front, one behind)
- Compulsory
- Compulsory
- Compulsory for all riders
- 18
- International driving permit advised; note that Turkey is in both Europe and Asia
- Use only allowed with hands-free kit
- Tow rope and tool kit must be carried

Ukraine (UA)

🚗	🚙	🛣	🏙
130	90	90	60

If towing

🚗	🚙	🛣	🏙
80	80	80	60

Speed limit in pedestrian zone 20 kph

- Compulsory in front and rear seats
- Under 12 not allowed in front seats
- 0.0%
- Compulsory
- Compulsory
- Optional
- Compulsory
- Compulsory for all riders
- Cars 18; motorbikes 16
- International driving permit; visa
- No legislation
- Tow rope and tool kit recommended

United Kingdom (GB)

🚗	🚙	🛣	🏙
112	112	96	48

If towing

🚗	🚙	🛣	🏙
96	96	80	48

- Compulsory in front seats and if fitted in rear seats
- Under 3 not allowed in front seats except with appropriate restraint, and in rear must use child restraint if available; 3–12 and under 150cm must use appropriate restraint or seat belt in front seats, and in rear if available
- 0.08%
- Recommended
- Recommended
- Recommended
- Recommended
- Compulsory for all riders
- 17 (16 for mopeds)
- Use only allowed with hands-free kit
- Driving is on the left

Ski resorts

The resorts listed are popular ski centres, therefore road access to most is normally good and supported by road clearing during snow falls. However, mountain driving is never predictable and drivers should make sure they take suitable snow chains as well as emergency provisions and clothing. Listed for each resort are: the atlas page and grid square; the altitude; the number of lifts; the season start and end dates; the nearest town (with its distance in km); and the telephone number of the local tourist information centre ('00' prefix required for calls from the UK).

Andorra

Pyrenees

Pas de la Casa / Grau Roig **146 B2** 2640m 31 lifts Dec–May •Andorra La Vella (30km) ☎+376 801060 ☐http://pas_grau.andorramania.com *Access via Envalira Pass (2407m), highest in Pyrenees, snow chains essential.*

Austria

Alps

A 24-hour driving conditions information line is provided by the Tourist Office of Austria www.austria.info +43 1 588 660

Bad Gastein **109 B4** 1002m 51 lifts Dec–Apr •Bad Hofgastein (6km) ☎+43 6432 85044 ☐www.skigastein.at *Snow report: +43 6432 64555.*

Bad Hofgastein **109 B4** 860m 51 lifts Dec–Apr •Salzburg (90km) ☎+43 6432 33930 ☐www.badhofgastein.com

Bad Kleinkirchheim **109 C4** 1100m 32 lifts Dec–Apr •Villach (35km) ☎+43 4240 8212 ☐www.badkleinkirchheim.com *Snowfone:+43 4240 8222. Near Ebene Reichenau.*

Ehrwald **108 B1** 1000m 22 lifts Dec–Apr •Imst (30km) ☎+43 5673 20000208 ☐www.tiscover.at/ehrwald *Weather report: +43 5673 3329*

Innsbruck **108 B2** 574m 75 lifts Dec–Apr •Innsbruck ☎+43 5125 9850 ☐www.innsbruck-tourismus.com *Motorway normally clear. The motorway through to Italy and through the Arlberg Tunnel West to Austria are both toll roads.*

Ischgl **107 B5** 1400m 42 lifts Dec–May •Landeck (25km) ☎+43 5444 52660 ☐www.ischgl.com *Car entry to resort prohibited between 2200hrs and 0600hrs.*

Kaprun **109 B3** 800m, 56 lifts Jan–Dec •Zell am See (10km) ☎+43 6542 7700

☐www.zellkaprun.at *Snowfone:+43 6547 73684.*

Kirchberg in Tyrol **109 B3** 860m 59 lifts Dec–Apr •Kitzbühel (6km) ☎+43 5357 2309 ☐www.kirchberg.at *Easily reached from Munich International Airport (120 km)*

Kitzbühel **109 B3** 800m 59 lifts Dec–Apr •Wörgl (40km) ☎+43 5356 777 ☐www.kitzbuehel.com

Lech/Oberlech **107 B5** 1450m 84 lifts Dec–Apr •Bludenz (50km) ☎+43 5583 21610 ☐www.Lech at *Roads normally cleared but keep chains accessible because of altitude. Road conditions report tel +43 5583 1515.*

Mayrhofen **108 B2** 630m 29 lifts Dec–Apr •Jenbach (35km) ☎+43 5285 67600 ☐www.mayrhofen. *Chains rarely required.*

Obertauern **109 B4** 1740m 26 lifts Nov–May •Radstadt (20km) ☎+43 6456 7252 ☐www.top-obertauern.com *Roads normally cleared but chains accessibility recommended Camper vans and caravans not allowed; park these in Radstadt*

Saalbach Hinterglemm **109 B** 1003m 52 lifts Dec–Apr •Zell am See (19km) ☎+43 6541 6800 68 ☐www.saalbach.com *Both villa centres are pedestrianised and there is a good ski bus service during the daytime*

St Anton am Arlberg **107 B5** 1304m 84 lifts Nov–May •Innsbruck (104km) ☎+43 5446 226 ☐www.stantonamarlberg.com *Snow report tel +43 5446 2565*

Schladming **109 B4** 2708m 86 lifts Nov–Apr •Schladming ☎+43 3687 22777 ☐www.schladming.com

Serfaus **108 B1** 1427m 53 lifts Dec–Apr •Landeck (30km) ☎+43 5476 62390 ☐www.serfaus.com *Cars banned from village, use world's only 'hover' powered underground railway.*

ölden 108 C2 1377m, 32 lifts
year •Imst (50km) ☎+43 5254
00 ☐www.soelden.com *Roads
rmally cleared but snow chains
commended because of altitude.
e route from Italy and the
uth over the Timmelsjoch via
bergurgl is closed in the winter
d anyone arriving from the
uth should use the Brenner Pass
otorway. Snow information tel
43 5254 2666.*

ell am See 109 B3 758m 57
s Dec–Mar •Zell am See ☎+43
42 7700 ☐www.zellkaprun.at
owfone +43 6542 73694 Low
titude, therefore good access
d no mountain passes to cross.

**ell im Zillertal (Zell am Ziller)
9 B3** 580m 47 lifts Dec–Apr
enbach (25km) ☎+43 5282
81 ☐www.tiscover.at/zell
owfone +43 5282 716526.

rs 107 B5 1720m 84 lifts
c–May •Bludenz (30km) ☎+43
83 2245 ☐www.lech.at *Roads
rmally cleared but keep chains
cessible because of altitude.
llage has garage with 24-hour
lf-service gas/petrol, breakdown
rvice and wheel chains supply.*

rance

lps

pe d'Huez 118 B3 1860m 87
s Dec–Apr •Grenoble (63km)
☎+33 4 76 11 44 44 ☐www.
pedhuez.com *Snow chains may
required on access road to
sort. Road report tel +33 4 76
44 50.*

voriaz 118 A3 2277m 38 lifts
c–May •Morzine (14km) ☎+33
50 74 02 11 ☐www.avoriaz.
m *Chains may be required for
cess road from Morzine. Car
e resort, park on edge of vil-
e. Horse-drawn sleigh service
ailable.*

amonix-Mont-Blanc 119 B3
35m 49 lifts Nov–May •Mar-
ny (38km) ☎+33 4 50 53 00 24
www.chamonix.com

Chamrousse 118 B2 1700m 26
lifts Dec–Apr •Grenoble (30km)
☎+33 4 76 89 92 65 ☐www.
chamrousse.com *Roads normally
cleared, keep chains accessible
because of altitude.*

Châtel 119 A3 2200m 40 lifts
Dec–Apr •Thonon Les Bains
(35km) ☎+33 4 50 73 22 44
☐www.chatel.com

Courchevel 118 B3 1850m 185
lifts Dec–Apr •Moûtiers (23km)
☎+33 4 79 08 00 29 ☐www.
courchevel.com *Roads normally
cleared but keep chains accessible. Traffic 'discouraged' within
the four resort bases. Traffic info:
+33 4 79 37 73 37.*

Flaine 118 A3 1800m 74 lifts
Dec–Apr •Cluses (25km) ☎+33
4 50 90 80 01 ☐www.flaine.com
*Keep chains accessible for D6
from Cluses to Flaine. Car access
for depositing luggage and passengers only. 1500-space car park
outside resort. Road conditions
report tel +33 4 50 25 20 50.
Near Sixt-Fer-á-Cheval.*

La Clusaz 118 B3 1100m 55 lifts
Dec–Apr •Annecy (32km) ☎+33 4
50 32 65 00 ☐www.laclusaz.com
*Roads normally clear but keep
chains accessible for final road
from Annecy.*

La Plagne 118 B3 2100m 110
lifts Dec–Apr Moûtiers (32km)
☎+33 4 79 09 79 79 ☐www.
la-plagne.com *Ten different centres up to 2100m altitude. Road
access via Bozel, Landry or Aime
normally cleared.*

Les Arcs 119 B3 2600m 77
lifts Dec–Apr •Bourg-St-Maurice
(15km) ☎+33 4 79 07 12 57
☐www.lesarcs.com *Three base
areas up to 2000 metres; keep
chains accessible. Pay parking at
edge of each base resort.*

Les Carroz d'Araches 118 A3
1140m 74 lifts Dec–Apr •Cluses
(13km) ☎+33 4 50 90 00 04
☐www.lescarroz.com

Les Deux-Alpes 118 C3 1650m
63 lifts Dec–May •Grenoble

(75km) ☎+33 4 76 79 22 00
☐www.les2alpes.com *Roads
normally cleared, however snow
chains recommended for D213 up
from valley road (N91).*

Les Gets 118 A3 1172m 53 lifts
Dec–May •Cluses (18km) ☎+33 4
50 75 80 80 ☐www.lesgets.com

Les Ménuires 118 B3 1815m
197 lifts Dec–Apr •Moûtiers
(27km) ☎+33 4 79 00 73 00
☐www.lesmenuires.com *Keep
chains accessible for N515A from
Moûtiers.*

Les Sept Laux 118 B3 1350m,
29 lifts Dec–Apr •Grenoble
(38km) ☎+33 4 76 08 17 86
☐www.les7laux.com *Roads
normally cleared, however keep
chains accessible for mountain
road up from the A41 motorway.
Near St Sorlin d'Arves.*

Megève 118 B3 2350m 117
lifts Dec–Apr •Sallanches (12km)
☎+33 4 50 21 27 28 ☐www.
megeve.com *Horse-drawn sleigh
rides available.*

Méribel 118 B3 1400m 197
lifts Dec–May •Moûtiers (18km)
☎+33 4 79 08 60 01
☐www.meribel.com *Keep chains
accessible for 18km to resort on
D90 from Moûtiers.*

Morzine 118 A3 1000m 217
lifts, Dec–May •Thonon-Les-Bains
(30km) ☎+33 4 50 74 72 72
☐www.morzine.com

Pra Loup 132 A2 1600m 53 lifts
Dec–Apr •Barcelonnette (10km)
☎+33 4 92 84 10 04 ☐www.
praloup.com *Roads normally
cleared but chains accessibility
recommended.*

Risoul 118 C3 1850m 58 lifts
Dec–Apr •Briançon (40km) ☎+33
4 92 46 02 60 ☐www.risoul.
com *Keep chains accessible. Near
Guillestre.*

St Gervais 118 B3 850m 121
lifts Dec–Apr •Sallanches (10km)
☎+33 4 50 47 76 08
☐www.st-gervais.com

Serre-Chevalier 118 C3 1350m
79 lifts Dec–May •Briançon
(10km) ☎+33 4 92 24 98 98
☐www.serre-chevalier.com *Made

up of 13 small villages along the
valley road, which is normally
cleared.*

Tignes 119 B3 2100m 97 lifts
Jan–Dec •Bourg St Maurice
(26km) ☎+33 4 79 40 04 40
☐www.tignes.net *Keep chains
accessible because of altitude.
Parking information tel +33 4 79
06 39 45.*

Val d'Isère 119 B3 1850m 97
lifts Nov–May •Bourg-St-Maurice
(30km) ☎+33 4 79 06 06
60 ☐www.valdisere.com *Roads
normally cleared but keep chains
accessible.*

Val Thorens 118 B3 2300m 197
lifts Nov–May •Moûtiers (37km)
☎+33 4 79 00 08 08 ☐www.
valthorens.com *Chains essential
– highest ski resort in Europe.
Obligatory paid parking on edge
of resort.*

Valloire 118 B3 1430m 36 lifts
Dec–May •Modane (20km)
☎+33 4 79 59 03 96
☐www.valloire.net *Road normally
clear up to the Col du Galbier,
to the south of the resort, which
is closed from 1st November to
1st June.*

Valmeinier 118 B3 2600m 32
lifts Dec–Apr •St Michel de Mau-
rienne (47km) ☎+33 4 79 59 53
69 ☐www.valmeinier.com *Access
from north on N9 / N902. Col du
Galbier, to the south of the resort
closed from 1st November to 1st
June. Near Valloire.*

Valmorel 118 B3 1400m 55 lifts
Dec–Apr •Moûtiers (15km) ☎+33
4 79 09 85 55 ☐www.valmorel.
com *Near St Jean-de-Belleville.*

Vars Les Claux 118 C3 1850m
58 lifts Dec–Apr •Briançon (40km)
☎+33 4 92 46 51 31 ☐www.
vars-ski.com *Four base resorts
up to 1850 metres. Keep chains
accessible. Road and weather
information tel +33 4 36 68 02 05
and +33 4 91 78 78 78. Snowfone
+33 492 46 51 04*

Villard-de-Lans 118 B2 1050m
29 lifts Dec–Apr •Grenoble
(32km) ☎+33 4 76 95 10 38
☐www.villard-de-lans.com

Pyrenees

Font-Romeu 146 B3 1800m 33
lifts Dec–Apr •Perpignan (87km)
☎+33 4 68 30 68 30
☐www.fontromeu.com *Roads
normally cleared but keep chains
accessible.*

St Lary-Soulan 145 B4 830m
32 lifts Dec–Apr •Tarbes (75km)
☎+33 5 62 39 50 81
☐www.saintlary.com *Access
roads constantly cleared of snow.*

Vosges

La Bresse-Hohneck 106 A1
900m 20 lifts Dec–Mar •Corni-
mont (6km) ☎+33 3 29 25 41 29
☐www.labresse-remy.com

Germany

Alps

**Garmisch-Partenkirchen 108
B2** 702m 38 lifts Dec–Apr
•Munich (95km) ☎+49 8821 180
700 ☐www.garmisch-parten-
kirchen.de *Roads usually clear,
chains rarely needed.*

Oberaudorf 108 B3 483m 21
lifts Dec–Apr •Kufstein (15km)
☎+49 8033 301 20 ☐www.ober-
audorf.de *Motorway normally kept
clear. Near Bayrischzell.*

Oberstdorf 107 B5 815m 31
lifts Dec–Apr •Sonthofen (15km)
☎+49 8322 7000 ☐www.oberst-
dorf.de *Snow information on tel
+49 8322 3035 or 1095 or 5757.*

Rothaargebirge

Winterberg 81 A4 700m 55 lifts
Dec–Mar •Brilon (30km) ☎+49
2981 925 00 ☐www.winterberg.
de *Roads usually cleared, chains
rarely required.*

Greece

Central Greece

**Mountain Parnassos: Kelaria-
Fterolakka 182 E4** 1750–1950m
14 lifts Dec–Apr •Amfiklia
☐Kelaria ☎+30 22340 22694,
Ftorolakka 22340 22373 ☐www.
parnassos-ski.gr

Mountain Parnassos: Gerondovrahos **182 E4** 1800–2390m 3 lifts Dec–Apr •Amfiklia ☎+30 29444 70371

Ipiros

Mountain Pindos: Karakoli **182 D3** 1350–1700m 1 lift Dec–Mar •Metsovo ☎+30 26560 41333

Mountain Pindos: Profitis Ilias **182 D3** 1500–1700m 3 lifts Dec–Mar •Metsovo ☎+30 26560 41095

Peloponnisos

Mountain Helmos: Kalavrita Ski Centre **184 A3** 1650–2340m 7 lifts Dec–Mar •Kalavrita ☎+30 26920 24451/24452 ⌂www.kalavrita-ski.gr/en/default.asp

Mountain Menalo: Oropedio Ostrakinos **184 B3** 1600m 3 lifts Dec–Mar •Tripoli ☎+30 27960 22227

Macedonia

Mountain Falakro: Agio Pneuma **183 B6** 1720m 3 lifts Dec–Mar •Drama ☎+30 25210 62224 ⌂www.falakro.gr

Mountain Vasilitsa: Vasilitsa **182 C3** 1750m 2 lifts Dec–Mar •Konitsa ☎+30 24620 84850 ⌂www.vasilitsa.com

Mountain Vermio: Seli **182 C4** 1500m 4 lifts Dec–Mar •Kozani ☎+30 23310 26237

Mountain Vermio: Tria-Pente Pigadia **182 C3** 1420–2005m 4 lifts Dec–Mar •Ptolemaida ☎+30 23320 44446

Mountain Verno: Vigla **182 C3** 1650–2000m 3 lifts Dec–Mar •Florina ☎+30 23850 22354

Mountain Vrondous: Lailias **183 B5** 1847m 3 lifts Dec–Mar •Serres ☎+30 23210 62400

Thessalia

Mountain Pilio: Agriolefkes **183 D5** 1500m 4 lifts Dec–Mar •Volos ☎+30 24280 73719

Italy
Alps

Bardonecchia **118 B3** 1312m 24 lifts Dec–Apr •Bardonecchia ☎+39 122 99137 Snowfone +39 122 907778 ⌂www.bardonecchia-ski.com *Resort reached through the 11km Frejus tunnel from France, roads normally cleared.*

Bórmio **107 C5** 1225m 16 lifts Dec–Apr •Tirano (40km) ☎+39 342 903300 ⌂www.bormio.com *Tolls payable in Ponte del Gallo Tunnel, open 0800hrs–2000hrs.*

Breuil-Cervinia **119 B4** 2050m 73 lifts Jan–Dec •Aosta (54km) ☎+39 166 940986 ⌂www.breuil-cervinia.it *Snow chains strongly recommended. Bus from Milan airport.*

Courmayeur **119 B3** 1224m 27 lifts Dec–Apr •Aosta (40km) ☎+39 165 842370 ⌂www.courmayeur.com *Access through the Mont Blanc tunnel from France. Roads constantly cleared.*

Limone Piemonte **133 A3** 1050m 29 lifts Dec–Apr •Cuneo (27km) ☎+39 171 925280 ⌂www.limonepiemonte.it *Roads normally cleared, chains rarely required. Snow report tel +39 171 926254.*

Livigno **107 C5** 1816m 33 lifts Dec–May •Zernez (CH) (27km) ☎+39 342 052200 ⌂www.aptlivigno.it *Keep chains accessible. La Drosa Tunnel from Zernez, Switzerland, is open only from 0800hrs to 2000hrs.*

Sestrière **119 C3** 2035m 91 lifts Dec–Apr •Oulx (22km) ☎+39 122 755444 ⌂www.sestriere.it *One of Europe's highest resorts; although roads are normally cleared keep chains accessible.*

Appennines

Roccaraso – Aremogna **169 B4** 1285m 31 lifts Dec–Apr •Castel di Sangro (7km) ☎+39 864 62210 ⌂www.roccaraso.it

Dolomites

Andalo – Fai della Paganella **121 A3** 1042m 22 lifts Dec–Apr •Trento (40km) ⌂www.paganella.net ☎+39 461 585588

Arabba **108 C2** 2500m 30 lifts Dec–Apr •Brunico (45km) ☎+39 436 780019 ⌂www.arabba.it *Roads normally cleared but keep chains accessible.*

Cortina d'Ampezzo **108 C3** 1224m 48 lifts Dec–Apr •Belluno (72km) ☎+39 436 866252 ⌂www.cortinadampezzo.it *Access from north on route 51 over the Cimabanche Pass may require chains.*

Corvara (Alta Badia) **108 C2** 1568m 54 lifts Dec–Apr •Brunico (38km) ☎+39 471 836176 ⌂www.altabadia.it/inverno *Roads normally clear but keep chains accessible.*

Madonna di Campiglio **121 A3** 1550m 60 lifts Dec–Apr •Trento (60km) ☎+39 465 447501 ⌂www.campiglio.net *Roads normally cleared but keep chains accessible.*

Moena di Fassa (Sorte/Ronchi) **108 C2** 1184m 29 lifts Dec–Apr •Bolzano (40km) ☎+39 462 602466 ⌂www.dolomitisuperski.com

Passo del Tonale **121 A3** 1883m 30 lifts Dec–Aug •Breno (50km) ☎+39 364 903838 ⌂www.adamelloski.com *Located on high mountain pass; keep chains accessible.*

Selva di Val Gardena/Wolkenstein Groden **108 C2** 1563m 82 lifts Dec–Apr •Bolzano (40km) ☎+39 471 792277 ⌂www.valgardena.it *Roads normally cleared but keep chains accessible.*

Norway

Hemsedal **47 B5** 650m 16 lifts Nov–May •Honefoss (150km) ☎+47 32 055030 ⌂www.hemsedal.com *Be prepared for extreme weather conditions.*

Trysil (Trysilfjellet) **49 A4** 465m 24 lifts Nov–May •Elverum (100km) ☎+47 62 451000 ⌂www.trysil.com *Be prepared for extreme weather conditions.*

Slovakia

Chopok **99 C3** 2024m 21 lifts Nov–May •Jasna ☎+421 48 991505 ⌂www.jasna.sk

Donovaly **99 C3** 1360m 15 lifts Nov–May •Ruzomberok ☎+421 48 4199900 ⌂www.parksnow.sk

Martinske Hole **98 B2** 1456m 7 lifts Nov–May •Zilina ☎+421 41 500 3429 ⌂www.martinske-hole.sk

Plejsy **99 C4** 912m 8 lifts Nov–May •Krompachy ☎+421 53 447 1121 ⌂www.plejsy.com

Strbske Pleso **99 B4** 1915m 8 lifts Nov–May •Poprad ☎+421 52 449 2343 ⌂www.parksnow.sk/tatry-leto

Rohace **99 B3** 1450m 4 lifts Nov–May •Liptovsky Mikulas ☎+421 43 5395320 ⌂www.rohace.sk

Slovenia
Julijske Alpe

Kanin **122 A2** 2289m 6 lifts Dec–May •Bovec ☎+386 5 3841 919 ⌂www.bovec.si

Kobla **122 A2** 1480m 6 lifts Dec–Apr •Bohinjska Bistrica ☎+386 4 5747 100 ⌂www.bohinj.si/kobla

Kranjska Gora **122 A2** 1620m 20 lifts Dec–Apr •Kranjska Gora ☎+386 4 5881 768 ⌂www.kranjska-gora.si

Vogel **122 A2** 1800m 9 lifts Dec–Apr •Bohinjska Bistrica ☎+386 4 5724 236 ⌂www.vogel.si

Kawiniske Savinjske Alpe

Krvavec **122 A3** 1970m 13 lifts Dec–May •Kranj ☎+386 4 2525 930 ⌂www.rtc-krvavec.si *Ski phone tel +386 4 1182 500*

Pohorje

Rogla **123 A4** 1517m 11 lifts Dec–May •Slovenska Bistrica ☎+386 3 7576 000 ⌂www.rogla.si

Spain
Pyrenees

Baqueira/Beret **145 B4** 1500m 24 lifts Dec–Apr •Viella (15km) ☎+34 973 649010 ⌂www.baqueira.es *Roads normally clear but keep chains accessible. Snowfone tel +34 973 639025. Near Salardú.*

Sistema Penibetico

Sierra Nevada **163 A4** 2102m 21 lifts Dec–May •Granada (32km) ☎+34 958 249100 ⌂www.sierranevadaski.com *Access road designed to be avalanche safe and is snow cleared. Snowfone +34 958 249119.*

Sweden

Idre Fjäll **199 D9** 710m 30 lifts Oct-May •Mora (140km) ☎+46 253 41000 ⌂www.idrefjall.se *Be prepared for extreme weather conditions.*

Sälen **49 A5** 360m 101 lifts Nov–May •Malung (70km) ☎+46 280 86070 ⌂www.skistar.com/english *Be prepared for extreme weather conditions.*

Switzerland
Alps

Adelboden **106 C2** 1353m 50 lifts Dec–Apr •Frutigen (15km) ☎+41 33 673 80 80 ⌂www.adelboden.ch

Arosa **107 C4** 1800m 16 lifts Dec–Apr •Chur (30km) ☎+41 81 378 70 20 ⌂www.arosa.ch *Roads cleared but keep chains accessible because of high altitude (1800m).*

Crans Montana **119 A4** 1500m 35 lifts Dec–Apr, Jul-Oct •Sierre (15km) ☎+41 27 485 04 04 ⌂www.crans-montana.ch *Roads normally cleared, however keep chains accessible for ascent from Sierre.*

Davos **107 C4** 1560m 54 lifts Nov–May •Davos ☎+41 81 415 21 21 ⌂www.davos.ch

Engelberg **106 C3** 1000m 26 lifts Nov–Jun •Luzern (39km) ☎+41 41 639 77 77 ⌂www.engelberg.ch *Straight access road normally cleared.*

Flums (Flumserberg) **107 B4** 1400m 17 lifts Dec–Apr •Buchs (25km) ☎+41 81 720 18 18 ⌂www.flumserberg.com *Roads normally cleared, but 1000-metre vertical ascent; keep chains accessible.*

Grindelwald **106 C3** 1034m 30 lifts Dec–Apr •Interlaken (20km) ☎+41 33 854 12 12 ⌂www.grindelwald.ch

Gstaad – Saanenland **106 C2** 1050m 66 lifts Dec–Apr •Gstaad ☎+41 33 748 81 81 ⌂www.gstaad.ch

Klosters **107 C4** 1191m 61 lifts Dec–Apr •Davos (10km) ☎+41 81 410 20 20 ⌂www.klosters.ch *Roads normally clear but keep chains accessible*

Leysin **119 A4** 1263m 19 lifts Dec–Apr •Aigle (6km) ☎+41 24 494 22 44 ⌂www.leysin.ch

Mürren **106 C2** 1650m 37 lifts Dec–Apr •Interlaken (18km) ☎+41 33 856 86 86 ⌂www.wengen-muerren.ch *No road access. Park in Strechelberg (1500 free places) and take the two-stage cable car.*

Nendaz **119 A4** 1365m 91 lifts Nov–Apr •Sion (16km) ☎+41 27 289 55 89 ⌂www.nendaz.ch *Roads normally cleared, however keep chains accessible for ascent from Sion. Near Vex.*

Saas-Fee **119 A4** 1800m 25 lifts Jan–Dec •Brig (35km) ☎+41 27 958 18 58 ⌂www.saas-fee.ch *Roads normally cleared but keep chains accessible.*

St Moritz **107 C4** 1856m 58 lifts Nov–May •Chur (89km) ☎+41 81 837 33 33 ⌂www.stmoritz.ch *Roads normally cleared but keep chains accessible.*

Samnaun **107 C5** 1846m 42 lifts Dec–May •Scuol (30km) ☎+41 81 868 58 58 ⌂www.samnaun.c *Roads normally cleared but keep chains accessible.*

Verbier **119 A4** 1500m 95 lifts Nov–May, Jun-Jul •Martigny (27km) ☎+41 27 775 38 88 ⌂www.verbier.ch *Roads normally cleared.*

Villars **119 A4** 1253m 37 lifts Nov–Apr, Jun-Jul •Montreux (35km) ☎+41 24 495 32 32 ⌂www.villars.ch *Roads normally cleared but keep chains accessible for ascent from N9. Near Bex.*

Wengen **106 C2** 1270m 37 lifts Dec–Apr •Interlaken (12km) ☎+41 33 855 14 14 ⌂www.wengen-muerren.ch *No road access. Park at Lauterbrunnen and take mountain railway.*

Zermatt **119 A4** 1620m 73 lifts all year •Brig (42km) ☎+41 27 966 81 00 ⌂www.zermatt.ch *Cars not permitted in resort, park in Täsch (3km) and use shuttle train.*

Turkey
North Anatolian Mountains

Uludag **186 B4** 2543m 14 lifts Dec–March •Bursa (36km) ☎+9 224 254 22 74 ⌂www.guideto-turkey.com/ski_centers

300 greatest sights of Europe

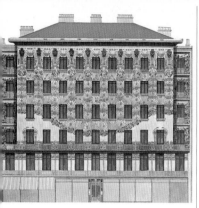

Maholicahaus, Vienna, Austria

Albania Shqipëria

www.albanian.com

Berat

Fascinating old town with picturesque Ottoman Empire buildings and traditional Balkan domestic architecture. 82 C1

Tirana Tiranë

Capital of Albania. Skanderbeg Square has main historic buildings. Also: 18c Haxhi Ethem Bey Mosque; Art Gallery (Albanian); National Museum of History. Nearby: medieval Krujë; Roman monuments. 182 B1

Austria Österreich

www.austria-tourism.at

Bregenz

Lakeside town bordering Germany, Liechtenstein, Switzerland. Locals, known as Vorarlbergers, have their own dialect. St Martinsturm 7th century tower, 17th century town hall, Kunsthaus Bregenz gallery of modern art, Vorarlberger Landesmuseum, Festspielhaus www.bregenz.ws 107 B4

Graz

University town, seat of imperial court to 1619. Historic centre around Hauptplatz. Imperial monuments: Burg; mausoleum of Ferdinand II; towers of 16c schloss; 17c schloss Eggenburg. Also: 16c Town Hall; Zeughaus; 15c cathedral. Museums: Old Gallery (Gothic, Flemish); New Gallery (good 19–20c). www.graztourismus.at 110 B2

Krems

On a hill above the Danube, medieval quarter has Renaissance mansions. Also: Gothic Piaristenkirche; Wienstadt Museum. www.krems.at 97 C3

Linz

Port on the Danube. Historic buildings are concentrated on Hauptplatz below the imperial 15c schloss. Notable: Baroque Old Cathedral; 16c Town Hall; New Gallery. www.linz.at 96 C2

Melk

Set on a rocky hill above the Danube, the fortified abbey is the greatest Baroque achievement in Austria – particularly the Grand Library and abbey church. www.stiftmelk.at 110 A2

Innsbruck

Old town is reached by Maria-Theresien-Strasse with famous views. Buildings: Goldenes Dachl (1490s); 18c cathedral; remains of Hofburg imperial residence; 16c Hofkirche (tomb of Maximilian I). www.innsbruck.info 108 B2

Salzburg

Set in subalpine scenery, the town was associated with powerful 16-17c prince-archbishops. The 17c cathedral has a complex of archiepiscopal buildings: the Residence and its gallery (excellent 16–19c); the 13c Franciscan Church (notable altar). Other sights: Mozart's birthplace; the Hohensalzburg fortress; the Collegiate Church of St Peter (cemetery, catacombs); scenic views from Mönchsberg and Hettwer Bastei. The Grosse Festspielhaus runs the Salzburg festival. www2.salzburg.info 109 B4

Salzkammergut

Natural beauty with 76 lakes (Wolfgangersee, Altersee, Gosausee, Traunsee, Grundlsee) in mountain scenery. Attractive villages (St Wolfgang) and towns (Bad Ischl, Gmunden) include Hallstatt, famous for Celtic remains. www.salzkammergut.at 109 B4

Vienna Wien

Capital of Austria. The historic centre lies within the Ring. Churches: Gothic St Stephen's Cathedral; 17c Imperial Vault; 14c Augustine Church; 14c Church of the Teutonic Order (treasure); 18c Baroque churches (Jesuit Church, Franciscan Church, St Peter, St Charles). Imperial residences: Hofburg; Schönbrunn. Architecture of Historicism on Ringstrasse (from 1857). Art Nouveau: Station Pavilions, Postsparkasse, Looshaus, Majolicahaus. Exceptional museums: Art History Museum (antiquities, old masters); Cathedral and Diocesan Museum (15c); Academy of Fine Arts (Flemish); Belvedere (Gothic, Baroque, 19–20c). www.wien.gv.at 111 A3

Belgium Belgique

www.visitbelgium.com

Antwerp Antwerpen

City with many tall gabled Flemish houses on the river. Heart of the city is Great Market with 16–17c guildhouses and Town Hall. 14–16c Gothic cathedral has Rubens paintings. Rubens also at the Rubens House and his burial place in St Jacob's Church. Excellent museums: Mayer van den Berg Museum (applied arts); Koninklijk Museum of Fine Arts (Flemish, Belgian). www.visitantwerp.be 79 A4

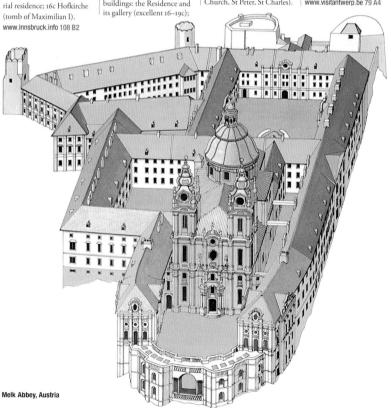

Melk Abbey, Austria

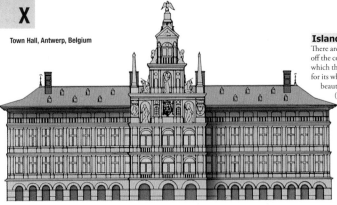

Town Hall, Antwerp, Belgium

Bruges Brugge

Well-preserved medieval town with narrow streets and canals. Main squares: the Market with 13c Belfort and covered market; the Burg with Basilica of the Holy Blood and Town Hall. The Groeninge Museum and Memling museum in St Jans Hospital show 15c Flemish masters. The Onze Lieve Vrouwekerk has a famous *Madonna and Child* by Michelangelo www.brugge.be **78 A3**

Brussels Bruxelles

Capital of Belgium. The Lower Town is centred on the enormous Grand Place with Hôtel de Ville and rebuilt guildhouses. Symbols of the city include the 'Manneken Pis' and Atomium (giant model of a molecule). The 13c Notre Dame de la Chapelle is the oldest church. The Upper Town contains: Gothic cathedral; Neoclassical Place Royale; 18c King's Palace; Royal Museums of Fine Arts (old and modern masters). Also: much Art Nouveau (Victor Horta Museum, Hôtel Tassel, Hôtel Solvay); Place du Petit Sablon and Place du Grand Sablon; 19c Palais de Justice. www.brusselsinternational.be **79 B4**

Ghent Gent

Medieval town built on islands surrounded by canals and rivers. Views from Pont St-Michel. The Graslei and Koornlei quays have Flemish guild houses. The Gothic cathedral has famous Van Eyck altarpiece. Also: Belfort; Cloth Market; Gothic Town Hall; Gravensteen. Museums: Bijloke Museum in beautiful abbey (provincial and applied art); Museum of Fine Arts (old masters). www.gent.be **79 A3**

Namur

Reconstructed medieval citadel is the major sight of Namur, which also has a cathedral and provincial museums. www.namur.be **79 B4**

Tournai

The Romanesque-Gothic cathedral is Belgium's finest (much excellent art). Fine Arts Museum has a good collection (15–20c). www.tournai.be **78 B3**

Bulgaria Bulgariya

www.bulgariatravel.org

Black Sea Coast

Beautiful unspoiled beaches (Zlatni Pyasŭtsi). The delightful resort Varna is popular. Nesebŭr is famous for Byzantine churches. Also: Danube Delta in Hungary. **17 D7**

Koprivshtitsa

Beautiful village known both for its half-timbered houses and links with the April Rising of 1876. Six house museums amongst which the Lyutov House and the Oslekov House, plus the birthplaces of Georgi Benkovski, Dimcho Debelyanov, Todor Kableshkov, and Lyuben Karavelov.

Plovdiv

City set spectacularly on three hills. The old town has buildings from many periods: 2c Roman stadium and amphitheatre; 14c Dzumaiya Mosque; 19c Koyumdjioglu House and Museum (traditional objects). Nearby: Bačkovo Monastery (frescoes). www.plovdiv.org **183 A6**

Rila

Bulgaria's finest monastery, set in the most beautiful scenery of the Rila mountains. The church is richly decorated with frescoes.

Sofia Sofiya

Capital of Bulgaria. Sights: exceptional neo-Byzantine cathedral; Church of St Sofia; 4c rotunda of St George (frescoes); Byzantine Boyana Church (frescoes) on panoramic Mount Vitoša. Museums: National Historical Museum (particularly for Thracian artefacts); National Art Gallery (icons, Bulgarian art). www.sofia.bg/en **17 D5**

Veliko Tŭrnovo

Medieval capital with narrow streets. Notable buildings: House of the Little Monkey; Hadji Nicoli Inn; ruins of medieval citadel; Baudouin Tower; churches of the Forty Martyrs and of SS Peter and Paul (frescoes); 14c Monastery of the Transfiguration. www.veliko-tarnovo.net **17 D6**

Croatia Hrvatska

www.croatia.hr

Dalmatia Dalmacija

Exceptionally beautiful coast along the Adriatic. Among its 1185 islands, those of the Kornati Archipelago and Brijuni Islands are perhaps the most spectacular. Along the coast are several attractive medieval and Renaissance towns, most notably Dubrovnik, Split, Šibenik, Trogir, Zadar. www.dalmacija.net **138 B2**

Dubrovnik

Surrounded by medieval and Renaissance walls, the city's architecture dates principally from 15–16c. Sights: many churches and monasteries including Church of St Vlah and Dominican monastery (art collection); promenade street of Stradun, Dubrovnik Museums; Renaissance Rector's Palace; Onofrio's fountain; Sponza Palace. The surrounding area has some 80 16c noblemen's summer villas. www.dubrovnik-online.com **139 C4**

Islands of Croatia

There are over 1,000 islands off the coast of Croatia among which there is Brač, known for its white marble and the beautiful beaches of Bol (www.bol.hr); Hvar (www.hvar.hr) is beautifully green with fields of lavender, marjoram, rosemary, sage and thyme; Vis (www.tz-vis.hr) has the beautiful towns of Komiža and Vis Town, with the Blue Cave on nearby Biševo. **123 & 137–138**

Istria Istra

Peninsula with a number of ancient coastal towns (Rovinj, Poreč, Pula, Piran in Slovene Istria) and medieval hill-top towns (Motovun). Pula has Roman monuments (exceptional 1c amphitheatre). Poreč has narrow old streets; the mosaics in 6c Byzantine basilica of St Euphrasius are exceptional. See also Slovenia. www.istra.com **122 B2**

Plitvička Jezera

Outstandingly beautiful world of water and woodlands with 16 lakes and 92 waterfalls interwoven by canyons. www.np-plitvicka-jezera.hr **123 C4**

Split

Most notable for the exceptional 4c palace of Roman Emperor Diocletian, elements of which are incorporated into the streets and buildings of the town itself. The town also has a cathedral (11c baptistry) and a Franciscan monastery. www.split.hr **138 B2**

Trogir

The 13–15c town centre is surrounded by medieval city walls. Romanesque-Gothic cathedral includes the chapel of Ivan the Blessed. Dominican and Benedictine monasteries house art collections. www.trogir-online.com **138 B2**

Zagreb

Capital city of Croatia with cathedral and Archbishop's Palace in Kaptol and to the west Gradec with Baroque palaces. Donji Grad is home to the Archaological Museum, Art Pavilion, Museum of Arts and Crafts, Ethnographic Museum, Mimara Museum and National Theatre. www.zagreb-touristinfo.hr **124 B1**

Czech Republic Česká Republika

www.czech.cz

Brno

Capital of Moravia. Sights: Vegetable Market and Old Town Hall; Capuchin crypt decorated with bones of dead monks; hill of St Peter with Gothic cathedral; Mies van der Rohe's buildings (Bata, Avion Hotel, Togendhat House). Museums: UPM (modern applied arts); Pražáků Palace (19c Czech art). www.brno.cz **97 B4**

České Budějovice

Famous for Budvar beer, the medieval town is centred on náměstí Přemysla Otokara II. The Black Tower gives fine views. Nearby: medieval Český Krumlov. www.c-budejovice.cz **96 C2**

Kutná Hora

A town with strong silver mining heritage shown in the magnificent Cathedral of sv Barbara which was built by the miners. See also the ossuary with 40,000 complete sets of bones moulded into sculptures and decorations. www.kutnohorsko.cz **97 B3**

Olomouc

Well-preserved medieval university town of squares and fountains. The Upper Square has the Town Hall. Also: 18c Holy Trinity; Baroque Church of St Michael. www.olomoucko.cz **98 B1**

Plzeň

Best known for Plzeňský Prazdroj (Pilsener Urquell), beer has been brewed here since 1295. An industrial town with eclectic architecture shown in the railway stations and the namesti Republiky (main square). www.zcu.cz/plzen **96 B1**

Prague Praha

Capital of Czech Republic and Bohemia. The Castle Quarter has a complex of buildings behind the walls (Royal Castle; Royal Palace; cathedral). The Basilica of St George has a fine Romanesque interior. The Belvedere is the best example of Renaissance architecture. Hradčani Square has aristocratic palaces and the National Gallery. The Little Quarter has many Renaissance (Wallenstein Palace) and Baroque mansions and the Baroque Church of St Nicholas. The Old Town has its centre at the Old Town Square with the Old Town

Hall (astronomical clock), Art Nouveau Jan Hus monument and Gothic Týn church. The Jewish quarter has 14c Staranova Synagogue and Old Jewish Cemetery. The Charles Bridge is famous. The medieval New Town has many Art Nouveau buildings and is centred on Wenceslas Square. www.prague.cz **84 B2**

Spas of Bohemia

Spa towns of Karlovy Vary (Carlsbad), Márianske Lázně (Marienbad) and Frantiskovy Lázně (Franzenbad). **83 B4**

Denmark Danmark

www.visitdenmark.com

Århus

Second largest city in Denmark with a mixture of old and new architecture that blends well, Århus has been dubbed the culture capital of Denmark with the Gothic Domkirke; Latin Quarter; 13th Century Vor Frue Kirke; Den Gamle By, open air museum of traditional Danish life; ARoS, Århus Art Museum. www.visitaarhus. dk **9 B3**

Copenhagen

København

Capital of Denmark. Old centre has fine early 20c Town Hall. Latin Quarter has 19c cathedral. 18c Kastellet has statue of the Little Mermaid nearby. The 17c Rosenborg Castle was a royal residence, as was the Christianborg (now government offices). Other popular sights: Nyhavn canal; Tivoli Gardens. Excellent art collections: Ny Carlsberg Glypotek; State Art Museum; National Museum. www.viscopenhagen.dk **61 D2**

Hillerød

Frederiksborg is a fine redbrick Renaissance castle set among three lakes. **61 D2**

Roskilde

Ancient capital of Denmark. The marvellous cathedral is burial place of the Danish monarchy. The Viking Ship Museum houses the remains of five 11c Viking ships excavated in the 1960s. www.visiroskilde.com **61 D2**

Estonia Eesti

www.visitestonia.com

Kuressaare

Main town on the island of Saaremaa with the 14c Kuressaare Kindlus. www.kuressaare.ee **8 C3**

Pärnu

Sea resort with an old town centre. Sights: 15c Red Tower; neoclassical Town Hall; St Catherine's Church. www.parnu.ee **8 C4**

Tallinn

Capital of Estonia. The old town is centred on the Town Hall Square. Sights: 15c Town Hall; Toompea Castle; Three Sisters houses. Churches: Gothic St Nicholas; 14c Church of the Holy Spirit; St Olaf's Church. www.tallinn.ee **8 C4**

Tartu

Historic town with 19c university. The Town Hall Square is surrounded by neoclassical buildings. Also: remains of 13c cathedral; Estonian National Museum. www.tartu.ee **8 C5**

Finland Suomi

http://virtual.finland.fi

Finnish Lakes

Area of outstanding natural beauty covering about one third of the country with thousands of lakes, of which Päijänne and Saimaa are the most important. Tampere, industrial centre of the region, has numerous museums, including the Sara Hildén Art Museum (modern). Savonlinna has the medieval Olavinlinna Castle. Kuopio has the Orthodox and Regional Museums. **8 A5**

Helsinki

Capital of Finland. The 19c neoclassical town planning between the Esplanade and Senate Square includes the Lutheran cathedral. There is also a Russian Orthodox cathedral. The Constructivist Stockmann Department Store is the largest in Europe. The main railway station is Art Nouveau. Gracious 20c buildings in Mannerheimintie avenue include Finlandiatalo by Alvar Aalto. Many good museums: Art Museum of the Ateneum (19–20c); National Museum; Museum of Applied Arts; Helsinki City Art Museum (modern Finnish); Open Air Museum (vernacular architecture); 18c fortress of Suomenlinna has several museums. www.hel.fi **8 B4**

Lappland (Finnish)

Vast unspoiled rural area. Lappland is home to thousands of nomadic Sámi living in a traditional way. The capital, Rovaniemi, was rebuilt after WWII; museums show Sámi history and culture. Nearby is the Arctic Circle with the famous Santa Claus Village. Inari is a centre of Sámi culture. See also Norway and Sweden. www.laplandfinland.com **192–193**

France

www.franceguide.com

Albi

Old town with rosy brick architecture. The vast Cathédrale Ste-Cécile (begun 13c) holds some good art. The Berbie Palace houses the Toulouse-Lautrec museum. www.mairie-albi.fr **130 B1**

Alps

Grenoble, capital of the French Alps, has a good 20c collection in the Museum of Painting and Sculpture. The Vanoise Massif has the greatest number of resorts (Val d'Isère, Courchevel). Chamonix has spectacular views on Mont Blanc, France's and Europe's highest peak. www.thealps.com **118 B2**

Amiens

France's largest Gothic cathedral has beautiful decoration. The Museum of Picardy has unique 16c panel paintings. www.amiens.fr **90 B2**

Arles

Ancient, picturesque town with Roman relics (1c amphitheatre), 11c cathedral, Archaeological Museum (Roman art). www.tourisme.ville-arles.fr **131 B3**

Avignon

Medieval papal capital (1309–77) with 14c walls and many ecclesiastical buildings. Vast Palace of the Popes has stunning frescoes. The Little Palace has fine Italian Renaissance painting. The 12–13c Bridge of St Bénézet is famous. www.ot-avignon.fr **131 B3**

Bourges

The Gothic Cathedral of St Etienne, one of the finest in France, has a superb sculptured choir. Also notable is the House of Jacques Coeur. www.bourgestourisme.com **103 B4**

Burgundy Bourgogne

Rural wine region with a rich Romanesque, Gothic and Renaissance heritage. The 12c cathedral in Autun and 12c basilica in Vézelay have fine Romanesque sculpture. Monasteries include 11c L'Abbaye de Cluny (ruins) and L'Abbaye de Fontenay. Beaune

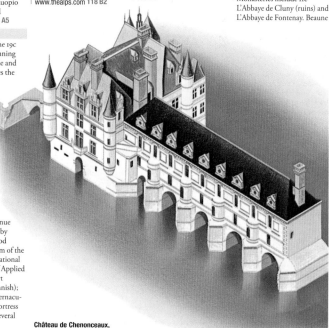

Abbaye aux Hommes, Caen, France

Château de Chenonceaux, Châteaux of the Loire, France

has beautiful Gothic Hôtel-Dieu and 15c Nicolas Rolin hospices. www.burgundy-tourism.com 104 B3

Brittany Bretagne

Brittany is famous for cliffs, sandy beaches and wild landscape. It is also renowned for megalithic monuments (Carnac) and Celtic culture. Its capital, Rennes, has the Palais de Justice and good collections in the Museum of Brittany (history) and Museum of Fine Arts. Also: Nantes; St-Malo. www.brittany-bretagne.com 100–101

Caen

City with two beautiful Romanesque buildings: Abbaye aux Hommes; Abbaye aux Dames. The château has two museums (15–20c painting; history). The *Bayeux Tapestry* is displayed in nearby Bayeux. www.ville-caen.fr 89 A3

Carcassonne

Unusual double-walled fortified town of narrow streets with an inner fortress. The fine Romanesque Church of St Nazaire has superb stained glass. www.carcassonne.org 130 B1

Chartres

The 12–13c cathedral is an exceptionally fine example of Gothic architecture (Royal Doorway, stained glass, choir screen). The Fine Arts Museum has a good collection. www.chartres.com 90 C1

Loire Valley

The Loire Valley has many 15–16c châteaux built amid beautiful scenery by French monarchs and members of their courts. Among the most splendid are Azay-le-Rideau, Chenonceaux and Loches. Also: Abbaye de Fontévraud. www.lvo.com 102 B2

Clermont-Ferrand

The old centre contains the cathedral built out of lava and Romanesque basilica. The Puy de Dôme and Puy de Sancy give spectacular views over some 60 extinct volcanic peaks (*puys*). www.ville-clermont-ferrand.fr 116 B3

Colmar

Town characterised by Alsatian half-timbered houses. The Unterlinden Museum has excellent German religious art including the famous Isenheim altarpiece. The Dominican church also has a fine altarpiece. www.ot-colmar.fr 106 A2

Corsica Corse

Corsica has a beautiful rocky coast and mountainous interior. Napoleon's birthplace of Ajaccio has: Fesch Museum with Imperial Chapel and a large collection of Italian art; Maison Bonaparte; cathedral. Bonifacio, a medieval town, is spectacularly set on a rock over the sea. www.visit-corsica.com 180

Côte d'Azur

The French Riviera is best known for its coastline and glamorous resorts. There are many relics of artists who worked here: St-Tropez has Musée de l'Annonciade; Antibes has 12c Château Grimaldi with the Picasso Museum; Cagnes has the Renoir House and Mediterranean Museum of Modern Art; St-Paul-de-Vence has the excellent Maeght Foundation and Matisse's Chapelle du Rosaire. Cannes is famous for its film festival. Also: Marseille, Monaco, Nice. www.cote.azur.fr 133 B3

Dijon

Great 15c cultural centre. The Palais des Ducs et des Etats is the most notable monument and contains the Museum of Fine Arts. Also: the Charterhouse of Champmol. www.dijon-tourism.com 105 B4

Disneyland Paris

Europe's largest theme park follows in the footsteps of its famous predecessors in the United States. www.disneylandparis.com 90 C2

Le Puy-en-Velay

Medieval town bizarrely set on the peaks of dead volcanoes. It is dominated by the Romanesque cathedral (cloisters). The Romanesque chapel of St-Michel is dramatically situated on the highest rock. www.ot-lepuyenvelay.fr 117 B3

Lyon

France's third largest city has an old centre and many museums including the Museum of the History of Textiles and the Museum of Fine Arts (old masters).

Marseilles Marseille

Second lagest city in France. Spectacular views from the 19c Notre-Dame-de-la-Garde. The Old Port has 11–12c Basilique St Victor (crypt, catacombs). Cantini Museum has major collection of 20c French art. Château d'If was the setting of Dumas' *The

Count of Monte Cristo. www.marseille-tourisme.com 131 B4

Mont-St-Michel

Gothic pilgrim abbey (11–12c) set dramatically on a steep rock island rising from mud flats and connected to the land by a road covered by the tide. The abbey is made up of a complex of buildings. www.e-mont-saint-michel.com 101 A4

Nancy

A centre of Art Nouveau. The 18c Place Stanislas was constructed by dethroned Polish king Stanislas. Museums: School of Nancy Museum (Art Nouveau furniture); Fine Arts Museum. www.ot-nancy.fr 92 C2

Nantes

Former capital of Brittany, with the 15c Château des ducs de Bretagne. The cathedral has a striking interior. www.nantes-tourisme.com 101 B4

Nice

Capital of the Côte d'Azur, the old town is centred on the old castle on the hill. The seafront includes the famous 19c Promenade des Anglais. The aristocratic quarter of the Cimiez Hill has the Marc Chagall Museum and the Matisse Museum. Also: Museum of Modern and Contemporary Art (especially neo-Realism and Pop Art). www.nicetourism.com 133 B3

Paris

Capital of France, one of Europe's most interesting cities. The Île de la Cité area, an island in the River Seine has the 12–13c Gothic Notre Dame (wonderful stained glass) and La Sainte-Chapelle (1240–48), one of the jewels of Gothic art. The Left Bank area: Latin Quarter with famous Sorbonne university; Museum of Cluny housing medieval art; the Panthéon; Luxembourg Palace and Gardens; Montparnasse, interwar artistic and literary centre; Eiffel Tower; Hôtel des Invalides with Napoleon's tomb. Right Bank: the great boulevards (Avenue des Champs-Élysées joining the Arc de Triomphe and Place de la Concorde); 19c Opéra Quarter; Marais, former aristocratic quarter of elegant mansions (Place des Vosges); Bois de Boulogne, the largest park in Paris; Montmartre, centre of 19c bohemianism, with the Basilique Sacré-Coeur. The Church of St Denis is the first gothic

church and the mausoleum of the French monarchy. Paris has three of the world's greatest art collections: The Louvre (to 19c, *Mona Lisa*), Musée d'Orsay (19–20c) and National Modern Art Museum in the Pompidou Centre. Other major museums include: Orangery Museum; Paris Museum of Modern Art; Rodin Museum; Picasso Museum. Notable cemeteries with graves of the famous: Père-Lachaise, Montmartre, Montparnasse. Near Paris are the royal residences of Fontainebleau and Versailles. www.paris.fr 90 C2

Pyrenees

Beautiful unspoiled mountain range. Towns include: delightful sea resorts of St-Jean-de-Luz and Biarritz; Pau, with access to the Pyrenees National Park; pilgrimage centre Lourdes. www.pyrenees-online.fr 144–145

Reims

Together with nearby Epernay, the centre of champagne production. The 13c Gothic cathedral is one of the greatest architectural achievements in France (stained glass by Chagall). Other sights: Palais du Tau with cathedral sculpture, 11c Basilica of St Rémi; cellars on Place St-Niçaise and Place des Droits-des-Hommes. www.reims-tourisme.com 91 B4

Rouen

Old centre with many half-timbered houses and 12–13c Gothic cathedral and the Gothic Church of St Maclou with its fascinating remains of a dance macabre on the former cemetery of Aître St-Maclou. The Fine Arts Museum has a good collection. www.mairie-rouen.fr 89 A5

St-Malo

Fortified town (much rebuilt) in a fine coastal setting. There is a magnificent boat trip along the river Rance to Dinan, a splendid well-preserved medieval town. www.saint-malo.fr 101 A3

Strasbourg

Town whose historic centre includes a well-preserved quarter of medieval half-timbered Alsatian houses, many of them set on the canal. The cathedral is one of the best in France. The Palais Rohan contains several museums. www.strasbourg.fr 93 C3

Toulouse

Medieval university town characterised by flat pink brick (Hôtel Assézat). The Basilique St Sernin, the largest Romanesque church in France, has many art treasures. Marvellous Church of the Jacobins holds the body of St Thomas Aquinas. www.ot-toulouse.fr 129 C4

Tours

Historic town centred on Place Plumereau. Good collections in the Guilds Museum and Fine Arts Museum. www.tours.fr 102 B2

Versailles

Vast royal palace built for Louis XIV, primarily by Mansart, set in large formal gardens with magnificent fountains. The extensive and much-imitated state apartments include the famous Hall of Mirrors and the exceptional Baroque chapel. www.chateauversailles.fr 90 C2

Vézère Valley Caves

A number of prehistoric sites, most notably the cave paintings of Lascaux (some 17,000 years old), now only seen in a duplicate cave, and the cave of Font de Gaume. The National Museum of Prehistory is in Les Eyzies. www.leseyzies.com 129 B4

Germany Deutschland

www.germany-tourism.de

Northern Germany

Aachen

Once capital of the Holy Roman Empire. Old town around the Münsterplatz with magnificent cathedral. An exceptionally rich treasure is in the Schatzkammer. The Town Hall is on the medieval Market. www.aachen.de 80 B2

Berlin

Capital of Germany. Sights include: the Kurfürstendamm avenue; Brandenburg Gate, former symbol of the division between East and West Germany; Tiergarten; Unter den Linden; 19c Reichstag. Berlin has many excellent art and history collections. Museum Island includes: Pergamon Museum (classical antiquity, Near and Far East, Islam); Bode Museum (Egyptian, Early Christian, Byzantine and European); Old National Gallery (19–20c German); Dahlem Museums: Picture Gallery (13–18c); Sculpture Collection (13–19c); Prints and Drawings Collection; Di

Brücke Museum (German Expressionism). Tiergarten Museums: New National Gallery (19–20c); Decorative Arts Museum; Bauhaus Archive. In the Kreuzberg area: Berlin Museum; Grupius Building with Jewish Museum and Berlin Gallery; remains of Berlin Wall and Checkpoint Charlie House. Schloss Charlottenburg houses a number of collections including the National Gallery's Romantic Gallery; the Egyptian Museum is nearby. www.berlin-tourist-information.de **74 B2**

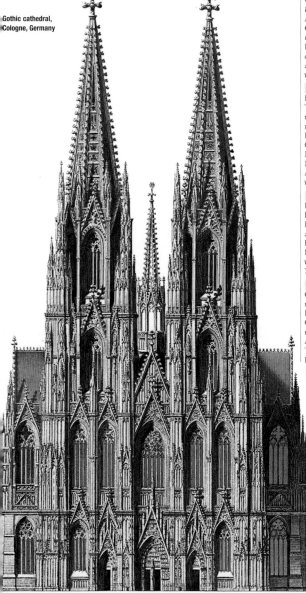

Gothic cathedral, Cologne, Germany

Cologne Köln
Ancient city with 13–19c cathedral (rich display of art). In the old town are the Town Hall and many Romanesque churches (Gross St Martin, St Maria im Kapitol, St Maria im Lyskirchen, St Ursula, St Georg, St Severin, St Pantaleon, St Apostolen).

Dresden
Historic centre with a rich display of Baroque architecture. Major buildings: Castle of the Electors of Saxony; 18c Hofkirche; Zwinger Palace with fountains and pavilions (excellent old masters); Albertinum with excellent Gallery of New Masters; treasury of Grünes Gewölbe. The Baroque-planned New Town contains the Japanese Palace and Schloss Pillnitz. www.dresden.de **84 A1**

Frankfurt
Financial capital of Germany. The historic centre around the Römerberg Square has 13–15c cathedral, 15c Town Hall, Gothic St Nicholas Church, Saalhof (12c chapel). Museums: Museum of Modern Art (post-war); State Art Institute. www.frankfurt.de **81 B4**

Hamburg
Port city with many parks, lakes and canals. The Kunsthalle has Old Masters and 19-20c German art. Buildings: 19c Town Hall; Baroque St Michael's Church. www.hamburg-tourismus.de **72 A3**

Hildesheim
City of Romanesque architecture (much destroyed). Principal sights: St Michael's Church; cathedral (11c interior, sculptured doors, St Anne's Chapel); superb 15c Tempelhaus on the Market Place. www.hildesheim.de **72 B2**

Lübeck
Beautiful old town built on an island and characterised by Gothic brick architecture. Sights: 15c Holsten Gate; Market with the Town Hall and Gothic brick St Mary's Church; 12–13c cathedral; St Ann Museum. www.luebeck-tourism.de **65 C3**

Mainz
The Electoral Palatinate schloss and Market fountain are Renaissance. Churches: 12c Romanesque cathedral; Gothic St Steven's (with stained glass by Marc Chagall). www.mainz.de **93 A4**

Marburg
Medieval university town with the Market Place

Museums: Diocesan Museum (religious art); Roman-German Museum (ancient history); Wallraf-Richartz/Ludwig Museum (14–20c art). www.koeln.de **80 B2**

and Town Hall, St Elizabeth's Church (frescoes, statues, 13c shrine), 15–16c schloss. www.marburg.de **81 B4**

Münster
Historic city with well-preserved Gothic and Renaissance buildings: 14c Town Hall; Romanesque-Gothic cathedral. The Westphalian Museum holds regional art. www.munster.de **71 C4**

Potsdam
Beautiful Sanssouci Park contains several 18–19c buildings including: Schloss Sanssouci; Gallery (European masters); Orangery; New Palace; Chinese Teahouse. www.potsdam.de **74 B2**

Rhein Valley Rheintal
Beautiful 80km gorge of the Rhein Valley between Mainz and Koblenz with rocks (Loreley), vineyards (Bacharach, Rüdesheim), white medieval towns (Rhens, Oberwesel) and castles. Some castles are medieval (Marksburg, Rheinfles, island fortress Pfalzgrafenstein) others were built or rebuilt in the 19c (Stolzenfles, Rheinstein). www.rheintal.de **80 B3**

Weimar
The Neoclassical schloss, once an important seat of government, now houses a good art collection. Church of SS Peter and Paul has a Cranach masterpiece. Houses of famous people: Goethe, Schiller, Liszt. The famous Bauhaus was founded at the School of Architecture and Engineering. www.weimar.de **82 B3**

Southern Germany

Alpine Road Deutsche Alpenstrasse
German Alpine Road in the Bavarian Alps, from Lindau on Bodensee to Berchtesgaden. The setting for 19c fairy-tale follies of Ludwig II of Bavaria (Linderhof, Hohenschwangau, Neuschwanstein), charming old villages (Oberammergau) and Baroque churches (Weiss, Ottobeuren). Garmisch-Partenkirchen has views on Germany's highest peak, the Zugspitze. www.deutsche-alpenstrasse.de **108 B2**

Augsburg
Attractive old city. The Town Hall is one of Germany's finest Renaissance buildings. Maximilianstrasse has several Renaissance houses and Rococo Schaezler Palace (good art collection). Churches:

Romanesque-Gothic cathedral; Renaissance St Anne's Church. The Fuggerei, founded 1519 as an estate for the poor, is still in use. www.augsburg.de **94 C2**

Bamberg
Well-preserved medieval town. The island, connected by two bridges, has the Town Hall and views of Klein Venedig. Romanesque-Gothic cathedral (good art) is on an exceptional square of Gothic, Renaissance and Baroque buildings – Alte Hofhaltung; Neue Residenz with State Gallery (German masters); Ratstube. www.bamberg.info **94 B2**

Black Forest
Schwarzwald
Hilly region between Basel and Karlsruhe, the largest and most picturesque woodland in Germany, with the highest summit, Feldberg, lake resorts (Titisee), health resorts (Baden-Baden) and clock craft (Triberg). Freiburg is regional capital. www.schwarzwald.de **93 C4**

Freiburg
Old university town with system of streams running through the streets. The Gothic Minster is surrounded by the town's finest buildings. Two towers remain of the medieval walls. The Augustine Museum has a good collection. www.freiburg.de **106 B2**

Heidelberg
Germany's oldest university town, majestically set on the banks of the river and romantically dominated by the ruined schloss. The Gothic Church of the Holy Spirit is on the Market Place with the Baroque Town Hall. Other sights include the 16c Knight's House and the Baroque Morass Palace with a museum of Gothic art. www.heidelberg.de **93 B4**

Lake Constance
Bodensee
Lake Constance, with many pleasant lake resorts. Lindau, on an island, has numerous gabled houses. Birnau has an 18c Rococo church. Konstanz (Swiss side) has the Minster set above the Old Town. www.bodensee.de **107 B4**

Munich München
Old town centred on the Marienplatz with 15c Old Town Hall and 19c New Town Hall. Many richly decorated churches: St Peter's (14c tower); Gothic red-brick

cathedral; Renaissance St Michael's (royal portraits on the façade); Rococo St Asam's. The Residenz palace consists of seven splendid buildings holding many art objects. Schloss Nymphenburg has a palace, park, botanical gardens and four beautiful pavilions. Superb museums: Old Gallery (old masters), New Gallery (18–19c), Lenbachhaus (modern German). Many famous beer gardens. www.muenchen.de **108 A2**

Nuremberg Nürnberg
Beautiful medieval walled city dominated by the 12c Kaiserburg. Romanesque-Gothic St Sebaldus Church and Gothic St Laurence Church are rich in art. On Hauptmarkt is the famous 14c Schöner Brunnen. Also notable is 15c Dürer House. The German National Museum has excellent German medieval and Renaissance art. www.nuernberg.de **94 B3**

Regensburg
Medieval city set majestically on the Danube. Views from 12c Steinerne Brücke. Churches: Gothic cathedral; Romanesque St Jacob's; Gothic St Blaisius; Baroque St Emmeram. Other sights: Old Town Hall (museum); Haidplatz; Schloss Thurn und Taxis; State Museum. www.regensburg.de **95 B4**

Romantic Road
Romantische Strasse
Romantic route between Aschaffenburg and Füssen, leading through picturesque towns and villages of medieval Germany. The most popular section is the section between Würzburg and Augsburg, centred on Rothenburg ob der Tauber. Also notable are Nördlingen, Harburg Castle, Dinkelsbühl, Creglingen. www.romantischestrasse.de **94 B2**

Rothenburg ob der Tauber
Attractive medieval walled town with tall gabled and half-timbered houses on narrow cobbled streets. The Market Place has Gothic-Renaissance Town Hall, Rattrinke-stube and Gothic St Jacob's Church (altarpiece). www.rothenburg.de **94 B2**

Speyer
The 11c cathedral is one of the largest and best Romanesque buildings in Germany. 12c Jewish Baths are well-preserved. www.speyer.de **93 B4**

Stuttgart
Largely modern city with old centre around the Old Schloss, Renaissance Alte Kanzlei, 15c Collegiate Church and Baroque New Schloss. Museums: Regional Museum; post-modern State Gallery (old masters, 20c German). The 1930s Weissenhofsiedlung is by several famous architects. www.stuttgart.de **94 C1**

Trier
Superb Roman monuments: Porta Nigra; Aula Palatina (now a church); Imperial Baths; amphitheatre. The Regional Museum has Roman artefacts. Also, Gothic Church of Our Lady; Romanesque cathedral. www.trier.de **92 B2**

Ulm
Old town with half-timbered gabled houses set on a canal. Gothic 14–19c minster has tallest spire in the world (161m). www.tourismus.ulm.de **94 C1**

Würzburg
Set among vineyard hills, the medieval town is centred on the Market Place with the Rococo House of the Falcon. The 18c episcopal princes' residence (frescoes) is magnificent. The cathedral is rich in art. Work of the great local Gothic sculptor, Riemenschneider, is in Gothic St Mary's Chapel, Baroque New Minster, and the Mainfränkisches Museum. www.wuerzburg.de **94 B1**

Great Britain
www.visitbritain.com

England

Bath
Elegant spa town with notable 18c architecture: Circus, Royal Crescent, Pulteney Bridge, Assembly Rooms; Pump Room. Also: well-preserved Roman baths; superb Perpendicular Gothic Bath Abbey. Nearby: Elizabethan Longleat House; exceptional 18c landscaped gardens at Stourhead. www.visitbath.co.uk **43 A4**

Brighton
Resort with a sea-front of Georgian, Regency and Victorian buildings with the Palace Pier, and an old town of narrow lanes. The main sight is the 19c Royal Pavilion in Oriental styles. www.brighton.co.uk **44 C3**

Bristol
Old port city with the fascinating Floating Harbour.

Major sights include Gothic 13–14c Church of St Mary Redcliffe and 19c Clifton Suspension Bridge. www.visitbristol.co.uk **43 A4**

Cambridge
City with university founded in the early 13c. Peterhouse (1284) is the oldest college. Most famous colleges were founded in 14–16c: Queen's, King's (with the superb Perpendicular Gothic 15–16c King's College Chapel), St John's (with famous 19c Bridge of Sighs), Trinity, Clare, Gonville and Caius, Magdalene. Museums: excellent Fitzwilliam Museum (classical, medieval, old masters). Kettle's Yard (20c British). www.visitcambridge.org **45 A4**

Canterbury
Medieval city and old centre of Christianity. The Norman-Gothic cathedral has many sights and was a major medieval pilgrimage site (as related in Chaucer's *Canterbury Tales*). St Augustine, sent to convert the English in 597, founded St Augustine's Abbey, now in ruins. www.canterbury.co.uk **45 B5**

Chatsworth
One of the richest aristocratic country houses in England (largely 17c) set in a large landscaped park. The palatial interior has some 175 richly furnished rooms and a major art collection. www.chatsworth-house.co.uk **40 B2**

Chester
Charming medieval city with complete walls. The Norman-Gothic cathedral has several abbey buildings. www.visitchester.co.uk **38 A4**

Cornish Coast
Scenic landscape of cliffs and sandy beaches (the north coast being a popular surfing destination) with picturesque villages (Fowey, Mevagissey). St Ives has the Tate Gallery with work of the St Ives Group. The island of St Michael's Mount holds a priory. www.cornwalltouristboard.co.uk **42 B1**

Dartmoor
Beautiful wilderness area in Devon with tors and its own breed of wild pony as well as free-ranging cattle and sheep. www.dartmoor-npa.gov.uk **42 B3**

Durham
Historic city with England's finest Norman cathedral and a

castle, both placed majestically on a rock above the river. www.durham.gov.uk **37 B5**

Eden Project
Centre showing the diversity of plant life on the planet, built in a disused clay pit. Two biomes, one with Mediterranean and Southern African focus and the larger featuring a waterfall, river and tropical trees plants and flowers. Outdoors also features plantations including bamboo and tea. www.edenproject.com **42 B2**

Hadrian's Wall
Built to protect the northernmost border of the Roman Empire in the 2c AD, the walls originally extended some 120km with castles every mile and 16 forts. Best-preserved walls around Hexam; forts at Housesteads and Chesters. www.hadrians-wall.org **37 A4**

Lake District
Beautiful landscape of lakes (Windermere, Coniston) and England's high peaks (Scafell Pike, Skiddaw, Old Man), famous for its poets, particularly Wordsworth. www.lake-district.gov.uk **36 B3**

Leeds Castle
One of the oldest and most romantic English castles, standing in the middle of a lake. Most of the present appearance dates from 19c. www.leeds-castle.com **45 B4**

Lincoln
Old city perched on a hill with narrow streets, majestically dominated by the Norman-Gothic cathedral and castle. www.visitlincolnshire.co.uk **40 B3**

Liverpool
City on site of port founded in 1207 and focused around 1846 Albert Dock, now a heritage attraction. Croxteth Hall and Country Park; Speke Hall; Sudley House; Royal Liver Building; Liverpool cathedral; Walker Art Gallery; University of Liverpool Art Gallery. www.visitliverpool.com **38 A4**

London
Capital of UK and Europe's largest city. To the east of the medieval heart of the city – now the largely modern financial district and known as the City of London – is the Tower of London (11c White Tower, Crown Jewels) and 1880s Tower Bridge. The popular heart of the city and its entertainment is the West End, around Piccadilly

Circus, Leicester Square and Trafalgar Square (Nelson's Column). Many sights of political and royal power: Whitehall (Banqueting House, 10 Downing Street, Horse Guards); Neo-Gothic Palace of Westminster (Houses of Parliament) with Big Ben; The Mall leading to Buckingham Palace (royal residence, famous ceremony of the Changing of the Guard). Numerous churches include: 13–16c Gothic Westminster Abbey (many tombs, Henry VII's Chapel); Wren's Baroque St Paul's Cathedral, St Mary-le-Bow, spire of St Bride's, St Stephen Walbrook. Museums of world fame: British Museum (prehistory, oriental and classical antiquity, medieval); Victoria and Albert Museum (decorative arts); National Gallery (old masters to 19c); National Portrait Gallery (historic and current British portraiture); Tate – Britain and Modern; Science Museum; Natural History Museum. Madame Tussaud's waxworks museum is hugely popular. Other sights include: London Eye, Kensington Palace; Greenwich with Old Royal Observatory (Greenwich meridian), Baroque Royal Naval College, Palladian Queen's House; Tudor Hampton Court Palace; Syon House. Nearby: Windsor Castle (art collection, St George's Chapel).
www.visitlondon.com **44 B3**

Longleat
One of the earliest and finest Elizabethan palaces in

Gothic cathedral (cutaway), Salisbury, England

England. The palace is richly decorated. Some of the grounds have been turned into a pleasure park, with the Safari Park, the first of its kind outside Africa.
www.longleat.co.uk **43 A4**

Manchester
Founded on a Roman settlement of 79AD and a main player in the Industrial Revolution. Victorian Gothic Town Hall; Royal Exchange; Cathedral. Many museums including Imperial War Museum North, Lowry Centre and Manchester Art Gallery.
www.visitmanchester.com **40 B1**

Newcastle
A key player in the Industrial Revolution with 12th century cathedral and many museums as well as strong railway heritage.
www.visitnewcastle.co.uk **37 B5**

Norwich
Medieval quarter has half-timbered houses. 15c castle keep houses a museum and gallery. Many medieval churches include the Norman-Gothic cathedral.
www.visitnorwich.co.uk **41 C5**

Oxford
Old university city. Earliest colleges date from 13c: University College; Balliol; Merton. 14–16c colleges include: New College; Magdalen; Christ Church (perhaps the finest). Other buildings: Bodleian Library; Radcliffe Camera; Sheldonian Theatre; cathedral. Good museums: Ashmolean

Museum (antiquity to 20c); Museum of Modern Art; Christ Church Picture Gallery (14–17c). Nearby: outstanding 18c Blenheim Palace.
www.visitoxford.org **44 B2**

Petworth
House (17c) with one of the finest country-house art collections (old masters), set in a huge landscaped park.
www.nationaltrust.org.uk **44 C3**

Salisbury
Pleasant old city with a magnificent 13c cathedral built in an unusually unified Gothic style. Nearby: Wilton House.
www.visitsalisburyuk.com **44 B2**

Stonehenge
Some 4000 years old, one of the most famous and haunting Neolithic monuments in Europe. Many other Neolithic sites are nearby.
www.english-heritage.org.uk **44 B2**

Stourhead
Early 18c palace famous for its grounds, one of the finest examples of neoclassical landscaped gardening, consist-

ing of a lake surrounded by numerous temples.
www.nationaltrust.org.uk **43 A4**

Stratford-upon-Avon
Old town of Tudor and Jacobean half-timbered houses, famed as the birth and burial place of William Shakespeare. Nearby: Warwick Castle.
www.shakespeare-country.co.uk **44 A2**

Wells
Charming city with beautiful 12–16c cathedral (west facade, scissor arches, chapter house, medieval clock). Also Bishop's Palace; Vicar's Close. **43 A4**

Winchester
Historic city with 11–16c cathedral (tombs of early English kings). Also: 13c Great Hall; Winchester College; St Cross almshouses.
www.visitwinchester.co.uk **44 B2**

York
Attractive medieval city surrounded by well-preserved walls with magnificent Gothic 13–15c Minster. Museums: York City Art Gallery (14–19c); Jorvik Viking Centre. Nearby: Castle Howard.
www.york-tourism.co.uk **40 B2**

Scotland

Edinburgh
Capital of Scotland, built on volcanic hills. The medieval Old Town is dominated by the castle set high on a volcanic rock (Norman St Margaret's Chapel, state apartments, Crown Room). Holyrood House (15c and 17c) has lavishly decorated state apartments and the ruins of Holyrood Abbey (remains of Scottish monarchs). The 15c cathedral has the Crown Spire and Thistle Chapel. The

New Town has good Georgian architecture (Charlotte Square, Georgian House). Excellent museums: Scottish National Portrait Gallery, National Gallery of Scotland; Scottish National Gallery of Modern Art.
www.edinburgh.org **35 C4**

Glamis Castle
In beautiful, almost flat landscaped grounds, 14c fortress, rebuilt 17c, gives a fairy-tale impression.
www.glamis-castle.co.uk **35 B5**

Glasgow
Scotland's largest city, with centre around George Square and 13–15c Gothic cathedral. The Glasgow School of Art is the masterpiece of Charles Rennie Mackintosh. Fine art collections: Glasgow Museum and Art Gallery; Hunterian Gallery; Burrell Collection.
www.seeglasgow.com **35 C3**

Loch Ness
In the heart of the Highlands, the lake forms part of the scenic Great Glen running from Inverness to Fort William. Famous as home of the fabled Loch Ness Monster (exhibition at Drumnadrochit). Nearby: ruins of 14–16c Urquhart Castle. **32 D2**
www.loch-ness-scotland.com

Wales

Caernarfon
Town dominated by a magnificent 13c castle, one of a series built by Edward I in Wales (others include Harlech, Conwy, Beaumaris, Caerphilly).
www.visitcaernarfon.com **38 A2**

Cardiff
Capital of Wales, most famous for its medieval castle, restored 19c in Greek, Gothic and Oriental styles. Also: National Museum and Gallery.
www.visitcardiff.info **39 C3**

Greece Ellas
www.gnto.gr

Athens Athina
Capital of Greece. The Acropolis, with 5c BC sanctuary complex (Parthenon, Propylaia, Erechtheion, Temple of Athena Nike), is the greatest architectural achievement of antiquity in Europe. The Agora was a public meeting place in ancient Athens. Plaka has narrow streets and small Byzantine churches (Kapnikarea). The Olympeum was

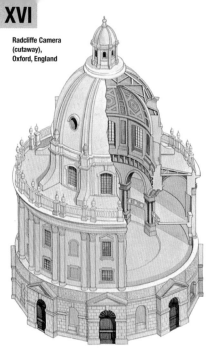

Radcliffe Camera (cutaway), Oxford, England

---

the largest temple in Greece. Also: Olympic Stadium; excellent collections of ancient artefacts (Museum of Cycladic and Ancient Greek Art; Acropolis Museum; National Archeological Museum; Benaki Museum). www.athens.gr **185 B4**

Corinth Korinthos
Ancient Corinth (ruins), with 5c BC Temple of Apollo, was in 44 BC made capital of Roman Greece by Julius Caesar. Set above the city, the Greek-built acropolis hill of Acrocorinth became the Roman and Byzantine citadel (ruins). **184 B3**

Crete Kriti
Largest Greek island, Crete was home to the great Minoan civilization (2800–1100 BC). The main relics are the ruined Palace of Knossos and Malia. Gortys was capital of the Roman province. Picturesque Rethimno has narrow medieval streets, a Venetian fortress and a former Turkish mosque. Matala has beautiful beaches and famous caves cut into cliffs. Iraklio (Heraklion), the capital, has a good Archeological Museum. **185 D6**

Delphi
At the foot of the Mount Parnassos, Delphi was the seat of the Delphic Oracle of Apollo, the most important oracle in Ancient Greece. Delphi was also a political meeting place and the site of the Pythian Games. The Sanctuary of Apollo consists of: Temple of Apollo, led to by the Sacred Way; Theatre; Stadium. The museum has a display of objects from the site (5c BC Charioteer). www.delphi.gr **182 E4**

Epidavros
Formerly a spa and religious centre focused on the Sanctuary of Asclepius (ruins). The enormous 4c BC theatre is probably the finest of all ancient theatres. www.ancientepidavros.org **184 B4**

Greek Islands
Popular islands with some of the most beautiful and spectacular beaches in Europe. The many islands are divided into various groups and individual islands: The major groups are the Kiklades and Dodekanisa in the Aegean Sea, the largest islands are Kerkyra (Corfu) in the Ionian Sea and Kriti. **182–185 & 188**

Meteora
The tops of bizarre vertical cylinders of rock and towering cliffs are the setting for 14c Cenobitic monasteries, until recently only accessible by baskets or removable ladders. Mega Meteoro is the grandest and set on the highest point. Roussánou has the most extraordinary site. Varlaám is one of the oldest and most beautiful, with the Ascent Tower and 16c church with frescoes. Aghiou Nikolaou also has good frescoes. **182 D3**

Mistras
Set in a beautiful landscape, Mistras is the site of a Byzantine city, now in ruins, with palaces, frescoed churches, monasteries and houses. **184 B3**

Mount Olympus
Oros Olymbos
Mount Olympus, mythical seat of the Greek gods, is the highest, most dramatic peak in Greece. **182 C4**

Mycenae Mikines
The citadel of Mycenae prospered between 1950 BC and 1100 BC and consists of the royal complex of Agamemnon: Lion Gate, royal burial site, Royal Palace, South House, Great Court. **184 B3**

Olympia
In a stunning setting, the Panhellenic Games were held here for a millennium. Ruins of the sanctuary of Olympia consist of the Doric temples of Zeus and Hera and the vast Stadium. There is also a museum (4c BC figure of Hermes). **184 B2**

Rhodes
One of the most attractive islands with wonderful sandy beaches. The city of Rhodes has a well-preserved medieval centre with the Palace of the Grand Masters and the Turkish Süleymaniye Mosque **188 C2**

Salonica Thessaloniki
Largely modern city with Byzantine walls and many fine churches: 8c Aghia Sofia; 11c Panaghia Halkeo; 14c Dodeka Apostoli; 14c Aghios Nikolaos Orfanos; 5c Aghios Dimitrios (largest in Greece, 7c Mosaics). www.thessalonikicity.gr **183 C5**

Hungary
Magyarország
www.hungarytourism.hu

Balaton
The 'Hungarian sea', famous for its holiday resorts: Balatonfüred, Tihany, Badacsonytomaj, Keszthely. www.balaton.hu **111 C4**

Budapest
Capital of Hungary on River Danube, with historic area centring on the Castle Hill of Buda district. Sights include: Matthias church; Pest district with late 19c architecture, centred on Ferenciek tere; neo-Gothic Parliament Building on river; Millennium Monument. The Royal Castle houses a number of museums: Hungarian National Gallery, Budapest History Museum; Ludwig Collection. Other museums: National Museum of Fine Arts (excellent Old and Modern masters); Hungarian National Museum (Hungarian history). Famous for public thermal baths: Király and Rudas baths, both made under Turkish rule; Gellért baths, the most visited. www.budapestinfo.hu **112 B3**

Esztergom
Medieval capital of Hungary set in scenic landscape. Sights: Hungary's largest basilica (completed 1856); royal palace ruins. www.esztergom.hu **112 B2**

Pécs
Attractive old town with Europe's fifth oldest university (founded 1367). Famous for Turkish architecture (Mosque of Gazi Kasim Pasha, Jakovali Hassan Mosque). www.pecs.hu **125 A4**

Sopron
Beautiful walled town with many Gothic and Renaissance houses. Nearby: Fertőd with the marvellous Eszergázy Palace. www.sopron.hu **111 B3**

Ireland
www.discoverireland.com

Northern Ireland

Antrim Coast
Spectacular coast with diverse scenery of glens (Glenarm, Glenariff), cliffs (Murlough Bay) and the famous Giant's Causeway, consisting of some 40,000 basalt columns. Carrickfergus Castle is the largest and best-preserved Norman castle in Ireland. www.northantrim.com **27 A4**

Belfast
Capital of Northern Ireland. Sights: Donegall Square with 18c Town Hall; neo-Romanesque Protestant cathedral; University Square; Ulster Museum (European painting). www.gotobelfast.com **27 B5**

Giant's Causeway
Spectacular and unique rock formations in the North Antrim coast, formed by volcanic activity 50–60 million years ago. World Heritage Site. www.northantrim.com **27 A4**

Republic of Ireland

Aran Islands
Islands with spectacular cliffs and notable pre-Christian and Christian sights, especially on Inishmore. www.visitaranislands.com **26 B2**

Cashel
Town dominated by the Rock of Cashel (61m) topped by ecclesiastical ruins including 13c cathedral; 15c Halls of the Vicars; beautiful Romanesque 12c Cormac's Chapel (fine carvings). www.connemar-tourism.org **29 B4**

Connemara
Beautiful wild landscape of mountains, lakes, peninsulas and beaches. Clifden is the capital. www.connemar-tourism.org **28 A1**

Cork
Pleasant city with its centre along St Patrick's Street and Grand Parade lined with fine 18c buildings. Churches: Georgian St Anne's Shandon (bell tower); 19c cathedral. www.corkcorp.ie **29 C3**

County Donegal
Rich scenic landscape of mystical lakes and glens and seascape of cliffs (Slieve League cliffs are the highest in Europe). The town of Donegal has a finely preserved Jacobean castle. www.donegaldirect.ie **26 B2**

Dublin
Capital of Ireland. City of elegant 18c neoclassical and Georgian architecture with gardens and parks (St Stephen's Green, Merrion Square with Leinster House – now seat of Irish parliament). City's main landmark, Trinity College (founded 1591), houses in its Old Library fine Irish manuscripts (7c Book of Durrow, 8c Book of Kells). Two Norman cathedrals: Christ Church; St Patrick's. Other buildings: originally medieval Dublin Castle with State Apartments; James Gandon's masterpieces: Custom House; Four Courts. Museums: National Museum (Irish history); National Gallery (old masters,

mpressionists, Irish painting); Guinness Brewery Museum; Dublin Writers' Museum (Joyce, Wilde, Yeats and others). www.visitdublin.com 30 A2

Glendalough

impressive ruins of an important early Celtic (6c) monastery with 9c cathedral, 12c St Kevin's Cross, oratory of St Kevin's Church. www.wicklow.com/glendalough 30 A2

Kilkenny

Charming medieval town, with narrow streets dominated by 12c castle (restored 19c). The 13c Gothic cathedral has notable tomb monuments. www.kilkenny.ie 30 B1

Newgrange

One of the best passage graves in Europe, the massive 4500-year-old tomb has stones richly decorated with patterns. www.knowth.com/newgrange 30 A2

Ring of Kerry

Route around the Iveragh peninsula with beautiful lakes (Lough Leane), peaks overlooking the coastline and islands (Valencia Island, Skelling). Also: Killarney; ruins of 15c Muckross Abbey. www.ringofkerrytourism.com 9 B2

Italy Italia

www.enit.it

Northern Italy

Alps

Wonderful stretch of the Alps running from the Swiss and French borders to Austria. The region of Valle d'Aosta is one of the most popular ski regions, bordered by the highest peaks of the Alps. www.thealps.com 108–109 & 119–120

Arezzo

Beautiful old town set on a hill dominated by 13c cathedral. Piazza Grande is surrounded by medieval and Renaissance palaces. Main sight: Piero della Francesca's frescoes in the choir of San Francesco. www.arezzocitta.com 135 B4

Assisi

Hill-top town that attracts crowds of pilgrims to the shrine of St Francis of Assisi at the Basilica di San Francesco, consisting of two churches, Lower and Upper, with superb frescoes (particularly Giotto's in the Upper). www.assisi.com 136 B1

Bologna

Elegant city with oldest uni-versity in Italy. Historical centre around Piazza Maggiore and Piazza del Nettuno with the Town Hall, Palazzo del Podestà, Basilica di San Petronio. Other churches: San Domenico; San Giacomo Maggiore. The two towers (one incomplete) are symbols of the city. Good collec-tion in the National Gallery (Bolognese). www.commune.bologna.it/bolognaturismo 135 A4

Dolomites Dolomiti

Part of the Alps, this mountain range spreads over the region of Trentino-Alto Adige, with the most picturesque scenery between Bolzano and Cortina d'Ampezzo. www.dolomiti.it 121 A4

Ferrara

Old town centre around Romanesque-Gothic cathedral and Palazzo Communale. Also: Castello Estense; Palazzo Schifanoia (frescoes); Palazzo dei Diamanti housing Pinacoteca Nazionale. www.ferraraturismo.it 121 C4

Florence Firenze

City with exceptionally rich medieval and Renaissance heritage. Piazza del Duomo has:13–15c cathedral (first dome since antiquity); 14c campanile; 11c baptistry (bronze doors). Piazza della Signoria has: 14c Palazzo Vecchio (frescoes); Loggia della Signoria (sculpture); 16c Uffizi Gallery with one of the world's greatest collections (13–18c). Other great paintings: Museo di San Marco; Palatine Gallery in 15–16c

Pitti Palace surrounded by Boboli Gardens. Sculpture: Cathedral Works Museum; Bargello Museum; Academy Gallery (Michelangelo's David). Among many other Renaissance palaces: Medici-Riccardi; Rucellai; Strozzi. The 15c church of San Lorenzo has Michelangelo's tombs of the Medici. Many churches have richly frescoed chapels: Santa Maria Novella, Santa Croce, Santa Maria del Carmine. The 13c Ponte Vecchio is one of the most famous sights. www.firenzeturismo.it 135 B4

Italian Lakes

Beautiful district at the foot of the Alps, most of the lakes with holiday resorts. Many lakes are surrounded by aristocratic villas (Maggiore, Como, Garda). 120–121

Mantua Mántova

Attractive city surrounded by three lakes. Two exceptional palaces: Palazzo Ducale (Sala del Pisanello; Camera degli Sposi, Castello San Giorgio); luxurious Palazzo Tè (brilliant frescoes). Also: 15c Church of Sant'Andrea; 13c law courts. www.mantova.com 121 B3

Milan Milano

Modern city, Italy's fashion and design capital (Corso and

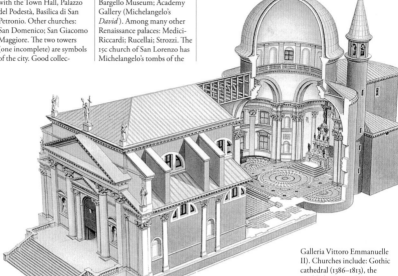

Il Redentore (cutaway), Venice, Italy

Galleria Vittoro Emmanuelle II). Churches include: Gothic cathedral (1386–1813), the world's largest (4c baptistry); Romanesque St Ambrose; 15c San Satiro; Santa Maria delle Grazie with Leonardo da Vinci's Last Supper in the convent refectory. Great art collections, Brera Gallery, Ambrosian Library, Museum of Contemporary Art. Castello Sforzesco (15c, 19c) also has a gallery. The famous La Scala theatre opened in 1778. Nearby: monastery at Pavia. www.milaninfotourist.com 120 B2

Romanesque cathedral, Pisa, Italy

Padua Pádova

Pleasant old town with arcaded streets. Basilica del Santo is a place of pilgrimage to the tomb of St Anthony. Giotto's frescoes in the Scrovegni chapel are exceptional. Also: Piazza dei Signori with Palazzo del Capitano; vast Palazzo della Ragione; church of the Eremitani (frescoes). www.turismopadova.it 121 B4

Parma

Attractive city centre, famous for Corregio's frescoes in the Romanesque cathedral and church of St John the Evangelist, and Parmigianino's frescoes in the church of Madonna della Steccata. Their works are also in the National Gallery. www.commune.parma.it 120 C3

Perúgia

Hill-top town centred around Piazza Quattro Novembre with the cathedral, Fontana Maggiore and Palazzo dei Priori. Also: Collegio di Cambio (frescoes); National Gallery of Umbria; many churches. www.perugiaonline.com 136 B1

Pisa

Medieval town centred on the Piazza dei Miracoli. Sights: famous Romanesque Leaning Tower, Romanesque cathedral (excellent façade, Gothic pulpit); 12–13c Baptistry; 13c Camposanto cloistered cemetery (fascinating 14c frescoes). www.commune.pisa.it 134 B3

Ravenna

Ancient town with exceptionally well-preserved Byzantine mosaics. The finest are in 5c Mausoleo di Galla Placidia and 6c Basilica di San Vitale. Good mosaics also in the basilicas of Sant'Apollinare in Classe and Sant'Apollinare Nuovo. www.turismo.ravenna.it 135 A5

Siena

Outstanding 13–14c medieval town centred on beautiful Piazza del Campo with Gothic Palazzo Publico (frescoes of secular life). Delightful Romanesque-Gothic Duomo (Libreria Piccolomini, baptistry, art works). Many other richly decorated churches. Fine Sienese painting in Pinacoteca Nazionale and Museo dell'Opera del Duomo. www.terresiena.it 135 B4

Turin Torino

City centre has 17-18c Baroque layout dominated by twin Baroque churches. Also:

15c cathedral (holds Turin Shroud); Palazzo Reale; 18c Superga Basilica; Academy of Science with two museums (Egyptian antiquities; European painting). www.commune.torino.it 119 B4

Urbino

Set in beautiful hilly landscape, Urbino's heritage is mainly due to the 15c court of Federico da Montefeltro at the magnificent Ducal Palace (notable Studiolo), now also a gallery. www.turismo.pesaurbino.it 136 B1

Venice Venezia

Stunning old city built on islands in a lagoon, with some 150 canals. The Grand Canal is crossed by the famous 16c Rialto Bridge and is lined with elegant palaces (Gothic Ca'd'Oro and Ca'Foscari, Renaissance Palazzo Grimani, Baroque Rezzonico). The district of San Marco has the core of the best known sights and is centred on Piazza San Marco with 11c Basilica di San Marco (bronze horses, 13c mosaics); Campanile (exceptional views) and Ducal Palace (connected with the prison by the famous Bridge of Sighs). Many churches (Santa Maria Gloriosa dei Frari, Santa Maria della Salute, Redentore, San Giorgio Maggiore, San Giovanni e Paolo) and scuole (Scuola di San Rocco, Scuola di San Giorgio degli Schiavoni) have excellent works of art. The Gallery of the Academy houses superb 14–18c Venetian art. The Guggenheim Museum holds 20c art. http://english.comune.venezia.it 122 B1

Verona

Old town with remains of 1c Roman Arena and medieval sights including the Palazzo degli Scaligeri; Arche Scaligere; Romanesque Santa Maria Antica; Castelvecchio; Ponte Scaliger. The 14c House of Juliet has associations with *Romeo and Juliet*. Many churches with fine art works (cathedral; Sant'Anastasia; basilica di San Zeno Maggiore). www.tourism.verona.it 121 B4

Vicenza

Beautiful town, famous for the architecture of Palladio, including the Olympic Theatre (extraordinary stage), Corso Palladio with many of his palaces, and Palazzo Chiericati. Nearby: Villa Rotonda, the most influential

of all Palladian buildings. www.vicenzae.org 121 B4

Southern Italy

Naples Napoli

Historical centre around Gothic cathedral (crypt). Spaccanapoli area has numerous churches (bizarre Cappella Sansevero, Gesù Nuovo, Gothic Santa Chiara with fabulous tombs). Buildings: 13c Castello Nuovo; 13c Castel dell'Ovo; 15c Palazzo Cuomo. Museums: National Archeological Museum (artefacts from Pompeii and Herculaneum); National Museum of Capodimonte (Renaissance painting). Nearby: spectacular coast around Amalfi; Pompeii; Herculaneum. www.inaples.it 170 C2

Orvieto

Medieval hill-top town with a number of monuments including the Romanesque-Gothic cathedral (façade, frescoes). www.commune.orvieto.tr.it 168 A2

Rome Roma

Capital of Italy, exceptionally rich in sights from many eras. Ancient sights: Colosseum; Arch of Constantine; Trajan's

Column; Roman and Imperial fora; hills of Palatino and Campidoglio (Capitoline Museum shows antiquities); Pantheon; Castel Sant' Angelo; Baths of Caracalla). Early Christian sights: catacombs (San Calisto, San Sebastiano, Domitilla); basilicas (San Giovanni in Laterano, Santa Maria Maggiore, San Paolo Fuori le Mura). Rome is known for richly decorated Baroque churches: il Gesù, Sant'Ignazio, Santa Maria della Vittoria, Chiesa Nuova. Other churches, often with art treasures: Romanesque Santa Maria in Cosmedin, Gothic Santa Maria Sopra Minerva, Renaissance Santa Maria del Popolo, San Pietro in Vincoli. Several Renaissance and Baroque palaces and villas house superb art collections (Palazzo Barberini, Palazzo Doria Pamphilj, Palazzo Spada, Palazzo Corsini, Villa Giulia, Galleria Borghese) and are beautifully frescoed (Villa Farnesina). Fine Baroque public spaces with fountains: Piazza Navona; Piazza di Spagna with the Spanish Steps; also Trevi Fountain. Nearby: Tivoli; Villa Adriana. Rome also contains the Vatican City (Città del Vaticano). www.romaturismo.com 168 B2

Volcanic Region

Region from Naples to Sicily. Mount Etna is one of the most famous European volcanoes. Vesuvius dominates the Bay of Naples and has at its foot two of Italy's finest Roman sites,

Pompeii and Herculaneum, both destroyed by its eruption in 79ad. Stromboli is one of the beautiful Aeolian Islands.

Sardinia Sardegna

Sardinia has some of the most beautiful beaches in Italy (Alghero). Unique are the nuraghi, some 7000 stone constructions (Su Nuraxi, Serra Orios), the remains of an old civilization (1500–400 BC) Old towns include Cagliari and Sássari. www.sardi.it 178–179

Palazzo Publico, Siena, Italy

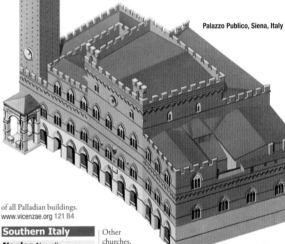

Sicily Sicilia

Surrounded by beautiful beaches and full of monuments of many periods, Sicily is the largest island in the Mediterranean. Taormina with its Greek theatre has one of the most spectacular beaches, lying under the mildly active volcano Mount Etna. Also: Agrigento; Palermo, Siracusa. www.regione.sicilia.it/turismo/web_turismo 176–177

Agrigento

Set on a hill above the sea and famed for the Valley of the Temples. The nine originally 5c BC Doric temples are Sicily's best-preserved Greek remains. www.agrigento-sicilia.it 176 B2

Palermo

City with Moorish, Norman and Baroque architecture, especially around the main squares (Quattro Canti, Piazza Pretoria, Piazza Bellini). Sights: remains of Norman palace (12c Palatine Chapel); Norman cathedral; Regional

Gallery (medieval); some ₂₀₀₀ preserved bodies in the ₂atacombs of the Cappuchin Convent. Nearby: 12c ₁orman Duomo di Monreale. ₁ww.commune.palermo.it ₁76 A2

₂yracuse Siracusa
₂uilt on an island connected ₂ the mainland by a bridge, ₂ old town has a 7c cathe-ral, ruins of the Temple of ₂pollo; Fountain of Arethusa; ₂rchaeological museum. On ₂e mainland: 5c BC Greek ₂heatre with seats cut out ₂f rock; Greek fortress of ₂uralus; 2c Roman amphi-₂heatre; 5–6c Catacombs of ₂t John.
₁ww.apt-siracusa.it
₁77 B4

₂atvia Latvija
₁ww.lv

₂iga
₂ell-preserved medieval town ₂entre around the cathedral. ₂ights: Riga Castle; medieval ₂lanseatic houses; Great Guild ₂lall; Gothic Church of St ₂eter; Art Nouveau buildings ₂ the New Town. Nearby: ₂aroque Rundale Castle.
₁ww.riga.lv 8 D4

₂ithuania Lietuva
₁ww.tourism.lt

₂ilnius
₂aroque old town with fine ₂rchitecture including: cathe-₂ral; Gediminas Tower; uni-₂ersity complex; Archbishop's ₂alace; Church of St Anne. ₂lso: remains of Jewish ₂fe; Vilnius Picture Gallery ₂6–19c regional); Lithuanian ₂ational Museum.
₁ww.vilnius.lt 13 A6

₂uxembourg
₁ww.ont.lu

₂uxembourg
₂apital of Luxembourg, built ₂ a rock with fine views. ₂ld town is around the Place ₂ Armes. Buildings: Grand ₂ucal Palace; fortifications of ₂ocher du Bock; cathedral. ₂luseum of History and Art ₂olds an excellent regional ₂ollection.
₁ww.ont.lu 92 B2

₂lacedonia Makedonija
₁ww.macedonia.org

₂kopje
₂istoric town with Turkish ₂tadel, fine 15c mosques, ori-₂tal bazaar, ancient bridge.

Superb Byzantine churches nearby. www.skopjeonline.com. mk 182 A3

Ohrid
Old town, beautifully set by a lake, with houses of wood and brick, remains of a Turkish citadel, many churches (two cathedrals; St Naum south of the lake). www.ohrid.org.mk 182 B2

Malta
www.visitmalta.com

Valletta
Capital of Malta. Historic walled city, founded in 16c by the Maltese Knights, with 16c Grand Master's Palace and a richly decorated cathedral. 175 C3

Monaco
www.visitmonaco.com

Monaco
Major resort area in a beauti-ful location. Sights include: Monte Carlo casino, Prince's Palace at Monaco-Ville; 19c cathedral; oceanographic museum.
www.visitmonaco.com 133 B3

The Netherlands Nederland
www.visitholland.com

Amsterdam
Capital of the Netherlands. Old centre has picturesque canals lined with distinctive elegant 17–18c merchants' houses. Dam Square has 15c New Church and Royal Palace. Other churches include Westerkerk. The Museumplein has three

Westerkerk,
Amsterdam,
Netherlands

world-famous museums: Rijksmuseum (several art collections including 15–17c painting); Van Gogh Museum; Municipal Museum (art from 1850 on). Other museums: Anne Frank House; Jewish Historical Museum; Rembrandt House.
www.visitamsterdam.nl 70 B1

Delft
Well-preserved old Dutch town with gabled red-roofed houses along canals. Gothic churches: New Church; Old Church. Famous for Delftware (two museums). www.delft.nl 70 B1

The Hague Den Haag
Seat of Government and of the royal house of the Netherlands. The 17c Mauritshuis houses the Royal Picture Gallery (excellent 15–18c Flemish and Dutch). Other good collections: Prince William V Gallery; Hesdag Museum; Municipal Museum www.denhaag.nl 70 B1

Haarlem
Many medieval gabled houses centred on the Great Market with 14c Town Hall and 15c Church of St Bavon. Museums: Frans Hals Museum; Teylers Museum. www.haarlem.nl 70 B1

Het Loo
Former royal palace and gar-dens set in a vast landscape (commissioned by future Queen of England, Mary Stuart).
www.paleishetloo.nl 70 B2

Keukenhof
Landscaped gardens, planted with bulbs of many varieties, are the largest flower gardens in the world.
www.keukenhof.nl 70 B1

Leiden
University town of beauti-ful gabled houses set along canals. The Rijksmuseum Van Oudheden is Holland's most important home to archaeological artefacts from the Antiquity. The 16c Hortus Botanicus is one of the oldest botanical gardens in Europe. The Cloth Hall with van Leyden's *Last Judgement*. www.leidenpromotie.nl 70 B1

Rotterdam
The largest port in the world. The Boymans-van Beuningen Museum has a huge and excel-lent decorative and fine art

collection (old and modern). Nearby: 18c Kinderdijk with 19 windmills.
www.rotterdam.nl 79 A4

Utrecht
Delightful old town cen-tre along canals with the Netherlands' oldest univer-sity and Gothic cathedral. Good art collections: Central Museum; National Museum. www.utrecht.nl 70 B2

Norway Norge
www.norway.no

Bergen
Norway's second city in a scenic setting. The Quay has many painted wooden medieval buildings. Sights: 12c Romanesque St Mary's Church; Bergenhus for-tress with 13c Haakon's Hall; Rosenkrantztårnet; Grieghallen; Rasmus Meyer Collection (Norwegian art); Bryggens Museum. www.visitbergen.com 46 B2

Lappland (Norwegian)
Vast land of Finnmark is home to the Sámi. Nordkapp is the northern point of Europe. Also Finland, Sweden. www.lappland.no 192–193

Norwegian Fjords
Beautiful and majestic land-scape of deep glacial valleys filled by the sea. The most thrilling fjords are between Bergen and Ålesund. www.fjords.com 46 & 198

Oslo
Capital of Norway with a modern centre. Buildings: 17c cathedral; 19c city hall, 19c royal palace; 19c Stortinget (housing parliament); 19c University; 13c Akershus (cas-tle); 12c Akerskirke (church). Museums: National Gallery; Munch Museum; Viking Ship Museum; Folk Museum (reconstructed buildings). www.visitoslo.com 48 C2

Stavkirker
Wooden medieval stave churches of bizarre pyramidal structure, carved with images from Nordic mythology. Best preserved in southern Norway.

Tromsø
Main arctic city of Norway with a university and two cathedrals.
www.destinasjontromso.no 192 C3

Trondheim
Set on the edge of a fjord, a modern city with the superb Nidaros cathedral (rebuilt 19c). Also: Stiftsgaard (royal

residence); Applied Arts
Museum.
www.trondheim.com 199 B7

Poland Polska

www.poland.pl

Częstochowa
Centre of Polish Catholicism,
with the 14c monastery of
Jasna Góra a pilgrimage
site to the icon of the Black
Madonna for six centuries.
86 B3

Gdańsk
Medieval centre with: 14c
Town Hall (state rooms);
Gothic brick St Mary's
Church, Poland's largest; Long
Market has fine buildings
(Artus Court); National Art
Museum. www.gdansk.pl 69 A3

Kraków
Old university city, rich in
architecture, centred on
superb 16c Marketplace with
Gothic-Renaissance Cloth
Hall containing the Art
Gallery (19c Polish), Clock
Tower, Gothic red-brick St
Mary's Church (altarpiece).
Czartoryski Palace has
city's finest art collection.
Wawel Hill has the Gothic
cathedral and splendid
Renaissance Royal Palace.
The former Jewish ghetto in
Kazimierz district has 16c Old
Synagogue, now a museum.
www.krakow.pl 99 A3

Poznań
Town centred on the Old
Square with Renaissance Town
Hall and Baroque mansions.
Also: medieval castle; Gothic
cathedral; National Museum
(European masters). www.plot.
poznan.pl 76 B1

Tatry
One of Europe's most delightful mountain ranges with
many beautiful ski resorts
(Zakopane). Also in Slovakia.
99 B3

Warsaw Warszawa
Capital of Poland, with many
historic monuments in the
Old Town with the Royal
Castle (museum) and Old
Town Square surrounded
by reconstructed 17–18c
merchants' houses. Several
churches including: Gothic
cathedral; Baroque Church
of the Nuns of Visitation.
Richly decorated royal palaces
and gardens: Neoclassical
Łazienki Palace; Baroque palace in Wilanów. The National
Museum has Polish and
European art.
www.warsawtour.pl
77 C6

Wrocław
Historic town centred on
the Market Square with 15c
Town Hall and mansions.
Churches: Baroque cathedral;
St Elizabeth; St Adalbert.
National Museum displays
fine art. Vast painting of
Battle of Racławice is specially
housed. www.wroclaw.pl 85 A5

Portugal

www.visitportugal.pt

Alcobaça
Monastery of Santa Maria,
one of the best examples of
a Cistercian abbey, founded
in 1147 (exterior 17–18c). The
church is Portugal's largest
(14c tombs). 154 A1

Algarve
Modern seaside resorts among
picturesque sandy beaches and
rocky coves (Praia da Rocha).
Old towns: Lagos; Faro.
www.rtalgarve.pt 160 B1

Batalha
Abbey is one of the mas-
terpieces of French Gothic
and Manueline architecture
(tombs, English Perpendicular
chapel, unfinished pantheon).
154 A2

Braga
Historic town with cathedral
and large Archbishop's Palace.
www.cm-braga.com.pt 148 A1

Coimbra
Old town with narrow streets
set on a hill. The Romanesque
cathedral is particularly
fine (portal). The university
(founded 1290) has a fascinating Baroque library. Also:
Museum of Machado de
Castro; many monasteries and
convents. 148 B1

Évora
Centre of the town, sur-
rounded by walls, has narrow
streets of Moorish character
and medieval and Renaissance
architecture. Churches:
12–13c Gothic cathedral; São
Francisco with a chapel decorated with bones of some 5000
monks; 15c Convent of Dos
Lóis. The Jesuit university was
founded in 1559. Museum of
Évora holds fine art (particularly Flemish and Portugese).
154 B3

Guimarães
Old town with a castle with
seven towers on a vast keep.
Churches: Romanesque
chapel of São Miguel; São
Francisco. Alberto Sampaio
Museum and Martins
Sarmento Museum are excel-
lent. 148 A1

Lisbon Lisboa
Capital of Portugal. Baixa
is the Neoclassical heart of
Lisbon with the Praça do
Comércio and Rossío squares.
São Jorge castle (Visigothic,
Moorish, Romanesque) is
surrounded by the medieval
quarters. Bairro Alto is famous
for *fado* (songs). Monastery
of Jerónimos is exceptional.
Churches: 12c cathedral; São
Vicente de Fora; São Roque
(tiled chapels); Torre de
Belém; Convento da Madre de
Deus. Museums: Gulbenkian
Museum (ancient, oriental,
European), National Museum
of Antique Art (old masters),
Modern Art Centre; Azulejo
Museum (decorative tiles).
Nearby: palatial monastic
complex Mafra; royal resort
Sintra. www.cm-lisboa.pt
154 A1

Porto
Historic centre with narrow
streets. Views from Clérigos
Tower. Churches: São
Francisco; cathedral. Soares
dos Reis Museum holds fine
and decorative arts (18–19c).
The suburb of Vila Nova de
Gaia is the centre for port
wine. www.portoturismo.pt
148 A1

Tomar
Attractive town with the
Convento de Cristo, founded
in 1162 as the headquarters of
the Knights Templar (Charola
temple, chapter house,
Renaissance cloisters). 154 A2

Romania

www.turism.ro

Bucovina
Beautiful region in northern
Romanian Moldova renowned
for a number of 15–16c
monasteries and their fresco
cycles. Of particular note
are Moldovita, Voroneţ and
Suceviţa. 17 B6

Bucharest Bucureşti
Capital of Romania with the
majority of sites along the
Calea Victoriei and centring
on Piaţa Revoluţiei with 19c
Romanian Athenaeum and
1930s Royal Palace housing
the National Art Gallery. The
infamous 1980s Civic Centre
with People's Palace is a symbol of dictatorial aggrandise-
ment. www.bucuresti.ro 17 C7

Carpathian
Mountains Carpaţii
The beautiful Carpathian
Mountains have several ski
resorts (Sinaia) and peaks
noted for first-rate mountain-
eering (Făgă raşuiui, Rodnei).

Danube Delta Europe's largest marshland, a spectacular
nature reserve. Travel in the
area is by boat, with Tulcea the
starting point for visitors. The
Romanian Black Sea Coast has
a stretch of resorts (Mamaia,
Eforie) between Constanţa
and the border, and well-
preserved Roman remains in
Histria. 17 B6

Transylvania
Transilvania
Beautiful and fascinating scenic region of medieval citadels
(Timişoara, Sibiu) provides a
setting for the haunting image
of the legendary Dracula
(Sighişoara, Braşov, Bran
Castle). Cluj-Napoca is the
main town. 17 B5

Russia Rossiya

www.russia.com

Moscow Moskva
Capital of Russia, with
many monuments. Within
the Kremlin's red walls
are: 15c Cathedral of the
Dormition; 16c Cathedral
of the Archangel; Cathedral
of the Annunciation (icons),
Armour Palace. Outside the
walls, Red Square has the
Lenin Mausoleum and 16c
St Basil's Cathedral. There
are a number of monaster-
ies (16c Novodevichi). Two
superb museums: Tretiakov
Art Gallery (Russian);
Pushkin Museum of Fine Art
(European). Kolomenskoe,
once a royal summer retreat,
has the Church of the
Ascension. The VDNKh is
a symbol of the Stalinist era.
www.moscow-guide.ru 9 E10

Novgorod
One of Russia's oldest towns,
centred on 15c Kremlin with
St Sophia Cathedral (iconos-
tasis, west door). Two other
cathedrals: St Nicholas; St
George. Museum of History,
Architecture and Art has notable icons and other artefacts.
www.novgorod.ru 9 C7

Petrodvorets
Grand palace with numerous
pavilions (Monplaisir) set in
beautiful parkland interwoven by a system of fountains,
cascades and waterways connected to the sea.
www.petrodvorets.ru 9 C6

Pushkin
(Tsarskoye Selo) Birthplace of
Alexander Pushkin, with the
vast Baroque Catherine Palace
– splendid state apartments,
beautiful gardens and lakes.
www.pushkin-town.net 9 C7

Saint Petersburg
Sankt Peterburg
Founded in 1703 with the
SS Peter and Paul Fortress
and its cathedral by Peter the
Great, and functioning as
seat of court and government
until 1918. Many of the most
famous sights are around
elegant Nevski Prospekt. The
Hermitage, one of the world's
largest and finest art collections is housed in five buildings including the Baroque
Winter and Summer palaces.
The Mikhailovsky Palace
houses the Russian Museum
(Russian art). Other sights:
neoclassical Admiralty; 19c St
Isaac's Cathedral and St Kazar
Cathedral; Vasilievsky Island
with 18c Menshikov Palace;
Alexander Nevsky Monastery
18c Smolny Convent. www.
spb.ru 9 C7

Sergiev Posad
(Zagorsk) Trinity St Sergius
monastery with 15c cathedral.
www.musobl.divo.ru 9 D11

Serbia Srbija

www.serbia-tourism.org

Belgrade Beograd
Capital of Serbia. The largely
modern city is set between
the Danube and Sava rivers.
The National Museum holds
European art. To the south
there are numerous fascinatin
medieval monasteries, richly
embellished with frescoes.
www.belgradetourism.org.yu
127 C2

Spain España

www.spaintour.com

Ávila
Medieval town with 2km-lon
11c walls. Pilgrimage site to
shrines to St Teresa of Ávila
(Convent of Santa Teresa,
Convent of the Incarnation).
www.avila.world-guides.com
150 B3

Barcelona
Showcase of Gothic ('Barri
Gòtic': cathedral; Santa Mari
del Mar; mansions on Carrer
de Montcada) and *modernista*
architecture ('Eixample' area
with Manzana de la Discòrdi
Sagrada Familia, Güell Park,
La Pedrera). Many elegant
boulevards (La Rambla,
Passeig de Gràcia). Museums
Modern Catalan Art; Picasso
Museum, Miró Museum;
Tàpies Museum. Nearby:
monastery of Montserrat
(Madonna); Figueres (Dali
Museum).
www.barcelonaturisme.com
147 C3

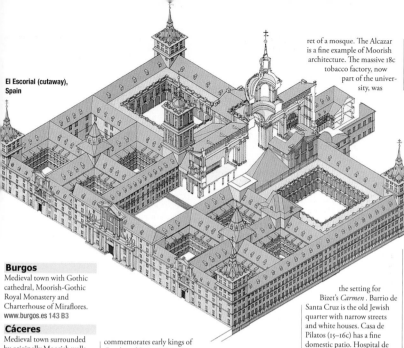

El Escorial (cutaway), Spain

Burgos
Medieval town with Gothic cathedral, Moorish-Gothic Royal Monastery and Charterhouse of Miraflores. www.burgos.es **143 B3**

Cáceres
Medieval town surrounded by originally Moorish walls and with several aristocratic palaces with solars. www.caceres.es **155 A4**

Córdoba
Capital of Moorish Spain with a labyrinth of streets and houses with tile-decorated patios. The 8–10c Mezquita is the finest mosque in Spain. A 16c cathedral was added at the centre of the building and a 17c tower replaced the minaret. The old Jewish quarter has 14c synagogue www.cordoba.es **156 C3**

El Escorial
Immense Renaissance complex of palatial and monastic buildings and mausoleum of the Spanish monarchs. www.patrimonionacional.es/escorial/escorial.htm **151 B3**

Granada
The Alhambra was hill-top palace-fortress of the rulers of the last Moorish kingdom and is the most splendid example of Moorish art and architecture in Spain. The complex has three principal parts: Alcazaba fortress (11c); Casa Real palace (14c, with later Palace of Carlos V); Generalife gardens. Also: Moorish quarter; gypsy quarter; Royal Chapel with good art in the sacristy. www.granadatur.com **163 A4**

León
Gothic cathedral has notable stained glass. Royal Pantheon

commemorates early kings of Castile and León. **142 B1**

Madrid
Capital of Spain, a mainly modern city with 17–19c architecture at its centre around Plaza Mayor. Sights: Royal Palace with lavish apartments; Descalzas Reales Convent (tapestries and other works); Royal Armoury museum. Spain's three leading galleries: Prado (15–18c); Queen Sofia Centre (20c Spanish, Picasso's *Guernica*); Thyssen-Bornemisza Museum (medieval to modern). www.munimadrid.es **151 B4**

Oviedo
Gothic cathedral with 12c sanctuary. Three Visigoth (9c) churches: Santullano, Santa María del Naranco, San Miguel de Lillo. www.ayto-oviedo.es **141 A5**

Palma
Situated on Mallorca, the largest and most beautiful of the Balearic islands, with an impressive Gothic cathedral. www.a-palma.es **166 B2**

Picos de Europa
Mountain range with river gorges and peaks topped by Visigothic and Romanesque churches. **142 A2**

Pyrenees
Unspoiled mountain range with beautiful landscape and villages full of Romanesque architecture (cathedral of

Jaca). The Ordesa National Park has many waterfalls and canyons. **144–145**

Salamanca
Delightful old city with some uniquely Spanish architecture: Renaissance Plateresque is famously seen on 16c portal of the university (founded 1215); Baroque Churrigueresque on 18c Plaza Mayo; both styles at the Convent of San Esteban. Also: Romanesque Old Cathedral; Gothic-Plateresque New Cathedral; House of Shells. www.salamanca.com **150 B2**

Santiago di Compostela
Medieval city with many churches and religious institutions. The famous pilgrimage to the shrine of St James the Apostle ends here in the magnificent cathedral, originally Romanesque with many later elements (18c Baroque façade). www.santiagoturismo.com **140 B2**

Segovia
Old town set on a rock with a 1c Roman aqueduct. Also: 16c Gothic cathedral; Alcázar (14–15c, rebuilt 19c); 12-sided 13c Templar church of Vera Cruz. www.viasegovia.com **151 B3**

Seville Sevilla
City noted for festivals and flamenco. The world's largest Gothic cathedral (15c) retains the Orange Court and mina-

ret of a mosque. The Alcazar is a fine example of Moorish architecture. The massive 18c tobacco factory, now part of the university, was the setting for Bizet's *Carmen* . Barrio de Santa Cruz is the old Jewish quarter with narrow streets and white houses. Casa de Pilatos (15–16c) has a fine domestic patio. Hospital de la Caridad has good Spanish painting. Nearby: Roman Italica with amphitheatre. www.sevilla.org **162 A2**

Tarragona
The city and its surroundings have some of the best-preserved Roman heritage in Spain. Also: Gothic cathedral (cloister); Archaeological Museum. www.tarragona.es **147 C2**

Toledo
Historic city with Moorish, Jewish and Christian sights. The small 11c mosque of El Cristo de la Luz is one of the earliest in Spain. Two synagogues have been preserved: Santa María la Blanca; El Tránsito. Churches: San Juan de los Reyes; Gothic cathedral (good artworks). El Greco's *Burial of the Count of Orgaz* is in the Church of Santo Tomé. More of his works are in the El Greco house and, with other art, in Hospital de Santa Cruz. www.toledo.es **151 C3**

Valencia
The old town has houses and palaces with elaborate façades. Also: Gothic cathedral and Lonja de la Seda church. www.comunitatvalenciana.com **159 B3**

Zaragoza
Town notable for Moorish architecture (11c Aljafería Palace). The Basilica de Nuestra Señora del Pilar, one

of two cathedrals, is highly venerated. www.zaragoza-ciudad.com **153 A3**

Slovenia Slovenija
www.slovenia-tourism.si

Istria Istra
Two town centres, Koper and Piran, with medieval and Renaissance squares and Baroque palaces. See also Croatia. www.slo-istra.com **122 B2**

Julian Alps Julijske Alpe
Wonderfully scenic section of the Alps with lakes (Bled, Bohinj), deep valleys (Planica, Vrata) and ski resorts (Kranjska Gora, Bohinjska Bistrica). **122 A2**

Karst Caves
Numerous caves with huge galleries, extraordinary stalactites and stalagmites, and underground rivers. The most spectacular are Postojna (the most famous, with Predjamski Castle nearby) and Škocjan. www.postojnska-jama.si **123 B3**

Ljubljana
Capital of Slovenia. The old town, dominated by the castle (good views), is principally between Prešeren Square and Town Hall (15c, 18c), with the Three Bridges and colonnaded market. Many Baroque churches (cathedral, St Jacob, St Francis, Ursuline) and palaces (Bishop's Palace, Seminary, Gruber Palace). Also: 17c Križanke church and monastery complex; National Gallery and Modern Gallery show Slovene art. www.ljubljana.si **123 A3**

Slovakia Slovenska Republika
www.slovakia-republika.com

Bratislava
Capital of Slovakia, dominated by the castle (Slovak National Museum, good views). Old Town centred on the Main Square with Old Town Hall and Jesuit Church. Many 18–19c palaces (Mirbach Palace, Pálffy Palace, Primate's Palace), churches (Gothic cathedral, Corpus Christi Chapel) and museums (Slovak National Gallery). www.bratislava.sk **111 A4**

Košice
Charming old town with many Baroque and neoclassical buildings and Gothic cathedral. www.kosice.sk **12 D4**

Spišské Podhradie
Region, east of the Tatry, full of picturesque medieval towns (Levoča, Kežmarok, Prešov) and architectural monuments (Spišský Castle). 99 B4

Tatry
Beautiful mountain region. Poprad is an old town with 19c villas. Starý Smokovec is a popular ski resort. See also Poland. www.tatry.sk 99 B3

Sweden Sverige
www.sweden.se

Abisko
Popular resort in the Swedish part of Lapland set in an inspiring landscape of lakes and mountains. www.abisko.nu 194 B9

Gothenburg Göteborg
Largest port in Sweden, the historic centre has 17–18c Dutch architectural character (Kronhuset). The Art Museum has interesting Swedish works. www.goteborg.com 60 B1

Gotland
Island with Sweden's most popular beach resorts (Ljugarn) and unspoiled countryside with churches in Baltic Gothic style (Dahlem, Bunge). Visby is a pleasant walled medieval town. www.gotland.se 57 C4

Lappland (Swedish)
Swedish part of Lappland with 18c Arvidsjaur the oldest preserved Sámi village. Jokkmokk is a Sámi cultural centre in fine scenery. Also Finland, Norway. www.lappland.se 192–193

Lund
Charming university city with medieval centre and a fine 12c Romanesque cathedral (14c astronomical clock, carved tombs). www.lund.se 61 D3

Malmö
Old town centre set among canals and squares dominated by a red-brick castle (museums) and a vast market square with Town Hall and Gothic Church of St Peter. www.malmo.se 61 D3

Mora
Delightful village on the shores of Siljan Lake in the heart of the Dalarna region, home to folklore and traditional crafts. www.mora.se 50 A1

Stockholm
Capital of Sweden built on a number of islands. The Old Town is largely on three islands with 17–18c houses, Baroque Royal Castle (apartments and museums), Gothic cathedral, parliament. Riddarholms church has tombs of the monarchy. Museums include: Modern Gallery (one of world's best modern collections); Nordiska Museet (cultural history); open-air Skansen (Swedish houses). Baroque Drottningholm Castle is the residence of the monarchy. www.stockholm.se 57 A4

Swedish Lakes
Beautiful region around the Vättern and Vänern Lakes. Siljan Lake is in the Dalarna region where folklore and crafts are preserved (Leksand, Mora, Rättvik). 55 B4

Uppsala
Appealing university town with a medieval centre around the massive Gothic cathedral. www.uppsala.se 51 C4

Switzerland Schweiz
www.myswitzerland.com

Alps
The most popular Alpine region is the Berner Oberland with the town of Interlaken a starting point for exploring the large number of picturesque peaks (Jungfrau). The valleys of the Graubünden have famous ski resorts (Davos, St Moritz). Zermatt lies below the highest and most recognizable Swiss peak, the Matterhorn. www.thealps.com 119 A4

Basle Basel
Medieval university town with Romanesque-Gothic cathedral (tomb of Erasmus). Superb collections: Art Museum; Museum of Contemporary Art. www.baseltourismus.ch 106 B2

Bern
Capital of Switzerland. Medieval centre has fountains, characteristic streets (Spitalgasse) and tower-gates. The Bärengraben is famed for its bears. Also: Gothic cathedral; good Fine Arts Museum. www.berne.ch 106 C2

Geneva Genève
Wonderfully situated on the lake with the world's highest fountain. The historic area is centred on the Romanesque cathedral and Place du Bourg du Four. Excellent collections: Art and History Museum;

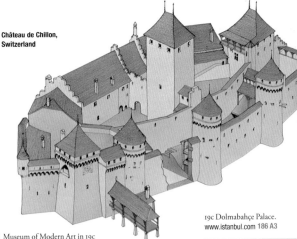
Château de Chillon, Switzerland

Museum of Modern Art in 19c Petit Palais. On the lake shore: splendid medieval Château de Chillon. www.geneva-tourism.ch 118 A3

Interlaken
Starting point for excursions to the most delightful part of the Swiss Alps, the Bernese Oberland, with Grindelwald and Lauterbrunnen – one of the most thrilling valleys leading up to the ski resort of Wengen with views on the Jungfrau. www.interlakentourism.ch 106 C2

Lucerne Luzern
On the beautiful shores of Vierwaldstättersee, a charming medieval town of white houses on narrow streets and of wooden bridges (Kapellbrücke, Spreuerbrücke). It is centred on the Kornmarkt with the Renaissance Old Town Hall and Am Rhyn-Haus (Picasso collection). www.luzern.org 106 C1

Zürich
Set on Zürichsee, the old quarter is around Niederdorf with 15c cathedral. Gothic Fraumünster has stained glass by Chagall. Museums: Swiss National Museum (history); Art Museum (old and modern masters); Bührle Foundation (Impressionists, Post-impressionists). www.zuerich.com 107 B3

Turkey Türkiye
www.tourismturkey.org

Istanbul
Divided by the spectcular Bosphorus, the stretch of water that separates Europe from Asia, the historic district is surrounded by the Golden Horn, Sea of Marmara and the 5c wall of Theodosius. Major sights: 6c Byzantine church of St Sophia (converted first to a mosque in 1453 and then a museum in 1934); 15c Topkapi Palace; treasury and Archaeological Museum; 17c Blue Mosque; 19c Bazaar; 16c Süleymaniye Mosque; 12c Kariye Camii; European district with Galata Tower and

19c Dolmabahçe Palace. www.istanbul.com 186 A3

Ukraine Ukraina
www.ukraine.com

Kiev Kyïv
Capital of Ukraine, known for its cathedral (11c, 17c) with Byzantine frescoes and mosaics. The Monastery of the Caves has churches, monastic buildings and catacombs. www.uazone.net/kiev 13 C9

Vatican City Città del Vaticano
www.vatican.va

Vatican City Città del Vaticano
Independent state within Rome. On Piazza San Pietro is the 15–16c Renaissance-Baroque Basilica San Pietro (Michelangelo's dome and Pietà), the world's most important Roman Catholic church. The Vatican Palace contains the Vatican Museums with many fine art treasures including Michelangelo's frescoes in the Sistine Chapel. www.vatican.va 168 B2

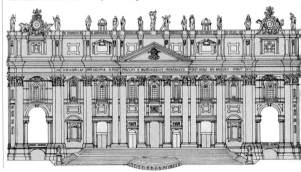
The facade of Basilica San Pietro, Vatican City

European politics and economics

EUROPEAN UNION MEMBERSHIP

1957 Founder members, Belgium, France, Italy, Germany, Luxembourg, Netherlands	
1973 Denmark, Ireland, UK	
1981 Greece	
1986 Portugal, Spain	
1990 East Germany, following German reunification	
1995 Austria, Finland, Sweden	
2004 Czech Republic, Cyprus, Estonia, Hungary, Latvia, Lithuania, Malta, Poland, Slovakia, Slovenia	
2007 Bulgaria, Romania	
Future candidates for EU membership	
Eurozone countries are outlined in yellow	

April 2005 when its former leader Jörg Haider left to set up the Alliance for Austria's Future.

Economy Has a well-developed market economy and high standard of living. The leading economic activity is the manufacture of metals and tourism. Dairy and livestock farming are the principal agricultural activities. To meet increased competition from both EU and Central European countries, particularly the new EU members, Austria will need to continue restructuring, emphasising knowledge-based sectors of the economy and encouraging greater labour flexibility.

Belarus

Area 207,600 sq km (80,154 sq miles)
Population 10,300,483
Capital Minsk (1,717,000)
Languages Belarusian, Russian (both official)
GDP 2005 US$7,600
Currency Belarussian ruble = 100 kopek
Government Republic
Head of state President Alexander Lukashenko, 1994
Head of government Prime Minister Sergei Sidorsky, 2003
Website http://government.by/eng/sovmin/index.htm
Events Belarus attained its independence in 1991. As a result of a referendum in 1996 the president increased his power at the expense of parliament. In 1997, Belarus signed a Union Treaty committing it to political and economic integration with Russia. Since his election in July 1994 as the country's first president, Alexander Lukashenko, has steadily consolidated his power through authoritarian means. Government restrictions on freedom of speech, the press and religion continue.
Economy Belarus continues to receive heavily discounted oil and natural gas from Russia. Agriculture, especially meat and dairy farming, is important.

Belgium *Belgique*

Area 30,528 sq km (11,786 sq miles)
Population 10,364,388
Capital Brussels/Bruxelles (964,000)
Languages Dutch, French, German (all official)
GDP 2005 US$31,800
Currency Euro = 100 cents
Government federal constitutional monarchy
Head of state King Albert II, 1993
Head of government Prime Minister Guy Verhofstadt, Flemish Liberal Democrats, 1999
Website www.belgium.be
Events In 1993 Belgium adopted a federal system of government, each of the regions having its own parliament. The socialist and liberal parties have two

Albania *Shqipëria*

Area 28,748 sq km (11,100 sq miles)
Population 3,563,112
Capital Tirana / Tiranë (380,400)
Languages Albanian (official), Greek, Vlach, Romani and Slavic
GDP 2005 US$4,900
Currency Lek = 100 Quindars
Government multiparty republic
Head of state President Alfred Moisiu, 2002
Head of government Prime Minister Sali Berisha, Democratic Party, 2005
Website www.parlament.al
Events In the 2005 general elections, the Democratic Party and its allies won a decisive victory on pledges of reducing crime and corruption, promoting economic growth, and decreasing the size of government. The election, and particularly the orderly transition of power, was considered an important step forward.
Economy Although the economy continues to grow, it is still one of the poorest in Europe. It is continuing to work toward joining NATO and the EU. With troops in Iraq and Afghanistan, it has been a strong supporter of the global war on terrorism. 56% of the workforce are engaged in agriculture. Private

ownership of land has been encouraged since 1991.

Andorra
Principat d'Andorra

Area 468 sq km (181 sq miles)
Population 70,549
Capital Andorra la Vella (20,300)
Languages Catalan (official), French, Castilian and Portuguese
GDP 2005 US$26,800
Currency Euro = 100 cents
Government independent state and co-principality
Head of state co-princes: Joan Enric Vives Sicilia, Bishop of Urgell, 2003 and Jacques Chirac (see France), 1995
Head of government Chief Executive Albert Pintat, 2005
Website www.andorra.ad
Events In 1993 a new democratic constitution was adopted that reduced the roles of the President of France and the Bishop of Urgell to purely constitutional figureheads.
Economy Tourism accounts for more than 80% of GDP with an estimated 11.6 million visiting annually, attracted by duty-free status and its summer and winter resorts. Agricultural production is limited (2% of the land is arable) and most food has to be imported. The prin-

cipal livestock activity is sheep raising. Manufacturing output consists mainly of cigarettes, cigars, and furniture.

Austria *Österreich*

Area 83,859 sq km (32,377 sq miles)
Population 8,184,691
Capital Vienna / Wien (1,807,000)
Languages German (official)
GDP 2005 US$32,900
Currency Euro = 100 cents
Government federal republic
Head of state President Heinz Fischer, Social Democrats, 2004
Head of government Federal Chancellor Wolfgang Schüssel, People's Party, 2000
Website www.austria.gv.at
Events In general elections in 1999, the extreme right Freedom Party, under Jörg Haider, made gains at the expense of the Social Democrats. He subsequently resigned as leader. People's Party electoral win in 2002 wasn't sufficient to form a government so a new government coalition was formed with the Freedom Party after failure of talks with the Social Democrats and the Greens. In July 2004 President Fischer's predecessor Thomas Klestil died of a heart attack one day before Heinz Fischer was due to take his place. The Freedom Party split in

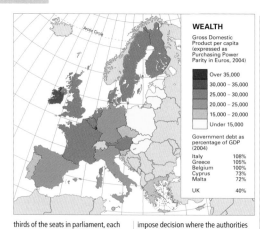

thirds of the seats in parliament, each main party is split into two – half for the Flemish and half for the Walloons.

Economy Belgium is a major trading nation with a modern, private-enterprise economy. The leading activity is manufacturing i.e. steel and chemicals. With few natural resources, it imports substantial quantities of raw materials and export a large volume of manufactures. Belgium began circulating the euro currency in January 2002.

Bosnia-Herzegovina
Bosna i Hercegovina

Area 51,197 sq km
(19,767 sq miles)
Population 4,025,476
Capital Sarajevo (737,350)
Languages Bosnian/Croatian/Serbian
GDP 2005 US$2,600
Currency Convertible Marka =
100 convertible pfenniga
Government federal republic
Head of state Chairman of the Presidency Ivo Miro Jovic, Croatian Democratic Union, 2005
Head of government Chairman of the Council of Ministers Adnan Terzic, Muslim Party of Democratic Action, 2002
Website www.fbihvlada.gov.ba
Events In 1992 a referendum approved independence from the Yugoslav federation. The Bosnian Serb population was against independence and in the resulting war occupied over two-thirds of the land. Croat forces seized other parts of the country. The 1995 Dayton Peace Accord ended the war and set up the Bosnian Muslim/Croat Federation and the Bosnian Serb Republic, each with their own president, government, parliament, military and police, there is also a central Bosnian government and rotating presidency the other members of which are Sulejman Tihic (Muslim Party of Democratic Action) and Borislav Paravac (Serb Democratic Party). The office of High Representative has the power to

impose decision where the authorities are unable to agree or where political or economic interests are affected. In 2005, Paddy Ashdown sacked Ivo Jovic's predecessor Dragan Covic. Eufor troops took over from the NATO-led force as peacekeepers in 2004.

Economy Excluding Macedonia, Bosnia was the least developed of the former republics of Yugoslavia. Currently receiving substantial aid, though this will be reduced.

Bulgaria *Bulgariya*

Area 110,912 sq km
(42,822 sq miles)
Population 7,450,349
Capital Sofia (1,187,000)
Languages
Bulgarian (official), Turkish
GDP 2005 US$9,000
Currency Lev = 100 stotinki
Government multiparty republic
Head of state
President Georgi Purvanov, Bulgarian Socialist Party, 2002
Head of government Prime Minister Sergei Stanishev, Bulgarian Socialist Party, 2005
Website www.president.bg/en
Events In 1990 the first non-communist president for 40 years, Zhelyu Zhelev, was elected. A new constitution in 1991 saw the adoption of free-market reforms. Former king Simeon Saxe-Coburg-Gotha was the first ex-monarch in post-communist eastern Europe to return to power. He leads a coalition government, has gained membership of NATO for Bulgaria and signed an accession treaty with the EU in April 2005 allowing for EU membership in 2007 subject to reforms being satisfactory. Parliament voted in early 2005 to withdraw troops from Iraq by the end of 2005. Elections in June 2005 were inclusive. Sergei Stanishev's Socialist Party was originally asked to form a government but after parliament rejected his choice of ministers,

the president asked the NMS to form a coalition.

Economy Bulgaria has experienced macroeconomic stability and strong growth since 1996 when a major economic downturn led to the fall of the then socialist government. Bulgaria has averaged 4% growth since 2000 and has begun to attract significant amounts of foreign direct investment. Manufacturing is the leading economic activity but has outdated technology. The main products are chemicals, metals, machinery and textiles. The valleys of the Maritsa are ideal for winemaking, plums and tobacco. Tourism is increasing rapidly.

Croatia *Hrvatska*

Area 56,538 sq km
(21,829 sq miles)
Population 4,495,904
Capital Zagreb (1,067,000)
Languages Croatian
GDP 2005 US$11,600
Currency Kuna = 100 lipas
Government
multiparty republic
Head of state
President Stjepan Mesic, 2000
Head of government
Prime Minister Ivo Sanader, Croatian Democratic Union, 2003
Website www.croatia.hr
Events A 1991 referendum voted overwhelmingly in favour of independence. Serb-dominated areas took up arms to remain in the federation. Serbia armed Croatian Serbs, war broke out between Serbia and Croatia, and Croatia lost much territory. In 1992 United Nations peacekeeping troops were deployed. Following the Dayton Peace Accord of 1995, Croatia and Yugoslavia established diplomatic relations. An agreement between the Croatian government and Croatian Serbs provided for the eventual reintegration of Krajina into Croatia in 1998. PM Sanader leads a minority government with the support of many smaller parties. Croatia is a partner-country with NATO and applied for EU membership in 2003. The start-date for accession talks has been postponed because of the lack of progress in arresting some war crimes suspects, particularly Gen Ante Gotvina.

Economy The wars have badly disrupted Croatia's relatively prosperous economy but it emerged from a mild recession in 2000 with tourism, banking, and public investments leading the way. Unemployment remains high, at about 18%, with structural factors slowing its decline. Croatia has a wide range of manufacturing industries, such as steel, chemicals, oil refining, and wood products. Agriculture is the principal employer. Crops include maize, soya beans, sugar beet and wheat.

Czech Republic
Česka Republica

Area 78,864 sq km
(30,449 sq miles)
Population 10,241,138
Capital Prague/Praha (1,203,000)
Languages Czech (official), Moravian
GDP 2005 US$18,100
Currency Czech Koruna = 100 haler
Government multiparty republic
Head of state President Václav Klaus, 2003
Head of government Prime Minister Jiri Paroubek, Czech Social Democratic Party, 2005
Website www.czech.cz
Events In 1992 the government agreed to the secession of the Slovak Republic, and on 1 January 1993 the Czech Republic was created. The Czech Republic was granted full membership of NATO in 1999 and joined the EU in May 2004. The opposition Civic Democratic Party, with their agenda of not ceding too much power to the EU, were the winners in the European elections of June 2004, as a result of which Prime Minister Vladimir Spidla resigned, to be replaced by Stanislav Gross, who then resigned in April 2005 over a financial scandal. An election to the Chamber of Deputies took place in June 2006, producing an evenly balanced result. Forming a stable government that will last four years will be difficult.

Economy The country has deposits of coal, uranium, iron ore, tin and zinc. Industries include chemicals, beer, iron and steel. Private ownership of land is gradually being restored. Agriculture employs 12% of the workforce. Inflation is under control. Privatisation of the state-owned telecommunications firm Cesky Telecom took place in 2005. Intensified restructuring among large enterprises, improvements in the financial sector, and effective use of available EU funds should strengthen output growth. Prague is now a major tourist destination.

Denmark *Danmark*

Area 43,094 sq km
(16,638 sq miles)
Population 5,432,335
Capital Copenhagen /
København (1,332,000)
Languages Danish (official)
GDP 2005 US$33,500
Currency Krone = 100 øre
Government parliamentary monarchy
Head of state Queen Margrethe II, 1972
Head of government Prime Minister Anders Fogh Rasmussen, Venstre (Left) Party, 2001
Website www.denmark.dk
Events In 1992 Denmark rejected the Maastricht Treaty, but reversed the

decision in a 1993 referendum. In 1998 the Amsterdam Treaty was ratified by a further referendum. Currency pegged to Euro but still independent. The government is a coalition formed with the Conservative Party. Anti-immigration policies are backed by the well-supported far-right Danish People's Party. The opposition Social Democrats were clear winners in the European elections of June 2004, though this could be down to opposition to the government's support for the war in Iraq, and snap elections in February 2005 gave Rasmussen's Venstre Party a second term in power.

Economy Danes enjoy a high standard of living with a thoroughly modern market economy featuring high-tech agriculture, up-to-date small-scale and corporate industry, comfortable living standards and a stable currency. Economic growth gained momentum in 2004 and the upturn accelerated through 2005. Denmark is self-sufficient in oil and natural gas. Services, including tourism, form the largest sector (63% of GDP). Farming employs only 4% of the workforce but is highly productive. Fishing is also important.

Estonia *Eesti*

Area 45,100 sq km
(17,413 sq miles)
Population 1,332,893
Capital Tallinn (392,000)
Languages Estonian (official), Russian
GDP 2005 US$16,400
Currency Kroon = 100 sents
Government multiparty republic
Head of state President Arnold Rüütel, Estonian People's Union, 2001
Head of government Prime Minister Andrus Ansip, Reform Party 2005
Website www.riik.ee/en
Events In 1992 Estonia adopted a new constitution and multiparty elections were held. Estonia joined NATO in March 2004 and the EU in May 2004. In June 2004 the value of the Kroon was fixed against the Euro with a view to joining in 2007.

Economy Privatisation and free-trade reforms have increased foreign investment and trade with the EU. Chief natural resources are oil shale and forests. The economy benefits from strong electronics and telecommunications sectors. The state budget is essentially in balance and public debt is low. Manufactures include petrochemicals, fertilisers and textiles.

Finland *Suomi*

Area 338,145 sq km
(130,557 sq miles)
Population 5,223,442
Capital Helsinki (558,000)
Languages Finnish, Swedish (both official)
GDP 2005 US$30,300

Currency Euro = 100 cents
Government multiparty republic
Head of state President Tarja Kaarina Halonen, 2000
Head of government Prime Minister Matti Vanhanen, Centre Party, 2003
Website www.government.fi
Events In 1986 Finland became a member of EFTA, and in 1995 joined the EU. A new constitution was established in March 2000. A coalition was set up between the Social Democrats and the Swedish Peoples' Party after a close election result in 2003.

Economy Forests are Finland's most valuable resource, with wood and paper products accounting for 35% of exports. Engineering, shipbuilding and textile industries have grown. Finland excels in high-tech exports and is a leading light in the telecoms industry. Farming employs 9% of the workforce. High unemployment is a persistent problem.

France

Area 551,500 sq km
(212,934 sq miles)
Population 60,656,178
Capital Paris (9,630,000)
Languages French (official), Breton, Occitan
GDP 2005 US$29,900
Currency Euro = 100 cents
Government multiparty republic
Head of state President Jacques Chirac, Assembly for the Republic, 1995
Head of government Prime Minister Dominique de Villepin, Democratie Liberale, 2005
Website www.elysee.fr
Events In 2002 voter apathy led to FN leader Jean-Marie Le Pen reaching second round of voting in presidential elections above Lionel Jospin, who resigned as PM after the presidential elections which Jacques Chirac won with 82% of the vote. As a result of their opposition to the 2003 war in Iraq, France and Germany have forged closer ties while relations with the UK and the US have been put under some strain. The US believes that France is being ungrateful for their assistance in WWII some 60 years before. The resounding 'no' vote in the referendum on the European constitution in May 2005 led both to the resignation of PM Jean-Pierre Raffarin and further decline in the relationship between Jacques Chirac and Tony Blair over the UK's rebate and Common Agricultural Policy subsidies for French farmers. Riots in October and November 2005 led to strong debates about integration and discrimination in France.

Economy France is a leading industrial nation. It is the world's fourth-largest manufacturer of cars. Industries include chemicals and steel. It is the leading producer of farm products in western Europe. Livestock and dairy farming are

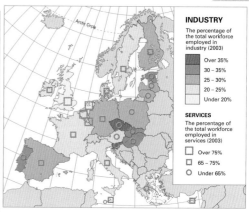

INDUSTRY
The percentage of the total workforce employed in industry (2003)
- Over 35%
- 30 – 35%
- 25 – 30%
- 20 – 25%
- Under 20%

SERVICES
The percentage of the total workforce employed in services (2003)
- Over 75%
- 65 – 75%
- Under 65%

vital sectors. It is the world's second-largest producer of cheese and wine. Tourism is a major industry.

Germany *Deutschland*

Area 357,022 sq km
(137,846 sq miles)
Population 82,431,390
Capital Berlin (3,387,000)
Languages German (official)
GDP 2005 US$29,700
Currency Euro = 100 cents
Government federal multiparty republic
Head of state President Horst Köehler, Christian Democratic Union, 2004
Head of government Chancellor Angela Merkel in coalition with SPD
Website www.deutschland.de
Events Germany is a major supporter of the European Union, and former chancellor Helmut Köhl was the driving force behind the creation of the Euro. During 2002, state elections in the former German Democratic Republic saw massive losses for the Social Democrats. As a result of their opposition to the 2003 war in Iraq Germany and France have forged closer ties. In July 2005, Schröder triggered early general elections, which took place in September 2005. The opposition Christian Democratic Union (CDU) and its sister party, the Christian Social Union (CSU), significantly lost momentum during the campaign and ultimately won only 1% more votes. Exit polls showed clearly that neither coalition group had won a majority of seats. On October 10, 2005, officials indicated that negotiations had concluded successfully and that the participating parties would form a Grand Coalition with Angela Merkel as Chancellor.

Economy Germany is one of the world's greatest economic powers. Services form the largest economic sector. Machinery and transport equipment account for 50% of exports. It is the world's third-

largest car producer. Other major products: ships, iron, steel, petroleum, tyres. It has the world's second-largest lignite mining industry. Other minerals: copper, potash, lead, salt, zinc, aluminium. Germany is the world's second-largest producer of hops and beer, and fifth-largest of wine. Other products: cheese and milk, barley, rye, pork.

Greece *Ellas*

Area 131,957 sq km
(50,948 sq miles)
Population 10,668,354
Capital Athens / Athina (3,116,000)
Languages Greek (official)
GDP 2005 US$22,800
Currency Euro = 100 cents
Government multiparty republic
Head of state President Karolos Papoulias, Panhellenic Socialist Movement (PASOK), 2005
Head of government Prime Minister Konstandinos Karamanlis, New Democracy Party, 2004
Website www.greece.gr
Events In 1981 Greece joined the EU and Andreas Papandreou became Greece's first socialist prime minister, 1981-89 and 1993-96. PM Costas Karamanlis is the nephew of former Greek president Constantine Karamanlis. The issue of Cyprus is still contentious in Greece's relations with Turkey, with the southern two-thirds still being Greek Cypriot and no agreement on unification yet reached. In July 2004 Greece unexpectedly won the European football championships. The 28th Olympiad took place in Greece in August 2004. Karolos Papoulias was nominated President by the PM in 2005.

Economy Greece is one of the poorest members of the European Union. Manufacturing is important. Products: textiles, cement, chemicals, metallurgy. Minerals: lignite, bauxite, chromite. Farmland covers 33% of Greece, grazing land 40%.

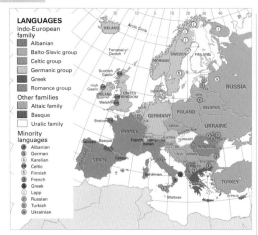

LANGUAGES

Indo-European family

- Albanian
- Balto-Slavic group
- Celtic group
- Germanic group
- Greek
- Romance group

Other families

- Altaic family
- Basque
- Uralic family

Minority languages

- Ⓐ Albanian
- Ⓓ German
- Ⓚ Karelian
- Ⓒ Celtic
- Ⓕ Finnish
- Ⓕ French
- Ⓖ Greek
- Ⓛ Lapp
- Ⓡ Russian
- Ⓣ Turkish
- Ⓤ Ukrainian

Major crops: tobacco, olives, grapes, cotton, wheat. Livestock are raised. Tourism provides 15% of GDP.

Hungary *Magyarorszàg*

Area 93,032 sq km
(35,919 sq miles)
Population 10,006,835
Capital Budapest (1,819,000)
Languages Hungarian (official)
GDP 2005 US$15,900
Currency Forint = 100 filler
Government
multiparty republic
Head of state
President Laszlo Solyom, 2005
Head of government
Prime Minister Ferenc Gyurcsany, 2004
Website
www.magyarorszag.hu/angol
Events In 1990 multiparty elections were won by the conservative Democratic Forum. In 1999 Hungary joined NATO. Former PM Peter Medgyessy narrowly avoided having to resign in 2002 when he admitted to having worked for the secret services in the late 70s/early 80s, but denied working for the KGB. He oversaw Hungary's accession to the European Union in May 2004 but resigned later in the year after arguments over a cabinet reshuffle with coalition co-members the Free Democrats. Hungary still has problems with discrimination against the Roma community, though in the European elections of 2004 a member of this ethnic group was elected for the first time. Hungary is aiming to adopt the Euro in 2010.
Economy Since the early 1990s, Hungary has adopted market reforms and privatisation programmes. Inflation has declined from 14% in 1998 to 3.7% in 2005. Germany is by far Hungary's largest economic partner. The manufacture of machinery and transport is the most valuable sector. Hungary's resources

include bauxite, coal and natural gas. Major crops include grapes for winemaking, maize, potatoes, sugar beet and wheat. Tourism is a growing sector.

Iceland *Ísland*

Area 103,000 sq km
(39,768 sq miles)
Population 296,737
Capital Reykjavik (114,500)
Languages Icelandic
GDP 2005 US$34,600
Currency Krona = 100 aurar
Government multiparty republic
Head of state
President Olafur Ragnar Grimsson, 1996
Head of government
Prime Minister Halldor Asgrimsson, Progressive Party, 2004
Website http://government.is
Events In 1944, a referendum decisively voted to sever links with Denmark, and Iceland became a fully independent republic. In 1946 it joined NATO. The USA maintained military bases on Iceland after WWII. In 1970 Iceland joined the European Free Trade Association. The extension of Iceland's fishing limits in 1958 and 1972 precipitated the "Cod War" with the UK. In 1977, the UK agreed not to fish within Iceland's 370km fishing limits. The continuing US military presence remains a political issue. David Oddson leader of the Independence Party stood down as PM in September 2004 and the leader of coalition partner the Progressive Party Halldor Asgrimsson took over the premiership.
Economy The economy remains sensitive to declining fish stocks as well as to fluctuations in world prices for its main exports: fish and fish products, aluminum, and ferrosilicon. There is low unemployment, and remarkably even distribution of income.

Ireland, Republic of *Eire*

Area 70,273 sq km
(27,132 sq miles)
Population 4,015,676
Capital Dublin (985,000)
Languages Irish, English (both official)
GDP 2005 US$34,100
Currency Euro = 100 cents
Government multiparty republic
Head of state
President Mary McAleese, 1997
Head of government Taoiseach Bertie Ahern, Fianna Fáil, 1997
Website www.irlgov.ie
Events In 1948 Ireland withdrew from the British Commonwealth and joined the European Community in 1973. The Anglo-Irish Agreement (1985) gave Ireland a consultative role in the affairs of Northern Ireland. Following a 1995 referendum, divorce was legalised. Abortion remains a contentious political issue. In 1997 elections Bertie Ahern became taoiseach and Mary McAleese became president. In the Good Friday Agreement of 1998 the Irish Republic gave up its constitutional claim to Northern Ireland and a North-South Ministerial Council was established. Sinn Fein got its first seats in the European elections of June 2004.
Economy Ireland has benefited greatly from its membership of the European Union. It joined in circulating the euro in 2002. Grants have enabled the modernisation of farming, which employs 14% of the workforce. Major products include cereals, cattle and dairy products, sheep, sugar beet and potatoes. Fishing is important. Traditional sectors, such as brewing, distilling and textiles, have been supplemented by high-tech industries, such as electronics. Tourism is the most important component of the service industry. The economy has also benefited from a rise in consumer spending, construction, and business investment.

Italy *Italia*

Area 301,318 sq km
(116,338 sq miles)
Population 58,103,033
Capital Rome / Roma (2,649,000)
Languages Italian (official)
GDP 2005 US$28,300
Currency Euro = 100 cents
Government social democracy
Head of state President Giorgio Napolitano, 2006
Head of government Romano Prodi, L'Unione, 2006
Website www.enit.it
Events In the 2006 general election, prime minister Silvio Berlusconi, leader of the centre-right House of Freedoms, was closely defeated by Romano Prodi, leader of the centre-left The Union. Prodi declared victory on 11 April. Berlusconi

was Italy's longest serving premier in half a century. The mandate of President Ciampi came to an end in May 2006, he declined to run again. Giorgio Napolitano was elected and his term officially started with a swearing-in ceremony on 15 May.
Economy Italy's main industrial region is the north-western triangle of Milan, Turin and Genoa. It is the world's eighth-largest car and steel producer. Machinery and transport equipment account for 37% of exports. Agricultural production is important. Italy is the world's largest producer of wine. Tourism is a vital economic sector. The economy experienced almost no growth in 2005 and unemployment remained at a high level.

Latvia *Latvija*

Area 64,589 sq km
(24,942 sq miles)
Population 2,290,237
Capital Riga (811,000)
Languages
Latvian (official), Russian
GDP 2005 US$12,800
Currency Lats = 100 santims
Government multiparty republic
Head of state
President Vaira Vike-Freiberga, 1999
Head of government
Prime Minister Aigars Kalvitis, People's Party, 2004
Website www.lv
Events In 1993 Latvia held its first multiparty elections. President Vaira Vike-Freiberga was re-elected for a second four-year term in June 2003. Latvia became a member of NATO and the EU in spring 2004. People applying for citizenship are now required to pass a Latvian language test, which has caused much upset amongst the one third of the population who are Russian speakers. As a result many are without citizenship, much like their compatriots in Estonia. PM Indulis Emsis was chosen as a result of the resignation of his predecessor just before Latvia's accession to the EU. After the resignation of the ruling minority coalition in October 2004 following rejection of Indulis Emsis' budget for 2005, a new 4-party coalition was approved by parliament in December.
Economy Latvia is a lower-middle-income country. The country has to import many of the materials needed for manufacturing. Latvia produces only 10% of the electricity it needs, and the rest has to be imported from Belarus, Russia and Ukraine. Manufactures include electronic goods, farm machinery and fertiliser. Farm exports include beef, dairy products and pork. The majority of companies, banks, and real estate have been privatised.

Liechtenstein

Area 157 sq km
(61 sq miles)
Population 33,717
Capital Vaduz (5,200)
Languages German (official)
GDP 2005 US$25,000
Currency Swiss franc = 100 centimes
Government independent principality
Head of state Prince Alois, 2004
Head of government Prime Minister
Ottmar Hasler, Progressive Citizens Party,
2001
Website www.liechtenstein.li/en
Events Women finally got the vote in
1984. The principality joined the UN
in 1990. In 2003 the people voted in a
referendum to give Prince Hans Adam
II new political powers, rendering the
country Europe's only absolute monarchy with the prince having power of
veto over the government. Its status
as a tax haven has been criticised as it
has been alleged that many billions are
laundered there each year. The law has
been reformed to ensure that anonymity
is no longer permitted when opening
a bank account. In August 2004 Prince
Hans Adam II transferred the day-to-day
running of the country to his son Prince
Alois, though he did not abdicate and
remains titular head of state. Following
elections in 2005, the government is
made up of 3 ministers from the Progressive Citizens Party and 2 from the
People's Union.
Economy Liechtenstein is the fourth-
smallest country in the world and one
of the richest per capita. Since 1945
it has rapidly developed a specialised
manufacturing base. It imports more
than 90% of its energy requirements.
The economy is widely diversified with a
large number of small businesses. Tourism is increasingly important.

Lithuania *Lietuva*

Area 65,200 sq km
(25,173 sq miles)
Population 3,596,617
Capital Vilnius (542,000)
Languages Lithuanian (official),
Russian, Polish
GDP 2005 US$13,700
Currency Litas = 100 centai
Government multiparty republic
Head of state President Valdas Adam-
kus, 2004
Head of government Premier Algirdas
Mykolas Brazauskas, Social Democratic
Party, 2001
Website www.lithuania.lt
Events The Soviet Union recognised
Lithuania as independent in September
1991. Valdas Adamkus regained the
presidency from Rolandus Paksas after
the latter was impeached in April 2004
after being found guilty of leaking clas-
sified material and unlawfully granting

citizenship to a Russian businessman
who had funded his election campaign.
His successor was also his predecessor.
Lithuania joined NATO in March 2004
and the EU in May 2004. In June 2004
Lithuania fixed the value of the Litas
against the Euro with a view to joining
in 2007.
Economy Lithuania is dependent on
Russian raw materials. Manufacturing
is the most valuable export sector and
major products include chemicals, electronic goods and machine tools. Dairy
and meat farming and fishing are also
important activities. More than 80% of
enterprises have been privatised.

Luxembourg

Area 2,586 sq km
(998 sq miles)
Population 468,571
Capital Luxembourg (76,300)
Languages Luxembourgian / Letzburg-
ish (official), French, German
GDP 2005 US$62,700
Currency Euro = 100 cents
Government constitutional monarchy
(or grand duchy)
Head of state Grand Duke Henri, 2000
Head of government Prime Minister
Jean-Claude Juncker, Christian Social
People's Party, 1995
Website www.luxembourg.lu/en
Events Following 1994 elections, the
Christian Social People's Party (CD)
and the Luxembourg Socialist Workers'
Party (SOC) formed a coalition govern-
ment, which lasted until 1999 and was
followed by a 5-year coalition with the
Democratic Party. Grand Duke Jean abdi-
cated in favour of his son Prince Henri
in October 2000. In general elections in
2004, the CD held on to power, again in
coalition with the SOC. In 2005 the people voted for the European constitution.
Economy It has a stable, high-income
economy, benefiting from its proximity
to France, Germany and Belgium. The
city of Luxembourg is a major centre of
European administration and finance.
Its strict laws on secrecy in banking
have meant that tax evasion and fraud
are prevalent. There are rich deposits
of iron ore, and is a major producer of
iron and steel. Other industries include
chemicals, textiles, tourism, banking and
electronics.

Former Yugoslav Republic of Macedonia *Makedonija*

Area 25,713 sq km
(9,927 sq miles)
Population 2,045,262
Capital Skoplje (477,400)
Languages Macedonian (official),
Albanian
GDP 2005 US$7,400
Currency Denar = 100 deni
Government multiparty republic

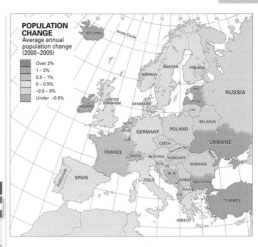

POPULATION CHANGE
Average annual
population change
(2000–2005)

Over 2%
1 – 2%
0.5 – 1%
0 – 0.5%
–0.5 – 0%
Under –0.5%

Head of state President Branko
Crvenkovski, Social Democrat Union,
2004
Head of government
Vlado Buckovski, Social Democrats, 2004
Website www.vlada.mk
Events In 1993 the UN accepted the
new republic as a member. Still retains
the FYR prefix due to Greek fears that
the name implies territorial ambitions
towards the Greek region named Macedonia. President Branko Crvenoski was
elected in April 2004 as a result of the
death in a plane crash of Boris Trajkovski.
He aims to continue the improvement of
the country with EU membership as the
goal. The government is a coalition of
Social Democrat Union and Democratic
Union for Integration (Albanian community). In August 2004, proposed expan-
sion of rights and local autonomy for
Albanians provoked riots by Macedonian
nationalists, but the ensuing referendum
was rendered invalid by a low turnout
and the measures went through.
Economy Macedonia is a developing
country. The poorest of the six former
republics of Yugoslavia, its economy was
devastated by UN trade damaged by
sanctions against Yugoslavia and by the
Greek embargo. The GDP is increasing
each year and successful privatisation in
2000 boosted the country's reserves to
over $700 Million. Manufactures, espe-
cially metals, dominate exports. Agriculture employs 17% of the workforce.
Major crops include cotton, fruits, maize,
tobacco and wheat.

Malta

Area 316 sq km
(122 sq miles)
Population 398,534
Capital Valetta (6,700)
Languages Maltese, English (both
official)

GDP 2005 US$18,800
Currency Maltese lira = 100 cents
Government multiparty republic
Head of state President Edward Fenech
Adami, Christian Democratic Nationalist
Party, 2004
Head of government Prime Minister
Lawrence Gonzi, Christian Democratic
Nationalist Party, 2004
Website www.gov.mt
Events In 1990 Malta applied to join
the EU. In 1997 the newly elected Malta
Labour Party pledged to rescind the
application. The Christian Democratic
Nationalist Party, led by the pro-Euro-
pean Edward Fenech Adami, regained
power in 1998 elections. Malta joined
the EU in May 2004.
Economy Malta produces only about
20% of its food needs, has limited fresh
water supplies and has few domestic
energy sources. Machinery and transport equipment account for more than
50% of exports. Malta's historic naval
dockyards are now used for commercial
shipbuilding and repair. Manufactures
include chemicals, electronic equipment and textiles. The largest sector is
services, especially tourism. Privatisation
of state-controlled companies and liber-
alisation of markets is still a contentious
issue.

Moldova

Area 33,851 sq km
(13,069 sq miles)
Population 4,455,421
Capital Chisinau (623,600)
Languages Moldovan / Romanian
(official)
GDP 2005 US$2,100
Currency Leu = 100 bani
Government multiparty republic
Head of state President Vladimir
Voronin, Communist Party, 2001

Head of government Prime Minister Vasile Tarlev, Communist Party, 2001
Website www.parliament.md/en.html
Events In 1994 a referendum rejected reunification with Romania and Parliament voted to join the CIS. A new constitution established a presidential parliamentary republic. In 2001 Vladimir Voronin was elected president - the first former Soviet state to elect a Communist as its president. The Transnistria region mainly inhabited by Russian and Ukrainian speakers declared independence from Moldova in 1990 fearing the impact of closer ties with Romania, this independence has never been recognised. Relations with Moscow have cooled in the last few years and Voronin is now actively seeking ties with the west.
Economy There is a favourable climate and good farmland but no major mineral deposits. Agriculture is important and major products include fruits and grapes for wine-making. Farmers also raise livestock, including dairy cattle and pigs. Moldova has to import materials and fuels for its industries. Exports include food, wine, tobacco and textiles. The economy remains vulnerable to higher fuel prices and poor agricultural weather.

Monaco

Area 1.5 sq km (0.6 sq miles)
Population 32,409
Capital Monaco-Ville (970)
Languages French (official), Italian, Monegasque
GDP 2005 US$27,000
Currency Euro = 100 cents
Government principality
Head of state Prince Albert II, 2005
Head of government Minister of State Jean-Paul Proust, 2005
Website www.monaco.gouv.mc
Events Monaco has been ruled by the Grimaldi family since the end of the 13th century and been under the protection of France since 1860.
Economy The chief source of income is tourism. The state retains monopolies in tobacco, the telephone network and the postal service. There is some light industry, including printing, textiles and postage stamps. Also a major banking centre, residents live tax free. The state has been accused of tolerating money laundering.

Montenegro *Crna Gora*

Area 13,812 sq km (5,333 sq miles)
Population 680,158
Capital Podgorica (160,100)
Languages Serbian (of the Ijekavian dialect)
GDP 2005 US$3,100
Currency Euro = 100 cents
Government federal republic

Head of state President of Montenegro Filip Vujanovic, 2003
Head of government Prime Minister Milo Djukanovic, Democratic Party of Socialists, 2002
Website www.montenegro.yu
Events In 1992 Montenegro went into federation with Serbia, first as Federal Republic of Yugoslavia, then as a looser State Union of Serbia and Montenegro. Montenegro formed its own economic policy and adopted the Deutschmark as its currency in 1999. It currently uses the euro, though it is not formally part of the Eurozone. In 2002, Serbia and Montenegro came to a new agreement regarding continued cooperation. On 21 May 2006, the status of the union was decided as 55.54% of voters voted for independence of Montenegro, narrowly passing the 55% threshold needed to validate the referendum under rules set by the EU. On 3 June 2006 the Parliament of Montenegro declared independence, formally confirming the result of the referendum on independence. Montenegro has begun the process of seeking international recognition as well as a seat at international organisations.
Economy A rapid period of urbanisation and industrialisation was created within the communism era of Montenegro. During 1993, two thirds of the Montenegrin population lived below the poverty line. Financial losses under the effects of the UN sanctions on the economy of Montenegro are estimated to be $6.39 billion - the second highest hyperinflation in the history of humankind. Today there is faster and more efficient privatisation, introduction of VAT and usage of the euro.

The Netherlands *Nederland*

Area 41,526 sq km (16,033 sq miles)
Population 16,407,491
Capital Amsterdam (1,105,000); administrative capital 's-Gravenhage (The Hague) (440,000)
Languages Dutch (official), Frisian
GDP 2005 US$30,500
Currency Euro = 100 cents
Government constitutional monarchy
Head of state Queen Beatrix, 1980
Head of government Prime Minister Jan Peter Balkenende, Christian Democrats, 2002
Website www.holland.com
Events A founding member of NATO and the EU. In 2002 Pim Fortuyn, leader of right wing anti-immigrant party Lijst Pim Fortuyn was assassinated. Subsequently Wim Kok lost power to Jan Peter Balkenende who formed a coalition cabinet with the Democrats-66 and VVD (Peoples' Party for Freedom and

Democracy). Like the French, the Dutch voters rejected the proposed European constitution in 2005.
Economy The Netherlands has prospered through its close European ties. Private enterprise has successfully combined with progressive social policies. It is highly industrialised. Products include aircraft, chemicals, electronics and machinery. Agriculture is intensive and mechanised, employing only 5% of the workforce. Dairy farming is the leading agricultural activity. It continues to be one of the leading European nations for attracting foreign direct investment.

Norway *Norge*

Area 323,877 sq km (125,049 sq miles)
Population 4,593,041
Capital Oslo (779,000)
Languages Norwegian (official), Lappish, Finnish
GDP 2005 US$42,400
Currency Krone = 100 øre
Government constitutional monarchy
Head of state King Harald V, 1991
Head of government Prime Minister Jens Stoltenberg, Labour, 2005
Website www.norge.no
Events In referenda in 1972 and 1994 Norway rejected joining the EU. A centre-left coalition, the Labour-led 'Red-Green Alliance' won closely contested elections in September 2005.
Economy Norway has one of the world's highest standards of living. Discovery of oil and gas in adjacent waters in the late 1960s boosted its economic fortunes, with its chief exports now oil and natural gas. Per capita, it is the world's largest producer of hydroelectricity. It is possible oil and gas will begin to run out in Norway in the next two decades but it has been saving its oil budget surpluses and is invested abroad in a fund, now valued at more than $150 billion. Major manufactures include petroleum products, chemicals, aluminium, wood pulp and paper. The chief farming activities are dairy and meat production, but Norway has to import food.

Poland *Polska*

Area 323,250 sq km (124,807 sq miles)
Population 38,635,144
Capital Warsaw / Warszawa (1,626,000)
Languages Polish (official)
GDP 2005 US$12,700
Currency Zloty = 100 groszy
Government multiparty republic
Head of state President Lech Kaczynski, Law and Justice (PiS), 2005
Head of government Prime Minister Kazimierz Marcinkiewicz, Law and Justice (PiS), 2005
Website www.poland.pl
Events In 1996 Poland joined the

Organisation for Economic Cooperation and Development. Poland joined NATO in 1999 and the EU in May 2004. The 2005 elections brought in President Kaczynski of the right-wing Law and Justice party – the party was established in 2001 by the Kaczynski twins. Poland sent about 2,000 troops to Iraq in support of the US, the new President stating these troops could continue their mission in Iraq beyond the current timetable.
Economy Of the workforce, 27% is employed in agriculture and 37% in industry. The GDP per capita roughly equals that of the three Baltic states. Poland is the world's fifth-largest producer of lignite and ships. Copper ore is also a vital resource. Manufacturing accounts for 24% of exports. Agriculture remains important. Major crops include barley, potatoes and wheat. Economic growth is slowly returning.

Portugal

Area 88,797 sq km (34,284 sq miles)
Population 10,566,212
Capital Lisbon / Lisboa (3,861,000)
Languages Portuguese (official)
GDP 2005 US$18,400
Currency Euro = 100 cents
Government multiparty republic
Head of state President Jorge Sampaio, Socialist Party, 1996
Head of government Jose Socrates, Socialist Party, 2005
Website www.portugal.gov.pt
Events In 1986 Portugal joined the EU. In 2002 the Social Democrat Party won the election and formed a coalition government with the Popular Party. The opposition Socialist Party were clear victors in European elections of June 2004, a result attributed in part to the ruling party's support for the war in Iraq Portugal hosted the Euro 2004 football championships. PM Barroso was chosen as president of EU Commission in July 2004 and consequently resigned his premiership. President Sampaio chose Lisbon mayor Pedro Santana Lopes to succeed him. The leader of the Socialists, Eduardo Ferro Rodrigues then resigned in protest saying Sampaio should have ordered elections. In the general election in February 2005, the Socialists won an outright majority under their new leader Jose Socrates.
Economy Portugal's commitment to the EU has seen the economy emerge from recession, but a poor educational system, in particular, has been an obstacle to greater productivity and growth. Manufacturing accounts for 33% of exports. Textiles, footwear and clothing are major exports. Portugal is the world's fifth-largest producer of tungsten and eighth-largest producer of wine. Olives, potatoes and wheat are also grown. Tourism is very important.

Romania

Area 238,391 sq km
(92,042 sq miles)
Population 22,329,977
Capital Bucharest / Bucuresti
(2,001,000)
Languages Romanian (official), Hungarian
GDP 2005 US$8,300
Currency Romanian leu = 100 bani
Government multiparty republic
Head of state President Traian Basescu, 2004
Head of government Calin Popescu-Tariceanu, 2004
Website www.gov.ro/engleza
Events A new constitution was introduced in 1991. Ion Iliescu, a former communist official, was re-elected in 2000, but barred from standing again in 2004, when he was replaced by Traian Basescu. Tariceanu's government is a centrist coalition. Romania joined NATO in March 2004 and signed its EU accession treaty in April 2005 and could become a member in 2007/08, depending on the pace of reform. The Romany minority still suffers from discrimination.
Economy In 2005, confidence in the economic process was emphasised whenthe government re-valued its currency, making 10,000 'old' Lei equal to 1 'new' Lei.

Russia *Rossiya*

Area 17,075,000 sq km
(6,592,800 sq miles)
Population 143,420,309
Capital Moscow / Moskva (8,367,000)
Languages Russian (official), and many others
GDP 2005 US$10,700
Currency Russian ruble = 100 kopeks
Government federal multiparty republic
Head of state President Vladimir Putin, 2000
Head of government Premier Mikail Fradkov, 2004
Website www.president.kremlin.ru/eng/
Events In 1992 the Russian Federation became a co-founder of the CIS (Commonwealth of Independent States). A new Federal Treaty was signed between the central government and the autonomous republics within the Russian Federation, Chechnya refused to sign and declared independence. In December 1993 a new democratic constitution was adopted. From 1994 to 1996, Russia fought a costly civil war in Chechnya which flared up again in 1999. Tycoons who have capitalised on the change to a capitalist system find themselves under criminal investigation. Putin re-elected March 2004, much criticism in the west of media bias towards him that left opponents little opportunity to broadcast their views, this also applied to parliamentary elections of December 2003. Putin has a very high level of control over parliament and appointed the PM Fradkov. The only privately owned national television station was closed in 2003. Moscow-backed Chechen president Kadryov assassinated in May 2004. In September 2004 Chechen separatists stormed a school in North Ossetia taking over 1000 children and adults hostage. Hundreds died when bombs were set off and a gun battle ensued.
Economy In 1993 mass privatisation began. By 1996, 80% of the Russian economy was in private hands. A major problem remains the size of Russia's foreign debt. It is reliant on world oil prices to keep its economy from crashing. Industry employs 46% of the workforce and contributes 48% of GDP. Mining is the most valuable activity. Russia is the world's leading producer of natural gas and nickel, the second largest producer of aluminium and phosphates. and the third-largest of crude oil, lignite and brown coal. Most farmland is still government-owned or run as collectives, with important products barley, oats, rye, potatoes, beef and veal.

San Marino

Area 61 sq km (24 sq miles)
Population 28,880
Capital San Marino (4,600)
Languages Italian (official)
GDP 2005 US$34,600
Currency Euro = 100 cents
Government multiparty republic
Head of state co-Chiefs of State: Captain Regent Gian Franco Terenzi and Captain Regent Loris Francini
Head of government Secretary of State for Foreign and Political Affairs Fabio Berardi, 2003
Website www.omniway.sm
Events World's smallest republic and perhaps Europe's oldest state, San Marino's links with Italy led to the adoption of the Euro. Its 60-member Great and General Council is elected every five years and headed by two captains-regent, who are elected by the council every six months.
Economy The economy is largely agricultural. Tourism is vital to the state's income, contributing over 50% of GDP. Also a tax haven used by many non-residents.

Serbia *Srbija*

Area 88,412 sq km
(34,137 sq miles)
Population 9,981,929
Capital Belgrade / Beograd (1,113,500)
Languages Serbian
GDP 2005 US$3,200
Currency Dinar = 100 paras
Government federal republic
Head of state President of Serbia Boris Tadic, Democratic Party, 2004
Head of government Prime Minister Vojislav Kostunica, Democratic Party, 2004
Website www.serbia-tourism.org
Events In 1989 Slobodan Milosevic became president of Serbia and called for the creation of a "Greater Serbia". Serbian attempts to dominate the Yugoslav federation led to the secession of Slovenia and Croatia in 1991 and to Bosnia-Herzegovina's declaration of independence in March 1992. Serbian aid to the Bosnian Serb campaign of "ethnic cleansing" in the civil war in Bosnia led the UN to impose sanctions on Serbia. In 1995 Milosevic signed the Dayton Peace Accord, which ended the Bosnian war. In 1997 Milosevic became president of Yugoslavia. In 1999, following the forced expulsion of Albanians from Kosovo, NATO bombed Yugoslavia, forcing withdrawal of Serbian forces from Kosovo. Kostunica won the elections of September 2000, but Milosevic refused to hand over power. After a week of civil unrest and increased support for Kostunica, Milosevic was finally ousted. From 2003 to 2006, Serbia was part of the State Union of Serbia and Montenegro. On 21 May 2006 Montenegro held a referendum to determine whether to terminate its union with Serbia. On 22 May state-certified results showed voters favouring independence. On 3 June, the Parliament of Montenegro declared Montenegro independent of the State Union, and on 5 June the National Assembly of Serbia declared Serbia the successor to the State Union.
Economy The lower-middle income economy was devastated by war and economic sanctions. Industrial production collapsed. Natural resources include bauxite, coal and copper. There is some oil and natural gas. Manufacturing includes aluminium, cars, machinery, plastics, steel and textiles. Agriculture is important.

Slovakia
Slovenska Republika

Area 49,012 sq km
(18,923 sq miles)
Population 5,431,363
Capital Bratislava (422,400)
Languages Slovak (official), Hungarian
GDP 2005 US$15,700
Currency Koruna = 100 halierov
Government multiparty republic
Head of state President Ivan Gasparovic, 2004
Head of government Prime Minister Mikulás Dzurinda, Democratic & Christian Union, 1998
Website www.slovakia.org
Events Slovakia joined NATO in March 2004 and the EU in May 2004. There is still a problem with the Romany population being deprived. The 17% turn-out for the European elections in June 2004 was the lowest of all 25 members.
Economy The transition from communism to private ownership has been painful with industrial output falling, unemployment and inflation rising. In 1995 the privatisation programme was suspended but major privatisations are nearly now complete with the banking sector almost completely in foreign hands. Manufacturing employs 33% of the workforce. Bratislava and Košice are the chief industrial cities. Major products include ceramics, machinery and steel. Farming employs 12% of the workforce. Crops include barley and grapes. Tourism is growing.

Slovenia *Slovenija*

Area 20,256 sq km
(7,820 sq miles)
Population 2,011,070
Capital Ljubljana (254,100)
Languages Slovene
GDP 2005 US$20,900
Currency Tolar = 100 stotin
Government multiparty republic
Head of state President Janez Drnovsek, Liberal Democrats of Slovenia, 2002
Head of government Prime Minister Janez Jansa, Slovenian Democratic Party, 2004
Website www.gov.si
Events In 1990 Slovenia declared itself independent, which led to brief fighting between Slovenes and the federal army. In 1992 the EU recognised Slovenia's independence. Janez Drnovsek was elected president in December 2002 and immediately stepped down as prime minister. Slovenia joined NATO in March 2004 and the EU in May 2004. In June 2004 the value of the Tolar was fixed against the Euro with a view to joining in 2007. Their reputation as a liberal nation has been somewhat scarred by the recent referendum overturning a parliamentary bill that restored citizenship of Slovenia to resident nationals of other former Yugoslav countries. The 2004 general election resulted in a coalition government of the Slovenian Democratic Party, New Slovenia, the People's Party and the Democratic Party of Pensioners.
Economy The transformation of a centrally planned economy and the fighting in other parts of former Yugoslavia have caused problems for Slovenia. Manufacturing is the leading activity. Major manufactures include chemicals, machinery, transport equipment, metal goods and textiles. Major crops include maize, fruit, potatoes and wheat.

Spain *España*

Area 497,548 sq km (192,103 sq miles)
Population 40,341,462
Capital Madrid (3,017,000)
Languages Castilian Spanish (official), Catalan, Galician, Basque
GDP 2005 US$25,100
Currency Euro = 100 cents
Government constitutional monarchy
Head of state King Juan Carlos, 1975
Head of government Prime Minister Jose Luis Rodriguez Zapatero, Socialist Party, 2004
Website www.la-moncloa.es
Events From 1959 the militant Basque organization ETA waged a campaign of terror but announced a ceasefire in 1998. Basque separatist party Batasuna was permanently banned in 2003 as it is thought to be the political wing of ETA. In March 2004 terrorist bombs exploded in Madrid killing 191 people, this was deemed to be the work of al Qaeda, though the then government were keen to persuade the people that it was the work of ETA. The country went to the polls three days later and voted Aznar out, largely seen as a reaction to his support of the US in Iraq and the sending of troops which was to blame for the bombing some three days earlier. The new PM subsequently withdrew all troops from Iraq. Although the ruling Socialist Party are short of a majority, Zapatero has pledged to govern through dialogue with others rather than form a coalition. In a referendum in 2005, Spanish voters voted for the proposed European constitution.
Economy Spain has rapidly transformed from a largely poor, agrarian society into a prosperous industrial nation. Agriculture now employs only 10% of the workforce. Spain is the world's third-largest wine producer. Other crops include citrus fruits, tomatoes and olives. Industries: cars, ships, chemicals, electronics, metal goods, steel, textiles.

Sweden *Sverige*

Area 449,964 sq km (173,731 sq miles)
Population 9,001,774
Capital Stockholm (1,612,000)
Languages Swedish (official), Finnish
GDP 2005 US$29,600
Currency Swedish krona = 100 ore
Government constitutional monarchy
Head of state King Carl XVI Gustaf, 1973
Head of government Prime Minister Göran Persson, Social Democratic Workers' Party (SSA), 1996
Website www.sweden.gov.se
Events In 1995 Sweden joined the European Union. The cost of maintaining Sweden's extensive welfare services has become a major political issue. In

September 2003 Sweden was shocked by the murder of popular minister Anna Lindh (a pro-Euro campaigner), reigniting discussion over the relaxed attitude to security. Days later Sweden said no to the Euro. Brand new Euro-sceptic party Junilistan came third in the European elections, exceeding all expectations and underlining Swedish ambivalence towards Europe.
Economy Sweden is a highly developed industrial country. It has rich iron ore deposits. Privately owned firms account for about 90% of industrial output. Steel is a major product, used to manufacture aircraft, cars, machinery and ships. Forestry and fishing are important. Agriculture accounts for only 2% of GDP and of jobs. The Swedish central bank focuses on price stability with its inflation target of 2%.

Switzerland *Schweiz*

Area 41,284 sq km (15,939 sq miles)
Population 7,489,370
Capital Bern (120,500)
Languages French, German, Italian, Romansch (all official)
GDP 2005 US$35,000
Currency Swiss Franc = 100 centimes
Government federal republic
Head of state President Samuel Schmid, 2005
Website www.gov.ch
Events Priding itself on their neutrality, Swiss voters rejected membership of the UN in 1986 and the EU in 1992 and 2001. However, Switzerland finally became a partner country of NATO in 1997 and joined the UN in 2002. The federal council is made up of seven federal ministers from whom the president is chosen on an annual basis. Prior to 2003 the allocation of posts was fixed between Free Democrats (2), Social Democrats (2), Christian Democrats (2) and Swiss People's Party (SVP) (1), however this changed after the elections of 2003 when the SVP increased their share of the vote to 28%, thereby becoming the largest party. The allocation was subsequently changed (after much debate) with the SVP taking an extra seat and the Christian Democrats losing one.
Economy Switzerland is wealthy and a stable modern market economy with low unemployment. Manufactures include chemicals, electrical equipment, machinery, precision instruments, watches and textiles. Livestock raising, notably dairy farming, is the chief agricultural activity. Tourism is important, and Swiss banks remain a safehaven for investors.

Turkey *Türkiye*

Area 774,815 sq km (299,156 sq miles)
Population 69,660,559
Capital Ankara (3,203,000)

Languages Turkish (official), Kurdish
GDP 2005 US$7,900
Currency New Turkish lira = 100 kurus
Government multiparty republic
Head of state President Ahmet Necdet Sezer, 2000
Head of government Prime Minister Recep Tayyip Erdogan, Justice and Development Party (AK), 2003
Website www.tourismturkey.org
Events The president is interested in greater freedom of expression. The PM is leader of the Islamist Justice & Development Party, though claims to be committed to secularism.
Economy Turkey is a lower-middle income developing country. Agriculture employs 47% of the workforce. Turkey is a leading producer of citrus fruits, barley, cotton, wheat, tobacco and tea. It is a major producer of chromium and phosphate fertilisers. Tourism is a vital source of foreign exchange. In January 2005, the New Turkish lira was introduced at a rate of 1 to 1,000,000 old Turkish lira. Privatisation sales are currently approaching $21 billion.

Ukraine *Ukraina*

Area 603,700 sq km (233,088 sq miles)
Population 47,425,336
Capital Kiev / Kyiv (2,621,000)
Languages Ukrainian (official), Russian
GDP 2005 US$6,800
Currency Hryvnia = 100 kopiykas
Government multiparty republic
Head of state President Viktor Yushchenko, 2005
Head of government Prime Minister Yuriy Yekhanurov, 2005
Website www.mfa.gov.ua/mfa/en
Events The Chernobyl disaster of 1986 contaminated large areas of Ukraine. Final independence was achieved in 1991 with the dissolution of the USSR. Leonid Kuchma was elected president in 1994. He continued the policy of establishing closer ties with the West and sped up the pace of privatisation. Ukraine is pushing for membership of NATO though reforms are required before this can happen. The election of November 2004 was thrown into turmoil after opposition presidential candidate Yushchenko was poisoned with dioxins and the result was declared as a victory for former PM, and pro-Russian, Viktor Yanukovich leading to accusations of electoral fraud and widespread demonstrations. After 10 days the Supreme Court declared the vote invalid and the elections were re-run, resulting in victory for the pro-west Yushchenko. In September 2005, bitter in-fighting, widespread accusations of corruption and lack of progress on economic reform led Mr Yushchenko to sack the entire cabinet and appoint Yuri Yekhanurov as acting

Prime Minister, subject to parliamentary approval.
Economy Ukraine is a lower-middle-income economy. Agriculture is important. It is the world's leading producer of sugar beet, the second-largest producer of barley, and a major producer of wheat. Ukraine has extensive raw materials, including coal (though many mines are exhausted), iron ore and manganese ore. Ukraine is reliant on oil and natural gas imports. The privatization of the Kryvoryzhstal steelworks in late 2005 produced $4.8 billion in windfall revenue for the government. Some of the proceeds were used to finance the budget deficit, some to recapitalize two state banks, some to retire public debt, and the rest may be used to finance future deficits.

United Kingdom

Area 241,857 sq km (93,381 sq miles)
Population 60,441,457
Capital London (8,089,000)
Languages English (official), Welsh (also official in Wales), Gaelic
GDP 2005 US$30,900
Currency Sterling (pound) = 100 pence
Government constitutional monarchy
Head of state Queen Elizabeth II, 1952
Head of government Prime Minister Tony Blair, Labour Party, 1997
Website www.parliament.uk
Events The United Kingdom of Great Britain and Northern Ireland is a union of four countries – England, Northern Ireland, Scotland and Wales. In 1997 referenda on devolution saw Scotland and Wales gain their own legislative assemblies. The Scottish assembly was given tax-varying power. The Good Friday Agreement of 1998 offered the best chance of peace in Northern Ireland for generation. In 2005 the IRA announced a permanent cessation of hostilities. Tony Blair controversially gave full support to Bush over the war in Iraq in 2003 The 2005 general election resulted in a reduced majority for Labour. Widesprea delight at London's winning the 2012 Olympics was shattered the following day when four suicide bombers hit the city's transport network killing 57 people.
Economy The UK is a major industrial and trading nation. The economy has become more service-centred and high-technology industries have grown in importance. A producer of oil, petroleu products, natural gas, potash, salt and lead. Agriculture employs only 2% of th workforce. Financial services and tourism are the leading service industries.

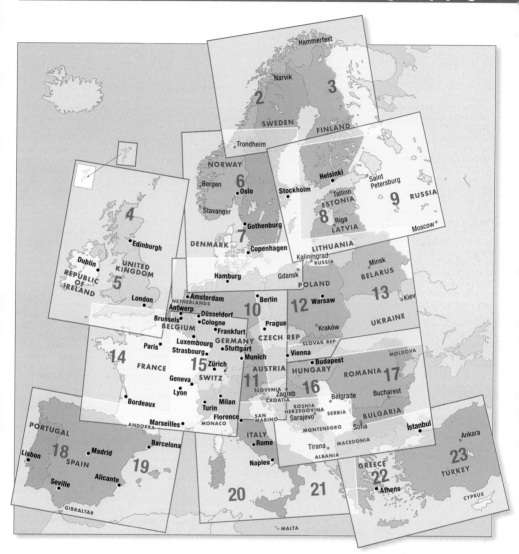

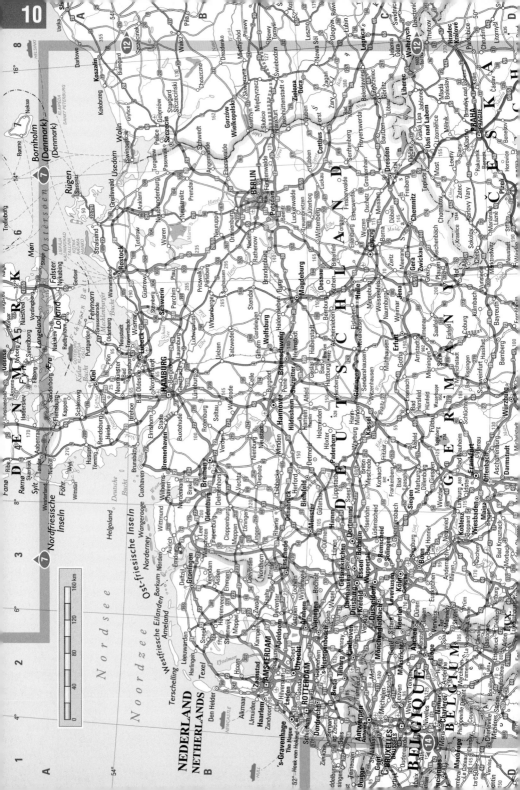

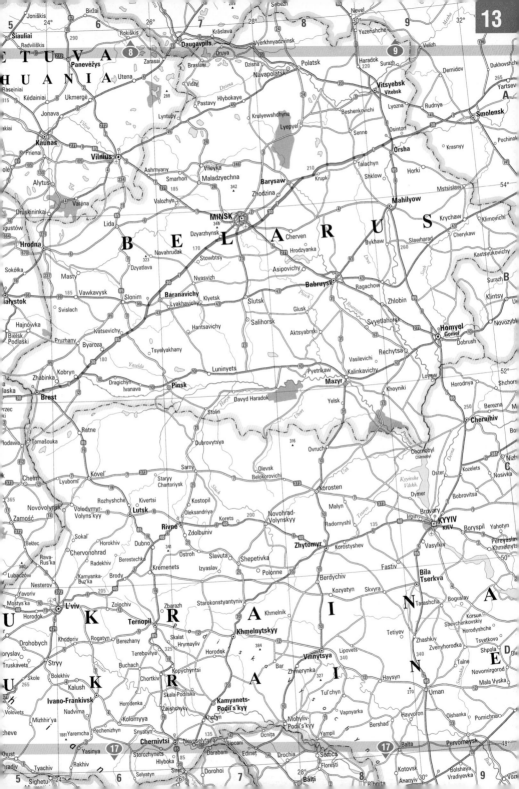

Key to road map pages

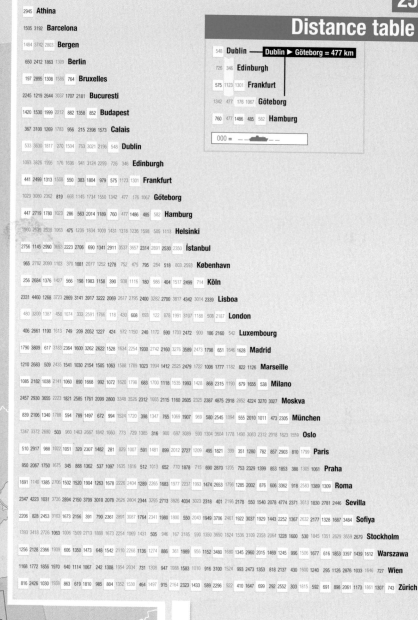

Distance table

Amsterdam

2945 **Athina**

1505 3192 **Barcelona**

1484 3742 2803 **Bergen**

650 2412 1863 1309 **Berlin**

197 2895 1308 1586 764 **Bruxelles**

2245 1219 2644 3037 1707 2181 **Bucuresti**

1420 1530 1999 2212 882 1358 852 **Budapest**

367 3100 1269 1783 956 215 2398 1573 **Calais**

533 3630 1817 270 1504 763 3021 2196 548 **Dublin**

1093 3826 1995 176 1696 941 3124 2299 726 346 **Edinburgh**

441 2499 1313 1508 550 383 1804 979 575 1123 1301 **Frankfurt**

1029 3080 2362 819 668 1145 1734 1550 1342 477 176 1067 **Göteborg**

447 2719 1780 1023 286 563 2014 1189 760 477 1486 485 582 **Hamburg**

1560 2636 2838 1063 475 1239 1834 1009 1431 1318 1236 1598 505 1113 **Helsinki**

2756 1145 2990 3653 2223 2706 690 1341 2911 3537 3657 2314 2891 2350 2350 **İstanbul**

965 2782 2090 1103 370 1081 2077 1252 1278 752 479 795 284 518 803 2593 **København**

256 2684 1376 1427 566 198 1983 1158 390 938 1116 180 986 404 1517 2499 714 **Köln**

2331 4460 1268 3723 2869 3141 3917 3222 2069 2617 2795 2400 3282 2700 3817 4342 3014 2339 **Lisboa**

480 3200 1387 458 1074 333 2591 1766 118 430 608 693 122 878 1991 3107 1188 508 2187 **London**

406 2661 1190 1613 209 209 2052 1227 424 972 1150 240 1172 590 1703 2472 900 186 2160 542 **Luxembourg**

1790 3809 617 3183 2364 1600 3262 2622 1528 1634 2254 1930 2742 2160 3276 3589 2473 1798 651 1646 1628 **Madrid**

1210 2683 509 2435 1541 1030 2154 1505 1063 1588 1789 1023 1994 1412 2525 2479 1722 1006 1777 1182 822 1126 **Marseille**

1085 2182 1038 2141 1060 890 1668 992 1072 1620 1798 683 1700 1118 1535 1993 1428 868 2315 1190 679 1655 538 **Milano**

2457 2930 3655 2223 1821 2585 1761 2099 2800 3348 3526 2312 1655 2115 1160 2605 2325 2387 4875 2918 2852 4224 3270 3027 **Moskva**

839 2106 1340 1788 594 789 1497 672 994 1524 1720 398 1347 765 1069 1907 969 580 2545 1094 555 2010 1011 473 2305 **München**

1347 3372 2680 503 960 1463 2667 1842 1660 773 729 1385 316 900 697 3089 590 1304 3804 1778 1490 3063 2312 2018 1823 1559 **Oslo**

510 2917 988 1922 1051 320 2307 1482 281 825 1007 591 1481 899 2012 2727 1209 495 1821 399 351 1280 782 857 2903 810 1799 **Paris**

950 2067 1750 1675 345 888 1362 537 1097 1635 1816 512 1013 652 770 1878 715 690 2870 1205 753 2329 1399 853 1853 386 1305 1061 **Praha**

1691 1140 1385 2706 1502 1520 1904 1263 1678 2226 2404 1289 2265 1683 1977 2237 1993 1474 2653 1796 1285 2002 876 606 3362 918 2583 1389 1309 **Roma**

2347 4223 1031 3736 2894 2150 3709 3010 2078 2626 2804 2344 3295 2713 3826 4034 3023 2318 401 2196 2178 550 1540 2078 4774 2371 3613 1830 2781 2446 **Sevilla**

2206 828 2453 3103 1673 2156 391 790 2361 2891 3087 1764 2341 1980 1800 550 2043 1949 3706 2461 1922 3037 1929 1443 2252 1367 2632 2177 1328 1687 3484 **Sofiya**

1393 3418 2726 1063 1006 1509 2713 1888 1673 2254 1069 1431 505 946 167 3185 590 1350 3650 1824 1536 3109 2358 2064 1228 1600 530 1845 1351 2629 3659 2679 **Stockholm**

1256 2128 2366 1909 606 1350 1473 648 1542 2110 2268 1136 1274 886 361 1989 956 1152 3480 1680 1345 2960 2015 1469 1245 996 1506 1677 616 1853 3397 1439 1612 **Warszawa**

1168 1772 1856 1970 640 1114 1067 242 1308 1954 2034 731 1308 947 1088 1583 1016 916 3100 1524 993 2473 1353 818 2137 410 1600 1240 295 1126 2876 1033 1646 727 **Wien**

816 2426 1030 1938 863 619 1810 985 804 1352 1530 464 1497 915 2164 2323 1433 589 2296 922 410 1647 699 292 2552 303 1815 592 691 898 2061 1173 1861 1307 743 **Zürich**

Distance table (legend box)

548 **Dublin** — Dublin ► Göteborg = 477 km

726 346 **Edinburgh**

575 1123 1301 **Frankfurt**

1342 477 176 1067 **Göteborg**

760 477 1486 485 582 **Hamburg**

000 = — — — 🚢 — —

km

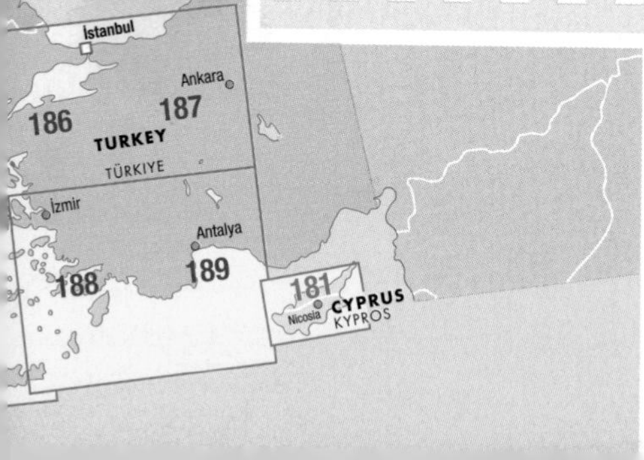

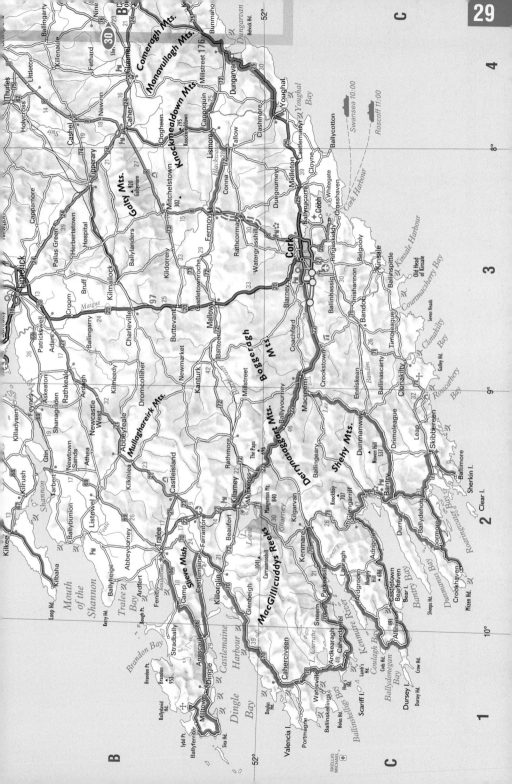

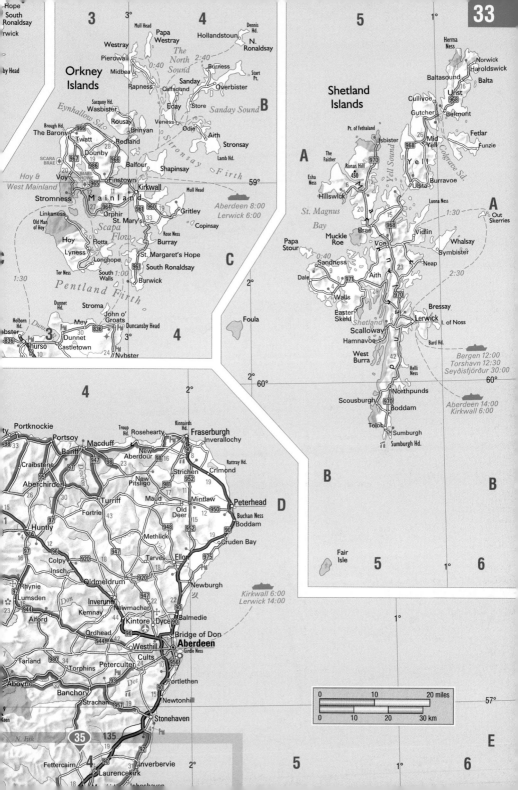

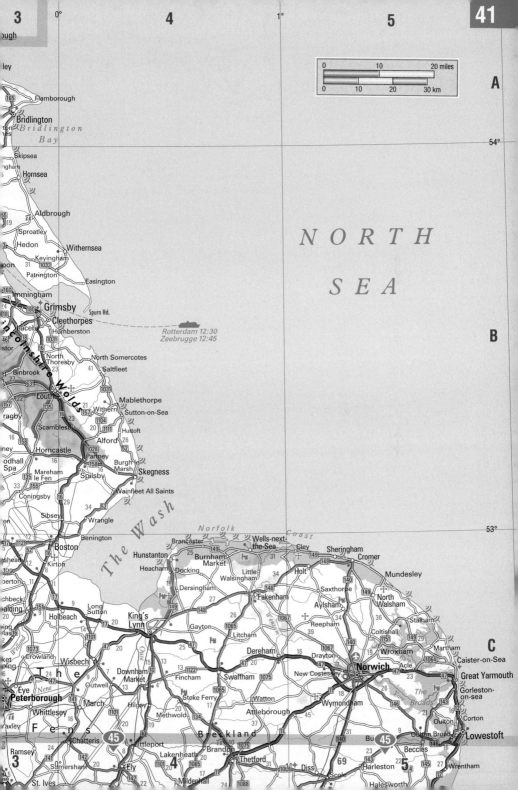

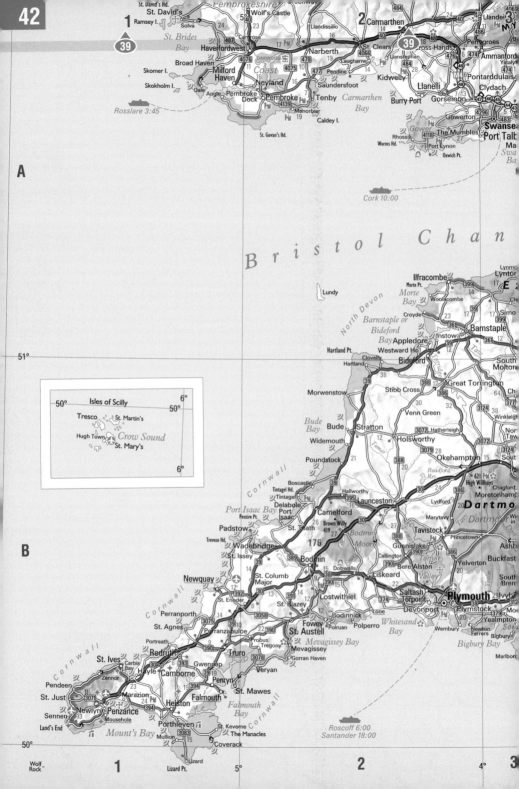

1 St. David's Hd.
St. David's
Ramsey I.
Solva

2 Carmarthen

3 Llandei
Penygroes
Ammanford
Ystalyf

Wolf's Castle
Camrose
Llandissilio
484
484
468
40
471
476
474
474 I

Haverfordwest
Narberth
St. Clears
ross-Hands
Pontardulais
Clydach
487
478
40
4066
48
45
Llanstephan
474
M4
703

Broad Haven
Milford Haven
Neyland
Saundersfoot
Laugharne
Kidwelly
Llanelli
Gorseinon
Gowerton
4076
478
4075
11
477
19
Pendine
28
Burry Port
4296

Skomer I.
Dale
Angle
Pembroke Dock
Pembroke
Tenby
Caldey I.
Gower
Swansea

Skokholm I.
4139
Manorbier
Carmarthen
Bay
The Mumbles
Port Talb
4118

Rosslare 3:45
St. Govan's Hd.
Rhossili
Worms Hd.
Port Eynon
Oxwich Pt.
Swa
Ba

A

Cork 10:00

B r i s t o l   C h a n

Lundy

Ilfracombe
Lynto
Lynmo
E
Morte Pt.
399
399

North Devon
Morte Bay
Woolacombe
14
Ch

Barnstaple or Bideford Bay
Croyde
Woolacombe
23
17
Simo
17
361
399

51°
Hartland Pt.
Clovelly
Hartland
Appledore
Westward Ho!
Instow
Barnstaple
12
361
South Molton

50° Isles of Scilly 6° 50°
Morwenstow
Bideford
38
Great Torrington
Ch
64
377

Tresco St. Martin's
Hugh Town
Crow Sound
St. Mary's
Stibb Cross
Venn Green
388
366
3124
38
Winkleigh
Nor
Taw

Bude Bay
Bude
Stratton
30
32
Hatherleigh
3072
3072

6°
Widemouth
Holsworthy
Tamar
3079
28
Okehampton
15
Sout
3124

Poundstock
21
388
20
Roadford Res.
High Willhays
621
Chagford
Moretonhamp

Boscastle
Tintagel Hd.
Tintagel
Delabole
Port Isaac
Hallworthy
Launceston
Lydford
386
Dartmo
Dartmo

Port Isaac Bay
Pentire Pt.
St. Teath
Camelford
Brown Willy
419
395
30
Marytavy
Tavistock
27
Princetown
Ashb

Padstow
Trevose Hd.
Wadebridge
Bodmin Moor
Gunnislake
Bere Alston
390
386
Yelverton
Buckfast

B
Newquay
St. Issey
Canal
389
Bodmin
176
Dobwalls
Callington
390
Saltash
Torpoint
22
Plymouth
Plymstock
Plymouth
South Bren

St. Columb Major
St. Enoder
14
14
15
Liskeard
374
Devonport
Yealmpton
312
379

Perranporth
St. Agnes
3075
392
12
13
St. Blazey
391
Lostwithiel
Looe
Polruan
Whitesand Bay
Wembury
Newton Ferrers
379

Cornwall
Portreath
Redruth
Perranzabuloe
3058
St. Austell
Fowey
Bodinnick
Polperro
Bigbury Bay
Marlbor
390
22
540
Probus
Tregony

St. Ives
Carbis Bay
Hayle
Camborne
Gwennap
Truro
Veryan
Mevagissey Bay
Mevagissey
Gorran Haven
393
390
3078

Pendeen
Zennor
24
Penryn
394
St. Mawes
Cornwall

St. Just
3071
Marazion
Helston
Falmouth
Falmouth Bay
3083
Newlyn
Penzance
Mousehole
394
Porthleven
St. Keverne
The Manacles

Sennen
Land's End
13
Mount's Bay
Mullion
3083
Coverack
15

Wolf Rock
Lizard Pt.
Lizard

Roscoff 6:00
Santander 18:00

1 5° **2** 4° **3**

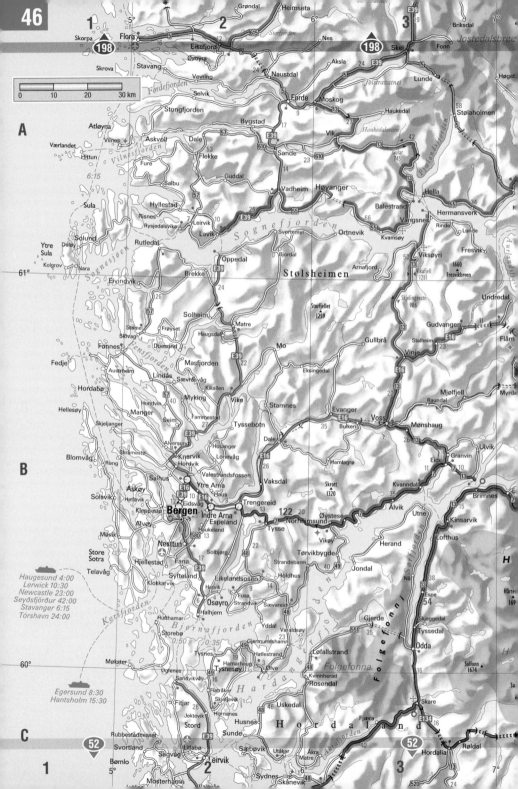

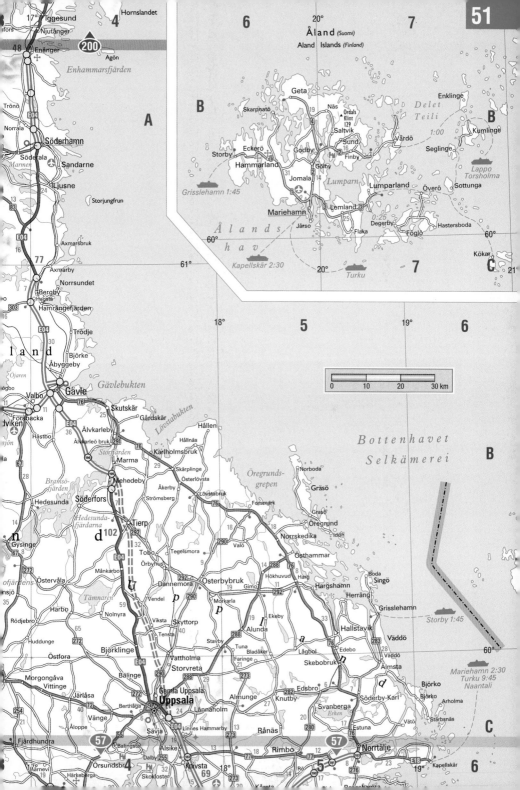

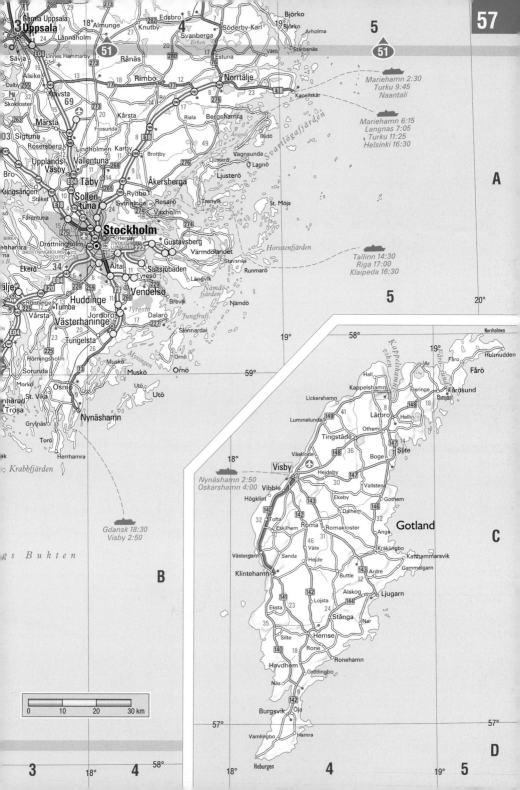

3 Gamla Uppsala
Uppsala 18° Almunge
Lannaholm Knutby Edsbro Söderby-Karl
4 Svanberga Björko
Björko Arholma **5**
51 E4 Linnés Hammarby Rånäs
273 280 Väto Stärbsnäs **51**
Dalby 255 Sävja Alsike Rimbo 77 Estuna
Knivsta Norrtälje Kapellskär Mariehamn 2:30
Skokloster 69 273 Rö Turku 9:45
263 Kårsta 795 Naantali
Märsta Frosunda 8 E18 Bergshamra Mariehamn 6:15
Sigtuna Riala Langnas 7:05
Rosersberg Lindholmen Karby Ljusterö Ångso Turku 11:25
Upplands Vallentuna Brottby 276 Ljustero Helsinki 16:30
Väsby 268 Ö Lagnö
Bro Täby Åkersberga St. Möja **A**
Kungsängen Sollentuna Rydbo Tranvik
Stäket Svinninge Resarö
Stockholm Vaxholm 274 Horstensfjärden
Hersby Tallinn 14:30
Drottningholm Gustavsberg Riga 17:00
Alta Värmdölandet Klaipeda 16:30
Ekerö Saltsjöbaden Stavsnäs
Tyresö Längvik Runmarö **5** 20°
Vendelsö Nämdö
Huddinge Brevik fjärden
Vårsta Jordbro Dalarö Nämdö
Västerhaninge Tungelsta Skinnardai Ornö
Hörningsholm Musko Ornö
Sorunda Muskö Ornö **58** Norsholmen 19° Fårö
Mörko Utö Hall Ar Fårö
St. Vika Utö Kappelshamn Fleringe Holmudden
Trosa Kappelshamnsviken Burge Fårösund
Grytnäs Lickershamn 148 18
Torö Lummelunda 149 41 Lärbro Hellvi
Herrhamra Väskinde 148 Othem
Krabbfjärden Visby 36 Boge 147 Slite
Nynäshamn Hejdeby 147
Nynäshamn 2:50 Vibble 30 Vallstena
Oskarshamn 4:00 Högklint Ekeby Gothem **C**
143 Dalhem 146
Gdansk 18:30 Tofta 142 Roma Anga
Visby 2:50 Eskilhem Romakloster
B Västergarn 46 Väte Kräklingbo
Sanda 31 Katthammarsvik
Hejde Ardre Gammelgarn
Klintehamn 143 Buttle 12
141 Alskog Ljugarn
Eksta Lojsta 142 144
23 24 Stånga
35 Nar
Silte Hemse
140 Rone
Havdhem 18 Ronehamn
Näs Grötlingbo
142
Burgsvik Öja **D**
Vamlingbo Hamra 57°
Hoburgen

0 10 20 30 km

Gotland

Horstensfjärden
Svartlögafjärden

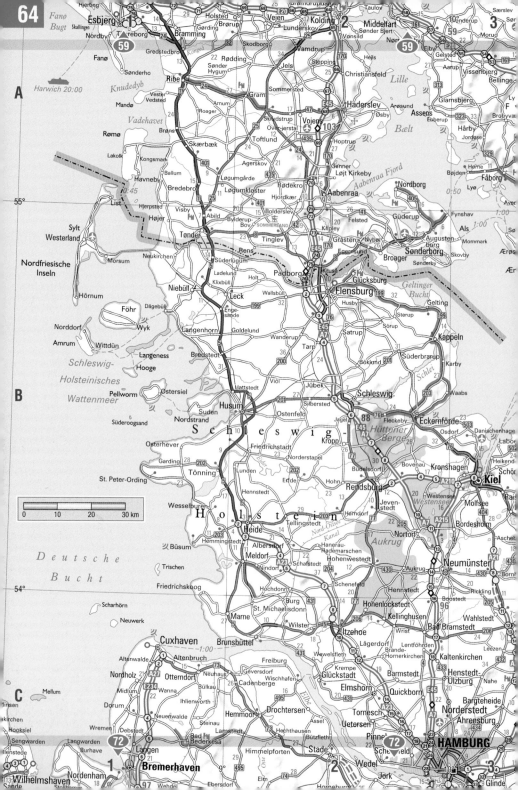

3 · 15° · 4 · 16° · 5

A

0 10 20 30 km

Simrishamn

killinge

Kolmsgattet

Ertholmene

Hammeren
Sandvig-Allinge
Tejn
Bornholm
(Danmark)
(Denmark) Rø Gudhjem
Hasle
Klemensker
Nyker Svaneke
Øster-
marie
benhavn 6:00 Rønne Nylars 38 Åkirkeby
28
Neksø
Pedersker
Snogebæk

55°

5:15

København 9:00
Malmö 9:00
Ystad 6:30

Jaroslawiec

J. Kopań

B

203 64 *Wieprza*

Darłowo Stary
Jaroslaw

Dąbki **Sławne**

Łazy J. Bukowo 68
203 32
Ostrowie
E28
6

Mielno J. Jamno Lejkowo
Sarbinowo Jamno

Ustronie **Koszalin** Sianów 203
Morskie 42 H Bonin 35 Nacław

Kołobrzeg 11 206 Manowo
Mrzeżyno 5 Dygowo Biesiekierz Rosnowo Mostowo
Niechorze 27 163 Niedalino 37 *Radew*
Rewal 102 162 Karlino 166 Dargiń **Bobolice**
Pobierowo 31 Gościno 19 167 25
Dziwnów 103 Gorawino 16 166 **Białogard** 169
Międzywodzie Cerkwica 18 E28 Rąbino **Tychowo** 171
Wolinski 102 Kamień 109 219 Tychówka 29 **Grzmiąca**
Kolczewo **Pomorski** Swierzno *Rega* Ryman Sławoborze 167 Białowąs
Międzyzdroje 32 105 Mechowo Rzesznikowo 23 **Barwice**
cle Lubin 107 15 **Gryfice** 33 Żabrowo 23 172
Wolin 13 Piaty 23 Sława Połczyn- 172
Haff E65 75 Golczewo 108 20 Resko Rusinowo 21 75 -Zdrój
Zalew 106 Ploty 152 **Świdwin** 35 Sława 16° Ostropole
Szczeciński Przybiernów Żabowo 18 Starogard 163
owe Warpno 3 15° 4 Brzeźno *Drawsko* 5

54°

C

219

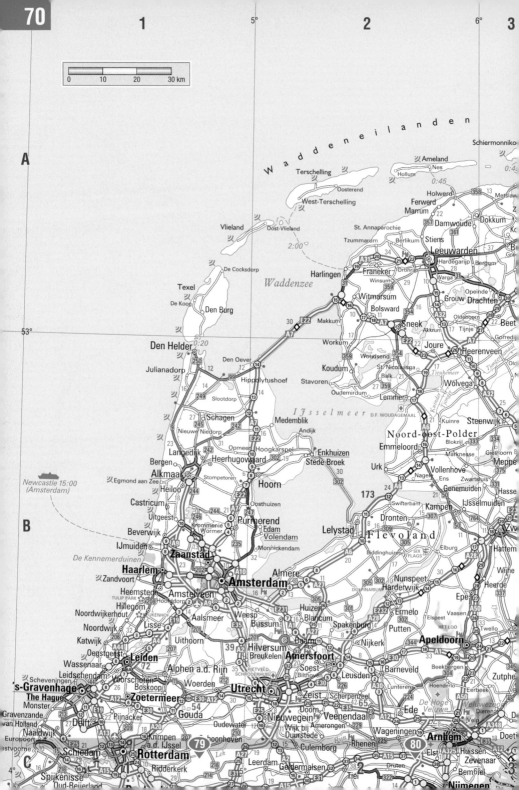

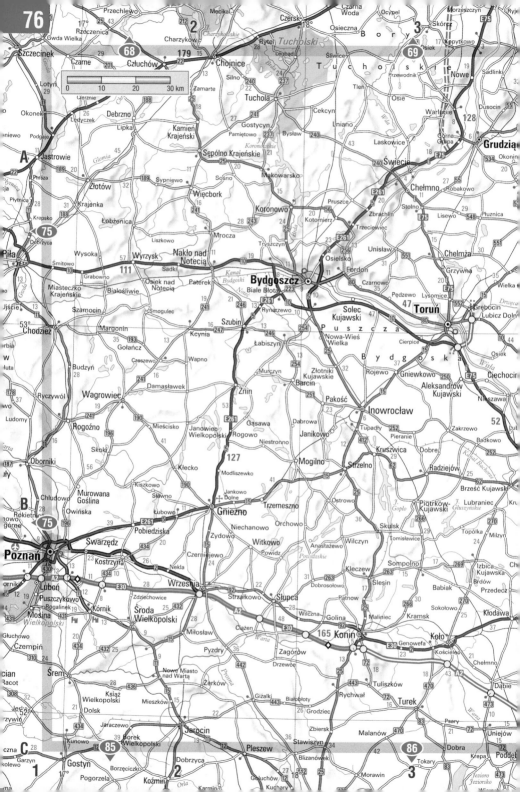

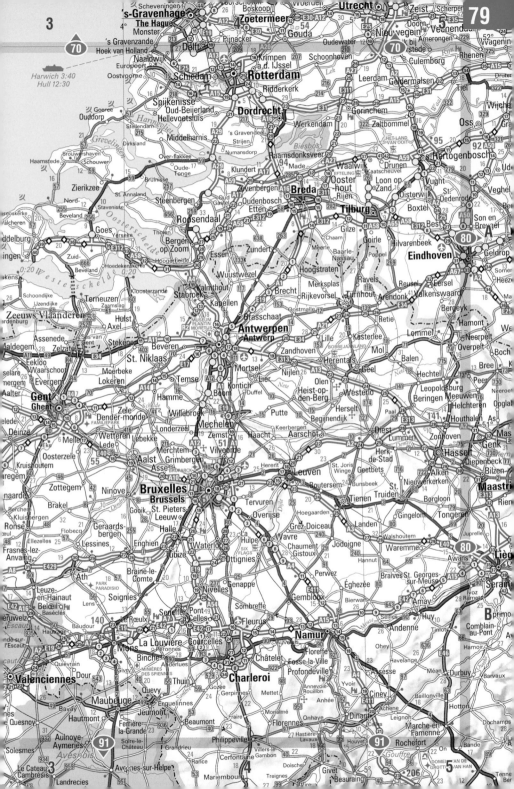

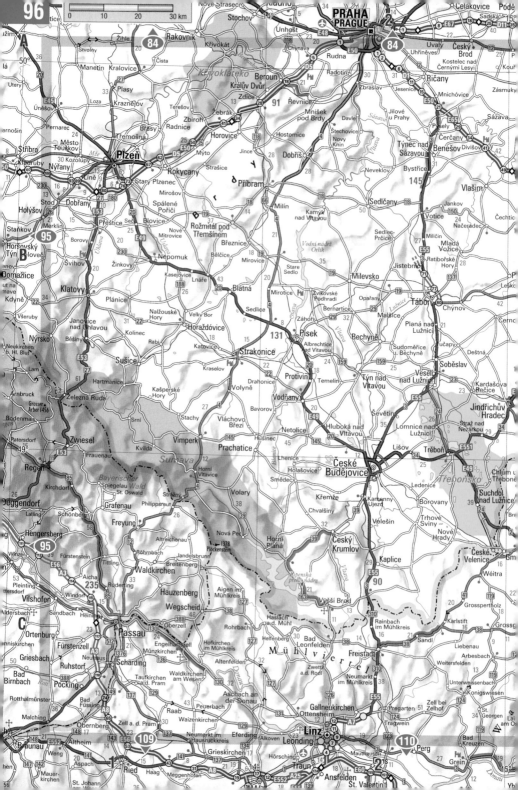

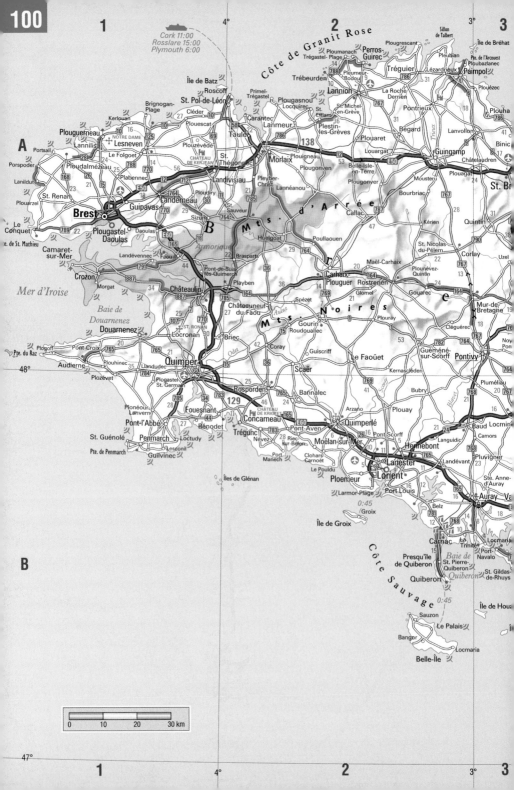

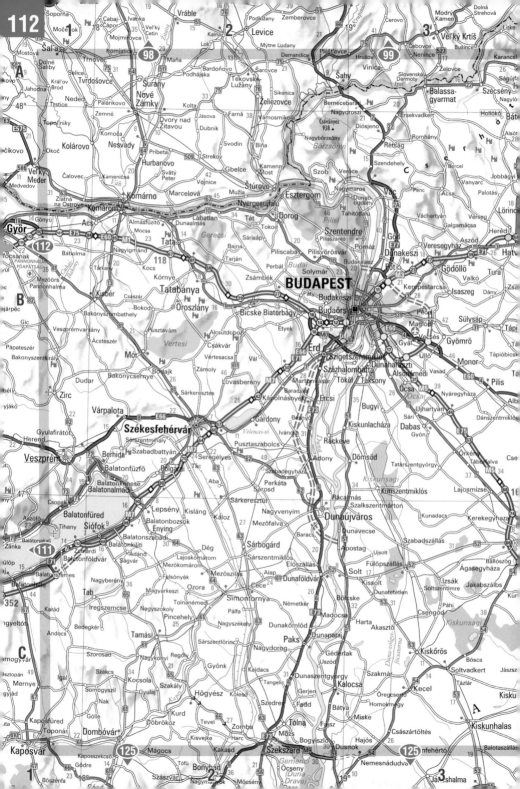

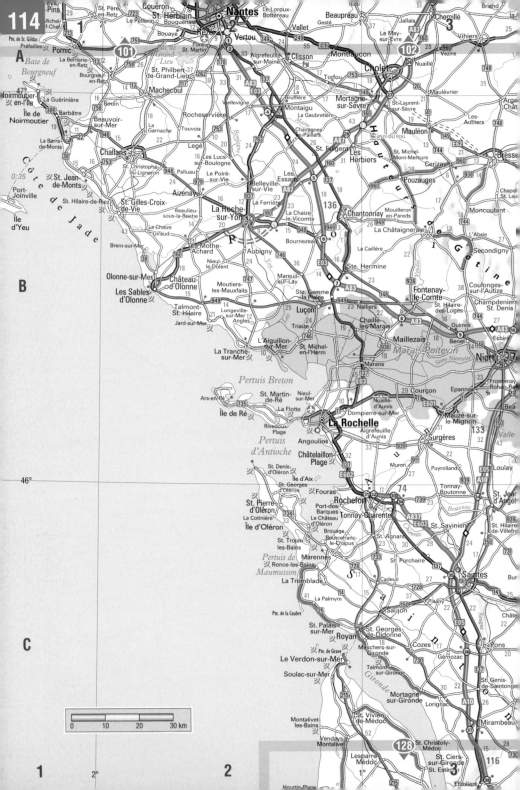

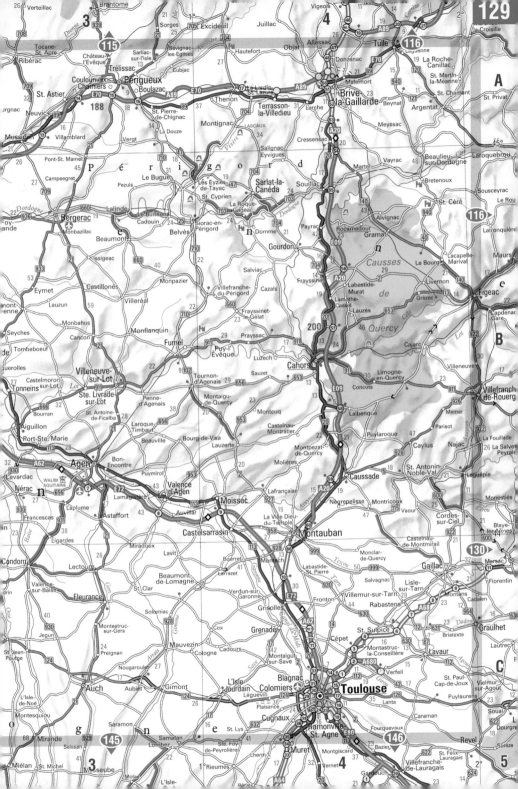

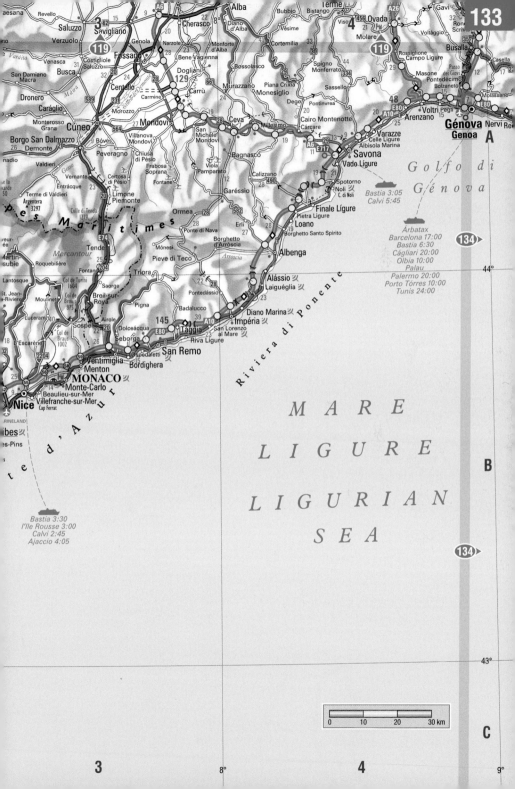

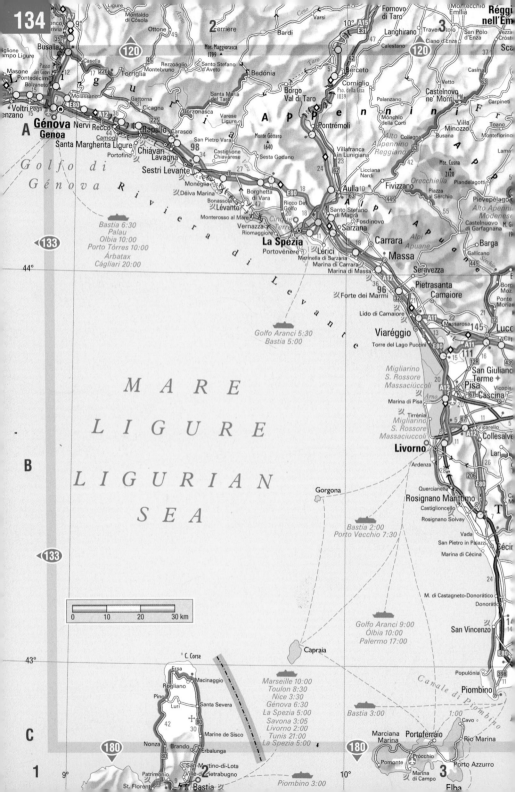

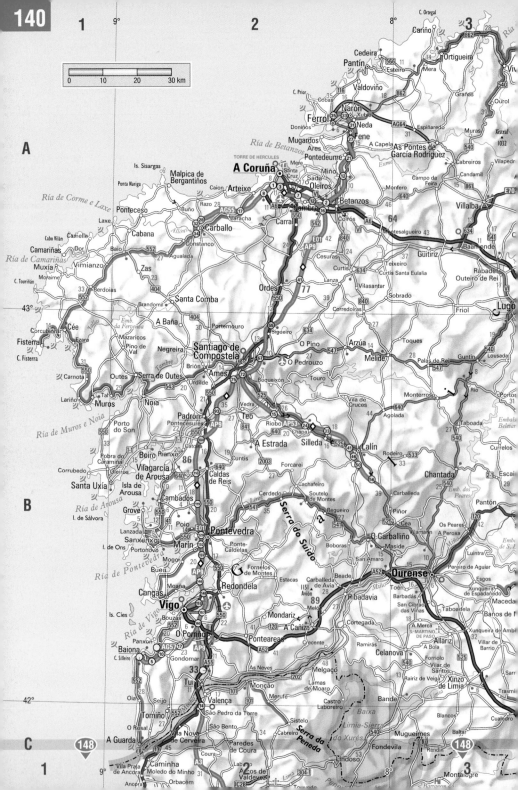

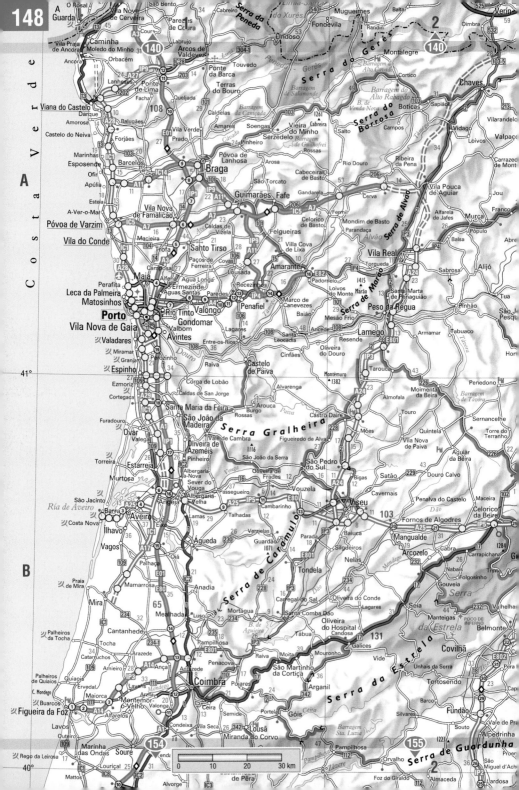

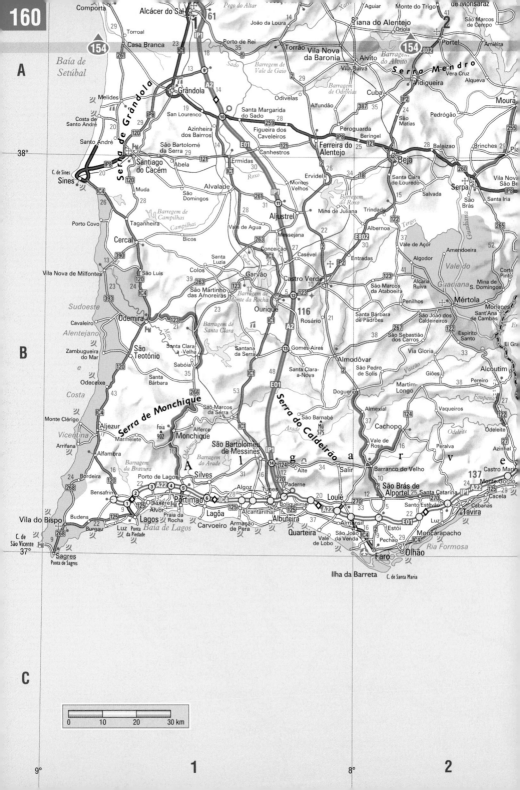

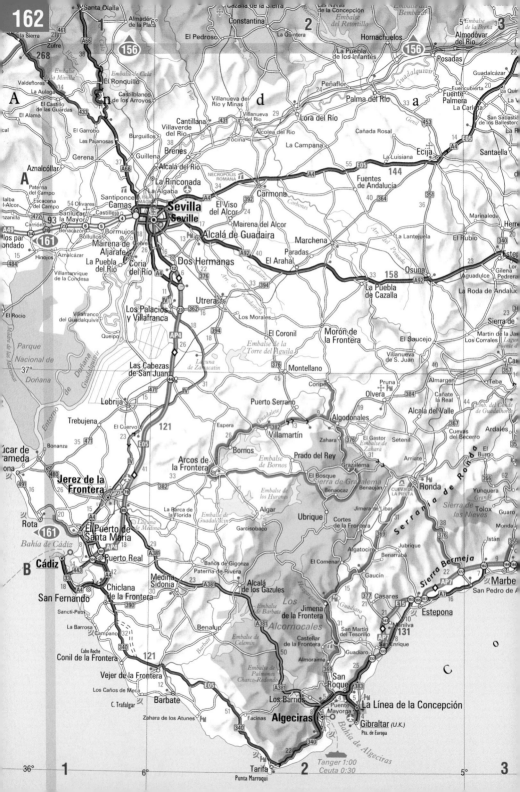

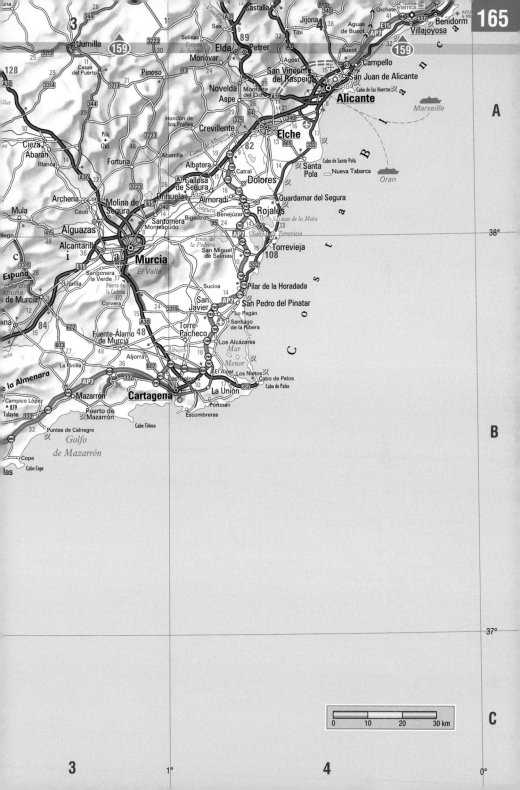

1

2° 2

A

40°

40°

Islas
Columbretes
(España)
(Spain)

Islas
Columbretes

1°

ISLAS
BALEARES

BALEARIC
ISLANDS

Port de Sóller

Deià

Valldemossa

Banyalbufar
Esporles
Estellencs
39
Puigpunyent
12
Sa Dragonera
710
Palma de
Mallorca
Andratx
Calvià
15
Port d'Andratx
13
PM1
Peguera 719
Palma
Can
Nova
Pastilla
Santa Ponsa
S'Arenal
Magaluf
Cap Enderrocat
Cap de Cala Figuera
Bahía
de Palma
Maó 6:30
Mallorca
Majorca

Barcelona 3:00

Valencia 6:00

Eivissa 2:15
Denia 9:00

Marra

25
711
Bu
So

B

Portinatx

Eivissa
Ibiza
Sant Miquel
8
Sant Joan Baptista
Santa Agnès
Pta. Grossa
Sant Carlos
Tagomago
Sant Antoni
733
Es Caná
Abat
39°
Sant
23
Santa Eulàlia des Riu
Rafel 731
Cala Llonga
16
Sant Josep
Eivissa
Ibiza
Palma de Mallorca 2:15
Barcelona 9:30
Es Vedrà
Cap
Sant Francesc
Llentrisca
de ses Salines
Punta Portás
Denia 4:00
S'Espardell
Valencia 3:15
S'Espalmador
0:25
Formentera
Sa Savina
Es Pujols
Sant Francesc de
Sant Ferran
Formentera
Nuestra Señora
Sa Verge des Pilar
C. de Barbària
Pta. Rotja

C

1

2° 2

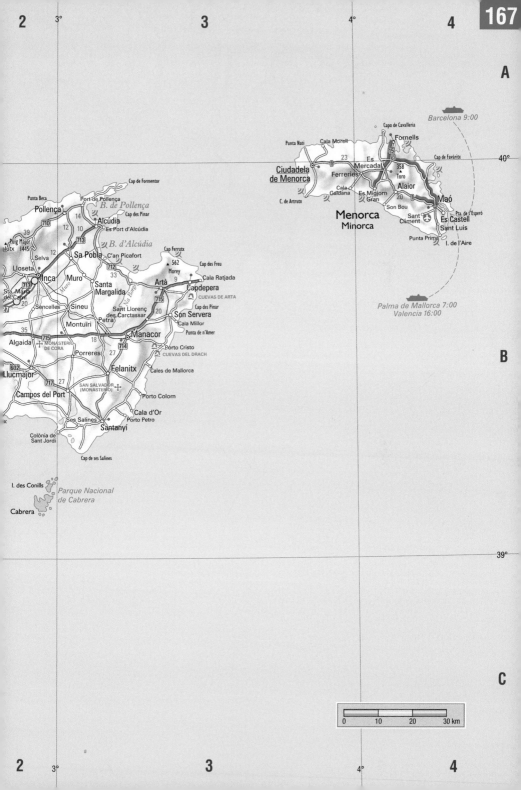

A

Barcelona 9:00

Capo de Cavalleria

Punta Nati Cala Morell Fornells

Es 15
23 Mercadal 19

Ciudadela Ferreries 358 Cap de Favàritx 40°
de Menorca Cala Toro
Galdana Es Migjorn Alaior
C. de Artrutx Gran 20
Son Bou Maó

Menorca Sant Es Castell
Minorca Climent Sant Luis
Pta. de l'Esperó
Punta Prima I. de l'Aire

Cap de Formentor

Port de Pollença

Punta Beca B. de Pollença
Pollença 14 Cap des Pinar
710 12 10 **Alcúdia**
39 713 Es Port d'Alcúdia
Puig Major B. d'Alcúdia
alutx 1445 12 Selva Cap Ferrutx
Lloseta 712 C'an Picafort ▲ 562 Cap des Freu
33 Morey
Sta. Maria **Inca** Muro Santa Artà 9 Cala Ratjada
del Camí Margalida **Capdepera**
20 Sencelles Sineu 715 CUEVAS DE ARTA
Palma de Mallorca 7:00
35 Petra Sant Llorenç Cap des Pinar Valencia 16:00
Algaida 715 Montuiri des Carctassar 20 **Són Servera**
MONASTERIO 18 **Manacor** Cala Millor
DE CORA 714 Punta de n'Amer
602 Porreres 27 Pórto Cristo
Llucmajor CUEVAS DEL DRACH

B

717 27 **Felanitx** Cales de Mallorca
SAN SALVADOR
(MONASTERIO)
Campos del Port Porto Colom
Cala d'Or
Ses Salines Porto Petro
Colònia de **Santanyí**
Sant Jordi
Cap de ses Salines

39°

I. des Conills Parque Nacional
de Cabrera
Cabrera

C

0 10 20 30 km

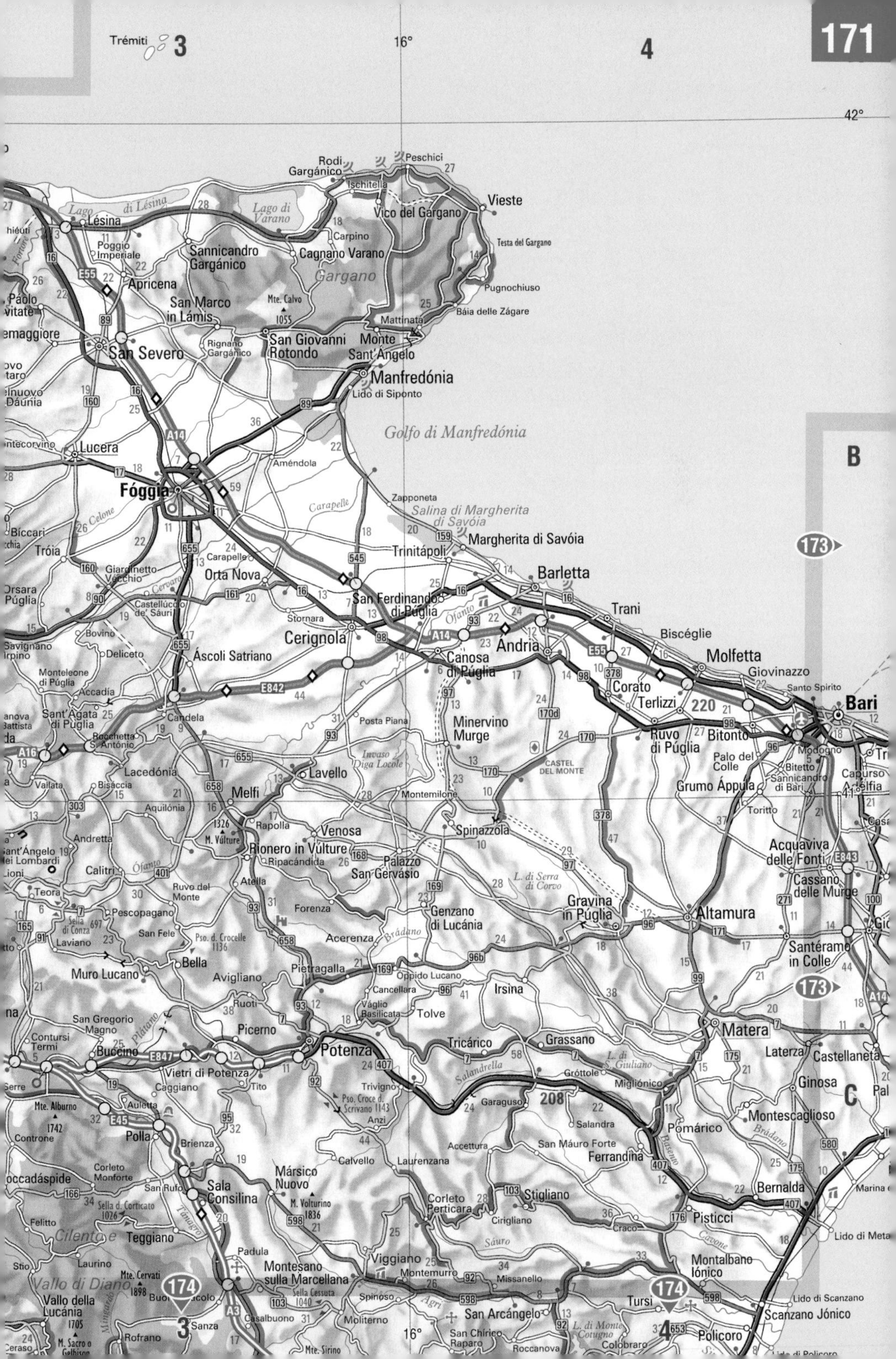

42°

Lago di Lésina
Lésina
Lago di Varano
Rodi Gargánico
Rodi Gargánico
Peschici
Ischitella
Vico del Gargano
Vieste
Poggio Imperiale
Sannicandro Gargánico
Carpino
Cagnano Varano
Testa del Gargano
Apricena
Gargano
Mte. Calvo
Pugnochiuso
San Marco in Lámis
Báia delle Zágare
Rignano Gargánico
Mattinata
San Giovanni Rotondo
Monte Sant'Angelo
San Severo
Manfredónia
Lido di Siponto
Lucera
Améndola
Golfo di Manfredónia

B

Fóggia
Carapelle
Zapponeta
Salina di Margherita di Savóia
Margherita di Savóia
Trinitápoli
Orta Nova
Barletta
Bíccari
Giardinetto Vecchio
San Ferdinando di Púglia
Trani
Tróia
Stornara
Biscéglie
Castelluccio de' Sáuri
Molfetta
Cerignola
Andria
Giovinazzo
Ávellino
Bovino
Áscoli Satriano
Canosa di Púglia
Corato
Santo Spirito
Delicato
Terlizzi
Bari
Sant'Agata di Púglia
Candela
Posta Piana
Minervino Murge
Ruvo di Púglia
Bitonto
Accadia
Palo del Colle
Lacedónia
Lavello
Montemilone
Grumo Áppula
Bisáccia
Castel del Monte
Modugno
Melfi
Rapolla
Venosa
Spinazzola
Bitetto
Sannicandro di Bari
Capurso
M. Vúlture
Acquaviva delle Fonti
Rionero in Vúlture
Ripacándida
Palazzo San Gervásio
L. di Serra di Corvo
Cassano delle Murge
Atella
Forenza
Genzano di Lucánia
Gravina in Púglia
Altamura
Ruvo del Monte
San Fele
Acerenza
Brádano
Santéramo in Colle
Pescopagano
Bella
Pietragalla
Oppido Lucano
Muro Lucano
Avigliano
Cancellara
Irsina
Matera
Ruoti
Váglio Basilicata
Tolve
Laterza
Castellaneta
Picerno
Tricárico
Grassano
Ginosa
Buccino
Potenza
Gróttole
Miglionico
Montescaglioso
Vietri di Potenza
Trivigno
Garaguso
Pómarico
Caggiano
Anzi
Salandra
San Máuro Forte
Ferrandina
Pollá
Brienza
Calvello
Laurenzana
Accettura
Corleto Monforte
Mársico Nuovo
Stigliano
Bernalda
Sala Consilina
M. Volturino
Cirigliano
Pisticci
Teggiano
Padula
Craco
Viggiano
Montalbano Iónico
Montesano sulla Marcellana
Montemurro
Missanello
Tursi
Scanzano Jónico
San Arcángelo
Policoro

174
173
208

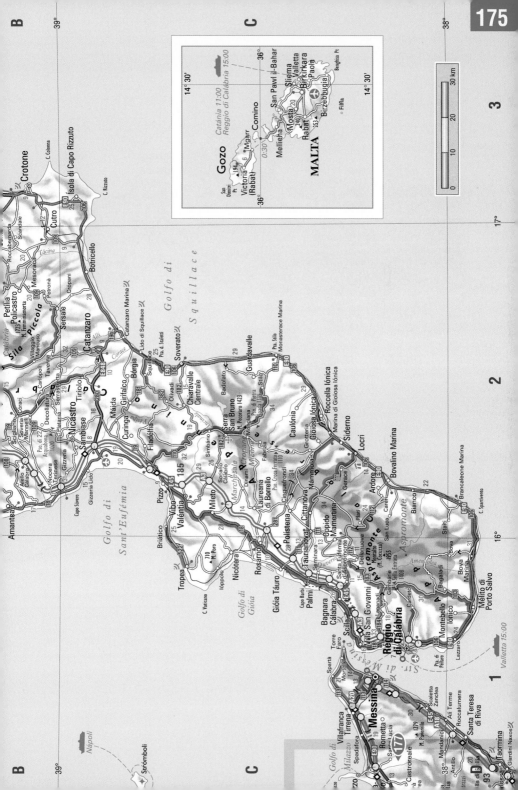

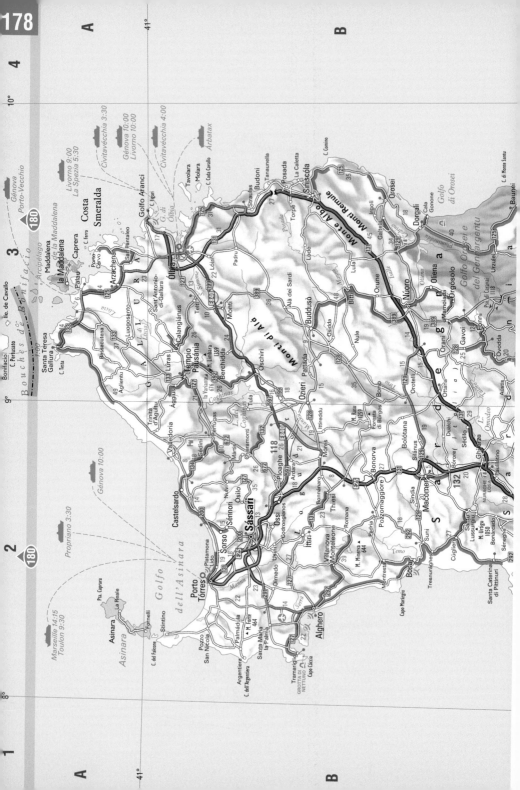

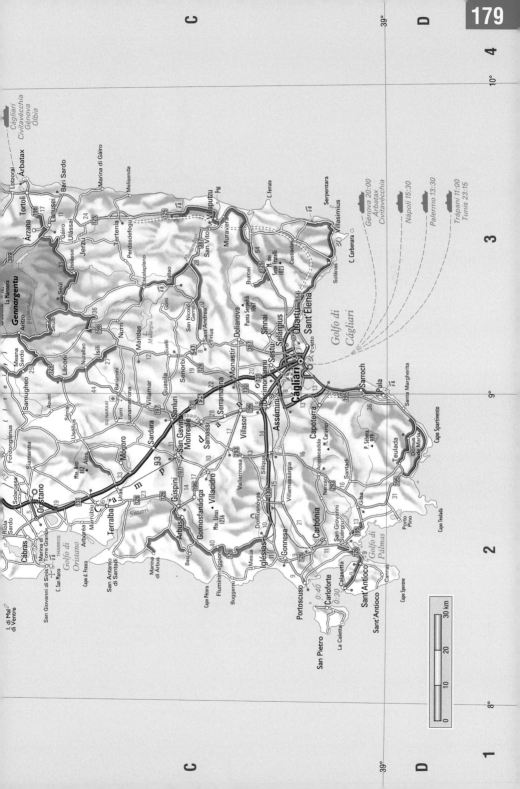

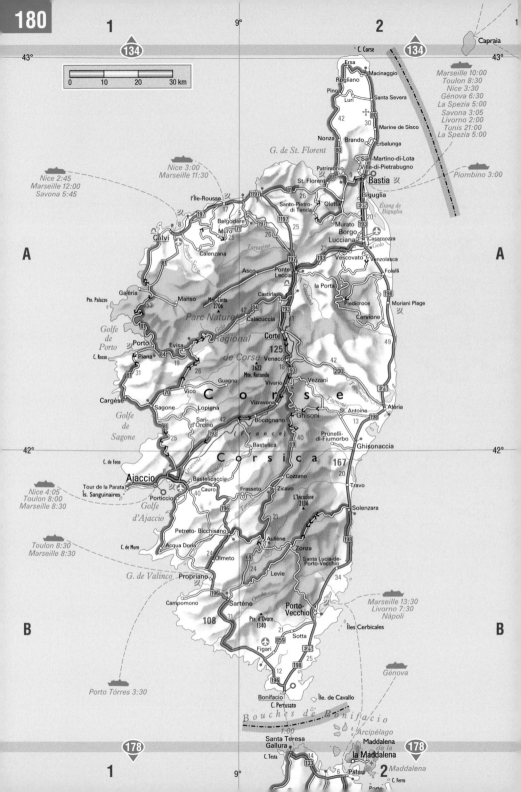

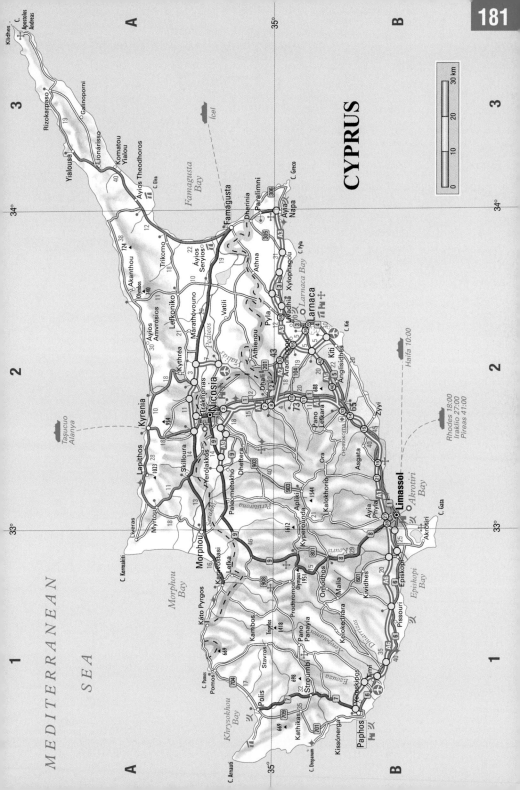

CYPRUS

MEDITERRANEAN SEA

Khrysokhou Bay

Morphou Bay

Famagusta Bay

Larnaca Bay

Akrotiri Bay

Episkopi Bay

Kládhes C.
Apóstolos
Andréas

Rizokárpaso
Yialoúsa
Komátou Yialou
Ayios Theodhoros
Galinopórni
Elonárisso
19
40
C. Elia

 Táşucu
Alanya

Icel

Famágusta
Paralímni
Ayía Napa
Dherínia
C. Greco

C. Kormakíti
Kyrenia
Lápithos
Nicosia
Trakhónas
Skilloúra
Kythréa
Ayios Amvrósios
Akánthou
Lefkóniko
Trikomo
Márathóvouno
Ayios Senyósi
Vatili
Athna
Xylophágou
Ladhiá
Pyla
Larnaca
Kiti
Anglísidh63
Zyví
Pano
Lefkara
Kalokhorió
Ayía Phyla
Limassol
Akrotíri
C. Gata

Mórphou
Léfka
Karavostási
Káto Pyrgos
Kámbos
Tripylos
Pano Panayía
Stavroús
Stroumbi
Kathikás
Kissónerga
Paphos
Pissoúri
Kívidhes
Kelokedhára
Omódhos
Prodhrómou
Olympus
1951
Apliki
Kyperoúnda
Dheftera
Yeróskos
Peristeróna
Dháli
Aradhippou
Athiénou
Pérgamos

C. Arnaúti
C. Pomos
Pomos
C. Drépanum

Haifa 10:00
Rhodes 18:00
Iráklio 27:00
Píreás 41:00

Pedieos
Seirahis
Idalis
Yialias
Kouris
Dhiarrizos
Ezousa
Khapotamí

30 km
0 10 20

7 18° 8 17° 9 16° 10 15° 11 14° 12

ARCTIC CIRCLE 66°30'

A

66°

B

65°

C

64°

D

7 18° 8 17° 9 16° 10 15° 11 14° 12 63°

Grímsey

3:30

Raufarhöfn 85

Kópasker

Öxarfjörður

Svalbarð

Pórshöfn

Hlíð

Fontur

177

Pistilfjörður

Bakkaflói

Skjálfandi

Ólafsfjörður

Húsavík 75 85 Asbyrgi

Bakkafjörður 85

Digranes

Dalvík Grenivík Björg

Haganes 82 83

Laxamýri

Jökulsárgljúfur

864

967

60

Vopnafjörður

Vopnafjörður

Húsey

Héraðsflói

34 46

82

Akureyri 24 85 87

Laugar

Reykjahlíð 38

Grímsstaðir

82

Sleðbrjótur

Glettinganes

Bakkagerði

30

Hrafnagil 1538

Mývatn 285 44

Lögurinn 94

64

Seyðisfjörður

Saurbær

Bláfjall 1222

Móðrudalur

77

Egilsstaðir 23 93

Neskaupstaður

Myri

Ódáðahraun

Herðubreið 1682

Hallormsstaður 931 27

32 92

35

Eskifjörður 92

Reyðarfjörður

SLAND

1460 Tröllaðyngja

Valþjófsstaður

69

86

Fáskrúðsfjörður

96

Stöðvarfjörður

1765 fsjökull

Snæfell 1833

Berufjörður

Breiðdalsvík

CELAND

Vatnajökull

Djúpivogur

146

Hantsholm 52:00
Lerwick 30:00
Tórshavn 17:00

Nesjahverfi

Höfn

Stokksnes

þórisvatn

Skaftafell

Gerði

192

LAKAGÍGAR

Hvannadalshnúkur 2119

Skaftafell 687

Skeiðarársandur

Ingólfshöfði

Búland 26 Kirkjubæjarklaustur

50 204

Langholt

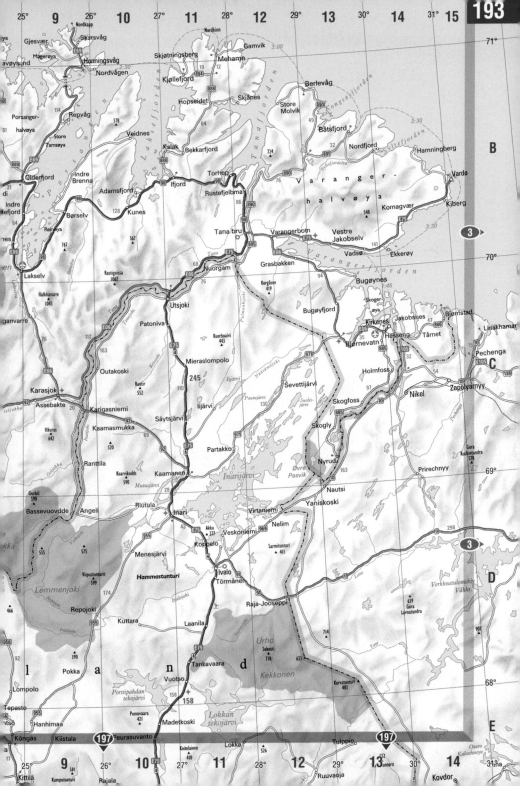

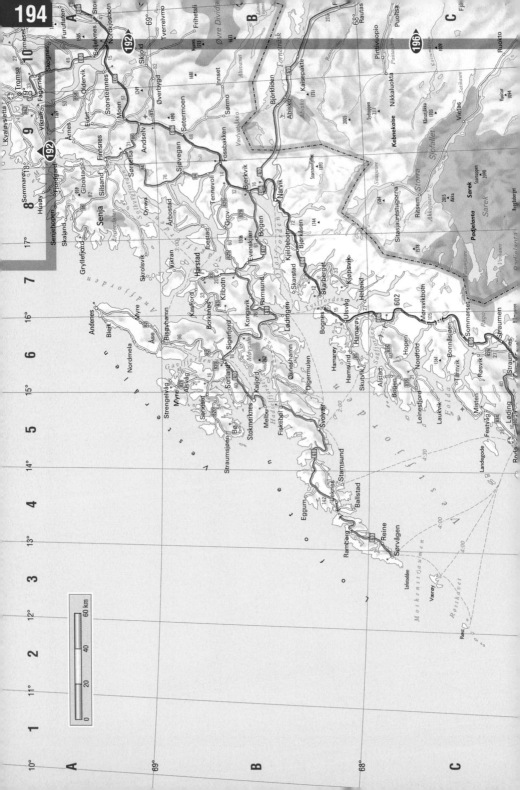

City plans

Motorway	**GENT** Destination
Major through route	Railway
Through route	Rail/bus station
Secondary road	⊖🅜🅤🅣 Underground, metro station
Dual carriageway	Cable car
Other road	† Abbey, cathedral
Tunnel	† Church of interest
Limited access / pedestrian road	✿ Synagogue
One-way street	⊞ Hospital
℗ Parking	POL Police station
A7 Motorway number	✉ Post office
447 National road number	𝑖 Tourist information
E45 European road number	Theatre Place of interest
Car ferry	British Embassy or Consulate

Approach maps

A10 Toll motorway – with motorway number	Secondary route dual carriageway
E51 Toll-free motorway – with European road number	96 single carriageway
	under construction tunnel
Pre-pay motorway – vignette required	Other road
	Car ferry
◇ Motorway services	**GIRONA** Destination
24 Motorway junction – full/restricted	Railway
	Estación Central Railway station
● Motorway junction name	Railway tunnel
Under construction	234 ▲ Height above sea level – in metres
Tunnel	✈ Airport
Major route dual carriageway	✈ Airfield
14 single carriageway	City plan coverage area
under construction tunnel	

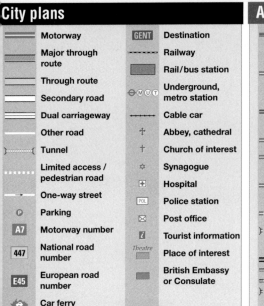

Alicante 0 km 0.5

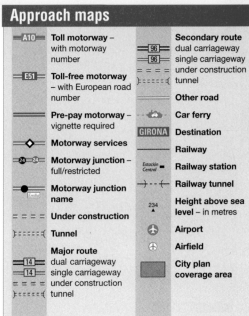

Antwerpen Antwerp 0 km 1

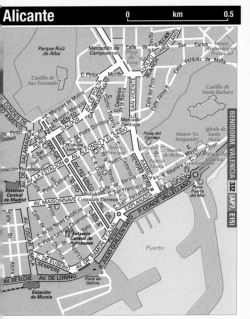

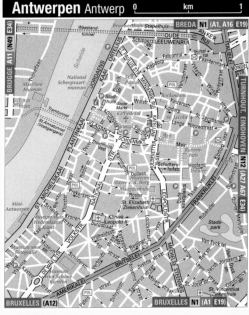

Amsterdam

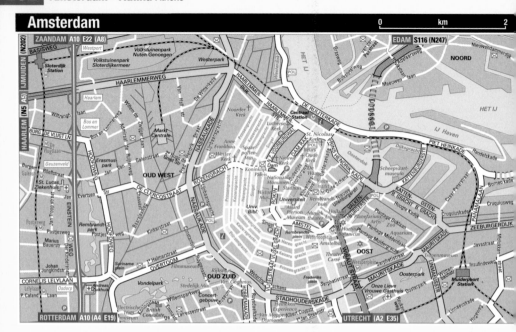

Athina Athens

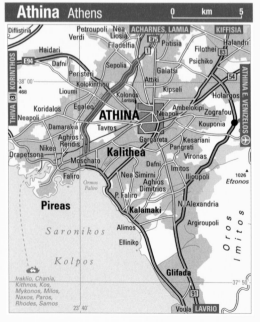

Athina Athens

Barcelona

0 km 5

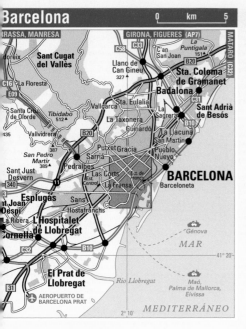

TERRASSA, MANRESA | GIRONA, FIGUERES (AP7) | MATARÓ (C32)

Sant Cugat del Vallès
Llano de Can Gineu
Sta. Coloma de Gramanet
Badalona
Sant Adrià de Besós
La Floresta
Santa Cruz de Olorde
Tibidabo 512▲
Vallvidrera
Vallcarca
Sta. Eulalia
La Sagrera
La Taxonera
Guinardó
La Llacuna
San Martin
Pueblo Nuevo
Putxet Gracia
Sarrià
Pedralbes
Les Corts
La Fransa
BARCELONA
Barceloneta
Esplugas
Sans
Hostafranchs
L'Hospitalet de Llobregat
Cornellà
El Prat de Llobregat
AEROPUERTO DE BARCELONA PRAT

Génova
MAR
41° 20'
Rio Llobregat
Maó, Palma de Mallorca, Eivissa
MEDITERRÁNEO
2° 10'

Barcelona

0 km 1

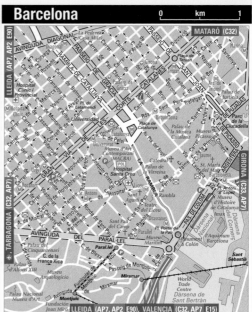

MATARÓ (C32)

LLEIDA (AP7) AP2 E90
GIRONA (C33, AP7)
TARRAGONA (C32, AP7)
LLEIDA (AP7, AP2 E90), VALENCIA (C32, AP7 E15)

La Pedrera (Casa Milà)
AVINGUDA DIAGONAL
PASSEIG DE GRÀCIA
RAMBLA DE CATALUNYA
GRAN VIA
Plaça de Catalunya
Catedral
La Rambla
Museu Picasso
Parc de la Ciutadella
PASSEIG DE COLOM
AVINGUDA DEL PARAL·LEL
Monument à Colón
Aquàrium de Barcelona
Montjuïc
Palau Nacional Museu d'Art
Fundació Joan Miró
World Trade Centre
Dàrsena de Sant Bertràn
Miramar

Bruxelles Brussels

0 km 1

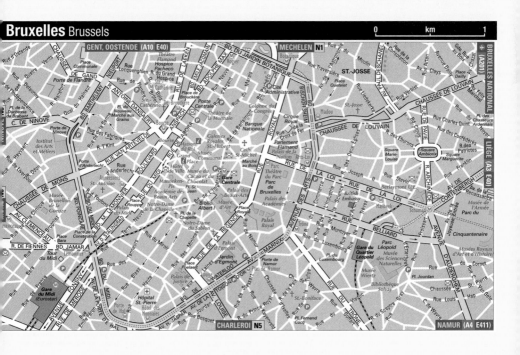

GENT, OOSTENDE (A10 E40) | MECHELEN N1 | BRUXELLES NATIONAL (A201)

BD DU JARDIN BOTANIQUE
ST.-JOSSE
CHAUSSÉE DE LOUVAIN
LIÈGE (A3 E40)
Square Ambiorix
CHAUSSÉE DE MONS
Gare Centrale
Parc de Bruxelles
RUE DE LA LOI
Parc du Cinquantenaire
Gare du Quartier Léopold
Gare du Midi (Eurostar)
CHARLEROI N5
NAMUR (A4 E411)

Berlin

0   km   5

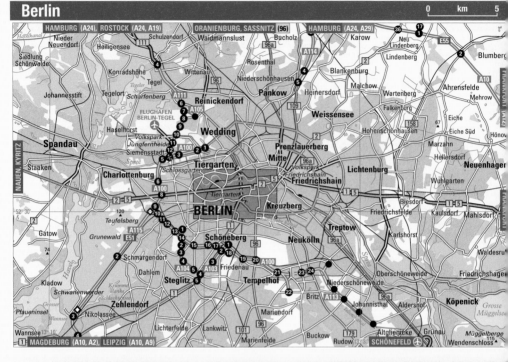

Berlin

0   km   1

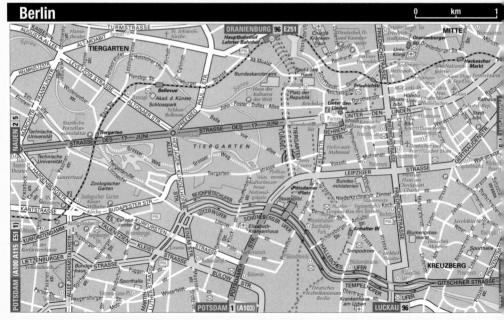

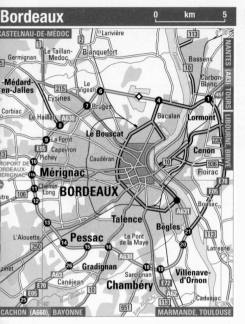

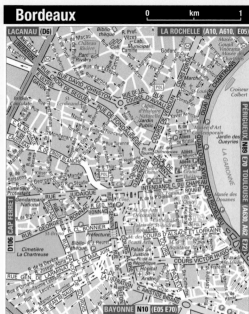

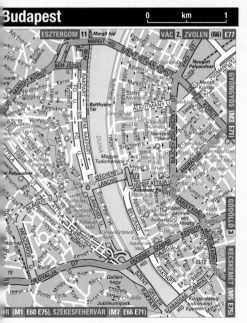

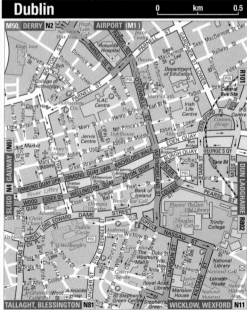

For **Cologne** see page 211
For **Copenhagen** see page 210

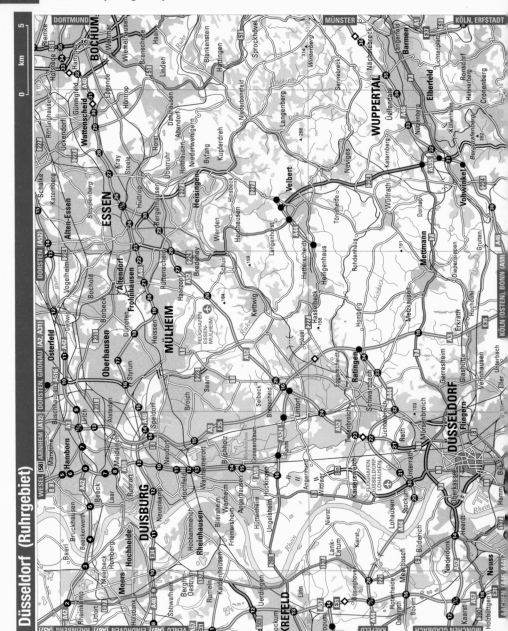

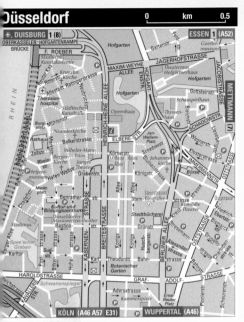

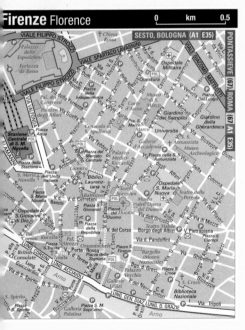

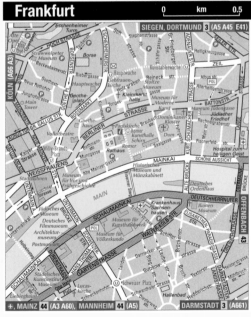

Genève Geneva

0 km 0,5

Göteborg Gothenburg

0 km

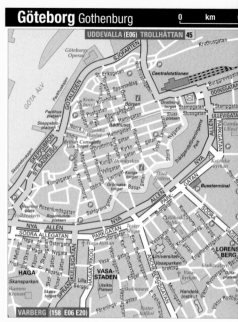

Hamburg

0 km 5

Hamburg

0 km

Helsinki

0   km   10

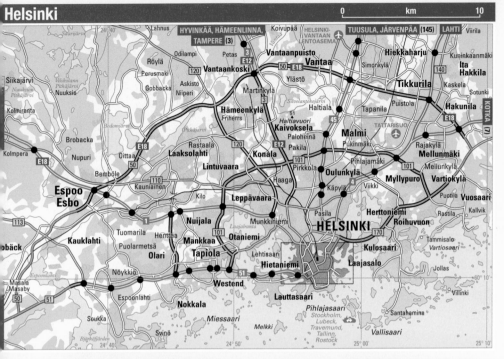

Helsinki

0   km   1

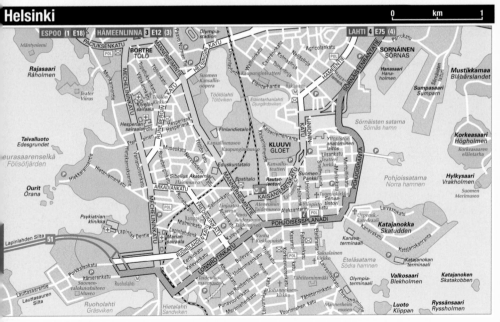

İstanbul

København Copenhagen

København Copenhagen

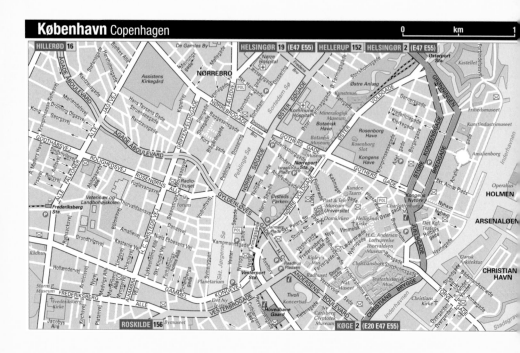

Köln Cologne

0   km   0.5

Luxembourg

0   km   0.5

Lisboa Lisbon

0   km   5

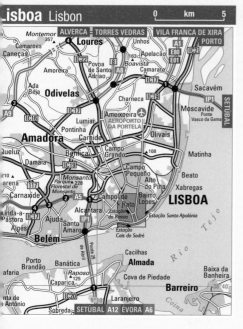

Lisboa Lisbon

0   km   1

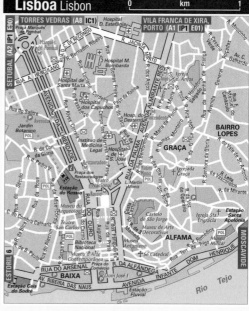

London

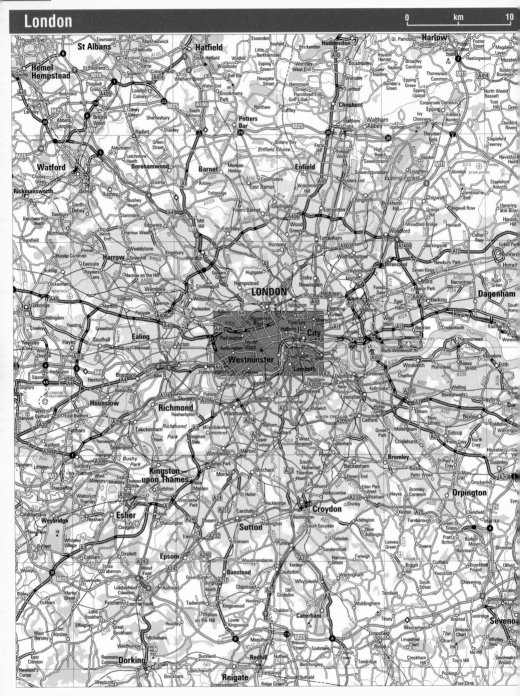

London

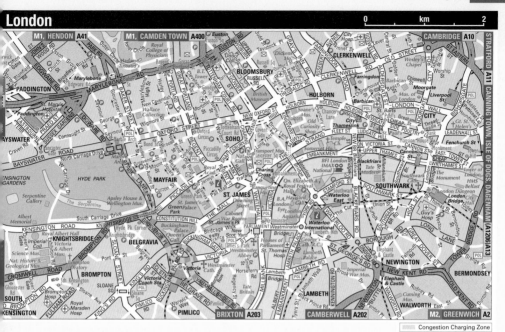

Congestion Charging Zone

Lyon

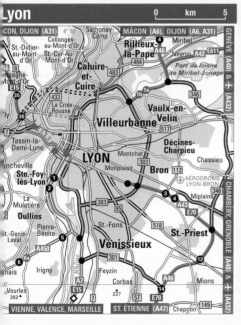

Lyon

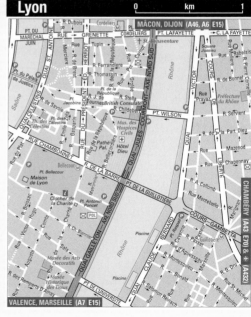

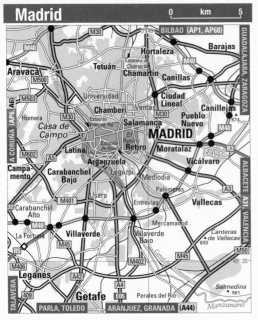

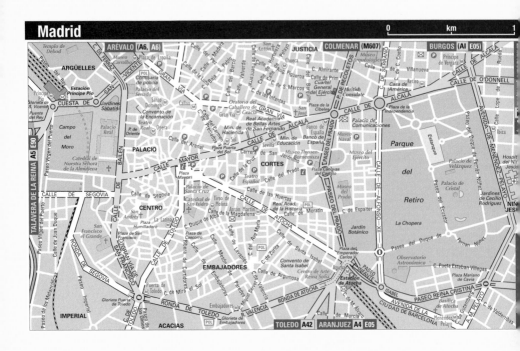

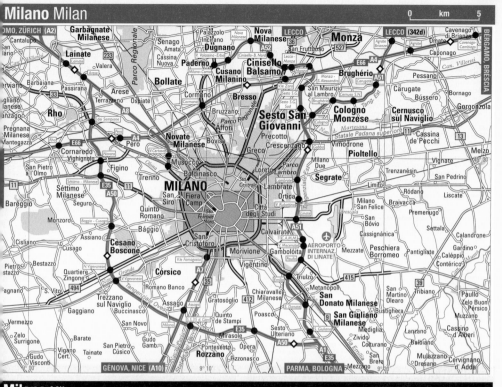

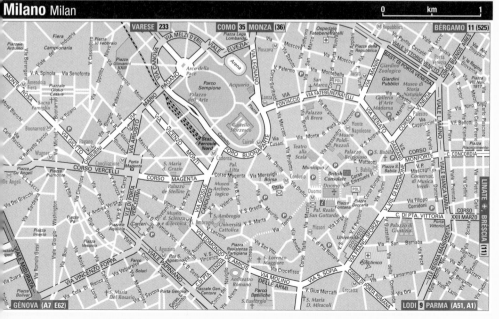

München Munich

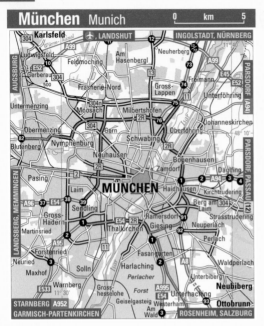

München Munich

Nápoli Naples

Nápoli Naples

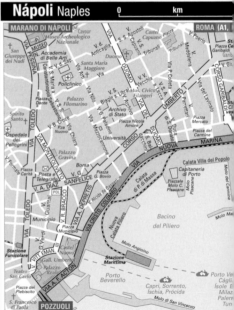

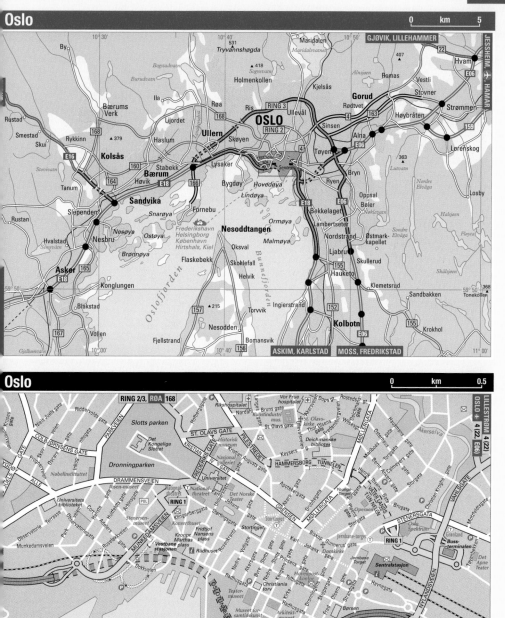

0 km 5

GJØVIK, LILLEHAMMER

JESSHEIM, HAMAR

By
Bognvatn
531
Tryvannshøgda
Maridalen
Maridalsvatnet
Hvam
22
418
Sognsvann
Holmenkollen
Kjelsås
Alnsjøen
Romsås
407
Vestli
E06
Burudvatn
Bærums Verk
Ila
Røa
Ris
RING 3
Ullevål
Gorud
Rødtvet
Stovner
Strømmen
Rustad
Lijordet
168
OSLO
4
163
Høybråten
159
Smestad
Rykkinn
168
Haslum
RING 2
Ullern
Skøyen
Sinsen
Alna
E06
Lørenskog
Skui
379
Kolsås
160
Vestbanen
4
Tøyen
363
Lutvatn
Nordre Elvåga
Losby
E16
Stabekk
Lysaker
Sentralstasjon
Bryn
Bærum
Bygdøy
Hovedøya
Ryen
Oppsal
Bøler
Tanum
164
Høvik
E18
166
Lindøya
E18
E06
Bekkelaget
Nøklevatn
Sandvika
Fornebu
Ormøya
Lambertseter
Østmark-kapellet
Søndre Elvåga
Flaytal
Sjøpenden
Snarøya
Nesoddtangen
Malmøya
Nordstrand
Nesøya
Frederikshavn Helsingborg København Hirtshals, Kiel
Oksval
Ljabru
Rustan
Nesbru
Ostøya
Flaskebekk
Skullerud
155
Skåljøen
Hvalstad
Semsvatn
Brønnøya
Skoklefall
Hauketo
Asker
165
Konglungen
Helvik
Klemetsrud
368
Tonekollen
E18
Blakstad
215
Torvvik
Ingierstrand
152
Sandbakken
167
Vollen
157
Nesodden
Kolbotn
155
Krokhol
Gjellumvatn
Fjellstrand
Bomansvik
156
E06

ASKIM, KARLSTAD   MOSS, FREDRIKSTAD

0 km 0.5

RING 2/3, RØA 168

LILLESTRØM 4 (22), OSLO + 4 (22) E06

KARLSTAD E18, FREDRIKSTAD E18 (E06)

Oslofjorden

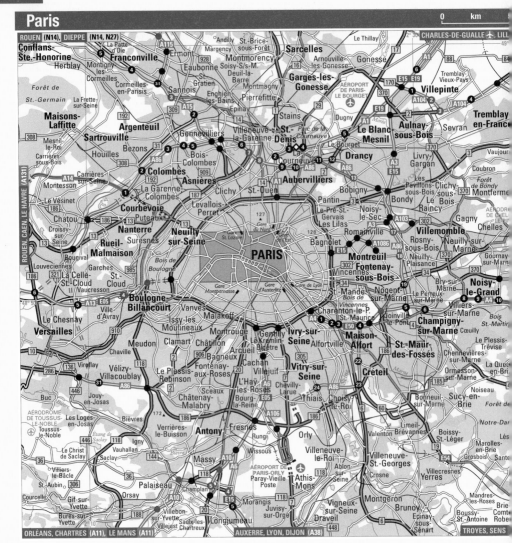

Paris

ROUEN (N14), DIEPPE (N14, N27)

CHARLES-DE-GUALLE ✈ LILL

Conflans-
Ste-Honorine
Herblay

Andilly St-Brice-
Mărgency sous-Forêt
Ermont
Franconville
Montigny-
les-
Cormeilles
Cormeilles-
en-Parisis
Sannois

La Patte
d'Oie
Eaubonne
St-
Gratien
Enghien-
les-Bains

Montmorency
Soisy-S/s-M.
Deuil-la-
Barre
Montmagny
Pierrefitte
Epinay

Sarcelles

Arnouville-
les-Gonesse
Gonesse

Garges-les-
Gonesse

Tremblay
Vieux-Pays

Villepinte

Tremblay
en-France

Forêt de
St-Germain
La Frette-
sur-Seine

Maisons-
Laffitte
Mesnil-
le-Roi
Sartrouville
Houilles
Bezons
Montesson

Argenteuil

Gennevilliers

Villeneuve-
la-Garenne
Stains

Dugny

St.-
Denis

La
Courneuve

AÉROPORT
DE PARIS-
LE BOURGET

Le Bourget

Le Blanc
Mesnil

Aulnay-
sous-Bois

Sevran

Vaujour

Carrières-
sous-Bois
Carrières-
sur-Seine
Le Vésinet
Chatou
Croissy-
s/Seine

Colombes
La Garenne-
Colombes

Bois-
Colombes
Asnières

Clichy
St-Ouen

Aubervilliers

Pantin
Le Pré-St-
Gervais
Les Lilas

Drancy

Bobigny

Les
Pavillons-
sous-Bois

Clichy-
sous-Bois

Livry-
Gargan

Forêt
de Bondy

Montferme

Nanterre
Courbevoie
Puteaux
Suresnes

Neuilly-
sur-Seine

Levallois-
Perret

Gare
St-Lazare
Gare
du Nord
Gare
de l'Est

Romainville

Noisy-
le-Sec

Rosny-
sous-Bois

Le Bois
Raincy

Gagny

Villemomble

Neuilly-
sur-
Marne

Chelles

Rueil-
Malmaison
Garches
St.-
Cloud
Bougival
Louveciennes
La Celle-
St-Cloud
Vaucresson

Bois de
Boulogne

PARIS

Bagnolet

Montreuil

Fontenay-
sous-Bois

Neuilly-
Plaisance

Gournay-
sur-Marne

Noisy-
le-Grand

Le Chesnay
Versailles

Boulogne-
Billancourt

Vanves
Issy-les-
Moulineaux
Malakoff

Gare
Montparnasse
Gare
d'Austerlitz

Gare
de Lyon

Vincennes
St-
Mandé
Bois de
Vincennes

Nogent-
sur-Marne

Le Perreux-
sur-Marne

Bry-sur-
Marne

Villiers-
sur-Marne

Champigny-
sur-Marne

St-Martin

Bois

Meudon
Chaville

Clamart
Châtillon
Montrouge

Gentilly
Le Kremlin-
Bicêtre

Ivry-sur-
Seine

Charenton-le-P.
St-Maurice

Joinville-
le-Pont

Maison-
Alfort

St-Maur-
des-Fossés

Cœuilly

Le Plessis-
Trévise

Chennevières-
sur-Marne

Viroflay
Vélizy-
Villacoublay
Le Plessis-
Robinson
Fontenay-
aux-Roses
Bagneux
Cachan
Villejuif

Vitry-sur-
Seine

Alfortville

Créteil

Ormesson-
sur-Marne

La Quee
en-Bri.

Buc
Jouy-
en-Josas
Sceaux
Bourg-
la-Reine
L'Haÿ-
les-Roses
Chevilly-
Larue
Thiais
Choisy-
le-Roi

Bonneuil-
sur-Marne

Sucy-en-
Brie

Forêt de

Châtenay-
Malabry

Noiseau

Notre-Dar

AÉRODROME
DE TOUSSUS-
LE-NOBLE
Toussus-
le-Noble
Les Loges-
en-Josas

Verrières-
le-Buisson
Antony
Fresnes
Rungis

Orly

Valenton

Limeil-
Brévannes

Boissy-
St-Léger

Lés
Marolles-
en-Brie

Santé

Le Christ
de Saclay
Saclay
Igny
Bièvres

Massy
Wissous

AÉROPORT DE
PARIS-ORLY
Paray-Vieille
Poste

Villeneuve-
le-Roi

Ablon-
sur-
Seine
Crosne

Villeneuve-
St-Georges

Yerres

Villecresnes

Boissy-
St-Antoine

Mandres-
les-Roses

Brie
Comte
Robe

Villiers-
le-Bâcle
St-Aubin
Vauhallan
Courcelle
Gif-sur-
Yvette
Bures-sur-
Yvette

Palaiseau
Orsay
Champlan
Villebon-
sur-Yvette
Saulx-les-
Villejust Chartreux

Morangis

Athis-
Mons

Juvisy-
sur-Orge

Vigneux-
sur-Seine
Draveil

Montgeron

Brunoy

Epinay-
sous-
Sénart

Boussy-
St-Antoine

Longjumeau

ORLÉANS, CHARTRES (A11), LE MANS (A11)   AUXERRE, LYON, DIJON (A38)   TROYES, SENS

Paris

0 — km — 1

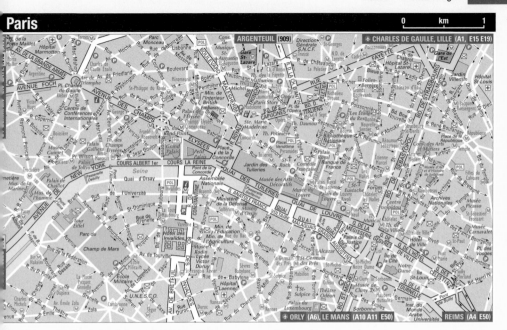

Praha Prague

0 — km — 5

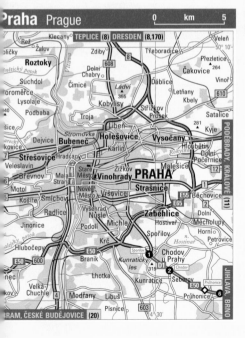

Praha Prague

0 — km — 1

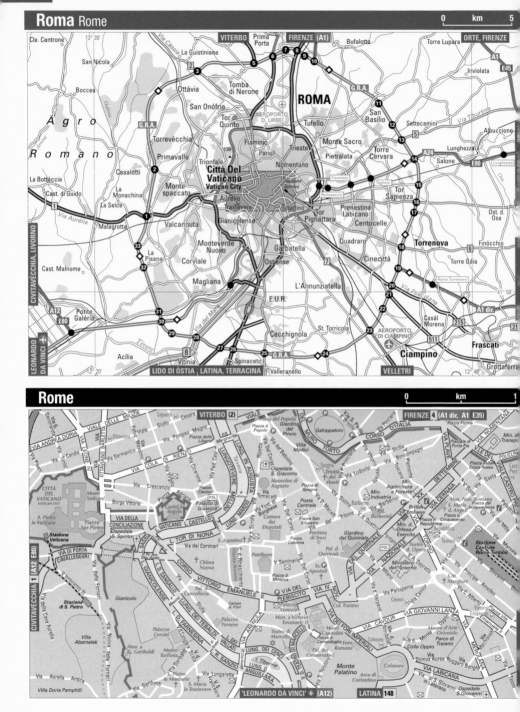

Stockholm

0 km 5

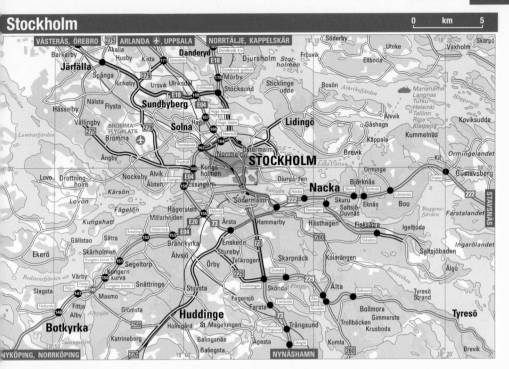

Stockholm

0 km 1

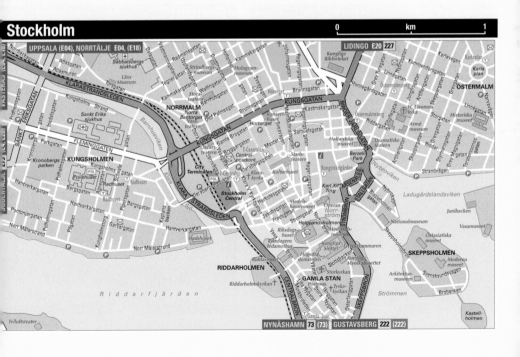

Strasbourg

Strasbourg

Sevilla Seville

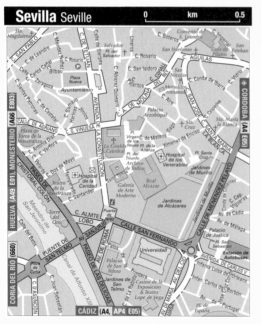

Stuttgart

Torino Turin

0 km 5

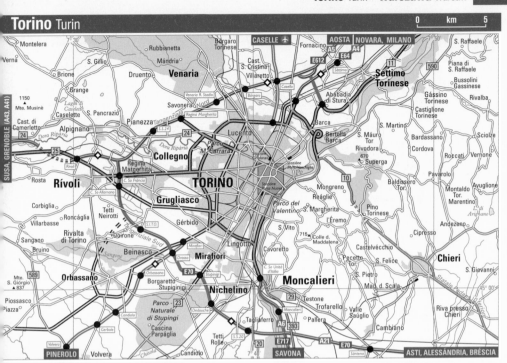

Torino Turin

0 km 1

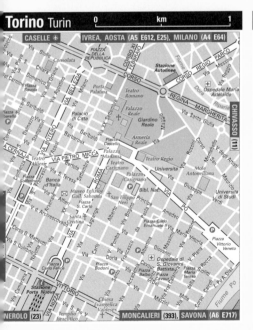

Warszawa Warsaw

0 km 1

For **Vienna** see page 224

Wien Vienna

0   km   1

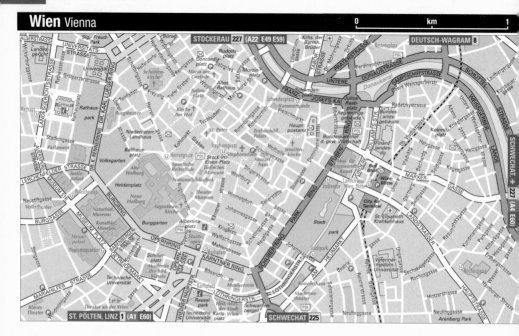

STOCKERAU **227** (A22 E49 E59)   DEUTSCH-WAGRAM **8**

ST. PÖLTEN, LINZ **1** (A1 E60)   SCHWECHAT **225**   SCHWECHAT ✈ **227** (A4 E60)

Wien Vienna

0   km   5

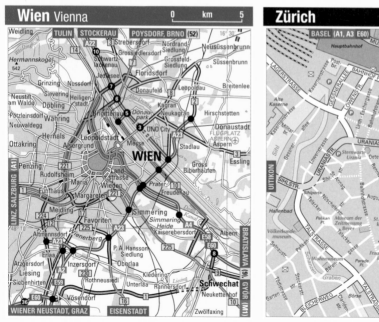

TULIN   STOCKERAU   POYSDORF, BRNO (52)

WIEN

WIENER NEUSTADT, GRAZ   EISENSTADT

BRATISLAVA (9), GYÖR (M1)

Schwechat

Zürich

0   km   0.5

BASEL (A1, A3 E60)   BÜLACH (A1b)

RAPPERSWIL **17**

	GB	F	D	I
(A)	Austria	Autriche	Österreich	Austria
(AL)	Albania	Albanie	Albanien	Albania
(AND)	Andorra	Andorre	Andorra	Andorra
(B)	Belgium	Belgique	Belgien	Belgio
(BG)	Bulgaria	Bulgarie	Bulgarien	Bulgaria
(BIH)	Bosnia-Herzegovina	Bosnie-Herzegovine	Bosnien-Herzegowina	Bosnia-Herzogovina
(BY)	Belarus	Belarus	Weissrussland	Bielorussia
(CG)	Montenegro	Monténégro	Montenegro	Montenegro
(CH)	Switzerland	Suisse	Schweiz	Svizzera
(CY)	Cyprus	Chypre	Zypern	Cipro
(CZ)	Czech Republic	République Tchèque	Tschechische Republik	Repubblica Ceca
(D)	Germany	Allemagne	Deutschland	Germania
(DK)	Denmark	Danemark	Dänemark	Danimarca
(E)	Spain	Espagne	Spanien	Spagna
(EST)	Estonia	Estonie	Estland	Estonia
(F)	France	France	Frankreich	Francia
(FIN)	Finland	Finlande	Finnland	Finlandia
(FL)	Liechtenstein	Liechtenstein	Liechtenstein	Liechtenstein
(FO)	Faeroe Islands	Îles Féroé	Färöer-Inseln	Isole Faroe
(GB)	United Kingdom	Royaume Uni	Grossbritannien und Nordirland	Regno Unito
(GBZ)	Gibraltar	Gibraltar	Gibraltar	Gibilterra
(GR)	Greece	Grèce	Greichenland	Grecia
(H)	Hungary	Hongrie	Ungarn	Ungheria

	GB	F	D	I
(HR)	Croatia	Croatie	Kroatien	Croazia
(I)	Italy	Italie	Italien	Italia
(IRL)	Ireland	Irlande	Irland	Irlanda
(IS)	Iceland	Islande	Island	Islanda
(L)	Luxembourg	Luxembourg	Luxemburg	Lussemburgo
(LT)	Lithuania	Lituanie	Litauen	Lituania
(LV)	Latvia	Lettonie	Lettland	Lettonia
(M)	Malta	Malte	Malta	Malta
(MC)	Monaco	Monaco	Monaco	Monaco
(MD)	Moldova	Moldavie	Moldawien	Moldavia
(MK)	Macedonia	Macédoine	Makedonien	Macedonia
(N)	Norway	Norvège	Norwegen	Norvegia
(NL)	Netherlands	Pays-Bas	Niederlande	Paesi Bassi
(P)	Portugal	Portugal	Portugal	Portogallo
(PL)	Poland	Pologne	Polen	Polonia
(RO)	Romania	Roumanie	Rumanien	Romania
(RSM)	San Marino	Saint-Marin	San Marino	San Marino
(RUS)	Russia	Russie	Russland	Russia
(S)	Sweden	Suède	Schweden	Svezia
(SK)	Slovak Republic	République Slovaque	Slowak Republik	Repubblica Slovacca
(SLO)	Slovenia	Slovénie	Slowenien	Slovenia
(SRB)	Serbia	Serbie	Serbien	Serbia
(TR)	Turkey	Turquie	Türkei	Turchia
(UA)	Ukraine	Ukraine	Ukraine	Ucraina

A

A Baña E 140 B2
A Bola E 140 B3
A Cañiza E 140 A2
A Capela E 140 A2
A Coruña E 140 A2
A Estrada E 140 B2
A Fonsagrada E 141 A3
A Guarda E 140 C2
A Gudiña E 141 B3
A Merca E 140 B3
A Peroxa E 140 B3
A Pontenova E 141 A3
A Rúa E 141 B3
A Teixeira E 141 B3
A Veiga E 141 B3
A-Ver-o-Mar P 148 A1
Aabybro DK 58 A2
Aach D 107 B4
Aachen D 80 B2
Aalborg DK 58 A2
Aalen D 94 C2
Aalestrup DK 58 B2
Aalsmeer NL 70 B1
Aalst B 79 B4
Aalten NL 71 C3
Aalter B 79 A3
Äänekoski FIN 8 A4
Aapajärvi FIN 197 B10
Aarau CH 106 B3
Aarberg CH 106 B2
Aarburg CH 106 B2
Aardenburg NL 79 A3
Aars DK 58 B2
Aarschot B 79 B4
Aba H 112 B2
Abádanes E 152 B1
Abades E 151 B3
Abadin E 141 A3
Abádszalók H 113 B4
Abaliget H 125 A4
Abana TR 23 A8
Abanilla E 165 A3
Abano Terme I 121 B4
Abarán E 165 A3
Abasár H 113 B4
Abbadia San Salvatore I 135 C4
Abbaue D 74 A2
Abbehausen D 72 A1
Abbekås S 66 A2
Abbeville F 90 A1
Abbey IRL 28 A3
Abbey Town GB 36 B3
Abbeydorney IRL 29 B2
Abbeyfeale IRL 29 B2
Abbeyleix IRL 30 B1
Abbiategrasso I 120 B1
Abborrträsk S 196 D2
Abbots Bromley GB 40 C2
Abbotsbury GB 43 B4
Abda H 111 B4
Abejar E 143 C4
Abela P 160 B1
Abelvær N 199 A8
Abenberg D 94 B2
Abenójar E 157 B3
Åbenrå DK 64 A2
Abensberg D 95 C3
Aberaeron GB 39 B2
Aberchirder GB 33 D4
Aberdare GB 39 C3
Aberdaron GB 38 B2
Aberdeen GB 33 D4
Aberdulais GB 39 C3
Aberdyfi GB 39 C3
Aberfeldy GB 35 B4

Aberffraw GB 38 A2
Aberfoyle GB 34 B3
Abergavenny GB 39 C3
Abergele GB 38 A3
Abergynolwyn GB 38 B3
Aberporth GB 39 B2
Abersoch GB 38 B2
Abertillery GB 39 C3
Abertura E 156 A2
Aberystwyth GB 39 B2
Abetone I 135 A3
Abfaltersbach A 109 C3
Abide, Çanakkale TR 186 B1
Abide, Kütahya TR 187 D4
Abiego E 145 B3
Abild DK 64 B1
Abingdon GB 44 B2
Abington GB 36 A3
Abisko S 194 B9
Abiul P 154 B2
Abla E 164 B2
Ablis F 90 C1
Abondance F 118 A3
Abony H 113 B4
Aboyne GB 33 D4
Abrantes P 154 B2
Abreiro P 148 A2
Abreschviller F 92 C3
Abrest F 117 A3
Abriès F 119 C3
Abrud RO 17 B5
Absdorf A 97 C3
Abtenau A 109 B4
Abtsgmünd D 94 C1
Abusejo E 149 B3
Åby, Kronoberg S 62 A2
Åby, Östergötland S 56 B2
Abyggeby S 51 B4
Åbytorp S 55 A6
Acate I 177 B3
Accadia I 171 B3
Accéglio I 132 A2
Accettura I 172 B2
Acciaroli I 170 C3
Accous F 145 A3
Accrington GB 40 B1
Accúmoli I 169 A3
Acedera E 156 A2
Acehúche E 155 B4
Acered E 152 A2
Acerenza I 172 B1
Acerno I 170 C3
Acerra I 170 C2
Aceuchal E 155 C4
Acharacle GB 34 B2
Acharnes GR 185 A4
Acharávi GR 182 D1
Achavanich GB 32 C3
Achene B 79 B5
Achenkirch A 108 B2
Achensee A 108 B2
Achenthal A 108 B2
Achentrias GR 185 E6
Acheux-en-Amienois F 90 A2
Achiltibuie GB 32 C1
Achim D 72 A2
Achladochori GR 183 B5
Achnasheen GB 32 D1
Achnashellach GB 32 D1
Achosnich GB 34 B1
Aci Castello I 177 B4
Aci Catena I 177 B4
Acipayam TR 189 B4
Acilia I 168 B2
Acireale I 177 B4
Acle GB 41 C5

Acqua Doria F 180 B1
Acquacadda I 179 C2
Acquanegra sul Chiese I 121 B3
Acquapendente I 168 A1
Acquasanta Terme I 136 C2
Acquasparta I 168 A2
Acquaviva I 135 B4
Acquaviva delle Fonti I 171 C4
Acquaviva Picena I 136 C2
Acqui Terme I 119 C5
Acquigny F 89 A5
Acri I 174 B2
Acs H 112 B2
Acsa H 112 B3
Ácsteszér H 112 B1
Acy-en-Multien F 90 B2
Ada SRB 126 B2
Adak S 195 E9
Ådalsbruk N 48 B3
Adamas GR 185 C5
Adamsfjord N 193 B10
Adamuz E 157 B3
Adana TR 23 C8
Ádánd H 112 C2
Adanero E 150 B3
Adare IRL 29 B3
Adaševci SRB 125 B5
Adeanueva de Ebro E 144 B2
Adelboden CH 106 C2
Adelebsen D 82 A1
Adélfia I 173 A2
Adelmannsfelden D 94 C2
Adelsheim D 94 B1
Adelsö S 57 A3
Ademuz E 152 B2
Adenau D 80 B2
Adendorf D 72 A3
Adinkerke B 78 A2
Adjud RO 17 B7
Adliswil CH 107 B3
Admont A 110 B1
Adneram N 52 A2
Adolfsström S 195 D7
Adony H 112 B2
Adorf, Hessen D 81 A4
Adorf, Sachsen D 83 B4
Adra E 164 C1
Adradas E 152 A1
Adrall E 147 B2
Adrano I 177 B3
Adria I 121 B5
Adrigole IRL 29 C2
Adwick le Street GB 40 B2
Adzaneta E 153 B3
Ærøskøbing DK 65 B3
Aesch CH 106 B2
Afandou GR 188 C3
Åfarnes N 198 C4
Affing D 94 C2
Affoltern CH 106 B3
Affric Lodge GB 32 D1
Afitos GR 183 D5
Åfjord N 199 B7
Aflenz Kurort A 110 B2
Afragóla I 170 C2
Afritz A 109 C4
Afyon TR 187 D5
Ağapınar TR 187 D5
Agay F 132 B2
Agazzano I 120 C2
Agde F 130 B2
Agdenes N 198 B6
Agen F 129 B3

Ager E 145 C4
Agerbæk DK 59 C1
Agerskov DK 64 A2
Agger DK 58 B1
Aggersund DK 58 A2
Aggius I 178 B3
Aggsbach Dorf A 97 C3
Aggsbach Markt A 97 C3
Aggtelek H 99 C4
Aghalee GB 27 B4
Aghia GR 182 D4
Aghia Anna GR 183 E5
Aghia Galini GR 185 D5
Aghia Marina, Dodekanisa GR 188 B1
Aghia Marina, Dodekanisa GR 188 D1
Aghia Paraskevi GR 186 C1
Aghia Pelagia GR 184 C3
Aghia Triada GR 184 B2
Aghio Theodori GR 184 B4
Aghiokambos GR 182 D4
Aghios Efstratios GR 183 D6
Aghios Kirikos GR 185 B7
Aghios Matheos GR 182 D1
Aghios Mironas GR 185 D6
Aghios Nikolaos GR 185 D6
Aghios Petros GR 182 D2
Agiči BIH 124 C2
Agira I 177 B3
Ağlasun TR 189 B5
Aglientu I 178 A3
Agnières F 118 C2
Agno CH 120 B1
Agnone I 170 B2
Agolada E 140 B2
Agon Coutainville F 88 A2
Ágordo I 121 A5
Agost E 165 A4
Agramón E 158 C2
Agramunt E 147 C2
Agreda E 144 C2
Agria GR 183 D5
Agrigento I 176 B2
Agrinio GR 182 E3
Agrón E 163 A4
Agrópoli I 170 C2
Agua Longa P 148 A1
Aguadulce, Almería E 164 C2
Aguadulce, Sevilla E 162 A3
Agualada E 140 A2
Aguarón E 152 A2
Aguas E 145 B3
Aguas Belas P 154 B2
Aguas de Busot E 159 C3
Aguas de Moura P 154 C2
Águas Frias P 148 A2
Águas Santas P 148 A1
Aguaviva E 153 B3
Aguaviva de la Vega E 152 A1
Agudo E 156 B3
Águeda P 148 B1
Aguessac F 130 A2
Agugliano I 136 B2
Aguiar P 154 C3
Aguiar da Beira P 148 B2
Aguilafuente E 151 A3
Aguilar de Campóo E 142 B2
Aguilar de la Frontera E 163 A3
Aguilas E 164 B3
Agunnaryd S 60 C4
Ağva TR 187 A4
Ahat TR 187 D4

Ahaus D 71 B3
Åheim N 198 C2
Ahigal E 149 B3
Ahigal de Villarino E 149 A3
Ahillones E 156 B2
Ahlbeck, Mecklenburg-Vorpommern D 66 C3
Ahlbeck, Mecklenburg-Vorpommern D 74 A3
Ahlen D 81 A3
Ahlhorn D 71 B5
Ahmetbey TR 186 A2
Ahmetler TR 188 A4
Ahmetli TR 188 A2
Ahoghill GB 27 B4
Ahola FIN 197 C11
Ahrensbök D 65 B3
Ahrensburg D 72 A3
Ahrenshoop D 66 B1
Ahun F 116 A2
Åhus S 63 C2
Ahvenselkä FIN 197 C11
Aibar E 144 B2
Aich D 95 C4
Aicha D 96 C1
Aichach D 94 C3
Aidone I 177 B3
Aiello Cálabro I 175 B2
Aigen im Mühlkreis A 96 C1
Aigle CH 119 A3
Aignan F 128 C3
Aignay-le-Duc F 104 B3
Aigre F 115 C4
Aigrefeuille-d'Aunis F 114 B3
Aigrefeuille-sur-Maine F 101 B4
Aiguablava E 147 C4
Aiguebelle F 118 B3
Aigueperse F 116 A3
Aigues-Mortes F 131 B3
Aigues-Vives F 130 B1
Aiguilles F 119 C3
Aiguillon F 129 B3
Aigurande F 103 C3
Ailefroide F 118 C3
Aillant-sur-Tholon F 104 B2
Ailly-sur-Noye F 90 B2
Ailly-sur-Somme F 90 B2
Aimargues F 131 B3
Aime F 118 B3
Ainaži LV 8 D4
Ainet A 109 C3
Ainhoa F 144 A2
Ainsa E 145 B4
Airaines F 90 B1
Aird GB 34 B2
Aird Asaig Tairbeart GB 31 B2
Airdrie GB 35 C4
Aire-sur-la-Lys F 78 B2
Aire-sur-l'Adour F 128 C2
Airole I 133 B3
Airolo CH 107 C3
Airvault F 102 C1
Aisey-sur-Seine F 104 B3
Aissey F 105 B5
Aisy-sur-Armançon F 104 B3
Aiterhofen D 95 C4
Aith, Orkney GB 33 B4
Aith, Shetland GB 33 A5
Aitona E 153 A4
Aitrach D 107 B5

Aiud RO 17 B5
Aix-en-Othe F 104 A2
Aix-en-Provence F 131 B4
Aix-les-Bains F 118 B4
Aixe-sur-Vienne F 115 C5
Aizenay F 114 B2
Aizkraukle LV 8 D4
Aizpute LV 8 D2
Ajac F 146 A3
Ajaccio F 180 B1
Ajain F 116 A1
Ajaureforsen S 195 E6
Ajdovščina SLO 122 B2
Ajka H 111 B4
Ajo E 143 A3
Ajofrin E 157 A4
Ajos FIN 196 D7
Ajuda P 155 C3
Akanthou CY 181 A2
Akarca TR 189 A4
Akasztó H 112 C3
Akçakoca TR 187 A6
Akçaova TR 187 A4
Akçay TR 189 C4
Aken D 83 A4
Åkerby S 51 B4
Åkernes N 52 B3
Åkers styckebruk S 56 A3
Åkersberga S 57 A4
Åkervik N 195 E4
Akhisar TR 186 D2
Åkirkeby DK 67 A3
Akköy TR 188 B2
Akkrum NL 70 A2
Akören TR 189 B7
Åkra N 52 A2
Akranes IS 190 C3
Åkrehamn N 52 A1
Akrotiri CY 181 B1
Aksaray TR 23 B8
Akşehir TR 189 A6
Akseki TR 189 B6
Aksla N 46 A3
Aksu TR 189 C5
Aktsyabrski BY 13 B8
Akureyri IS 191 B7
Åkvåg N 53 B5
Akyazı TR 187 B5
Ål N 47 B5
Ala I 121 B4
Alà dei Sardi I 178 B3
Alà di Stura I 119 B4
Ala-Nampa FIN 197 C9
Alaçam TR 23 A8
Alaçatı TR 188 A1
Alaejos E 150 A2
Alagna Valsésia I 119 B4
Alagón E 144 C2
Alaior E 167 B4
Alájar E 161 B3
Alakurtti RUS 197 C13
Alakylä FIN 196 B7
Alameda E 163 A3
Alameda de la Sagra E 151 B4
Alamedilla E 163 A4
Alaminos E 151 B5
Alandroal P 155 C3
Alange E 156 B1
Alaniemi FIN 197 D8
Alanís E 156 B2
Alanno I 169 A3
Alansbro S 200 D3
Alanya TR 189 C7

Alap H 112 C2
Alaquáso E 159 B3
Alar del Rey E 142 B2
Alaraz E 150 B2
Alarcón E 158 B1
Alaró E 167 B2
Alaşehir TR 188 A3
Alássio I 133 A4
Alatoz E 158 B2
Alatri I 169 B3
Alavus FIN 8 A3
Alba E 152 B2
Alba I 119 C5
Alba Adriática I 136 C2
Alba de Tormes E 150 B2
Alba de Yeltes E 149 B3
Alba-Iulia RO 17 B5
Albacete E 158 C2
Albæk DK 58 A3
Albaida E 159 C3
Albala del Caudillo E 156 A1
Albaladejo E 158 C1
Albalat E 159 B3
Albalate de Cinca E 145 C4
Albalate de las Nogueras E 152 B1
Albalate del Arzobispo E 153 A3
Albalete de Zorita E 151 B5
Alban F 130 B1
Albánchez E 164 B2
Albanchez de Ubeda E 163 A4
Albano Laziale I 168 B2
Albanyà E 147 B3
Albaredo d'Adige I 121 B4
Albares E 151 B4
Albarracín E 152 B2
Albatana E 158 C2
Albatarrec E 153 A4
Albatera E 165 A4
Albbruck D 106 B3
Albedin E 163 A3
Albelda de Iregua E 143 B4
Albenga I 133 A4
Albens F 118 B2
Ålberga, *Södermanland* S 56 A2
Ålberga, *Södermanland* S 56 B2
Albergaria-a-Nova P 148 B1
Albergaria-a-Velha P 148 B1
Albergaria dos Doze P 154 B2
Alberge P 154 C2
Alberic E 159 B3
Albernoa P 160 B2
Alberobello I 173 B3
Alberoni I 122 B1
Albersdorf D 64 B2
Albersloh D 81 A3
Albert F 90 A2
Albertirsa H 112 B3
Albertville F 118 B3
Alberuela de Tubo E 145 C3
Albi F 130 B1
Albidona I 174 B2
Albinia I 168 A1
Albino I 120 B2
Albinshof D 66 C2
Albires E 142 B1
Albisola Marina I 133 A4
Albocácer E 153 B4
Albolote E 163 A4
Albondón E 164 C1
Alborea E 158 B2
Albox E 164 B2
Albrechtice nad Vltavou CZ 96 B2
Albstadt D 107 A4
Albufeira P 160 B1
Albuñol E 164 C1
Albuñuelas E 163 B4
Alburquerque E 155 B3
Alby, *Öland* S 63 B4
Alby, *Västernorrland* S 200 D1
Alcácer do Sal P 154 C2
Alcáçovas P 154 C2
Alcadozo E 158 C2
Alcafoces P 155 B3
Alcains P 155 B3
Alcalá de Guadaira E 162 A2
Alcalá de Gurrea E 144 B3
Alcalá de Henares E 151 B4
Alcalá de la Selva E 153 B3
Alcalá de los Gazules E 162 B2
Alcalá de Xivert E 153 B4
Alcalá del Júcar E 158 B2
Alcalá del Río E 162 A2
Alcalá del Valle E 162 B2
Alcalá la Real E 163 A4
Álcamo I 176 B1
Alcampell E 145 C4
Alcanadre E 144 B1
Alcanar E 153 B4
Alcanede P 154 B2
Alcanena P 154 B2
Alcañices E 149 A3
Alcántara E 155 B4
Alcantarilha P 160 B1
Alcantarilla E 165 B3
Alcañz E 153 A3
Alcara il Fusi I 177 A3
Alcaracejos E 156 B3
Alcaraz E 158 C1
Alcaria Ruiva P 160 B2
Alcarraz E 153 A4
Alcaudete E 163 A3
Alcaudete de la Jara E 150 C3
Alcázar de San Juan E 157 A4
Alcazarén E 150 A3
Alcester GB 44 A2
Alcoba E 157 A3
Alcobaça P 154 B1
Alcobendas E 151 B4
Alcocer E 151 B5
Alcochete P 154 C2
Alcoentre P 154 B2
Alcolea, *Almería* E 164 C2
Alcolea, *Córdoba* E 156 C3
Alcolea de Calatrava E 157 B3
Alcolea de Cinca E 145 C4
Alcolea de Tajo E 150 C2
Alcolea del Pinar E 152 A1
Alcolea del Rio E 162 A2
Alcollarin E 156 A2
Alconchel E 155 C3
Alconera E 155 C4
Alcontar E 164 B2
Alcora E 153 B3
Alcorcón E 151 B4
Alcorisa E 153 B3
Alcossebre E 153 B4
Alcoutim P 160 B2
Alcover E 147 C2
Alcoy E 159 C3
Alcsútdoboz H 112 B2
Alcubierre E 145 C3
Alcubilla de Avellaneda E 143 C3
Alcubilla de Nogales E 141 B5
Alcubillas E 157 B4
Alcublas E 159 B3
Alcúdia E 167 B3
Alcudia de Guadix E 164 B1
Alcuéscar E 155 B4
Aldbrough GB 41 B3
Aldea de Trujillo E 156 A2
Aldea del Cano E 155 B4
Aldea del Fresno E 151 B3
Aldea del Obispo E 149 B3
Aldea del Rey E 157 B4
Aldea Real E 151 A3
Aldeacentenera E 156 A2
Aldeadávila de la Ribera E 149 A3
Aldealcorvo E 151 A4
Aldealuenga de Santa Maria E 151 A4
Aldeamayor de San Martin E 150 A3
Aldeanueva de Barbarroya E 150 C2
Aldeanueva de San Bartolomé E 156 A2
Aldeanueva del Camino E 149 B4
Aldeanueva del Codonal E 150 A3
Aldeapozo E 144 C1
Aldeaquemada E 157 B4
Aldearrubia E 150 A2
Aldeaseca de la Frontera E 150 B2
Aldeasoña E 151 A3
Aldeatejada E 150 B2
Aldeavieja E 150 B3
Aldeburgh GB 45 A5
Aldehuela E 152 B2
Aldehuela de Calatañazor E 143 C4
Aldeia da Serra P 155 C3
Aldeia do Bispo P 149 B3
Aldeia do Mato P 154 B2
Aldeia Gavinha P 154 B1
Aldeire E 164 B1
Aldenhoven D 80 B2
Aldersbach D 95 C5
Aldershot GB 44 B3
Aldudes F 144 A2
Åled S 60 C2
Aledo E 165 B3
Alegria E 143 B4
Aleksa Šantić SRB 126 B1
Aleksandrovac SRB 127 C3
Aleksandrów Kujawski PL 76 B3
Aleksandrów Łódźki PL 86 A3
Ålem S 62 B4
Alençon F 89 B4
Alenquer P 154 B1
Alenya F 146 B3
Aléria F 180 A2
Alès F 131 A3
Áles I 179 C2
Alessándria I 120 C1
Alessándria della Rocca I 176 B2
Alessano I 173 C4
Ålesund N 198 C3
Alet-les-Bains F 146 B3
Alexandria GB 34 C3
Alexandria GR 182 C4
Alexandria RO 17 D6
Alexandroupoli GR 183 C7
Aleyrac F 131 A3
Alézio I 173 B4
Alfacar E 163 A4
Alfaiates P 149 B3
Alfajarin E 153 A3
Alfambra E 152 B2
Alfambra P 160 B1
Alfândega da Fé P 149 A3
Alfarela de Jafes P 148 A2
Alfarelos P 148 B1
Alfarim P 154 C1
Alfarnate E 163 B3
Alfaro E 144 B2
Alfarrás E 145 C4
Alfaz del Pi E 159 C3
Alfedena I 169 B4
Alfeizarão P 154 B1
Alfeld, *Bayern* D 95 B3
Alfeld, *Niedersachsen* D 72 C2
Alfena P 148 A1
Alferce P 160 B1
Alfhausen D 71 B4
Alfonsine I 135 A5
Alford, *Aberdeenshire* GB 33 D4
Alford, *Lincolnshire* GB 41 B4
Alforja E 147 C1
Alfoz E 141 A3
Alfreton GB 40 B2
Alfta S 50 A3
Alfundão P 160 A1
Algaida E 167 B2
Algar E 162 B2
Älgarås S 55 B5
Ålgård N 52 B1
Algarinejo E 163 A3
Algarrobo E 163 B3
Algatocin E 162 B2
Algeciras E 162 B2
Algemesí E 159 B3
Algés P 154 C1
Algete E 151 B4
Alghero I 178 B2
Älghult S 62 A3
Alginet E 159 B3
Algodonales E 162 B2
Algodor E 151 C4
Algodor P 160 B2
Algora E 151 B5
Algoso P 149 A3
Algoz P 160 B1
Älgsjö S 200 B3
Alguaire E 145 C4
Alguazas E 165 A3
Algutsrum S 63 B4
Algyő H 126 A2
Alhama de Almería E 164 C2
Alhama de Aragón E 152 A2
Alhama de Granada E 163 B4
Alhama de Murcia E 165 B3
Alhambra E 157 B4
Alhandra P 154 C1
Alhaurin de la Torre E 163 B3
Alhaurín el Grande E 163 B3
Alhendin E 163 A4
Alhóndiga E 151 B5
Ali Terme I 177 A4
Alia E 156 A2
Ália I 176 B2
Aliaga E 153 B3
Aliağa TR 186 D1
Alibunar SRB 127 B2
Alicante E 165 A4
Alicún de Ortega E 164 B1
Alife I 170 B2
Alija del Infantado E 141 B5
Alijó P 148 A2
Alimena I 177 B3
Alingsås S 60 B2
Alinyà E 147 B2
Aliseda E 155 B4
Aliveri GR 185 A5
Alixan F 117 C5
Aljaraque E 161 B2
Aljezur P 160 B1
Aljorra E 165 B3
Aljubarrota P 154 B2
Aljucen E 155 B4
Aljustrel P 160 B1
Alken B 79 B5
Alkmaar NL 70 B1
Alkoven A 96 C2
Allaines F 103 A3
Allaire F 101 B3
Allanche F 116 B2
Alland A 111 A3
Allariz E 140 B3
Allassac F 129 A4
Allauch F 131 B4
Alleen N 52 B3
Allègre F 117 B3
Allemont F 118 B3
Allendale Town GB 37 B4
Allendorf D 81 B4
Allentsteig A 97 C3
Allepuz E 153 B3
Allersberg D 95 B3
Allershausen D 95 C3
Alles E 142 A2
Allevard F 118 B3
Allgunnen S 62 A3
Allihies IRL 29 C1
Allingåbro DK 58 B3
Allmannsdorf D 107 B4
Allo E 144 B1
Alloa GB 35 B4
Allogny F 103 B4
Ålloluokta S 196 B2
Allones, *Eure et Loire* F 90 C1
Allones, *Maine-et-Loire* F 102 B2
Allonnes F 102 B2
Allons F 128 B2
Allos F 132 A2
Allstedt D 82 A3
Alltwalis GB 39 C2
Allumiere I 168 A1
Almaceda P 155 B3
Almacelles E 145 C4
Almachar E 163 B3
Almada P 154 C1
Almadén E 156 B3
Almadén de la Plata E 161 B3
Almadenejos E 156 B3
Almadrones E 151 B5
Almagro E 157 B4
Almajano E 144 C1
Almansa E 159 C2
Almansil P 160 B1
Almanza E 142 B1
Almaraz E 150 C2
Almargen E 162 B2
Almarza E 143 C4
Almásfüzitő H 112 B2
Almassora E 159 B3
Almazán E 152 A1
Almazul E 152 A1
Alme D 81 A4
Almedina E 158 C1
Almedinilla E 163 A3
Almeida E 149 A3
Almeida P 149 B3
Almeirim P 154 B2
Almelo NL 71 B3
Almenar E 145 C4
Almenar de Soria E 152 A1
Almenara E 159 B3
Almendra P 149 B2
Almendral E 155 C4
Almendral de la Cañada E 150 B3
Almendralejo E 155 C4
Almenno San Bartolomeo I 120 B2
Almere NL 70 B2
Almería E 164 C2
Almerimar E 164 C2
Almese I 119 B4
Almexial P 160 B2
Älmhult S 63 B2
Almiropotamos GR 185 A5
Almiros GR 182 D4
Almodôvar P 160 B1
Almodóvar del Campo E 157 B3
Almodóvar del Pinar E 158 B2
Almodóvar del Río E 162 A2
Almofala P 148 B2
Almogia E 163 B3
Almoharin E 156 A1
Almonacid de la Sierra E 152 A2
Almonacid de Toledo E 157 A4
Almonaster la Real E 161 B3
Almondsbury GB 43 A4
Almonte E 161 B3
Almoradí E 165 A4
Almoraima E 162 B2
Almorox E 150 B3
Almoster P 154 B2
Almsele S 200 B3
Älmsta S 51 C5
Almudena E 164 A3
Almudévar E 145 B3
Almuñécar E 163 B4
Almunge S 51 C5
Almuradiel E 157 B4
Almussafes E 159 B3
Almvik S 62 A4
Alness GB 32 D2
Alnmouth GB 37 A5
Alnwick GB 37 A5
Åloppe S 51 C4
Álora E 163 B3
Alos d'Ensil E 146 B2
Alosno E 161 B2
Alozaina E 162 B3
Alpbach A 108 B2
Alpedrete de la Sierra E 151 B4
Alpedrinha P 148 B2
Alpen D 80 A2
Alpera E 159 C2
Alphen aan de Rijn NL 70 B1
Alpiarça P 154 B2
Alpignano I 119 B4
Alpirsbach D 93 C4
Alpu TR 187 C5
Alpuente E 159 B2
Alqueva P 160 A2
Alquézar E 145 B4
Als DK 58 B3
Alsasua E 144 B1
Alsdorf D 80 B2
Alselv DK 59 C1
Alsfeld D 81 B5
Alsike S 57 A3
Alskog S 57 C4
Alsleben D 83 A3
Alsónémedi H 112 B3
Alsótold H 112 B3
Alsóújlak H 111 B3
Alstad N 194 C6
Alstätte D 71 B3
Alsterbro S 62 B3
Alstermo S 62 B3
Alston GB 37 B4
Alsvåg N 194 B6
Alsvik N 194 C5
Alt Ruppin D 74 B1
Alta N 192 C7
Älta S 57 A4
Altamura I 172 B2
Altarejos E 158 B1
Altaussee A 109 B4
Altavilla Irpina I 170 B2
Altavilla Silentina I 170 C3
Altdöbern D 84 A2
Altdorf CH 107 C3
Altdorf D 95 C4
Altdorf bei Nürnberg D 95 B3
Alte P 160 B1
Altea E 159 C3
Altedo I 121 C4
Alten-weddingen D 73 B4
Altena D 81 A3
Altenau D 82 A2
Altenberg D 84 B1
Altenberge D 71 B4
Altenbruch D 64 C1
Altenburg D 83 B4
Altenfelden A 96 C1
Altengronau D 82 B1
Altenheim D 93 C3
Altenhundem D 81 A4
Altenkirchen, *Mecklenburg-Vorpommern* D 66 B2
Altenkirchen, *Radom* D 81 B3
Altenkunstadt D 82 B3
Altenmarkt A 110 B1
Altenmarkt D 109 A3
Altenmarkt im Pongall A 109 B4
Altensteig D 93 C4
Altentreptow D 74 A2
Altenwalde D 64 C1
Alter do Chão P 155 B3
Altfraunhofen D 95 C4
Altheim A 109 A4
Altheim D 94 B1
Althofen A 110 C1
Altınoluk TR 186 C1
Altınova TR 186 C1
Altıntaş TR 187 C5
Altınyaka TR 189 C5
Altınyayla TR 189 B4
Altkirch F 106 B2
Altlandsberg D 74 B2
Altlewin D 74 B3
Altmannstein D 95 C3
Altmorschen D 82 A1
Altmunster A 109 B4
Altnaharra GB 32 C2
Alto Campoó E 142 A2
Altofonte I 176 A2
Altomonte I 174 B2
Alton, *Hampshire* GB 44 B3
Alton, *Staffordshire* GB 40 C2
Altopáscio I 135 B3
Altötting D 109 A3
Altreichenau D 96 C1
Altshausen D 107 B4
Altstätten CH 107 B4
Altura E 159 B3
Altusried D 107 B5
Alūksne LV 8 D5
Alunda S 51 B5
Alustante E 152 B2
Alva GB 35 B4
Alvaiázere P 154 B2
Alvalade P 160 B1
Älvängen S 60 B2
Alvarenga P 148 B1
Alvares P 154 A2
Alvdal N 199 C7
Älvdalen S 49 A6
Alverca P 154 C1
Alversund N 46 B2
Alvesta S 62 B2
Alvignac F 129 B4
Alvignano I 170 B2
Ålvik N 46 B3
Alvik S 50 B1
Alvimare F 89 A4
Alviobeira P 154 B2
Alvito P 160 A2
Älvkarleby S 51 B4
Älvkarleö bruk S 51 B4
Alvor P 160 B1
Alvorge P 154 B2
Alvøy N 46 B2
Älvros S 199 C11
Alvsbacka S 55 A4
Älvsbyn S 196 D4
Älvsered S 60 B2
Alwernia PL 86 B3
Alwinton GB 37 A4
Alyth GB 35 B4
Alytus LT 13 A6
Alzénau D 93 A5
Alzey D 93 B4
Alzira E 159 B3
Alzonne F 146 A3
Amadora P 154 C1
Åmål S 55 A3
Amalfi I 170 C2
Amaliada GR 184 B2
Amance F 105 B5
Amancey F 105 B5
Amándola I 136 C2
Amantea I 175 B2
Amarante P 148 A1
Amareleja P 161 A2
Amares P 148 A1
Amaseno I 169 B3
Amasra TR 187 A7
Amatrice I 169 A3
Amay B 79 B5
Ambarnyy RUS 3 D13
Ambazac F 115 C5
Ambelonas GR 182 D4
Amberg D 95 B3
Ambérieu-en-Bugey F 118 B2
Ambérieux-en-Dombes F 117 A4
Ambert F 117 B3
Ambés F 128 A2
Ambjörby S 49 B5
Ambjörnarp S 60 B3
Amble GB 37 A5
Ambleside GB 36 B4
Ambleteuse F 78 B1
Amboise F 102 B2
Ambrières-les-Vallées F 88 B3
Amden CH 107 B4
Amel B 80 B2
Amélia I 168 A2
Amélie-les-Bains-Palalda F 146 B3
Amelinghausen D 72 A3
Amendoa P 154 B2
Amendoeira P 160 B2
Améndola I 171 B3
Amendolara I 174 B2
Amer E 147 B3
Amerongen NL 70 B2
Amersfoort NL 70 B2
Amersham GB 44 B3
Ames E 140 B2
Amesbury GB 44 B2
Amfiklia GR 182 E4
Amfilochia GR 182 E3
Amfipoli GR 183 C5
Amfissa GR 184 A3
Amieira, *Évora* P 155 C3
Amieira, *Portalegre* P 154 B3
Amieiro P 148 B1
Amiens F 90 B2
Amindeo GR 182 C3
Åminne S 60 B3
Åmli N 53 B4
Amlwch GB 38 A2
Ammanford GB 39 C3
Ammarnäs S 195 E7
Åmmeberg S 55 B5
Amorbach D 94 B1
Amorebieta E 143 A4
Amorgos GR 185 C6
Amorosa P 148 A1
Amorosi I 170 B2
Åmot, *Buskerud* N 48 C1
Åmot, *Telemark* N 53 A3
Åmot S 50 B3
Åmotfors S 54 A3
Åmotsdal N 53 A4
Amou F 128 C2
Ampezzo I 122 A1
Ampfing D 95 C4
Ampflwang A 109 A4
Amplepuis F 117 B4
Amposta E 153 B4
Ampthill GB 44 A3
Ampudia E 142 C2
Ampuero E 143 A3
Amriswil CH 107 B4
Åmsele S 200 B5
Amstelveen NL 70 B1
Amsterdam NL 70 B1
Amstetten A 110 A1
Amtzell D 107 B4
Amulree GB 35 B4

Amurrio E 143 A4
Amusco E 142 B2
An t-Ob GB 31 B1
Åna-Sira N 52 B2
Anacapri I 170 C2
Anadia P 148 B1
Anadon E 152 B2
Anafi GR 185 C6
Anagni I 169 B3
Anamur TR 23 C7
Ananyiv UA 17 B8
Anascaul IRL 29 B1
Ånäset S 2 D7
Anastażewo PL 76 B3
Anaya de Alba E 150 B2
Ança P 148 B1
Ancaster GB 40 C3
Ancede P 148 A1
Ancenis F 101 B4
Ancerville F 91 C5
Anchuras E 156 A3
Ancona I 136 B2
Ancora P 148 A1
Ancrum GB 35 C5
Ancy-le-Franc F 104 B3
Andalo I 121 A3
Åndalsnes N 198 C4
Andance F 117 B4
Andau A 111 B4
Andebu N 53 A6
Andeer CH 107 C4
Andelfingen CH 107 B3
Andelot F 105 A4
Andelot-en-Montagne F 105 C4
Andenes N 194 A7
Andenne B 79 B5
Anderlues B 79 B4
Andermatt CH 107 C3
Andernach D 80 B3
Andernos-les-Bains F 128 B1
Anderslöv S 66 A2
Anderstorp S 60 B3
Andijk NL 70 B2
Andoain E 144 A1
Andocs H 112 C1
Andolsheim F 106 A2
Andorra E 153 B3
Andorra La Vella AND 146 B2
Andosilla E 144 B2
Andover GB 44 B2
Andratx E 166 B2
Andreapol RUS 9 D8
Andreas GB 36 B2
Andréspol PL 86 A3
Andrest F 145 A4
Andretta I 172 B1
Andrezieux-Bouthéon F 117 B4
Ándria I 171 B4
Andrijevica CG 16 D3
Andritsena GR 184 B2
Andros GR 185 B5
Andrychów PL 99 B3
Andselv N 194 A9
Andújar E 157 B3
Anduze F 131 A2
Åneby N 48 B2
Aneby S 62 A2
Añes E 143 A3
Anet F 90 C1
Anfo I 121 B3
Ang S 62 A2
Anga S 57 C4
Angaïs F 145 A3
Ånge, *Jämtland* S 199 B11
Ånge, *Västernorrland* S 200 D1
Angeja P 148 B1
Ängelholm S 61 C2
Angeli FIN 193 D9
Ängelsberg S 50 C3
Anger A 110 B2
Angera I 120 B1
Angermünde D 74 A3
Angern A 97 C4
Angers F 102 B1
Angerville F 90 C2
Anghiari I 135 B5
Angle GB 39 C1
Anglès E 147 C3
Anglés, *Tarn* F 130 B1
Angles, *Vendée* F 114 B2
Angles sur l'Anglin F 115 B4
Anglesola E 147 C2
Anglet F 128 C1
Anglisidhes CY 181 B2
Anglure F 91 C3
Angoulême F 115 C4
Angoulins F 114 B2
Angsö S 56 A2
Angueira P 149 A3
Angües E 145 B3
Anguiano E 143 B4
Anguillara Sabazia I 168 A2
Anguillara Véneta I 121 B4
Anhée B 79 B4
Anholt DK 60 C1
Aniane F 130 B2
Aniche F 78 B3
Änimskog S 54 B3
Anina RO 16 C4
Anixi GR 182 D3
Anizy-le-Château F 91 B3
Anjalankoski FIN 8 B5
Anjan S 199 B9
Ankara TR 187 C7
Ankaran SLO 122 B2
Ankarsrum S 62 A4
Ankerlia N 192 C4
Anklam D 66 C2
Ankum D 71 B4
Anlauftal A 109 B4
Anlezy F 104 C2
Ånn S 199 B9
Annaberg A 110 B2
Annaberg-Buchholz D 83 B5
Annaberg im Lammertal A 109 B4
Annaburg D 83 A5
Annahütte D 84 A1
Annalong GB 27 B5
Annan GB 36 B3
Anndalsvågen N 195 E3
Anneberg, *Halland* S 60 B2
Anneberg, *Jönköping* S 62 A2
Annecy F 118 B3
Annelund S 60 B3
Annemasse F 118 A3
Annenskiy Most RUS 9 B10
Annerstad S 60 C3
Annestown IRL 30 B1
Annevoie-Rouillon B 79 B4
Annonay F 117 B4
Annot F 132 B2
Annweiler D 93 B3
Ano Poroia GR 183 B5
Ano Siros GR 185 B5
Añora E 156 B3
Anould F 106 A1
Anquela del Ducado E 152 B1
Anröchte D 81 A4
Ans DK 59 B2
Ansager DK 59 C1
Ansbach D 94 B2
Anse F 117 B4
Anserœul B 79 B3
Ansfelden A 110 A1
Ansião P 154 B2
Ansó E 144 B3
Ansoain E 144 B2
Anstruther GB 35 B5
Antalya TR 189 C5
Antas E 164 B3
Antegnate I 120 B2
Antequera E 163 A3
Anterselva di Mezzo I 108 C3
Antibes F 132 B3
Antigüedad E 142 C2
Antillo I 177 B4
Antirio GR 184 A2
Antnäs S 196 D4
Antoing B 79 B3
Antonin PL 86 A1
Antrain F 88 B2
Antrim GB 27 B4
Antrodoco I 169 A3
Antronapiana I 119 A5
Anttis S 196 B5
Antuzede P 148 B1
Antwerp = Antwerpen B 79 A4
Antwerpen = Antwerp B 79 A4
Anversa d'Abruzzi I 169 B3
Anvin F 78 B2
Anzat-le-Luguet F 116 B3
Anzi I 172 B1
Ánzio I 168 B2
Anzola d'Emilia I 135 A4
Anzón E 144 C2
Aoiz E 144 B2
Aosta I 119 B4
Apalhão P 155 B3
Apátfalva H 126 A2
Apatin SRB 125 B5
Apatity RUS 3 C13
Apc H 112 B3
Apécchio I 136 B1
Apeldoorn NL 70 B2
Apen D 71 A4
Apenburg D 73 B4
Apensen D 72 A2
Apiro I 136 B2
Apliki CY 181 B2
Apolda D 82 A3
Apolonia GR 185 C5
Apostag H 112 C2
Äppelbo S 49 B6
Appennino I 136 C2
Appenzell CH 107 B4
Appiano I 108 C2
Appingedam NL 71 A3
Appleby-in-Westmorland GB 37 B4
Applecross GB 31 B3
Appledore GB 42 A2
Appoigny F 104 B2
Apremont-la-Forêt F 92 C1
Aprica I 120 A3
Apricena I 171 B3
Aprigliano I 174 B2
Aprília I 168 B2
Apt F 131 B4
Apúlia P 148 A1
Aquiléia I 122 B2
Aquilónia I 172 B1
Aquino I 169 B3
Ar S 57 C4
Arabayona E 150 A2
Arabba I 108 C2
Araç TR 23 A7
Aracena E 161 B3
Arachova GR 184 A3
Aračinovo MK 182 A3
Arad RO 126 A3
Aradac SRB 126 B2
Aradhippou CY 181 B2
Aragnouet F 145 B4
Aragona I 176 B2
Aramits F 144 A3
Aramon F 131 B3
Aranda de Duero E 143 C3
Aranda de Moncayo E 152 A2
Arandjelovac SRB 127 C2
Aranjuez E 151 B4
Arantzazu E 143 B4
Aranzueque E 151 B4
Aras de Alpuente E 159 B2
Arauzo de Miel E 143 C3
Arazede P 148 B1
Arbas F 145 B4
Árbatax I 179 C3
Arbeca E 147 C1
Arberg D 94 B2
Arbesbach A 96 C2
Arboga S 56 A1
Arbois F 105 C4
Arbon CH 107 B4
Arboréa I 179 C2
Arbório I 119 B5
Årbostad N 194 B8
Arbrå S 50 A3
Arbroath GB 35 B5
Arbùcies E 147 C3
Arbuniel E 163 A4
Arbus I 179 C2
Arc-en-Barrois F 105 B3
Arc-et-Senans F 105 B4
Arc-lès-Gray F 105 B4
Arc-sur-Tille F 105 B4
Arcachon F 128 B1
Arce I 169 B3
Arcen NL 80 A2
Arces-Dilo F 104 A2
Arcévia I 136 B1
Arcey F 106 B1
Archanes GR 185 D6
Archangelos GR 188 C3
Archena E 165 A3
Archez E 163 B4
Archiac F 115 C3
Archidona E 163 A3
Archiestown GB 32 D3
Archivel E 164 A3
Arcidosso I 135 C4
Arcille I 135 C4
Arcis-sur-Aube F 91 C4
Arco I 121 B3
Arcones E 151 A4
Arcos E 143 B3
Arcos de Jalón E 152 A1
Arcos de la Frontera E 162 B2
Arcos de la Sierra E 152 B1
Arcos de las Salinas E 159 B2
Arcos de Valdevez P 148 A1
Arcozelo P 148 B2
Arcusa E 145 B4
Arcy-sur-Cure F 104 B2
Ardagh IRL 29 B2
Årdal N 52 A2
Ardala S 55 B4
Ardales E 162 B3
Årdalstangen N 47 A4
Ardara I 178 B2
Ardara IRL 26 B2
Ardarroch GB 31 B3
Ardbeg GB 34 C1
Ardcharnich GB 32 D1
Ardchyle GB 34 B3
Ardee IRL 27 C4
Arden DK 58 B2
Ardentes F 103 C3
Ardenza I 134 B3
Ardersier GB 32 D2
Ardes F 116 B3
Ardessie GB 32 D1
Ardez CH 107 C5
Ardfert IRL 29 B2
Ardgay GB 32 D2
Ardglass GB 27 B5
Ardgroom IRL 29 C2
Ardhasig GB 31 B2
Ardino BG 183 B7
Ardisa E 144 B3
Ardkearagh IRL 29 C1
Ardlui GB 34 B3
Ardlussa GB 34 B2
Ardón E 142 B1
Ardooie B 78 B3
Ardore I 175 C2
Ardre S 57 C4
Ardres F 78 B1
Ardrishaig GB 34 B2
Ardrossan GB 34 C3
Are N 52 A1
Åre S 199 B10
Areia Branca P 154 B1
Aremark N 54 A2
Arenales de San Gregorio E 157 A4
Arenas E 163 B3
Arenas de Iguña E 142 A2
Arenas de San Juan E 157 A4
Arenas de San Pedro E 150 B2
Arenas del Rey E 163 B4
Arendal N 53 B4
Arendonk B 79 A5
Arengosse F 128 B2
Arentorp S 55 B3
Arenys de Mar E 147 C3
Arenys de Munt E 147 C3
Arenzano I 133 A4
Areo E 146 B2
Areopoli GR 184 C3
Ares E 140 A2
Arès F 128 B1
Ares del Maestrat E 153 B3
Aresvika N 198 B5
Arette F 144 A3
Aretxabaleta E 143 A4
Arevalillo E 150 B2
Arévalo E 150 A3
Arez P 155 B3
Arezzo I 135 B4
Arfeuilles F 117 A3
Argalasti GR 183 D5
Argallón E 156 B2
Argamasilla de Alba E 157 A4
Argamasilla de Calatrava E 157 B3
Arganda E 151 B4
Arganil P 148 B1
Argasion GR 184 B1
Argegno I 120 B2
Argelès-Gazost F 145 A3
Argelès-sur-Mer F 146 B4
Argent-sur-Sauldre F 103 B4
Argenta I 121 C4
Argentan F 89 B3
Argentat F 116 B1
Argentera I 132 A2
Argenteuil F 90 C2
Argenthal D 93 B3
Argentiera I 178 B2
Argenton-Château F 102 C1
Argenton-sur-Creuse F 103 C3
Argentona E 147 C3
Argentré F 102 A1
Argentré-du-Plessis F 101 A4
Argıthani TR 189 A6
Argirades GR 182 D1
Argos GR 184 B3
Argos Orestiko GR 182 C3
Argostoli GR 184 A1
Argote E 143 B4
Arguedas E 144 B2
Argueil F 90 B1
Arholma S 51 C6
Århus DK 59 B3
Ariano Irpino I 170 B3
Ariano nel Polésine I 121 C5
Aribe E 144 B2
Aridea GR 182 C4
Arienzo I 170 B2
Arild S 61 C2
Arileod GB 34 B1
Arinagour GB 34 B1
Ariño E 153 A3
Arinthod F 118 A2
Arisaig GB 34 B2
Arisgotas E 157 A4
Aritzo I 179 C3
Ariza E 152 A1
Årjäng S 54 A3
Arjeplog S 195 D8
Arjona E 157 C3
Arjonilla E 157 C3
Arkasa GR 188 D2
Arkelstorp S 63 B2
Arklow IRL 30 B2
Arkösund S 56 B2
Ärla S 56 A2
Arlanc F 117 B3
Arlanzón E 143 B3
Arlebosc F 117 B4
Arlena di Castro I 168 A1
Arles F 131 B3
Arles-sur-Tech F 146 B3
Arló H 113 A4
Arlon B 92 B1
Armação de Pera P 160 B1
Armadale, *Highland* GB 31 B3
Armadale, *West Lothian* GB 35 C4
Armagh GB 27 B4
Armamar P 148 A2
Armenistis GR 185 B7
Armeno I 119 B5
Armenteros E 150 B2
Armentières F 78 B2
Armilla E 163 A4
Armiñón E 143 B4
Armoy GB 27 A4
Armuña de Tajuña E 151 B4
Armutlu, *Bursa* TR 186 B3
Armutlu, *İzmır* TR 188 A2
Arnac-Pompadour F 115 C5
Arnafjord N 46 A3
Arnage F 102 B2
Arnas F 117 A4
Årnäs S 55 B4
Arnay-le-Duc F 104 B3
Arnborg DK 59 B2
Arnbruck D 95 B4
Arnea GR 183 C5
Arneberg, *Hedmark* N 48 A2
Arneberg, *Hedmark* N 49 B4
Arneburg D 73 B5
Arnedillo E 144 B1
Arnedo E 144 B1
Arneguy F 144 A2
Arnés E 153 B4
Árnes IS 190 A4
Årnes, *Akershus* N 48 B3
Årnes, *Troms* N 194 A9
Arnfels A 110 C2
Arnhem NL 70 C2
Arnissa GR 182 C3
Arno S 56 B3
Arnold GB 40 B2
Arnoldstein A 109 C4
Arnsberg D 81 A4
Arnschwang D 95 B4
Arnsdorf D 84 A1
Årnset N 198 B6
Arnside GB 37 B4
Arnstadt D 82 B2
Arnstein D 94 B1
Arnstorf D 95 C4
Arnum DK 59 C1
Aroche E 161 B3
Ároktő H 113 B4
Arolla CH 119 A4
Arolsen D 81 A5
Arona I 119 B5
Åros N 54 A1
Arosa CH 107 C4
Arosa P 148 A1
Årøsund DK 59 C2
Arouca P 148 B1
Årøysund N 54 A1
Arpajon F 90 C2
Arpajon-sur-Cère F 116 C2
Arpela FIN 196 C7
Arpino I 169 B3
Arquata del Tronto I 136 C2
Arques F 78 B2
Arques-la-Bataille F 89 A5
Arquillos E 157 B4
Arraia-Maeztu E 143 B4
Arraiolos P 154 C2
Arrancourt F 92 C2
Arras F 78 B2
Arrasate E 143 A4
Årre DK 59 C1
Arreau F 145 B4
Arredondo E 143 A3
Arrens-Marsous F 145 B3
Arriate E 162 B2
Arrifana P 160 B1
Arrigorriaga E 143 A4
Arriondas E 142 A1
Arroba de los Montes E 157 A3
Arrochar GB 34 B3
Arromanches-les-Bains F 88 A3
Arronches P 155 B3
Arroniz E 144 B1
Arrou F 103 A3
Arroya E 142 B2
Arroya de Cuéllar E 150 A3
Arroyal E 142 B2
Arroyo de la Luz E 155 B4
Arroyo de San Servan E 155 C4
Arroyo del Ojanco E 164 A2
Arroyomolinos de León E 161 A3
Arroyomolinos de Montánchez E 156 A1
Arruda dos Vinhos P 154 C1
Ars-en-Ré F 114 B2
Ars-sur-Moselle F 92 B2
Arsac F 128 B2
Arsiè I 121 B4
Arsiero I 121 B4
Årslev DK 59 C3
Ársoli I 169 A3
Årsunda S 50 B3
Artà E 167 B3
Arta GR 182 D3
Artajona E 144 B2
Artegna I 122 A2
Arteixo E 140 A2
Artemare F 118 B2
Arten I 121 A4
Artena I 169 B2
Artenay F 103 A3
Artern D 82 A3
Artés E 147 C2
Artesa de Segre E 147 C2
Arth CH 107 B3
Arthez-de-Béarn F 145 A3
Arthon-en-Retz F 101 B4
Arthurstown IRL 30 B2
Artieda E 144 B3
Artix F 145 A3
Artotina GR 182 E4
Artsyz UA 17 B8
Artziniega E 143 A3
Arudy F 145 A3
Arundel GB 44 C3
Årup DK 59 C3
Arveyres F 128 B2
Arvidsjaur S 196 D2
Arvieux F 118 C3
Arvika S 54 A3
Åryd, *Blekinge* S 63 B3
Åryd, *Kronoberg* S 62 B2
Arzachena I 178 A3
Arzacq-Arraziguet F 128 C2
Árzana I 179 C3
Arzano F 100 B2
Aržano HR 138 B2
Arzberg D 95 A4
Arzignano I 121 B4
Arzila P 148 B1
Arzl im Pitztal A 108 B1
Arzúa E 140 B2
As B 80 A1
Aš CZ 83 B4
Ås N 54 A1
As Neves E 140 B2
As Nogais E 141 B3
As Pontes de García Rodríguez E 140 A3
Åsa S 60 B2
Aşağıçiğil TR 189 A6
Ašanja SRB 127 C2
Åsarna S 199 C11
Åsarøy N 52 A2
Åsarp S 55 B4
Asasp F 145 A3
Åsbro S 55 A6
Åsby, *Halland* S 60 B2
Åsby, *Östergötland* S 62 A3
Asbygri IS 191 A9
Ascain F 144 A2
Ascea I 172 B1
Ascha D 95 B4
Aschach an der Donau A 96 C2
Aschaffenburg D 93 B5
Aschbach Markt A 110 A1
Ascheberg, *Nordrhein-Westfalen* D 81 A3
Ascheberg, *Schleswig-Holstein* D 65 B3
Aschendorf D 71 A4
Aschersleben D 82 A3
Asciano I 135 B4
Ascó E 153 A4
Asco F 180 A2
Áscoli Piceno I 136 C2
Áscoli Satriano I 171 B3
Ascona CH 120 A1
Ascot GB 44 B3
Ascoux F 103 A4
Åse N 194 A6
Åseda S 62 A3
Åsele S 200 B3
Åsen N 199 B8
Åsen S 49 A5
Asendorf D 72 B2
Asenovgrad BG 183 A6
Åsensbruk S 54 B3
Åseral N 52 B3
Asfeld F 91 B4
Ásgarður IS 190 B1
Åsgårdstrand N 54 A1
Asgate CY 181 B2
Ash, *Kent* GB 45 B5
Ash, *Surrey* GB 44 B3
Åshammar S 50 B3
Ashbourne GB 40 B2
Ashbourne IRL 30 A2
Ashburton GB 43 B3
Ashby-de-la-Zouch GB 40 C2
Ashchurch GB 44 B1
Åsheim N 199 D8
Ashford GB 45 B4
Ashington GB 37 A5
Ashley GB 38 B4
Ashmyany BY 13 A6
Ashton Under Lyne GB 40 B1
Ashwell GB 44 A3
Asiago I 121 B4
Asipovichy BY 13 B8
Aska FIN 197 B9
Askam-in-Furness GB 36 B3
Askeaton IRL 29 B3
Asker N 48 C2

Askersund S 55 B5
Åskilje S 200 B3
Askim N 54 A2
Askland S 53 B4
Åsköping S 56 A2
Askvoll N 46 A2
Åsljunga S 61 C3
Asmunti FIN 197 D9
Asnæs DK 61 D1
Ásola I 120 B3
Asolo I 121 B4
Asos GR 184 A1
Ascthalom H 126 A1
Aspach A 109 A4
Aspang Markt A 111 B3
Aspariegos E 149 A4
Asparn an der Zaya A 97 C4
Aspatria GB 36 B3
Aspberg S 55 A4
Aspe E 165 A4
Aspet F 145 A4
Åspö S 63 B3
Aspres-sur-Buëch F 132 A1
Aspsele S 200 C4
Assaa DK 58 A3
Assafora P 154 C1
Asse B 79 B4
Assebakte N 193 C9
Assel D 72 A2
Asselborn L 92 A1
Assémini I 179 C2
Assen NL 71 B3
Assenede B 79 A3
Assens, Aarhus Amt. DK 58 B3
Assens, Fyns Amt. DK 59 C2
Assesse B 79 B5
Assisi I 136 B1
Åsskard N 198 B5
Assling D 108 B3
Asso I 120 B2
Asson F 145 A3
Åssoro I 177 B3
Assumar P 155 B3
Åsta N 48 A3
Astaffort F 129 B3
Astakos GR 184 A2
Asten NL 80 A1
Asti I 119 C5
Astipalea GR 188 C1
Astorga E 141 B4
Åstorp S 61 C2
Åsträsk S 200 B5
Astudillo E 142 B2
Asuni I 179 C2
Ásványráró H 111 B4
Aszód H 112 B3
Aszófö H 111 C4
Atabey TR 189 B5
Atalaia P 154 B3
Atalandi GR 182 E4
Ataljo P 154 C2
Åtány H 113 B4
Atanzón E 151 B4
Atarfe E 163 A4
Atça TR 188 B3
Ateca E 152 A2
Atella I 172 B1
Atessa I 169 A4
Ath B 79 B3
Athboy IRL 30 A2
Athea IRL 29 B2
Athenry IRL 28 A3
Athens = Athina GR 185 B4
Atherstone GB 40 C2
Athienou CY 181 A2
Athies F 90 B2
Athies-sous-Laon F 91 B3
Athina = Athens GR 185 B4
Athleague IRL 28 A3
Athlone IRL 28 A4
Athna CY 181 A2
Athy IRL 30 B2
Atienza E 151 A5
Atina I 169 B3
Atkár H 113 B3
Atlanti TR 189 A7
Atna N 199 D7
Ätorp S 55 A5
Åträ N 47 C5
Åtran S 60 B2
Atri I 169 A3
Atripalda I 170 C2
Atsiki GR 183 D7
Attendorn D 81 A3
Attichy F 90 B3
Attigliano I 168 A2
Attigny F 91 B4
Attleborough GB 41 C5
Åtvidaberg S 56 B1
Atzendorf D 73 C4
Au, Steiermark A 110 B2
Au, Vorarlberg A 107 B4
Au, Bayern D 108 A2
Au, Bayern D 95 C3
Aub D 94 B2
Aubagne F 132 B1
Aubel B 80 B1
Aubenas F 117 C4
Aubenton F 91 B4
Auberive F 105 B4

Aubeterre-sur-Dronne F 128 A3
Aubiet F 129 C3
Aubigné F 115 B3
Aubigny F 114 B2
Aubigny-au-Bac F 78 B3
Aubigny-en-Artois F 78 B2
Aubigny-sur-Nère F 103 B4
Aubin F 130 A1
Auborne CH 105 C5
Aubrac F 116 C2
Aubusson F 116 B2
Auch F 129 C3
Auchencairn GB 36 B3
Auchinleck GB 36 A2
Auchterarder GB 35 B4
Auchtermuchty GB 35 B4
Auchtertyre GB 31 B3
Auchy-au-Bois F 78 B2
Audenge F 128 B1
Auderville F 88 A2
Audierne F 100 A1
Audincourt F 106 B1
Audlem GB 38 B4
Audruicq F 78 B2
Audun-le-Roman F 92 B1
Audun-le-Tiche F 92 B1
Aue, Nordrhein-Westfalen D 81 A4
Aue, Sachsen D 83 B4
Auerbach, Bayern D 95 B3
Auerbach, Sachsen D 83 B4
Auffach A 108 B3
Augher GB 27 B3
Aughnacloy GB 27 B4
Aughrim IRL 30 B2
Augignac F 115 C4
Augsburg D 94 C2
Augusta I 177 B4
Augusten-borg DK 64 B2
Augustfehn D 71 A4
Augustów PL 12 B5
Aukrug D 64 B2
Auktsjaur S 196 D2
Auldearn GB 32 D3
Aulendorf D 107 B4
Auletta I 172 B1
Aulla I 134 A2
Aullène F 180 B2
Aulnay F 115 B3
Aulnoye-Aymeries F 79 B3
Ault F 90 A1
Aultbea GB 31 B3
Aulum DK 59 B1
Aulus-les-Bains F 146 B2
Auma D 83 B3
Aumale F 90 B1
Aumetz F 92 B1
Aumont-Aubrac F 116 C3
Aunay-en-Bazois F 104 B2
Aunay-sur-Odon F 88 A3
Aune N 199 A10
Auneau F 90 C1
Auneuil F 90 B1
Auning DK 58 B3
Aunsterra N 199 A9
Aups F 132 B2
Aura D 82 B1
Auray F 100 B3
Aurdal N 47 B6
Aure D 198 B5
Aurich D 71 A4
Aurignac F 145 A4
Aurillac F 116 C2
Auriol F 132 B1
Auritz-Burguette E 144 B2
Aurlandsvangen N 47 B4
Auronzo di Cadore I 109 C3
Auros F 128 B2
Auroux F 117 C3
Aurskog N 48 C3
Aursmoen N 48 C3
Ausónia I 169 B3
Aussernvillgraten A 109 C3
Austad N 52 B3
Austbygda N 47 B5
Aústis I 178 B3
Austmarka N 49 B4
Austre Moland N 53 B4
Austre Vikebygd N 52 A1
Austrheim N 46 B1
Auterive F 146 A2
Autheuil-Authouillet F 89 A5
Authon F 132 A2
Authon-du-Perche F 102 A2
Autol E 144 B2
Autreville F 92 C1
Autrey-lès-Gray F 105 B4
Autti FIN 197 C10
Autun F 104 C3
Auty-le-Châtel F 103 B4
Auvelais B 79 B4
Auvillar F 129 B3
Auxerre F 104 B2
Auxi-le-Château F 78 B2
Auxon F 104 A2
Auxonne F 105 B4
Auxy F 104 C3
Auzances F 116 A2
Auzon F 117 B3

Auzon F 117 B3
Availles-Limouzine F 115 B4
Avaldsnes N 52 A1
Avallon F 104 B2
Avantas GR 183 C7
Avaviken S 195 E9
Avebury GB 44 B2
Aveiras de Cima P 154 B2
Aveiro P 148 B1
Avelgem B 79 B3
Avellino I 170 C2
Avenches CH 106 C2
Aversa I 170 C2
Avesnes-le-Comte F 78 B2
Avesnes-sur-Helpe F 91 A3
Avesta S 50 B3
Avetrana I 173 B3
Avezzano I 169 A3
Avià E 147 B2
Aviano I 122 A1
Aviemore GB 32 D3
Avigliana I 119 B4
Avigliano I 172 B1
Avignon F 131 B3
Ávila E 150 B3
Avilés E 141 A5
Avilley F 105 B5
Avintes P 148 A1
Avinyo E 147 C2
Avioth F 92 B1
Avis P 154 B3
Avize F 91 C4
Avlonari GR 185 A5
Ávola I 177 C4
Avon F 90 C2
Avonmouth GB 43 A4
Avord F 103 B4
Avranches F 88 B2
Avril F 92 B1
Avrillé F 102 B1
Avtovac BIH 139 B4
Awans B 79 B5
Ax-les-Thermes F 146 B2
Axams A 108 B2
Axat F 146 B3
Axbridge GB 43 A4
Axel NL 79 A3
Axmarby S 51 B4
Axmarsbruk S 51 A4
Axminster GB 43 B3
Axvall S 55 B4
Ay F 91 B4
Aya E 144 A1
Ayamonte E 161 B2
Ayancık TR 23 A8
Ayaş TR 187 B7
Aydın TR 188 B2
Ayelo de Malferit E 159 C3
Ayer CH 119 A4
Ayerbe E 144 B3
Ayette F 78 B2
Ayia Napa CY 181 B2
Ayia Phyla CY 181 B2
Áyios Amvrósios CY 181 A2
Áyios Seryios CY 181 A2
Áyios Theodhoros CY 181 A2
Ayirkirikçi TR 187 C5
Aylesbury GB 44 B3
Ayllón E 151 A4
Aylsham GB 41 C5
Ayna E 158 C1
Ayódar E 159 B3
Ayora E 159 B2
Ayr GB 36 A2
Ayrancı TR 23 C7
Ayrancılar TR 188 A2
Ayron F 115 B4
Aysgarth GB 37 B4
Ayton GB 35 C5
Aytos BG 17 D7
Ayvacık TR 186 C1
Ayvalık TR 186 C1
Aywaille B 80 B1
Azaila E 153 A3
Azambuja P 154 B2
Azambujeira P 154 B2
Azanja SRB 127 C2
Azannes-et-Soumazannes F 92 B1
Azanúy-Alins E 145 C4
Azaruja P 155 C3
Azay-le-Ferron F 115 B5
Azay-le-Rideau F 102 B2
Azcoitia E 143 A4
Aze F 117 A4
Azeiteiros P 155 B3
Azenhas do Mar P 154 C1
Azinhaga P 154 B2
Azinheira dos Bairros P 160 A1
Aznalcázar E 161 B3
Aznalcóllar E 161 B3
Azóia P 154 B2
Azpeitia E 144 A1
Azuaga E 156 B2
Azúebar E 159 B3
Azuel E 157 B3
Azuqueca de Henares E 151 B4
Azur F 128 C1
Azzano Décimo I 122 B1

B

Baad A 107 A5
Baamonde E 140 A3
Baar CH 107 B3
Baarle-Nassau B 79 A4
Baarn NL 70 B2
Babadag RO 17 C8
Babadağ TR 188 B3
Babaeski TR 186 A2
Babayevo RUS 9 C9
Babenhausen, Bayern D 107 A5
Babenhausen, Hessen D 93 B4
Babiak PL 76 B3
Babice PL 86 B3
Babigoszcz PL 75 A3
Babimost PL 75 B4
Babina Greda HR 125 B4
Babócsa H 124 A3
Bábolna H 112 B1
Baborów PL 86 B2
Baboszewo PL 77 B5
Babót H 111 B4
Babruysk BY 13 B8
Babsk PL 87 A4
Bač SRB 125 B5
Bač SRB 31 A2
Bacares E 164 B2
Bacău RO 17 B7
Baccarat F 92 C2
Bacharach D 93 A3
Backa S 50 B2
Bačka Palanka SRB 126 B1
Bačka Topola SRB 126 B1
Backaryd S 63 B3
Backe S 200 C2
Bačko Gradište SRB 126 B2
Bačko Novo Selo SRB 125 B5
Bačko Petrovo Selo SRB 126 B2
Bácoli I 170 C2
Bacqueville-en-Caux F 89 A5
Bácsalmás H 126 A1
Bácsbokod H 125 A5
Bad Abbach D 95 C4
Bad Aibling D 108 B3
Bad Bederkesa D 72 A1
Bad Bentheim D 71 B4
Bad Bergzabern D 93 B3
Bad Berka D 82 B3
Bad Berleburg D 81 A4
Bad Berneck D 95 A3
Bad Bevensen D 73 A3
Bad Bibra D 82 A3
Bad Birnbach D 95 C5
Bad Blankenburg D 82 B3
Bad Bleiberg A 109 C4
Bad Brambach D 83 B4
Bad Bramstedt D 64 C2
Bad Breisig D 80 B3
Bad Brückenau D 82 B1
Bad Buchau D 107 A4
Bad Camberg D 81 B4
Bad Doberan D 65 B4
Bad Driburg D 81 A5
Bad Düben D 83 A4
Bad Dürkheim D 93 B4
Bad Dürrenberg D 83 A4
Bad Dürrheim D 107 A3
Bad Elster D 83 B4
Bad Endorf D 109 B3
Bad Essen D 71 B5
Bad Fischau A 111 B3
Bad Frankenhausen D 82 A3
Bad Freienwalde D 74 B3
Bad Friedrichshall D 93 B5
Bad Füssing D 95 C5
Bad Gandersheim D 82 A2
Bad Gastein A 109 B4
Bad Gleichenberg A 110 C2
Bad Goisern A 109 B4
Bad Gottleuba D 84 B1
Bad Hall A 110 A1
Bad Harzburg D 82 A2
Bad Herrenalb D 93 C4
Bad Hersfeld D 82 B1
Bad Hofgastein A 109 B4
Bad Homburg D 81 B4
Bad Honnef D 80 B3
Bad Hönningen D 80 B3
Bad Iburg D 71 B5
Bad Ischl A 109 B4
Bad Karlshafen D 81 A5

Bad Kemmeriboden CH 106 C2
Bad Kissingen D 82 B2
Bad Kleinen D 65 C4
Bad Kohlgrub D 108 B2
Bad König D 93 B5
Bad Königshofen D 82 B2
Bad Köstritz D 83 B4
Bad Kreuzen A 110 A1
Bad Kreuznach D 93 B3
Bad Krozingen D 106 B2
Bad Laasphe D 81 B4
Bad Langensalza D 82 A2
Bad Lauchstädt D 83 A3
Bad Lausick D 83 A4
Bad Lauterberg D 82 A2
Bad Leonfelden A 96 C2
Bad Liebenwerda D 83 A5
Bad Liebenzell D 93 C4
Bad Lippspringe D 81 A4
Bad Meinberg D 81 A4
Bad Mergentheim D 94 B1
Bad Mitterndorf A 109 B4
Bad Münder D 72 B2
Bad Münster D 93 B3
Bad Münstereifel D 80 B2
Bad Muskau D 84 A2
Bad Nauheim D 81 B4
Bad Nenndorf D 72 B2
Bad Neuenahr-Ahrweiler D 80 B3
Bad Neustadt D 82 B2
Bad Oeynhausen D 72 B1
Bad Oldesloe D 65 C3
Bad Orb D 81 B5
Bad Peterstal D 93 C4
Bad Pyrmont D 72 C2
Bad Radkersburg A 110 C2
Bad Ragaz CH 107 C4
Bad Rappenau D 93 B5
Bad Reichenhall D 109 B3
Bad Saarow-Pieskow D 74 B3
Bad Sachsa D 82 A2
Bad Säckingen D 106 B2
Bad Salzdetfurth D 72 B3
Bad Salzig D 81 B3
Bad Salzuflen D 72 B1
Bad Salzungen D 82 B2
Bad Sankt Leonhard A 110 C1
Bad Sassendorf D 81 A4
Bad Schandau D 84 B2
Bad Schmiedeberg D 83 A4
Bad Schönborn D 93 B4
Bad Schussenried D 107 A4
Bad Schwalbach D 81 B4
Bad Schwartau D 65 C3
Bad Segeberg D 64 C3
Bad Soden D 81 B4
Bad Soden-Salmünster D 81 B5
Bad Sooden-Allendorf D 82 A1
Bad Sulza D 83 A3
Bad Sülze D 66 B1
Bad Tatzmannsdorf A 111 B3
Bad Tennstedt D 82 A2
Bad Tölz D 108 B2
Bad Urach D 94 C1
Bad Vellach A 110 C1
Bad Vilbel D 81 B4
Bad Waldsee D 107 B4
Bad Wiessee D 108 B2
Bad Wildungen D 81 A5
Bad Wimpfen D 93 B5
Bad Windsheim D 94 B2
Bad Wörishofen D 108 A1
Bad Wurzach D 107 B4
Bad Zwesten D 81 A5
Bad Zwischenahn D 71 A5
Badacsonytomaj H 111 C4
Badajoz E 155 C4
Badalona E 147 C3
Badalucco I 133 B3
Bádames E 143 A3
Baden A 111 A3
Baden-Baden D 93 C4
Bádenas E 152 A2
Badenweiler D 106 B2
Baderna HR 122 B2
Badia Polésine I 121 B4
Badia Pratáglia I 135 B4
Badia Tedalda I 135 B5
Bädkowo PL 76 B3
Badljevina HR 124 B3
Badolato I 175 C2
Badonviller F 92 C2
Badovinci SRB 127 C1
Badules E 152 A2
Bække DK 59 C2

Bækmarksbro DK 58 B1
Baells E 145 C4
Bælum DK 58 B3
Baena E 163 A3
Baesweiler D 80 B2
Baeza E 157 C4
Baflo NL 71 A3
Baga E 147 B2
Bagaladi I 175 C1
Bagarasi TR 188 B2
Bagenkop DK 65 B3
Baggetorp S 56 A2
Bagh a Chaisteil GB 31 C1
Bagheria I 176 A2
Bagn N 47 B6
Bagnacavallo I 135 A4
Bagnáia I 168 A2
Bagnara Cálabra I 175 C1
Bagnasco I 133 A4
Bagnères-de-Bigorre F 145 A4
Bagnères-de-Luchon F 145 B4
Bagni del Másino I 120 A2
Bagni di Lucca I 134 A3
Bagni di Rabbi I 121 A3
Bagni di Tivoli I 168 B2
Bagno di Romagna I 135 B4
Bagnoles-de-l'Orne F 89 B3
Bagnoli dei Trigno I 170 B2
Bagnoli di Sopra I 121 B4
Bagnoli Irpino I 170 C3
Bagnolo Mella I 120 B3
Bagnols-en-Forêt F 132 B2
Bagnols-sur-Cèze F 131 A3
Bagnorégio I 168 A2
Bagolino I 121 B3
Bagrationovsk RUS 12 A4
Bagrdan SRB 127 C3
Báguena E 152 A2
Bahabón de Esguava E 143 C3
Bahillo E 142 B2
Báia delle Zágare I 171 B4
Baia Domizia I 169 B3
Baia Mare RO 17 B5
Baião P 148 A1
Baiano I 170 C2
Baiersbronn D 93 C4
Baiersdorf D 94 B3
Baignes-Ste.-Radegonde F 115 C3
Baigneux-les-Juifs F 104 B3
Baildon GB 40 B2
Bailén E 157 B4
Băile Herculane RO 16 C4
Bäilesti RO 17 C5
Bailleul F 78 B2
Baillonville B 79 B5
Bains F 117 B3
Bains-les-Bains F 105 A5
Bainton GB 40 B3
Baio E 140 A2
Baiona E 140 B2
Bais F 89 B3
Baiso I 134 A3
Baiuca P 148 B1
Baja H 125 A4
Bajánsenye H 111 C3
Bajina Bašta SRB 127 D1
Bajmok SRB 126 B1
Bajna H 112 B2
Bajovo Polje MNE 139 B4
Bajša SRB 126 B1
Bak H 111 C3
Bakar HR 123 B3
Bakewell GB 40 B2
Bakio E 143 A4
Bakkafjörður IS 191 A11
Bakkagerði IS 191 B12
Bakken N 48 B3
Baklan TR 189 B4
Bäckowa PL 85 B4
Bakonybél H 111 B4
Bakonycsernye H 112 B2
Bakonyjákó H 111 B4
Bakonyszentkirály H 111 B4
Bakonyszombathely H 112 B1
Bakov nad Jizerou CZ 84 B2
Baks H 113 C4
Baksa H 125 B4
Bakum D 71 B5
Bala GB 38 B3
Bâlâ TR 23 B7
Balaguer E 145 C4
Balassagyarmat H 112 A3
Balástya H 113 C4
Balatonakali H 111 C4
Balatonalmádi H 112 B2
Balatonboglár H 111 C4
Balatonbozsok H 112 C2

Balatonederics H 111 C4
Balatonfenyves H 111 C4
Balatonföldvár H 112 C1
Balatonfüred H 112 C1
Balatonfüzfő H 112 B2
Balatonkenese H 112 B2
Balatonkiliti H 112 C2
Balatonlelle H 111 C4
Balatonszabadi H 112 C2
Balatonszemes H 111 C4
Balatonszentgyörgy H 111 C4
Balazote E 158 C1
Balbeggie GB 35 B4
Balbigny F 117 B4
Balboa E 141 B4
Balbriggan IRL 30 A2
Balchik BG 17 D8
Balçova TR 188 A2
Baldock GB 44 B3
Bale HR 122 B2
Baleira E 141 A3
Baleizao P 160 A2
Balen B 79 A5
Balerma E 164 C2
Balestrand N 46 A3
Balestrate I 176 A2
Balfour GB 33 B4
Bälganet S 63 B3
Balıkesir TR 186 C2
Balıklıçeşme TR 186 B2
Bälinge S 51 C4
Balingen D 107 A3
Balingsta S 56 A3
Balintore GB 32 D3
Balizac F 128 B2
Balk NL 70 B2
Balkbrug NL 71 B3
Balla IRL 28 A2
Ballachulish GB 34 B2
Ballaghaderreen IRL 26 C2
Ballancourt-sur-Essonne F 90 C2
Ballantrae GB 36 A2
Ballao I 179 C3
Ballasalla GB 36 B2
Ballater GB 32 D3
Ballen DK 59 C3
Ballenstedt D 82 A3
Ballerias E 145 C3
Balleroy F 88 A3
Ballerup DK 61 D2
Ballesteros de Calatrava E 157 B4
Ballı TR 186 B2
Ballina IRL 26 B1
Ballinalack IRL 30 A1
Ballinamore IRL 26 B3
Ballinascarty IRL 29 C3
Ballinasloe IRL 28 A3
Ballindine IRL 28 A3
Balling DK 58 B1
Ballingarry, *Limerick* IRL 29 B3
Ballingarry, *Tipperary* IRL 30 B1
Ballingeary IRL 29 C2
Ballinhassig IRL 29 C3
Ballinluig GB 35 B4
Ballino I 121 B3
Ballinrobe IRL 28 A2
Ballinskellings IRL 29 C1
Ballinspittle IRL 29 C3
Ballintra IRL 26 B2
Ballivor IRL 30 A2
Ballobar E 153 A4
Ballon F 102 A2
Ballon IRL 30 B2
Ballószög H 112 C3
Ballsh AL 182 C1
Ballstad N 194 B4
Ballum DK 64 A1
Ballybay IRL 27 B4
Ballybofey IRL 26 B3
Ballybunion IRL 29 B2
Ballycanew IRL 30 B2
Ballycarry GB 27 B5
Ballycastle GB 27 A4
Ballycastle IRL 26 B1
Ballyclare GB 27 B5
Ballyconneely IRL 28 A1
Ballycotton IRL 29 C3
Ballycroy IRL 26 B1
Ballydehob IRL 29 C2
Ballyferriter IRL 29 B1
Ballygawley GB 27 B3
Ballygowan GB 27 B5
Ballyhaunis IRL 28 A3
Ballyheige IRL 29 B2
Ballyjamesduff IRL 27 C3
Ballylanders IRL 29 B3
Ballylynan IRL 30 B1
Ballymahon IRL 28 A4
Ballymena GB 27 B4
Ballymoe IRL 28 A3
Ballymoney GB 27 A4
Ballymore IRL 28 A4
Ballymote IRL 26 B2
Ballynacorra IRL 29 C3
Ballynagore IRL 30 A1
Ballynahinch GB 27 B5
Ballynure GB 27 B5
Ballyragget IRL 30 B1
Ballysadare IRL 26 B2
Ballyshannon IRL 26 B2
Ballyvaghan IRL 28 A2
Ballyvourney IRL 29 C2
Ballywalter GB 27 B5
Balmaclellan GB 36 A2
Balmaseda E 143 A3
Balmazújváros H 113 B5
Balme I 119 B4
Balmedie GB 33 D4
Balmuccia I 119 B5
Balna-paling GB 32 D2
Balneario de Panticosa E 145 B3
Balotaszállás H 126 A1
Balsa P 148 A2
Balsareny E 147 C2
Balsorano-Nuovo I 169 B3
Bålsta S 57 A3
Balsthal CH 106 B2
Balta UA 17 A8
Baltanás E 142 C2
Baltar E 140 C3
Baltasound GB 33 A6
Bălţi MD 17 B7
Baltimore IRL 29 C2
Baltinglass IRL 30 B2
Baltiysk RUS 69 A4
Baltów PL 87 A5
Balugães P 148 A1
Balve D 81 A3
Balvi LV 8 D5
Balvicar GB 34 B2
Balya TR 186 C2
Balzo I 136 C2
Bamberg D 94 B2
Bamburgh GB 37 A5
Banatska Palanka SRB 127 C3
Banatski Brestovac SRB 127 C2
Banatski Despotovac SRB 126 B2
Banatski Dvor SRB 126 B2
Banatski-Karlovac SRB 127 B3
Banatsko Arandjelovo SRB 126 A2
Banatsko-Novo Selo SRB 127 C2
Banaz TR 187 D4
Banbridge GB 27 B4
Banbury GB 44 A2
Banchory GB 33 D4
Bande B 79 B5
Bande E 140 B3
Bandholm DK 65 B4
Bandırma TR 186 B2
Bandol F 132 B1
Bandon IRL 29 C3
Bañeres E 159 C3
Banff GB 33 D4
Bangor F 100 B2
Bangor, *Down* GB 27 B5
Bangor, *Gwynedd* GB 38 A2
Bangor IRL 26 B1
Bangsund N 199 A8
Banie PL 74 A3
Banja Koviljača SRB 127 C1
Banja Luka BIH 124 C3
Banja Vručica BIH 125 C3
Banjaloka SLO 123 B3
Banjani SRB 127 C1
Banka SK 98 C1
Bankekind S 56 B1
Bankend GB 36 A3
Bankeryd S 62 A2
Bankfoot GB 35 B4
Banloc RO 126 B3
Bannalec F 100 B2
Bannes F 91 C3
Bannockburn GB 35 B4
Bañobárez E 149 B3
Bañon E 152 B2
Banon F 132 A1
Baños E 149 B4
Baños de Gigonza E 162 B2
Baños de la Encina E 157 B4
Baños de Molgas E 140 B3
Baños de Rio Tobia E 143 B4
Baños de Valdearados E 143 C3
Bánov CZ 98 C1
Banova Jaruga HR 124 B2
Bánovce nad Bebravou SK 98 C2
Banovići BIH 139 A4
Banoviči Selo BIH 139 A4
Bánréve H 99 C4
Bansin D 66 C3
Banská Belá SK 98 C2
Banská Bystrica SK 99 C3
Banská Štiavnica SK 98 C2
Bansko BG 183 B5
Banstead GB 44 B3
Banteer IRL 29 B3
Bantheville F 91 B5
Bantry IRL 29 C2
Bantzenheim F 106 B2
Banyalbufar E 166 B2
Banyoles E 147 B3
Banyuls-sur-Mer F 146 B4
Bapaume F 90 A2
Bar CG 16 D3
Bar UA 13 D7
Bar-le-Duc F 91 C5
Bar-sur-Aube F 104 A3
Bar-sur-Seine F 104 A3
Barabhas GB 31 A2
Barači BIH 138 A2
Baracs H 112 C2
Baracska H 112 B2
Barahona E 151 A5
Barajes de Melo E 151 B5
Barakaldo E 143 A4
Baralla E 141 B3
Barañain E 144 B2
Baranavichy BY 13 B7
Báránd H 113 B5
Baranda SRB 127 B2
Baranello I 170 B2
Baranów Sandomierski PL 87 B5
Baraqueville F 130 A1
Barasoain E 144 B2
Barbacena P 155 C3
Barbadás E 140 B3
Barbadillo E 149 B4
Barbadillo de Herreros E 143 B3
Barbadillo del Mercado E 143 B3
Barbadillo del Pez E 143 B3
Barban HR 123 B3
Barbarano Vicento I 121 B4
Barbariga HR 122 C2
Barbaros TR 186 B2
Barbastro E 145 B4
Barbate E 162 B2
Barbatona E 152 A1
Barbâtre F 114 B1
Barbazan F 145 A4
Barbeitos E 141 A3
Barbentane F 131 B3
Barberino di Mugello I 135 A4
Barbezieux-St. Hilaire F 115 C3
Barbonne-Fayel F 91 C3
Barbotan-les-Thermes F 128 C2
Barby D 73 C4
Barca de Alva P 149 A3
Bárcabo E 145 B4
Barcarrota E 155 C4
Barcellona-Pozzo di Gotto I 177 A4
Barcelona E 147 C3
Barcelonette F 132 A2
Barcelos P 148 A1
Barcena de Pie de Concha E 142 A2
Bárcena del Monasterio E 141 A4
Barchfeld D 82 B2
Barcin PL 76 B2
Barcino PL 68 A1
Bárcis I 122 A1
Barco P 148 B2
Barcones E 151 A5
Barcs H 124 B3
Barcus F 144 A3
Bardejov SK 12 D4
Bårdesø DK 59 C3
Bardi I 120 C2
Bardney GB 40 B3
Bardo PL 85 B4
Bardolino I 121 B3
Bardonécchia I 118 B3
Bardoňovo SK 112 A2
Barèges F 145 B4
Barenstein D 83 B5
Barentin F 89 A4
Barenton F 88 B3
Barevo BIH 138 A3
Barfleur F 88 A2
Barga I 134 A3
Bargas E 151 C3
Barge I 119 C4
Bargemon F 132 B2
Barghe I 120 B3
Bargoed GB 39 C3
Bargrennan GB 36 A2
Bargteheide D 64 C3
Barham GB 45 B5
Bari I 173 A2
Bari Sardo I 179 C3
Barič Draga HR 137 A4
Barilović HR 123 B4
Barisciano I 169 A3
Barjac F 131 A3
Barjols F 132 B1
Barjon F 105 B3
Bårkåker N 54 A1
Barkald N 199 D7
Barkowo, *Dolnośląskie* PL 85 A4
Barkowo, *Pomorskie* PL 68 B2
Bârlad RO 17 B7
Barles F 132 A2
Barletta I 171 B4
Barlinek PL 75 B4
Barmouth GB 38 B2
Barmstedt D 64 C2
Barnard Castle GB 37 B5
Barnarp S 62 A2
Bärnau D 95 B4
Bärnbach A 110 B2
Barneberg D 73 B4
Barnenitz D 74 B1
Barnet GB 44 B3
Barnetby le Wold GB 40 B3
Barneveld NL 70 B2
Barneville-Carteret F 88 A2
Barnoldswick GB 40 B1
Barnowko PL 75 B3
Barnsley GB 40 B2
Barnstädt D 83 A3
Barnstaple GB 42 A2
Barnstorf D 72 B1
Barntrup D 72 C2
Baron F 90 B2
Baronissi I 170 C2
Barqueiro P 154 B2
Barquinha P 154 B2
Barr F 93 C3
Barr GB 36 A2
Barra P 148 B1
Barracas E 159 A3
Barraco E 150 B3
Barrado E 150 B2
Barrafranca I 177 B3
Barranco do Velho P 160 B2
Barrancos P 161 A3
Barrax E 158 B1
Barrbaar D 94 C2
Barre-des-Cevennes F 130 A2
Barreiro P 154 C1
Barreiros E 141 A3
Barrême F 132 B2
Barret-le-Bas F 132 A1
Barrhead GB 34 C3
Barrhill GB 36 A2
Barrio de Nuesra Señora E 142 B1
Barrow-in-Furness GB 36 B3
Barrow upon Humber GB 40 B3
Barrowford GB 40 B1
Barruecopardo E 149 A3
Barruelo de Santullán E 142 B2
Barruera E 145 B4
Barry GB 39 C3
Bårse DK 65 A4
Barsinghausen D 72 B2
Barssel D 71 A4
Barth D 66 B1
Bartholomä D 94 C1
Bartin TR 187 A7
Barton upon Humber GB 40 B3
Barúmini I 179 C2
Baruth D 74 B2
Barvaux B 80 B1
Barver D 72 B1
Barwatd PL 99 B3
Barwice PL 68 B1
Barysaw BY 13 A8
Barzana E 141 A5
Bârzava RO 16 B4
Bárzio I 120 B2
Bas E 147 B3
Bašaid SRB 126 B2
Basaluzzo I 120 C1
Basarabeasca MD 17 B8
Basauri E 143 A4
Baschi I 168 A2
Baschurch GB 38 B4
Basconcillos del Tozo E 143 B3
Bascones de Ojeda E 142 B2
Basécles B 79 B3
Basel CH 106 B2
Basélice I 170 B2
Basildon GB 45 B4
Basingstoke GB 44 B2
Baška CZ 98 B2
Baška HR 123 C3
Baška Voda HR 138 B2
Bäsksjö S 200 B3
Baslow GB 40 B2
Başmakçı TR 189 B5
Basovizza I 122 B2
Bassacutena I 178 A3
Bassano del Grappa I 121 B4
Bassano Romano I 168 A2
Bassecourt CH 106 B2
Bassella E 147 B2
Bassevuovdde N 193 D9
Bassou F 104 B2
Bassoues F 128 C3
Bassum D 72 B1
Båstad S 61 C2
Bastardo I 136 C1
Bastelica F 180 A2
Bastelicaccia F 180 B1
Bastia F 180 A2
Bastia I 136 B1
Bastogne B 92 A1
Baston GB 40 C3
Bastuträsk S 200 B6
Bata H 125 A4
Batajnica SRB 127 C2
Batak BG 183 B6
Batalha P 154 B2
Bátaszék H 125 A4
Batea E 153 A4
Batelov CZ 97 B3
Bath GB 43 A4
Bathgate GB 35 C4
Batida H 126 A2
Batignano I 135 C4
Batina HR 125 B4
Bátka SK 99 C4
Batković BIH 125 C5
Batley GB 40 B2
Batnfjordsøra N 198 C4
Batočina SRB 127 C3
Bátonyterenye H 113 B3
Batrina HR 125 B3
Båtsfjord N 193 B13
Båtskärsnäs S 196 D6
Battaglia Terme I 121 B4
Bätterkinden CH 106 B2
Battice B 80 B1
Battipáglia I 170 C2
Battle GB 45 C4
Battonya H 126 A3
Batuša SRB 127 C3
Bátya H 112 C2
Bau I 179 C2
Baud F 100 B2
Baudour B 79 B3
Baugé F 102 B1
Baugy F 103 B4
Bauma CH 107 B3
Baume-les-Dames F 105 B5
Baumholder D 93 B3
Baunatal D 81 A5
Baunei I 178 B3
Bauska LV 8 D4
Bautzen D 84 A2
Bavanište SRB 127 C2
Bavay F 79 B3
Bavilliers F 106 B1
Bavorov CZ 96 B2
Bawdsey GB 45 A5
Bawinkel D 71 B4
Bawtry GB 40 B2
Bayat TR 187 D5
Bayel F 105 A3
Bayeux F 88 A3
Bayındır TR 188 A2
Bayon F 92 C2
Bayonne F 128 C1
Bayons F 132 A2
Bayramiç TR 186 C1
Bayreuth D 95 B3
Bayrischzell D 108 B3
Baza E 164 B2
Bazas F 128 B2
Baziege F 146 A2
Bazoches-les-Gallerandes F 103 A4
Bazoches-sur-Hoëne F 89 B4
Bazzano I 135 A4
Beaconsfield GB 44 B3
Beade E 140 B2
Beadnell GB 37 A5
Beaminster GB 43 B4
Bearsden GB 34 C3
Beas E 161 B3
Beas de Segura E 164 A2
Beasain E 144 A1
Beattock GB 36 A3
Beaubery F 117 A4
Beaucaire F 131 B3
Beaufort F 118 B3
Beaufort IRL 29 B2
Beaufort-en Vallée F 102 B1
Beaugency F 103 B3
Beaujeu, *Alpes-de-Haute-Provence* F 132 A2
Beaujeu, *Rhône* F 117 A4
Beaulac F 128 B2
Beaulieu F 103 B4
Beaulieu GB 44 C2
Beaulieu-sous-la-Roche F 114 B2
Beaulieu-sur-Dordogne F 129 B4
Beaulieu-sur-Mer F 133 B3
Beaulon F 104 C2
Beauly GB 32 D2
Beaumaris GB 38 A2
Beaumesnil F 89 A4
Beaumetz-lès-Loges F 78 B2
Beaumont B 79 B4
Beaumont F 129 B3
Beaumont-de-Lomagne F 129 C3
Beaumont-du-Gâtinais F 103 A4
Beaumont-en-Argonne F 91 B5
Beaumont-Hague F 88 A2
Beaumont-la-Ronce F 102 B2
Beaumont-le-Roger F 89 A4
Beaumont-sur-Oise F 90 B2
Beaumont-sur-Sarthe F 102 A2
Beaune F 105 B3
Beaune-la-Rolande F 103 A4
Beaupréau F 101 B5
Beauraing B 91 A4
Beaurepaire F 117 B5
Beaurepaire-en-Bresse F 105 C4
Beaurières F 132 A1
Beauvais F 90 B2
Beauval F 90 A2
Beauville F 129 B3
Beauvoir-sur-Mer F 114 B1
Beauvoir-sur-Niort F 114 B3
Beba Veche RO 126 A2
Bebertal D 73 B4
Bebington GB 38 A3
Bebra D 82 B1
Bebrina HR 125 B3
Beccles GB 45 A5
Becedas E 150 B2
Beceite E 153 B4
Bečej SRB 126 B2
Becerreá E 141 B3
Becerril de Campos E 142 B2
Bécherel F 101 A4
Bechhofen D 94 B2
Bechyně CZ 96 B2
Becilla de Valderaduey E 142 B1
Beckfoot GB 36 B3
Beckingham GB 40 B3
Beckum D 81 A4
Beco P 154 B2
Bécon-les-Granits F 102 B1
Bečov nad Teplou CZ 83 B4
Becsehely H 111 C3
Bedale GB 37 B5
Bedames E 143 A3
Bédar E 164 B3
Bédarieux F 130 B2
Bédarrides F 131 A3
Bedburg D 80 B2
Beddgelert GB 38 A2
Beddingestrand S 66 A2
Bédée F 101 A4
Bedegkér H 112 C2
Beden TR 189 C7
Bedford GB 44 A3
Będków PL 87 A3
Bedlington GB 37 A5
Bedlno PL 77 B4
Bedmar E 163 A4
Bédoin F 131 A4
Bedónia I 134 A2
Bedretto CH 107 C3
Bedsted DK 58 B1
Bedum NL 71 A3
Bedwas GB 39 C3
Bedworth GB 40 C2
Będzin PL 86 B3
Beek en Donk NL 80 A1
Beekbergen NL 70 B2
Beelen D 71 C5
Beelitz D 74 B1
Beer GB 43 B3
Beerfelde D 74 B3
Beerfelden D 93 B4
Beernem B 78 A3
Beeskow D 74 B3
Beetsterzwaag NL 70 A3
Beetzendorf D 73 B4
Beflelay CH 106 B2
Begaljica SRB 127 C2
Bégard F 100 A2
Begejci SRB 126 B2
Begijar E 157 C4
Begijnendijk B 79 A4
Begndal N 48 B1
Begues E 147 C2
Beguildy GB 39 B3
Begur E 147 C4
Beho B 80 B1
Behringen D 82 A2
Beilen NL 71 B3
Beilngries D 95 B3
Beine-Nauroy F 91 B4
Beinwil CH 106 B3
Beiseförth D 82 A1
Beith GB 34 C3
Beitostølen N 47 A5
Beiuş RO 16 B5
Beja P 160 A2
Béjar E 149 B4
Bekçiler TR 189 C4
Békés H 113 C5
Békéscsaba H 113 C5
Bekilli TR 189 A4
Bekkarfjord N 193 B11
Bela SK 98 B2
Bela Crkva SRB 127 C3
Belá nad Radbuzou CZ 95 B4
Bělá Pod Bezdězem CZ 84 B2
Bélâbre F 115 B5
Belalcázar E 156 B2
Belanovica SRB 127 C2
Bélapátfalva H 113 A4
Belcaire F 146 B2
Bełchatów PL 86 A3
Belchite E 153 A3
Bělčice CZ 96 B1

Belcoo GB 26 B3
Belecke D 81 A4
Beled H 111 B4
Belej HR 123 C3
Beleño E 142 A1
Bélesta F 146 B2
Belevi TR 188 A2
Belfast GB 27 B5
Belford GB 37 A5
Belfort F 106 B1
Belgentier F 132 B1
Belgern D 83 A5
Belgioioso I 120 B2
Belgodère F 180 A2
Belgooly IRL 29 C3
Belgrade = Beograd SRB 127 C2
Belhade F 128 B2
Beli Manastir HR 125 B4
Belica HR 124 A2
Belin-Bèliet F 128 B2
Belinchón E 151 B4
Belišće HR 125 B4
Bělkovice-Lašt'any CZ 98 B1
Bell-lloc d'Urgell E 153 A4
Bella I 172 B1
Bellac F 115 B5
Bellágio I 120 B2
Bellananagh IRL 27 C3
Bellano I 120 A2
Bellária I 136 A1
Bellavary IRL 26 C1
Belle-Isle-en-Terre F 100 A2
Belleau F 90 B3
Belleek GB 26 B2
Bellegarde, *Gard* F 131 B3
Bellegarde, *Loiret* F 103 B4
Bellegarde-en-Diois F 132 A1
Bellegarde-en-Marche F 116 B2
Bellegarde-sur-Valserine F 118 A2
Bellême F 89 B4
Bellenaves F 116 A3
Bellentre F 118 B3
Bellevaux F 118 A3
Bellevesvre F 105 C4
Belleville F 117 A4
Belleville-sur-Vie F 114 B2
Bellevue-la-Montagne F 117 B3
Belley F 118 B2
Bellheim D 93 B4
Bellinge DK 59 C3
Bellingham GB 37 A4
Bellinzago Novarese I 120 B1
Bellinzona CH 120 A2
Bello E 152 B2
Bellpuig d'Urgell E 147 C2
Bellreguart E 159 C3
Bellsbank GB 36 A2
Belltall E 147 C2
Belluno I 121 A5
Bellver de Cerdanya E 146 B2
Bellvis E 147 C1
Bélmez E 156 B2
Belmez de la Moraleda E 163 A4
Belmont GB 33 A6
Belmont-de-la-Loire F 117 A4
Belmont-sur-Rance F 130 B1
Belmonte, *Asturias* E 141 A4
Belmonte, *Cuenca* E 158 B1
Belmonte P 148 B2
Belmonte de San José E 153 B3
Belmonte de Tajo E 151 B4
Belmullet IRL 26 B1
Belobresça RO 127 C3
Belœil B 79 B3
Belogradchik BG 16 D5
Belokorovichi UA 13 C8
Belorado E 143 B3
Belotič SRB 127 C1
Bělotín CZ 98 B1
Belovo BG 183 A6
Belozersk RUS 9 C10
Belp CH 106 C2
Belpasso I 177 B3
Belpech F 146 A2
Belper GB 40 B2
Belsay GB 37 A5
Belsk Duzy PL 87 A4
Beltinci SLO 111 C3
Beltra IRL 26 C1
Belturbet IRL 27 B3
Beluša SK 98 B2
Belvedere Marittimo I 174 B1
Belver de Cinca E 153 A4
Belver de los Montes E 142 C1
Belvès F 129 B3
Belvezet F 130 A2
Belvis de la Jara E 150 C3
Belvis de Monroy E 150 C2
Belyy RUS 9 E8
Belz F 100 B2
Bełżec PL 13 C5
Belzig D 73 B5
Bembibre E 141 B4
Bembridge GB 44 C2
Bemmel NL 80 A1
Bemposta, *Bragança* P 149 A3
Bemposta, *Santarém* P 154 B2
Benabarre E 145 B4
Benacazón E 161 B3
Benaguacil E 159 B3
Benahadux E 164 C2
Benalmádena E 163 B3
Benalúa de Guadix E 164 B1
Benalúa de las Villas E 163 A4
Benalup E 162 B2
Benamargosa E 163 B3
Benamaurel E 164 B2
Benameji E 163 A3
Benamocarra E 163 B3
Benaocaz E 162 B2
Benaoján E 162 B2
Benarrabá E 162 B2
Benasque E 145 B4
Benátky nad Jizerou CZ 84 B2
Benavente E 142 B1
Benavente P 154 C2
Benavides de Órbigo E 141 B5
Benavila P 154 B3
Bendorf D 81 B3
Bene Vagienna I 133 A3
Benedikt SLO 110 C2
Benejama E 159 C3
Benejúzar E 165 A4
Benešov CZ 96 B2
Bénestroff F 92 C2
Benet F 114 B3
Bénévent-l'Abbaye F 116 A1
Benevento I 170 B2
Benfeld F 93 C3
Benfica P 154 B2
Bengtsfors S 54 A3
Bengtsheden S 50 B2
Beničanci HR 125 B4
Benicarló E 153 B4
Benicássim E 153 B4
Benidorm E 159 C3
Benifaió E 159 B3
Beniganim E 159 C3
Benington GB 41 B4
Benisa E 159 C4
Benkovac HR 137 A4
Benllech GB 38 A2
Benneckenstein D 82 A2
Bénodet F 100 B1
Benquerencia de la Serena E 156 B2
Bensafrim P 160 B1
Bensbyn S 196 D5
Bensdorf D 73 B5
Benshausen D 82 B2
Bensheim D 93 B4
Bentley GB 44 B3
Bentwisch D 65 B5
Beočin SRB 126 B1
Beograd = Belgrade SRB 127 C2
Beragh GB 27 B3
Beranga E 143 A3
Berat AL 182 C1
Bérat F 146 A2
Beratzhausen D 95 B3
Bérbaltavár H 111 B3
Berbegal E 145 C3
Berbenno di Valtellina I 120 A2
Berberana E 143 B3
Bercedo E 143 A3
Bercel H 112 B3
Bercenay-le-Hayer F 91 C3
Berceto I 134 A2
Berchem B 79 B3
Berchidda I 178 B3
Berching D 95 B3
Berchtesgaden D 109 B4
Bérchules E 163 B4
Bercianos de Aliste E 149 A3
Berck F 78 B1
Berclaire d'Urgell E 147 C1
Berdoias E 140 A1
Berducedo E 141 A4
Berdún E 144 B3
Berdychiv UA 13 D8
Bere Alston GB 42 B2
Bere Regis GB 43 B4
Bereguardo I 120 B2
Berehommen N 53 A3
Berehove UA 16 A5
Berek BIH 124 B3
Beremend H 125 B4
Berestechko UA 13 C6
Berettyóújfalu H 113 B5
Berezhany UA 13 D6
Berezivka UA 17 B9
Berezna UA 13 C9
Berg D 95 B3
Berg N 195 E3
Berg S 56 B2
Berg im Gau D 95 C3
Berga, *Sachsen-Anhalt* D 82 A3
Berga, *Thüringen* D 83 B4
Berga E 147 B2
Berga S 62 A4
Bergama TR 186 C2
Bérgamo I 120 B2
Bergara E 143 A4
Bergby S 51 B4
Berge, *Brandenburg* D 74 B1
Berge, *Niedersachsen* D 71 B4
Berge, *Telemark* N 53 A4
Berge, *Telemark* N 53 A4
Bergeforsen S 200 D3
Bergen, *Mecklenburg-Vorpommern* D 66 B2
Bergen, *Niedersachsen* D 72 B2
Bergen, *Niedersachsen* D 73 B3
Bergen N 46 B2
Bergen NL 70 B1
Bergen op Zoom NL 79 A4
Bergerac F 129 B3
Bergères-lés-Vertus F 91 C4
Bergeyk NL 79 A5
Berghausen D 93 C4
Bergheim D 80 B2
Berghem S 60 B2
Bergisch Gladbach D 80 B3
Bergkamen D 81 A3
Bergkvara S 63 B4
Berglern D 95 C3
Bergnäset S 196 D5
Bergneustadt D 81 A3
Bergs slussar S 56 B1
Bergsäng S 49 B5
Bergshamra S 57 A4
Bergsjö S 200 E3
Bergsviken S 196 D4
Bergtheim D 94 B2
Bergues F 78 B2
Bergum NL 70 A2
Bergün Bravuogn CH 107 C4
Bergwitz D 83 A4
Berhida H 112 B2
Beringel P 160 A2
Beringen B 79 A5
Berja E 164 C2
Berkåk N 199 C7
Berkeley GB 43 A4
Berkenthin D 65 C3
Berkhamsted GB 44 B3
Berkheim D 107 A5
Berkhof D 72 B2
Berkovići BIH 139 B4
Berkovitsa BG 17 D5
Berlanga E 156 B2
Berlanga de Duero E 151 A5
Berlevåg N 193 B13
Berlikum NL 70 A2
Berlin D 74 B2
Berlstedt D 82 A3
Bermeo E 143 A4
Bermillo de Sayago E 149 A3
Bern CH 106 C2
Bernalda I 174 A2
Bernardos E 150 A3
Bernartice, *Jihočeský* CZ 96 B2
Bernartice, *Vychodočeský* CZ 85 B3
Bernau, *Baden-Württemberg* D 106 B3
Bernau, *Bayern* D 109 B3
Bernau, *Brandenburg* D 74 B2
Bernaville F 90 A2
Bernay F 89 A4
Bernburg D 83 A3
Berndorf A 111 B3
Berne D 72 A1
Bernecebarati H 112 A2
Bernhardsthal A 97 C4
Bernkastel-Kues D 92 B3
Bernolakovo SK 111 A4
Bernsdorf D 84 A2
Bernstadt D 84 A2
Bernstein A 111 B3
Bernués E 145 B3
Beromünster CH 106 B3
Beroun CZ 96 B2
Berovo MK 182 B4
Berre-l'Etang F 131 B4
Berriedale GB 32 C3
Berriew GB 39 B3
Berrocal E 161 B3
Bersenbrück D 71 B4
Bershad' UA 13 D8
Berthåga S 51 C4
Berthelming F 92 C2
Bertincourt F 90 A2
Bertinoro I 135 A5
Bertogne B 92 A1
Bertrix B 91 B5
Berufjörður IS 191 C11
Berville-sur-Mer F 89 A4
Berwick-upon-Tweed GB 37 A4
Berzasca RO 16 C4
Berzence H 124 A3
Berzocana E 156 A2
Besalú E 147 B3
Besançon F 105 B5
Besenfeld D 93 C4
Besenyötelek H 113 B4
Besenyszög H 113 B4
Beshenkovichi BY 13 A8
Besigheim D 93 C5
Běšiny CZ 96 B1
Beška SRB 126 B2
Beşkonak TR 189 B6
Besle F 101 B4
Besnyö H 112 B2
Bessais-le-Fromental F 103 C4
Bessan F 130 B2
Besse-en-Chandesse F 116 B2
Bessé-sur-Braye F 102 B2
Bessèges F 131 A3
Bessines-sur-Gartempe F 115 B5
Best NL 79 A5
Bestorp S 56 B1
Betanzos E 140 A2
Betelu E 144 A2
Bétera E 159 B3
Beteta E 152 B1
Béthenville F 91 B4
Bethesda GB 38 A2
Béthune F 78 B2
Beton-Bazoches F 90 C3
Bettembourg L 92 B2
Betterdorf L 92 B2
Bettna S 56 B2
Béttola I 120 C2
Bettona I 136 B1
Bettyhill GB 32 C2
Betws-y-Coed GB 38 A3
Betxi E 159 B3
Betz F 90 B2
Betzdorf D 81 B3
Beuil F 132 A2
Beulah GB 39 B3
Beuzeville F 89 A4
Bevagna I 136 C1
Bevens-bruk S 56 A1
Beveren B 79 A4
Beverley GB 40 B3
Bevern D 81 A5
Beverstedt D 72 A1
Beverungen D 81 A5
Beverwijk NL 70 B1
Bex CH 119 A4
Bexhill GB 45 C4
Beyazköy TR 186 A2
Beychevelle F 128 A2
Beydağ TR 188 A3
Beyeğaç TR 188 B3
Beykoz TR 186 A4
Beynat F 129 A4
Beyoğlu TR 186 A4
Beypazarı TR 187 B6
Beyşehir TR 189 B6
Bezas E 152 B2
Bezau A 107 B4
Bezdan SRB 125 B4
Bèze F 105 B4
Bezenet F 116 A2
Bezhetsk RUS 9 D10
Béziers F 130 B2
Bezzecca I 121 B3
Biadki PL 85 A5
Biała, *Łódzkie* PL 77 C4
Biała, *Opolskie* PL 85 B5
Biała Podlaska PL 13 B5
Biała Rawska PL 87 A4
Białaczów PL 87 A4
Biale Błota PL 76 A2
Białobłoty PL 76 B2
Białobrzegi PL 87 A4
Białogard PL 67 C4
Białośliwie PL 76 A2
Białowąs PL 68 B1
Biały Bór PL 68 B1
Białystok PL 13 B5
Biancavilla I 177 B3
Bianco I 175 C2
Biandrate I 119 B5
Biar E 159 C3
Biarritz F 144 A2
Bias F 128 B1
Biasca CH 120 A1
Biatorbágy H 112 B2
Bibbiena I 135 B4
Bibbona I 134 B3
Biberach, *Baden-Württemberg* D 107 A4
Biberach, *Baden-Württemberg* D 93 C4
Bibinje HR 137 A4
Bibione I 122 B2
Biblis D 93 B4
Bibury GB 44 B2
Bicaj AL 182 B2
Biccari I 171 B3
Bicester GB 44 B2
Bichl D 108 B2
Bichlbach A 108 B1
Bicorp E 159 B3
Bicos P 160 B1
Bicske H 112 B2
Bidache F 128 C1
Bidart F 144 A2
Biddinghuizen NL 70 B2
Biddulph GB 40 B1
Bideford GB 42 A2
Bidford-on-Avon GB 44 A2
Bidjovagge N 192 C6
Bie S 56 A2
Bieber D 81 B5
Biebersdorf D 74 C2
Biedenkopf D 81 B4
Biel CH 106 B2
Biel E 144 B3
Bielany Wroclawskie PL 85 A4
Bielawa PL 85 B4
Bielawy PL 77 B4
Bielefeld D 72 B1
Biella I 119 B5
Bielsa E 145 B4
Bielsk PL 77 B4
Bielsk Podlaski PL 13 B5
Bielsko-Biała PL 99 B3
Bienenbuttel D 72 A3
Bieniow PL 84 A3
Bienservida E 158 C1
Bienvenida E 156 B1
Bierdzany PL 86 B2
Bierné F 102 B1
Biersted DK 58 A2
Bierun PL 86 B3
Bierutów PL 85 A5
Bierwart B 79 B5
Bierzwina PL 75 A4
Bierzwnik PL 75 A4
Biescas E 145 B3
Biesenthal D 74 B2
Biesiekierz PL 67 B5
Bietigheim-Bissingen D 93 C5
Bièvre B 91 B5
Bieżuń PL 77 B4
Biga TR 186 B2
Bigadiç TR 186 C3
Biganos F 128 B2
Bigas P 148 B2
Bigastro E 165 A4
Bigbury GB 42 B3
Biggar GB 36 A3
Biggin Hill GB 45 B4
Biggleswade GB 44 A3
Bignasco CH 119 A5
Biguglia F 180 A2
Bihać BIH 124 C1
Biharnagybajom H 113 B5
Bijeljani BIH 139 B4
Bijeljina BIH 125 C5
Bijuesca E 152 A2
Bila Tserkva UA 13 D9
Bilaj HR 137 A4
Bilbao E 143 A4
Bilcza PL 87 B4
Bildudalur IS 190 B2
Bileća BIH 139 C4
Bilecik TR 187 B4
Biled RO 126 B2
Biłgoraj PL 12 C5
Bilhorod-Dnistrovskyy UA 17 B9
Bílina CZ 84 B1
Bilisht AL 182 C2
Bilje HR 125 B4
Billdal S 60 B1
Billerbeck D 71 C4
Billericay GB 45 B4
Billesholm S 61 C2
Billingborough GB 40 C3
Billinge S 61 D3
Billingham GB 37 B5
Billinghay GB 41 B3
Billingsfors S 54 B3
Billingshurst GB 44 B3
Billom F 116 B3
Billsta S 200 C4
Billund DK 59 C2
Bílovec CZ 98 B2
Bilstein D 81 A4
Bilthoven NL 70 B2
Bilto N 192 C5
Bilzen B 80 B1
Bíňa SK 112 B2
Binaced E 145 C4
Binasco I 120 B2
Binbrook GB 41 B3
Binche B 79 B4
Bindlach D 95 B3
Bindslev DK 58 A3
Binefar E 145 C4
Bingen D 93 B3
Bingham GB 40 C3
Bingley GB 40 B2
Bingsjö S 50 A2
Binic F 100 A3
Binz D 66 B2
Biograd na Moru HR 137 B4
Bionaz I 119 B4
Bioska SRB 127 D1
Birda RO 126 B3
Birdlip GB 44 B1
Biri N 48 B2
Birkeland N 53 B4
Birkenfeld, *Baden-Württemberg* D 93 C4
Birkenfeld, *Rheinland-Pfalz* D 92 B3
Birkenhead GB 38 A3
Birkerød DK 61 D2
Birkfeld A 110 B2
Birkirkara M 175 C3
Birmingham GB 40 C2
Birr IRL 28 A4
Birresborn D 80 B2
Birstein D 81 B5
Biržai LT 8 D4
Birzebbugia M 175 C3
Bisáccia I 172 A1
Bisacquino I 176 B2
Bisbal de Falset E 153 A4
Biscarosse F 128 B1
Biscarosse Plage F 128 B1
Biscarrués E 144 B3
Biscéglie I 171 B4
Bischheim F 93 C3
Bischofsheim D 82 B1
Bischofshofen A 109 B4
Bischofswerda D 84 A2
Bischofswiesen D 109 B3
Bischofszell CH 107 B4
Bischwiller F 93 C3
Bisenti I 169 A3
Bishop Auckland GB 37 B5
Bishop's Castle GB 39 B4
Bishops Lydeard GB 43 A3
Bishop's Stortford GB 45 B4
Bishop's Waltham GB 44 C2
Bisignano I 174 B2
Bisingen D 93 C4
Biskupice-Oławskie PL 85 A5
Biskupiec PL 69 B4
Bismark D 73 B4
Bismo N 198 D5
Bispgården S 200 C2
Bispingen D 72 A2
Bissen L 92 B2
Bissendorf D 71 B5
Bisserup DK 65 A4
Bistango I 119 C5
Bistarac Donje BIH 139 A4
Bistrica BIH 124 C3
Bistrica ob Sotli SLO 123 A4
Bistriţa RO 17 B6
Bitburg D 92 B2
Bitche F 93 B3
Bitetto I 171 B4
Bitola MK 182 B3
Bitonto I 171 B4
Bitschwiller F 106 B2
Bitterfeld D 83 A4
Bitti I 178 B3
Biville-sur-Mer F 89 A5
Bivona I 176 B2
Biwer L 92 B2
Bizeljsko SLO 123 A4
Bizovac HR 125 B4
Bjåen N 52 A3
Bjärnum S 61 C3
Bjärred S 61 D3
Bjästa S 200 C4
Bjelland, *Vest-Agder* N 52 B2
Bjelland, *Vest-Agder* N 52 B3
Bjelovar HR 124 B2
Bjerkreim N 52 B2
Bjerkvik N 194 B8
Bjerreby DK 65 B3
Bjerregrav DK 58 B2
Bjerringbro DK 59 B2
Bjøberg N 47 B5
Bjøllånes N 195 D5
Björbo S 50 B1
Bjordal N 46 A2
Björg IS 191 B8
Bjørkåsen N 194 B7
Björke, *Gävleborg* S 51 B4
Björke, *Östergötland* S 56 B1
Bjørkelangen N 48 C3
Björketorp S 60 B2
Björkholmen S 196 C2
Björkliden S 194 B9
Björklinge S 51 B4
Björko, *Stockholm* S 51 C6
Björkö, *Västra Götaland* S 60 B1
Björköby S 62 A2
Björkvik S 56 B2
Bjørn N 195 D3
Björna S 200 C4
Björneborg S 55 A5
Björnerod S 54 A2
Bjørnevatn N 193 C13
Björnlunda S 56 A3
Bjørnstad N 193 C14
Björsäter S 56 B2
Bjurberget S 49 B4
Bjurholm S 200 C5
Bjursås S 50 B2
Bjurtjärn S 55 A5
Bjuv S 61 C2

Blachownia PL **86** B2
Blackburn GB **38** A4
Blackpool GB **38** A3
Blackstad S **62** A4
Blackwater IRL **30** B2
Blackwaterfoot GB **34** C2
Blacy F **91** C4
Bladåker S **51** B5
Blaenau Ffestiniog GB **38** B3
Blaenavon GB **39** C3
Blaengarw GB **39** C3
Blagaj BIH **124** B2
Blagaj BIH **139** B3
Blagdon GB **43** A4
Blagnac F **129** C4
Blagoevgrad BG **183** A5
Blaichach D **107** B5
Blain F **101** B4
Blainville-sur-l'Eau F **92** C2
Blair Atholl GB **35** B4
Blairgowrie GB **35** B4
Blajan F **145** A4
Blakeney GB **39** C4
Blakstad N **53** B4
Blâmont F **92** C2
Blanca E **165** A3
Blancos E **140** C3
Blandford Forum GB **43** B4
Blanes E **147** C3
Blangy-sur-Bresle F **90** B1
Blankaholm S **62** A4
Blankenberge B **78** A3
Blankenburg D **82** A2
Blankenfelde D **74** B2
Blankenhain D **82** B3
Blankenheim D **80** B2
Blanquefort F **128** B2
Blansko CZ **97** B4
Blanzac F **115** C4
Blanzy F **104** C3
Blaricum NL **70** B2
Blarney IRL **29** C3
Blascomillán E **150** B2
Blascosancho E **150** B3
Błaszki PL **86** A2
Blatná CZ **96** B1
Blatné SK **111** A4
Blatnice CZ **98** C1
Blatnika BIH **139** A3
Blato HR **138** C2
Blato na Cetini HR **138** B2
Blatten CH **119** A4
Blattnicksele S **195** E8
Blatzheim D **80** B2
Blaubeuren D **94** C1
Blaufelden D **94** B1
Blaustein D **94** C1
Blaydon GB **37** B5
Blaye F **128** A2
Blaye-les-Mines F **130** A1
Blázquez E **156** B2
Bleckede D **73** A3
Blecua E **145** B3
Bled SLO **123** A3
Bleiburg A **110** C1
Bleichenbach D **81** B5
Bleicherode D **82** A2
Bleik N **194** A6
Bleikvassli N **195** E4
Bléneau F **104** B1
Blentarp S **61** D3
Blera I **168** A2
Blérancourt F **90** B3
Bléré F **102** B2
Blesle F **116** B3
Blessington IRL **30** A2
Blet F **103** C4
Bletchley GB **44** B3
Bletterans F **105** C4
Blidö S **57** A4
Blidsberg S **60** B3
Blieskastel D **92** B3
Bligny-sur-Ouche F **104** B3
Blikstorp S **55** B5
Blinisht AL **182** B1
Blinja HR **124** B2
Blizanówek PL **76** C3
Bliżyn PL **87** A4
Blois F **103** B3
Blokhus DK **58** A2
Blokzijl NL **70** B2
Blombacka S **55** A4
Blomberg D **72** C2
Blomskog S **54** A3
Blomstermåla S **62** B4
Blomvåg N **46** B1
Blönduós IS **190** B5
Błonie PL **77** B5
Blonville-sur-Mer F **89** A4
Blötberget S **50** B2
Blovice CZ **96** B1
Bloxham GB **44** A2
Blšany CZ **83** B5
Bludenz A **107** B4
Bludov CZ **97** B4
Blumberg D **107** B3
Blyberg S **49** A6
Blyth, *Northumberland* GB **37** A5
Blyth, *Nottinghamshire* GB **40** B2
Blyth Bridge GB **35** C4
Blythburgh GB **45** A5
Blythe Bridge GB **40** C1
Bø, *Nordland* N **194** B5
Bø, *Telemark* N **53** A5
Boa Vista P **154** B2
Boal E **141** A4
Boan CG **139** C5
Boario Terme I **120** B3
Boat of Garten GB **32** D3
Boba H **111** B4
Bobadilla, *Logroño* E **143** B4
Bobadilla, *Málaga* E **163** A3
Bobadilla del Campo E **150** A2
Bobadilla del Monte E **151** B4
Bóbbio I **120** C2
Bóbbio Pellice I **119** C4
Bobigny F **90** C2
Bobingen D **94** C2
Böblingen D **93** C5
Bobolice PL **68** B1
Boboras E **140** B2
Boboshevo BG **182** A4
Bobowa PL **99** B4
Bobrová CZ **97** B4
Bobrovitsa UA **13** C9
Bobrowice PL **75** C4
Bobrówko PL **75** B4
Boca de Huérgano E **142** B2
Bocairent E **159** C3
Bočar SRB **126** B2
Bocchigliero I **174** B2
Boceguillas E **151** A4
Bochnia PL **99** B4
Bocholt B **80** A1
Bocholt D **80** A2
Bochov CZ **83** B5
Bochum D **80** A3
Bockara S **62** A4
Bockenem D **72** B3
Bockfliess A **97** C4
Bockhorn D **71** A5
Bočna SLO **123** A3
Bocognano F **180** A2
Boconád H **113** B4
Bőcs H **113** A4
Boczów PL **75** B3
Böda, *Dalarnas* S **50** A2
Böda, *Öland* S **62** A5
Boda, *Stockholm* S **51** B5
Boda, *Värmland* S **55** A4
Boda, *Västernorrland* S **200** D2
Boda Glasbruk S **63** B3
Bodafors S **62** A2
Bodajk H **112** B2
Boddam, *Aberdeenshire* GB **33** D5
Boddam, *Shetland* GB **33** B5
Boddin D **73** A4
Bödefeld-Freiheit D **81** A4
Boden S **196** D4
Bodenmais D **95** B5
Bodenteich D **73** B3
Bodenwerder D **72** C2
Bodiam GB **45** B4
Bodinnick GB **42** B2
Bodio CH **120** A1
Bodjani SRB **125** B5
Bodmin GB **42** B2
Bodø N **194** C5
Bodonal de la Sierra E **161** A3
Bodrum TR **188** B2
Bodstedt D **66** B1
Bodträskfors S **196** C3
Bodzanów PL **77** B5
Bodzanowice PL **86** B2
Bodzechów PL **87** B5
Bodzentyn PL **87** B4
Boecillo E **150** A3
Boëge F **118** A3
Boën F **117** B3
Bogács H **113** B4
Bogadmindszent H **125** B4
Bogajo E **149** B3
Bogarra E **158** C1
Bogarre E **163** A4
Bogatić SRB **127** C1
Bogatynia PL **84** B2
Boğazkale TR **23** A8
Boğazlıyan TR **23** B8
Bogda RO **126** B3
Bogdaniec PL **75** B4
Boge S **57** C4
Bogen D **95** C4
Bogen, *Nordland* N **194** B7
Bogen, *Nordland* N **194** C6
Bogen S **49** B4
Bogense DK **59** C3
Bognanco Fonti I **119** A5
Bognelv N **192** B6
Bognes N **194** B7
Bogno CH **120** A2
Bognor Regis GB **44** C3
Bogoria PL **87** B5
Bograngen S **49** B4
Boguchwaly PL **69** B5
Bogumiłowice PL **86** A3
Boguslav UA **13** D9
Boguszów-Gorce PL **85** B4
Bogyiszló H **112** C2
Bohain-en-Vermandois F **91** B3
Böheimkirchen A **110** A2
Bohinjska Bistrica SLO **122** A2
Böhlen D **83** A4
Böhmenkirch D **94** C1
Bohmte D **71** B5
Bohonal de Ibor E **150** C2
Böhönye H **124** A3
Bohumin CZ **98** B2
Boiro E **140** B2
Bois-d'Amont F **105** C5
Boisseron F **131** B3
Boitzenburg D **74** A2
Boixols E **147** B2
Boizenburg D **73** A3
Bojadła PL **75** C4
Bojano I **170** B2
Bojanowo PL **85** A4
Bøjden DK **64** A3
Bojkovice CZ **98** B1
Bojná SK **98** C2
Bojnice SK **98** C2
Boka SRB **126** B2
Böklund D **64** B2
Bokod H **112** B2
Böksholm S **62** A2
Boksitogorsk RUS **9** C8
Bol HR **138** B2
Bolaños de Calatrava E **157** B4
Bolayır TR **186** B1
Bolbec F **89** A4
Bölcske H **112** C2
Bolderslev DK **64** B2
Boldog H **112** B3
Boldva H **113** A4
Böle S **196** D4
Bolea E **145** B3
Bolekhiv UA **13** D5
Bolesławiec PL **84** A3
Boleszkowice PL **74** B3
Bolewice PL **75** B5
Bólgheri I **134** B3
Bolhrad UA **17** C8
Boliden S **200** B6
Bolimów PL **77** B5
Boliqueime P **160** B1
Boljevci SRB **127** C2
Boljkovci SRB **127** C2
Bolków PL **85** B4
Bollebygd S **60** B2
Bollène F **131** A3
Bólliga E **152** B1
Bollnäs S **50** A3
Bollstabruk S **200** D3
Bollullos E **161** B3
Bollullos par del Condado E **161** B3
Bologna I **135** A4
Bologne F **105** A4
Bolognetta I **176** B2
Bolognola I **136** C2
Bologoye RUS **9** D9
Bolótana I **178** B2
Bolsena I **168** A1
Bolshaya Vradiyevka UA **17** B9
Bolsover GB **40** B2
Bolstad S **54** B3
Bolsward NL **70** A2
Boltaña E **145** B4
Boltenhagen D **65** C4
Boltigen CH **106** C2
Bolton GB **38** A4
Bolu TR **187** B6
Bolungavík IS **190** A2
Bolvadin TR **187** D6
Bóly H **125** B4
Bolzaneto I **133** A4
Bolzano I **108** C2
Bomba I **169** A4
Bombarral P **154** B1
Bömenzien D **73** B4
Bomlitz D **72** B2
Bømlo N **52** A1
Bøn N **48** B3
Bon-Encontre F **129** B3
Bona F **104** B2
Bonaduz CH **107** C4
Bonanza E **161** C3
Boñar E **142** B1
Bonarbridge GB **32** D2
Bonárcado I **178** B2
Bonares E **161** B3
Bonäs S **50** A1
Bonassola I **134** A2
Bonawe GB **34** B2
Bondal N **53** A4
Bondeno I **121** C4
Bondorf D **93** C4
Bondstorp S **60** B3
Bo'ness GB **35** B4
Bonete E **158** C2
Bonifacio F **180** B2
Bonigen CH **106** C2
Bonin PL **67** B5
Bonn D **80** B3
Bonnánaro I **178** B2
Bonnåsjøen N **194** C6
Bonnat F **116** A1
Bonndorf D **106** B3
Bonnétable F **102** A2
Bonnétage F **106** B1
Bonneuil-les-Eaux F **90** B2
Bonneuil-Matours F **115** B4
Bonneval F **103** A3
Bonneval-sur-Arc F **119** B4
Bonneville F **118** A3
Bonnières-sur-Seine F **90** B1
Bonnieux F **131** B4
Bönnigheim D **93** B5
Bonny-sur-Loire F **103** B4
Bonnyrigg GB **35** C4
Bono E **145** B4
Bono I **178** B3
Bonorva I **178** B2
Bønsnes N **48** B2
Bonyhád H **125** A4
Boom B **79** A4
Boos F **89** A5
Boostedt D **64** B3
Bootle, *Cumbria* GB **36** B3
Bootle, *Merseyside* GB **38** A3
Bopfingen D **94** C2
Boppard D **81** B3
Boqueixón E **140** B2
Bor CZ **95** B4
Bor S **62** A2
Bor SRB **16** C5
Bor TR **23** C8
Boran-sur-Oise F **90** B2
Borås S **60** B2
Borba P **155** C3
Borbona I **169** A3
Borča SRB **127** C2
Borci BIH **139** B4
Borculo NL **71** B3
Bordány H **126** A1
Bordeaux F **128** B2
Bordeira P **160** B1
Bordesholm D **64** B3
Borðeyri IS **190** B4
Bordighera I **133** B3
Bording DK **59** B2
Bordón E **153** B3
Bore I **120** C2
Borehamwood GB **44** B3
Borek Strzeliński PL **85** B5
Borek Wielkopolski PL **76** C2
Boreland GB **36** A3
Borello I **135** A5
Borensberg S **56** B1
Borgafjäll S **199** A12
Borgarnes IS **190** C4
Borgentreich D **81** A5
Börger D **71** B4
Borger NL **71** B3
Borggård S **56** B1
Borghamn S **55** B5
Borghetta di Vara I **134** A2
Borghetto d'Arróscia I **133** A3
Borghetto Santo Spirito I **133** A4
Borgholm S **62** B4
Borghorst D **71** B4
Bórgia I **175** C2
Borgloon B **79** B5
Børglum DK **58** A2
Borgo F **180** A2
Borgo a Mozzano I **134** B3
Borgo alla Collina I **135** B4
Borgo Pace I **135** B5
Borgo San Dalmazzo I **133** A3
Borgo San Lorenzo I **135** B4
Borgo Val di Taro I **134** A2
Borgo Valsugana I **121** A4
Borgo Vercelli I **119** B5
Borgoforte I **121** B3
Borgofranco d'Ivrea I **119** B4
Borgomanero I **119** B5
Borgomasino I **119** B4
Borgonovo Val Tidone I **120** B2
Borgorose I **169** A3
Borgosésia I **119** B5
Borgstena S **60** B3
Borgue GB **36** B2
Borgund N **47** A4
Borgvik S **55** A3
Borja E **144** C2
Bork D **80** A3
Borken D **80** A2
Borkenes N **194** B7
Børkop DK **59** C2
Borkowice PL **87** A4
Borkowo PL **77** B5
Borkum D **71** A3
Borlänge S **50** B2
Borlu TR **186** D3
Bormes-les-Mimosas F **132** B2
Bórmio I **107** C5
Bormujos E **161** B3
Borna D **83** A4
Borne NL **71** B3
Borne Sulinowo PL **68** B1
Bornes P **149** A2
Bornheim D **80** B2
Bornhöved D **64** B3
Börnicke D **74** B1
Bornos E **162** B2
Borobia E **152** A2
Borodino RUS **9** E9
Borohrádek CZ **85** B4
Boronów PL **86** B2
Bórore I **178** B2
Borosźow PL **86** B2
Borota H **126** A1
Boroughbridge GB **40** A2
Borovany CZ **96** C2
Borovichi RUS **9** C8
Borovnica SLO **123** B3
Borovo HR **125** B4
Borovsk RUS **9** E10
Borovy CZ **96** B1
Borowa PL **85** A5
Borox E **151** B4
Borrby S **66** A3
Borre DK **65** B5
Borre N **54** A1
Borredá E **147** B2
Borrenes E **141** B4
Borriol E **159** A3
Borris DK **59** C1
Borris IRL **30** B2
Borris-in-Ossory IRL **28** B4
Borrisokane IRL **28** B3
Borrisoleigh IRL **28** B4
Borrowdale GB **36** B3
Børrud N **49** C4
Borşa RO **17** B6
Borsdorf D **83** A4
Børselv N **193** B9
Borsfa H **111** C3
Borský Mikuláš SK **98** C1
Borsodivánka H **113** B4
Borsodnádasd H **113** A4
Bort-les-Orgues F **116** B2
Börte N **53** A3
Borth GB **39** B2
Börtnan S **199** C10
Børtnes N **47** B6
Boruja Kościelne PL **75** B5
Borup DK **61** D1
Boryslav UA **13** D5
Boryspil UA **13** C9
Boryszyn PL **75** B4
Borzęciczki PL **85** A5
Borzęcin PL **77** B5
Borzonasca I **134** A2
Borzyszkowy PL **68** A2
Borzytuchom PL **68** A2
Bosa I **178** B2
Bošáca SK **98** C1
Bosanci HR **123** B4
Bosanska Dubica BIH **124** B2
Bosanska Gradiška BIH **124** B3
Bosanska Kostajnica BIH **124** B2
Bosanska Krupa BIH **124** C2
Bosanski Brod BIH **125** B3
Bosanski Novi BIH **124** B2
Bosanski Petrovac BIH **124** C2
Bosanski Šamac BIH **125** B4
Bosansko Grahovo BIH **138** A2
Bošany SK **98** C2
Bösárkány H **111** B4
Bosau D **65** B3
Bósca H **112** C3
Boscastle GB **42** B2
Bosco I **120** C1
Bosco Chiesanuova I **121** B4
Bösdorf D **65** B3
Bösel D **71** A4
Bosham GB **44** C3
Bösingfeld D **72** B2
Bosjön S **49** C5
Boskoop NL **70** B1
Boskovice CZ **97** B4
Bošnjaci HR **125** B4
Bošnjane SRB **127** D3
Bossast E **145** B4
Bossolasco I **133** A4
Boštanj SLO **123** A4
Boston GB **41** C3
Bostrak N **53** A4
Böszénfa H **125** A3
Bot E **153** A4
Botajica BIH **125** C4
Bøte By DK **65** B4
Bothel GB **36** B3
Boticas P **148** A2
Botilsäter S **55** A4
Botngård N **198** B6
Botoš SRB **126** B2
Botoşani RO **17** B7
Botricello I **175** C2
Botsmark S **200** B6
Bottendorf D **81** A4
Bottesford GB **40** C3
Bottnaryd S **60** B3
Bottrop D **80** A2
Botunje SRB **127** C3
Bötzingen D **106** A2
Bouaye F **101** B4
Bouça P **149** A2
Boucau F **128** C1
Bouchain F **78** B3
Bouchoir F **90** B2
Boudreville F **105** B3
Boudry CH **106** C1
Bouesse F **103** C3
Bouguenais F **101** B4
Bouhy F **104** B2
Bouillargues F **131** B3
Bouillon B **91** B5
Bouilly F **104** A2
Bouin F **114** B2
Boulay-Moselle F **92** B2
Boulazac F **129** A3
Boule-d'Amont F **146** B3
Bouligny F **92** B1
Boulogne-sur-Gesse F **145** A4
Boulogne-sur-Mer F **78** B1
Bouloire F **102** B2
Bouquemaison F **78** B2
Bourbon-Lancy F **104** C2
Bourbon-l'Archambault F **104** C2
Bourbonne-les-Bains F **105** B4
Bourbourg F **78** B2
Bourbriac F **100** A2
Bourcefranc-le-Chapus F **114** C2
Bourdeaux F **131** A4
Bouresse F **115** B4
Bourg F **128** A2
Bourg-Achard F **89** A4
Bourg-Argental F **117** B4
Bourg-de-Péage F **117** B5
Bourg-de-Thizy F **117** A4
Bourg-de-Visa F **129** B3
Bourg-en-Bresse F **118** A2
Bourg-et-Comin F **91** B3
Bourg-Lastic F **116** B2
Bourg-Madame F **146** B2
Bourg-St. Andéol F **131** A3
Bourg-St. Maurice F **119** B3
Bourganeuf F **116** B1
Bourges F **103** B4
Bourgneuf-en-Retz F **114** A2
Bourgogne F **91** B4
Bourgoin-Jallieu F **118** B2
Bourgtheroulde F **89** A4
Bourgueil F **102** B2
Bourmont F **105** A4
Bourne GB **40** C3
Bournemouth GB **43** B5
Bourneville F **89** A4
Bournezeau F **114** B2
Bourran F **129** B3
Bourret F **129** C4
Bourron-Marlotte F **90** C2
Bourton-on-The-Water GB **44** B2
Boussac F **116** A2
Boussens F **145** A4
Boutersem B **79** B4
Bouttencourt F **90** B1
Bouvières F **131** A4
Bouvron F **101** B4
Bouxwiller F **93** C3
Bouzas E **140** B2
Bouzonville F **92** B2
Bova I **175** D1
Bova Marina I **175** D1
Bovalino Marina I **175** C2
Bovallstrand S **54** B2
Bovec SLO **122** A2
Bóveda E **141** B3
Bóvegno I **120** B3
Bovenau D **64** B2
Bovenden D **82** A1
Bøverdal N **198** D5
Bóves I **133** A3
Bovey Tracey GB **43** B3
Bovino I **171** B3
Bøvlingbjerg DK **58** B1
Bovolenta I **121** B4
Bovolone I **121** B4
Bowes GB **37** B5
Bowmore GB **34** C1
Bowness-on-Windermere GB **36** B4
Box GB **43** A4
Boxberg, *Baden-Württemberg* D **94** B1
Boxberg, *Sachsen* D **84** A2
Boxholm S **55** B6
Boxmeer NL **80** A1
Boxtel NL **79** A5
Boyabat TR **23** A8
Boyalica TR **187** B4
Boyle IRL **26** C2
Bozan TR **187** C6
Božava HR **137** A3
Bozburun TR **188** C3
Bozcaada TR **186** C1
Bozdoğan TR **188** B3
Božepole Wielkie PL **68** A2
Boževac SRB **127** C3
Boži Dar CZ **83** B4
Božice CZ **97** C4
Bozkır TR **189** B7

Bozouls F 130 A1
Bozova TR 189 B5
Bozüyük TR 187 C5
Bózzolo I 121 B3
Bra I 119 C4
Braås S 62 A3
Brabrand DK 59 B3
Bracadale GB 31 B2
Bracciano I 168 A2
Bracieux F 103 B3
Bräcke S 199 C12
Brackenheim D 93 B5
Brackley GB 44 A2
Bracklin IRL 27 C4
Bracknell GB 44 B3
Brackwede D 72 C1
Braco GB 35 B4
Brad RO 16 B5
Bradford GB 40 B2
Bradford on Avon GB 43 A4
Bradina BIH 139 B4
Brådland N 52 B2
Brae GB 33 A5
Brædstrup DK 59 C2
Braemar GB 32 D3
Braemore GB 32 D1
Braga P 148 A1
Bragança P 149 A3
Brăila RO 17 C7
Braine F 91 B3
Braine-le-Comte B 79 B4
Braintree GB 45 B4
Braives B 79 B5
Brake D 72 A1
Brakel B 79 B3
Brakel D 81 A5
Bräkne-Hoby S 63 B3
Brålanda S 54 B3
Bralin PL 86 A1
Brallo di Pregola I 120 C2
Bram F 146 A3
Bramafan F 132 B2
Bramberg am Wildkogel A 109 B3
Bramdrupdam DK 59 C2
Bramming DK 59 C1
Brampton GB 37 B4
Bramsche D 71 B4
Branca I 136 B1
Brancaleone Marina I 175 D2
Brancaster GB 41 C4
Brand, *Nieder Östereich* A 96 C3
Brand, *Vorarlberg* A 107 B4
Brand-Erbisdorf D 83 B5
Brandbu N 48 B2
Brande DK 59 C2
Brande-Hornerkirchen D 64 C2
Brandenberg A 108 B2
Brandenburg D 73 B5
Brandis D 83 A4
Brando F 180 A2
Brandomil E 140 A2
Brandon GB 45 A4
Brandshagen D 66 B2
Brandval N 49 B4
Brandýs nad Labem CZ 84 B2
Branice PL 98 A1
Braničevo SRB 127 C3
Braniewo PL 69 A4
Branik SLO 122 B2
Brankovina SRB 127 C1
Branky CZ 98 B1
Branne F 128 B2
Brannenburg-Degerndorf D 108 B3
Brantôme F 115 C4
Branzi I 120 A2
Bras d'Asse F 132 B2
Braskereidfoss N 48 B3
Braslaw BY 13 A7
Braşov RO 17 C6
Brasparts F 100 A2
Brassac, *Charente* F 115 C3
Brassac, *Tarn* F 130 B1
Brassac-les-Mines F 116 B3
Brasschaat B 79 A4
Brastad S 54 B2
Břasy CZ 96 B1
Brąszewice PL 86 A2
Bratislava SK 111 A4
Brattfors S 55 A5
Brattvåg N 198 C3
Bratunac BIH 127 C1
Braubach D 81 B3
Braunau A 95 C5
Braunfels D 81 B4
Braunlage D 82 A2
Braunsbedra D 83 A3
Braunschweig D 73 B3
Bray IRL 30 A2
Bray Dunes F 78 A2
Bray-sur-Seine F 90 C3
Bray-sur-Somme F 90 B2
Brazatortas E 157 B3
Brazey-en-Plaine F 105 B4
Brbinj HR 137 A4
Brčko BIH 125 C4
Brdani SRB 127 D2
Brdów PL 76 B3
Brea de Tajo E 151 B4
Brécey F 88 B2
Brechen D 81 B4
Brechin GB 35 B5
Brecht B 79 A4
Brecketfeld D 80 A3
Břeclav CZ 97 C4
Brecon GB 39 C3
Brécy F 103 B4
Breda E 147 C3
Breda NL 79 A4
Bredaryd S 60 B3
Bredbyn S 200 C4
Breddin D 73 B5
Bredebro DK 64 A1
Bredelar D 81 A4
Bredenfelde D 74 A2
Bredsjö S 50 C1
Bredstedt D 64 B1
Bredsten DK 59 C2
Bredträsk S 200 C4
Bredviken S 195 D5
Bree B 80 A1
Bregana HR 123 B4
Breganze I 121 B4
Bregenz A 107 B4
Bréhal F 88 B2
Brehna D 83 A4
Breidenbach F 93 B3
Breiðdalsvík IS 191 C11
Breil-sur-Roya F 133 B3
Breisach D 106 A2
Breitenbach CH 106 B2
Breitenbach D 81 B5
Breitenberg D 96 C1
Breitenfelde D 73 A3
Breitengussbach D 94 B2
Breivikbotn N 192 B6
Brejning DK 59 C2
Brekke N 46 A2
Brekken N 199 C8
Brekkestø N 53 B4
Brekkvasselv N 199 A10
Brekstad N 198 B6
Breland N 53 B3
Brem-sur-Mer F 114 B2
Bremanger N 198 D1
Bremen D 72 A1
Bremerhaven D 72 A1
Bremervörde D 72 A2
Bremgarten CH 106 B3
Bremsnes N 198 B4
Brenderup DK 59 C2
Brenes E 162 A2
Brengova SLO 110 C2
Brenna PL 98 B2
Breno I 120 B3
Brénod F 118 A2
Brensbach D 93 B4
Brentwood GB 45 B4
Brescello I 121 C3
Bréscia I 120 B3
Breskens NL 79 A3
Bresles F 90 B2
Bresnica SRB 127 D2
Bressana I 120 B2
Bressanone I 108 C2
Bressuire F 102 C1
Brest BY 13 B5
Brest F 100 A1
Brest HR 122 B2
Brestač SRB 127 C1
Brestanica SLO 123 A4
Brestova HR 123 B3
Brestovac HR 125 B3
Bretenoux F 129 B4
Breteuil, *Eure* F 89 B4
Breteuil, *Oise* F 90 B2
Brétigny-sur-Orge F 90 C2
Bretten D 93 B4
Bretteville-sur-Laize F 89 A3
Brettheim D 94 B2
Breuil-Cervinia I 119 B4
Breukelen NL 70 B2
Brevik N 53 A5
Brevik, *Stockholm* S 57 A4
Brevik, *Västra Götaland* S 55 B5
Breza BIH 139 A4
Brežice SLO 123 B4
Bréziers F 132 A2
Breznica HR 124 A2
Breznica Našička HR 125 B4
Březnice CZ 96 B1
Brezno SK 99 C3
Brezolles F 89 B5
Březová nad Svitavou CZ 97 B4
Brezová pod Bradlom SK 98 C1
Brezovica SK 99 B4
Brezovica SLO 123 A3
Brezovo Polje Selo BIH 125 C4
Briançon F 118 C3
Brianconnet F 132 B2
Briare F 103 B4
Briatexte F 129 C4
Briático I 175 C2
Briaucourt F 105 A4
Bribir HR 123 B3
Bricquebec F 88 A2
Bridge of Cally GB 35 B4
Bridge of Don GB 33 D4
Bridge of Earn GB 35 B4
Bridge of Orchy GB 34 B3
Bridgend, *Argyll & Bute* GB 34 C1
Bridgend, *Bridgend* GB 39 C3
Bridgnorth GB 39 B4
Bridgwater GB 43 A4
Břidličná CZ 98 B1
Bridlington GB 41 A3
Bridport GB 43 B4
Brie-Comte-Robert F 90 C2
Briec F 100 A1
Brienne-le-Château F 91 C4
Brienon-sur-Armançon F 104 B2
Brienz CH 106 C3
Brienza I 172 B1
Briesen D 74 B3
Brieskow Finkenheerd D 74 B3
Brietlingen D 72 A3
Brieva de Cameros E 143 B4
Briey F 92 B1
Brig CH 119 A5
Brigg GB 40 B3
Brighouse GB 40 B2
Brightlingsea GB 45 B5
Brighton GB 44 C3
Brignogan-Plage F 100 A1
Brignoles F 132 B2
Brigstock GB 40 C3
Brihuega E 151 B5
Brijuni HR 122 C2
Brillon-en-Barrois F 91 C5
Brilon D 81 A4
Brimnes N 46 B3
Brinches P 160 A2
Bríndisi I 173 B3
Brinje HR 123 B4
Brinon-sur-Beuvron F 104 B2
Brinon-sur-Sauldre F 103 B4
Brinyan GB 33 B3
Brión E 140 B2
Briones E 143 B4
Brionne F 89 A4
Brioude F 117 B3
Brioux-sur-Boutonne F 115 B3
Briouze F 89 B3
Briscous F 144 A2
Brisighella I 135 A4
Brissac-Quincé F 102 B1
Brissago CH 120 A1
Bristol GB 43 A4
Brive-la-Gaillarde F 129 A4
Briviesca E 143 B3
Brixham GB 43 B3
Brixlegg A 108 B2
Brjánslækur IS 190 B2
Brka BIH 125 C4
Brnaze HR 138 B2
Brněnec CZ 97 B4
Brno CZ 97 B4
Bro S 57 A3
Broad Haven GB 39 C1
Broadclyst GB 43 B3
Broadford GB 31 B3
Broadford IRL 28 B3
Broadstairs GB 45 B5
Broadstone GB 43 B4
Broadway GB 44 A2
Broager DK 64 B2
Broaryd S 60 B3
Broby S 61 C4
Brobyværk DK 59 C3
Bročanac BIH 138 B3
Brocas F 128 B2
Brock D 71 B4
Brockel D 72 A2
Brockenhurst GB 44 C2
Broczyno PL 75 A5
Brod MK 182 B3
Brod na Kupi HR 123 B3
Brodalen S 54 B2
Broddbo S 50 C3
Brodek u Přerova CZ 98 B1
Broden-bach D 80 B3
Brodick GB 34 C2
Brodnica PL 69 B4
Brodnica Graniczna PL 68 A3
Brodowe Łąki PL 77 A6
Brody, *Lubuskie* PL 75 B4
Brody, *Lubuskie* PL 84 A2
Brody, *Mazowieckie* PL 77 B5
Brody UA 13 C6
Broglie F 89 B4
Brójce PL 75 B4
Brokind S 56 B1
Brolo I 177 A3
Brome D 73 B3
Bromley GB 45 B4
Bromölla S 63 B2
Bromont-Lamothe F 116 B2
Brömsebro S 63 B3
Bromsgrove GB 44 A1
Bromyard GB 39 B4
Bronchales E 152 B2
Bronco E 149 B3
Brønderslev DK 58 A2
Broni I 120 B2
Brønnøysund N 195 E3
Brøns DK 59 C1
Bronte I 177 B3
Bronzani Mejdan BIH 124 C2
Bronzolo I 121 A4
Broons F 101 A3
Broquies F 130 A1
Brora GB 32 C3
Brørup DK 59 C2
Brösarp S 63 C2
Brostrud N 47 B5
Brotas P 154 C2
Brötjärna S 50 B2
Broto E 145 B3
Brottby S 57 A4
Brøttum N 48 A2
Brou F 103 A3
Brouage F 114 C2
Brough GB 37 B4
Broughshane GB 27 B4
Broughton GB 35 C4
Broughton-in-Furness GB 36 B3
Broumov CZ 85 B4
Broût-Vernet F 116 A3
Brouvelieures F 106 A1
Brouwershaven NL 79 A3
Brovary UA 13 C9
Brovst DK 58 A2
Brownhills GB 40 C2
Brozas E 155 B4
Brozzo I 120 B3
Brtnice CZ 97 B3
Brtonigla HR 122 B2
Bruay-la-Buissière F 78 B2
Bruchhausen-Vilsen D 72 B2
Bruchsal D 93 B4
Bruck, *Bayern* D 95 B4
Brück, *Brandenburg* D 74 B1
Bruck an der Grossglocknerstrasse A 109 B3
Bruck an der Leitha A 111 A3
Bruck an der Mur A 110 B2
Brückl A 110 C1
Bruckmühl D 108 B2
Brue-Auriac F 132 B1
Brüel D 65 C4
Bruen CH 107 C3
Bruère-Allichamps F 103 C4
Bruff IRL 29 B3
Bruflat N 47 B6
Brugg CH 106 B3
Brugge B 78 A3
Brüggen D 80 A2
Brühl D 80 B2
Bruinisse NL 79 A4
Brûlon F 102 B1
Brumano I 120 B2
Brumath F 93 C3
Brummen NL 70 B3
Brumov-Bylnice CZ 98 B2
Brumunddal N 48 B2
Brunau D 73 B4
Brunehamel F 91 B4
Brünen D 80 A2
Brunete E 151 B3
Brunflo S 199 B11
Brunico I 108 C2
Brunkeberg N 53 A4
Brunn D 74 A2
Brunnen CH 107 C3
Brunsbüttel D 64 C2
Brunssum NL 80 B1
Bruntál CZ 98 B1
Brušane HR 137 A4
Brusasco I 119 B5
Brusio CH 120 A3
Brusno SK 99 C3
Brusque F 130 B1
Brussels = Bruxelles B 79 B4
Brusson I 119 B4
Brüssow D 74 A3
Brusy PL 68 B2
Bruton GB 43 A4
Bruvno HR 138 A1
Bruvoll N 48 B3
Bruxelles = Brussels B 79 B4
Bruyères F 106 A1
Bruz F 101 A4
Bruzaholm S 62 A3
Brwinów PL 77 B5
Brynamman GB 39 C3
Bryncrug GB 39 B2
Bryne N 52 B1
Brynmawr GB 39 C3
Bryrup DK 59 B2
Brzeg PL 85 B5
Brzeg Dolny PL 85 A4
Brześć Kujawski PL 76 B3
Brzesko PL 99 B4
Brzeszcze PL 99 B3
Brzezie PL 68 B1
Brzeziny, *Łódzkie* PL 87 A3
Brzeziny, *Wielkopolskie* PL 86 A2
Brzeźnica PL 84 A3
Brzežnica Nowa PL 86 A3
Brzeźno PL 75 A4
Brzotin SK 99 C4
Brzozie Lubawskie PL 69 B4
Bua S 60 B2
Buarcos P 148 B1
Buaveg N 52 A1
Bubbio I 119 C5
Bubry F 100 B2
Buca TR 188 A2
Bucak TR 189 B5
Bučany SK 98 C1
Buccheri I 177 B3
Buccino I 172 B1
Bucelas P 154 C1
Buch, *Bayern* D 94 C2
Buch, *Bayern* D 95 C4
Buchach UA 13 D6
Bucharest = Bucureşti RO 17 C7
Buchbach D 95 C4
Buchboden A 107 B4
Buchen, *Baden-Württemberg* D 94 B1
Büchen, *Schleswig-Holstein* D 73 A3
Buchenberg D 107 B5
Buchères F 104 A3
Buchholz D 72 A2
Buchloe D 108 A1
Buchlovice CZ 98 B1
Buchlyvie GB 34 B3
Bucholz D 73 A5
Buchs CH 107 B4
Buchy F 89 A5
Bückeburg D 72 B2
Buckfastleigh GB 42 B3
Buckhaven GB 35 B4
Buckie GB 33 D4
Buckingham GB 44 A3
Buckley GB 38 A3
Bückwitz D 73 B5
Bučovice CZ 97 B5
Bucsa H 113 B5
Bucureşti = Bucharest RO 17 C7
Bucy-lés-Pierreport F 91 B3
Buczek PL 86 A3
Bud N 198 C3
Budakalasz H 112 B3
Budakeszi H 112 B2
Budal N 199 C7
Budaörs H 112 B2
Budapest H 112 B3
Budča SK 99 C3
Buddusò I 178 B3
Bude GB 42 B2
Budeč CZ 97 B3
Büdelsdorf D 64 B2
Budens P 160 B1
Búðardalur IS 190 B4
Budia E 151 B5
Budimlić-Japra BIH 124 C2
Büdingen D 81 B5
Budinšćina HR 124 A2
Budišov CZ 98 B1
Budleigh Salterton GB 43 B3
Budmerice SK 98 C1
Budoni I 178 B3
Búdrio I 135 A4
Budva CG 16 D3
Budyně nad Ohří CZ 84 B2
Budziszewice PL 87 A3
Budzyń PL 76 B1
Bue N 52 B1
Bueña E 152 B2
Buenache de Alarcón E 158 B1
Buenache de la Sierra E 152 B2
Buenaventura E 150 B3
Buenavista de Valdavia E 142 B2
Buendia E 151 B5
Bueu E 140 B2
Buezo E 143 B3
Bugac H 112 C3
Bugarra E 159 B3
Bugeat F 116 B1
Buggerru I 179 C2
Bugojno BIH 138 A3
Bugøyfjord N 193 C13
Bugøynes N 193 C13
Bugyi H 112 B3
Buharkent TR 188 B3
Bühl, *Baden-Württemberg* D 93 C4
Bühl, *Bayern* D 107 B5
Bühlertal D 93 C4
Bühlertann D 94 B1
Buia I 122 A2
Builth Wells GB 39 B3
Buin N 47 B6
Buis-les-Baronnies F 131 A4
Buitenpost NL 70 A3
Buitrago del Lozoya E 151 B4
Bujalance E 157 C3
Bujaraloz E 153 A3
Buje HR 122 B2
Bujedo E 143 B3
Bük H 111 B3
Buk PL 75 B5
Bükkösd H 125 A3
Bükkzsérc H 113 B4
Bukovci SLO 124 A1
Bukowiec PL 75 B5
Bukowina Tatrzańska PL 99 B4
Bukownica PL 86 A2
Bukowno PL 86 B3
Bülach CH 107 B3
Búland IS 191 D7
Buldan TR 188 A3
Bulgnéville F 105 A4
Bulgurca TR 188 A2
Bülkau D 64 C1
Bulken N 46 B3
Bulkowo PL 77 B5
Bullas E 164 A3
Bulle CH 106 C2
Büllingen B 80 B2
Bullmark S 200 B6
Bulqizë AL 182 B2
Buna BIH 139 B3
Bunahowen IRL 26 B1
Bunbeg IRL 26 A2
Bunclody IRL 30 B2
Buncrana IRL 27 A3
Bunde, *Niedersachsen* D 71 A4
Bünde, *Nordrhein-Westfalen* D 72 B1
Bundoran IRL 26 B2
Bunessan GB 34 B1
Bungay GB 45 A5
Bunge S 57 C5
Bunić HR 123 C4
Bunmahon IRL 30 B1
Bunnyconnellan IRL 26 B1
Buño E 140 A2
Buñol E 159 B3
Bunratty IRL 29 B3
Bunsbeek B 79 B4
Buñuel E 144 C2
Bunyola E 166 B2
Buonabitácolo I 172 B1
Buonalbergo I 170 B2
Buonconvento I 135 B4
Buonvicino I 174 B1
Burano I 122 B1
Burbach D 81 B4
Burcei I 179 C3
Burdons-sur-Rognon F 105 A4
Burdur TR 189 B5
Bureå S 2 D7
Burela E 141 A3
Büren D 81 A4
Büren an der Aare CH 106 B2
Burford GB 44 B2
Burg, *Cottbus* D 84 A2
Burg, *Magdeburg* D 73 B4
Burg, *Schleswig-Holstein* D 64 C2
Burg auf Fehmarn D 65 B4
Burg Stargard D 74 A2
Burgas BG 17 D7
Burgau A 111 B3
Burgau D 94 C2
Burgau P 160 B1
Burgbernheim D 94 B2
Burgdorf CH 106 B2
Burgdorf D 72 B3
Burgebrach D 94 B2
Bürgel D 83 B3
Burgess Hill GB 44 C3
Burgh le Marsh GB 41 B4
Burghaslach D 94 B2
Burghausen D 109 A3
Burghead GB 32 D3
Burgheim D 94 C3
Búrgio I 176 B2
Burgkirchen D 109 A3
Burgkunstadt D 82 B3
Burglengenfeld D 95 B4
Burgo P 148 B1
Burgoberbach D 94 B2
Burgohondo E 150 B3
Burgos E 143 B3
Burgsinn D 82 B1
Burgstädt D 83 B4
Burgstall D 73 B4
Burgsvik S 57 C4
Burgui E 144 B3
Burguillos E 162 A2
Burguillos de Toledo E 151 C4
Burguillos del Cerro E 155 C4
Burhaniye TR 186 C1
Burhave D 71 A5
Burie F 114 C3
Burjassot E 159 B3
Burk D 94 B2
Burkhardtsdorf D 83 B4
Burlada E 144 B2
Burladingen D 107 A4

Burlage D 71 A4
Burness GB 33 B4
Burnham GB 44 B3
Burnham Market GB 41 C4
Burnham-on-Crouch GB 45 B4
Burnham-on-Sea GB 43 A4
Burniston GB 40 A3
Burnley GB 40 B1
Burntisland GB 35 B4
Burón E 142 A1
Buronzo I 119 B5
Burovac SRB 127 C3
Burow D 74 A2
Burravoe GB 33 A5
Burrel AL 182 B2
Burret F 146 B2
Burriana E 159 B3
Burry Port GB 39 C2
Bürs A 107 B4
Bursa TR 186 B4
Burseryd S 60 B3
Bürstadt D 93 B4
Burton GB 37 B4
Burton Agnes GB 41 A3
Burton Bradstock GB 43 B4
Burton Latimer GB 44 A3
Burton upon Stather GB 40 B3
Burton upon Trent GB 40 C2
Burträsk S 200 B6
Burujón E 151 C3
Burwell GB 45 A4
Burwick GB 33 C4
Bury GB 40 B1
Bury St. Edmunds GB 45 A4
Burzenin PL 86 A2
Busachi I 179 B2
Busalla I 134 A1
Busana I 134 A3
Busano I 119 B4
Busca I 133 A3
Busch D 73 B4
Buševec HR 124 B2
Bushat AL 182 B1
Bushey GB 44 B3
Bushmills GB 27 A4
Bušince SK 112 A3
Buskhyttan S 56 B2
Busko-Zdrój PL 87 B4
Busot E 159 C3
Busovača BIH 139 A3
Busquistar E 163 B4
Bussang F 106 B1
Busseto I 120 C3
Bussière-Badil F 115 C4
Bussière-Poitevine F 115 B4
Bussolengo I 121 B3
Bussoleno I 119 B4
Bussum NL 70 B2
Busto Arsízio I 120 B1
Büsum D 64 B1
Butera I 177 B3
Butgenbach B 80 B2
Butler's Bridge IRL 27 B3
Butryny PL 77 A5
Bütschwil CH 107 B4
Buttermere GB 36 B3
Buttevant IRL 29 B3
Buttle S 57 C4
Buttstädt D 82 A3
Butzbach D 81 B4
Bützfleth D 72 A2
Bützow D 65 C4
Buxières-les-Mines F 104 C1
Buxtehude D 72 A2
Buxton GB 40 B2
Buxy F 104 C3
Büyükçekmece TR 186 A3
Büyükkariştiran TR 186 A2
Büyükorhan TR 186 C3
Buzançais F 103 C3
Buzancy F 91 B4
Buzău RO 17 C7
Buzet HR 122 B2
Buziaş RO 126 B3
Buzsák H 111 C4
Buzy F 145 A3
By S 50 B3
Byala BG 17 D6
Byaroza BY 13 B6
Byczyna PL 86 A2
Bydalen S 199 B10
Bydgoszcz PL 76 A3
Bygdin N 47 A5
Bygdsiljum S 200 B6
Bygland N 53 B3
Byglandsfjord N 53 B3
Bygstad N 46 A2
Bykhaw BY 13 B9
Bykle N 52 A3
Bylderup-Bov DK 64 B2
Byrkjedal N 52 B2
Byrkjelo N 198 D3
Byrum DK 58 A3
Byšice CZ 84 B2
Byske S 2 D7
Býškovice CZ 98 B1
Bysław PL 76 A2
Bystré CZ 97 B4
Bystrice, *Středočeský* CZ 98 B2
Bystřice, *Středočeský* CZ 96 B2
Bystřice n Pernštejnem CZ 97 B4
Bystřice pod Hostýnem CZ 98 B1
Bystrzyca Kłodzka PL 85 B4
Bytča SK 98 B2
Bytnica PL 75 B4
Bytom PL 86 B2
Bytom Odrzański PL 85 A3
Bytów PL 68 A2
Byxelkrok S 62 A5
Bzenec CZ 98 C1
Bzince SK 98 C1

C

Cabacos P 154 B2
Cabaj-Čápor SK 98 C2
Cabana E 140 A2
Cabanac-et-Villagrains F 128 B2
Cabañaquinta E 142 A1
Cabanas P 160 B2
Cabañas de Yepes E 151 C4
Cabañas del Castillo E 156 A2
Cabanelles E 147 B3
Cabanes E 153 B4
Cabanillas E 144 B2
Čabar HR 123 B3
Cabasse F 132 B2
Cabdella E 146 B2
Cabeceiras de Basto P 148 A1
Cabeço de Vide P 155 B3
Cabella Ligure I 120 C2
Cabeza del Buey E 156 B2
Cabeza la Vaca E 161 A3
Cabezamesada E 151 C4
Cabezarados E 157 B3
Cabezarrubias del Puerto E 157 B3
Cabezas del Villar E 150 B2
Cabezas Rubias E 161 B2
Cabezón E 142 C2
Cabezón de la Sal E 142 A2
Cabezón de Liébana E 142 A2
Cabezuela E 151 A4
Cabezuela del Valle E 149 B4
Cabo de Gata E 164 C2
Cabo de Palos E 165 B4
Cabolafuenta E 152 A1
Cabourg F 89 A3
Cabra E 163 A3
Cabra P 148 B2
Cabra del Santo Cristo E 163 A4
Cabrach GB 32 D3
Cábras I 179 C2
Cabreiro P 140 C2
Cabreiros E 140 A3
Cabrejas E 152 B1
Cabrela P 154 C2
Cabrillas E 149 B3
Cabuna HR 125 B3
Cacabelos E 141 B4
Čačak SRB 127 D2
Cáccamo I 176 B2
Caccuri I 174 B2
Cacela P 160 B2
Cacém P 154 C1
Cáceres E 155 B4
Cachafeiro E 140 B2
Cachopo P 160 B2
Čachtice SK 98 C1
Cacin E 163 A4
Čačinci HR 125 B3
Cadafais P 154 C1
Cadalen F 129 C5
Cadalso E 149 B3
Cadaqués E 147 B4
Cadaval P 154 B1
Cadavedo E 141 A4
Čadavica BIH 138 A2
Čadca SK 98 B2
Cadéac F 145 B4
Cadelbosco di Sopra I 121 C3
Cadenazzo CH 120 A1
Cadenberge D 64 C2
Cadenet F 131 B4
Cadeuil F 114 C3
Cádiar E 164 C1
Cadillac F 128 B2
Cádiz E 162 B1
Čadjavica HR 125 B3
Cadouin F 129 B3
Cadours F 129 C4
Cadrete E 152 A3
Caen F 89 A3
Caerleon GB 39 C4
Caernarfon GB 38 A2
Caerphilly GB 39 C3
Caersws GB 39 B3
Cafede P 155 B3
Çağa TR 187 B7
Caggiano I 172 B1
Cagli I 136 B1
Cágliari I 179 C3
Čaglin HR 125 B3
Cagnano Varano I 171 B3
Cagnes-sur-Mer F 132 B3
Caher IRL 29 B4
Caherciveen IRL 29 C1
Caherdaniel IRL 29 C1
Cahors F 129 B4
Cahul MD 17 C8
Caiazzo I 170 B2
Caion E 140 A2
Cairndow GB 34 B3
Cairnryan GB 36 B1
Cairo Montenotte I 133 A4
Caister-on-Sea GB 41 C5
Caistor GB 41 B3
Caivano I 170 C2
Cajarc F 129 B4
Čajniče BIH 139 B5
Çakırlar TR 189 C5
Çakmak TR 187 C6
Čakovec HR 124 A2
Çal TR 189 A4
Cala E 161 B3
Cala d'Or E 167 B3
Cala Galdana E 167 B3
Cala Gonone I 178 B3
Cala Llonga E 166 C1
Cala Millor E 167 B3
Cala Morell E 167 A3
Cala Ratjada E 167 B3
Calabritto I 172 B1
Calaceite E 153 B4
Calacuccia F 180 A2
Calaf E 147 C2
Calafat RO 17 C5
Calafell E 147 C2
Calahonda, *Granada* E 163 B4
Calahonda, *Málaga* E 163 B3
Calahorra E 144 B2
Calais F 78 B1
Calalzo di Cadore I 109 C3
Calamocha E 152 B2
Calamonte E 155 C4
Calanais GB 31 A2
Calañas E 161 B3
Calanda E 153 B3
Calangiánus I 178 B3
Călăraşi RO 17 C7
Calascibetta I 177 B3
Calasetta I 179 C2
Calasparra E 164 A3
Calatafimi I 176 B1
Calatayud E 152 A2
Calatorao E 152 A2
Calau D 84 A1
Calbe D 73 C4
Calcena E 152 A2
Calcinelli I 136 B1
Calco I 120 B2
Caldaro sulla strada del Vino I 121 A4
Caldarola I 136 B2
Caldas da Rainha P 154 B1
Caldas de Boì E 145 B4
Caldas de Malavella E 147 C3
Caldas de Reis E 140 B2
Caldas de San Jorge P 148 B1
Caldas de Vizela P 148 A1
Caldaso de los Vidrios E 150 B3
Caldbeck GB 36 B3
Caldearenas E 145 B3
Caldelas P 148 A1
Calders E 147 C2
Caldes de Montbui E 147 C3
Caldicot GB 39 C4
Caldirola I 120 C2
Caledon GB 27 B4
Calella, *Barcelona* E 147 C3
Calella, *Girona* E 147 C4
Calenzana F 180 A1
Calera de León E 161 A3
Calera y Chozas E 150 C3
Caleruega E 143 C3
Caleruela E 150 C2
Cales de Mallorca E 167 B3
Calestano I 134 A3
Calfsound GB 33 B4
Calgary GB 34 B1
Calimera I 173 B4
Calitri I 172 B1
Calizzano I 133 A4
Callac F 100 A2
Callan IRL 30 B1
Callander GB 35 B3
Callas F 132 B2
Calliano, *Piemonte* I 119 B5
Calliano, *Trentino Alto Adige* I 121 B4
Callington GB 42 B2
Callosa de Ensarriá E 159 C3
Callosa de Segura E 165 A4
Callús E 147 C2
Čalma SRB 127 B1
Calmbach D 93 C4
Calne GB 43 A5
Calolziocorte I 120 B2
Calonge E 147 C4
Čalovec SK 112 B1
Calpe E 159 C4
Caltabellotta I 176 B2
Caltagirone I 177 B3
Caltanissetta I 177 B3
Caltavuturo I 176 B2
Çaltılıbük TR 186 C3
Caltojar E 151 A5
Caluire-et-Cuire F 117 B4
Caluso I 119 B4
Calvello I 172 B1
Calvi F 180 A1
Calviá E 166 B2
Calvinet F 116 C2
Calvisson F 131 B3
Calvörde D 73 B4
Calw D 93 C4
Calzada de Calatrava E 157 B4
Calzada de Valdunciel E 150 A2
Calzadilla de los Barros E 155 C4
Cam GB 43 A4
Camaiore I 134 B3
Camarasa E 145 C4
Camarena E 151 B3
Camarès F 130 B1
Camaret-sur-Aigues F 131 A3
Camaret-sur-Mer F 100 A1
Camarillas E 153 B3
Camariñas E 140 A1
Camarma E 151 B4
Camarzana de Tera E 141 B4
Camas E 162 A1
Camastra I 176 B2
Cambados E 140 B2
Cambarinho P 148 B1
Camberley GB 44 B3
Cambil E 163 A4
Cambligeu F 78 B2
Cambo-les-Bains F 144 A2
Camborne GB 42 B1
Cambrai F 78 B3
Cambre E 140 A2
Cambridge GB 45 A4
Cambrils E 147 C2
Cambs D 65 C4
Camburg D 83 A3
Camden GB 44 B3
Cameleño E 142 A2
Camelford GB 42 B2
Çameli TR 189 B4
Camelle E 140 A1
Camerano I 136 B2
Camerino I 136 B2
Camerota I 172 B1
Camigliatello Silano I 174 B2
Caminha P 148 A1
Caminomorisco E 149 B3
Caminreal E 152 B2
Camisano Vicentino I 121 B4
Camlıdere TR 187 B7
Cammarata I 176 B2
Camogli I 134 A2
Camors F 100 B3
Camp IRL 29 B2
Campagna I 172 B1
Campagnano di Roma I 168 A2
Campagnático I 135 C4
Campan F 145 A4
Campana I 174 B2
Campanario E 156 B2
Campanillas E 163 B3
Campano E 162 B1
Campaspero E 151 A3
Campbeltown GB 34 C2
Campello E 165 A4
Campelos P 154 B1
Campi Bisénzio I 135 B4
Campi Salentina I 173 B4
Campico López E 165 B3
Campíglia Marittima I 134 B3
Campillo de Altobuey E 158 B2
Campillo de Aragón E 152 A2
Campillo de Arenas E 163 A4
Campillo de Llerena E 156 B2
Campillos E 162 A3
Câmpina RO 17 C6
Campli I 136 C2
Campo E 145 B4
Campo da Feira E 140 A3
Campo de Bacerros E 141 B3
Campo de Caso E 142 A1
Campo de Criptana E 157 A4
Campo Ligure I 133 A4
Campo Lugar E 156 A2
Campo Maior P 155 B3
Campo Molino I 133 A3
Campo Real E 151 B4
Campo Túres I 108 C2
Campobasso I 170 B2
Campobello di Licata I 176 B2
Campobello di Mazara I 176 B1
Campodársego I 121 B4
Campodolcino I 120 A2
Campofelice di Roccella I 176 B2
Campofiorito I 176 B2
Campofórmido I 122 A2
Campofranco I 176 B2
Campofrio E 161 B3
Campogalliano I 121 C3
Campolongo I 109 C3
Campomanes E 141 A5
Campomarino I 170 B3
Campomono F 180 B1
Camporeale I 176 B2
Camporeggiano I 136 B1
Camporrells E 145 C4
Camporrobles E 158 B2
Campos P 148 A2
Campos del Port E 167 B3
Camposa P 148 A1
Camposampiero I 121 B4
Camposanto I 121 C4
Camposines E 153 A4
Campotéjar E 163 A4
Campotosto I 169 A3
Camprodón E 147 B3
Campsegret F 129 B3
Camrose GB 39 C1
Camuñas E 157 A4
Çamyolu TR 189 C7
Çan TR 186 B2
Can Pastilla E 166 B2
C'an Picafort E 167 B3
Cana I 135 C4
Cañada del Hoyo E 158 B2
Cañada Rosal E 162 A2
Cañadajuncosa E 158 B1
Čanak HR 123 C4
Çanakkale TR 186 B1
Canal San Bovo I 121 A4
Canale I 119 C4
Canales, *Asturias* E 141 B5
Canales, *Castellón de la Plana* E 159 B3
Canals E 159 C3
Cañamares E 152 B1
Cañamero E 156 A2
Cañar E 163 B4
Cañate la Real E 162 B2
Cañaveral E 155 B4
Cañaveral de León E 161 A3
Cañaveras E 152 B1
Cañaveruelas E 151 B5
Canazei I 108 C2
Cancale F 88 B2
Cancellara I 172 B1
Cancello ed Arnone I 170 B2
Cancon F 129 B3
Canda E 141 B4
Candamil E 140 A3
Candanchu E 145 B3
Çandarlı TR 186 D1
Candas E 141 A5
Candasnos E 153 A4
Candé F 101 B4
Candela I 172 A1
Candelario E 150 B2
Candeleda E 150 B2
Cándia Lomellina I 120 B1
Candide Casamazzagno I 109 C3
Candin E 141 B4
Candosa P 148 B2
Canecas P 154 C1
Canelli I 119 C5
Canena E 157 B4
Canencia E 151 B4
Canero E 141 A4
Canet F 130 B2
Canet de Mar E 147 C3
Canet d'en Berenguer E 159 B3
Canet-Plage F 146 B4
Cañete E 158 A2
Cañete de las Torres E 163 A3
Canfranc E 145 B3
Cangas, *Lugo* E 141 A3
Cangas, *Pontevedra* E 140 B2
Cangas de Narcea E 141 A4
Cangas de Onís E 142 A1
Canha P 154 C2
Canhestros P 160 A1
Canicattì I 176 B2
Canicattini Bagni I 177 B4
Canicosa de la Sierra E 143 C3
Caniles E 164 B2
Canillas de Aceituno E 163 B3
Canino I 168 A1
Canisy F 88 A2
Cañizal E 150 A2
Cañizo E 142 C1
Canjáyar E 164 C2
Çankırı TR 23 A7
Cannai I 179 C2
Cannara I 136 B1
Cánnero Riviera I 120 A1
Cannes F 132 B3
Canneto, *Sicilia* I 177 A3
Canneto, *Toscana* I 135 B3
Canneto sull'Oglio I 120 B3
Cannich GB 32 D2
Cannóbio I 120 A1
Cannock GB 40 C1
Canonbie GB 36 A4
Canosa di Púglia I 171 B4
Cantalapiedra E 150 A2
Cantalejo E 151 A4
Cantalgallo E 161 A3
Cantalice I 169 A2
Cantalpino E 150 A2
Cantalupo in Sabina I 168 A2
Cantanhede P 148 B1
Cantavieja E 153 B3
Čantavir SRB 126 B1
Canterbury GB 45 B5
Cantiano I 136 B1
Cantillana E 162 A2
Cantiveros E 150 B3
Cantoria E 164 B2
Cantù I 120 B2
Canvey GB 45 B4
Cany-Barville F 89 A4
Canyet de Mar E 147 C3
Caol GB 34 B2
Cáorle I 122 B1
Caorso I 120 B2
Cap-de-Pin F 128 B2
Cap Ferret F 128 B1
Capáccio I 172 B1
Capaci I 176 A2
Capálbio I 168 A1
Capánnori I 134 B3
Caparde BIH 139 A4
Caparroso E 144 B2
Capbreton F 128 C1
Capdenac-Gare F 116 C2
Capdepera E 167 B3
Capel Curig GB 38 A3
Capellades E 147 C2
Capena I 168 A2
Capendu F 146 A3
Capestang F 130 B2
Capestrano I 169 A3
Capileira E 163 B4
Capinha P 148 B2
Ca'Pisani I 122 C1
Capistrello I 169 B3
Capizzi I 177 B3
Čaplje BIH 124 C2
Čapljina BIH 139 B3
Capo di Ponte I 120 A3
Caposile I 122 B1
Capoterra I 179 C2
Cappamore IRL 29 B3
Cappeln D 71 B5
Cappoquin IRL 29 B4
Capracotta I 169 B4
Capránica I 168 A2
Caprarola I 168 A2
Capretta I 135 C5
Capri I 170 C2
Capriati a Volturno I 170 B2
Caprino Veronese I 121 B3
Captieux F 128 B2
Cápua I 170 B2
Capurso I 173 A2
Capvern F 145 A4
Carabaña E 151 B4
Carabias E 151 A4
Caracal RO 17 C6
Caracenilla E 152 B1
Caráglio I 133 A3
Caraman F 146 A2
Caramánico Terme I 169 A4
Caranga E 141 A4
Caranguejeira P 154 B2
Caransebeş RO 16 C5
Carantec F 100 A2
Carapelle I 171 B3
Carasco I 134 A2
Carate Brianza I 120 B2
Caravaca de la Cruz E 164 A3
Caravággio I 120 B2
Carbajal E 163 B3
Carbajo E 155 B3
Carballeda E 140 B3
Carballeda de Avia E 140 B2
Carballo E 140 A2
Carbis Bay GB 42 B1
Carbon-Blanc F 128 B2

Carbonera de Frentes	E	143	C4
Carboneras	E	164	C3
Carboneras de Guadazaón	E	158	B2
Carbonero el Mayor	E	151	A3
Carboneros	E	157	B4
Carbónia	I	179	C2
Carbonin	I	108	C3
Carbonne	F	146	A2
Carbost, *Highland*	GB	31	B2
Carbost, *Highland*	GB	31	B2
Carcaboso	E	149	B3
Carcabuey	E	163	A3
Carcaixent	E	159	B3
Carcans	F	128	A1
Carcans-Plage	F	128	A1
Carção	P	149	A3
Carcar	E	144	B2
Cárcare	I	133	A4
Carcassonne	F	146	A3
Carcastillo	E	144	B2
Carcedo de Burgos	E	143	B3
Carcelén	E	159	B2
Carcès	F	132	B2
Carchelejo	E	163	A4
Çardak, *Çanakkale*	TR	186	B1
Çardak, *Denizli*	TR	189	B4
Cardedeu	E	147	C3
Cardeña	E	157	B3
Cardenete	E	158	B2
Cardeñosa	E	150	B3
Cardeto	I	175	C1
Cardiff	GB	39	C3
Cardigan	GB	39	B2
Cardona	E	147	C2
Cardosos	P	154	B2
Carei	RO	16	B5
Carentan	F	88	A2
Carentoir	F	101	B3
Careri	I	175	C2
Carevdar	HR	124	A2
Cargèse	F	180	A1
Carhaix-Plouguer	F	100	A2
Caria	P	148	B2
Cariati	I	174	B2
Carignan	F	91	B5
Carignano	I	119	C4
Cariñena	E	152	A2
Carini	I	176	A2
Cariño	E	140	A3
Carínola	I	170	B1
Carisbrooke	GB	44	C2
Carlabhagh	GB	31	A2
Carlepont	F	90	B3
Carlet	E	159	B3
Carlingford	IRL	27	B4
Carlisle	GB	36	B4
Carloforte	I	179	C2
Carlópoli	I	175	B2
Carlow	D	65	C3
Carlow	IRL	30	B2
Carlton	GB	40	C2
Carluke	GB	35	C4
Carmagnola	I	119	C4
Carmarthen	GB	39	C2
Carmaux	F	130	A1
Carmena	E	150	C3
Cármenes	E	142	B1
Carmine	I	133	A3
Carmona	E	162	A2
Carmonita	E	155	B4
Carmyllie	GB	35	B5
Carnac	F	100	B2
Carndonagh	IRL	27	A3
Carnew	IRL	30	B2
Carnforth	GB	37	B4
Cárnia	I	122	A2
Carnlough	GB	27	B5
Carno	GB	39	B3
Carnon Plage	F	131	B2
Carnota	E	140	B1
Carnoustie	GB	35	B5
Carnwath	GB	35	C4
Carolei	I	174	B2
Carolinensiel	D	71	A4
Carolles	F	88	B2
Carona	I	120	A2
Caronía	I	177	A3
Carovigno	I	173	B3
Carovilli	I	170	B2
Carpaneto Piacentino	I	120	C2
Carpegna	I	135	B5
Carpenédolo	I	121	B3
Carpentras	F	131	A4
Carpi	I	121	C3
Carpignano Sésia	I	119	B5
Carpineti	I	134	A3
Carpineto Romano	I	169	B3
Cărpiniş	RO	126	B2
Carpino	I	171	B3
Carpinone	I	170	B2
Carpio	E	150	A2
Carquefou	F	101	B4
Carqueiranne	F	132	B2
Carral	E	140	A2
Carranque	E	151	B4
Carrapichana	P	148	B2
Carrara	I	134	A3
Carraroe	IRL	28	A2
Carrascalejo	E	156	A2
Carrascosa del Campo	E	151	B5
Carratraca	E	162	B3
Carrazeda de Ansiães	P	148	A2
Carrazedo de Montenegro	P	148	A2
Carrbridge	GB	32	D3
Carregal do Sal	P	148	B1
Carreña	E	142	A2
Carrick	IRL	26	B2
Carrick-on-Shannon	IRL	26	C2
Carrick-on-Suir	IRL	30	B1
Carrickart	IRL	26	A3
Carrickfergus	GB	27	B5
Carrickmacross	IRL	27	C4
Carrigallen	IRL	27	C3
Carrión	E	161	B3
Carrión de Calatrava	E	157	A4
Carrión de los Condes	E	142	B2
Carrizo de la Ribera	E	141	B5
Carrizosa	E	157	B5
Carro	F	131	B4
Carrocera	E	142	B1
Carros	F	133	B3
Carrouge	CH	106	C1
Carrouges	F	89	B3
Carrù	I	133	A3
Carry-le-Rouet	F	131	B4
Carryduff	GB	27	B5
Carsóli	I	169	A3
Carsphairn	GB	36	A2
Cartagena	E	165	B4
Cártama	E	163	B3
Cartaxo	P	154	B2
Cartaya	E	161	B2
Carteret	F	88	A2
Cartes	E	142	A2
Carúnchio	I	170	B2
Carviçães	P	149	A3
Carvin	F	78	B2
Carvoeira	P	154	B1
Carvoeiro	P	160	B1
Casa Branca, *Portalegre*	P	154	C3
Casa Branca, *Setúbal*	P	154	C2
Casa Castalda	I	136	B1
Casa l'Abate	I	173	B4
Casabermeja	E	163	B3
Casacalenda	I	170	B2
Casaio	E	141	B4
Casàl di Principe	I	170	B2
Casalarreina	E	143	B4
Casalbordino	I	169	A4
Casalborgone	I	119	B4
Casalbuono	I	174	A1
Casalbuttano ed Uniti	I	120	B2
Casale Monferrato	I	119	B5
Casalécchio di Reno	I	135	A4
Casalina	I	136	C1
Casalmaggiore	I	121	C3
Casalnuovo Monterotaro	I	170	B3
Casaloldo	I	121	B3
Casalpusterlengo	I	120	B2
Casamássima	I	173	B2
Casamicciola Terme	I	170	C1
Casamozza	F	180	A2
Casar de Cáceres	E	155	B4
Casar de Palomero	E	149	B3
Casarabonela	E	162	B3
Casarano	I	173	B4
Casarejos	E	143	C3
Casares	E	162	B2
Casares de las Hurdes	E	149	B3
Casariche	E	163	A3
Casarrubios del Monte	E	151	B3
Casas de Don Pedro	E	156	A2
Casas de Fernando Alonso	E	158	B1
Casas de Haro	E	158	B1
Casas de Juan Gil	E	159	B2
Casas de Millán	E	155	B4
Casas de Reina	E	156	B2
Casas de Ves	E	159	B2
Casas del Juan Núñez	E	158	B2
Casas del Puerto	E	159	C2
Casas del Rio	E	159	B2
Casas-Ibáñez	E	158	B2
Casas Nuevas	E	164	B3
Casasimarro	E	158	B1
Casasola	E	150	B3
Casasola de Arión	E	150	A2
Casasuertes	E	142	A2
Casatejada	E	150	C2
Casavieja	E	150	B3
Casazza	I	120	B2
Cascais	P	154	C1
Cascante	E	144	C2
Cascante del Rio	E	152	B2
Cáscia	I	169	A3
Casciana Terme	I	134	B3
Cáscina	I	134	B3
Cáseda	E	144	B2
Casekow	D	74	A3
Casella	I	134	A2
Caselle Torinese	I	119	B4
Casemurate	I	135	A5
Casenove	I	136	C1
Caseres	E	153	A4
Caserío Benali	E	159	B3
Caserta	I	170	B2
Casével	P	160	B1
Cashel	IRL	29	B4
Casillas	E	150	B3
Casillas de Coria	E	155	B4
Casina	I	134	A3
Casinos	E	159	B3
Čáslav	CZ	97	B3
Cásola Valsénio	I	135	A4
Cásole d'Elsa	I	135	B4
Cásoli	I	169	A4
Casória	I	170	C2
Caspe	E	153	A3
Cassà de la Selva	E	147	C3
Cassagnas	F	130	A2
Cassagnes-Bégonhès	F	130	A1
Cassano allo Iónio	I	174	B2
Cassano d'Adda	I	120	B2
Cassano delle Murge	I	171	C4
Cassano Magnago	I	120	B1
Cassano Spinola	I	120	C1
Cassel	F	78	B2
Cassíbile	I	177	C4
Cassine	I	119	C5
Cassino	I	169	B3
Cassis	F	132	B1
Cassolnovo	I	120	B1
Cassuéjouls	F	116	C2
Častá	SK	98	C1
Castagnaro	I	121	B4
Castagneto Carducci	I	134	B3
Castagnola	CH	120	A1
Castalla	E	159	C3
Castañar de Ibor	E	156	A2
Castanheira de Pêra	P	154	A2
Cástano Primo	I	120	B1
Castasegna	CH	120	A2
Castéggio	I	120	B2
Casteição	P	148	B2
Castejón	E	144	B2
Castejón de Monegros	E	153	A3
Castejón de Sos	E	145	B4
Castejón de Valdejasa	E	144	C3
Castèl Baronia	I	172	A1
Castel Bolognese	I	135	A4
Castel d'Aiano	I	135	A3
Castel d'Ario	I	121	B3
Castel de Cabra	E	153	B3
Castél del Monte	I	169	A3
Castel del Piano	I	135	C4
Castel di Iúdica	I	177	B3
Castel di Rio	I	135	A4
Castèl di Sangro	I	169	B4
Castél di Tora	I	169	A2
Castèl Frentano	I	169	A4
Castel San Gimignano	I	135	B4
Castèl San Giovanni	I	120	B2
Castèl San Pietro Terme	I	135	A4
Castél Sant'Elia	I	168	A2
Castél Volturno	I	170	B1
Castelbuono	I	177	B3
Casteldáccia	I	176	A2
Casteldelfino	I	132	A3
Castelfidardo	I	136	B2
Castelfiorentino	I	135	B3
Castelforte	I	169	B3
Castelfranco Emília	I	121	C4
Castelfranco in Miscano	I	170	B3
Castelfranco Véneto	I	121	B4
Casteljaloux	F	128	B3
Castell Arquato	I	120	C2
Castell de Cabres	E	153	B4
Castell de Castells	E	159	C3
Castell de Ferro	E	163	B4
Castellabate	I	170	C2
Castellammare del Golfo	I	176	A1
Castellammare di Stábia	I	170	C2
Castellamonte	I	119	B4
Castellana Grotte	I	173	B3
Castellane	F	132	B2
Castellaneta	I	173	B2
Castellaneta Marina	I	173	B2
Castellar	E	157	B4
Castellar de la Frontera	E	162	B2
Castellar de la Ribera	E	147	B2
Castellar de Santiago	E	157	B4
Castellar del Vallés	E	147	C3
Castellarano	I	135	A3
Castell'Azzara	I	135	C4
Castellbell i Villar	E	147	C2
Castelldans	E	153	A4
Castelldefels	E	147	C2
Castelleone	I	120	B2
Castellet	E	147	C2
Castelletto di Brenzone	I	121	B3
Castellfollit de la Roca	E	147	B3
Castellfollit de Riubregos	E	147	C2
Castellfort	E	153	B3
Castellina in Chianti	I	135	B4
Castellina Marittima	I	134	B3
Castelló de Farfaña	E	145	C4
Castelló de la Plana	E	159	B3
Castello d'Empùries	E	147	B4
Castello di Fiemme	I	121	A4
Castello Tesino	I	121	A4
Castelloli	E	147	C2
Castellón de Rugat	E	159	C3
Castellote	E	153	B3
Castellterçol	E	147	C3
Castellúcchio	I	121	B3
Castellúccio de'Sáuri	I	171	B3
Castelluccio Inferiore	I	174	B1
Castelmassa	I	121	B4
Castelmáuro	I	170	B2
Castelmoron-sur-Lot	F	129	B3
Castelnau-de-Médoc	F	128	A2
Castelnau-de-Montmirail	F	129	C4
Castelnau-Magnoac	F	145	A4
Castelnau-Montratier	F	129	B4
Castelnaudary	F	146	A2
Castelnou	E	153	A3
Castelnovo ne'Monti	I	134	A3
Castelnuovo Berardenga	I	135	B4
Castelnuovo della Dáunia	I	170	B3
Castelnuovo di Garfagnana	I	134	A3
Castelnuovo di Val di Cécina	I	135	B3
Castelnuovo Don Bosco	I	119	B4
Castelnuovo Scrivia	I	120	C1
Castelo Branco, *Bragança*	P	149	A3
Castelo Branco, *Castelo Branco*	P	155	B3
Castelo de Paiva	P	148	A1
Castelo de Vide	P	155	B3
Castelo do Neiva	P	148	A1
Castelo Mendo	P	149	B3
Castelraimondo	I	136	B2
Castelsantángelo	I	136	C2
Castelsaraceno	I	174	A1
Castelsardo	I	178	B2
Castelsarrasin	F	129	B4
Castelserás	E	153	B3
Casteltérmini	I	176	B2
Castelvecchio Subéquo	I	169	A3
Castelvetrano	I	176	B1
Castenédolo	I	120	B3
Castets	F	128	C1
Castiádas	I	179	C3
Castiglion Fibocchi	I	135	B4
Castiglion Fiorentino	I	135	B4
Castiglioncello	I	134	B3
Castiglione	I	169	A3
Castiglione Chiavarese	I	134	A2
Castiglione d'Adda	I	120	B2
Castiglione dei Pepoli	I	135	A4
Castiglione del Lago	I	135	B5
Castiglione della Pescáia	I	135	C3
Castiglione delle Stiviere	I	121	B3
Castiglione di Sicilia	I	177	B4
Castiglione d'Órcia	I	135	B4
Castiglione Messer Marino	I	170	B2
Castiglione Messer Raimondo	I	169	A3
Castil de Peones	E	143	B3
Castilblanco	E	156	A2
Castilblanco de los Arroyos	E	161	B4
Castilfrío de la Sierra	E	144	C1
Castilgaleu	E	145	B4
Castilisar	E	144	B2
Castilleja	E	161	B3
Castillejar	E	164	B2
Castillejo de Martin Viejo	E	149	B3
Castillejo de Mesleón	E	151	A4
Castillejo de Robledo	E	151	A4
Castillo de Bayuela	E	150	B3
Castillo de Locubín	E	163	A4
Castillon-la-Bataille	F	128	B2
Castillon-Len-Couserans	F	146	B2
Castillonès	F	129	B3
Castillonroy	E	145	C4
Castilruiz	E	144	C1
Castione	CH	120	A2
Castions di Strada	I	122	B2
Castirla	F	180	A2
Castle Cary	GB	43	A4
Castle Douglas	GB	36	B3
Castlebar	IRL	28	A2
Castlebellingham	IRL	27	C4
Castleblaney	IRL	27	B4
Castlebridge	IRL	30	B2
Castlecomer	IRL	30	B1
Castlederg	GB	27	B3
Castledermot	IRL	30	B2
Castleford	GB	40	B2
Castleisland	IRL	29	B2
Castlemaine	IRL	29	B2
Castlemartyr	IRL	29	C3
Castlepollard	IRL	30	A1
Castlerea	IRL	28	A3
Castleton	GB	40	B2
Castletown, *Highland*	GB	32	C3
Castletown, *Isle of Man*	GB	36	B2
Castletown Bearhaven	IRL	29	C2
Castletownroche	IRL	29	B3
Castlewellan	GB	27	B5
Casto	I	120	B3
Castrejón	E	150	A2
Castrelo del Valle	E	141	B3
Castres	F	130	B1
Castricum	NL	70	B1
Castries	F	131	B2
Castrignano del Capo	I	173	C4
Castril	E	164	B2
Castrillo de Duero	E	151	A4
Castrillo de la Vega	E	143	C3
Castrillo de Onielo	E	142	C2
Castro	E	142	A2
Castro	I	173	B4
Castro-Caldelas	E	141	B3
Castro Daire	P	148	B2
Castro de Rey	E	141	A3
Castro dei Volsci	I	169	B3
Castro del Río	E	163	A3
Castro Laboreiro	P	140	B2
Castro Marim	P	160	B2
Castro-Urdiales	E	143	A3
Castro Verde	P	160	B1
Castrocabón	E	141	B5
Castrocaro Terme	I	135	A4
Castrocontrigo	E	141	B4
Castrofilippo	I	176	B2
Castrogonzaio	E	142	B1
Castrojeriz	E	142	B2
Castromonte	E	142	C1
Castromudarra	E	142	B1
Castronuevo	E	142	C1
Castronuño	E	150	A2
Castropol	E	141	A3
Castroreale	I	177	A4
Castroserracin	E	151	A4
Castroverde	E	141	A3
Castroverde de Campos	E	142	C1
Castroverde de Cerrato	E	142	C2
Castrovíllari	I	174	B2
Castuera	E	156	B2
Catadau	E	159	B3
Cataéggio	I	120	A2
Çatalca	TR	186	A3
Catallar	TR	189	C5
Çatalzeytin	TR	23	A8
Catánia	I	177	B4
Catanzaro	I	175	C2
Catanzaro Marina	I	175	C2
Catarroja	E	159	B3
Catarruchos	P	148	B1
Catcleugh	GB	37	A4
Catenanuova	I	177	B3
Caterham	GB	44	B3
Cati	E	153	B4
Čatići	BIH	139	A4
Catignano	I	169	A3
Catillon	F	91	A3
Catoira	E	140	B2
Caton	GB	37	B4
Catral	E	165	A4
Catterick	GB	37	B5
Cattólica	I	136	B1
Cattólica Eraclea	I	176	B2
Catton	GB	37	B4
Caudebec-en-Caux	F	89	A4
Caudete	E	159	C3
Caudete de las Fuentes	E	159	B2
Caudiel	E	159	B3
Caudiès-de-Fenouillèdes	F	146	B3
Caudry	F	91	A3
Caulkerbush	GB	36	B3
Caulnes	F	101	A3
Caulónia	I	175	C2
Caumont-l'Evente	F	88	A3
Caunes-Minervois	F	146	A3
Cauro	F	180	B1
Caussade	F	129	B4
Causse-de-la-Selle	F	130	B2
Cauterets	F	145	B3
Cava de Tirreni	I	170	C2
Cavaglia	I	119	B5
Cavaillon	F	131	B4
Cavalaire-sur-Mer	F	132	B2
Cavaleiro	P	160	B1
Cavalese	I	121	A4
Cavallermaggiore	I	119	C4
Cavallino	I	122	B1
Cavan	IRL	27	C3
Cavárzere	I	121	B5
Çavdarhisar	TR	187	C4
Çavdır	TR	189	B4
Cavernais	P	148	B2
Cavezzo	I	121	C4
Cavignac	F	128	A2
Čavle	HR	123	B3
Cavo	I	134	C3
Cavour	I	119	C4
Cawdor	GB	32	D3
Çay	TR	187	D6
Çaycuma	TR	187	A7
Cayeux-sur-Mer	F	78	B1
Çayırhan	TR	187	B6
Cayiralan	TR	23	B8
Caylus	F	129	B4
Cayres	F	117	C3
Cazalilla	E	157	C4
Cazalla de la Sierra	E	156	C2
Cazals	F	129	B4
Cazanuecos	E	142	B1
Cazaubon	F	128	C2
Cazaux	F	128	B1
Cazavet	F	146	A2
Cazères	F	146	A2
Cazin	BIH	124	C1
Cazis	CH	107	C4
Čazma	HR	124	B2
Cazo	E	142	A1
Cazorla	E	164	B2
Cazouls-lès-Béziers	F	130	B2
Cea, *León*	E	142	B1
Cea, *Orense*	E	140	B3
Ceánuri	E	143	A4
Ceauce	F	88	B3
Cebolla	E	150	C3
Čebovce	SK	112	A3
Cebreros	E	150	B3
Čečava	BIH	125	C3
Ceccano	I	169	B3
Cece	H	112	C2
Cecenowo	PL	68	A2
Čechtice	CZ	96	B3
Čechtín	CZ	97	B3
Cécina	I*	134	B3
Ceclavín	E	155	B4
Cedégolo	I	120	A3
Cedeira	E	140	A2
Cedillo	E	155	B3
Cedillo del Condado	E	151	B4
Cedrillas	E	153	B3
Cedynia	PL	74	B3
Cée	E	140	B1
Cefalù	I	177	A3
Céggia	I	122	B1
Cegléd	H	113	B3
Ceglédbercel	H	112	B3
Céglie Messápica	I	173	B3

Cehegín E 164 A3
Ceilhes-et-Rocozels F 130 B2
Ceinos de Campos E 142 B1
Ceira P 148 B1
Čejč CZ 97 C4
Cekcyn PL 76 A3
Cela BIH 124 C2
Čelákovice CZ 84 B2
Celano I 169 A3
Celanova E 140 B3
Celbridge IRL 30 A2
Čelebič BIH 138 B2
Celenza Valfortore I 170 B2
Čelić BIH 125 C4
Čelinac BIH 124 C3
Celje SLO 123 A4
Cella E 152 B2
Celldömölk H 111 B4
Celle D 72 B3
Celle Ligure I 133 A4
Celles B 79 B4
Celles-sur-Belle F 115 B3
Cellino San Marco I 173 B3
Celorico da Beira P 148 B2
Celorico de Basto P 148 A1
Çeltik TR 187 C6
Çeltikçi TR 189 B5
Cemaes GB 38 A2
Cembra I 121 A4
Čemerno BIH 139 B4
Cenad RO 126 A2
Cencenighe Agordino I 121 A4
Cenei RO 126 B2
Ceneselli I 121 B4
Cenicero E 143 B4
Cenicientos E 150 B3
Censeau F 105 C5
Čenta SRB 126 B2
Centallo I 133 A3
Centelles E 147 C3
Cento I 121 C4
Centúripe I 177 B3
Cepeda la Mora E 150 B2
Cépet F 129 C4
Čepin HR 125 B4
Čepinski Martinci HR 125 B4
Cepovan SLO 122 A2
Ceprano I 169 B3
Čeralije HR 125 B3
Cerami I 177 B3
Cerano I 120 B1
Cérans Foulletourte F 102 B2
Ceraso I 172 B1
Cerbaia I 135 B4
Cerbère F 146 B4
Cercadillo E 151 A5
Cercal, *Lisboa* P 154 B1
Cercal, *Setúbal* P 160 B1
Čerčany CZ 96 B2
Cerceda E 151 B4
Cercedilla E 151 B3
Cercemaggiore I 170 B2
Cercs E 147 B2
Cercy-la-Tour F 104 C2
Cerda I 176 B2
Cerdedo E 140 B2
Cerdeira P 149 B2
Cerdon F 103 B4
Cerea I 121 B4
Ceres GB 35 B5
Ceres I 119 B4
Cerese I 121 B3
Ceresole-Reale I 119 B4
Cereste F 132 B1
Céret F 146 B3
Cerezo de Abajo E 151 A4
Cerezo de Riotirón E 143 B3
Cerfontaine B 79 B4
Cergy F 90 B2
Cerignola I 171 B3
Cérilly F 103 C4
Cerisiers F 104 A2
Cerizay F 114 B3
Çerkeş TR 23 A7
Çerkezköy TR 186 A3
Cerkije SLO 123 A3
Cerknica SLO 123 B3
Cerkno SLO 122 A2
Cerkwica PL 67 B4
Cerna HR 125 B4
Černá Hora CZ 97 B4
Cernavodă RO 17 C8
Cernay F 106 B2
Cerne Abbas GB 43 B4
Cernégula E 143 B3
Cernik HR 124 B3
Cernóbbio I 120 B2
Černošin CZ 95 B4
Cernovice CZ 96 B2
Cérons F 128 B2
Cerovlje HR 123 B3
Cerovo SK 99 C3
Cerqueto I 135 C5
Cerralbo E 149 B3
Cerreto d'Esi I 136 B1
Cerreto Sannita I 170 B2
Cerrigydrudion GB 38 A3
Cërrik AL 182 B1
Cerro Muriano E 156 B3
Certaldo I 135 B4
Certosa di Pésio I 133 A3
Cerva P 148 A2
Cervaro I 169 B3
Cervatos de la Cueza E 142 B2
Červena Řečice CZ 97 B3
Červená-Skala SK 99 C4
Cervená Voda CZ 97 A4
Cerveny Kostelec CZ 85 B4
Cervera E 147 C2
Cervera de la Cañada E 152 A2
Cervera de Pisuerga E 142 B2
Cervera del Llano E 158 B1
Cervera del Río Alhama E 144 B2
Cervéteri I 168 B2
Cérvia I 135 A5
Cerviá de les Garriques E 147 C1
Cervignano del Friuli I 122 B2
Cervinara I 170 B2
Cervione F 180 A2
Cervo E 141 A3
Cervon F 104 B2
Cesana Torinese I 119 C3
Cesarica HR 137 A4
Cesarò I 177 B3
Cesena I 135 A5
Cesenático I 135 A5
Cēsis LV 8 D4
Česká Belá CZ 97 B3
Česká Kamenice CZ 84 B2
Česká Lípa CZ 84 B2
Česká Skalice CZ 85 B4
Česká Třebová CZ 97 B4
České Budějovice CZ 96 C2
České Velenice CZ 96 C2
Český Brod CZ 96 A2
Český Dub CZ 84 B2
Český Krumlov CZ 96 C2
Český Těšin CZ 98 B2
Češljeva Bara SRB 127 C3
Çeşme TR 188 A1
Cessenon F 130 B2
Cesson-Sévigné F 101 A4
Cestas F 128 B2
Čestobrodica SRB 127 D2
Cesuras E 140 A2
Cetin Grad HR 123 B4
Cetina E 152 A2
Cetinje CG 16 D3
Cetraro I 174 B1
Ceuti E 165 A3
Ceva I 133 A4
Cevico de la Torre E 142 C2
Cevico Navero E 142 C2
Cevins F 118 B3
Cévio CH 119 A5
Cevizli TR 189 B6
Cewice PL 68 A2
Ceylan TR 189 C4
Ceyrat F 116 B3
Ceyzériat F 118 A2
Chaam NL 79 A4
Chabanais F 115 C4
Chabeuil F 117 C5
Chabielice PL 86 A3
Chablis F 104 B2
Châbons F 118 B2
Chabówka PL 99 B3
Chabreloche F 117 B3
Chabris F 103 B3
Chagford GB 42 B3
Chagny F 105 C3
Chagoda RUS 9 C9
Chaherrero E 150 B3
Chailland F 88 B3
Chaillé-les-Marais F 114 B2
Chailles F 103 B3
Chailley F 104 A2
Chalabre F 146 B3
Chalais F 128 A3
Chalamont F 118 B2
Châlette-sur-Loing F 103 A4
Chalindrey F 105 B4
Challacombe GB 42 A3
Challans F 114 B2
Challes-les-Eaux F 118 B2
Chalmazel F 117 B3
Chalmoux F 104 C2
Chalon-sur-Saône F 105 C3
Chalonnes-sur-Loire F 102 B1
Châlons-en-Champagne F 91 C4
Chalupy PL 69 A3
Châlus F 115 C4
Cham CH 106 B3
Cham D 95 B4
Chamberet F 116 B1
Chambéry F 118 B2
Chambilly F 117 A4
Chambley F 92 B1
Chambly F 90 B2
Chambois F 89 B4
Chambon-sur-Lac F 116 B2
Chambon-sur-Voueize F 116 A2
Chambord F 103 B3
Chamborigaud F 131 A2
Chamboulive F 116 B1
Chamerau D 95 B4
Chamonix-Mont Blanc F 119 B3
Chamoux-sur-Gelon F 118 B3
Champagnac-le-Vieux F 117 B3
Champagney F 106 B1
Champagnole F 105 C4
Champagny-Mouton F 115 B4
Champaubert F 91 C3
Champdeniers-St. Denis F 114 B3
Champdieu F 117 B4
Champdôtre F 105 B4
Champeix F 116 B3
Champéry CH 119 A3
Champigne F 102 B1
Champignelles F 104 B2
Champigny-sur-Veude F 102 B2
Champlitte-et-le-Prelot F 105 B4
Champoluc I 119 B4
Champoly F 117 B3
Champorcher I 119 B4
Champrond-en-Gâtine F 89 B5
Champs-sur-Tarentaine F 116 B2
Champs-sur-Yonne F 104 B2
Champtoceaux F 101 B4
Chamrousse F 118 B2
Chamusca P 154 B2
Chanac F 130 A2
Chanaleilles F 117 C3
Chandler's Ford GB 44 C2
Chandra GR 185 D7
Chandrexa de Queixa E 141 B3
Chañe E 150 A3
Changy F 117 A3
Chania GR 185 D5
Channes F 104 B3
Chantada E 140 B3
Chantelle F 116 A3
Chantenay-St. Imbert F 104 C2
Chanteuges F 117 B3
Chantilly F 90 B2
Chantonnay F 114 B2
Chão de Codes P 154 B2
Chaource F 104 A3
Chapa E 140 B2
Chapareillan F 118 B2
Chapel en le Frith GB 40 B2
Chapelle Royale F 103 A3
Chapelle-St. Laurent F 102 C1
Charbonnat F 104 C3
Chard GB 43 B4
Charenton-du-Cher F 103 C4
Charlbury GB 44 B2
Charleroi B 79 B4
Charlestown IRL 26 C2
Charlestown of Aberlour GB 32 D3
Charleville IRL 29 B3
Charleville-Mézières F 91 B4
Charlieu F 117 A4
Charlottenberg S 49 C4
Charlton Kings GB 44 B1
Charly F 90 C3
Charmes F 92 C2
Charmes-sur-Rhône F 117 C4
Charmey CH 106 C2
Charminster GB 43 B4
Charmont-en-Beauce F 103 A4
Charny F 104 B2
Charolles F 117 A4
Chârost F 103 C4
Charquemont F 106 B1
Charrin F 104 C2
Charroux F 115 B4
Chartres F 90 C1
Charzykow PL 68 B2
Chasseneuil-sur-Bonnieure F 115 C4
Chassigny F 105 B4
Château-Arnoux F 132 A2
Château-Chinon F 104 B2
Château-d'Oex CH 106 C2
Château-d'Olonne F 114 B2
Château-du-Loir F 102 B2
Château-Gontier F 102 B1
Château-la-Vallière F 102 B2
Château-Landon F 103 A4
Château-l'Evêque F 129 A3
Château-Porcien F 91 B4
Château-Renault F 102 B2
Château-Salins F 92 C2
Château-Thierry F 91 B3
Châteaubernard F 115 C3
Châteaubourg F 101 A4
Châteaubriant F 101 B4
Châteaudun F 103 A3
Châteaugiron F 101 A4
Châteaulin F 100 A1
Châteaumeillant F 103 C4
Châteauneuf, *Nièvre* F 104 B2
Châteauneuf, *Saône-et-Loire* F 117 A4
Châteauneuf-de-Randon F 117 C3
Châteauneuf-d'Ille-et-Vilaine F 88 B2
Châteauneuf-du-Faou F 100 A2
Châteauneuf-du-Pape F 131 A3
Châteauneuf-en-Thymerais F 89 B5
Châteauneuf la-Forêt F 116 B1
Châteauneuf-le-Rouge F 132 B1
Châteauneuf-sur-Charente F 115 C3
Châteauneuf-sur-Cher F 103 C4
Châteauneuf-sur-Loire F 103 B4
Châteauneuf-sur-Sarthe F 102 B1
Châteauponsac F 115 B5
Châteauredon F 132 A2
Châteaurenard, *Bouches du Rhône* F 131 B3
Châteaurenard, *Loiret* F 104 B1
Châteauroux F 103 C3
Châteauroux-les-Alpes F 118 C3
Châteauvillain F 105 A3
Châtel F 119 A3
Châtel-Censoir F 104 B2
Châtel-de-Neuvre F 116 A3
Châtel-Montagne F 117 A3
Châtel-St. Denis CH 106 C1
Châtel-sur-Moselle F 92 C2
Châtelaillon-Plage F 114 B2
Châtelaudren F 100 A3
Châtelet B 79 B4
Châtelguyon F 116 B3
Châtellerault F 115 B4
Châtelus-Malvaleix F 116 A2
Châtenois F 105 A4
Châtenois-les-Forges F 106 B1
Chatham GB 45 B4
Châtillon I 119 B4
Châtillon-Coligny F 103 B4
Châtillon-en-Bazois F 104 B2
Châtillon-en-Diois F 118 C2
Châtillon-sur Chalaronne F 117 A4
Châtillon-sur-Indre F 103 C3
Châtillon-sur-Loire F 103 B4
Châtillon-sur-Marne F 91 B3
Châtillon-sur-Seine F 104 B3
Châtres F 91 C3
Chatteris GB 45 A4
Chatton GB 37 A5
Chauchina E 163 A4
Chaudes-Aigues F 116 C3
Chaudrey F 91 C4
Chauffailles F 117 A4
Chaulnes F 90 B2
Chaument Gistoux B 79 B4
Chaumergy F 105 C4
Chaumont F 105 A4
Chaumont-en-Vexin F 90 B1
Chaumont-Porcien F 91 B4
Chaumont-sur-Aire F 91 C5
Chaumont-sur-Loire F 103 B3
Chaunay F 115 B4
Chauny F 90 B3
Chaussin F 105 C4
Chauvigny F 115 B4
Chavagnes-en-Paillers F 114 B2
Chavanges F 91 C4
Chaves P 148 A2
Chavignon F 91 B3
Chazelles-sur-Lyon F 117 B4
Chazey-Bons F 118 B2
Cheadle, *Greater Manchester* GB 40 B1
Cheadle, *Staffordshire* GB 40 C2
Cheb CZ 83 B4
Chebsara RUS 9 C11
Checa E 152 B2
Chęciny PL 87 B4
Cheddar GB 43 A4
Cheddleton GB 40 B1
Chef-Boutonne F 115 B3
Cheles E 155 C3
Chella E 159 B3
Chelles F 90 C2
Chełm PL 13 C5
Chełmno, *Kujawsko-Pomorskie* PL 76 A3
Chełmno, *Wielkopolskie* PL 76 B3
Chelmsford GB 45 B4
Chelmuzhi RUS 9 A9
Chełmża PL 76 A3
Cheltenham GB 44 B1
Chelva E 159 B2
Chémery F 103 B3
Chemery-sur-Bar F 91 B4
Chemillé F 102 B1
Chemin F 105 C4
Chemnitz D 83 B4
Chénerailles F 116 A2
Cheniménil F 105 A5
Chenonceaux F 103 B3
Chenôve F 105 B3
Chepelare BG 183 B6
Chepstow GB 39 C4
Chera E 159 B3
Cherasco I 119 C4
Cherbonnières F 115 C3
Cherbourg F 88 A2
Cherchiara di Calábria I 174 B2
Cherepovets RUS 9 C10
Chernihiv UA 13 C9
Chernivtsi UA 17 A6
Chernobyl = Chornobyl UA 13 C9
Chernyakhovsk RUS 12 A4
Chéroy F 104 A1
Cherven BY 13 B8
Chervonohrad UA 13 C6
Cherykaw BY 13 B9
Chesham GB 44 B3
Cheshunt GB 44 B3
Chessy-lès-Pres F 104 A2
Cheste E 159 B3
Chester GB 38 A4
Chester-le-Street GB 37 B5
Chesterfield GB 40 B2
Chevagnes F 104 C2
Chevanceaux F 115 C3
Chevillon F 91 C5
Chevilly F 103 A3
Chew Magna GB 43 A4
Chézery-Forens F 118 A2
Chialamberto I 119 B4
Chiampo I 121 B4
Chianale I 119 C4
Chianciano Terme I 135 B4
Chiaramonte Gulfi I 177 B3
Chiaramonti I 178 B2
Chiaravalle I 136 B2
Chiaravalle Centrale I 175 C2
Chiaréggio I 120 A2
Chiari I 120 B2
Chiaromonte I 174 A2
Chiasso CH 120 B2
Chiávari I 134 A2
Chiavenna I 120 A2
Chiché F 102 C1
Chichester GB 44 C3
Chiclana de la Frontera E 162 B1
Chiclana de Segura E 164 A1
Chiddingfold GB 44 B3
Chieri I 119 B4
Chiesa in Valmalenco I 120 A2
Chieti I 169 A4
Chieti Scalo I 169 A4
Chiéuti I 171 B3
Chigwell GB 45 B4
Chiliomodi GR 184 B3
Chillarón de Cuenca E 152 B1
Chillarón del Rey E 151 B5
Chilleurs-aux-Bois F 103 A4
Chillón E 156 B3
Chilluevar E 164 B1
Chiloeches E 151 B4
Chimay B 91 A4
Chimeneas E 163 A4
Chinchilla de Monte Aragón E 158 C2
Chinchón E 151 B4
Chingford GB 45 B4
Chinon F 102 B2
Chióggia I 122 B1
Chiomonte I 119 B3
Chipiona E 161 C3
Chippenham GB 43 A4
Chipping Campden GB 44 A2
Chipping Norton GB 44 B2
Chipping Ongar GB 45 B4
Chipping Sodbury GB 43 A4
Chirac F 130 A2
Chirbury GB 39 B3
Chirens F 118 B2
Chirivel E 164 B2
Chirk GB 38 B3
Chirnside GB 35 C5
Chişinău = Khisinev MD 17 B8
Chişineu Criş RO 113 C5
Chissey-en-Morvan F 104 B3
Chiusa I 108 C2
Chiusa di Pésio I 133 A3
Chiusa Sclàfani I 176 B2
Chiusaforte I 122 A2
Chiusi I 135 B4
Chiva E 159 B3
Chivasso I 119 B4
Chlewiska PL 87 A4
Chludowo PL 75 B5
Chlum u Třeboně CZ 96 C2
Chlumec nad Cidlinou CZ 84 B3
Chmielnik PL 87 B4
Chobienia PL 85 A4
Chobienice PL 75 B4
Choceň CZ 97 A4
Choceń PL 77 B4
Chochołow PL 99 B3
Chocianów PL 85 A3
Chociw PL 86 A3
Chociwel PL 75 A4
Choczewo PL 68 A2
Chodaków PL 77 B5
Chodecz PL 77 B4
Chodov CZ 83 B4
Chodzież PL 75 B5
Chojna PL 74 B3
Chojnice PL 68 B2
Chojno, *Kujawsko-Pomorskie* PL 77 B4
Chojno, *Wielkopolskie* PL 75 B5
Chojnów PL 85 A3
Cholet F 114 A3
Chomérac F 117 C4
Chomutov CZ 83 B5
Chop UA 12 D5
Chora GR 184 B2
Chora Sfakion GR 185 D5
Chorges F 132 A2
Chorley GB 38 A4
Chornobyl = Chernobyl UA 13 C9
Chortkiv UA 13 D6
Chorzele PL 77 A5
Chorzew PL 86 A2
Chorzów PL 86 B2
Choszczno PL 75 A4
Chotěboř CZ 97 B3
Chouilly F 91 B4
Chouto P 154 B2
Chouzy-sur-Cisse F 103 B3
Chozas de Abajo E 142 B1
Chrast, *Vychodočeský* CZ 97 B3
Chrást, *Západočeský* CZ 96 B1
Chrastava CZ 84 B2
Chřibská CZ 84 B2
Christchurch GB 44 C2
Christiansfeld DK 59 C2
Chroberz PL 87 B4
Chropyně CZ 98 B1
Chrudim CZ 97 B3
Chrzanów PL 86 B3
Chtelnica SK 98 C1
Chudovo RUS 9 C7
Chueca E 157 A4
Chulmleigh GB 42 B3
Chur CH 107 C4
Church Stretton GB 39 B4
Churriana E 163 B3
Churwalden CH 107 C4
Chvalšiny CZ 96 C2
Chwaszczyno PL 69 A3
Chynava CZ 96 A2
Chýnov CZ 96 B2
Çinarcık TR 186 B4
Ciacova RO 126 B3
Ciadîr-Lunga MD 17 B8
Ciadoncha E 143 B3
Cianciana I 176 B2
Ciano d'Enza I 134 A3
Ciążen PL 76 B2
Cibakhaza H 113 C4
Ciborro P 154 C2
Cicagna I 134 A2
Cicciano I 170 C2
Ciciliano I 169 B2
Cicognolo I 120 B3
Cidadelhe P 149 B2
Cide TR 23 A7
Cidones E 143 C4
Ciechanów, *Dolnośląskie* PL 85 A4

Creeve	GB	27	B4
Creglingen	D	94	B2
Creil	F	90	B2
Creissels	F	130	A2
Crema	I	120	B2
Cremeaux	F	117	B3
Crémenes	E	142	B1
Crémieu	F	118	B2
Cremlingen	D	73	B3
Cremona	I	120	B3
Creney	F	91	C4
Črenšovci	SLO	111	C3
Créon	F	128	B2
Crepaja	SRB	127	B2
Crépey	F	92	C1
Crépy	F	91	B3
Crépy-en-Valois	F	90	B2
Cres	HR	123	C3
Crescentino	I	119	B5
Crespino	I	121	C4
Crespos	E	150	B3
Cressage	GB	39	B4
Cressensac	F	129	A4
Cressia	F	105	C4
Crest	F	117	C5
Cresta	CH	107	C4
Créteil	F	90	C2
Creully	F	88	A3
Creussen	D	95	B3
Creutzwald	F	92	B2
Creuzburg	D	82	A2
Crevalcore	I	121	C4
Crèvecœur-le-Grand	F	90	B2
Crevillente	E	165	A4
Crévola d'Ossola	I	119	A5
Crewe	GB	38	A4
Crewkerne	GB	43	B4
Criales	E	143	B3
Crianlarich	GB	34	B3
Criccieth	GB	38	B2
Crickhowell	GB	39	C3
Cricklade	GB	44	B2
Crieff	GB	35	B4
Criel-sur-Mer	F	90	A1
Crikvenica	HR	123	B3
Crillon	F	90	B1
Crimmitschau	D	83	B4
Crimond	GB	33	D5
Crinitz	D	84	A1
Cripán	E	143	B4
Criquetot-l'Esneval	F	89	A4
Crispiano	I	173	B3
Crissolo	I	119	C4
Cristóbal	E	149	B4
Crivitz	D	73	A4
Črna	SLO	110	C1
Crna Bara, *Srbija*	SRB	127	C1
Crna Bara, *Vojvodina*	SRB	126	B2
Crnac	HR	125	B3
Crnča	SRB	127	C1
Crni Lug	BIH	138	A2
Crni Lug	HR	123	B3
Črni Vrh	SLO	123	B3
Crnjelovo Donje	BIH	125	C5
Črnomelj	SLO	123	B4
Crocketford	GB	36	A3
Crocq	F	116	B2
Crodo	I	119	A5
Croglin	GB	37	B4
Crolly	IRL	26	A2
Cromarty	GB	32	D2
Cromer	GB	41	C5
Cronat	F	104	C2
Crookhaven	IRL	29	C2
Crookstown	IRL	29	C3
Croom	IRL	29	B3
Cropalati	I	174	B2
Crópani	I	175	C2
Crosbost	GB	31	A2
Crosby	GB	38	A3
Crosía	I	174	B2
Cross-Hands	GB	39	C2
Crossakiel	IRL	27	C3
Crosshaven	IRL	29	C3
Crosshill	GB	36	A2
Crossmolina	IRL	26	B1
Crotone	I	175	B3
Crottendorf	D	83	B4
Crouy	F	90	B3
Crowborough	GB	45	B4
Crowland	GB	41	C3
Crowthorne	GB	44	B3
Croyde	GB	42	A2
Croydon	GB	44	B3
Crozon	F	100	A1
Cruas	F	117	C4
Cruceni	RO	126	A3
Crúcoli	I	174	B3
Cruden Bay	GB	33	D5
Crudgington	GB	38	B4
Cruis	F	132	A1
Crumlin	GB	27	B4
Cruseilles	F	118	A3
Crusheen	IRL	28	B3
Cruz de Incio	E	141	B3
Crvenka	SRB	126	B1
Črveny Kamen	SK	98	B2
Csabacsüd	H	113	C4
Csabrendek	H	111	B4
Csákánydoroszló	H	111	C3
Csákvár	H	112	B2
Csanádapáca	H	113	C4
Csanádpalota	H	126	A2
Csány	H	113	B3
Csanytelek	H	113	C4
Csapod	H	111	B3
Császár	H	112	B2
Császártöltés	H	112	C3
Csávoly	H	125	A5
Csemö	H	113	B3
Csengöd	H	112	C3
Csépa	H	113	C4
Csepreg	H	111	B3
Cserkeszölö	H	113	C4
Csernely	H	113	A4
Csesztreg	H	111	C3
Csökmö	H	113	B5
Csököly	H	124	A3
Csokonyavisonta	H	124	A3
Csólyospálos	H	113	C3
Csongrád	H	113	C4
Csopak	H	112	C1
Csorna	H	111	B4
Csorvás	H	113	C4
Csurgo	H	124	A3
Cuacos de Yuste	E	150	B2
Cualedro	E	140	C3
Cuanca de Campos	E	142	B1
Cuba	P	160	A2
Cubel	E	152	A2
Cubelles	E	147	C2
Cubillos	E	143	C4
Cubillos del Sil	E	141	B4
Cubjac	F	129	A3
Cubo de la Solana	E	152	A1
Çubuk	TR	23	A7
Cuckfield	GB	44	B3
Cucuron	F	131	B4
Cudillero	E	141	A4
Cuéllar	E	151	A3
Cuenca	E	152	B1
Cuers	F	132	B2
Cuerva	E	157	A3
Cueva de Agreda	E	144	C2
Cuevas Bajas	E	163	A3
Cuevas de San Clemente	E	143	B3
Cuevas de San Marcos	E	163	A3
Cuevas del Almanzora	E	164	B3
Cuevas del Becerro	E	162	B2
Cuevas del Campo	E	164	B2
Cuevas del Valle	E	150	B2
Cuges-les-Pins	F	132	B1
Cúglieri	I	178	B2
Cugnaux	F	129	C4
Cuijk	NL	80	A1
Cuinzier	F	117	A4
Cuiseaux	F	105	C4
Cuisery	F	105	C4
Culan	F	103	C4
Culemborg	NL	79	A5
Cúllar	E	164	B2
Cullaville	GB	27	B4
Cullera	E	159	B3
Cullivoe	GB	33	A5
Cullompton	GB	43	B3
Cully	CH	106	C1
Culoz	F	118	B2
Cults	GB	33	D4
Cumbernauld	GB	35	C4
Cumbres de San Bartolomé	E	161	A3
Cumbres Mayores	E	161	A3
Cumiana	I	119	C4
Čumić	SRB	127	C2
Cumnock	GB	36	A2
Çumra	TR	23	C7
Cúneo	I	133	A3
Cunlhat	F	117	B3
Čunski	HR	123	C3
Cuntis	E	140	B2
Cuorgnè	I	119	B4
Cupar	GB	35	B4
Cupello	I	170	A2
Cupra Maríttima	I	136	B2
Cupramontana	I	136	B2
Čuprija	SRB	127	D3
Curinga	I	175	C2
Currelos	E	140	B3
Currie	GB	35	C4
Curtea de Argeş	RO	17	C6
Curtici	RO	126	A3
Curtis	E	140	A2
Curtis Santa Eulalia	E	140	A2
Čurug	SRB	126	B2
Cusano Mutri	I	170	B2
Cushendall	GB	27	A4
Cusset	F	117	A3
Cussy-les-Forges	F	104	B3
Custines	F	92	C2
Cutanda	E	152	B2
Cutro	I	175	B2
Cutrofiano	I	173	B4
Cuts	F	90	B3
Cuvilly	F	90	B2
Cuxhaven	D	64	C1
Cvikov	CZ	84	B2
Cwmbran	GB	39	C3
Cybinka	PL	75	B3
Czacz	PL	75	B5
Czajków	PL	86	A2
Czaplinek	PL	75	A5
Czarlin	PL	69	A3
Czarna-Dąbrówka	PL	68	A2
Czarna Woda	PL	68	B3
Czarnca	PL	87	B3
Czarne	PL	68	B1
Czarnków	PL	75	B5
Czarnowo	PL	76	A3
Czarnozyly	PL	86	A2
Czarny Bór	PL	85	B4
Czarny-Dunajec	PL	99	B3
Czarny Las	PL	86	A1
Czchow	PL	99	B4
Czechowice-Dziedzice	PL	98	B2
Czempiń	PL	75	B5
Czermno	PL	87	A4
Czernichow	PL	99	B3
Czerniejewo	PL	76	B2
Czernikowo	PL	76	B3
Czersk	PL	68	B2
Czerwieńsk	PL	75	B4
Czerwionka-Leszczyny	PL	86	B2
Częstochowa	PL	86	B3
Czeszewo	PL	76	B2
Człopa	PL	75	A5
Człuchów	PL	68	B2
Czołpino	PL	68	A2

D

Daaden	D	81	B3
Dabas	H	112	B3
Dąbie	PL	76	B3
Dąbki	PL	67	B5
Dabo	F	92	C3
Dabrowa	PL	76	B2
Dąbrowa Górnicza	PL	86	B3
Dąbrowa Tarnowska	PL	87	B4
Dąbrowice	PL	77	B4
Dabrowno	PL	77	A5
Dachau	D	108	A2
Dačice	CZ	97	B3
Daday	TR	23	A7
Dağ	TR	189	B5
Dagali	N	47	B5
Dägebüll	D	64	B1
Dagmersellen	CH	106	B2
Dahlen	D	83	A4
Dahlenburg	D	73	A3
Dahme	D	83	A5
Dahn	D	93	B3
Dähre	D	73	B3
Daikanvik	S	195	E7
Dail bho Dheas	GB	31	A2
Dailly	GB	36	A2
Daimiel	E	157	A4
Daingean	IRL	30	A1
Đakovica	SRB	16	D4
Đakovo	HR	125	B4
Dal, *Akershus*	N	48	B3
Dal, *Telemark*	N	47	C5
Dala-Floda	S	50	B1
Dala-Husby	S	50	B2
Dala-Järna	S	50	B1
Dalaas	A	107	B5
Dalabrog	GB	31	B1
Dalaman	TR	188	C3
Dalarö	S	57	A4
Dalbeattie	GB	36	B3
Dalby	DK	59	C3
Dalby, *Skåne*	S	61	D3
Dalby, *Uppsala*	S	57	A3
Dalby, *Värmland*	S	49	B4
Dale, *Pembrokeshire*	GB	39	C1
Dale, *Shetland*	GB	33	A5
Dale, *Hordaland*	N	46	B2
Dale, *Sogn og Fjordane*	N	46	A2
Dalen, *Akershus*	N	48	C3
Dalen, *Telemark*	N	53	A4
Daleszyce	PL	87	B4
Dalhalvaig	GB	32	C3
Dalheim	L	92	B2
Dalhem	S	57	C4
Dalias	E	164	C2
Dalj	HR	125	B4
Dalkeith	GB	35	C4
Dalkey	IRL	30	A2
Dalmally	GB	34	B3
Dalmellington	GB	36	A2
Dalmose	DK	65	A4
Daløy	N	46	A1
Dalry, *Dumfries & Galloway*	GB	34	C3
Dalry, *North Ayrshire*	GB	36	A2
Dalrymple	GB	36	A2
Dals Långed	S	54	B3
Dals Rostock	S	54	B3
Dalseter	N	47	A6
Dalsjöfors	S	60	B3
Dalskog	S	54	B3
Dalston	GB	36	B4
Dalstorp	S	60	B3
Dalton-in-Furness	GB	36	B3
Daluis	F	132	A2
Dalum	D	71	B4
Dalum	S	60	B3
Dalvík	IS	191	B7
Dalwhinnie	GB	32	E2
Dalyan	TR	188	C3
Damasi	GR	182	D4
Damasławek	PL	76	B2
Damazan	F	129	B3
Dammarie-les-Lys	F	90	C2
Dammartin-en-Goële	F	90	B2
Damme	D	71	B5
Damnica	PL	68	A2
Dampierre	F	105	B4
Dampierre-sur-Salon	F	105	B4
Damüls	A	107	B4
Damville	F	89	B5
Damvillers	F	92	B1
Damwoude	NL	70	A2
Danasjö	S	195	E7
Danbury	GB	45	B4
Dangé-St. Romain	F	102	C2
Dångebo	S	63	B3
Dangers	F	89	B5
Dangeul	F	89	B4
Danilovgrad	CG	16	D3
Danischenhagen	D	64	B3
Daniszyn	PL	85	A5
Danjoutin	F	106	B1
Dannas	S	60	B3
Dannemarie	F	106	B2
Dannemora	S	51	B4
Dannenberg	D	73	A4
Dánszentmiklós	H	112	B3
Dány	H	112	B3
Daoulas	F	100	A1
Darabani	RO	17	A7
Darány	H	125	B3
Darda	HR	125	B4
Dardesheim	D	73	C3
Darfeld	D	71	B4
Darfo	I	120	B3
Dargiń	PL	68	A1
Dargun	D	66	C1
Darlington	GB	37	B5
Darłowo	PL	68	A1
Darmstadt	D	93	B4
Darney	F	105	A5
Daroca	E	152	A2
Darque	P	148	A1
Darragh	IRL	28	B2
Dartford	GB	45	B4
Dartington	GB	43	B3
Dartmouth	GB	43	B3
Darton	GB	40	B2
Daruvar	HR	124	B3
Darvas	H	113	B5
Darvel	GB	36	A2
Darwen	GB	38	A4
Dassel	D	82	A1
Dassow	D	65	C3
Datça	TR	188	C2
Datteln	D	80	A3
Dattenfeld	D	81	B3
Daugard	DK	59	C2
Daugavpils	LV	8	E5
Daumeray	F	102	B1
Daun	D	80	B2
Daventry	GB	44	A2
Davle	CZ	96	B2
Davor	HR	124	B3
Davos	CH	107	C4
Davutlar	TR	188	B2
Davyd Haradok	BY	13	B7
Dawlish	GB	43	B3
Dax	F	128	C1
Dazkırı	TR	189	B4
De Cocksdorp	NL	70	A1
De Haan	B	78	A3
De Koog	NL	70	A1
De Panne	B	78	A2
De Wijk	NL	71	B3
Deal	GB	45	B5
Deauville	F	89	A4
Deba	E	143	A4
Debar	MK	182	B2
Dębe	PL	77	B5
Dębica	PL	87	B5
Dębnica Kaszubska	PL	68	A2
Dębno	PL	74	B3
Dębołęka	PL	86	A2
Dębowa Łaka	PL	69	B4
Debrc	SRB	127	C1
Debrecen	H	113	B5
Debrznica	PL	75	B4
Debrzno	PL	68	B2
Debstedt	D	72	A1
Decazeville	F	130	A1
Dechtice	SK	98	C1
Decima	I	168	B2
Decimomannu	I	179	C2
Děčín	CZ	84	B2
Decize	F	104	C2
Decollatura	I	175	B2
Decs	H	125	A4
Deddington	GB	44	B2
Dedeler	TR	187	B5
Dedelow	D	74	A2
Dedemli	TR	189	B7
Dedemsvaart	NL	71	B3
Dédestapolcsány	H	113	A4
Dedovichi	RUS	9	D6
Deeping St. Nicholas	GB	41	C3
Dég	H	112	C2
Degaña	E	141	B4
Degeberga	S	61	D4
Degerby	FIN	51	B7
Degerfors	S	55	A5
Degerhamn	S	63	B4
Degernes	N	54	A2
Deggendorf	D	95	C4
Deggingen	D	94	C1
Dego	I	133	A4
Degolados	P	155	B3
Dehesas de Guadix	E	164	B1
Dehesas Viejas	E	163	A4
Deia	E	166	B2
Deining	D	95	B3
Deinze	B	79	B3
Déiva Marina	I	134	A2
Dej	RO	17	B5
Deje	S	55	A4
Delabole	GB	42	B2
Delary	S	61	C3
Delbrück	D	81	A4
Delčevo	MK	182	B4
Delden	NL	71	B3
Deleitosa	E	156	A2
Delekovec	HR	124	A2
Delémont	CH	106	B2
Delft	NL	70	B1
Delfzijl	NL	71	A3
Délia	I	176	B2
Delianuova	I	175	C1
Deliblato	SRB	127	C3
Delice	TR	23	B7
Deliceto	I	171	B3
Delitzsch	D	83	A4
Dellach	A	109	C4
Delle	F	106	B2
Delme	F	92	C2
Delmen-horst	D	72	A1
Delnice	HR	123	B3
Delsbo	S	200	E2
Delvin	IRL	30	A1
Delvinë	AL	182	D2
Demandice	SK	112	A2
Demen	D	73	A4
Demidov	RUS	13	A9
Demigny	F	105	C3
Demirci	TR	186	C3
Demirköy	TR	186	A2
Demirtaş	TR	186	B4
Demmin	D	66	C2
Demonte	I	133	A3
Demyansk	RUS	9	D8
Den Burg	NL	70	A1
Den Ham	NL	71	B3
Den Helder	NL	70	B1
Den Oever	NL	70	B2
Denain	F	78	B3
Denbigh	GB	38	A3
Dender-monde	B	79	A4
Denekamp	NL	71	B4
Denholm	GB	35	C5
Denia	E	159	C4
Denizli	TR	188	B4
Denkendorf	D	95	C3
Denklingen	D	81	B3
Denny	GB	35	B4
Denta	RO	126	B3
Déols	F	103	C3
Derbent	TR	188	A3
Derby	GB	40	C2
Derecske	H	113	B5
Dereköy	TR	186	A2
Derenberg	D	82	A2
Derinkuyu	TR	23	B8
Dermbach	D	82	B2
Dermulo	I	121	A4
Deronje	SRB	125	B5
Derrygonnelly	GB	26	B3
Derrylin	GB	27	B3
Derry/Londonderry	GB	27	B3
Dersingham	GB	41	C4
Deruta	I	136	C1
Dervaig	GB	34	B1
Derval	F	101	B4
Derveni	GR	184	A3
Derventa	BIH	125	C3
Dervock	GB	27	A4
Desana	I	119	B5
Descartes	F	102	C2
Desenzano del Garda	I	121	B3
Deset	N	48	A3
Deševa	BIH	139	B4
Desfina	GR	184	A3
Desimirovac	SRB	127	C2
Désio	I	120	B2
Deskati	GR	182	D3
Deskle	SLO	122	A2
Desná	CZ	84	B3
Dešov	CZ	97	C3
Despotovac	SRB	127	C3
Despotovo	SRB	126	B1
Dessau	D	83	A4
Deštná	CZ	96	B2
Destriana	E	141	B4
Désulo	I	179	B3
Desvres	F	78	B1
Deszk	H	126	A2
Deta	RO	126	B3
Detmold	D	72	C1
Dětřichov	CZ	98	B1
Dettelbach	D	94	B2
Dettingen, *Baden-Württemberg*	D	107	B4
Dettingen, *Baden-Württemberg*	D	94	C1
Dettwiller	F	93	C3
Detva	SK	99	C3
Deurne	NL	80	A1
Deutsch Wagram	A	111	A3
Deutschkreutz	A	111	B3
Deutschlandsberg	A	110	C2
Deva	RO	16	C5
Dévaványa	H	113	B4
Devecikonağı	TR	186	C3
Devecser	H	111	B4
Develi	TR	23	B8
Deventer	NL	70	B3
Devil's Bridge	GB	39	B3
Devin	BG	183	B6
Devinska Nova Ves	SK	111	A3
Devizes	GB	43	A5
Devonport	GB	42	B2
Devrek	TR	187	A6
Devrekâni	TR	23	A7
Đevrske	HR	137	B4
Dewsbury	GB	40	B2
Deza	E	152	A1
Dežanovac	HR	124	B3
Dezzo	I	120	B3
Dhali	CY	181	A2
Dheftera	CY	181	A2
Dherinia	CY	181	A2
Diamante	I	174	B1
Dianalund	DK	61	D1
Diano d'Alba	I	119	C5
Diano Marina	I	133	B4
Dicomano	I	135	B4
Didcot	GB	44	B2
Didimoticho	GR	186	A1
Die	F	118	C2
Diebling	F	92	B2
Dieburg	D	93	B4
Diego del Carpio	E	150	B2
Diekirch	L	92	B2
Diélette	F	88	A2
Diémoz	F	118	B2
Dienten am Hochkönig	A	109	B3
Diepenbeck	B	79	B5
Diepholz	D	71	B5
Dieppe	F	89	A5
Dierberg	D	74	A1
Dierdorf	D	81	B3
Dieren	NL	70	B3
Dierhagen	D	66	B1
Diesdorf	D	73	B3
Diessen	D	108	B2
Diest	B	79	B5
Dietenheim	D	94	C2
Dietfurt	D	95	B3
Dietikon	CH	106	B3
Dietzenbach	D	93	A4
Dieue-sur-Meuse	F	92	B1
Dieulefit	F	131	A4
Dieulouard	F	92	C2
Dieuze	F	92	C2
Diever	NL	71	B3
Diez	D	81	B4
Diezma	E	163	A4
Differdange	L	92	B1
Digermulen	N	194	B6
Dignac	F	115	C4
Dignano	I	122	A1
Digne-les-Bains	F	132	A2
Digny	F	89	B5
Digoin	F	104	C2
Dijon	F	105	B4
Dikanäs	S	195	E7
Dikili	TR	186	C1
Diksmuide	B	78	A2
Dilar	E	163	A4
Dillenburg	D	81	B4
Dillingen, *Bayern*	D	94	C2
Dillingen, *Saarland*	D	92	B2
Dilsen	B	80	A1
Dimaro	I	121	A3
Dimitrovgrad	BG	183	A7
Dimitsana	GR	184	B3
Dinami	I	175	C2
Dinan	F	101	A3
Dinant	B	79	B4
Dinar	TR	189	A5
Dinard	F	101	A3
Dinek	TR	187	C6
Dingden	D	80	A2
Dingelstädt	D	82	A2
Dingle	IRL	29	B1
Dingle	S	54	B2
Dingolfing	D	95	C4
Dingtuna	S	56	A2
Dingwall	GB	32	D2
Dinkelsbühl	D	94	B2
Dinkelscherben	D	94	C2
Dinklage	D	71	B5
Dinslaken	D	80	A2
Dinxperlo	NL	80	A2
Diö	S	63	B2
Diósgyör	H	113	A4
Diósjeno	H	112	B3
Diou	F	104	C2
Dippen	GB	34	C2

Dipperz D 82 B1
Dippoldiswalde D 84 B1
Dirdal N 52 B2
Dirksland NL 79 A4
Dirlewang D 108 B1
Dischingen D 94 C2
Disentis CH 107 C3
Diso I 173 B4
Diss GB 45 A5
Dissen D 71 B5
Distington GB 36 B3
Ditzingen D 93 C5
Ditzum D 71 A4
Divača SLO 122 B2
Dives-sur-Mer F 89 A3
Divín SK 99 C3
Divion F 78 B2
Divišov CZ 96 B2
Divonne les Bains F 118 A3
Dixmont F 104 A2
Dizy-le-Gros F 91 B4
Djúpivogur IS 191 C11
Djupvasshytta N 198 C4
Djura S 50 B1
Djurås S 50 B2
Djurmo S 50 B2
Djursdala S 62 A3
Dlouhá Loucka CZ 98 B1
Długowola PL 87 A5
Dmitrov RUS 9 D10
Dno RUS 9 D6
Doade E 141 B3
Dobanovci SRB 127 C2
Dobbertin D 73 A5
Dobbiaco I 108 C3
Dobczyce PL 99 B4
Dobele LV 8 D3
Döbeln D 83 A5
Doberlug-Kirchhain D 83 A5
Dobern D 84 A2
Dobersberg A 97 C3
Dobiegniew PL 75 B4
Dobieszyn PL 87 A5
Doboj BIH 125 C4
Dobošnica BIH 125 C4
Doboz H 113 C5
Dobrá CZ 98 B2
Dobra, *Wielkopolskie* PL 76 C3
Dobra, *Zachodnio-Pomorskie* PL 74 A3
Dobra, *Zachodnio-Pomorskie* PL 75 A4
Dobrá Niva SK 99 C3
Dobřany CZ 96 B1
Dobre PL 76 B3
Dobre Miasto PL 69 B5
Dobreta-Turnu-Severin RO 16 C5
Dobri H 111 C3
Dobrica SRB 126 B2
Dobrich BG 17 D7
Dobrinishta BG 183 B5
Dobříš CZ 96 B2
Dobro E 143 B3
Dobrodzień PL 86 B2
Döbrököz H 112 C2
Dobromierz PL 85 B4
Dobrosołowo PL 76 B3
Dobroszyce PL 85 A5
Dobrovnik SLO 111 C3
Dobrush BY 13 B9
Dobruška CZ 85 B4
Dobrzany PL 75 A4
Dobrzen Wielki PL 86 B1
Dobrzyca, *Wielkopolskie* PL 75 A5
Dobrzyca, *Wielkopolskie* PL 85 A5
Dobrzyca, *Zachodnio-Pomorskie* PL 67 B4
Dobrzyń nad Wisłą PL 77 B4
Dobšiná SK 99 C4
Dobwalls GB 42 B2
Dochamps B 80 B1
Docking GB 41 C4
Docksta S 200 C4
Doddington GB 37 A4
Döderhult S 62 A4
Doesburg NL 70 B3
Doetinchem NL 71 C3
Doğanhisar TR 189 A6
Dogliani I 133 A3
Dogueno P 160 B2
Dois Portos P 154 B1
Doische B 91 A4
Dojč SK 98 C1
Dokka N 48 B2
Dokkedal DK 58 B3
Dokkum NL 70 A2
Dokležovje SLO 111 C3
Doksy CZ 84 B2
Dokuz TR 189 A7
Dol-de-Bretagne F 88 B2
Dolancourt F 104 A3
Dolceácqua I 133 B3
Dole F 105 B4
Dølemo N 53 B4
Dolenja vas SLO 123 B3
Dolenjske Toplice SLO 123 B4
Dolfor GB 39 B3
Dolgarrog GB 38 A3
Dolgellau GB 38 B3
Doliana GR 182 D2
Dolianova I 179 C3
Dolice PL 75 A4
Doljani HR 138 A2
Döllach im Mölltal A 109 C3
Dolle D 73 B4
Dollnstein D 94 C3
Dollot F 104 A2
Döllstadt D 82 A2
Dolná Strehová SK 99 C3
Dolné Saliby SK 111 A4
Dolni Benešov CZ 98 B2
Dolni Bousov CZ 84 B3
Dolni Kounice CZ 97 B4
Dolni Kralovice CZ 97 B3
Dolni Újezd CZ 97 B4
Dolni Žandov CZ 95 A4
Dolný Kubín SK 99 B3
Dolo I 121 B5
Dolores E 165 A4
Dolovo SRB 127 C2
Dölsach A 109 C3
Dolsk PL 76 B2
Dolwyddelan GB 38 A3
Domaljevac BIH 125 B4
Domaniç TR 187 C4
Domaniža SK 98 B2
Domanovići BIH 139 B3
Domašov CZ 85 B5
Domaszék H 126 A1
Domaszków PL 85 B4
Domaszowice PL 86 A1
Domat-Ems CH 107 C4
Domažlice CZ 95 B4
Dombås N 198 C6
Dombasle-sur-Meurthe F 92 C2
Dombegyház H 126 A3
Dombóvár H 112 C2
Domène F 118 B2
Domérat F 116 A2
Domfessel F 92 C3
Domfront F 88 B3
Domfront-en-Champagne F 102 A2
Domingão P 154 B2
Domingo Pérez, *Granada* E 163 A4
Domingo Pérez, *Toledo* E 150 C3
Dömitz D 73 A4
Dommartin F 91 C4
Dommartin-le-Franc F 91 C4
Domme F 129 B4
Dommitzsch D 83 A4
Domodóssola I 119 A5
Domokos GR 182 D4
Domoszló H 113 B4
Dompaire F 105 A5
Dompierre-du-Chemin F 88 B2
Dompierre-sur-Besbre F 104 C2
Dompierre-sur-Mer F 114 B2
Domrémy-la-Pucelle F 92 C1
Dömsöd H 112 B3
Domsure F 118 A2
Dómus de Maria I 179 D2
Domusnóvas I 179 C2
Domvena GR 184 A3
Domžale SLO 123 A3
Don Alvaro E 155 C4
Don Benito E 156 B2
Doña Mencía E 163 A3
Donado E 141 B4
Donaghadee GB 27 B5
Donaueschingen D 106 B3
Donauwörth D 94 C2
Doncaster GB 40 B2
Donegal IRL 26 B2
Donestebe-Santesteban E 144 A2
Donges F 101 B3
Dongo I 120 A2
Donington GB 41 C3
Doniños E 140 A2
Donja Bebrina HR 125 B4
Donja Brela HR 138 B2
Donja Dubica BIH 125 B4
Donja Dubrava HR 124 A2
Donja Kupčina HR 123 B4
Donja Šatornja SRB 127 C2
Donja Stubica HR 124 B1
Donje Brišnik BIH 138 B3
Donje Stative HR 123 B4
Donji-Andrijevci HR 125 B4
Donji Kazanci BIH 138 B2
Donji Koričáni BIH 138 A3
Donji Lapac HR 124 C1
Donji Malovan BIH 138 B3
Donji Miholjac HR 125 B4
Donji Mosti HR 124 A2
Donji Poloj HR 123 B4
Donji-Rujani BIH 138 B2
Donji Srb HR 138 A2
Donji Svilaj BIH 125 B4
Donji Tovarnik SRB 127 C1
Donji Vakuf BIH 138 A3
Donnalucata I 177 C3
Donnemarie-Dontilly F 90 C3
Donnersbach A 110 B1
Donnersbachwald A 109 B5
Donnerskirchen A 111 B3
Donorático I 134 B3
Donostia-San Sebastián E 144 A2
Donovaly SK 99 C3
Donzenac F 129 A4
Donzère F 131 A3
Donzy F 104 B2
Doonbeg IRL 29 B2
Doorn NL 70 B2
Dor E 140 A1
Dorchester GB 43 B4
Dørdal N 53 B5
Dordrecht NL 79 A4
Dörenthe D 71 B4
Dores GB 32 D2
Dorf Mecklenburg D 65 C4
Dorfen D 95 C4
Dorfgastein A 109 B4
Dorfmark D 72 B2
Dorgali I 178 B3
Dorking GB 44 B3
Dormagen D 80 A2
Dormánd H 113 B4
Dormans F 91 B3
Dornava SLO 124 A1
Dornbirn A 107 B4
Dornburg D 83 A3
Dorndorf D 82 B2
Dornecy F 104 B2
Dornes F 104 C2
Dornhan D 93 C4
Dornie GB 31 B3
Dornoch GB 32 D2
Dornum D 71 A4
Dorog H 112 B2
Dorohoi RO 17 B7
Dorotea S 200 B2
Dorotowo PL 69 B5
Dörpen D 71 B4
Dorsten D 80 A2
Dortan F 118 A2
Dortmund D 80 A3
Doruchów PL 86 A2
Dorum D 64 C1
Dörverden D 72 B2
Dörzbach D 94 B1
Dos Aguas E 159 B3
Dos Hermanas E 162 A2
Dos-Torres E 156 B3
Dosbarrios E 151 C4
Döşemealtı TR 189 B5
Dospat BG 183 B6
Dötlingen D 72 B1
Dottignies B 78 B3
Döttingen CH 106 B3
Douai F 78 B3
Douarnenez F 100 A1
Douchy F 104 B2
Douchy-les-Mines F 78 B3
Doucier F 105 C4
Doudeville F 89 A4
Doué-la-Fontaine F 102 B1
Douglas, *Isle of Man* GB 36 B2
Douglas, *South Lanarkshire* GB 36 A3
Doulaincourt F 91 C5
Doulevant-le-Château F 91 C4
Doullens F 90 A2
Dounby GB 33 B3
Doune GB 35 B3
Dounreay GB 32 C3
Dour B 79 B3
Dourdan F 90 C2
Dourgne F 146 A3
Dournazac F 115 C4
Douro Calvo P 148 B2
Douvaine F 118 A3
Douvres-la-Délivrande F 89 A3
Douzy F 91 B5
Dover GB 45 B5
Dovje SLO 109 C4
Dovre N 198 D6
Downham Market GB 41 C4
Downhill GB 27 A4
Downpatrick GB 27 B5
Dowra IRL 26 B2
Doxato GR 183 B6
Doyet F 116 A2
Dozule F 89 A3
Drača SRB 127 C2
Dračevo BIH 139 C4
Dračevo MK 182 B3
Drachten NL 70 A3
Draga SLO 123 B3
Drăgăşani RO 17 C6
Dragatuš SLO 123 B4
Dragichyn BY 13 B6
Draginja SRB 127 C1
Dragocvet SRB 127 D3
Dragolovci BIH 125 C3
Dragoni I 170 B2
Dragør DK 61 D2
Dragotina HR 124 B2
Dragotinja BIH 124 B2
Dragozetići HR 123 B3
Draguignan F 132 B2
Drahnsdorf D 74 C2
Drahonice CZ 96 B2
Drahovce SK 98 C1
Drama GR 183 B6
Drammen N 54 A1
Drangedal N 53 A5
Drangsnes IS 190 B4
Dransfeld D 82 A1
Dranske D 66 B2
Draperstown GB 27 B4
Drassburg A 111 B3
Drávaszabolcs H 125 B4
Dravograd SLO 110 C2
Drawno PL 75 A4
Drawsko Pomorskie PL 75 A4
Drayton GB 41 C5
Drązdżewo PL 77 A6
Draženov CZ 95 B4
Draževac SRB 127 C2
Dražice HR 123 B3
Drebkau D 84 A2
Dreieich D 93 A4
Dreisen D 93 B4
Drenovci HR 125 C4
Drensteinfurt D 81 A3
Dresden D 84 A1
Dretyń PL 68 A1
Dreux F 89 B5
Dřevohostice CZ 98 B1
Drevsjø N 199 D9
Drewitz D 73 B5
Drezdenko PL 75 B4
Drežnica HR 123 B4
Drežnik-Grad HR 123 C4
Drietona SK 98 C1
Driffield GB 40 A3
Drimnin GB 34 B2
Drimoleague IRL 29 C2
Dringenberg D 81 A5
Drinić BIH 138 A2
Drinjača BIH 139 A5
Drinovci BIH 138 B3
Driopida GR 185 B5
Drivstua N 198 C6
Drlače SRB 127 C1
Drnholec CZ 97 C4
Drniš HR 138 B2
Drnje HR 124 A2
Drnovice CZ 97 B4
Dro I 121 B3
Drøbak N 54 A1
Drobin PL 77 B5
Drochia MD 17 A7
Drochtersen D 64 C2
Drogheda IRL 30 A2
Drohobych UA 13 D5
Droitwich Spa GB 44 A1
Drołtowice PL 85 A5
Dromahair IRL 26 B2
Dromcolliher IRL 29 B3
Dromore, *Down* GB 27 B4
Dromore, *Tyrone* GB 27 B3
Dromore West IRL 26 B2
Dronero I 133 A3
Dronfield GB 40 B2
Drongan GB 36 A2
Dronninglund DK 58 A3
Dronrijp NL 70 A2
Dronten NL 70 B2
Drosendorf A 97 C3
Drösing A 97 C4
Drottningholm S 57 A3
Droué F 103 A3
Drulingen F 92 C3
Drumbeg GB 32 C1
Drumcliff IRL 26 B2
Drumgask GB 32 D2
Drumkeeran IRL 26 B2
Drummore GB 36 B2
Drumnadrochit GB 32 D2
Drumquin GB 27 B3
Drumshanbo IRL 26 B2
Drumsna IRL 26 C2
Drunen NL 79 A5
Druskininkai LT 13 A5
Druten NL 80 A1
Druya BY 13 A7
Družetići SRB 127 C2
Drvar BIH 138 A2
Drvenik HR 138 B3
Drwalew PL 77 C6
Drymen GB 34 B3
Drynoch GB 31 B2
Drzewce PL 76 B2
Drzewiany PL 68 B1
Drzewica PL 87 A4
Dualchi I 178 B2
Duas Igrejas P 149 A3
Dub SRB 127 D1
Dubá CZ 84 B2
Dubăsari MD 17 B8
Duben D 74 C2
Dübendorf CH 107 B3
Dubi CZ 84 B1
Dubica HR 124 B2
Dublin IRL 30 A2
Dubna RUS 9 D10
Dubňany CZ 98 C1
Dubnica nad Váhom SK 98 C2
Dubnik SK 112 B2
Dubno UA 13 C6
Dubodiel SK 98 C2
Dubona SRB 127 C2
Dubovac SRB 127 C3
Dubovic BIH 124 C2
Dubranec HR 124 B1
Dubrava HR 124 B2
Dubrave BIH 125 C4
Dubravica HR 123 B4
Dubravica SRB 127 C3
Dubrovnik HR 139 C4
Dubrovytsya UA 13 C7
Ducey F 88 B2
Duchcov CZ 84 B1
Ducherow D 74 A2
Dučina SRB 127 C2
Duclair F 89 A4
Dudar H 112 B1
Duddington GB 40 C3
Duderstadt D 82 A2
Dudeştii Vechi RO 126 A2
Dudley GB 40 C1
Dueñas E 142 C2
Duesund N 46 B2
Dueville I 121 B4
Duffel B 79 A4
Duffield GB 40 C2
Dufftown GB 32 D3
Duga Resa HR 123 B4
Dugi Rat HR 138 B2
Dugny-sur-Meuse F 92 B1
Dugo Selo HR 124 B2
Dugopolje HR 138 B2
Duino I 122 B2
Duisburg D 80 A2
Dukat AL 182 C1
Dukovany CZ 97 B4
Duleek IRL 30 A2
Dülken D 80 A2
Dülmen D 80 A3
Dulovo BG 17 D7
Dulpetorpet N 49 B4
Dulverton GB 43 A3
Dumbarton GB 34 C3
Dümerek TR 187 C6
Dumfries GB 36 A3
Dumlupınar TR 187 D4
Dümpelfeld D 80 B2
Dun Laoghaire IRL 30 A2
Dun-le-Palestel F 116 A1
Dun-les-Places F 104 B3
Dun-sur-Auron F 103 C4
Dun-sur-Meuse F 91 B5
Dunaalmás H 112 B2
Dunabogdány H 112 B3
Dunafalva H 125 A4
Dunaföldvár H 112 C2
Dunaharaszti H 112 B3
Dunajská Streda SK 111 B4
Dunakeszi H 112 B3
Dunakiliti H 111 B4
Dunakömlöd H 112 C2
Dunapataj H 112 C2
Dunaszekcsö H 125 A4
Dunaszentgyorgy H 112 C2
Dunatetétlen H 112 C3
Dunaújváros H 112 C2
Dunavecse H 112 C2
Dunbar GB 35 B5
Dunbeath GB 32 C3
Dunblane GB 35 B4
Dunboyne IRL 30 A2
Dundalk IRL 27 B4
Dundee GB 35 B5
Dundrennan GB 36 B3
Dundrum GB 27 B5
Dunfanaghy IRL 26 A3
Dunfermline GB 35 B4
Dungannon GB 27 B4
Dungarvan IRL 29 B4
Dungiven GB 27 B4
Dunglow IRL 26 B2
Dungourney IRL 29 C3
Duninowo PL 68 A1
Dunkeld GB 35 B4
Dunker S 56 A2
Dunkerque = Dunkirk F 78 A2
Dunkineely IRL 26 B2
Dunkirk = Dunkerque F 78 A2
Dunlavin IRL 30 A2
Dunleer IRL 27 C4
Dunlop GB 36 A2
Dunloy GB 27 A4
Dunmanway IRL 29 C2
Dunmore IRL 28 A3
Dunmore East IRL 30 B2
Dunmurry GB 27 B4
Dunnet GB 32 C3
Dunningen D 107 A3
Dunoon GB 34 C3
Duns GB 35 C5
Dunscore GB 36 A3
Dunsford GB 43 B3
Dunshaughlin IRL 30 A2
Dunstable GB 44 B3
Dunster GB 43 A3
Dunvegan GB 31 B2
Duplek SLO 110 C2
Dupnitsa BG 17 D5
Durach D 107 B5
Durağan TR 23 A8
Durak TR 186 C3
Durana E 143 B4
Durance F 128 B3
Durango E 143 A4
Durankulak BG 17 D8
Duras F 128 B3
Durban-Corbières F 146 B3
Dürbheim D 107 A3
Durbuy B 79 B5
Dúrcal E 163 B4
Đurdjenovac HR 125 B4
Đurdjevac HR 124 A3
Đurdjevik BIH 139 A4
Düren D 80 B2
Durham GB 37 B5
Đurinci SRB 127 C2
Durlach D 93 C4
Đurmanec HR 124 A1
Durness GB 32 C2
Dürnkrut A 97 C4
Dürrboden CH 107 C4
Dürrenboden CH 107 C3
Durrës AL 182 B1
Durrow IRL 30 B1
Durrus IRL 29 C2
Dursunbey TR 186 C3
Durtal F 102 B1
Durup DK 58 B1
Durusu TR 186 A3
Dusina BIH 139 B3
Dusnok H 112 C2
Dusocin PL 69 B3
Düsseldorf D 80 A2
Dusslingen D 93 C5
Duszniki PL 75 B5
Duszniki-Zdrój PL 85 B4
Dutovlje SLO 122 B2
Duvebo S 55 B5
Duved S 199 B9
Düzağac TR 187 D5
Düzce TR 187 B6
Dvärsätt S 199 B11
Dvor HR 124 B2
Dvorce CZ 98 B1
Dvorníky SK 98 C1
Dvory nad Žitavou SK 112 B2
Dvůr Králové nad Labem CZ 85 B3
Dybvad DK 58 A3
Dyce GB 33 D4
Dygowo PL 67 B4
Dykehead GB 35 B4
Dymchurch GB 45 B5
Dymer UA 13 C9
Dyrnes N 198 B4
Dywity PL 69 B5
Džanići BIH 139 B3
Dziadowa Kłoda PL 86 A1
Działdowo PL 77 A5
Działoszyce PL 87 B4
Działoszyn PL 86 A2
Dziemiany PL 68 A2
Dzierząznia PL 77 B5
Dzierzgoń PL 69 B4
Dzierzgowo PL 77 A5
Dzierżoniów PL 85 B4
Dzisna BY 13 A8
Dziwnów PL 67 B3
Dźwierzuty PL 77 A5
Dzyarzhynsk BY 13 B7
Dzyatlava BY 13 B6

E

Ea E 143 A4
Eaglesfield GB 36 A3
Ealing GB 44 B3
Eardisley GB 39 B3
Earl Shilton GB 40 C2
Earls Barton GB 44 A3
Earlston GB 35 C5
Easington GB 41 B4
Easky IRL 26 B2
East Calder GB 35 C4
East Dereham GB 41 C4
East Grinstead GB 45 B4
East Ilsley GB 44 B2
East Kilbride GB 36 A2
East Linton GB 35 C5
East Markham GB 40 B3
East Wittering GB 44 C3
Eastbourne GB 45 C4
Easter Skeld GB 33 A5
Eastleigh GB 44 C2
Easton GB 43 B4
Eaton Socon GB 44 A3
Eaux-Bonnes F 145 B3
Eauze F 128 C3
Ebberup DK 59 C2
Ebbs A 108 B3
Ebbw Vale GB 39 C3
Ebeleben D 82 A2
Ebeltoft DK 59 B3
Eben im Pongau A 109 B4
Ebene Reichenau A 109 C4
Ebensee A 109 B4
Ebensfeld D 94 A2
Eberbach D 93 B4
Ebergötzen D 82 A2
Ebermann-Stadt D 94 B3
Ebern D 82 B2
Eberndorf A 110 C1
Ebersbach D 84 A2
Ebersberg D 108 A2
Ebersdorf, *Bayern* D 82 B3
Ebersdorf, *Niedersachsen* D 72 A2

Eberstein A 110 C1
Eberswalde D 74 B2
Ebnat-Kappel CH 107 B4
Éboli I 170 C3
Ebrach D 94 B2
Ebreichsdorf A 111 B3
Ebreuil F 116 A3
Ebstorf D 72 A3
Ecclefechan GB 36 A3
Eccleshall GB 40 C1
Eceabat TR 186 B1
Echallens CH 106 C1
Echauri E 144 B2
Echinos GR 183 B7
Echiré F 114 B3
Échirolles F 118 B2
Echourgnac F 128 A3
Echt NL 80 A1
Echte D 82 A2
Echternach L 92 B2
Ecija E 162 A2
Ečka SRB 126 B2
Eckartsberga D 82 A3
Eckelshausen D 81 B4
Eckental D 94 B3
Eckernförde D 64 B2
Eckerö FIN 51 B6
Eckington GB 40 B2
Éclaron F 91 C4
Écommoy F 102 B2
Écouché F 89 B3
Ecouis F 90 B1
Ecséd H 113 B3
Ecsegfalva H 113 B4
Écueillé F 103 B3
Ed S 54 B2
Eda S 49 C4
Eda glasbruk S 49 C4
Edam NL 70 B2
Edane S 55 A3
Edderton GB 32 D2
Ede NL 70 B2
Edebäck S 49 B5
Edebo S 51 B5
Edelény H 99 C4
Edelschrott A 110 B2
Edemissen D 72 B3
Edenbridge GB 45 B4
Edenderry IRL 30 A1
Edenkoben D 93 B4
Edesheim D 93 B4
Edessa GR 182 C4
Edewecht D 71 A4
Edgeworthstown IRL 30 A1
Edinburgh GB 35 C4
Edineţ MD 17 A7
Edirne TR 186 A1
Edland N 52 A3
Edolo I 120 A3
Edøy N 198 B5
Edremit TR 186 C2
Eds bruk S 56 B2
Edsbro S 51 C5
Edsbyn S 50 A2
Edsele S 200 C2
Edsleskog S 54 A3
Edsvalla S 55 A4
Eekloo B 79 A3
Eemshaven NL 71 A3
Eerbeek NL 70 B3
Eersel NL 79 A5
Eferding A 96 C2
Effiat F 116 A3
Efteløt N 53 A5
Egeln D 73 C4
Eger H 113 B4
Egerbakta H 113 B4
Egernsund DK 64 B2
Egersund N 52 B2
Egerszólát H 113 B4
Egervár H 111 C3
Egg A 107 B4
Egg D 107 A5
Eggby S 55 B4
Eggedal N 47 B6
Eggenburg A 97 C3
Eggenfelden D 95 C4
Eggesin D 74 A3
Eggum N 194 B4
Egham GB 44 B3
Éghezée B 79 B4
Egiertowo PL 68 A3
Egilsstaðir IS 191 B11
Egina GR 185 B4
Eginio GR 182 C4
Egio GR 184 A3
Égletons F 116 B2
Egling D 108 B2
Eglinton GB 27 A3
Eglisau CH 107 B3
Égliseneuve-d'Entraigues F 116 B2
Eglofs D 107 B4
Egmond aan Zee NL 70 B1
Egna I 121 A4
Egosthena GR 184 A4
Egremont GB 36 B3
Eğridir TR 189 B5
Egtved DK 59 C2
Eguilles F 131 B4
Eguilly-sous-Bois F 104 A3
Éguzon-Chantôme F 103 C3
Egyek H 113 B4
Egyházasrádóc H 111 B3
Ehekirchen D 94 C3
Ehingen D 94 C1
Ehra-Lessien D 73 B3
Ehrang D 92 B2
Ehrenfriedersdorf D 83 B4
Ehrenhain D 83 B4
Ehrenhausen A 110 C2
Ehringshausen D 81 B4
Ehrwald A 108 B1
Eibar E 143 A4
Eibelstadt D 94 B2
Eibenstock D 83 B4
Eibergen NL 71 B3
Eibiswald A 110 C2
Eichenbarleben D 73 B4
Eichendorf D 95 C4
Eichstätt D 95 C3
Eickelborn D 81 A4
Eide, *Hordaland* N 46 B3
Eide, *Møre og Romsdal* N 198 C4
Eidet N 194 A9
Eidfjord N 46 B4
Eidsberg N 54 A2
Eidsbugarden N 47 A5
Eidsdal N 198 C4
Eidsfoss N 53 A6
Eidskog N 49 B4
Eidsvåg, *Hordaland* N 46 B2
Eidsvåg, *Møre og Romsdal* N 198 C5
Eidsvoll N 48 B3
Eikefjord N 46 A2
Eikelandsosen N 46 B2
Eiken N 52 B3
Eikesdal N 198 C5
Eikstrand N 53 A5
Eilenburg D 83 A4
Eilsleben D 73 B4
Eina N 48 B2
Einbeck D 82 A1
Eindhoven NL 79 A5
Einsiedeln CH 107 B3
Einville-au-Jard F 92 C2
Eisenach D 82 B2
Eisenberg, *Rheinland-Pfalz* D 93 B4
Eisenberg, *Thüringen* D 83 B3
Eisenerz A 110 B1
Eisenhüttenstadt D 74 B3
Eisenkappel A 110 C1
Eisenstadt A 111 B3
Eisentratten A 109 C4
Eisfeld D 82 B2
Eisleben D 82 A3
Eislingen D 94 C1
Eitensheim D 95 C3
Eiterfeld D 82 B1
Eitorf D 80 B3
Eivindvik N 46 B2
Eivissa = Ibiza E 166 C1
Eixo P 148 B1
Ejby DK 59 C2
Ejea de los Caballeros E 144 B2
Ejstrupholm DK 59 C2
Ejulve E 153 B3
Eke B 79 B3
Ekeby, *Gotland* S 57 C4
Ekeby, *Skåne* S 61 D2
Ekeby, *Uppsala* S 51 B5
Ekeby-Almby S 56 A1
Ekenäs S 55 B4
Ekenässjön S 62 A3
Ekerö S 57 A3
Eket S 61 C3
Eketorp S 63 B4
Ekevik S 56 B2
Ekkerøy N 193 B14
Ekshärad S 49 B5
Eksingedal N 46 B2
Eksjö S 62 A2
Eksta S 57 C4
Ekträsk S 200 B5
El Alamo, *Madrid* E 151 B4
El Alamo, *Sevilla* E 161 B3
El Algar E 165 B4
El Almendro E 161 B2
El Alquián E 164 C2
El Arahal E 162 A2
El Arenal E 150 B2
El Arguellite E 164 A2
El Astillero E 143 A3
El Ballestero E 158 C1
El Barco de Ávila E 150 B2
El Berrón E 142 A1
El Berrueco E 151 B4
El Bodón E 149 B3
El Bonillo E 158 C1
El Bosque E 162 B2
El Bullaque E 157 A3
El Burgo E 162 B3
El Burgo de Ebro E 153 A3
El Burgo de Osma E 151 A4
El Burgo Ranero E 142 B1
El Buste E 144 C2
El Cabaco E 149 B3
El Callejo E 143 A3
El Campillo E 161 B3
El Campillo de la Jara E 156 A2
El Cañavete E 158 B1
El Carpio E 157 C3
El Carpio de Tajo E 150 C3
El Casar E 151 B4
El Casar de Escalona E 150 B3
El Castillo de las Guardas E 161 B3
El Centenillo E 157 B4
El Cerro E 149 B4
El Cerro de Andévalo E 161 B3
El Comenar E 162 B2
El Coronil E 162 A2
El Crucero E 141 A4
El Cubo de Tierra del Vino E 149 A4
El Cuervo E 162 B1
El Ejido E 164 C2
El Escorial E 151 B3
El Espinar E 151 B3
El Frago E 144 B3
El Franco E 141 A4
El Frasno E 152 A2
El Garrobo E 161 B3
El Gastor E 162 B2
El Gordo E 150 C2
El Grado E 145 B4
El Granado E 161 B2
El Grao de Castelló E 159 B4
El Grau E 159 C3
El Higuera E 163 A3
El Hijate E 164 B2
El Hontanar E 152 B2
El Hoyo E 157 B4
El Madroño E 161 B3
El Maillo E 149 B3
El Masnou E 147 C3
El Mirón E 150 B2
El Molar E 151 B4
El Molinillo E 157 A3
El Morell E 147 C2
El Muyo E 151 A4
El Olmo E 151 A4
El Palo E 163 B3
El Pardo E 151 B4
El Payo E 149 B3
El Pedernoso E 158 B1
El Pedroso E 162 A2
El Peral E 158 B2
El Perelló, *Tarragona* E 153 B4
El Perelló, *Valencia* E 159 B3
El Picazo E 158 B1
El Pinell de Bray E 153 A4
El Piñero E 150 A2
El Pla de Santa Maria E 147 C2
El Pobo E 153 B3
El Pobo de Dueñas E 152 B2
El Pont d'Armentera E 147 C2
El Port de la Selva E 147 B4
El Port de Llançà E 146 B4
El Port de Sagunt E 159 B3
El Prat de Llobregat E 147 C3
El Provencio E 158 B1
El Puente E 143 A3
El Puente del Arzobispo E 150 C2
El Puerto E 141 A4
El Puerto de Santa María E 162 B1
El Real de la Jara E 161 B3
El Real de San Vincente E 150 B3
El Robledo E 157 A3
El Rocio E 161 B3
El Rompido E 161 B2
El Ronquillo E 161 B3
El Royo E 143 C4
El Rubio E 162 A3
El Sabinar E 164 A2
El Saler E 159 B3
El Salobral E 158 C2
El Saucejo E 162 A2
El Serrat AND 146 B2
El Temple E 144 C3
El Tiemblo E 150 B3
El Toboso E 157 A5
El Tormillo E 145 C3
El Torno E 149 B4
El Valle de las Casas E 142 B1
El Vellón E 151 B4
El Vendrell E 147 C2
El Villar de Arnedo E 144 B1
El Viso E 156 B3
El Viso del Alcor E 162 A2
Élancourt F 90 C1
Elassona GR 182 D4
Elati GR 182 D3
Elbasan AL 182 B2
Elbeuf F 89 A4
Elbingerode D 82 A2
Elbląg PL 69 A4
Elburg NL 70 B2
Elche E 165 A4
Elche de la Sierra E 158 C1
Elchingen D 94 C2
Elda E 159 C3
Eldena D 73 A4
Eldingen D 72 B3
Elefsina GR 185 A4
Elek H 113 C5
Elemir SRB 126 B2
Eleutheroupoli GR 183 C6
Elgå N 199 C8
Elgin GB 32 D3
Elgoibar E 143 A4
Elgol GB 31 B2
Elgshøa N 49 A4
Elie GB 35 B5
Elizondo E 144 A2
Ełk PL 12 B5
Elkhovo BG 17 D7
Ellenberg D 94 B2
Ellesmere GB 38 B4
Ellesmere Port GB 38 A4
Ellezelles B 79 B3
Ellingen D 94 B2
Ellmau A 109 B3
Ellon GB 33 D4
Ellös S 54 B2
Ellrich D 82 A2
Ellwangen D 94 C2
Elm CH 107 C4
Elm D 72 A2
Elmadağ TR 23 B7
Elmalı TR 189 C4
Elmshorn D 64 C2
Elmstein D 93 B3
Elne F 146 B3
Elnesvågen N 198 C4
Elorrio E 143 A4
Elöszállás H 112 C2
Elouda GR 185 D6
Éloyes F 105 A5
Elphin GB 32 C1
Els Castells E 147 B2
Elsdorf D 80 B2
Elsenfeld D 93 B5
Elsfleth D 72 A1
Elspeet NL 70 B2
Elst NL 70 C2
Elstead GB 44 B3
Elster D 83 A4
Elsterberg D 83 B4
Elsterwerda D 83 A5
Elstra D 84 A2
Eltmann D 94 B2
Eltville D 93 A4
Elvas P 155 C3
Elvebakken N 192 C7
Elven F 101 B3
Elverum N 48 B3
Elvington GB 40 B3
Elxleben D 82 A2
Ely GB 45 A4
Elzach D 106 A3
Elze D 72 B2
Emådalen S 50 A1
Embleton GB 37 A5
Embonas GR 188 C2
Embrun F 132 A2
Embún E 144 B3
Emden D 71 A4
Emecik TR 188 C2
Emet TR 186 C4
Emirdağ TR 187 C6
Emlichheim D 71 B3
Emmaboda S 63 B3
Emmaljunga S 61 C3
Emmeloord NL 70 B2
Emmen CH 106 B3
Emmen NL 71 B3
Emmendingen D 106 A2
Emmer-Compascuum NL 71 B4
Emmerich D 80 A2
Emmern D 72 B2
Emőd H 113 B4
Émpoli I 135 B3
Emsbüren D 71 B4
Emsdetten D 71 B4
Emsfors S 62 A4
Emskirchen D 94 B2
Emstek D 71 B5
Emsworth GB 44 C3
Emyvale IRL 27 B4
Enafors S 199 B9
Enånger S 51 A4
Encamp AND 146 B2
Encarnaçao P 154 C1
Encinas de Abajo E 150 B2
Encinas de Esgueva E 142 C2
Encinas Reales E 163 A3
Encinasola E 161 A3
Encio E 143 B3
Enciso E 144 B1
Enden N 199 D7
Endingen D 106 A2
Endrinal E 149 B4
Endröd H 113 C4
Enebakk N 54 A2
Eneryda S 63 B2
Enese H 111 B4
Enez TR 183 C8
Enfield IRL 30 A2
Eng A 108 B2
Enge-sande D 64 B1
Engelberg CH 106 C3
Engelhartszell A 96 C1
Engelskirchen D 80 B3
Engen D 107 B3
Enger N 48 B2
Engerdal N 199 D8
Engerneset N 49 A4
Engesvang DK 59 B2
Enghien B 79 B4
Engstingen D 94 C1
Engter D 71 B5
Enguera E 159 C3
Enguidanos E 158 B2
Enkenbach D 93 B3
Enkhuizen NL 70 B2
Enklinge FIN 51 B7
Enköping S 56 A3
Enna I 177 B3
Ennezat F 116 B3
Ennigerloh D 81 A4
Enningdal N 54 B2
Ennis IRL 28 B3
Enniscorthy IRL 30 B2
Enniskean IRL 29 C3
Enniskillen GB 27 B3
Ennistimon IRL 28 B2
Enns A 110 A1
Eno FIN 9 A7
Enontekiö FIN 196 A6
Ens NL 70 B2
Enschede NL 71 B3
Ensdorf D 95 B3
Ensisheim F 106 B2
Enstaberga S 56 B2
Enstone GB 44 B2
Entlebuch CH 106 B3
Entrácque I 133 A3
Entradas P 160 B1
Entrains-sur-Nohain F 104 B2
Entrambasaguas E 143 A3
Entrambasmestas E 143 A3
Entraygues-sur-Truyère F 116 C2
Entre-os-Rios P 148 A1
Entrevaux F 132 B2
Entrin Bajo E 155 C4
Entroncamento P 154 B2
Entzheim F 93 C3
Envermeu F 89 A5
Enviken S 50 B2
Enying H 112 C2
Enzingerboden A 109 B3
Enzklösterle D 93 C4
Épagny F 90 B3
Epalinges CH 106 C1
Epannes F 114 B3
Epanomi GR 182 C4
Epe D 71 B4
Epe NL 70 B2
Épernay F 91 B3
Épernon F 90 C1
Epfig F 93 C3
Epierre F 118 B3
Épila E 152 A2
Épinac F 104 C3
Épinal F 105 A5
Episcopia I 174 A2
Episkopi CY 181 B1
Epitalio GR 184 B2
Epoisses F 104 B3
Eppenbrunn D 93 B3
Eppendorf D 83 B5
Epping GB 45 B4
Eppingen D 93 B4
Epsom GB 44 B3
Epworth GB 40 B3
Eraclea I 122 B1
Eraclea Mare I 122 B1
Erba I 120 B2
Erbach, *Baden-Württemberg* D 94 C1
Erbach, *Hessen* D 93 B4
Erbalunga F 180 A2
Erbendorf D 95 B4
Érchie I 173 B3
Ercolano I 170 C2
Ercsi H 112 B2
Érd H 112 B2
Erdek TR 186 B2
Erdemli TR 23 C8
Erdevik SRB 126 B1
Erding D 95 C3
Erdötelek H 113 B4
Erdut HR 125 B5
Erdweg D 95 C3
Ereğli, *Konya* TR 23 C8
Ereğli, *Zonguldak* TR 187 A6
Erenkaya TR 189 B7
Eresfjord N 198 C5
Eresos GR 183 D7
Eretria GR 185 A4
Erfde D 64 B2
Erfjord N 52 A2
Erfstadt D 80 B2
Erfurt D 82 B3
Ērgli LV 8 D4
Ergoldsbach D 95 C4
Eriboll GB 32 C2
Érice I 176 A1
Ericeira P 154 C1
Eriksberg S 195 E6
Eriksmåla S 62 B3
Eringsboda S 63 B3
Eriswil CH 106 B2
Erithres GR 185 A4
Erkelenz D 80 A2
Erkner D 74 B2
Erkrath D 80 A2
Erla E 144 B3
Erlangen D 94 B3
Erli I 133 A4
Erlsbach A 109 C3
Ermelo NL 70 B2
Ermenak TR 23 C7
Ermenonville F 90 B2
Ermezinde P 148 A1
Ermidas P 160 A1
Ermioni GR 184 B4
Ermoupoli GR 185 B5
Ermsleben D 82 A3
Erndtebrück D 81 B4
Ernée F 88 B3
Ernestinovo HR 125 B4
Ernstbrunn A 97 C4
Erolzheim D 107 A5
Erquelinnes B 79 B4
Erquy F 101 A3
Erra P 154 C2
Erratzu E 144 A2
Errindlev DK 65 B4
Erro E 144 B2
Ersa F 180 A2
Érsekcsanád H 125 A4
Ersekë AL 182 C2
Érsekvadkert H 112 B3
Ersmark S 200 C6
Erstein F 93 C3
Erstfeld CH 107 C3
Ertebølle DK 58 B2
Ertingen D 107 A4
Ervedal, *Coimbra* P 148 B1
Ervedal, *Portalegre* P 154 B3
Ervenik HR 138 A1
Ervidel P 160 B1
Ervy-le-Châtel F 104 A2
Erwitte D 81 A4
Erxleben D 73 B4
Erzsébet H 125 A4
Es Caná E 166 B1
Es Castell E 167 B4
Es Mercadal E 167 B4
Es Migjorn Gran E 167 B4
Es Port d'Alcúdia E 167 B3
Es Pujols E 166 C1
Es Soleràs E 153 A4
Esbjerg DK 59 C1
Esbly F 90 C2
Escacena del Campo E 161 B3
Escairón E 140 B3
Escalada E 143 B3
Escalante E 143 A3
Escalaplano I 179 C3
Escalona E 150 B3
Escalona del Prado E 151 A3
Escalonilla E 150 C3
Escalos de Baixo P 155 B3
Escalos de Cima P 155 B3
Escamilla E 152 B1
Escañuela E 157 C3
Escatrón E 153 A3
Esch-sur-Alzette L 92 B1
Esch-sur-Sûre L 92 B1
Eschach D 107 B4
Eschau D 94 B1
Eschede D 72 B3
Eschenau D 95 B3
Eschenbach D 95 B3
Eschenz CH 107 B3
Eschershausen D 72 C2
Eschwege D 82 A2
Eschweiler D 80 B2
Escobasa de Almazán E 152 A1
Escoeuilles F 78 B1
Escombreras E 165 B4
Escos F 144 A2
Escource F 128 B1
Escragnolles F 132 B2
Escrick GB 40 B2
Escurial E 156 A2
Escurial de la Sierra E 149 B4
Esens D 71 A4
Esgos E 140 B3
Esher GB 44 B3
Eskdalemuir GB 36 A3
Eskifjörður IS 191 B12
Eskilhem S 57 C4
Eskilsäter S 55 B4
Eskilstrup DK 65 B4
Eskilstuna S 56 A2
Eskipazar TR 187 B7
Eskişehir TR 187 C5
Eslarn D 95 B4
Eslava E 144 B2
Eslida E 159 B3
Eslohe D 81 A4
Eslöv S 61 D3
Eşme TR 188 A3
Espa N 48 B3
Espalion F 130 A1
Esparragalejo E 155 C4
Esparragosa del Caudillo E 156 B2
Esparragossa de la Serena E 156 B2
Esparreguera E 147 C2
Esparron F 132 B1

Espe N 46 B3
Espedal N 52 B2
Espejo, *Alava* E 143 B3
Espejo, *Córdoba* E 163 A3
Espeland N 46 B2
Espelkamp D 72 B1
Espeluche F 131 A3
Espeluy E 157 B4
Espera E 162 B2
Esperança P 155 B3
Espéraza F 146 B3
Espéria I 169 B3
Espevær N 52 A1
Espiel E 156 B2
Espinama E 142 A2
Espiñaredo E 140 A3
Espinasses F 132 A2
Espinelves E 147 C3
Espinhal P 154 A2
Espinho P 148 A1
Espinilla E 142 A2
Espinosa de Cerrato E 143 C3
Espinosa de los Monteros E 143 A3
Espinoso del Rey E 156 A3
Espirito Santo P 160 B2
Espluga de Francolí E 147 C2
Esplús E 145 C4
Espolla E 146 B3
Espoo FIN 8 B4
Esporles E 166 B2
Esposende P 148 A1
Espot E 146 B2
Esquedas E 145 B3
Esquivias E 151 B4
Essay F 89 B4
Essen B 79 A4
Essen, *Niedersachsen* D 71 B4
Essen, *Nordrhein-Westfalen* D 80 A3
Essenbach D 95 C4
Essertaux F 90 B2
Essingen D 94 C2
Esslingen D 94 C1
Essoyes F 104 A3
Estacas E 140 B2
Estadilla E 145 B4
Estagel F 146 B3
Estaires F 78 B2
Estang F 128 C2
Estarreja P 148 B1
Estartit E 147 B4
Estavayer-le-Lac CH 106 C1
Este I 121 B4
Esteiro E 140 A2
Estela P 148 A1
Estella E 144 B1
Estellencs E 166 B2
Estepa E 162 A3
Estépar E 143 B3
Estepona E 162 B2
Esternay F 91 C3
Esterri d'Aneu E 146 B2
Esterwegen D 71 B4
Estissac F 104 A2
Estivadas E 140 B3
Estivareilles F 116 A2
Estivella E 159 B3
Estói P 160 B2
Estopiñán E 145 C4
Estoril P 154 C1
Estoublon F 132 B2
Estrée-Blanche F 78 B2
Estrées-St. Denis F 90 B2
Estrela P 155 C3
Estremera E 151 B4
Estremoz P 155 C3
Estuna S 51 C5
Esyres F 102 B2
Esztergom H 112 B2
Etables-sur-Mer F 100 A3
Étain F 92 B1
Étalans F 105 B5
Etalle B 92 B1
Étampes F 90 C2
Etang-sur-Arroux F 104 C3
Étaples F 78 B1
Etauliers F 128 A2
Etili TR 186 C1
Etna N 48 B1
Etne N 52 A1
Etoges F 91 C3
Etoliko GR 184 A2
Eton GB 44 B3
Etréaupont F 91 B3
Étréchy F 90 C2
Étrépagny F 90 B1
Étretat F 89 A4
Étrœungt F 91 A3
Étroubles I 119 B4
Ettal D 108 B2
Ettelbruck L 92 B2
Etten NL 79 A4
Ettenheim D 106 A2
Ettington GB 44 A2
Ettlingen D 93 C4
Ettringen D 108 A1
Etuz F 105 B4
Etxarri-Aranatz E 144 B1
Etyek H 112 B2
Eu F 90 A1
Euerdorf D 82 B2
Eulate E 144 B1
Eupen B 80 B2
Europoort NL 79 A4
Euskirchen D 80 B2
Eutin D 65 B3
Evanger N 46 B3
Évaux-les-Bains F 116 A2
Evciler, *Afyon* TR 189 A4
Evciler, *Çanakkale* TR 186 C1
Evenskjær N 194 B7
Evenstad N 48 A3
Evercreech GB 43 A4
Evergem B 79 A3
Everöd S 61 D4
Eversberg D 81 A4
Everswinkel D 71 C4
Evertsberg S 49 A5
Evesham GB 44 A2
Évian-les-Bains F 118 A3
Evisa F 180 A1
Evje N 53 B3
Evolène CH 119 A4
Évora P 154 C3
Evoramonte P 155 C3
Evran F 101 A4
Evrecy F 89 A3
Évreux F 89 A5
Évron F 102 A1
Évry F 90 C2
Ewell GB 44 B3
Ewersbach D 81 B4
Excideuil F 115 C5
Exeter GB 43 B3
Exmes F 89 B4
Exminster GB 43 B3
Exmouth GB 43 B3
Eydehamn N 53 B4
Eye, *Peterborough* GB 41 C3
Eye, *Suffolk* GB 45 A5
Eyemouth GB 35 C5
Eyguians F 132 A1
Eyguières F 131 B4
Eygurande F 116 B2
Eylie F 145 B4
Eymet F 129 B3
Eymoutiers F 116 B1
Eynsham GB 44 B2
Eyrarbakki IS 190 D4
Eystrup D 72 B2
Ezaro E 140 B1
Ezcaray E 143 B4
Ezcároz E 144 B2
Ezine TR 186 C1
Ezmoriz P 148 B1

F

Fabara E 153 A4
Fábbrico I 121 C3
Fåberg N 48 A2
Fabero E 141 B4
Fábiánsebestyén H 113 C4
Fåborg DK 64 A3
Fabrègues F 130 B2
Fabriano I 136 B1
Fabrizia I 175 C2
Facha P 148 A1
Facinas E 162 B2
Fačkov SK 98 B2
Fadagosa P 155 B3
Fadd H 112 C2
Faédis I 122 A2
Faenza I 135 A4
Fafe P 148 A1
Fagagna I 122 A2
Făgăras RO 17 C6
Fågelberget S 199 A11
Fågelfors S 62 A3
Fågelmara S 63 B3
Fågelsta S 55 B6
Fagerås S 55 A4
Fagerheim N 47 B4
Fagerhøy N 48 A1
Fagerhult S 62 A3
Fagerlund N 48 B2
Fagernes, *Oppland* N 47 B6
Fagernes, *Troms* N 192 C3
Fagersanna S 55 B5
Fagersta S 50 B2
Fåglavik S 55 B4
Fagnano Castello I 174 B2
Fagnières F 91 C4
Faido CH 107 C3
Fains F 91 C5
Fairford GB 44 B2
Fairlie GB 34 C3
Fajsz H 112 C2
Fakenham GB 41 C4
Fåker S 199 B11
Fakse DK 65 A5
Fakse Ladeplads DK 65 A5
Falaise F 89 B3
Falcade I 121 A4
Falcarragh IRL 26 A2
Falces E 144 B2
Fălciu RO 17 B8
Falconara I 177 B3
Falconara Marittima I 136 B2
Falcone I 177 A4
Faldingworth GB 40 B3
Falerum S 56 B2
Făleşti MD 17 B7
Falkenberg, *Bayern* D 95 B4
Falkenberg, *Bayern* D 95 C4
Falkenberg, *Brandenburg* D 83 A5
Falkenberg S 60 C2
Falkensee D 74 B2
Falkenstein, *Bayern* D 95 B4
Falkenstein, *Sachsen* D 83 B4
Falkenthal D 74 B2
Falkirk GB 35 B4
Falkland GB 35 B4
Falköping S 55 B4
Fall D 108 B2
Falla S 56 B1
Fallingbostel D 72 B2
Falmouth GB 42 B1
Falset E 147 C1
Fălticeni RO 17 B7
Falun S 50 B2
Famagusta CY 181 A2
Fammestad N 46 B2
Fana N 46 B2
Fanano I 135 A3
Fanari GR 182 D3
Fanjeaux F 146 A3
Fano I 136 B2
Fântânele RO 126 A3
Fara in Sabina I 168 A2
Fara Novarese I 119 B5
Faramontanos de Tábara E 149 A4
Farasdues E 144 B2
Fårbo S 62 A4
Fareham GB 44 C2
Färentuna S 57 A3
Färgelanda S 54 B2
Färila S 200 E1
Faringdon GB 44 B2
Faringe S 51 C5
Farini I 120 C2
Fariza E 149 A3
Färjestaden S 63 B4
Farkadona GR 182 D4
Farkasfa H 111 C3
Farlete E 153 A3
Färlöv S 61 C4
Farmos H 113 B3
Farnă SK 112 B2
Färnäs S 50 B1
Farnborough GB 44 B3
Farnese I 168 A1
Farnham GB 44 B3
Farnroda D 82 B2
Faro P 160 B2
Fåro S 57 C5
Fårösund S 57 C5
Farra d'Alpago I 122 A1
Farranfore IRL 29 B2
Farre DK 59 B2
Farsala GR 182 D4
Farsø DK 58 B2
Farsund N 52 B2
Farum DK 61 D2
Fårup DK 58 B2
Fasana I 172 B1
Fasano I 173 B3
Fáskrúðsfjörður IS 191 C11
Fassberg D 72 B3
Fastiv UA 13 C8
Fastnäs S 49 B5
Fátima P 154 B2
Fatmomakke S 195 E6
Fättjaur S 195 E6
Faucogney-et-la-Mer F 105 B5
Fauguerolles F 128 B3
Faulenrost D 74 A1
Faulquemont F 92 B2
Fauquembergues F 78 B2
Fauske N 194 C6
Fauville-en-Caux F 89 A4
Fauvillers B 92 B1
Fåvang N 48 A2
Favara E 159 B3
Favara I 176 B2
Faverges F 118 B3
Faverney F 105 B5
Faversham GB 45 B4
Favignana I 176 B1
Fawley GB 44 C2
Fay-aux-Loges F 103 B4
Fayence F 132 B2
Fayet F 130 B1
Fayl-Billot F 105 B4
Fayón E 153 A4
Fearn GB 32 D3
Fécamp F 89 A4
Feda N 52 B2
Fedje N 46 B1
Feeny GB 27 B3
Fegen S 60 B3
Fegyvernek H 113 B4
Fehrbellin D 74 B1
Fehring A 111 C3
Feichten A 108 B1
Feiring N 48 B3
Feistritz im Rosental A 110 C1
Feketić SRB 126 B1
Felanitx E 167 B3
Feld am See A 109 C4
Feldbach A 110 C2
Feldberg D 74 A2
Feldkirch A 107 B4
Feldkirchen in Kärnten A 109 C5
Feldkirchen-Westerham D 108 B2
Felgueiras P 148 A1
Felitto I 172 B1
Félix E 164 C2
Felixstowe GB 45 B5
Felizzano I 119 C5
Felletin F 116 B2
Fellingsbro S 56 A1
Felnac RO 126 A3
Felnémet H 113 B4
Felpéc H 111 B4
Fels am Wagram A 97 C3
Felsberg D 81 A5
Felsönyék H 112 C2
Felsöszentiván H 126 A1
Felsöszentmárton H 125 B3
Felsözsolca H 113 A4
Felsted DK 64 B2
Feltre I 121 A4
Femsjö S 60 C3
Fenagh IRL 26 B3
Fene E 140 A2
Fenestrelle I 119 B4
Fénétrange F 92 C3
Feneu F 102 B1
Fengersfors S 54 B3
Fenit IRL 29 B2
Fensmark DK 65 A4
Fenwick GB 36 A2
Feolin Ferry GB 34 C1
Ferbane IRL 28 A4
Ferdinandovac HR 124 A3
Ferdinandshof D 74 A2
Fère-Champenoise F 91 C3
Fère-en-Tardenois F 91 B3
Ferentillo I 168 A2
Ferentino I 169 B3
Feres GR 183 C8
Feria E 155 C4
Feričanci HR 125 B3
Ferizli TR 187 B5
Ferla I 177 B3
Ferlach A 110 C1
Ferleiten A 109 B3
Fermil P 148 A2
Fermo I 136 B2
Fermoselle E 149 A3
Fermoy IRL 29 B3
Fernán Nuñéz E 163 A3
Fernán Peréz E 164 C2
Fernancabellero E 157 A4
Fernão Ferro P 154 C1
Fernay-Voltaire F 118 A3
Ferndown GB 43 B5
Ferness GB 32 D3
Fernhurst GB 44 B3
Ferns IRL 30 B2
Ferpécle CH 119 A4
Ferrals-les-Corbières F 146 A3
Ferrandina I 172 B2
Ferrara I 121 C4
Ferrara di Monte Baldo I 121 B3
Ferreira E 141 A3
Ferreira do Alentejo P 160 A1
Ferreira do Zêzere P 154 B2
Ferreras de Abajo E 141 C4
Ferreras de Arriba E 141 C4
Ferreries E 167 B4
Ferreruela E 152 A2
Ferreruela de Tabara E 149 A3
Ferret CH 119 B4
Ferrette F 106 B2
Ferriere I 120 C2
Ferrière-la-Grande F 79 B3
Ferrières, *Hautes-Pyrénées* F 145 A3
Ferrières, *Loiret* F 103 A4
Ferrières, *Oise* F 90 B2
Ferrières-sur-Sichon F 117 A3
Ferrol E 140 A2
Ferryhill GB 37 B5
Fertörakos H 111 B3
Fertöszentmiklós H 111 B3
Ferwerd NL 70 A2
Festieux F 91 B3
Festøy N 198 C3
Festvåg N 194 C5
Feteşti RO 17 C7
Fethard, *Tipperary* IRL 29 B4
Fethard, *Wexford* IRL 30 B2
Fethiye TR 188 C4
Fetsund N 48 C3
Fettercairn GB 35 B5
Feucht D 95 B3
Feuchtwangen D 94 B2
Feudingen D 81 B4
Feuges F 91 C4
Feuquières F 90 B1
Feurs F 117 B4
Fevik N 53 B4
Ffestiniog GB 38 B3
Fiamignano I 169 A3
Fiano I 119 B4
Ficarazzi I 176 A2
Ficarolo I 121 C4
Fichtelberg D 95 A3
Ficulle I 135 C5
Fidenza I 120 C3
Fidjeland N 52 B2
Fieberbrunn A 109 B3
Fier AL 182 C1
Fiera di Primiero I 121 A4
Fiesch CH 119 A5
Fiesso Umbertiano I 121 C4
Figari F 180 B2
Figeac F 116 C2
Figeholm S 62 A4
Figgjo N 52 B1
Figline Valdarno I 135 B4
Figols E 145 B4
Figueira da Foz P 148 B1
Figueira de Castelo Rodrigo P 149 B3
Figueira dos Caveleiros P 160 A1
Figueiredo P 154 B3
Figueiredo de Alva P 148 B2
Figueiró dos Vinhos P 154 B2
Figueres E 147 B3
Figueroles E 153 B3
Figueruela de Arriba E 141 C4
Filadélfia I 175 C2
Fil'akovo SK 99 C3
Filderstadt D 94 C1
Filey GB 41 A3
Filiaşi RO 17 C5
Filiates GR 182 D2
Filiatra GR 184 B2
Filipstad S 55 A5
Filisur CH 107 C4
Fillan N 198 B5
Filotio GR 185 B6
Filottrano I 136 B2
Filskov DK 59 C2
Filton GB 43 A4
Filtvet N 54 A1
Filzmoos A 109 B4
Finale Emilia I 121 C4
Finale Lígure I 133 A4
Fiñana E 164 B2
Finby FIN 51 B7
Fincham GB 41 C4
Finchingfield GB 45 B4
Findhorn GB 32 D3
Findochty GB 33 D4
Finike TR 189 C5
Finkenberg A 108 B2
Finnea IRL 27 C3
Finneidfjord N 195 D4
Finnerödja S 55 B5
Finnskog N 49 B4
Finnsnes N 194 A9
Finntorp S 54 A3
Finócchio I 168 B2
Finsjö S 62 A4
Finsland N 52 B3
Finspång S 56 B1
Finsterwalde D 84 A1
Finsterwolde NL 71 A4
Finstown GB 33 B3
Fintona GB 27 B3
Fionnphort GB 34 B1
Fiorenzuola d'Arda I 120 C2
Firenze = Florence I 135 B4
Firenzuola I 135 A4
Firmi F 130 A1
Firminy F 117 B4
Firmo I 174 B2
Fischamend Markt A 111 A3
Fischbach A 110 B2
Fischbach D 93 B3
Fischbeck D 73 B5
Fischen D 107 B5
Fishbourne GB 44 C2
Fishguard GB 39 C2
Fiskardo GR 184 A1
Fiskebäckskil S 54 B2
Fiskebøl N 194 B5
Fismes F 91 B3
Fisterra E 140 B1
Fitero E 144 B2
Fitjar N 46 C2
Fiuggi I 169 B3
Fiumata I 169 A3
Fiumefreddo Brúzio I 174 B2
Fiumefreddo di Sicília I 177 B4
Fiumicino I 168 B2
Fivemiletown GB 27 B3
Fivizzano I 134 A3
Fjæra N 46 C3
Fjälkinge S 63 B2
Fjällåsen S 196 B3
Fjällbacka S 54 B2
Fjärdhundra S 56 A2
Fjellerup DK 58 B3
Fjerritslev DK 58 A2
Fjordgard N 194 A8
Fjugesta S 55 A5
Flå N 47 B6
Flåbygd N 53 A4
Flaça E 147 B3
Flace F 117 A4
Fladungen D 82 B2
Flaine F 118 A3
Flaka FIN 51 B7
Flåm N 46 B4
Flamatt CH 106 C2
Flamborough GB 41 A3
Flammersfeld D 81 B3
Flassans-sur-Issole F 132 B2
Flatdal N 53 A4
Flateby N 48 C3
Flateland N 52 A3
Flateyri IS 190 A2
Flatøydegard N 47 B6
Flatråker N 46 C2
Flattach A 109 C4
Flatvarp S 62 A4
Flauenskjold DK 58 A3
Flavigny-sur-Moselle F 92 C2
Flavy-le-Martel F 90 B3
Flawil CH 107 B4
Flayosc F 132 B2
Flechtingen D 73 B4
Fleckeby D 64 B2
Fleet GB 44 B3
Fleetmark D 73 B4
Fleetwood GB 38 A3
Flehingen D 93 B4
Flekke N 46 A2
Flekkefjord N 52 B2
Flen S 56 A2
Flensburg D 64 B2
Fleringe S 57 C4
Flerohopp S 62 B3
Flers F 88 B3
Flesberg N 47 C6
Fleurance F 129 C3
Fleuré F 115 B4
Fleurier CH 105 C5
Fleurus B 79 B4
Fleury, *Hérault* F 130 B2
Fleury, *Yonne* F 104 B2
Fleury-les-Aubrais F 103 B3
Fleury-sur-Andelle F 89 A5
Fleury-sur-Orne F 89 A3
Flieden D 81 B5
Flimby GB 36 B3
Flims CH 107 C4
Flines-lèz-Raches F 78 B3
Flint GB 38 A3
Flirey F 92 C1
Flirsch A 108 B1
Flisa N 49 B4
Flisby S 62 A2
Fliseryd S 62 A4
Flix E 153 A4
Flixecourt F 90 A2
Flize F 91 B4
Flobecq B 79 B3
Floby S 55 B4
Floda S 60 B2
Flodden GB 37 A4
Flogny-la-Chapelle F 104 B2
Flöha D 83 B5
Flonheim D 93 B4
Florac F 130 A2
Floreffe B 79 B4
Florence = Firenze I 135 B4
Florennes B 79 B4
Florensac F 130 B2
Florentin F 129 C5
Florenville B 91 B5
Flores de Avila E 150 B2
Floresta I 177 B3
Floreşti MD 17 B8
Florídia I 177 B4
Florina GR 182 C3
Florø N 46 A2
Flörsheim D 93 A4
Floss D 95 B4
Fluberg N 48 B2
Flúðir IS 190 C5
Flühli CH 106 C3
Flumet F 118 B3
Fluminimaggiore I 179 C2
Flums CH 107 B4
Flyeryd S 63 B3
Flygsfors S 62 B3
Foča BIH 139 B4
Foça TR 186 D1
Fochabers GB 32 D3
Focşani RO 17 C7
Foel GB 38 B3
Foeni RO 126 B2
Fogdö S 56 A2
Fóggia I 171 B3
Foglianise I 170 B2
Föglö FIN 51 B7
Fohnsdorf A 110 B1

Foiano della Chiana I 135 B4
Foix F 146 B2
Fojnica BIH 139 B3
Fojnica BIH 139 B4
Fokstua N 198 C6
Földeák H 126 A2
Foldereid N 199 A9
Főldes H 113 B5
Folegandros GR 185 C5
Folelli F 180 A2
Folgaria I 121 B4
Folgosinho P 148 B2
Folgoso de la Ribera E 141 B4
Folgoso do Courel E 141 B3
Foligno I 136 C1
Folkärna S 50 B3
Folkestad N 198 C3
Folkestone GB 45 B5
Follafoss N 199 B8
Folldal N 198 C6
Follebu N 48 A2
Follina I 121 B5
Föllinge S 199 B11
Follónica I 135 C3
Fölsbyn S 54 A3
Foncebadón E 141 B4
Foncine-le-Bas F 105 C5
Fondevila E 140 C2
Fondi I 169 B3
Fondo I 121 A4
Fonelas E 164 B1
Fonfría, *Teruel* E 152 B2
Fonfría, *Zamora* E 149 A3
Fonn N 46 A3
Fonnes N 46 B1
Fonni I 178 B3
Font-Romeu F 146 B3
Fontaine F 91 C4
Fontaine de Vaucluse F 131 B4
Fontaine-Française F 105 B4
Fontaine-le-Dun F 89 A4
Fontainebleau F 90 C2
Fontan F 133 A3
Fontanarejo E 157 A3
Fontane I 133 A3
Fontanélice I 135 A4
Fontanières F 116 A2
Fontanosas E 157 B3
Fonteblanda I 168 A1
Fontenay-le-Comte F 114 B3
Fontenay-Trésigny F 90 C2
Fontevrault-l'Abbaye F 102 B2
Fontiveros E 150 B3
Fontoy F 92 B1
Fontpédrouse F 146 B3
Fontstown IRL 30 A2
Fonyód H 111 C4
Fonz E 145 B4
Fonzaso I 121 A4
Fóppolo I 120 A2
Föra S 62 A4
Forbach D 93 C4
Forbach F 92 B2
Forcall E 153 B3
Forcalquier F 132 B1
Forcarei E 140 B2
Forchheim D 94 B3
Forchtenau A 111 B3
Forchtenberg D 94 B1
Ford GB 34 B2
Førde, *Hordaland* N 52 A1
Førde, *Sogn og Fjordane* N 46 A2
Förderstedt D 83 A3
Førdesfjorden N 52 A1
Fordham GB 45 A4
Fordingbridge GB 44 C2
Fordon PL 76 A3
Fordongiánus I 179 C2
Forenza I 172 B1
Foresta di Búrgos I 178 B2
Forfar GB 35 B5
Forges-les-Eaux F 90 B1
Foria I 172 B1
Forío I 170 C1
Forjães P 148 A1
Førland N 52 B3
Forlì I 135 A5
Forlimpopoli I 135 A5
Formazza I 119 A5
Formby GB 38 A3
Formerie F 90 B1
Fórmia I 169 B3
Formígine I 135 A3
Formigliana I 119 B5
Formiguères F 146 B3
Fornalutx E 166 B2
Fornåsa S 56 B1
Fornelli I 178 B2
Fornells E 167 A4
Fornelos de Montes E 140 B2
Fornes E 163 B4
Forneset N 192 C3
Forni Avoltri I 109 C3
Forni di Sopra I 122 A1
Forni di Sotto I 122 A1
Forno, *Piemonte* I 119 B4
Forno, *Piemonte* I 119 B5
Forno Alpi-Gráie I 119 B4
Forno di Zoldo I 121 A5
Fornos de Algodres P 148 B2
Fornovo di Taro I 120 C3
Foros do Arrão P 154 B2
Forráskút H 126 A1
Forres GB 32 D3
Forriolo E 140 B3
Fors S 50 B3
Forsand N 52 B2
Forsbacka S 51 B3
Forserum S 62 A2
Forshaga S 55 A4
Forsheda S 60 B3
Forsinain GB 32 C3
Førslev DK 65 A4
Förslöv S 61 C2
Forsmark, *Uppsala* S 51 B5
Forsmark, *Västerbotten* S 195 E6
Forsmo S 200 C3
Forsnäs S 195 D9
Forsnes N 198 B5
Forssa FIN 8 B3
Forssjöbruk S 56 B2
Forst D 84 A2
Forsvik S 55 B5
Fort Augustus GB 32 D2
Fort-Mahon-Plage F 78 B1
Fort William GB 34 B2
Fortanete E 153 B3
Forte dei Marmi I 134 B3
Fortezza I 108 C2
Forth GB 35 C4
Fortrie GB 33 D4
Fortrose GB 32 D2
Fortun N 47 A4
Fortuna E 165 A3
Fortuneswell GB 43 B4
Forvik N 195 E3
Fos F 145 B4
Fos-sur-Mer F 131 B3
Fosdinovo I 134 A3
Foss N 47 B6
Fossacésia I 169 A4
Fossano I 133 A3
Fossato di Vico I 136 B1
Fossbakken N 194 B8
Fosse-la-Ville B 79 B4
Fossombrone I 136 B1
Fot H 112 B3
Fouchères F 104 A3
Fouesnant F 100 B1
Foug F 92 C1
Fougères F 88 B2
Fougerolles F 105 B5
Foulain F 105 A4
Fountainhall GB 35 C5
Fouras F 114 C2
Fourchambault F 104 B2
Fourmies F 91 A4
Fourna GR 182 D3
Fournels F 116 C3
Fourni GR 188 B1
Fournols F 117 B3
Fourques F 146 B3
Fourquevaux F 146 A2
Fours F 104 C2
Fowey GB 42 B2
Foxdale GB 36 B2
Foxford IRL 26 C1
Foyers GB 32 D2
Foynes IRL 29 B2
Foz E 141 A3
Foz do Arelho P 154 B1
Foz do Giraldo P 155 B3
Foza I 121 B4
Frabosa Soprana I 133 A3
Frades de la Sierra E 149 B4
Fraga E 153 A4
Fragagnano I 173 B3
Frailes E 163 A4
Fraire B 79 B4
Fraize F 106 A1
Framlingham GB 45 A5
Frammersbach D 94 A1
Framnes N 54 A1
França P 141 C4
Francaltroff F 92 C2
Francavilla al Mare I 169 A4
Francavilla di Sicília I 177 B4
Francavilla Fontana I 173 B3
Francavilla in Sinni I 174 A2
Francescas F 129 B3
Franco P 148 A2
Francofonte I 177 B3
Francos E 151 A4
Frändefors S 54 B3
Franeker NL 70 A2
Frangy F 118 A2
Frankenau D 81 A4
Frankenberg, *Hessen* D 81 A4
Frankenberg, *Sachsen* D 83 B5
Frankenburg A 109 A4
Frankenfels A 110 B2
Frankenmarkt A 109 B4
Frankenthal D 93 B4
Frankfurt, *Brandenburg* D 74 B3
Frankfurt, *Hessen* D 81 B4
Frankrike S 199 B10
Fränsta S 200 D2
Františkovy Lázně CZ 83 B4
Franzburg D 66 B1
Frascati I 168 B2
Frasdorf D 109 B3
Fraserburgh GB 33 D4
Frashër AL 182 C2
Frasne F 105 C5
Frasnes-lez-Anvaing B 79 B3
Frasseto F 180 B2
Frastanz A 107 B4
Fratel P 155 B3
Fratta Todina I 135 C5
Frauenau D 96 C1
Frauenfeld CH 107 B3
Frauenkirchen A 111 B3
Frauenstein D 83 B5
Frauental A 110 C2
Frayssinet F 129 B4
Frayssinet-le-Gélat F 129 B4
Frechas P 149 A2
Frechen D 80 B2
Frechilla E 142 B2
Freckenhorst D 71 C4
Fredeburg D 81 A4
Fredelsloh D 82 A1
Fredeng N 48 B2
Fredensborg DK 61 D2
Fredericia DK 59 C2
Frederiks DK 59 B2
Frederikshavn DK 58 A3
Frederikssund DK 61 D2
Frederiksværk DK 61 D2
Fredrika S 200 B4
Fredriksberg S 50 B1
Fredriksdal S 62 A2
Fredrikstad N 54 A1
Fregenal de la Sierra E 161 A3
Fregene I 168 B2
Freiberg D 83 B5
Freiburg, *Baden-Württemberg* D 106 B2
Freiburg, *Niedersachsen* D 64 C2
Freienhagen D 81 A5
Freienhufen D 84 A1
Freiensteinau D 81 B5
Freihung D 95 B3
Freilassing D 109 B3
Freisen D 92 B3
Freising D 95 C3
Freistadt A 96 C2
Freital D 84 A1
Freixedas P 149 B2
Freixo de Espada à Cinta P 149 A3
Fréjus F 132 B2
Fremdingen D 94 C2
Frenštát pod Radhoštěm CZ 98 B2
Freren D 71 B4
Freshford IRL 30 B1
Freshwater GB 44 C2
Fresnay-sur-Sarthe F 89 B4
Fresne-St. Mamès F 105 B4
Fresneda de la Sierra E 152 B1
Fresneda de la Sierra Tiron E 143 B3
Fresnedillas E 151 B3
Fresnes-en-Woevre F 92 B1
Fresno Alhandiga E 150 B2
Fresno de la Ribera E 150 A2
Fresno de la Vega E 142 B1
Fresno de Sayago E 149 A4
Fresnoy-Folny F 90 B1
Fresnoy-le-Grand F 91 B3
Fressenville F 90 A1
Fresvik N 46 A3
Fréteval F 103 B3
Fretigney F 105 B4
Freudenberg, *Baden-Württemberg* D 94 B1
Freudenberg, *Nordrhein-Westfalen* D 81 B3
Freudenstadt D 93 C4
Freux B 92 B1
Frévent F 78 B2
Freyburg D 83 A3
Freyenstein D 73 A5
Freyming-Merlebach F 92 B2
Freystadt D 95 B3
Freyung D 96 C1
Frias de Albarracin E 152 B2
Fribourg CH 106 C2
Frick CH 106 B3
Fridafors S 63 B2
Fridaythorpe GB 40 A3
Friedberg A 111 B3
Friedberg, *Bayern* D 94 C2
Friedberg, *Hessen* D 81 B4
Friedeburg D 71 A4
Friedewald D 82 B1
Friedland, *Brandenburg* D 74 B3
Friedland, *Mecklenburg-Vorpommern* D 74 A2
Friedland, *Niedersachsen* D 82 A1
Friedrichroda D 82 B2
Friedrichsdorf D 81 B4
Friedrichshafen D 107 B4
Friedrichskoog D 64 B1
Friedrichstadt D 64 B2
Friedrichswalde D 74 A2
Friesach A 110 C1
Friesack D 73 B5
Friesenheim D 93 C3
Friesoythe D 71 A4
Friggesund S 200 E2
Frigiliana E 163 B4
Frihetsli N 192 D3
Frillesås S 60 B2
Frinnaryd S 62 A2
Frinton-on-Sea GB 45 B5
Friockheim GB 35 B5
Friol E 140 A3
Fristad S 60 B2
Fritsla S 60 B2
Fritzlar D 81 A5
Frizington GB 36 B3
Frödinge S 62 A4
Froges F 118 B2
Frohburg D 83 A4
Frohnhausen D 81 B4
Frohnleiten A 110 B2
Froissy F 90 B2
Frombork PL 69 A4
Frome GB 43 A4
Frómista E 142 B2
Fröndenberg D 81 A3
Fronsac F 128 B2
Front I 119 B4
Fronteira P 155 B3
Frontenay-Rohan-Rohan F 114 B3
Frontenhausen D 95 C4
Frontignan F 130 B2
Fronton F 129 C4
Fröseke S 62 B3
Frosinone I 169 B3
Frosolone I 170 B2
Frosta N 199 B7
Frøstrup DK 58 A1
Frosunda S 57 A4
Frouard F 92 C2
Frövi S 56 A1
Frøyset N 46 B2
Fruges F 78 B2
Frutigen CH 106 C2
Frýdek-Místek CZ 98 B2
Frýdlant CZ 84 B3
Frydlant nad Ostravicí CZ 98 B2
Frygnowo PL 77 A5
Fryšták CZ 98 B1
Fucécchio I 135 B3
Fuencaliente, *Ciudad Real* E 157 A4
Fuencaliente, *Ciudad Real* E 157 B3
Fuencemillán E 151 B4
Fuendejalón E 144 C2
Fuengirola E 163 B3
Fuenlabrada E 151 B4
Fuenlabrada de los Montes E 156 A3
Fuensalida E 151 B3
Fuensanta E 164 B3
Fuensanta de Martos E 163 A4
Fuente al Olmo de Iscar E 150 A3
Fuente-Alamo E 158 C2
Fuente-Álamo de Murcia E 165 B3
Fuente Dé E 142 A2
Fuente de Cantos E 155 C4
Fuente de Santa Cruz E 150 A3
Fuente del Arco E 156 B2
Fuente del Conde E 163 A3
Fuente del Maestre E 155 C4
Fuente el Fresno E 157 A4
Fuente el Saz de Jarama E 151 B4
Fuente el Sol E 150 A3
Fuente Obejuna E 156 B2
Fuente Palmera E 162 A2
Fuente-Tójar E 163 A3
Fuente Vaqueros E 163 A4
Fuentealbilla E 158 B2
Fuentecén E 151 A4
Fuenteguinaldo E 149 B3
Fuentelapeña E 150 A2
Fuentelcésped E 151 A4
Fuentelespino de Haro E 158 B1
Fuentelespino de Moya E 158 B2
Fuentenovilla E 151 B4
Fuentepelayo E 151 A3
Fuentepinilla E 151 A5
Fuenterroble de Salvatierra E 150 B2
Fuenterrobles E 158 B2
Fuentes E 158 B1
Fuentes de Andalucía E 162 A2
Fuentes de Ebro E 153 A3
Fuentes de Jiloca E 152 A2
Fuentes de la Alcarria E 151 B5
Fuentes de León E 161 A3
Fuentes de Nava E 142 B2
Fuentes de Oñoro E 149 B3
Fuentes de Ropel E 142 B1
Fuentesauco, *Segovia* E 151 A3
Fuentesaúco, *Zamora* E 150 A2
Fuentespalda E 153 B4
Fuentespina E 151 A4
Fuentidueña E 151 A4
Fuentidueña de Tajo E 151 B4
Fuerte del Rey E 157 C4
Fügen A 108 B2
Fuglebjerg DK 65 A4
Fuglevik N 54 A1
Fuhrberg D 72 B2
Fulda D 82 B1
Fulgatore I 176 B1
Fully CH 119 A4
Fulnek CZ 98 B1
Fülöpszállás H 112 C3
Fulpmes A 108 B2
Fulunäs S 49 A5
Fumay F 91 B4
Fumel F 129 B3
Funäsdalen S 199 C9
Fundão P 148 B2
Funzie GB 33 A6
Furadouro P 148 B1
Fure N 46 A2
Fürstenau, *Niedersachsen* D 71 B4
Furstenau, *Nordrhein-Westfalen* D 81 A5
Fürstenberg D 74 A2
Fürstenfeld A 111 B3
Fürstenfeldbruck D 108 A2
Fürstenstein D 96 C1
Fürstenwalde D 74 B3
Fürstenwerder D 74 A2
Fürstenzell D 96 C1
Furta H 113 B5
Fürth, *Bayern* D 94 B2
Fürth, *Hessen* D 93 B4
Furth im Wald D 95 B4
Furtwangen D 106 A3
Furuby S 62 B3
Furudal S 50 A2
Furuflaten N 192 C4
Furulund S 61 D3
Furusjö S 60 B3
Fusa N 46 B2
Fuscaldo I 174 B2
Fusch an der Grossglocknerstrasse A 109 B3
Fushë Arrëz AL 182 A2
Fushë-Krujë AL 182 B1
Fusina I 122 B1
Fusio CH 107 C3
Füssen D 108 B1
Fustiñana E 144 B2
Futog SRB 126 B1
Futrikelv N 192 C3
Füzesabony H 113 B4
Füzesgyarmat H 113 B5
Fužine HR 123 B3
Fyllinge S 61 C2
Fynshav DK 64 B2
Fyresdal N 53 A4

G

Gaaldorf A 110 B1
Gabaldón E 158 B2
Gabarret F 128 C2
Gabčíkovo SK 111 B4
Gąbin PL 77 B4
Gabriac F 130 A1
Gabrovo BG 17 D6
Gaby I 119 B4
Gacé F 89 B4
Gacko BIH 139 B4
Gäddede S 199 A11
Gadebusch D 65 C4
Gadmen CH 106 C3
Gádor E 164 C2
Gádoros H 113 C4
Gael F 101 A3
Gærum DK 58 A3
Găeşti RO 17 C6
Gaeta I 169 B3
Gafanhoeira P 154 C2
Gaflenz A 110 B1
Gagarin RUS 9 E9
Gaggenau D 93 C4
Gagliano Castelferrato I 177 B3
Gagliano del Capo I 173 C4
Gagnet S 50 B2
Gaibanella I 121 C4
Gaildorf D 94 B1
Gaillac F 129 C4
Gaillefontaine F 90 B1
Gaillon F 89 A5
Gainsborough GB 40 B3
Gairloch GB 31 B3
Gairlochy GB 34 B3
Gáiro I 179 C3
Gaj HR 124 B3
Gaj SRB 127 C3
Gaja-la-Selve F 146 A2
Gajanejos E 151 B5
Gajary SK 97 C4
Gajdobra SRB 126 B1
Galan F 145 A4
Galanta SK 111 A4
Galapagar E 151 B3
Galápagos E 151 B4
Galaroza E 161 B3
Galashiels GB 35 C5
Galatas GR 185 B4
Galaţi RO 17 C8
Galatina I 173 B4
Galatista GR 183 C5
Galátone I 173 B4
Galaxidi GR 184 A3
Galdakao E 143 A4
Galeata I 135 B4
Galende E 141 B4
Galera E 164 B2
Galéria F 180 A1
Galgamácsa H 112 B3
Galgate GB 38 A4
Galgon F 128 B2
Galices P 148 B2
Galinduste E 150 B2
Galinoporni CY 181 A3
Galisteo E 155 B4
Galków PL 87 A3
Gallarate I 120 B1
Gallardon F 90 C1
Gallegos de Argañán E 149 B3
Gallegos del Solmirón E 150 B2
Galleguillos de Campos E 142 B1
Galleno I 135 B3
Galliate I 120 B1
Gallicano I 134 A3
Gállio I 121 B4
Gallipoli I 173 B3
Gallipoli = Gelibolu TR 186 B1
Gällivare S 196 B3
Gallizien A 110 C1
Gallneukirchen A 96 C2
Gällö S 199 C12
Gallocanta E 152 B2
Gällstad S 60 B3
Gallur E 144 C2
Galmisdale GB 31 C2
Galmpton GB 43 B3
Galston GB 36 A2
Galta N 52 A1
Galtelli I 178 B3
Galten DK 59 B2
Galtür A 107 C5
Galve de Sorbe E 151 A4
Galveias P 154 B2
Gálvez E 157 A3
Galway IRL 28 A2
Gamaches F 90 B1
Gámbara I 120 B3
Gambárie I 175 C1
Gambassi Terme I 135 B3
Gambatesa I 170 B2
Gambolò I 120 B1
Gaming A 110 B2
Gamla Uppsala S 51 C4
Gamleby S 62 A4
Gamlingay GB 44 A3
Gammelgarn S 57 C4
Gammelstad S 196 D5
Gammertingen D 107 A4
Gams CH 107 B4
Gamvik, *Finnmark* N 192 B6
Gamvik, *Finnmark* N 193 A12
Gan F 145 A3
Gáname E 149 A3
Ganda di Martello I 108 C1
Gandarela P 148 A1
Ganddal N 52 B1
Ganderkesee D 72 A1
Gandesa E 153 A4
Gandía E 159 C3
Gandino I 120 B2
Gandrup DK 58 A3
Ganges F 130 B2
Gånghester S 60 B3
Gangi I 177 B3
Gangkofen D 95 C4

Gorinchem NL 79 A4
Goring GB 44 B2
Goritsy RUS 9 D10
Göritz D 74 A2
Gorízia I 122 B2
Górki PL 77 B4
Gorleben D 73 A4
Gorleston-on-sea GB 41 C5
Gørlev DK 61 D1
Görlitz D 84 A2
Górliz E 143 A4
Görmin D 66 C2
Górna Grupa PL 69 B3
Gorna Oryakhovitsa BG 17 D6
Gornja Gorevnica SRB 127 D2
Gornja Ploča HR 137 A4
Gornja Radgona SLO 110 C2
Gornja Sabanta SRB 127 D3
Gornja Trešnjevica SRB 127 C2
Gornja Tuzla BIH 125 C4
Gornje Polje CG 139 C4
Gornje Ratkovo BIH 124 C2
Gornji Grad SLO 123 A3
Gornji Humac HR 138 B2
Gornji Jasenjani BIH 139 B3
Gornji Kamengrad BIH 124 C2
Gornji Kneginec HR 124 A2
Gornji Kosinj HR 123 C4
Gornji Milanovac SRB 127 C2
Gornji Podgradci BIH 124 B3
Gornji Ravno BIH 138 B3
Gornji Sjenicak HR 124 B1
Gornji Vakuf BIH 138 B3
Górno PL 87 B4
Görömböly H 113 A4
Górowo Iławeckie PL 69 A5
Gorran Haven GB 42 B2
Gorredijk NL 70 A3
Gorron F 88 B3
Gorseinon GB 39 C2
Gort IRL 28 A3
Gortin GB 27 B3
Görzke D 73 B5
Gorzkowice PL 86 A3
Górzno, *Kujawsko-Pomorskie* PL 77 A4
Górzno, *Zachodnio-Pomorskie* PL 75 A4
Gorzów Śląski PL 86 A2
Gorzów Wielkopolski PL 75 B4
Górzyca PL 74 B3
Gorzyce PL 98 B2
Górzyn, *Lubuskie* PL 84 A2
Gorzyń, *Wielkopolskie* PL 75 B4
Gorzyno PL 68 A2
Gosaldo I 121 A4
Gosau A 109 B4
Gosberton GB 41 C3
Gościcino PL 68 A3
Gościęcin PL 86 B2
Gościm PL 75 B4
Gościno PL 67 B4
Gosdorf A 110 C2
Gosforth GB 36 B3
Goslar D 82 A2
Goslice PL 77 B4
Gospič HR 137 A4
Gosport GB 44 C2
Goss Ilsede D 72 B3
Gössäter S 55 B4
Gossau CH 107 B4
Gössnitz D 83 B4
Gössweinstein D 95 B3
Gostivar MK 182 B2
Gostkow PL 77 C4
Göstling an der Ybbs A 110 B1
Gostomia PL 75 A5
Gostycyn PL 76 A2
Gostyń PL 85 A5
Gostynin PL 77 B4
Goszczyn PL 87 A4
Göta S 54 B3
Göteborg = Gothenburg S 60 B1
Götene S 55 B4
Gotha D 82 B2
Gothem S 57 C4
Gothenburg = Göteborg S 60 B1
Gotse Delchev BG 183 B5
Gottersdorf D 95 C4
Göttingen D 82 A1
Gottne S 200 C4
Götzis A 107 B4
Gouarec F 100 A2
Gouda NL 70 B1
Goudhurst GB 45 B4
Goumenissa GR 182 C4
Goura GR 184 B3
Gourdon F 129 B4
Gourgançon F 91 C4
Gourin F 100 A2
Gournay-en-Bray F 90 B1
Gourock GB 34 C3
Gouveia P 148 B2
Gouvy B 80 B1
Gouzeacourt F 90 A3
Gouzon F 116 A2
Govedari HR 138 C3
Govérnolo I 121 B3
Gowarczów PL 87 A4
Gowerton GB 39 C2
Gowidlino PL 68 A2
Gowran IRL 30 B1
Goyatz D 74 B3
Göynük, *Antalya* TR 189 C5
Göynük TR 187 B5
Gozdnica PL 84 A3
Gozdowo PL 77 B4
Gozee B 79 B4
Graal-Müritz D 65 B5
Grabenstätt D 109 B3
Grabhair GB 31 A2
Gråbo S 60 B2
Grabovac HR 138 B2
Grabovac SRB 127 C2
Grabovci SRB 127 C1
Grabow D 73 A4
Grabów PL 77 B4
Grabow nad Pilicą PL 87 A5
Grabów nad Prosną PL 86 A2
Grabowno PL 76 A2
Grabs CH 107 B4
Gračac HR 138 A1
Gračanica BIH 125 C4
Graçay F 103 B3
Grad SLO 111 C3
Gradac BIH 139 C4
Gradac CG 139 B5
Gradac HR 138 B3
Gradačac BIH 125 C4
Gradec HR 124 B2
Gradefes E 142 B1
Grades A 110 C1
Gradil P 154 C1
Gradina CG 139 B5
Gradina HR 124 B3
Gradisca d'Isonzo I 122 B2
Gradište HR 125 B4
Grado E 141 A4
Grado I 122 B2
Grærup Strand DK 59 C1
Græsted DK 61 C2
Grafenau D 96 C1
Gräfenberg D 95 B3
Gräfenhainichen D 83 A4
Grafenschlag A 97 C3
Grafenstein A 110 C1
Gräfenthal D 82 B3
Grafentonna D 82 A2
Grafenwöhr D 95 B3
Grafing D 108 A2
Grafling D 95 C4
Gräfsnäs S 54 B3
Gragnano I 170 C2
Grahovo SLO 122 A2
Graiguenamanagh IRL 30 B2
Grain GB 45 B4
Grainau D 108 B2
Graja de Iniesta E 158 B2
Grajera E 151 A4
Gram DK 59 C2
Gramais A 108 B1
Gramat F 129 B4
Gramatneusiedl A 111 A3
Grambow D 74 A3
Grammichele I 177 B3
Gramsh AL 182 C2
Gramzow D 74 A3
Gran N 48 B2
Granada E 163 A4
Granard IRL 27 C3
Grañas E 140 A3
Granátula de Calatrava E 157 B4
Grancey-le-Château F 105 B4
Grand-Champ F 100 B3
Grand Couronne F 89 A5
Grand-Fougeray F 101 B4
Grandas de Salime E 141 A4
Grandcamp-Maisy F 88 A2
Grândola P 160 A1
Grandpré F 91 B4
Grandrieu B 79 B4
Grandrieu F 117 C3
Grandson CH 106 C1
Grandvillars F 106 B1
Grandvilliers F 90 B1
Grañén E 145 C3
Grangärde S 50 B1
Grange IRL 26 B2
Grange-over-Sands GB 36 B4
Grangemouth GB 35 B4
Granges-de Crouhens F 145 B4
Granges-sur-Vologne F 106 A1
Grängesberg S 50 B1
Gräningen D 73 B5
Granitola-Torretta I 176 B1
Granja, *Évora* P 155 C3
Granja, *Porto* P 148 A1
Granja de Moreruela E 142 C1
Granja de Torrehermosa E 156 B2
Gränna S 55 B5
Grannäs, *Västerbotten* S 195 E7
Grannäs, *Västerbotten* S 195 E8
Granö S 200 B5
Granollers E 147 C3
Granowiec PL 85 A5
Granowo PL 75 B5
Gransee D 74 A2
Gransherad N 53 A5
Grantham GB 40 C3
Grantown-on-Spey GB 32 D3
Grantshouse GB 35 C5
Granville F 88 B2
Granvin N 46 B3
Gräsås S 60 C2
Grasbakken N 193 B12
Grasberg D 72 A2
Grasmere GB 36 B3
Gräsmyr S 200 C5
Grasö S 51 B5
Grassano I 172 B2
Grassau D 109 B3
Grasse F 132 B2
Grassington GB 40 A2
Gråsten DK 64 B2
Grästorp S 54 B3
Gratkorn A 110 B2
Gråträsk S 196 D2
Gratwein A 110 B2
Graulhet F 129 C4
Graus E 145 B4
Grávalos E 144 B2
Gravberget N 49 B4
Grave NL 80 A1
Gravedona I 120 A2
Gravelines F 78 A2
Gravellona Toce I 119 B5
Gravendal S 50 B1
Gravens DK 59 C2
Gravesend GB 45 B4
Graveson F 131 B3
Gravina in Púglia I 172 B2
Gray F 105 B4
Grayrigg GB 37 B4
Grays GB 45 B4
Grayshott GB 44 B3
Graz A 110 B2
Grazalema E 162 B2
Grążawy PL 69 B4
Grazzano Visconti I 120 C2
Greåker N 54 A2
Great Dunmow GB 45 B4
Great Malvern GB 39 B4
Great Torrington GB 42 B2
Great Waltham GB 45 B4
Great Yarmouth GB 41 C5
Grebbestad S 54 B2
Grebenstein D 81 A5
Grębocice PL 85 A4
Grębocin PL 76 A3
Greding D 95 B3
Gredstedbro DK 59 C1
Greenhead GB 37 B4
Greenisland GB 27 B5
Greenlaw GB 35 C5
Greenock GB 34 C3
Greenway GB 39 C2
Greenwich GB 45 B4
Grefrath D 80 A2
Greifenburg A 109 C4
Greiffenberg D 74 A2
Greifswald D 66 B2
Grein A 110 A1
Greipstad N 53 B3
Greiz D 83 B4
Grenaa DK 58 B3
Grenade F 129 C4
Grenade-sur-l'Adour F 128 C2
Grenchen CH 106 B2
Grendi N 53 B3
Grenivík IS 191 B7
Grenoble F 118 B2
Gréoux-les-Bains F 132 B1
Gresenhorst D 66 B1
Gressoney-la-Trinité I 119 B4
Gressoney-St.-Jean I 119 B4
Gressthal D 82 B2
Gressvik N 54 A1
Gresten A 110 B2
Gretna GB 36 B3
Greussen D 82 A2
Greve in Chianti I 135 B4
Greven, *Mecklenburg-Vorpommern* D 73 A3
Greven, *Nordrhein-Westfalen* D 71 B4
Grevena GR 182 C3
Grevenbroich D 80 A2
Grevenbrück D 81 A4
Grevenmacher L 92 B2
Grevesmühlen D 65 C4
Grevestrand DK 61 D2
Grevie S 61 C2
Greystoke GB 36 B4
Greystones IRL 30 A2
Grez-Doiceau B 79 B4
Grez-en-Bouère F 102 B1
Grèzec F 129 B4
Grezzana I 121 B4
Grgar SLO 122 A2
Grgurevci SRB 127 B1
Gries A 108 B2
Gries in Sellrain A 108 B2
Griesbach D 96 C1
Griesheim D 93 B4
Grieskirchen A 109 A4
Griffen A 110 C1
Grignan F 131 A3
Grignano I 122 B2
Grigno I 121 A4
Grignols F 128 B2
Grignon F 118 B3
Grijota E 142 B2
Grijpskerk NL 71 A3
Grillby S 56 A3
Grimaud F 132 B2
Grimbergen B 79 B4
Grimma D 83 A4
Grimmen D 66 B2
Grimmialp CH 106 C2
Grimsås S 60 B3
Grimsby GB 41 B3
Grimslöv S 62 B2
Grímsstaðir IS 191 B9
Grimstad N 53 B4
Grimstorp S 62 A2
Grindavík IS 190 D3
Grindelwald CH 106 C3
Grindheim N 52 B3
Grindsted DK 59 C1
Griñón E 151 B4
Gripenberg S 62 A2
Gripsholm S 56 A3
Grisolles F 129 C4
Grisslehamn S 51 B5
Gritley GB 33 C4
Grizebeck GB 36 B3
Grndina BIH 124 C2
Gröbming A 109 B4
Gröbzig D 83 A3
Grocka SRB 127 C2
Gröditz D 83 A5
Gródki PL 77 A5
Grodków PL 85 B5
Grodziec PL 76 B3
Grodzisk Mazowiecki PL 77 B5
Groenlo NL 71 B3
Groesbeek NL 80 A1
Grohote HR 138 B2
Groitzsch D 83 A4
Groix F 100 B2
Grójec PL 77 C5
Grom PL 77 A5
Gromiljca BIH 139 B4
Grömitz D 65 B3
Gromnik PL 99 B4
Gromo I 120 B2
Gronau, *Niedersachsen* D 72 B2
Gronau, *Nordrhein-Westfalen* D 71 B4
Grønbjerg DK 59 B1
Grönenbach D 107 B5
Grong N 199 A9
Grönhögen S 63 B4
Groningen D 73 C4
Groningen NL 71 A3
Grønnestrand DK 58 A2
Grono CH 120 A2
Grönskåra S 62 A3
Grootegast NL 71 A3
Gropello Cairoli I 120 B1
Grorud N 48 C2
Grósio I 120 A3
Grošnica SRB 127 D2
Gross Beeren D 74 B2
Gross Berkel D 72 B2
Gross-botwar D 94 C1
Gross-Dölln D 74 A2
Gross-Gerau D 93 B4
Grosshartmansdorf D 83 B5
Gross Kreutz D 74 B1
Gross Lafferde D 72 B3
Gross Leuthen D 74 B3
Gross Muckrow D 74 B3
Gross Oesingen D 72 B3
Gross Reken D 80 A3
Gross Sarau D 65 C3
Gross Särchen D 84 A2
Gross Schönebeck D 74 B2
Gross Umstadt D 93 B4
Gross Warnow D 73 A4
Gross-Weikersdorf A 97 C3
Gross-Welle D 73 A5
Gross Wokern D 65 C5
Grossalmerode D 82 A1
Grossarl A 109 B4
Grossbodungen D 82 A2
Grossburgwedel D 72 B2
Grosschönau D 84 B2
Grossenbrode D 65 B4
Grossenehrich D 82 A2
Grossengottern D 82 A2
Grossenhain D 83 A5
Grossenkneten D 71 B5
Grossenlüder D 81 B5
Grossensee D 72 A3
Grossenzersdorf A 111 A3
Grosseto I 135 C4
Grossgerungs A 96 C2
Grossglobnitz A 97 C3
Grosshabersdorf D 94 B2
Grossharras A 97 C4
Grosshöchstetten CH 106 C2
Grosskrut A 97 C4
Grosslohra D 82 A2
Grossmehring D 95 C3
Grossostheim D 93 B5
Grosspertholz A 96 C2
Grosspetersdorf A 111 B3
Grosspostwitz D 84 A2
Grossraming A 110 B1
Grossräschen D 84 A2
Grossrinderfeld D 94 B1
Grossröhrsdorf D 84 A2
Grossschirma D 83 B5
Grossschweinbarth A 97 C4
Grosssiegharts A 97 C3
Grosssölk A 109 B4
Grosswarasdorf A 111 B3
Grosswilfersdorf A 110 B2
Grostenquin F 92 C2
Grosuplje SLO 123 B3
Grotli N 198 C4
Grötlingbo S 57 C4
Grottáglie I 173 B3
Grottaminarda I 170 B3
Grottammare I 136 C2
Grotte di Castro I 168 A1
Grotteria I 175 C2
Gróttole I 172 B2
Grouw NL 70 A2
Grov N 194 B8
Grova N 53 A4
Grove E 140 B2
Grua N 48 B2
Grube D 65 B4
Grubišno Polje HR 124 B3
Grude BIH 138 B3
Grudovo BG 17 D7
Grudusk PL 77 A5
Grudziądz PL 69 B3
Grue N 49 B4
Gruissan F 130 B2
Grullos E 141 A4
Grumo Áppula I 171 B4
Grums S 55 A4
Grünau im Almtal A 109 B4
Grünberg D 81 B4
Grünburg A 110 B1
Grundarfjörður IS 190 C2
Gründau D 81 B5
Gründelhardt D 94 B1
Grundforsen S 49 A4
Grundlsee A 109 B4
Grundsund S 54 B2
Grunewald D 84 A1
Grungedal N 53 A3
Grunow D 74 B3
Grünstadt D 93 B4
Gruvberget S 50 A3
Gruyères CH 106 C2
Gruža SRB 127 D2
Grybów PL 99 B4
Grycksbo S 50 B2
Gryfice PL 67 C4
Gryfino PL 74 A3
Gryfów Śląski PL 84 A3
Gryllefjord N 194 A8
Grymyr N 48 B2
Gryt S 56 B2
Grytgöl S 56 B1
Grythyttan S 55 A5
Grytnäs S 57 B3
Grzmiąca PL 68 B1
Grzybno PL 74 A3
Grzywna PL 76 A3
Gschnitz A 108 B2
Gschwend D 94 C1
Gstaad CH 106 C2
Gsteig CH 119 A4
Guadahortuna E 163 A4
Guadalajara E 151 B4
Guadalaviar E 152 B2
Guadalcanal E 156 B2
Guadalcázar E 162 A3
Guadalix de la Sierra E 151 B4
Guadálmez E 156 B3
Guadalupe E 156 A2
Guadamur E 151 C3
Guadarrama E 151 B3
Guadiaro E 162 B2
Guadix E 164 B1
Guagnano I 173 B3
Guagno F 180 A1
Guajar-Faragüit E 163 B4
Gualchos E 163 B4
Gualdo Tadino I 136 B1
Gualtieri I 121 C3
Guarcino I 169 B3
Guarda P 149 B2
Guardamar del Segura E 165 A4
Guardão P 148 B1
Guardavalle I 175 C2
Guardea I 168 A2
Guárdia I 172 B1
Guárdia Sanframondi I 170 B2
Guardiagrele I 169 A4
Guardiarégia I 170 B2
Guardias Viejas E 164 C2
Guardiola de Bergueda E 147 B2
Guardo E 142 B2
Guareña E 156 B1
Guaro E 162 B3
Guarromán E 157 B4
Guasila I 179 C3
Guastalla I 121 C3
Gubbhögen S 199 A12
Gúbbio I 136 B1
Guben D 74 C3
Gubin PL 74 C3
Gudå N 199 B8
Gudavac BIH 124 C2
Guddal N 46 A2
Güderup DK 64 B2
Gudhem S 55 B4
Gudhjem DK 67 A3
Gudovac HR 124 B2
Gudow D 73 A3
Güdül TR 187 B7
Gudvangen N 46 B3
Guebwiller F 106 B2
Guéjar-Sierra E 163 A4
Guéméné-Penfao F 101 B4
Guéméné-sur-Scorff F 100 A2
Güeñes E 143 A3
Guer F 101 B3
Guérande F 101 B3
Guéret F 116 A1
Guérigny F 104 B2
Guesa E 144 B2
Gueugnon F 104 C3
Guglionesi I 170 B2
Gühlen Glienicke D 74 A1
Guia P 154 B2
Guichen F 101 B4
Guidizzolo I 121 B3
Guidónia-Montecélio I 168 B2
Guiglia I 135 A3
Guignes F 90 C2
Guijo E 156 B3
Guijo de Coria E 149 B3
Guijo de Santa Bábera E 150 B2
Guijuelo E 150 B2
Guildford GB 44 B3
Guillaumes F 132 A2
Guillena E 162 A1
Guillestre F 118 C3
Guillos F 128 B2
Guilsfield GB 38 B3
Guilvinec F 100 B1
Guimarães P 148 A1
Guincho P 154 C1
Guînes F 78 B1
Guingamp F 100 A2
Guipavas F 100 A1
Guisborough GB 37 B5
Guiscard F 90 B3
Guiscriff F 100 A2
Guise F 91 B3
Guisona E 147 C2
Guitiriz E 140 A3
Guîtres F 128 A2
Gujan-Mestras F 128 B1
Gulbene LV 8 D5
Gulçayır TR 187 C6
Guldborg DK 65 B4
Gullabo S 63 B3
Gullane GB 35 B5
Gullbrå N 46 B3
Gullbrandstorp S 61 C2
Gulleråsen S 50 A2
Gullhaug N 53 A6
Gullringen S 62 A3
Gullspång S 55 B5
Gullstein N 198 B5
Güllük TR 188 B2
Gülnar TR 23 C7
Gülpınar TR 186 C1
Gülşehir TR 23 B8
Gulsvik N 48 B1
Gülübovo BG 183 A7
Gumiel de Hizán E 143 C3
Gummersbach D 81 A3
Gümüldür TR 188 A2
Gümüşhaciköy TR 23 A8
Gümüşova TR 187 B5
Gundel-fingen D 106 A2
Gundelfingen D 94 C2
Gundelsheim D 93 B5
Gunderschoffen F 93 C3
Gundertshausen A 109 A3
Gundinci HR 125 B4
Gündoğmuş TR 189 C7
Güney, *Burdur* TR 189 B4
Güney, *Denizli* TR 188 A4
Gunja HR 125 C4
Günlüce TR 188 C3
Gunnarn S 195 E8
Gunnarsbyn S 196 C4
Gunnarskog S 49 C4
Gunnebo S 62 A4
Gunnislake GB 42 B2
Günselsdorf A 111 B3
Guntersblum D 93 B4
Guntersdorf A 97 C4

Guntin E 140 B3
Günyüzü TR 187 C6
Günzburg D 94 C2
Gunzenhausen D 94 B2
Güre, *Balıkesir* TR 186 C1
Güre, *Uşak* TR 186 D4
Gurk A 110 C1
Gurrea de Gállego E 144 B3
Gürsu TR 186 B4
Gušće HR 124 B2
Gusev RUS 12 A5
Gúspini I 179 C2
Gusselby S 56 A1
Güssing A 111 B3
Gusswerk A 110 B2
Gustav Adolf S 49 B5
Gustavsberg S 57 A4
Gustavsfors S 54 A3
Güstrow D 65 C5
Gusum S 56 B2
Gutcher GB 33 A5
Gutenstein A 110 B2
Gütersloh D 81 A4
Guttannen CH 106 C3
Guttaring A 110 C1
Guttau D 84 A2
Güttingen CH 107 B4
Gützkow D 66 C2
Guzów PL 77 B5
Gvardeysk RUS 12 A4
Gvarv N 53 A5
Gvozd CG 139 C5
Gvozdansko HR 124 B2
Gwda Wielka PL 68 B1
Gwennap GB 42 B1
Gy F 105 B4
Gyál H 112 B3
Gyarmat H 111 B4
Gyé-sur-Seine F 104 A3
Gyékényes H 124 A3
Gyljen S 196 C5
Gylling DK 59 C3
Gyoma H 113 C4
Gyömöre H 111 B4
Gyömrö H 112 B3
Gyón H 112 B3
Gyöngyfa H 125 B3
Gyöngyös H 113 B3
Gyöngyöspata H 113 B3
Gyönk H 112 C2
Györ H 111 B4
Györszemere H 111 B4
Gypsera CH 106 C2
Gysinge S 51 B3
Gyttorp S 55 A5
Gyula H 113 C5
Gyulafirátót H 112 B1
Gyulaj H 112 C2

H

Haacht B 79 B4
Haag, *Nieder Östereich* A 110 A1
Haag, *Ober Östereich* A 109 A4
Haag D 108 A3
Haaksbergen NL 71 B3
Haamstede NL 79 A3
Haan D 80 A3
Haapajärvi FIN 3 E9
Haapsalu EST 8 C3
Haarlem NL 70 B1
Habas F 128 C2
Habay B 92 B1
Habo S 62 A2
Håbol S 54 B3
Habry CZ 97 B3
Habsheim F 106 B2
Hachenburg D 81 B3
Hacıbektaş TR 23 B8
Hacılar TR 23 B8
Hacinas E 143 C3
Hackås S 199 C11
Hacketstown IRL 30 B2
Hackthorpe GB 37 B4
Hadamar D 81 B4
Hädanberg S 200 C4
Haddington GB 35 C5
Hadersdorf am Kamp A 97 C3
Haderslev DK 59 C2
Haderup DK 59 B1
Hadım TR 23 C7
Hadleigh, *Essex* GB 45 B4
Hadleigh, *Suffolk* GB 45 A4
Hadlow GB 45 B4
Hadmersleben D 73 B4
Hadsten DK 59 B3
Hadsund DK 58 B3
Hadžići BIH 139 B4
Hægebostad N 52 B3
Hægeland N 53 B3
Hafnarfjörður IS 190 C4
Hafnir IS 190 D3
Hafslo N 47 A4
Haganj HR 124 B2
Hagby S 63 B4
Hage D 71 A4
Hagen, *Niedersachsen* D 72 A1
Hagen, *Nordrhein-Westfalen* D 80 A3
Hagenbach D 93 B4
Hagenow D 73 A4
Hagetmau F 128 C2
Hagfors S 49 B5
Häggenås S 199 B11
Hagondange F 92 B2
Hagsta S 51 B4
Haguenau F 93 C3
Hahnbach D 95 B3
Hahnslätten D 81 B4
Hahót H 111 C3
Haiger D 81 B4
Haigerloch D 93 C4
Hailsham GB 45 C4
Hainburg A 111 A3
Hainfeld A 110 A2
Hainichen D 83 B5
Hajdúböszörmény H 113 B5
Hajdučica SRB 126 B2
Hajdúdorogo H 113 B5
Hajdúnánás H 113 B5
Hajdúszoboszló H 113 B5
Hajnáčka SK 113 A3
Hajnówka PL 13 B5
Hajós H 112 C3
Håkafot S 199 A11
Hakkas S 196 C4
Håksberg S 50 B2
Halaszi H 111 B4
Halberstadt D 82 A3
Halberton GB 43 B3
Hald Ege DK 58 B2
Haldem D 71 B5
Halden N 54 A2
Haldensleben D 73 B4
Halenbeck D 73 A5
Halesowen GB 40 C1
Halesworth GB 45 A5
Halfing D 109 B3
Halhjem N 46 B2
Håliden S 49 B5
Halifax GB 40 B2
Häljelöt S 56 B2
Halkida GR 185 A4
Halkirk GB 32 C3
Hall S 57 C4
Hall in Tirol A 108 B2
Hälla S 200 C3
Hallabro S 63 B3
Hällabrottet S 56 A1
Halland GB 45 C4
Hällaryd, *Blekinge* S 63 B2
Hallaryd, *Kronoberg* S 61 C3
Hällberga S 56 A2
Hällbybrunn S 56 A2
Halle B 79 B4
Halle, *Nordrhein-Westfalen* D 72 B1
Halle, *Sachsen-Anhalt* D 83 A3
Hålleberga S 62 B3
Hällefors S 55 A5
Hälleforsnäs S 56 A2
Hallein A 109 B4
Hällekis S 55 B4
Hallen, *Jämtland* S 199 B11
Hållen, *Uppsala* S 51 B4
Hallenberg D 81 A4
Hällestad S 56 B1
Hällevadsholm S 54 B2
Hällevik S 63 B2
Hälleviksstrand S 54 B2
Hallingby N 48 B2
Hallingeberg S 62 A4
Hallingen N 47 B6
Hällnäs, *Norrbotten* S 195 D9
Hållnäs, *Uppsala* S 51 B4
Hällnäs, *Västerbotten* S 200 B5
Hallormsstaður IS 191 B11
Hallsberg S 56 A1
Hållsta S 56 A2
Hallstahammar S 56 A2
Hallstatt A 109 B4
Hallstavik S 51 B5
Halltorp S 63 B4
Halluin F 78 B3
Hallviken S 199 B12
Hallworthy GB 42 B2
Halmstad S 61 C2
Hals DK 58 A3
Halsa N 198 B5
Halstead GB 45 B4
Haltdalen N 199 C8
Haltern D 80 A3
Haltwhistle GB 37 B4
Halvarsgårdarna S 50 B2
Halver D 80 A3
Halvrimmen DK 58 A2
Ham F 90 B3
Hamar N 48 B3
Hamarhaug N 46 B2
Hamarøy N 194 B6
Hambach F 92 B3
Hambergen D 72 A1
Hambergsund S 54 B2
Hambledon GB 44 C2
Hambuhren D 72 B2
Hamburg D 72 A3
Hamdibey TR 186 C2
Hamdorf D 64 B2
Hämeenlinna FIN 8 B4
Hameln = Hamlin D 72 B2
Hamersleben D 73 B4
Hamidiye TR 187 C5
Hamilton GB 36 A2
Hamina FIN 8 B5
Hamlagrø N 46 B3
Hamlin = Hameln D 72 B2
Hamm D 81 A3
Hammar S 55 B5
Hammarland FIN 51 B6
Hammarö S 55 A4
Hammarstrand S 200 C2
Hamme B 79 A4
Hammel DK 59 B2
Hammelburg D 82 B1
Hammelspring D 74 A2
Hammenhög S 66 A3
Hammerdal S 199 B12
Hammerfest N 192 B7
Hammershøj DK 58 B2
Hammerum DK 59 B2
Hamminkeln D 80 A2
Hamnavoe GB 33 A5
Hamneda S 60 C3
Hamningberg N 193 B14
Hamoir B 80 B1
Hamont B 80 A1
Hámor H 113 A4
Hamra, *Gävleborg* S 199 D12
Hamra, *Gotland* S 57 D4
Hamrångefjärden S 51 B4
Hamstreet GB 45 B4
Hamsund N 194 B6
Han TR 187 C5
Han Knežica BIH 124 B2
Han Pijesak BIH 139 A4
Hanaskog S 61 C4
Hanau D 81 B4
Händelöp S 62 A4
Handlová SK 98 C2
Hanerau-Hademarschen D 64 B2
Hånger S 60 B3
Hanhimaa FIN 197 B8
Hanken S 55 B5
Hankensbüttel D 73 B3
Hanko FIN 8 C3
Hannover D 72 B2
Hannut B 79 B5
Hansnes N 192 C3
Hanstedt D 72 A3
Hanstholm DK 58 A1
Hantsavichy BY 13 B7
Hanušovice CZ 85 B4
Haparanda S 196 D7
Haradok BY 13 A8
Harads S 196 C4
Häradsbäck S 63 B2
Häradsbygden S 50 B2
Harbo S 51 B4
Harboør DK 58 B1
Harburg, *Bayern* D 94 C2
Harburg, *Hamburg* D 72 A2
Hårby DK 59 C3
Harc H 112 C2
Hardegarijp NL 70 A2
Hardegsen D 82 A1
Hardelot Plage F 78 B1
Hardenbeck D 74 A2
Hardenberg NL 71 B3
Harderwijk NL 70 B2
Hardheim D 94 B1
Hardt D 106 A3
Hareid N 198 C3
Haren D 71 B4
Haren NL 71 A3
Harestua N 48 B2
Harfleur F 89 A4
Harg S 51 B5
Hargicourt F 90 B3
Hargnies F 91 A4
Hargshamn S 51 B5
Härja S 55 B4
Harkány H 125 B4
Härkeberga S 56 A3
Harkebrügge D 71 A4
Harlech GB 38 B2
Harleston GB 45 A5
Hårlev DK 65 A5
Harlingen NL 70 A2
Harlösa S 61 D3
Harlow GB 45 B4
Harmancık TR 186 C4
Harmånger S 200 E3
Härnevi S 56 A3
Härnösand S 200 D3
Haro E 143 B4
Haroldswick GB 33 A6
Háromfa H 124 A3
Haroué F 92 C2
Harpenden GB 44 B3
Harplinge S 60 C2
Harpstedt D 72 B1
Harrogate GB 40 A2
Harrow GB 44 B3
Härryda S 60 B2
Harsefeld D 72 A2
Harsewinkel D 71 C5
Hârşova RO 17 C7
Harstad N 194 B7
Harsum D 72 B2
Harsvik N 199 A7
Harta H 112 C3
Hartberg A 110 B2
Hartburn GB 37 A5
Hartennes F 90 B3
Hartest GB 45 A4
Hartha D 83 A4
Hartland GB 42 B2
Hartlepool GB 37 B5
Hartmanice CZ 96 B1
Hartmannsdorf A 110 B2
Harvassdal N 195 E5
Harwell GB 44 B2
Harwich GB 45 B5
Harzgerode D 82 A3
Häselgehr A 108 B1
Haselünne D 71 B4
Hasköy TR 186 A1
Haslach D 106 A3
Haslach an der Mühl A 96 C2
Hasle DK 67 A3
Haslemere GB 44 B3
Haslev DK 65 A4
Hasloch D 94 B1
Hasparren F 144 A2
Hassela S 200 D2
Hasselfelde D 82 A2
Hasselfors S 55 A5
Hasselt B 79 B5
Hasselt NL 70 B3
Hassfurt D 94 A2
Hassleben D 74 A2
Hässleholm S 61 C3
Hasslö S 63 B3
Hassloch D 93 B4
Hästbo S 51 B4
Hastersboda FIN 51 B7
Hästholmen S 55 B5
Hastière-Lavaux B 79 B4
Hastigrow GB 32 C3
Hastings GB 45 C4
Hästveda S 61 C3
Hasvik N 192 B6
Hatfield, *Hertfordshire* GB 44 B3
Hatfield, *South Yorkshire* GB 40 B3
Hatherleigh GB 42 B2
Hathersage GB 40 B2
Hatlestrand N 46 B2
Hattem NL 70 B3
Hatten D 71 A5
Hatten F 93 C3
Hattfjelldal N 195 E4
Hatting DK 59 C2
Hattingen D 80 A3
Hattstadt F 106 A2
Hattstedt D 64 B2
Hatvan H 112 B3
Hatvik N 46 B2
Hau D 80 A2
Haudainville F 92 B1
Hauganes IS 191 B7
Haugastøl N 47 B4
Hauge N 52 B2
Haugesund N 52 A1
Haughom N 52 B2
Haugsdal N 46 B2
Haugsdorf A 97 C4
Haukedal N 46 A3
Haukeland N 46 B2
Haukeligrend N 52 A3
Haukeliseter N 52 A3
Haukipudas FIN 3 D9
Haulerwijk NL 71 A3
Haunersdorf D 95 C4
Haus N 46 B2
Hausach D 106 A3
Hausham D 108 B2
Hausmannstätten A 110 C2
Hausvik N 52 B2
Haut-Fays B 91 A5
Hautajärvi FIN 197 C12
Hautefort F 129 A4
Hauterives F 117 B5
Hauteville-Lompnès F 118 B2
Hautmont F 79 B3
Hautrage B 79 B3
Hauzenberg D 96 C1
Havant GB 44 C3
Havdhem S 57 C4
Havdrup DK 61 D2
Havelange B 79 B5
Havelberg D 73 B5
Havelte NL 70 B3
Haverfordwest GB 39 C2
Haverhill GB 45 A4
Havering GB 45 B4
Håverud S 54 B3
Havířov CZ 98 B2
Havixbeck D 71 C4
Havlíčkův Brod CZ 97 B3
Havndal DK 58 B3
Havneby DK 64 A1
Havnebyen DK 61 D1
Havnsø DK 61 D1
Havøysund N 193 A8
Havran TR 186 C2
Havrebjerg DK 61 D1
Havsa TR 186 A1
Havstenssund S 54 B2
Havza TR 23 A8
Hawes GB 37 B4
Hawick GB 35 C5
Hawkhurst GB 45 B4
Hawkinge GB 45 B5
Haxey GB 40 B3
Hay-on-Wye GB 39 B3
Hayange F 92 B2
Haydarlı TR 189 A5
Haydon Bridge GB 37 B4
Hayle GB 42 B1
Haymana TR 187 C7
Hayrabolu TR 186 A2
Haysyn UA 13 D8
Hayvoron UA 13 D8
Haywards Heath GB 44 C3
Hazebrouck F 78 B2
Hazlov CZ 83 B4
Heacham GB 41 C4
Headcorn GB 45 B4
Headford IRL 28 A2
Heanor GB 40 B2
Héas F 145 B4
Heathfield GB 45 C4
Hebden Bridge GB 40 B1
Heberg S 60 C2
Heby S 51 C3
Hechingen D 93 C4
Hechlingen D 94 C2
Hecho E 144 B3
Hechtel B 79 A5
Hechthausen D 72 A2
Heckelberg D 74 B2
Heckington GB 41 C3
Hecklingen D 82 A3
Hed S 56 A1
Hedalen N 48 B1
Hedared S 60 B2
Heddal N 53 A5
Hédé F 101 A4
Hede S 199 C10
Hedekas S 54 B2
Hedemora S 50 B2
Hedenäset S 196 C6
Hedensted DK 59 C2
Hedersleben D 82 A3
Hedesunda S 51 B4
Hedge End GB 44 C2
Hedon GB 41 B3
Heede D 71 B4
Heek D 71 B4
Heemstede NL 70 B1
Heerde NL 70 B3
Heerenveen NL 70 B2
Heerhugowaard NL 70 B1
Heerlen NL 80 B1
Heeze NL 80 A1
Heggenes N 47 A6
Hegra N 199 B8
Hegyeshalom H 111 B4
Hegyközség H 111 B3
Heia N 199 A9
Heide D 64 B2
Heidelberg D 93 B4
Heiden D 80 A2
Heidenau D 84 B1
Heidenheim D 94 C2
Heidenreichstein A 97 C3
Heikendorf D 64 B3
Heikkilä FIN 197 C12
Heilam GB 32 C2
Heiland N 53 B4
Heilbad Heiligenstadt D 82 A2
Heilbronn D 93 B5
Heiligenblut A 109 B3
Heiligendamm D 65 B4
Heiligendorf D 73 B3
Heiligengrabe D 73 A5
Heiligenhafen D 65 B3
Heiligenhaus D 80 A2
Heiligenkreuz A 111 C3
Heiligenstadt D 94 B3
Heiloo NL 70 B1
Heilsbronn D 94 B2
Heim N 198 B6
Heimburg D 82 A2
Heimdal N 199 B7
Heinerscheid L 92 A2
Heinersdorf D 74 B3
Heining D 96 C1
Heiningen D 94 C1
Heinola FIN 8 B5
Heinsberg D 80 A2
Heist-op-den-Berg B 79 A4
Hejde S 57 C4
Hejdeby S 57 C4
Hejls DK 59 C2
Hejnice CZ 84 B3
Hel PL 69 A3
Helchteren B 79 A5
Heldburg D 82 B2
Heldrungen D 82 A3
Helechosa E 156 A3
Helensburgh GB 34 B3
Helfenberg A 96 C2
Helgen N 53 A5
Helgeroa N 53 B5
Hella IS 190 D5
Hella N 46 A3
Helland N 194 B7
Hellas S 55 B3
Helle N 52 B2
Helleland N 52 B2
Hellendoorn NL 71 B3
Hellenthal D 80 B2
Hellesøy N 46 B1
Hellesylt N 198 C3
Hellevoetsluis NL 79 A4
Helligskogen N 192 C4
Hellín E 158 C2
Hellissandur IS 190 C2
Hellnar IS 190 C2
Hellum DK 58 A3
Hellvi S 57 C4
Hellvik N 52 B1
Helm-brechts D 83 B3
Helmond NL 80 A1
Helmsdale GB 32 C3
Helmsley GB 37 B5
Helmstedt D 73 B3
Hel'pa SK 99 C3
Helsa D 82 A1
Helsby GB 38 A4
Helsingborg S 61 C2
Helsinge DK 61 C2
Helsingør DK 61 C2
Helsinki FIN 8 B4
Helston GB 42 B1
Hemau D 95 B3
Hemavan S 195 E6
Hemel Hempstead GB 44 B3
Hemer D 81 A3
Héming F 92 C2
Hemmet DK 59 C1
Hemmingstedt D 64 B2
Hemmoor D 64 C2
Hemnes N 54 A2
Hemnesberget N 195 D4
Hemse S 57 C4
Hemsedal N 47 B5
Hemslingen D 72 A2
Hemsworth GB 40 B2
Hen N 48 B2
Henån S 54 B2
Hendaye F 144 A2
Hendek TR 187 B5
Hendungen D 82 B2
Henfield GB 44 C3
Hengelo, *Gelderland* NL 71 B3
Hengelo, *Overijssel* NL 71 B3
Hengersberg D 95 C5
Hengoed GB 39 C3
Hénin-Beaumont F 78 B2
Henley-on-Thames GB 44 B3
Hennan S 200 D1
Henne Strand DK 59 C1
Henneberg D 82 B2
Hennebont F 100 B2
Hennigsdorf D 74 B2
Hennset N 198 B5
Hennstedt, *Schleswig-Holstein* D 64 B2
Hennstedt, *Schleswig-Holstein* D 64 B2
Henrichemont F 103 B4
Henryków PL 85 B5
Henrykowo PL 69 A5
Hensås N 47 A5
Henstedt-Ulzburg D 64 C2
Heppenheim D 93 B4
Herad, *Buskerud* N 47 B6
Herad, *Vest-Agder* N 52 B2
Heradsbygd N 48 B3
Heraklion = Iraklio GR 185 D6
Herálec CZ 97 B4
Herand N 46 B3
Herbault F 103 B3
Herbern D 81 A3
Herbertstown IRL 29 B3
Herbeumont B 91 B5
Herbignac F 101 B3
Herbisse F 91 C4
Herbitzheim F 92 B3
Herbolzheim D 106 A2
Herborn D 81 B4
Herbrechtingen D 94 C2
Herby PL 86 B2
Herceg-Novi CG 16 D3
Hercegovać HR 124 B3
Hercegszántó H 125 B4
Herchen D 80 B3
Heréd H 112 B3
Hereford GB 39 B4
Herefoss N 53 B4
Hereke TR 187 B4
Herencia E 157 A4
Herend H 111 B4
Herent B 79 B4
Herentals B 79 A4
Hérépian F 130 B2
Herfølge DK 61 D2
Herford D 72 B1
Herguijuela E 156 A2
Héric F 101 B4
Héricourt F 106 B1
Héricourt-en-Caux F 89 A4
Hérimoncourt F 106 B1
Heringsdorf D 65 B4
Herisau CH 107 B4
Hérisson F 103 C4
Herk-de-Stad B 79 B5
Herlufmagle DK 65 A4
Hermagor A 109 C4
Hermannsburg D 72 B3
Hermansverk N 46 A3
Heřmanův Městec CZ 97 B3

Herment F 116 B2
Hermeskeil D 92 B2
Hermisende E 141 C4
Hermonville F 91 B3
Hermsdorf D 83 B3
Hernani E 144 A2
Hernansancho E 150 B3
Herne D 80 A3
Herne Bay GB 45 B5
Hernes N 48 B3
Herning DK 59 B1
Herøya N 53 A5
Herramelluri E 143 B3
Herräng S 51 B5
Herre N 53 A5
Herrenberg D 93 C4
Herrera E 162 A3
Herrera de Alcántara E 155 B3
Herrera de los Navarros E 152 A2
Herrera de Pisuerga E 142 B2
Herrera del Duque E 156 A2
Herrerias E 161 B2
Herreros del Suso E 150 B2
Herrestad S 54 B2
Herrhamra S 57 B3
Herritslev DK 65 B4
Herrlisheim F 93 C3
Herrljunga S 55 B4
Herrnhut D 84 A2
Herrsching D 108 A2
Hersbruck D 95 B3
Hersby S 57 A4
Herscheid D 81 A3
Herselt B 79 A4
Herso GR 182 B4
Herstal B 80 B1
Herstmonceux GB 45 C4
Herten D 80 A3
Hertford GB 44 B3
Hervás E 149 B4
Hervik N 52 A1
Herxheim D 93 B4
Herzberg, *Brandenburg* D 74 B1
Herzberg, *Brandenburg* D 83 A5
Herzberg, *Niedersachsen* D 82 A2
Herzebrock D 81 A4
Herzfelde D 74 B2
Herzlake D 71 B4
Herzogenaurach D 94 B2
Herzogenbuchsee CH 106 B2
Herzogenburg A 110 A2
Herzsprung D 73 A5
Hesby N 52 A1
Hesdin F 78 B2
Hesel D 71 A4
Heskestad N 52 B2
Hessdalen N 199 C8
Hesselager DK 65 A3
Hesseng N 193 C13
Hessisch Lichtenau D 82 A1
Hessisch-Oldendorf D 72 B2
Hestra S 60 B3
Heswall GB 38 A3
Hetlevik N 46 B2
Hettange-Grande F 92 B2
Hetton-le-Hole GB 37 B5
Hettstedt D 82 A3
Heuchin F 78 B2
Heudicourt-sous-les-Côtes F 92 C1
Heunezel F 105 A5
Heuqueville F 89 A4
Heves H 113 B4
Héviz H 111 C4
Hexham GB 37 B4
Heysham GB 36 B4
Heytesbury GB 43 A4
Hidas H 125 A4
Hieflau A 110 B1
Hiendelaencina E 151 A5
Hiersac F 115 C4
High Bentham GB 37 B4
High Hesket GB 37 B4
High Wycombe GB 44 B3
Highclere GB 44 B2
Highley GB 39 B4
Higuera de Arjona E 157 C4
Higuera de Calatrava E 163 A3
Higuera de la Serena E 156 B2
Higuera de la Sierra E 161 B3
Higuera de Vargas E 155 C4
Higuera la Real E 161 A3
Higuers de Llerena E 156 B1
Higueruela E 158 C2
Hijar E 153 A3
Hilchenbach D 81 A4
Hildburghausen D 82 B2
Hilden D 80 A2
Hilders D 82 B1
Hildesheim D 72 B2
Hilgay GB 41 C4
Hillared S 60 B3
Hille D 72 B1
Hillegom NL 70 B1
Hillerød DK 61 D2
Hillerstorp S 60 B3
Hillesheim D 80 B2
Hillestad N 53 A6
Hillmersdorf D 83 A5
Hillsborough GB 27 B4
Hillswick GB 33 A5
Hilpoltstein D 95 B3
Hilpoltstein D 94 B3
Hilvarenbeek NL 79 A5
Hilversum NL 70 B2
Himarë AL 182 C1
Himbergen D 73 A3
Himesháza H 125 A4
Himmelberg A 109 C5
Himmelpforten D 72 A2
Himód H 111 B4
Hinckley GB 40 C2
Hindås S 60 B2
Hindelang D 108 B1
Hindelbank CH 106 B2
Hinderavåg N 52 A1
Hindhead GB 44 B3
Hinjosa del Valle E 156 B1
Hinnerup DK 59 B3
Hinneryd S 61 C3
Hinojal E 155 B4
Hinojales E 161 B3
Hinojos E 161 B3
Hinojosa del Duque E 156 B2
Hinojosas de Calatrava E 157 B3
Hinterhornbach A 108 B1
Hinterriss A 108 B2
Hintersee A 109 B4
Hintersee D 74 A3
Hinterstoder A 110 B1
Hintertux A 108 B2
Hinterweidenthal D 93 B3
Hinwil CH 107 B3
Hios GR 185 A7
Hippolytushoef NL 70 B1
Hirschaid D 94 B2
Hirschau D 95 B3
Hirschfeld D 83 A5
Hirschhorn D 93 B4
Hirsingue F 106 B2
Hirson F 91 B4
Hirtshals DK 58 A2
Hirvaskoski FIN 197 D10
Hirzenhain D 81 B5
Hisarcık TR 186 C4
Hishult S 61 C3
Hissjön S 200 C6
Hitchin GB 44 B3
Hitra N 198 B5
Hittarp S 61 C2
Hittisau A 107 B4
Hittun N 46 A1
Hitzacker D 73 A4
Hjallerup DK 58 A3
Hjällstad S 49 B5
Hjältevad S 62 A3
Hjärnarp S 61 C2
Hjartdal N 53 A4
Hjellestad N 46 B2
Hjelmeland N 52 A2
Hjelset N 198 C4
Hjerkinn N 198 C6
Hjerm DK 58 B1
Hjerpsted DK 64 A1
Hjerting DK 59 C1
Hjo S 55 B5
Hjordkær DK 64 A2
Hjørring DK 58 A2
Hjorted S 62 A4
Hjortkvarn S 56 B1
Hjortnäs S 50 B1
Hjortsberga S 62 B2
Hjukse N 53 A5
Hjuksebø N 53 A5
Hjulsjö S 55 A5
Hliník nad Hronom. SK 98 C2
Hlinsko CZ 97 B3
Hlío IS 191 A10
Hlohovec SK 98 C1
Hluboká nad Vltavou CZ 96 B2
Hlučín CZ 98 B2
Hlyboka UA 17 A6
Hlybokaye BY 13 A7
Hniezdne SK 99 B4
Hnilec SK 99 C4
Hnúšťa SK 99 C3
Hobol H 125 A3
Hobro DK 58 B2
Hobscheid L 92 B1
Hocalar TR 189 A4
Hochdonn D 64 B2
Hochdorf CH 106 B3
Hochfelden F 93 C3
Hochspeyer D 93 B3
Höchst im Odenwald D 93 B5
Höchstadt, *Bayern* D 94 B2
Höchstädt, *Bayern* D 94 C2
Hochstenbach D 81 B3
Höckendorf D 83 B5
Hockenheim D 93 B4
Hoddesdon GB 44 B3
Hodejov SK 99 C3
Hodenhagen D 72 B2
Hodkovice CZ 84 B3
Hódmezővásárhely H 113 C4
Hodnet GB 38 B4
Hodonín CZ 98 C1
Hodslavice CZ 98 B2
Hoedekenskerke NL 79 A3
Hoegaarden B 79 B4
Hoek van Holland NL 79 A4
Hoenderlo NL 70 B2
Hof D 83 B3
Hof N 53 A6
Hofbieber D 82 B1
Hoff GB 37 B4
Hofgeismar D 81 A5
Hofheim, *Bayern* D 82 B2
Hofheim, *Hessen* D 93 A4
Hofkirchen im Mühlkreis A 96 C1
Höfn IS 191 C10
Hofors S 50 B3
Hofsós IS 190 B6
Hofstad N 199 A7
Höganäs S 61 C2
Högbo S 51 B3
Hogdal S 54 A2
Høgebru N 46 A4
Högfors S 50 C2
Högklint S 57 C4
Högsäter S 54 B3
Högsby S 62 A4
Högsjö S 56 A1
Hogstad S 55 B6
Högyész H 112 C2
Hohen Neuendorf D 74 B2
Hohenau A 97 C4
Hohenberg A 110 B2
Hohenbucko D 83 A5
Hohenburg D 95 B3
Hohendorf D 66 B1
Hohenems A 107 B4
Hohenhameln D 72 B3
Hohenhausen D 72 B1
Hohenkirchen D 71 A4
Hohenlinden D 108 A2
Hohenlockstedt D 64 C2
Hohenmölsen D 83 A4
Hohennauen D 73 B5
Hohenseeden D 73 B5
Hohentauern A 110 B1
Hohentengen D 106 B3
Hohenwepel D 81 A5
Hohenwestedt D 64 B2
Hohenwutzen D 74 B3
Hohenzieritz D 74 A2
Hohn D 64 B2
Hohne D 72 B3
Hohnstorf D 73 A3
Højer DK 64 B1
Højslev Stby DK 58 B2
Hok S 62 A2
Hökerum S 60 B3
Hökhuvud S 51 B5
Hokksund N 53 A5
Hökön S 63 B2
Hol N 47 B5
Hólar IS 190 B6
Holašovice CZ 96 C2
Holbæk, *Aarhus Amt.* DK 58 B3
Holbæk, *Vestsjællands Amt.* DK 61 D1
Holbeach GB 41 C4
Holdenstedt D 73 B3
Holdhus N 46 B2
Holdorf D 71 B5
Holeby DK 65 B4
Hølen N 54 A1
Hølervasseter N 47 B6
Holešov CZ 98 B1
Holguera E 155 B4
Holíč SK 98 C1
Holice CZ 97 A3
Holice SK 111 B4
Höljes S 49 B4
Hollabrunn A 97 C4
Hollandstoun GB 33 B4
Høllen N 53 B3
Hollfeld D 95 B3
Hollókő H 112 B3
Hollstadt D 82 B2
Hollum NL 70 A2
Höllviksnäs S 66 A1
Holm N 195 E3
Hólmavík IS 190 B4
Holmbukt N 192 B5
Holme-on-Spalding-Moor GB 40 B3
Holmedal S 54 A2
Holmegil N 54 A2
Holmen N 48 B2
Holmes Chapel GB 38 A4
Holmestrand N 54 A1
Holmfirth GB 40 B2
Holmfoss N 193 C14
Holmsbu N 54 A1
Holmsjö S 63 B3
Holmsund S 200 C6
Holmsveden S 50 A3
Holmudden S 57 C5
Hölö S 57 A3
Holøydal N 199 C8
Holsbybrunn S 62 A3
Holseter N 48 A1
Holsljunga S 60 B2
Holstebro DK 59 B1
Holsted DK 59 C1
Holsworthy GB 42 B2
Holt D 64 B2
Holt, *Norfolk* GB 41 C5
Holt, *Wrexham* GB 38 A4
Holt IS 190 D6
Holt N 53 B4
Holten NL 71 B3
Holtwick D 71 B4
Holum N 52 B3
Holwerd NL 70 A2
Holycross IRL 29 B4
Holyhead GB 38 A2
Holýšov CZ 95 B5
Holywell GB 38 A3
Holywood GB 27 B5
Holzdorf D 83 A5
Holzhausen D 72 B1
Holzheim D 94 C2
Holzkirchen D 108 B2
Holzminden D 81 A5
Holzthaleben D 82 A2
Homberg, *Hessen* D 81 A5
Homberg, *Hessen* D 81 B5
Homburg D 93 B3
Hommelstø N 195 E3
Hommersåk N 52 B1
Homokmegy H 112 C3
Homokszentgyörgy H 124 A3
Homyel = Gomel BY 13 B9
Honaz TR 188 B4
Hondarribia E 144 A2
Hondón de los Frailes E 165 A4
Hondschoote F 78 B2
Hönebach D 82 B1
Hønefoss N 48 B2
Honfleur F 89 A4
Høng DK 61 D1
Honiton GB 43 B3
Hönningen D 80 B2
Honningsvåg N 193 B9
Hönö S 60 B1
Honrubia E 158 B1
Hontalbilla E 151 A3
Hontheim D 92 A2
Hontianske-Nemce SK 98 C2
Hontoria de la Cantera E 143 B3
Hontoria de Valdearados E 143 C3
Hontoria del Pinar E 143 C3
Hoofddorp NL 70 B1
Hoogerheide NL 79 A4
Hoogeveen NL 71 B3
Hoogezand-Sappemeer NL 71 A3
Hoogkarspel NL 70 B2
Hoogkerk NL 71 A3
Hoogstede D 71 B3
Hoogstraten B 79 A4
Hook GB 44 B3
Hooksiel D 71 A5
Höör S 61 D3
Hoorn NL 70 B2
Hope GB 38 A3
Hope under Dinmore GB 39 B4
Hopen N 194 C6
Hopfgarten A 108 B3
Hopfgarten in Defereggen A 109 C3
Hopseidet N 193 B11
Hopsten D 71 B4
Hoptrup DK 59 C2
Hora Svatého Sebestiána CZ 83 B5
Horaždóvice CZ 96 B1
Horb am Neckar D 93 C4
Horbelev DK 65 B5
Hørby DK 58 A3
Hörby S 61 D3
Horcajada de la Torre E 158 A1
Horcajo de los Montes E 156 A3
Horcajo de Santiago E 151 C4
Horcajo-Medianero E 150 B2
Horche E 151 B4
Horda S 62 A2
Hordabø N 46 B1
Hordalia N 52 A2
Hordvik N 46 B2
Hořesedly CZ 83 B5
Horezu RO 17 C6
Horgen CH 107 B3
Horgoš SRB 126 A1
Horia RO 126 A3
Hořice CZ 84 B3
Horjul SLO 123 A3
Horka D 84 A2
Hörken S 50 B1
Horki BY 13 A9
Hörle S 60 B4
Horn A 97 C3
Horn D 81 A4
Horn N 48 B2
Horn S 62 A3
Horna E 158 C2
Horná Mariková SK 98 B2
Horná Streda SK 98 C1
Horná Štrubna SK 98 C2
Horná Súča SK 98 C1
Hornachos E 156 B1
Hornachuelos E 162 A2
Hornanes N 46 C2
Hornbæk, *Aarhus Amt.* DK 58 B2
Hornbæk, *Frederiksværk* DK 61 C2
Hornberg D 106 A3
Hornburg D 73 B3
Horncastle GB 41 B3
Horndal S 50 B3
Horndean GB 44 C2
Horne, *Fyns Amt.* DK 64 A3
Horne, *Ribe Amt.* DK 59 C1
Hörnebo S 55 B5
Horneburg D 72 A2
Hörnefors S 200 C5
Horní Bečva CZ 98 B2
Horni Benešov CZ 98 B1
Horni Cerekev CZ 97 B3
Horní Jiřetín CZ 83 B5
Horní Lomná CZ 98 B2
Horni Maršov CZ 85 B3
Horní Planá CZ 96 C2
Horni Slavkov CZ 83 B4
Horni Vltavice CZ 96 C1
Hornindal N 198 D3
Hørning DK 59 B3
Hörningsholm S 57 A3
Hornnes N 53 B3
Horno D 84 A2
Hornos E 164 A2
Hornoy-le-Bourg F 90 B1
Hornsea GB 41 B3
Hornsjø N 48 A2
Hornslet DK 59 B3
Hornstein A 111 B3
Hörnum D 64 B1
Hornum DK 58 B2
Horný Tisovnik SK 99 C3
Horodenka UA 13 D6
Horodnya UA 13 C9
Horodok, *Khmelnytskyy* UA 13 D7
Horodok, *Lviv* UA 13 D5
Horokhiv UA 13 C6
Horovice CZ 96 B1
Horred S 60 B2
Hörröd S 61 D4
Hörsching A 110 A1
Horsens DK 59 C2
Horsham GB 44 B3
Hørsholm DK 61 D2
Horslunde DK 65 B4
Horšovský Týn CZ 95 B4
Horst NL 80 A2
Horstel D 71 B4
Horsten D 71 A4
Horstmar D 71 B4
Hort H 113 B3
Horta P 148 A2
Horten N 54 A1
Hortezuela E 151 A5
Hortiguela E 143 B3
Hortobágy H 113 B5
Horton in Ribblesdale GB 37 B4
Hørve DK 61 D1
Hörvik S 63 B2
Horwich GB 38 A4
Hosanger N 46 B2
Hösbach D 93 A5
Hosena D 84 A2
Hosenfeld D 81 B5
Hosingen L 92 A2
Hosio FIN 197 D8
Hospental CH 107 C3
Hospital IRL 29 B3
Hossegor F 128 C1
Hosszuhetény H 125 A4
Hostal de Ipiés E 145 B3
Hoštálkova CZ 98 B1
Hostalric E 147 C3
Hostens F 128 B2
Hostěradice CZ 97 C4
Hostinné CZ 85 B3
Hostomice CZ 96 B2
Hostouň CZ 95 B4
Hotagen S 199 B11
Hoting S 200 B2
Hotolisht AL 182 B2
Hotton B 79 B5
Houdain F 78 B2
Houdan F 90 C1
Houdelaincourt F 92 C1
Houeillès F 128 B3
Houffalize B 92 A1
Houghton-le-Spring GB 37 B5
Houlberg DK 59 B2
Houlgate F 89 A3
Hounslow GB 44 B3
Hourtin F 128 A1
Hourtin-Plage F 128 A1
Houthalen B 79 A5
Houyet B 79 B4
Hov DK 59 C3
Hov N 48 B2
Hova S 55 B5
Høvåg N 53 B4
Hovborg DK 59 C1
Hovda N 47 B6
Hovden N 52 A3
Hove GB 44 C3
Hovedgård DK 59 C2
Hovelhof D 81 A4
Hoven DK 59 C1
Hovet N 47 B5
Hovingham GB 40 A3
Hovmantorp S 62 B3
Hovsta S 56 A1
Howden GB 40 B3
Howe D 72 A3
Höxter D 81 A5
Hoya D 72 B2
Hoya de Santa Maria E 161 B3
Hoya-Gonzalo E 158 C2
Høyanger N 46 A3
Hoyerswerda D 84 A2
Høyjord N 53 A6
Hoylake GB 38 A3
Høylandet N 199 A9
Hoym D 82 A3
Høymyr N 47 C6
Hoyo de Manzanares E 151 B4
Hoyo de Pinares E 150 B3
Hoyocasero E 150 B3
Hoyos E 149 B3
Hoyos del Espino E 150 B2
Hrabusiče SK 99 C4
Hradec Králové CZ 85 B3
Hradec nad Moravicí CZ 98 B1
Hrádek CZ 97 C4
Hrádek nad Nisou CZ 84 B2
Hradište SK 98 C2
Hrafnagil IS 191 B7
Hrafnseyri IS 190 B2
Hranice, *Severomoravsky* CZ 98 B1
Hranice, *Západočeský* CZ 83 B4
Hranovnica SK 99 C4
Hrasnica BIH 139 B4
Hrastnik SLO 123 A4
Hřensko CZ 84 B2
Hriňová SK 99 C3
Hrisoupoli GR 183 C6
Hrochov CZ 97 B4
Hrochův Tynec CZ 97 B3
Hrodna BY 13 B5
Hrodzyanka BY 13 B8
Hronov CZ 85 B4
Hronský Beňadik SK 98 C2
Hrotovice CZ 97 B4
Hrtkovci SRB 127 C1
Hrun IS 190 A5
Hrušov SK 112 A3
Hrušovany nad Jevišovkou CZ 97 C4
Hřuštin SK 99 B3
Hrvaćani BIH 124 C3
Hrvace HR 138 B2
Hrymayliv UA 13 D7
Huben A 109 C3
Hückel-hoven D 80 A2
Hückeswagen D 80 A3
Hucknall GB 40 B2
Hucqueliers F 78 B1
Huddersfield GB 40 B2
Huddinge S 57 A3
Hüddunge S 51 B3
Hude D 72 A1
Hudiksvall S 200 E3
Huélago E 163 A4
Huélamo E 152 B2
Huelgoat F 100 A2
Huelma E 163 A4
Huelva E 161 B3
Huéneja E 164 B2
Huércal de Almeria E 164 C2
Huércal-Overa E 164 B3
Huerta de Abajo E 143 B3
Huerta de Valdecarabanos E 151 C4
Huerta del Rey E 143 C3
Huertahernando E 152 B1
Huesa E 164 B1
Huesca E 145 B3
Huéscar E 164 B2
Huete E 151 B5
Huétor Tájar E 163 A3
Hüfingen D 106 B3
Hufthamar N 46 B2
Hugh Town GB 42 B1
Huglfing D 108 B2
Huissen NL 70 C2
Huittinen FIN 8 B3
Huizen NL 70 B2
Hulín CZ 98 B1
Hüls D 80 A2
Hulsig DK 58 A3
Hulst NL 79 A4

Hult S 62 A3
Hulta S 56 B2
Hulteby S 55 A5
Hulterstad S 63 B4
Hultsfred S 62 A3
Humanes E 151 B4
Humberston GB 41 B3
Humble DK 65 B3
Humenné SK 12 D4
Humilladero E 163 A3
Humlebæk DK 61 D2
Humlum DK 58 B1
Hummelsta S 56 A2
Humpolec CZ 97 B3
Humshaugh GB 37 A4
Hundåla N 195 E3
Hundested DK 61 D1
Hundorp N 48 A1
Hundvåg N 52 A1
Hundvin N 46 B2
Hunedoara RO 17 C5
Hünfeld D 82 B1
Hungen D 81 B4
Hungerford GB 44 B2
Hunndalen N 48 B2
Hunnebostrand S 54 B2
Hunstanton GB 41 C4
Huntingdon GB 44 A3
Huntley GB 39 C4
Huntly GB 33 D4
Hünxe D 80 A2
Hurbanovo SK 112 B2
Hürbel D 107 A4
Hurdal N 48 B3
Hurezani RO 17 C5
Hurlford GB 36 A2
Hurstbourne Tarrant GB 44 B2
Hurstpierpoint GB 44 C3
Hürth D 80 B2
Hurum N 47 A5
Hurup DK 58 B1
Húsafell IS 190 C5
Húsavík IS 191 A8
Husbands Bosworth GB 44 A2
Husby D 64 B2
Husby DK 59 B1
Husey IS 191 B11
Huşi RO 17 B8
Husina BIH 139 A4
Husinec CZ 96 B1
Husinish GB 31 B1
Huskvarna S 62 A2
Husnes N 46 C2
Husøy N 194 A8
Hustad N 198 C4
Hüsten D 81 A3
Hustopeče CZ 97 C4
Hustopeče nad Bečvou CZ 98 B1
Husum D 64 B2
Husum S 200 C5
Husvika N 195 E3
Huta PL 75 B5
Hutovo BIH 139 C3
Hüttenberg A 110 C1
Hüttlingen D 94 C2
Huttoft GB 41 B4
Hutton Cranswick GB 40 B3
Hüttschlag A 109 B4
Huttwil CH 106 B2
Huy B 79 B5
Hüyük TR 189 B6
Hval N 48 B2
Hvåle N 47 B6
Hvaler N 54 A2
Hvalpsund DK 58 B2
Hvammstangi IS 190 B5
Hvammur IS 190 B6
Hvanneyri IS 190 C4
Hvar HR 138 B2
Hvarnes N 53 A5
Hveragerði IS 190 D4
Hvidbjerg DK 58 B1
Hvide Sande DK 59 C1
Hvittingfoss N 53 A6
Hvolsvöllur IS 190 D5
Hybe SK 99 B3
Hycklinge S 62 A3
Hydra GR 185 B4
Hyen N 198 D2
Hyères F 132 B2
Hyéres Plage F 132 B2
Hylestad N 52 A3
Hylke DK 59 C2
Hyllestad N 46 A2
Hyllstofta S 61 C3
Hyltebruk S 60 B3
Hynnekleiv N 53 B4
Hythe, *Hampshire* GB 44 C2
Hythe, *Kent* GB 45 B5
Hyvinkää FIN 8 B4

I

Iam RO 127 B3
Iaşi RO 17 B7
Iasmos GR 183 B7
Ibahernando E 156 A2
Ibarranguelua E 143 A4
Ibbenbüren D 71 B4
Ibeas de Juarros E 143 B3
Ibestad N 194 B8
Ibi E 159 C3
Ibiza = Eivissa E 166 C1
İbradı TR 189 B6
İbriktepe TR 186 A1
Ibros E 157 B4
Ibstock GB 40 C2
İçel TR 23 C8
Ichenhausen D 94 C2
Ichtegem B 78 A3
Ichtershausen D 82 B2
Idanha-a-Novo P 155 B3
Idar-Oberstein D 93 B3
Idd N 54 A2
Idiazábal E 144 B1
Idivuoma S 196 A4
Idkerberget S 50 B2
Idön S 51 B5
Idre S 199 D9
Idrija SLO 123 A3
Idritsa RUS 9 D6
Idstein D 81 B4
Idvor SRB 126 B2
Iecca Mare RO 126 B2
Ielsi I 170 B2
Ieper = Ypres B 78 B2
Ierapetra GR 185 D6
Ierissos GR 183 C5
Iesi I 136 B2
Ifjord N 193 B11
Ig SLO 123 B3
Igal H 112 C1
Igea E 144 B1
Igea Marina I 136 A1
Igelfors S 56 B1
Igersheim D 94 B1
Iggesund S 200 E3
Iglesias E 143 B3
Iglésias I 179 C2
Igls A 108 B2
İğneada TR 186 A2
Igny-Comblizy F 91 B3
Igorre E 143 A4
Igoumenitsa GR 182 D2
Igries E 145 B3
Igualada E 147 C2
Igüeña E 141 B4
Iguerande F 117 A4
Iharosberény H 124 A3
Ihl'any SK 99 B4
Ihlienworth D 64 C1
Ihringen D 106 A2
Ihrlerstein D 95 C3
İhsaniye TR 187 C5
Ii FIN 197 D8
Iijärvi FIN 193 C11
Iisalmi FIN 3 E10
IJmuiden NL 70 B1
IJsselmuiden NL 70 B2
IJzendijke NL 79 A3
Ikast DK 59 B2
Ikervár H 111 B3
il Castagno I 135 B3
Ilandža SRB 126 B2
Ilanz CH 107 C4
Ilava SK 98 C2
Iława PL 69 B4
Ilche E 145 C4
Ilchester GB 43 B4
Ilfeld D 82 A2
Ilfracombe GB 42 A2
Ilgaz TR 23 A7
Ilgın TR 189 A6
Ílhavo P 148 B1
Ilica TR 186 C2
Ilidža BIH 139 B4
Ilijaš BIH 139 B4
Ilirska Bistrica SLO 123 B3
Ilkeston GB 40 C2
Ilkley GB 40 B2
Illana E 151 B5
Illano E 141 A4
Illar E 164 C2
Illas E 141 A5
Illats F 128 B2
Ille-sur-Têt F 146 B3
Illertissen D 94 C2
Illescas E 151 B4
Illfurth F 106 B2
Illichivsk UA 17 B9
Illiers-Combray F 89 B5
Illkirch-Graffenstaden F 93 C3
Illmersdorf D 74 C2
Illmitz A 111 B3
Íllora E 163 A4
Illueca E 152 A2
Ilmajoki FIN 8 A3
Ilmenau D 82 B2
Ilminster GB 43 B4
Ilok HR 126 B1
Ilomantsi FIN 9 A7
Iłow PL 77 B5
Iłowa PL 84 A3
Iłowo-Osada PL 77 A5
Ilsenburg D 82 A2
Ilshofen D 94 B1
Ilz A 110 B2
Iłża PL 87 A5
Imatra FIN 9 B6
Imielin PL 86 B3
Imingen N 47 B5
Immeln S 63 B2
Immenhausen D 81 A5
Immenstadt D 107 B5
Immingham GB 41 B3
Ímola I 135 A4
Imon E 151 A5
Imotski HR 138 B3
Impéria I 133 B4
Imphy F 104 C2
İmroz TR 183 C7
Imsland N 52 A1
Imst A 108 B1
Inagh IRL 28 B2
Inari FIN 193 D10
Inca E 167 B2
Inchnadamph GB 32 C2
Incinillas E 143 B3
Indal S 200 D3
Indjija SRB 127 B2
Indre Arna N 46 B2
Indre Billefjord N 193 B9
Indre Brenna N 193 B9
İnebolu TR 23 A7
İnecik TR 186 B2
İnegöl TR 187 B4
Inerthal CH 107 B3
Infiesto E 142 A1
Ingatorp S 62 A3
Ingedal N 54 A2
Ingelheim D 93 B4
Ingelmunster B 78 B3
Ingelstad S 62 B2
Ingleton GB 37 B4
Ingolfsland N 47 C5
Ingolstadt D 95 C3
Ingrandes, *Maine-et-Loire* F 101 B5
Ingrandes, *Vienne* F 102 C2
Ingwiller F 93 C3
Inhisar TR 187 B5
Iniesta E 158 B2
Inishannon IRL 29 C3
Inishcrone IRL 26 B1
Inke H 124 A3
Inndyr N 195 C5
Innellan GB 34 C3
Innerleithen GB 35 C4
Innermessan GB 36 B2
Innertkirchen CH 106 C3
Innervillgraten A 109 C3
Innsbruck A 108 B2
Innset N 194 B9
Innvik N 198 D3
İnönü TR 187 C5
Inowłódz PL 87 A4
Inowrocław PL 76 B3
Ins CH 106 B2
Insch GB 33 D4
Insjön S 50 B2
Ińsko PL 75 A4
Instow GB 42 A2
Intepe TR 186 B1
Interlaken CH 106 C2
Intragna CH 120 A1
Introbio I 120 B2
Inverallochy GB 33 D5
Inveran GB 32 D2
Inveran IRL 28 A2
Inveraray GB 34 B2
Inverbervie GB 35 B5
Invergarry GB 32 D2
Invergordon GB 32 D2
Invergowrie GB 35 B4
Inverkeilor GB 35 B5
Inverkeithing GB 35 B4
Invermoriston GB 32 D2
Inverness GB 32 D2
Inveruno I 120 B1
Inverurie GB 33 D4
Ioannina GR 182 D2
Iolanda di Savoia I 121 C4
Ion Corvin RO 17 C7
Ióppolo I 175 C1
Ios GR 185 C6
Ipati GR 182 E4
İpsala TR 186 B1
Ipswich GB 45 A5
Iraklia GR 183 B5
Iraklio = Heraklion GR 185 D6
Irdning A 110 B1
Iregszemcse H 112 C2
Irgoli I 178 B3
Irig SRB 127 B1
Ironbridge GB 39 B4
Irpin UA 13 C9
Irrel D 92 B2
Irsina I 172 B2
Irthlingborough GB 44 A3
Iruela E 141 B4
Irún E 144 A2
Irurita E 144 A2
Irurzun E 144 B2
Irvine GB 36 A2
Irvinestown GB 27 B3
Is-sur-Tille F 105 B4
Isaba E 144 B3
Isabela E 157 B4
Ísafjörður IS 190 A2
Isane N 198 D2
Isaszeg H 112 B3
Isbister GB 33 A5
Íscar E 150 A3
İscehisar TR 187 D5
Ischgl A 107 B5
Íschia I 170 C1
Ischia di Castro I 168 A1
Ischitella I 171 B3
Isdes F 103 B4
Ise N 54 A2
Iselle I 119 A5
Iseltwald CH 106 C2
Isen D 108 A3
Isenbüttel D 73 B3
Iseo I 120 B3
Iserlohn D 81 A3
Isérnia I 170 B2
Isfjorden N 198 C4
Ishëm AL 182 B1
Işıklı TR 189 A4
Isigny-sur-Mer F 88 A2
Ísili I 179 C3
İskilip TR 23 A8
Isla Canela E 161 B2
Isla Cristina E 161 B2
Islares E 143 A3
Isle Of Whithorn GB 36 B2
Isleham GB 45 A4
Ismaning D 108 A2
Isna P 154 B3
Isnestoften N 192 B6
Isny D 107 B5
Isoba E 142 A1
Isokylä FIN 197 C10
Isokylä S 196 B5
Isola F 132 A3
Isola del Gran Sasso d'Itália I 169 A3
Ísola del Liri I 169 B3
Ísola della Scala I 121 B4
Isola delle Fémmine I 176 A2
Ísola di Capo Rizzuto I 175 C3
Isona E 147 B2
Ispagnac F 130 A2
Isparta TR 189 B5
Isperikh BG 17 D7
Íspica I 177 C3
Isselburg D 80 A2
Issigeac F 129 B3
Issogne I 119 B4
Issoire F 116 B3
Issoncourt F 91 C5
Issoudun F 103 C4
Issum D 80 A2
Issy-l'Evêque F 104 C2
Istán E 162 B3
İstanbul TR 186 A3
Istebna PL 98 B2
Ístia d'Ombrone I 135 C4
Istiea GR 183 E5
Istres F 131 B3
Istvándi H 125 A3
Itea GR 184 A3
Ithaki GR 184 A1
Itoiz E 144 B2
Ítrabo E 163 B4
Itri I 169 B3
Ittireddu I 178 B2
Íttiri I 178 B2
Itzehoe D 64 C2
Ivalo FIN 193 D11
Iván H 111 B3
Ivanava BY 13 B6
Ivančice CZ 97 B4
Ivančna Gorica SLO 123 B3
Iváncsa H 112 B2
Ivanec HR 124 A2
Ivanić Grad HR 124 B2
Ivanjska BIH 124 C3
Ivanka SK 98 C2
Ivankovo HR 125 B4
Ivano-Frankivsk UA 13 D6
Ivanovice na Hané CZ 98 B1
Ivanska HR 124 B2
Ivatsevichy BY 13 B6
Ivaylovgrad BG 183 B8
Iveland N 53 B3
Ivoz Ramet B 79 B5
Ivrea I 119 B4
İvrindi TR 186 C2
Ivry-en-Montagne F 104 B3
Ivry-la-Bataille F 90 C1
Ivybridge GB 42 B3
Iwaniska PL 87 B5
Iwiny PL 85 A3
Iwuy F 78 B3
Ixworth GB 45 A4
Izarra E 143 B4
Izbica Kujawska PL 76 B3
Izbište SRB 127 B3
Izeda P 149 A3
Izegem B 78 B3
Izernore F 118 A2
Izmayil UA 17 C8
İzmir TR 188 A2
İzmit = Kocaeli TR 187 B4
Iznájar E 163 A3
Iznalloz E 163 A4
Iznatoraf E 164 A1
İznik TR 187 B4
Izola SLO 122 B2
Izsák H 112 C3
Izsófalva H 99 C4
Izyaslav UA 13 C7

J

Jabalquinto E 157 B4
Jablanac HR 123 C3
Jablanica BIH 139 B3
Jablonec nad Jizerou CZ 84 B3
Jablonec nad Nisou CZ 84 B3
Jablonica SK 98 C1
Jablonka PL 99 B3
Jabłonna PL 77 B5
Jablonné nad Orlicí CZ 97 A4
Jablonne Podještědi CZ 84 B2
Jablonov nad Turňou SK 99 C4
Jabłonowo Pomorskie PL 69 B4
Jablúnka CZ 98 B1
Jablunkov CZ 98 B2
Jabučje SRB 127 C2
Jabugo E 161 B3
Jabuka SRB 127 C2
Jabukovac HR 124 B2
Jaca E 145 B3
Jáchymov CZ 83 B4
Jacobidrebber D 72 B1
Jade D 71 A5
Jäderfors S 50 B3
Jädraås S 50 B3
Jadraque E 151 B5
Jægerspris DK 61 D1
Jaén E 163 A4
Jagare BIH 124 C3
Jagel D 64 B2
Jagenbach A 96 C3
Jagodina SRB 127 D3
Jagodnjak HR 125 B4
Jagodzin PL 84 A3
Jagstheim D 94 B2
Jagstzell D 94 B2
Jahodna SK 111 A4
Jajce BIH 138 A3
Ják H 111 B3
Jakabszálbs H 112 C3
Jäkkvik S 195 D8
Jakobsnes N 193 C14
Jakovlje HR 124 B1
Jakšic HR 125 B3
Jakubany SK 99 B4
Jalance E 159 B2
Jalasjärvi FIN 8 A3
Jalhay B 80 B1
Jaligny-sur-Besbre F 117 A3
Jallais F 102 B1
Jalón E 159 C3
Jâlons F 91 C4
Jamena SRB 125 C5
Jamilena E 163 A4
Jämjö S 63 B3
Jamnička Kiselica HR 124 B1
Jamno PL 67 B5
Jamoigne B 92 B1
Jämsä FIN 8 B4
Jämshög S 63 B2
Jamu Mare RO 126 B3
Janakkala FIN 8 B4
Jandelsbrunn D 96 C1
Jänickendorf D 74 B2
Janikowo PL 76 B3
Janja BIH 125 C5
Janjina HR 138 C3
Janki, *Łódzkie* PL 86 A3
Janki, *Mazowieckie* PL 77 B5
Jankov CZ 96 B2
Jankowo Dolne PL 76 B2
Jánoshalma H 126 A1
Jánosháza H 111 B4
Jánoshida H 113 B4
Jánossomorja H 111 B4
Janovice nad Uhlavou CZ 96 B1
Janów PL 86 B3
Janowiec Wielkopolski PL 76 B2
Janowo PL 77 A5
Jänsmässholmen S 199 B10
Janville F 103 A3
Janzé F 101 B4
Jarabá SK 99 C3
Jaraczewo PL 76 C2
Jarafuel E 159 B2
Jaraicejo E 156 A2
Jaraíz de la Vera E 150 B2
Jarak SRB 127 C1
Jarandilla de la Vera E 150 B2
Jaray E 152 A1
Järbo S 50 B3
Jard-sur-Mer F 114 B2
Jaren N 48 B2
Jargeau F 103 B4
Jarkovac SRB 126 B2
Järlåsa S 51 C4
Jarmen D 66 C2
Järna S 57 A3
Jarnac F 115 C3
Järnäs S 200 C5
Järnforsen S 62 A3
Jarny F 92 B1
Jarocin PL 76 C2
Jaroměř CZ 85 B3
Jaroměřice nad Rokytnou CZ 97 B3
Jaroslav CZ 97 A4
Jaroslavice CZ 97 C4
Jarosław PL 12 C5
Jaroslawiec PL 68 A1
Jarošov nad Nežarkou CZ 96 B3
Järpås S 55 B3
Järpen S 199 B10
Jarrow GB 37 B5
Järso FIN 51 B6
Järvenpää FIN 8 B4
Jarvorník CZ 85 B4
Järvsö S 200 E2
Jarzé F 102 B1
Jaša Tomic SRB 126 B2
Jasenak HR 123 B4
Jasenica BIH 124 C2
Jasenice HR 137 A4
Jasenovac HR 124 B2
Jasenovo SRB 127 C3
Jasień PL 84 A3
Jasienica PL 84 A2
Jasło PL 12 D4
Jásova SK 112 B2
Jasseron F 118 A2
Jastarnia PL 69 A3
Jastrebarsko HR 123 B4
Jastrowie PL 68 B1
Jastrzębia-Góra PL 68 A3
Jastrzębie Zdrój PL 98 B2
Jászals-Lószentgyörgy H 113 B4
Jászapáti H 113 B4
Jászárokszállás H 113 B3
Jászberény H 113 B3
Jászdózsa H 113 B4
Jászfényszaru H 113 B3
Jászjakóhalma H 113 B4
Jászkarajenő H 113 B4
Jászkisér H 113 B4
Jászladány H 113 B4
Jászszentlászló H 113 C3
Jásztelek H 113 B4
Játar E 163 B4
Jättendal S 200 E3
Jatznick D 74 A2
Jaun CH 106 C2
Jausiers F 132 A2
Jávea E 159 C4
Jävenitz D 73 B4
Javerlhac F 115 C4
Javier E 144 B2
Javorani BIH 124 C3
Javorina SK 99 B4
Javron F 89 B3
Jawor PL 85 A4
Jaworzno PL 86 B3
Jaworzyna Śl. PL 85 B4
Jayena E 163 B4
Jażow PL 84 A2
Jebel RO 126 B3
Jebjerg DK 58 B2
Jedburgh GB 35 C5
Jedlinsk PL 87 A5
Jedlnia PL 87 A5
Jedlnia Letnisko PL 87 A5
Jednorożec PL 77 A6
Jedovnice CZ 97 B4
Jędrychow PL 69 B4
Jędrzejów PL 87 B4
Jedwabno PL 77 A5
Jeesiö FIN 197 B9
Jegłownik PL 69 A4
Jegun F 129 C3
Jēkabpils LV 8 D4
Jektevik N 46 C2
Jektvik N 195 D4
Jelcz-Laskowice PL 85 A5
Jelenec SK 98 C2
Jelenia Góra PL 85 B3
Jelgava LV 8 D3
Jelka SK 111 A4
Jelling DK 59 C2
Jels DK 59 C2
Jelsa HR 138 B2
Jelsa N 52 A2
Jelšava SK 99 C4
Jemgum D 71 A4
Jemnice CZ 97 B3
Jena D 82 B3
Jenaz CH 107 C4
Jenbach A 108 B2
Jenikow PL 75 A4
Jennersdorf A 111 C3
Jenny S 62 A4
Jerchel D 73 B4
Jeres del Marquesado E 164 B1
Jerez de la Frontera E 162 B1
Jerez de los Caballeros E 155 C4
Jerica E 159 B3
Jerichow D 73 B5
Jerka PL 75 B5
Jermenovci SRB 126 B3
Jerslev DK 58 A3
Jerte E 150 B2
Jerup DK 58 A3
Jerxheim D 73 B3
Jerzmanowice PL 87 B3
Jerzu I 179 C3
Jerzwałd PL 69 B4
Jesberg D 81 B5
Jesenice, *Středočeský* CZ 83 B5
Jesenice, *Středočeský* CZ 96 B2
Jesenice SLO 109 C5
Jeseník CZ 85 B5
Jesenké SK 99 C4
Jésolo I 122 B1
Jessen D 83 A4

Jessenitz D 73 A4
Jessheim N 48 B3
Jessnitz D 83 A4
Jesteburg D 72 A2
Jeumont F 79 B4
Jeven-stedt D 64 B2
Jever D 71 A4
Jevičko CZ 97 B4
Jevišovice CZ 97 C3
Jevnaker N 48 B2
Jezerane HR 123 B4
Jezero BIH 138 A3
Jezero HR 123 B4
Jezów PL 87 A3
Jičín CZ 84 B3
Jičiněves CZ 84 B3
Jihlava CZ 97 B3
Jijona E 159 C3
Jilemnice CZ 84 B3
Jílové CZ 84 B2
Jílové u Prahy CZ 96 B2
Jimbolia RO 126 B2
Jimena E 163 A4
Jimena de la Frontera E 162 B2
Jimera de Libar E 162 B2
Jimramov CZ 97 B4
Jince CZ 96 B1
Jindřichovice CZ 83 B4
Jindřichův Hradec CZ 96 B3
Jirkov CZ 83 B5
Jistebnice CZ 96 B2
Joachimsthal D 74 B2
João da Loura P 154 C2
Jobbágyi H 112 B3
Jochberg A 109 B3
Jockfall S 196 C5
Jódar E 163 A4
Jodoigne B 79 B4
Joensuu FIN 9 A6
Joesjö S 195 E5
Jœuf F 92 B1
Jõgeva EST 8 C5
Johann-georgen-stadt D 83 B4
Johannishus S 63 B3
Johanniskirchen D 95 C4
Johansfors S 63 B3
John o'Groats GB 32 C3
Johnshaven GB 35 B5
Johnstone GB 34 C3
Johnstown IRL 30 B1
Jõhvi EST 8 C5
Joigny F 104 B2
Joinville F 91 C5
Jokkmokk S 196 C2
Jöllenbeck D 72 B1
Jomala FIN 51 B6
Jönåker S 56 B2
Jonava LT 13 A6
Jonchery-sur-Vesle F 91 B3
Jondal N 46 B3
Jondalen N 53 A5
Joniškis LT 8 D3
Jönköping S 62 A2
Jonkowo PL 69 B5
Jønnbu N 53 A5
Jonsberg S 56 B2
Jonsered S 60 B2
Jonstorp S 61 C2
Jonzac F 114 C3
Jorba E 147 C2
Jordanów PL 99 B3
Jordanów Śląski PL 85 B4
Jordanowo PL 75 B4
Jordbro S 57 A4
Jordbrua N 195 D5
Jördenstorf D 66 C1
Jordet N 49 A4
Jordøse DK 59 C3
Jork D 72 A2
Jörlanda S 60 B1
Jormlien S 199 A10
Jormvattnet S 199 A11
Jörn S 200 A6
Jørpeland N 52 A2
Jorquera E 158 B2
Jošan HR 123 C4
Jošavka BIH 124 C3
Josipdol HR 123 B4
Josipovac HR 125 B4
Jössefors S 54 A3
Josselin F 101 B3
Jøssund N 199 A7
Jostedal N 47 A4
Jósvafö H 99 C4
Jou P 148 A2
Jouarre F 90 C3
Joué-lès-Tours F 102 B2
Joué-sur-Erdre F 101 B4
Joure NL 70 B2
Joutseno FIN 9 B6
Joutsijärvi FIN 197 C10
Joux-la-Ville F 104 B2
Jouy F 90 C1
Jouy-le-Châtel F 90 C3
Jouy-le-Potier F 103 B3
Joyeuse F 131 A3
Joze F 116 B3
Juan-les-Pins F 132 B3
Juankoski FIN 8 A6
Jübek D 64 B2
Jubera E 144 B1
Jubrique E 162 B2
Jüchsen D 82 B2
Judaberg N 52 A1
Judenburg A 110 B1
Juelsminde DK 59 C3
Jugon-les-Lacs F 101 A3
Juillac F 129 A4
Juillan F 145 A4
Juist D 71 A4
Jukkasjärvi S 196 B3
Jule N 199 A10
Julianadorp NL 70 B1
Julianstown IRL 30 A2
Jülich D 80 B2
Jullouville F 88 B2
Jumeaux F 117 B3
Jumièges F 89 A4
Jumilhac-le-Grand F 115 C5
Jumilla E 159 C2
Jumisko FIN 197 C11
Juncosa E 153 A4
Juneda E 147 C1
Jung S 55 B4
Jungingen D 93 C5
Junglingster L 92 B2
Juniville F 91 B4
Junosuando S 196 B5
Junqueira P 149 A2
Junsele S 200 C2
Juoksengi S 196 C6
Juoksenki FIN 196 C6
Juprelle B 80 B1
Jurata PL 69 A3
Jurbarkas LT 12 A5
Jurjevo HR 123 C3
Jūrmala LV 8 D3
Jurmu FIN 197 D10
Juromenha P 155 C3
Jursla S 56 B2
Jussac F 116 C2
Jussey F 105 B4
Jussy F 90 B3
Juta H 125 A3
Jüterbog D 74 C2
Juuka FIN 3 E11
Juuma FIN 197 C12
Juvigny-le-Terte F 88 B2
Juvigny-sous-Andaine F 89 B3
Juzennecourt F 105 A3
Jyderup DK 61 D1
Jyrkänkoski FIN 197 C12
Jyväskylä FIN 8 A4

K

Kaamanen FIN 193 C11
Kaamasmukka FIN 193 C10
Kaaresuvanto FIN 192 D6
Kaarssen D 73 A4
Kaatscheuvel NL 79 A5
Kaba H 113 B5
Kåbdalis S 196 C3
Kačarevo SRB 127 C2
Kács H 113 B4
Kadan CZ 83 B5
Kadarkút H 125 A3
Kadınhanı TR 189 A7
Kaduy RUS 9 C10
Kåfalla S 56 A1
Kåfjord N 192 C7
Kåfjordbotn N 192 C4
Kågeröd S 61 D3
Kahl D 93 A5
Kahla D 82 B3
Kainach bei Voitsberg A 110 B2
Kaindorf A 110 B2
Kainulasjärvi S 196 C5
Kairala FIN 197 B10
Kaisepakte S 192 D3
Kaisersesch D 80 B3
Kaiserslautern D 93 B3
Kaisheim D 94 C2
Kajaani FIN 3 D10
Kajárpéc H 111 B4
Kajdacs H 112 C2
Kakanj BIH 139 A4
Kakasd H 125 A4
Kaklik TR 189 B4
Kakolewo PL 85 A4
Kál H 113 B4
Kalajoki FIN 3 D8
Kalak N 193 B11
Kalamata = Kalamata GR 184 B3
Kalamata = Kalamata GR 184 B3
Kalambaka GR 182 D3
Kalamria GR 182 C4
Kalandra GR 183 D5
Kälarne S 200 D2
Kalavrita GR 184 A3
Kalbe D 73 B4
Kalce SLO 123 B3
Káld H 111 B4
Kale, *Antalya* TR 189 C4
Kale, *Denizli* TR 188 B3
Kalecik TR 23 A7
Kalefeld D 82 A2
Kalesija BIH 139 A4
Kalety PL 86 B2
Kalevala RUS 3 D12
Kalhovd N 47 B5
Kali HR 137 A4
Kalimnos GR 188 C2
Kaliningrad RUS 69 A5
Kalinkavichy BY 13 B8
Kalinovac HR 124 A3
Kalinovik BIH 139 B4
Kalinovo SK 99 C3
Kalirachi GR 183 C6
Kaliska, *Pomorskie* PL 68 A3
Kaliska, *Pomorskie* PL 68 B3
Kalisko PL 86 A3
Kalisz PL 86 A2
Kalisz Pomorski PL 75 A4
Kalix S 196 D6
Kaljord N 194 B6
Kalkan TR 189 C4
Kalkar D 80 A2
Kalkım TR 186 C2
Kall D 80 B2
Kall S 199 B10
Källby S 55 B4
Kållered S 60 B2
Kållerstad S 60 B3
Kallinge S 63 B3
Kallmünz D 95 B3
Kallo FIN 196 B7
Kallsedet S 199 B9
Källvik S 56 B3
Kalmar S 63 B4
Kalmthout B 79 A4
Kalná SK 112 A2
Kalo Nero GR 184 B2
Kalocsa H 112 C2
Kalokhorio CY 181 B2
Kaloni GR 186 C1
Káloz H 112 C2
Kals A 109 B3
Kalsdorf A 110 C2
Kaltbrunn CH 107 B4
Kaltenbach A 108 B2
Kaltenkirchen D 64 C2
Kaltennordheim D 82 B2
Kalundborg DK 61 D1
Kalush UA 13 D6
Kalv S 60 B3
Kalvåg N 198 D1
Kalvehave DK 65 A5
Kalwang A 110 B1
Kalwaria-Zebrzydowska PL 99 B3
Kalyazin RUS 9 D10
Kam H 111 B3
Kaman TR 23 B7
Kamares GR 185 C5
Kambos CY 181 A1
Kamen D 81 A3
Kamenice CZ 97 B3
Kamenice nad Lipou CZ 96 B3
Kameničná SK 112 B2
Kamenný Most SK 112 B2
Kamenny Ujezd CZ 96 C2
Kamenska HR 124 B3
Kamensko HR 138 B2
Kamenz D 84 A2
Kamičak BIH 124 C2
Kamień PL 87 A4
Kamień Krajeński PL 76 A2
Kamień Pomorski PL 67 C3
Kamieniec Ząbk PL 85 B4
Kamienka SK 99 B4
Kamienna Góra PL 85 B4
Kamieńsk PL 86 A3
Kamiros Skala GR 188 C2
Kamnik SLO 123 A3
Kamp-Lintfort D 80 A2
Kampen NL 70 B2
Kampinos PL 77 B5
Kampor HR 123 C3
Kamyanets-Podil's'kyy UA 13 D7
Kamyanka-Buz'ka UA 13 C6
Kamýk n Vltavou CZ 96 B2
Kanal SLO 122 A2
Kanalia GR 182 D4
Kandalaksha RUS 3 C13
Kandanos GR 185 D4
Kandel D 93 B4
Kandern D 106 B2
Kandersteg CH 106 C2
Kandıra TR 187 A5
Kandila GR 184 B3
Kandyty PL 69 A5
Kanfanar HR 122 B2
Kangasala FIN 8 B4
Kangos S 196 B5
Kangosjärvi FIN 196 B6
Kaniów PL 75 C3
Kanjiža SRB 126 A2
Kankaanpää FIN 8 B3
Kannus FIN 3 E8
Kanturk IRL 29 B3
Kapaklı TR 186 A2
Kapellen A 110 B2
Kapellen B 79 A4
Kapellskär S 57 A5
Kapfenberg A 110 B2
Kapfenstein A 110 C2
Kaplice CZ 96 C2
Kapljuh BIH 124 C2
Kápolna H 113 B4
Kápolnásnyék H 112 B2
Kaposfö H 125 A3
Kaposfüred H 125 A3
Kaposszekcsö H 125 A4
Kaposvár H 125 A3
Kapp N 48 B2
Kappel D 93 C3
Kappeln D 64 B2
Kappelshamn S 57 C4
Kappl A 107 B5
Kappstad S 55 A4
Kaprun A 109 B3
Kaptol HR 125 B3
Kapuvár H 111 B4
Karaadilli TR 189 A5
Karabiğa TR 186 B2
Karabük TR 187 A7
Karaburun TR 186 D1
Karacabey TR 186 B3
Karacaköy TR 186 A3
Karacaören TR 189 A5
Karacasu TR 188 B3
Karácsond H 113 B4
Karád H 112 C1
Karahallı TR 189 A4
Karaisali TR 23 C8
Karaman, *Balıkesir* TR 186 C3
Karaman, *Karaman* TR 23 C7
Karamanlı TR 189 B4
Karamürsel TR 187 B4
Karan SRB 127 D1
Karancslapujto H 113 A3
Karaova TR 188 B2
Karapınar TR 23 C7
Karasjok N 193 C9
Karasu TR 187 A5
Karataş, *Adana* TR 23 C8
Karataş, *Manisa* TR 188 A3
Karatoprak TR 188 B2
Karavostasi CY 181 A1
Karbenning S 50 B3
Kårberg S 55 B5
Kårböle S 199 D12
Karby D 64 B2
Karby DK 58 B1
Kårby, *Kalmar* S 62 A4
Karby, *Stockholm* S 57 A4
Karcag H 113 B4
Karczów PL 86 B1
Karczowiska PL 85 A4
Kardamena GR 188 C2
Kardamila GR 185 A7
Kardamili GR 184 C3
Kardašova Rečice CZ 96 B2
Kardis S 196 C6
Karditsa GR 182 D3
Kärdla EST 8 C3
Kardoskút H 113 C4
Karesuando S 192 D6
Kargı TR 23 A8
Kargopol RUS 9 B11
Kargowa PL 75 B4
Karigasniemi FIN 193 C9
Karise DK 65 A5
Karistos GR 185 A5
Karkkila FIN 8 B4
Karlholmsbruk S 51 B4
Karlino PL 67 B4
Karlobag HR 137 A4
Karlovac HR 123 B4
Karlovasi GR 188 B1
Karlovčic SRB 127 C2
Karlovice CZ 85 B5
Karlovo BG 17 D6
Karlovy Vary CZ 83 B4
Karłowice PL 86 B1
Karlsborg S 55 B5
Karlshamn S 63 B2
Karlshöfen D 72 A2
Karlshus N 54 A1
Karlskoga S 55 A5
Karlskrona S 63 B3
Karlsrud N 47 B5
Karlsruhe D 93 B4
Karlstad S 55 A4
Karlstadt D 94 B1
Karlstetten A 110 A2
Karlstift A 96 C2
Karlstorp S 62 A3
Karmacs H 111 C4
Karmin PL 85 A5
Kärna S 60 B1
Karnobat BG 17 D7
Karojba HR 122 B2
Karow D 73 A5
Karpacz PL 85 B3
Karpathos GR 188 D2
Karpenisi GR 182 E3
Karpuzlu TR 188 B2
Kärrbo S 56 A2
Karrebaeksminde DK 65 A4
Karshult S 60 B3
Karsin PL 68 B2
Kårsta S 57 A4
Karstädt D 73 A4
Kartal TR 186 B4
Kartitsch A 109 C3
Kartuzy PL 68 A3
Karungi S 196 C6
Karunki FIN 196 C7
Karup DK 59 B2
Karviná CZ 98 B2
Kås DK 58 A2
Kaş TR 189 C4
Kasaba TR 189 C4
Kašava CZ 98 B1
Kåseberga S 66 A3
Kasejovice CZ 96 B1
Kasfjord N 194 B7
Kashin RUS 9 D10
Kašina HR 124 B2
Kasina-Wielka PL 99 B4
Kaskinen FIN 8 A2
Kašperské Hory CZ 96 B1
Kassandrino GR 183 C5
Kassel D 81 A5
Kassiopi GR 182 D1
Kastamonu TR 23 A7
Kastav HR 123 B3
Kaštel-Stari HR 138 B2
Kaštel Zegarski HR 138 A1
Kasteli GR 185 D4
Kastellaun D 93 A3
Kastelli GR 185 D6
Kasterlee B 79 A4
Kastl D 95 B3
Kastlösa S 63 B4
Kastorf D 65 C3
Kastoria GR 182 C3
Kastorio GR 184 B3
Kastraki GR 185 C6
Kastrosikia GR 182 D2
Kastsyukovichy BY 13 B10
Kaszaper H 113 C4
Katakolo GR 184 B2
Katapola GR 185 C6
Katastari GR 184 B1
Katerbow D 74 B1
Katerini GR 182 C4
Kathikas CY 181 B1
Kätkesuando S 196 A6
Katlenburg-Lindau D 82 A2
Kato Achaia GR 184 A2
Káto Pyrgos CY 181 A1
Katouna GR 182 E3
Katovice CZ 96 B1
Katowice PL 86 B3
Katrineberg S 50 A3
Katrineholm S 56 B2
Kattarp S 61 C2
Kattavia GR 188 D2
Katthammarsvik S 57 C4
Kattilstorp S 55 B4
Katwijk NL 70 B1
Kąty Wrocławskie PL 85 A4
Katymár H 125 A5
Katzenelnbogen D 81 B3
Katzhütte D 82 B3
Kaub D 93 A3
Kaufbeuren D 108 B1
Kauhajoki FIN 8 A3
Kauhava FIN 8 A3
Kaukonen FIN 196 B7
Kauliranta FIN 196 C6
Kaulsdorf D 82 B3
Kaunas LT 13 A5
Kaunisvaara S 196 B6
Kaupanger N 47 A4
Kautokeino N 192 C7
Kautzen A 97 C3
Kavadarci MK 182 B4
Kavajë AL 182 B1
Kavakköy TR 186 B1
Kavaklı TR 186 A2
Kavaklıdere TR 188 B3
Kavala GR 183 C6
Kavarna BG 17 D8
Kävlinge S 61 D3
Kawcze PL 68 A1
Kaxås S 199 B10
Kaxholmen S 62 A2
Käylä FIN 197 C12
Kaymakçı TR 188 A3
Kaymaz TR 187 C6
Kaynarca TR 187 A5
Käyrämö FIN 197 C9
Kayseri TR 23 B8
Kaysersberg F 106 A2
Kazanlŭk BG 17 D6
Kazár H 113 A3
Kazimierza Wielka PL 87 B4
Kazincbarcika H 113 A4
Kaźmierz PL 75 B5
Kcynia PL 76 A2
Kdyně CZ 95 B5
Kea GR 185 B5
Keadow IRL 26 B2
Keady GB 27 B4
Kecel H 112 C3
Keçiborlu TR 189 B5
Kecskemét H 113 C3
Kėdainiai LT 13 A5
Kędzierzyn-Koźle PL 86 B2
Keel IRL 28 A1
Keenagh IRL 28 A4
Keerbergen B 79 A4
Kefalos GR 188 C1
Kefken TR 187 A5
Keflavík IS 190 C3
Kegworth GB 40 C2
Kehl D 93 C3
Kehrigk D 74 B2
Keighley GB 40 B2
Keila EST 8 C4
Keillmore GB 34 C2
Keiss GB 32 C3
Keith GB 33 D4
Kelankylä FIN 197 D10
Kelberg D 80 B2
Kelbra D 82 A3
Kelč CZ 98 B1
Kelchsau A 108 B3
Këlcyrë AL 182 C2
Keld GB 37 B4
Kelebia H 126 A1
Kelekçi TR 188 B4
Kelemér H 99 C4
Keles TR 186 C4
Kelheim D 95 C3
Kell D 92 B2
Kellas GB 32 D3
Kellinghusen D 64 C2
Kelloselkä FIN 197 C11
Kells GB 27 B4
Kells IRL 27 C4
Kelmis B 80 B2
Kelokedhara CY 181 B1
Kelottijärvi FIN 192 D6
Kelsall GB 38 A4
Kelso GB 35 C5
Kelsterbach D 93 A4
Keltneyburn GB 35 B3
Kelujärvi FIN 197 B10
Kemaliye TR 188 A3
Kemalpaşa TR 188 A2
Kematen A 108 B2
Kemberg D 83 A4
Kemer, *Antalya* TR 189 C5
Kemer, *Burdur* TR 189 B5
Kemer, *Muğla* TR 189 C4
Kemerkaya TR 187 D6
Kemeten A 111 B3
Kemi FIN 196 D7
Kemijärvi FIN 197 C10
Keminmaa FIN 196 D7
Kemnath D 95 B3
Kemnay GB 33 D4
Kemnitz, *Brandenburg* D 74 B1
Kemnitz, *Mecklenburg-Vorpommern* D 66 B2
Kempen D 80 A2
Kempsey GB 39 B4
Kempten D 107 B5
Kemptthal CH 107 B3
Kendal GB 37 B4
Kenderes H 113 B4
Kengyel H 113 B4
Kenilworth GB 44 A2
Kenmare IRL 29 C2
Kenmore GB 35 B4
Kennacraig GB 34 C2
Kenyeri H 111 B4
Kenzingen D 106 A2
Kepez TR 186 B1
Kępice PL 68 A1
Kępno PL 86 A2
Kepsut TR 186 C3
Keramoti GR 183 C6
Keräntöjärvi S 196 B6
Keratea GR 185 B4
Kerava FIN 8 B4
Kerecsend H 113 B4
Kerekegyhaza H 112 C3
Kerepestarcsa H 112 B3
Keri GR 184 B1
Kérien F 100 A2
Kerkafalva H 111 C3
Kerken D 80 A2
Kerkrade NL 80 B2
Kerkyra GR 182 D1
Kerlouan F 100 A1
Kernascléden F 100 A2
Kernhof A 110 B2
Kerns CH 106 C3
Kerpen D 80 B2
Kerrysdale GB 31 B3
Kerta H 111 B4
Kerteminde DK 59 C3
Kerzers CH 106 C2
Keşan TR 186 B1
Kesgrave GB 45 A5
Kesh GB 26 B3
Keskin TR 23 B7
Kesselfall A 109 B3
Kestenga RUS 3 D12
Keswick GB 36 B3
Keszthely H 111 C4
Kétegyháza H 113 C5
Kéthely H 111 C4
Kętrzyn PL 12 A4
Kettering GB 44 A3
Kettlewell GB 40 A1
Kęty PL 99 B3
Ketzin D 74 B1
Keula D 82 A2
Keuruu FIN 8 A4
Kevelaer D 80 A2
Kevermes H 113 C5
Kevi SRB 126 B1
Keyingham GB 41 B3
Keynsham GB 43 A4
Kežmarok SK 99 B4
Kharmanli BG 183 B7
Khaskovo BG 183 B7
Khimki RUS 9 E10
Khisinev = Chişinău MD 17 B8
Khmelnik UA 13 D7
Khmelnytskyy UA 13 D7
Khodoriv UA 13 D6
Kholm RUS 9 D7
Khotyn UA 13 D7
Khoyniki BY 13 C8
Khust UA 17 A5

Khvoynaya RUS 9 C9
Kınık, *Antalya* TR 188 C4
Kınık, *İzmir* TR 186 C2
Kırıkkale TR 23 B7
Kırka TR 187 C5
Kırkağaç TR 186 C2
Kırklareli TR 186 A2
Kırşehir TR 23 B8
Kıyıköy TR 186 A3
Kızılcabölük TR 188 B4
Kızılcadağ TR 189 B4
Kızılcahamam TR 23 A7
Kızılırmak TR 23 A7
Kızılkaya TR 189 B5
Kızılkuyu TR 187 D6
Kızılören, *Afyon* TR 189 A5
Kızılören, *Konya* TR 189 B7
Kiato GR 184 A3
Kibæk DK 59 B1
Kiberg N 193 B14
Kicasalih TR 186 A1
Kičevo MK 182 B2
Kidderminster GB 39 B4
Kidlington GB 44 B2
Kidsgrove GB 40 B1
Kidwelly GB 39 C2
Kiefersfelden D 108 B3
Kiel D 64 B3
Kielce PL 87 B4
Kiełczygłów PL 86 A3
Kielder GB 37 A4
Kiełpino PL 68 A3
Kielpiny PL 77 A4
Kierinki FIN 197 B8
Kiernozia PL 77 B4
Kierspe D 81 A3
Kietrz PL 86 B2
Kietz D 74 B3
Kiev = Kyyiv UA 13 C9
Kiezmark PL 69 A3
Kiffisia GR 185 A4
Kifino Selo BIH 139 B4
Kihlanki FIN 196 B6
Kihlanki S 196 B6
Kiistala FIN 197 B8
Kije PL 87 B4
Kijevo HR 138 B2
Kikallen N 46 B2
Kikinda SRB 126 B2
Kil N 53 B5
Kil, *Örebro* S 55 A6
Kil, *Värmland* S 55 A4
Kila S 55 A3
Kilafors S 50 A3
Kilb Rabenstein A 110 A2
Kilbaha IRL 29 B2
Kilbeggan IRL 30 A1
Kilberry GB 34 C2
Kilbirnie GB 34 C3
Kilboghamn N 195 D4
Kilbotn N 194 B7
Kilchattan GB 34 C2
Kilchoan GB 34 B1
Kilcock IRL 30 A2
Kilconnell IRL 28 A3
Kilcormac IRL 28 A4
Kilcreggan GB 34 C3
Kilcullen IRL 30 A2
Kilcurry IRL 27 B4
Kildare IRL 30 A2
Kildinstroy RUS 3 B13
Kildonan GB 32 C3
Kildorrery IRL 29 B3
Kilegrend N 53 A4
Kilen N 53 A4
Kilgarvan IRL 29 C2
Kiliya UA 17 C8
Kilkee IRL 29 B2
Kilkeel GB 27 B4
Kilkenny IRL 30 B1
Kilkieran IRL 28 A2
Kilkinlea IRL 29 B2
Kilkis GR 182 B4
Killadysert IRL 29 B2
Killala IRL 26 B1
Killaloe IRL 28 B3
Killarney IRL 29 B2
Killashandra IRL 27 B3
Killashee IRL 28 A4
Killearn GB 34 B3
Killeberg S 61 C4
Killeigh IRL 30 A1
Killenaule IRL 29 B4
Killimor IRL 28 A3
Killin GB 34 B3
Killinaboy IRL 28 B2
Killinge S 196 B3
Killinick IRL 30 B2
Killorglin IRL 29 B2
Killucan IRL 30 A1
Killybegs IRL 26 B2
Killyleagh GB 27 B5
Kilmacrenan IRL 26 A3
Kilmacthomas IRL 30 B1
Kilmaine IRL 28 A2
Kilmallock IRL 29 B3
Kilmarnock GB 36 A2
Kilmartin GB 34 B2
Kilmaurs GB 36 A2
Kilmeadan IRL 30 B1
Kilmeedy IRL 29 B3
Kilmelford GB 34 B2
Kilmore Quay IRL 30 B2
Kilmuir GB 32 D2
Kilnaleck IRL 27 C3
Kilninver GB 34 B2
Kilpisjärvi FIN 192 C4
Kilrea GB 27 B4
Kilrush IRL 29 B2
Kilsmo S 56 A1
Kilsyth GB 35 C3
Kiltoom IRL 28 A3
Kilwinning GB 36 A2
Kimasozero RUS 3 D12
Kimi GR 185 A5
Kimolos GR 185 C5
Kimovsk RUS 9 E10
Kimratshofen D 107 B5
Kimry RUS 9 D10
Kimstad S 56 B1
Kinbrace GB 32 C3
Kincardine GB 35 B4
Kincraig GB 32 D3
Kindberg A 110 B2
Kindelbruck D 82 A3
Kingarrow IRL 26 B2
Kingisepp RUS 9 C6
King's Lynn GB 41 C4
Kingsbridge GB 43 B3
Kingsclere GB 44 B2
Kingscourt IRL 27 C4
Kingsteignton GB 43 B3
Kingston, *Greater London* GB 44 B3
Kingston, *Moray* GB 32 D3
Kingston Bagpuize GB 44 B2
Kingston upon Hull GB 40 B3
Kingswear GB 43 B3
Kingswood GB 43 A4
Kington GB 39 B3
Kingussie GB 32 D2
Kinloch, *Highland* GB 31 B2
Kinloch, *Highland* GB 32 C2
Kinloch Rannoch GB 35 B3
Kinlochbervie GB 32 C1
Kinlochewe GB 32 D1
Kinlochleven GB 34 B3
Kinlochmoidart GB 34 B2
Kinloss GB 32 D3
Kinlough IRL 26 B2
Kinn N 48 B2
Kinna S 60 B2
Kinnared S 60 B3
Kinnarp S 55 B4
Kinne-Kleva S 55 B4
Kinnegad IRL 30 A1
Kinnitty IRL 28 A4
Kinrooi B 80 A1
Kinross GB 35 B4
Kinsale IRL 29 C3
Kinsarvik N 46 B3
Kintarvie GB 31 A2
Kintore GB 33 D4
Kinvarra IRL 28 A3
Kioni GR 184 A1
Kiparissia GR 184 B2
Kipfenburg D 95 C3
Kippen GB 35 B3
Kiraz TR 188 A3
Kirazlı TR 186 B1
Kirberg D 81 B4
Kirchbach in Steiermark A 110 C2
Kirchberg CH 106 B2
Kirchberg, *Baden-Württemberg* D 94 B1
Kirchberg, *Rheinland-Pfalz* D 93 B3
Kirchberg am Wechsel A 110 B2
Kirchberg an der Pielach A 110 A2
Kirchberg in Tirol A 109 B3
Kirchbichl A 108 B3
Kirchdorf, *Bayern* D 96 C1
Kirchdorf, *Mecklenburg-Vorpommern* D 65 C4
Kirchdorf, *Niedersachsen* D 72 B1
Kirchdorf an der Krems A 109 B5
Kirchdorf in Tirol A 109 B3
Kirchenlamitz D 83 B3
Kirchenthumbach D 95 B3
Kirchhain D 81 B4
Kirchheim, *Baden-Württemberg* D 94 C1
Kirchheim, *Bayern* D 108 A1
Kirchheim, *Hessen* D 81 B5
Kirchheim-bolanden D 93 B4
Kirchhundem D 81 A4
Kirchlintein D 72 B2
Kirchschlag A 111 B3
Kirchweidach D 109 A3
Kirchzarten D 106 B2
Kircubbin GB 27 B5
Kireç TR 186 C3
Kirillov RUS 9 C11
Kirishi RUS 9 C8
Kirk Michael GB 36 B2
Kirkbean GB 36 B3
Kirkbride GB 36 B3
Kirkby GB 38 A4
Kirkby Lonsdale GB 37 B4
Kirkby Malzeard GB 40 A2
Kirkby Stephen GB 37 B4
Kirkbymoorside GB 37 B6
Kirkcaldy GB 35 B4
Kirkcolm GB 36 B1
Kirkconnel GB 36 A2
Kirkcowan GB 36 B2
Kirkcudbright GB 36 B2
Kirke Hyllinge DK 61 D1
Kirkehamn N 52 B2
Kirkelly IRL 26 C2
Kirkenær N 49 B4
Kirkenes N 193 C14
Kirkham GB 38 A4
Kirkintilloch GB 35 C3
Kirkjubæjarklaustur IS 191 D7
Kirkkonummi FIN 8 B4
Kirkmichael GB 35 B4
Kirkoswald GB 36 A2
Kirkpatrick Fleming GB 36 A3
Kirkton of Glenisla GB 35 B4
Kirkwall GB 33 C4
Kirkwhelpington GB 37 A5
Kirn D 93 B3
Kirovsk RUS 3 C13
Kirriemuir GB 35 B5
Kirton GB 41 C3
Kirton in Lindsey GB 40 B3
Kirtorf D 81 B5
Kiruna S 196 B3
Kisa S 62 A3
Kisač SRB 126 B1
Kisbér H 112 B2
Kiseljak BIH 139 B4
Kisielice PL 69 B4
Kisköre H 113 B4
Kiskőrös H 112 C3
Kiskunfélegyháza H 113 C3
Kiskunhalas H 112 C3
Kiskunlacháza H 112 B2
Kiskunmajsa H 113 C3
Kisláng H 112 C2
Kisslegg D 107 B4
Kissolt H 112 C3
Kissónerga CY 181 B1
Kist D 94 B1
Kistanje HR 138 B1
Kistelek H 113 C3
Kisterenye H 113 A3
Kisújszállás H 113 B4
Kisvárda H 16 A5
Kisvejke H 112 C2
Kiszkowo PL 76 B2
Kiszombor H 126 A2
Kitee FIN 9 A7
Kithnos GR 185 B5
Kiti CY 181 B2
Kitkiöjärvi S 196 B6
Kitkiöjoki S 196 B6
Kittelfjäll S 195 E6
Kittendorf D 74 A1
Kittilä FIN 196 B7
Kittlitz D 84 A2
Kittsee A 111 A4
Kitzbühel A 109 B3
Kitzingen D 94 B2
Kiuruvesi FIN 3 E10
Kivertsi UA 13 C6
Kividhes CY 181 B1
Kivik S 63 C2
Kivotos GR 182 C3
Kjeldebotn N 194 B7
Kjellerup DK 59 B2
Kjellmyra N 49 B4
Kjøllefjord N 193 B11
Kjopmannskjaer N 54 A1
Kjøpsvik N 194 B7
Kľačno SK 98 C2
Kladanj BIH 139 A4
Kläden D 73 B4
Klädesholmen S 60 B1
Kladnice HR 138 B2
Kladno CZ 84 B2
Kladruby CZ 95 B4
Klagenfurt A 110 C1
Klågerup S 61 D3
Klagstorp S 66 A2
Klaipėda LT 8 E2
Klaistow D 74 B1
Klaksvík FO 4 A3
Klana HR 123 B3
Klanac HR 123 C4
Klanjec HR 123 A4
Klardorf D 95 B4
Klarup DK 58 A3
Klašnice BIH 124 C3
Klässbol S 55 A3
Klášterec nad Ohří CZ 83 B5
Kláštor pod Znievom SK 98 C2
Klatovy CZ 96 B1
Klaus an der Pyhrnbahn A 110 B1
Klazienaveen NL 71 B3
Klecko PL 76 B2
Kleczew PL 76 B3
Klein Plasten D 74 A1
Klein Sankt Paul A 110 C1
Kleinsölk A 109 B4
Kleinzell A 110 B2
Klejtrup DK 58 B2
Klek SRB 126 B2
Klemensker DK 67 A3
Klenak SRB 127 C1
Klenci pod Cerchovem CZ 95 B4
Klenica PL 75 C4
Klenje SRB 127 C1
Klenoec MK 182 B2
Klenovec SK 99 C3
Klenovica HR 123 B3
Klenovnik HR 124 A2
Kleppe N 52 B1
Kleppestø N 46 B2
Kleptow D 74 A2
Kleszewo PL 77 B6
Kleve D 80 A2
Klevshult S 60 B4
Klewki PL 77 A5
Kličevac SRB 127 C3
Kliening A 110 C1
Klietz D 73 B5
Klikuszowa PL 99 B3
Klimkovice CZ 98 B2
Klimontów PL 87 B5
Klimovichi BY 13 B9
Klimpfjäll S 195 E5
Klin RUS 9 D10
Klinča Sela HR 123 B4
Klingenbach A 111 B3
Klingenberg D 93 B5
Klingenmunster D 93 B4
Klingenthal D 83 B4
Klinken D 73 A4
Klintehamn S 57 C4
Kliny PL 87 A4
Klipley DK 64 B2
Klippan S 61 C3
Klis HR 138 B2
Klitmøller DK 58 A1
Klitten S 49 A6
Klixbüll D 64 B1
Kljajićevo SRB 126 B1
Ključ BIH 138 A2
Klobouky CZ 97 C4
Kłobuck PL 86 B2
Klockestrand S 200 D3
Kłodawa, *Lubuskie* PL 75 B4
Kłodawa, *Wielkopolskie* PL 76 B3
Kłodzko PL 85 B4
Kløfta N 48 B3
Klokkarvik N 46 B2
Klokkerholm DK 58 A3
Klokočov SK 98 B2
Kłomnice PL 86 B3
Klonowa PL 86 A2
Kloosterzande NL 79 A4
Kłopot PL 74 B3
Klos AL 182 B2
Kloštar Ivanić HR 124 B2
Kloster D 66 B2
Kloster DK 59 B1
Klösterle A 107 B5
Klostermansfeld D 82 A3
Klosterneuburg A 97 C4
Klosters CH 107 C4
Kloten CH 107 B3
Klötze D 73 B4
Klöverträsk S 196 D4
Klövsjö S 199 C11
Kluczbork PL 86 B2
Kluczewo PL 75 A5
Kluisbergen B 79 B3
Klundert NL 79 A4
Klutz D 65 C4
Klwów PL 87 A4
Klyetsk BY 13 B7
Knaben N 52 B2
Knaften S 200 B4
Knapstad N 54 A2
Knäred S 61 C3
Knaresborough GB 40 A2
Knarvik N 46 B2
Knebel DK 59 B3
Knebworth GB 44 B3
Knesebeck D 73 B3
Knesselare B 78 A3
Knežak SLO 123 B3
Kneževi Vinogradi HR 125 B4
Kneževo HR 125 B4
Knić SRB 127 D2
Knighton GB 39 B3
Knin HR 138 A2
Knislinge S 61 C4
Knittelfeld A 110 B1
Knivsta S 57 A3
Knock IRL 28 A3
Knocktopher IRL 30 B1
Knokke-Heist B 78 A3
Knowle GB 44 A2
Knurów PL 86 B2
Knutby S 51 C5
Knutsford GB 38 A4
Kobarid SLO 122 A2
København = Copenhagen DK 61 D2
Kobenz A 110 B1
Kobersdorf A 111 B3
Kobiernice PL 99 B3
Kobierzyce PL 85 B4
Kobilje SLO 111 C3
Kobiór PL 86 B2
Koblenz CH 106 B3
Koblenz D 81 B3
Kobryn BY 13 B6
Kobylanka PL 75 A3
Kobylin PL 85 A5
Kobylniki PL 77 B5
Kocaali TR 187 A5
Kocaaliler TR 189 B5
Kocaeli = İzmit TR 187 B4
Kočani MK 182 B4
Koçarlı TR 188 B2
Koceljevo SRB 127 C1
Kočerin BIH 138 B3
Kočevje SLO 123 B3
Kočevska Reka SLO 123 B3
Kochel am see D 108 B2
Kocs H 112 B2
Kocsér H 113 B3
Kocsola H 112 C2
Koczala PL 68 B2
Kodal N 53 A6
Kode S 60 B1
Kodersdorf D 84 A2
Kodrab PL 86 A3
Koekelare B 78 A2
Kofçaz TR 186 A2
Köflach A 110 B2
Køge DK 61 D2
Kohlberg D 95 B4
Kohtla-Järve EST 8 C5
Köinge S 60 B2
Kojetín CZ 98 B1
Kökar FIN 51 C7
Kokava SK 99 C3
Kokkola FIN 3 E8
Kokori BIH 124 C3
Kokoski PL 69 A3
Koksijde B 78 A2
Kola BIH 124 C3
Kola RUS 3 B13
Köla S 54 A3
Kołacin PL 87 A3
Kolari FIN 196 B6
Kolárovo SK 112 B1
Kolašin CG 16 D3
Kolbäck S 56 A2
Kolbacz PL 75 A3
Kolbeinsstaðir IS 190 C3
Kolbermoor D 108 B3
Kolbnitz A 109 C4
Kolbotn N 54 A1
Kolbu N 48 B2
Kolby Kås DK 59 C3
Kolczewo PL 67 C3
Kolczyglowy PL 68 A2
Kolding DK 59 C2
Kölesd H 112 C2
Kolgrov N 46 A1
Kolín CZ 97 A3
Kolind DK 59 B3
Kolinec CZ 96 B1
Koljane HR 138 B2
Kølkær DK 59 B2
Kölleda D 82 A3
Kollum NL 70 A3
Köln = Cologne D 80 B2
Koło PL 76 B3
Kołobrzeg PL 67 B4
Kolochau D 83 A5
Kolomyya UA 13 D6
Kolonowskie PL 86 B2
Koloveč CZ 95 B5
Kolpino RUS 9 C7
Kolrep D 73 A5
Kölsillre S 199 C12
Kolsko PL 75 C4
Kolsva S 56 A1
Kolta SK 112 A2
Kolunič BIH 138 A2
Koluszki PL 87 A3
Kolut SRB 125 B4
Kolvereid N 199 A8
Kølvrå DK 59 B2
Komadi H 113 B5
Komagvær N 193 B14
Komarica BIH 125 C3
Komárno SK 112 B2
Komárom H 112 B2
Komatou Yialou CY 181 A3
Komboti GR 182 D3
Komen SLO 122 B2
Komin HR 138 B3
Komiža HR 138 B2
Komjáti H 99 C4
Komjatice SK 112 A2
Komletinci HR 125 B4
Komló, *Baranya* H 125 A4
Kömlo, *Heves* H 113 B4
Komoča SK 112 B2
Komorniki PL 75 B5
Komorzno PL 86 A2
Komotini GR 183 B7
Konak SRB 126 B2
Konakovo RUS 9 D10
Konarzyny PL 68 B2
Kondias GR 183 D7
Kondopaga RUS 9 A9
Kondorfa H 111 C3
Kondoros H 113 C4
Konevo RUS 9 A11
Køng DK 65 A4
Konga S 63 B3
Köngäs FIN 196 B7
Kongerslev DK 58 B3
Kongsberg N 53 A5
Kongshamn N 53 B4
Kongsmark DK 64 A1
Kongsmoen N 199 A9
Kongsvik N 194 B7
Kongsvinger N 48 B3
Konice CZ 97 B4
Konie PL 77 C5
Koniecpol PL 86 B3
Königs Wusterhausen D 74 B2
Königsberg D 82 B2
Königsbronn D 94 C2
Königsbrück D 84 A1
Königsbrunn D 94 C2
Königsdorf D 108 B2
Königsee D 82 B3
Königshorst D 74 B1
Königslutter D 73 B3
Königssee D 109 B3
Königstein, *Hessen* D 81 B4
Königstein, *Sachsen* D 84 B2
Königstetten A 97 C4
Königswartha D 84 A2
Konigswiesen A 96 C2
Königswinter D 80 B3
Konin PL 76 B3
Konispol AL 182 D2
Konitsa GR 182 C2
Köniz CH 106 C2
Konjevići BIH 139 A5
Konjevrate HR 138 B2
Konjic BIH 139 B3
Konjščina HR 124 A2
Könnern D 83 A3
Konnerud N 53 A6
Konopiska PL 86 B2
Konotop PL 75 C4
Końskie PL 87 A4
Konsmo N 52 B3
Konstancin-Jeziorna PL 77 B6
Konstantynów Łódźki PL 86 A3
Konstanz D 107 B4
Kontich B 79 A4
Kontiolahti FIN 9 A6
Konya TR 189 B7
Konz D 92 B2
Kópasker IS 191 A9
Kópavogur IS 190 C4
Kopčany SK 98 C1
Koper SLO 122 B2
Kopervik N 52 A1
Kópháza H 111 B3
Kopice PL 85 B5
Kopidlno CZ 84 B3
Köping S 56 A1
Köpingebro S 66 A2
Köpingsvik S 62 B4
Köpmanholmen S 200 C4
Koppang N 48 A3
Koppangen N 192 C4
Kopparberg S 50 C1
Koppelo FIN 193 D11
Koppom S 54 A3
Koprivlen BG 183 B5
Koprivna BIH 125 C4
Koprivnica HR 124 A2
Kopřivnice CZ 98 B2
Köprübaşı TR 186 D3
Koprzywnica PL 87 B5
Kopstal L 92 B2
Kopychyntsi UA 13 D6
Kopytkowo PL 69 B3
Korbach D 81 A4
Körbecke D 81 A4
Korçë AL 182 C2
Korčula HR 138 C3
Korczyców PL 75 B3
Korenita SRB 127 C1
Korets UA 13 C7
Korfantów PL 85 B5
Körfez TR 187 B4
Korgen N 195 D4
Korinth DK 64 A3
Korinthos = Corinth GR 184 B3
Korita BIH 138 A2
Korita HR 139 C3
Korithi GR 184 B1
Korkuteli TR 189 B5
Körmend H 111 B3
Korne PL 68 A2
Korneuburg A 97 C4
Kornevo RUS 69 A5
Kórnik PL 76 B2
Kornsjø N 54 B2
Környe H 112 B2
Koromačno HR 123 C3
Koroni GR 184 C2
Koronos GR 185 B6
Koronowo PL 76 A2
Körösladány H 113 C5
Köröstarcsa H 113 C5
Korosten UA 13 C8
Korostyshev UA 13 C8
Korpikå S 196 D6
Korpikylä FIN 196 C6
Korpilombolo S 196 C6
Korsberga, *Jönköping* S 62 A3
Korsberga, *Skaraborg* S 55 B5
Korshavn N 54 A1
Korskrogen S 200 E1
Korsnäs S 50 B2
Korsør DK 65 A4

La Galera E 153 B4
La Garde-Freinet F 132 B2
La Garnache F 114 B2
La Garriga E 147 C3
La Garrovilla E 155 C4
La Gaubretière F 114 B2
La Gineta E 158 B1
La Granadella, *Alicante* E 159 C4
La Granadella, *Lleida* E 153 A4
La Grand-Combe F 131 A3
La Grande-Croix F 117 B4
La Grande-Motte F 131 B3
La Granja d'Escarp E 153 A4
La Granjuela E 156 B2
La Grave F 118 B3
La Gravelle F 101 A4
La Guardia E 151 C4
La Guardia de Jaén E 163 A4
La Guerche-de-Bretagne F 101 B4
La Guerche-sur-l'Aubois F 104 C1
La Guérinière F 114 B1
La Haba E 156 B2
La Haye-du-Puits F 88 A2
La Haye-Pesnel F 88 B2
La Herlière F 78 B2
La Hermida E 142 A2
La Herrera E 158 C1
La Higuera E 158 C2
La Hiniesta E 149 A4
La Horcajada E 150 B2
La Horra E 143 C3
La Hulpe B 79 B4
La Hutte F 89 B4
La Iglesuela E 150 B3
La Iglesuela del Cid E 153 B3
La Iruela E 164 B2
La Javie F 132 A2
La Jonchère-St. Maurice F 116 A1
La Jonquera E 146 B3
La Lantejuela E 162 A2
La Línea de la Concepción E 162 B2
La Llacuna E 147 C2
La Londe-les-Maures F 132 B2
La Loupe F 89 B5
La Louvière B 79 B4
La Luisiana E 162 A2
La Machine F 104 C2
la Maddalena I 178 A3
La Mailleraye-sur-Seine F 89 A4
La Malène F 130 A2
La Mamola E 163 B4
La Manresana dels Prats E 147 C2
La Masadera E 145 C3
La Mata E 150 C3
La Mata de Ledesma E 149 A4
La Mata de Monteagudo E 142 B1
La Meilleraye-de-Bretagne F 101 B4
La Ménitré F 102 B1
La Mojonera E 164 C2
La Mole F 132 B2
La Molina E 147 B2
La Monnerie-le-Montel F 117 B3
La Morera E 155 C4
La Mothe-Achard F 114 B2
La Mothe-St. Héray F 115 B3
La Motte-Chalançon F 131 A4
La Motte-du-Caire F 132 A2
La Motte-Servolex F 118 B2
La Mudarra E 142 C2
La Muela E 152 A2
La Mure F 118 C2
La Nava E 161 B3
La Nava de Ricomalillo E 156 A3
La Nava de Santiago E 155 B4
La Neuve-Lyre F 89 B4
La Neuveville CH 106 B2
La Nocle-Maulaix F 104 C2
La Nuez de Arriba E 143 B3
La Paca E 164 B3
La Pacaudière F 117 A3
La Palma d'Ebre E 153 A4
La Palma del Condado E 161 B3
La Palme F 146 B4
La Palmyre F 114 C2
La Parra E 155 C4
La Pedraja de Portillo E 150 A3
La Peraleja E 152 B1
La Petit-Pierre F 93 C3
La Pinilla E 165 B3
La Plagne F 118 B3
La Plaza E 141 A4
La Pobla de Lillet E 147 B2
La Pobla de Vallbona E 159 B3
La Pobla Llarga E 159 B3
La Pola de Gordón E 142 B1
la Porta F 180 A2
La Pouëze F 102 B1
La Póveda de Soria E 143 B4
La Preste F 146 B3
La Primaube F 130 A1
La Puebla de Almoradie E 157 A4
La Puebla de Cazalla E 162 A2
La Puebla de los Infantes E 162 A2
La Puebla de Montalbán E 150 C3
La Puebla de Roda E 145 B4
La Puebla de Valdavia E 142 B2
La Puebla de Valverde E 152 B3
La Puebla del Río E 162 A1
La Pueblanueva E 150 C3
La Puerta de Segura E 164 A2
La Punt CH 107 C4
La Quintana E 162 A3
La Quintera E 162 A2
La Rábita, *Granada* E 164 C1
La Rábita, *Jaén* E 163 A3
La Rambla E 163 A3
La Reale I 178 A2
La Redondela E 161 B2
La Réole F 128 B2
La Riera E 141 A4
La Riera de Gaià E 147 C2
La Rinconada E 162 A1
La Rivière-Thibouville F 89 A4
La Robla E 142 B1
La Roca de la Sierra E 155 B4
La Roche CH 106 C2
La Roche-Bernard F 101 B3
La Roche-Canillac F 116 B1
La Roche-Chalais F 128 A3
La Roche Derrien F 100 A2
La Roche-des-Arnauds F 132 A1
La Roche-en-Ardenne B 80 B1
La Roche-en-Brénil F 104 B3
La Roche-Guyon F 90 B1
La Roche-Posay F 115 B4
La Roche-sur-Foron F 118 A3
La Roche-sur-Yon F 114 B2
La Rochebeaucourt-et-Argentine F 115 C4
La Rochefoucauld F 115 C4
La Rochelle F 114 B2
La Rochette F 131 A4
La Roda, *Albacete* E 158 B1
La Roda, *Oviedo* E 141 A4
La Roda de Andalucía E 162 A3
La Roque-Gageac F 129 B4
La Roque-Ste. Marguerite F 130 A2
La Roquebrussanne F 132 B1
La Rubia E 143 C4
La Sagrada E 149 B3
La Salceda E 151 A4
La Salle F 118 C3
la Salute di Livenza I 122 B1
La Salvetat-Peyralés F 130 A1
La Salvetat-sur-Agout F 130 B1
La Sarraz CH 105 C5
La Seca E 150 A3
La Selva del Camp E 147 C2
La Senia E 153 B4
La Serra E 147 C2
La Seu d'Urgell E 146 B2
La Seyne-sur-Mer F 132 B1
La Solana E 157 B4
La Souterraine F 116 A1
La Spézia I 134 A2
La Storta I 168 B2
La Suze-sur-Sarthe F 102 B2
La Teste F 128 B1
La Thuile I 119 B3
La Toba E 152 B2
La Toledana E 157 A3
La Torre de Cabdella E 146 B1
La Torre de Esteban Hambrán E 151 B3
La Torre del l'Espanyol E 153 A4
La Torresaviñán E 152 B1
La Tour d'Aigues F 132 B1
La Tour de Peilz CH 106 C1
La Tour-du-Pin F 118 B2
La Tranche-sur-Mer F 114 B2
La Tremblade F 114 C2
La Trimouille F 115 B5
La Trinité F 100 B2
La Trinité-Porhoët F 101 A3
La Turballe F 101 B3
La Uña E 142 A1
La Unión E 165 B4
La Vall d'Uixó E 159 B3
La Vecilla de Curueño E 142 B1
La Vega, *Asturias* E 141 A5
La Vega, *Asturias* E 142 A1
La Vega, *Cantabria* E 142 A2
La Velilla E 151 A4
La Velles E 150 A2
La Ventosa E 152 B1
La Victoria E 162 A3
La Vid E 151 A4
La Vilavella E 159 B3
La Vilella Baixa E 147 C1
La Villa de Don Fadrique E 157 A4
La Ville Dieu-du-Temple F 129 B4
La Villedieu F 115 B3
La Voulte-sur-Rhône F 117 C4
La Wantzenau F 93 C3
La Yesa E 159 B3
La Zubia E 163 A4
Laa an der Thaya A 97 C4
Laage D 65 C5
Laanila FIN 193 D11
Laatzen D 72 B2
Laban IRL 28 A3
Labastide-Murat F 129 B4
Labastide-Rouairoux F 130 B1
Labastide-St. Pierre F 129 C4
Lábatlan H 112 B2
Labenne F 128 C1
Labin HR 123 B3
Łabiszyn PL 76 B2
Lablachère F 131 A3
Lábod H 124 A3
Laboe D 64 B3
Labouheyre F 128 B2
Łabowa PL 99 B4
Labrit F 128 B2
Labros E 152 A2
Labruguière F 130 B1
Labrujo P 148 A1
L'Absie F 114 B3
Laç AL 182 B1
Lacalahorra E 164 B1
Lacanau F 128 B1
Lacanau-Océan F 128 A1
Lacanche F 104 B3
Lacapelle-Marival F 129 B4
Laćarak SRB 127 B1
Lacaune F 130 B1
Laceby GB 41 B3
Lacedónia I 172 A1
Láces I 108 C1
Lachania GR 188 D2
Lachen CH 107 B3
Lachendorf D 72 B3
Lachowice PL 99 B3
Łack PL 77 B4
Läckeby S 62 B4
Läckö S 55 B4
Lacock GB 43 A4
Láconi I 179 C3
Lacq F 145 A3
Lacroix-Barrez F 116 C2
Lacroix-St. Ouen F 90 B2
Lacroix-sur-Meuse F 92 C1
Łacznik PL 86 B1
Lad H 125 A3
Ladbergen D 71 B4
Lądek-Zdrój PL 85 B4
Ladelund D 64 B2
Ladendorf A 97 C4
Ladignac-le-Long F 115 C5
Ladispoli I 168 B2
Ladoeiro P 155 B3
Ladon F 103 B4
Ladushkin RUS 69 A5
Ladybank GB 35 B4
Laer D 71 B4
Lærdalsøyri N 47 A4
Lafkos GR 183 D5
Lafnitz A 111 B3
Lafrançaise F 129 B4
Lagan S 60 C3
Laganadi I 175 C1
Lagarde F 146 A2
Lagares, *Coimbra* P 148 B2
Lagares, *Porto* P 148 A1
Lagaro I 135 A4
Lagartera E 150 C2
Lågbol S 51 B5
Lage D 72 C1
Lägerdorf D 64 C2
Lagg GB 34 C2
Laggan GB 32 D2
Laggartorp S 55 A5
Łagiewniki PL 85 B4
Láglio I 120 B2
Lagnieu F 118 B2
Lagny-sur-Marne F 90 C2
Lago, *Calabria* I 175 B2
Lago, *Veneto* I 121 B5
Lagôa P 160 B1
Lagoaça P 149 A3
Lagonegro I 174 A1
Lagos GR 183 B7
Lagos P 160 B1
Lagosanto I 121 C5
Łagów, *Lubuskie* PL 75 B4
Łagów, *Świętokrzyskie* PL 87 B5
Lagrasse F 146 A3
Laguardia E 143 B4
Laguarres E 145 B4
Laguenne F 116 B1
Laguépie F 129 B4
Laguiole F 116 C2
Laguna de Duera E 150 A3
Laguna de Negrillos E 142 B1
Laguna del Marquesado E 152 B2
Lagundo I 108 C2
Lagunilla E 149 B3
Laharie F 128 B1
Lahden D 71 B4
Laheycourt F 91 C5
Lahnstein D 81 B3
Laholm S 61 C3
Lahr D 93 C3
Lahti FIN 8 B4
Laichingen D 94 C1
L'Aigle F 89 B4
Laignes F 104 B3
Laiguéglia I 133 B4
L'Aiguillon-sur-Mer F 114 B2
Laimbach am Ostrong A 97 C3
Laina E 152 A1
Lainio S 196 B5
Lairg GB 32 C2
Laissac F 130 A1
Laisvall S 195 D8
Láives I 121 A4
Lajkovac SRB 127 C2
Lajoskomárom H 112 C2
Lajosmizse H 112 B3
Lak H 99 C4
Lakenheath GB 45 A4
Lakitelek H 113 C4
Lakki GR 185 D4
Lakolk DK 64 A1
Łąkorz PL 69 B4
Lakšárska Nová Ves SK 98 C1
Lakselv N 193 B8
Laksfors N 195 E4
Laktaši BIH 124 C3
Lalapaşa TR 186 A1
L'Albagès E 153 A4
Lalbenque F 129 B4
L'Alcudia E 159 B3
L'Aldea E 153 B4
Lalín E 140 B2
Lalinde F 129 B3
Lalizolle F 116 A3
Lalley F 118 C2
Lalling D 95 C5
Lalm N 198 D6
L'Alpe-d'Huez F 118 B3
Laluque F 128 C1
Lam D 95 B5
Lama dei Peligni I 169 A4
Lama Mocogno I 135 A3
Lamadrid E 142 A2
Lamagistére F 129 B3
Lamarche F 105 A4
Lamarche-sur-Saône F 105 B4
Lamargelle F 105 B3
Lamarosa P 154 B2
Lamarque F 128 A2
Lamas P 148 B1
Lamas de Moaro P 140 B2
Lamastre F 117 C4
Lambach A 109 A4
Lamballe F 101 A3
Lamberhurst GB 45 B4
Lambesc F 131 B4
Lambia GR 184 B2
Lambley GB 37 B4
Lambourn GB 44 B2
Lamego P 148 A2
L'Ametlla de Mar E 153 B4
Lamia GR 182 E4
Lammhult S 62 A2
Lamothe-Cassel F 129 B4
Lamothe-Montravel F 128 B3
Lamotte-Beuvron F 103 B4
Lampertheim D 93 B4
Lampeter GB 39 B2
L'Ampolla E 153 B4
Lamprechtshausen A 109 B3
Lamsfeld D 74 C3
Lamspringe D 72 C3
Lamstedt D 72 A2
Lamure-sur-Azergues F 117 A4
Lana I 108 C2
Lanaja E 145 C3
Lanarce F 117 C3
Lanark GB 36 A3
Lancaster GB 37 B4
Lanchester GB 37 B5
Lanciano I 169 A4
Lancing GB 44 C3
Lancon-provence F 131 B4
Lancova Vas SLO 124 A1
Landau, *Bayern* D 95 C4
Landau, *Rheinland-Pfalz* D 93 B4
Landeck A 108 B1
Landen B 79 B5
Landerneau F 100 A1
Landeryd S 60 B3
Landesbergen D 72 B2
Landete E 158 B2
Landévant F 100 B2
Landévennec F 100 A1
Landivisiau F 100 A1
Landivy F 88 B2
Landl A 108 B3
Landön S 199 B11
Landos F 117 C3
Landouzy-le-Ville F 91 B4
Landquart CH 107 C4
Landrecies F 91 A3
Landreville F 104 A3
Landriano I 120 B2
Lands-berg D 83 A4
Landsberg D 108 A1
Landsbro S 62 A2
Landscheid D 92 B2
Landshut D 95 C4
Landskrona S 61 D2
Landstuhl D 93 B3
Lanesborough IRL 28 A4
Lanester F 100 B2
Lanestosa E 143 A3
Langå DK 59 B2
Langa de Duero E 151 A4
Langada GR 185 A7
Langadas GR 183 C5
Langadia GR 184 B3
Langangen N 53 A5
Långared S 60 A2
Långaröd S 61 D3
Långaryd S 60 B3
Långås S 60 C2
Långasjö S 63 B3
Langau A 97 C3
Langeac F 117 B3
Langeais F 102 B2
Langedijk NL 70 B1
Langeln D 73 C3
Langelsheim D 72 C3
Langemark-Poelkapelle B 78 B2
Langen, *Hessen* D 93 B4
Langen, *Niedersachsen* D 72 A1
Langenau D 94 C2
Langenberg D 81 A4
Langenbruck CH 106 B2
Langenburg D 94 B1
Längenfeld A 108 B1
Langenfeld D 80 A2
Langenhorn D 64 B1
Langenlois A 97 C3
Langenlonsheim D 93 B3
Langennaudorf D 83 A5
Langenneufnach D 94 C2
Langenthal CH 106 B2
Langenzenn D 94 B2
Langeoog D 71 A4
Langeskov DK 59 C3
Langesund N 53 A5
Langewiesen D 82 B2
Långflon S 49 A4
Langförden D 71 B5
Langhagen D 73 A5
Länghem S 60 B3
Langhirano I 120 C3
Langholm GB 36 A4
Langholt IS 191 D7
Långlöt S 62 B4
Langnau CH 106 C2
Langø DK 65 B4
Langogne F 117 C3
Langon F 128 B2
Langquaid D 95 C4
Långrådna S 56 B2
Langreo E 142 A1
Langres F 105 B4
Långsele S 200 C3
Långserud S 54 A3
Langset N 48 B3
Långshyttan S 50 B3
Langstrand N 192 B7
Långträsk S 196 D3
Langueux F 101 A3
Languidic F 100 B2
Längvik S 57 A4
Langwarden D 71 A5
Langwathby GB 37 B4
Langwedel D 72 B2
Langweid D 94 C2
Langwies CH 107 C4
Lanheses P 148 A1
Lanięta PL 77 B4
Lanildut F 100 A1
Lanjarón E 163 B4
Lanmeur F 100 A2
Lanna, *Jönköping* S 60 B3
Lanna, *Örebro* S 55 A5
Lännaholm S 51 C4
Lannavaara S 196 A4
Lannéanou F 100 A2
Lannemezan F 145 A4
Lanneuville-sur-Meuse F 91 B5
Lannilis F 100 A1
Lannion F 100 A2
Lanouaille F 115 C5
Lansjärv S 196 C5
Lanškroun CZ 97 B4
Lanslebourg-Mont-Cenis F 119 B3
Lanta F 129 C4
Lantadilla E 142 B2
Lanton F 128 B1
Lantosque F 133 B3
Lanusei I 179 C3
Lanúvio I 168 B2
Lanvollon F 100 A3
Lánycsók H 125 A4
Lanz D 73 A4
Lanza E 140 A2
Lanzada E 140 B2
Lanzahita E 150 B3
Lanžhot CZ 97 C4
Lanzo Torinese I 119 B4
Laole SRB 127 C3
Laon F 91 B3
Laons F 89 B5
Lapalisse F 117 A3
Łapczyna Wola PL 87 B3
Lapeyrade F 128 B2
Lapeyrouse F 116 A2
Lapford GB 42 B3
Lapithos CY 181 A2
Laplume F 129 B3
Lapoutroie F 106 A2
Lapovo SRB 127 C3
Läppe S 56 A1
Lappeenranta FIN 8 B6
Lappoluobbal N 192 C7
Lappträsk S 196 C6
Lapseki TR 186 B1
Lapua FIN 8 A3
L'Àquila I 169 A3
Laracha E 140 A2
Laragh IRL 30 A2
Laragne-Montéglin F 132 A1
l'Arboç E 147 C2
L'Arbresle F 117 B4
Lärbro S 57 C4
Larceveau F 144 A2
Larche, *Alpes-de-Haute-Provence* F 132 A2
Larche, *Corrèze* F 129 A4
Lårdal N 53 A4
Lardosa P 155 B3
Laredo E 143 A3
Largentière F 131 A3
L'Argentière-la-Bessée F 118 C3
Largs GB 34 C3
Lari I 134 B3
Lariño E 140 B1
Larino I 170 B2
Larisa GR 182 D4
Larkhall GB 36 A3
Larkollen N 54 A1
Larmor-Plage F 100 B2
Larnaca CY 181 B2
Larne GB 27 B5
Larochette L 92 B2
Laroque d'Olmes F 146 B2
Laroque-Timbaut F 129 B3
Laroquebrou F 116 C2
Larouco E 141 B3
Larraga E 144 B2
Larrau F 144 A3
Larrazet F 129 C4
Larsnes N 198 C2
Laruns F 145 A3
Larva E 164 B1
Larvik N 53 A6
Las Arenas E 142 A2
Las Cabezadas E 151 A4
Las Cabezas de San Juan E 162 B2
Las Correderas E 157 B4

Las Cuevas de Cañart E 153 B3
Las Gabias E 163 A4
Las Herencias E 150 C3
Las Labores E 157 A4
Las Mesas E 158 B1
Las Minas E 164 A3
Las Navas E 163 A3
Las Navas de la Concepción E 156 C2
Las Navas del Marqués E 150 B3
Las Navillas E 157 A3
Las Negras E 164 C3
Las Pajanosas E 161 B3
Las Pedroñas E 158 B1
Las Planes d'Hostoles E 147 B3
Las Rozas, *Cantabria* E 142 B2
Las Rozas, *Madrid* E 151 B4
Las Uces E 149 A3
Las Veguillas E 149 B4
Las Ventas con Peña Aguilera E 157 A3
Las Ventas de San Julián E 150 B2
Las Villes E 153 B4
Lasalle F 131 A2
Lasarte E 144 A1
Låsby DK 59 B2
Łasin PL 69 B4
Lask PL 86 A3
Laska PL 68 B2
Łaskarzow PL 87 A5
Laško SLO 123 A4
Laskowice PL 76 A3
Laspaules E 145 B4
Laspuña E 145 B4
Lassan D 66 C2
Lassay-les-Châteaux F 89 B3
Lasseube F 145 A3
Lassigny F 90 B2
Lastovo HR 138 C2
Lastras de Cuéllar E 151 A3
Lästringe S 56 B3
Lastrup D 71 B4
Latasa E 144 B2
Látera I 168 A1
Laterza I 171 C4
Lathen D 71 B4
Latheron GB 32 C3
Latiano I 173 B3
Latina I 169 B2
Latisana I 122 B2
Látky SK 99 C3
Latrónico I 174 A2
Latronquière F 116 C2
Latterbach CH 106 C2
Laubach D 81 B4
Laubert F 117 C3
Laucha D 83 A3
Lauchhammer D 84 A1
Lauchheim D 94 C2
Lauda-Königshofen D 94 B1
Laudal N 52 B3
Lauder GB 35 C5
Lauenau D 72 B2
Lauenburg D 73 A3
Lauf D 95 B3
Laufach D 94 A1
Laufen CH 106 B2
Laufen D 109 B3
Lauffen D 93 B5
Laugar IS 191 B8
Laugarás IS 190 C5
Laugarbakki IS 190 B5
Laugarvatn IS 190 C5
Laugharne GB 39 C2
Lauingen D 94 C2
Laujar de Andarax E 164 C2
Laukaa FIN 8 A4
Lauker S 196 D2
Laukvik N 194 C5
Launceston GB 42 B2
Launois-sur-Vence F 91 B4
Laupheim D 94 C1
Lauragh IRL 29 C2
Laureana di Borrello I 175 C2
Laurencekirk GB 35 B5
Laurencetown IRL 28 A3
Laurenzana I 172 B1
Lauria I 174 A1
Laurière F 116 A1
Laurieston GB 36 B2
Laurino I 172 B1
Lausanne CH 106 C1
Laussonne F 117 C4
Lauta D 84 A2
Lautenthal D 82 A2
Lauterach A 107 B4
Lauterbach D 81 B5
Lauterbrunnen CH 106 C2
Lauterecken D 93 B3
Lauterhofen D 95 B3
Lautrec F 130 B1
Lauvsnes N 199 A7
Lauvvik N 52 B2
Lauzerte F 129 B4
Lauzès F 129 B4
Lauzun F 129 B3
Lavagna I 134 A2
Laval F 102 A1
Lavamünd A 110 C1
Lavara GR 186 A1
Lavardac F 129 B3
Lavaris P 148 B1
Lavarone I 121 B4
Lavau F 104 B1
Lavaur F 129 C4
Lavelanet F 146 B2
Lavello I 172 A1
Lavelsloh D 72 B1
Lavenham GB 45 A4
Laveno I 120 B1
Lavezzola I 135 A4
Laviano I 172 B1
Lavik N 46 A2
Lavilledieu F 131 A3
Lavinio-Lido di Enea I 168 B2
Lavis I 121 A4
Lavit F 129 C3
Lavoncourt F 105 B4
Lavos P 148 B1
Lavoûter-Chilhac F 117 B3
Lavradio P 154 C1
Lavre P 154 C2
Lavrio GR 185 B5
Lawers GB 35 B3
Ławy PL 75 B3
Laxå S 55 B5
Laxamýri IS 191 B8
Laxe E 140 A2
Laxey GB 36 B2
Laxford Bridge GB 32 C1
Laxhall S 55 B4
Laxsjö S 199 B11
Laxtjarn S 49 B6
Laxvik S 61 C2
Laxviken S 199 B11
Laza E 141 B3
Lazarevac SRB 127 C2
Lazarevo SRB 126 B2
Lazise I 121 B3
Łaziska Grn. PL 86 B2
Lazkao E 144 A1
Lázně Bělohrad CZ 84 B3
Lázně Bohdaneč CZ 97 A3
Lázně Kynžvart CZ 95 A4
Lazonby GB 37 B4
Łazy PL 67 B5
Lazzaro I 175 D1
Le Bar-sur-Loup F 132 B2
Le Barp F 128 B2
Le Béage F 117 C4
Le Beausset F 132 B1
Le Bessat F 117 B4
Le Blanc F 115 B5
Le Bleymard F 130 A2
Le Boullay-Mivoye F 89 B5
Le Boulou F 146 B3
Le Bourg F 129 B4
Le Bourg-d'Oisans F 118 B3
Le Bourget-du-Lac F 118 B2
Le Bourgneuf-la-Forêt F 101 A5
Le Bousquet d'Orb F 130 B2
Le Brassus CH 105 C5
Le Breuil F 117 A3
Le Breuil-en-Auge F 89 A4
Le Brusquet F 132 A2
Le Bry CH 106 C2
Le Bugue F 129 B3
Le Buisson F 129 B3
Le Caloy F 128 C2
Le Cap d'Agde F 130 B2
Le Cateau Cambrésis F 91 A3
Le Caylar F 130 B2
Le Cayrol F 116 C2
Le Chambon-Feugerolles F 117 B4
Le Chambon-sur-Lignon F 117 B4
Le Château d'Oléron F 114 C2
Le Châtelard F 118 B3
Le Châtelet F 103 C4
Le Chatelet-en-Brie F 90 C2
Le Chesne F 91 B4
Le Cheylard F 117 C4
Le Collet-de-Deze F 131 A2
Le Conquet F 100 A1
Le Creusot F 104 C3
Le Croisic F 101 B3
Le Crotoy F 78 B1
Le Deschaux F 105 C4
Le Donjon F 117 A3
Le Dorat F 115 B5
Le Faou F 100 A1
Le Faoüet F 100 A2
Le Folgoet F 100 A1
Le Fossat F 146 A2
Le Fousseret F 146 A2
Le Fugeret F 132 A2
Le Gault-Soigny F 91 C3
Le Grand-Bornand F 118 B3
Le-Grand-Bourg F 116 A1
Le Grand-Lucé F 102 B2
Le Grand-Pressigny F 102 C2
Le Grand-Quevilly F 89 A5
Le Grau-du-Roi F 131 B3
Le Havre F 89 A4
Le Hohwald F 93 C3
Le Houga F 128 C2
Le Lardin-St. Lazare F 129 A4
Le Lauzet-Ubaye F 132 A2
Le Lavandou F 132 B2
Le Lion-d'Angers F 102 B1
Le Locle CH 106 B1
Le Loroux-Bottereau F 101 B4
Le Louroux-Béconnais F 101 B5
Le Luc F 132 B2
Le Lude F 102 B2
Le Malzieu-Ville F 116 C3
Le Mans F 102 A2
Le Mas-d'Azil F 146 A2
Le Massegros F 130 A2
Le May-sur-Evre F 101 B5
Le Mayet-de-Montagne F 117 A3
Le Mêle-sur-Sarthe F 89 B4
Le Ménil F 105 A5
Le Merlerault F 89 B4
Le Mesnil-sur-Oger F 91 C4
Le Miroir F 105 C4
Le Molay-Littry F 88 A3
Le Monastier-sur-Gazeille F 117 C3
Le Monêtier-les-Bains F 118 C3
Le Mont-Dore F 116 B2
Le Mont-St. Michel F 88 B2
Le Montet F 116 A3
Le Muret F 128 B2
Le Muy F 132 B2
Le Neubourg F 89 A4
Le Nouvion-en-Thiérache F 91 A3
Le Palais F 100 B2
Le Parcq F 78 B2
Le Péage-de-Roussillon F 117 B4
Le Pellerin F 101 B4
Le Perthus F 146 B3
Le Pertuis F 117 B4
Le Petit-Bornand F 118 B3
Le Poët F 132 A1
Le Poirè-sur-Vie F 114 B2
Le Pont CH 105 C5
Le Pont-de-Montvert F 130 A2
Le Porge F 128 B1
Le Porge-Océan F 128 B1
Le Portel F 78 B1
Le Pouldu F 100 B2
Le Pouliguen F 101 B3
le Prese I 120 A3
Le Puy-en-Velay F 117 B3
Le Puy-Ste. Réparade F 131 B4
Le Quesnoy F 79 B3
Le Rayol F 132 B2
Le Rœulx B 79 B4
Le Rouget F 116 C2
Le Rozier F 130 A2
Le Russey F 106 B1
Le Sel-de-Bretagne F 101 B4
Le Sentier CH 105 C5
Le Souquet F 128 C1
Le Teil F 131 A3
Le Teilleul F 88 B3
Le Temple-de-Bretagne F 101 B4
Le Theil F 89 B4
Le Thillot F 106 B1
Le Touquet-Paris-Plage F 78 B1
Le Touvet F 118 B2
Le Translay F 90 B1
Le Tréport F 90 A1
Le Val F 132 B2
Le Val-André F 101 A3
Le Val-d'Ajol F 105 B5
Le Verdon-sur-Mer F 114 C2
Le Vernet F 132 A2
Le Vigan F 130 B2
le Ville I 135 B5
Le Vivier-sur-Mer F 88 B2
Lea GB 40 B3
Leadburn GB 35 C4
Leadhills GB 36 A3
Leap IRL 29 C2
Leatherhead GB 44 B3
Łeba PL 68 A2
Lebach D 92 B2
Lebekke B 79 A4
Lébény H 111 B4
Łebno PL 68 A3
Leboreiro E 140 B3
Lębork PL 68 A2
Lebrija E 162 B1
Lebring A 110 C2
Lebus D 74 B3
Lebusa D 83 A5
Leca da Palmeira P 148 A1
Lecce I 173 B4
Lecco I 120 B2
Lécera E 153 A3
Lećevica HR 138 B2
Lech A 107 B5
Lechbruck D 108 B1
Lechena GR 184 B2
Lechlade GB 44 B2
Lechovice CZ 97 C4
Leciñena E 145 C3
Leck D 64 B1
Lectoure F 129 C3
Łęczyca, *Łódzkie* PL 77 B4
Łęczyca, *Zachodnio-Pomorskie* PL 75 A4
Ledaña E 158 B2
Ledbury GB 39 B4
Lede B 79 B3
Ledeč nad Sazavou CZ 97 B3
Ledenice CZ 96 C2
Ledesma E 149 A3
Lédignan F 131 B3
Lédigos E 142 B2
Ledmore GB 32 C2
Lednice CZ 97 C4
Lednicke-Rovné SK 98 B2
Lędyczek PL 68 B1
Lędziny PL 86 B3
Leeds GB 40 B2
Leek GB 40 B1
Leek NL 71 A3
Leenaun IRL 28 A2
Leens NL 71 A3
Leer D 71 A4
Leerdam NL 79 A5
Leerhafe D 71 A4
Leese D 72 B2
Leeuwarden NL 70 A2
Leezen D 64 C3
Lefka CY 181 A1
Lefkada GR 182 E2
Lefkimis GR 182 D2
Lefkoniko CY 181 A2
Leganés E 151 B4
Legau D 107 B5
Legbąd PL 68 B2
Legé F 114 B2
Lège-Cap-Ferret F 128 B1
Legionowo PL 77 B5
Léglise B 92 B1
Legnago I 121 B4
Legnano I 120 B1
Legnaro I 121 B4
Legnica PL 85 A4
Łęgowo PL 69 A3
Legrad HR 124 A2
Léguevin F 129 C4
Legutiano E 143 B4
Lehesten D 82 B3
Lehnice SK 111 A4
Lehnin D 74 B1
Lehrberg D 94 B2
Lehre D 73 B3
Lehrte D 72 B2
Lehsen D 73 A4
Leibnitz A 110 C2
Leicester GB 40 C2
Leiden NL 70 B1
Leidschendam NL 70 B1
Leigh GB 38 A4
Leighlinbridge IRL 30 B2
Leighton Buzzard GB 44 B3
Leignon B 79 B5
Leikanger N 198 C2
Leimen D 93 B4
Leinefelde D 82 A2
Leinesfjord N 194 C6
Leintwardine GB 39 B4
Leipojärvi S 196 B4
Leipzig D 83 A4
Leira, *Nordland* N 195 D4
Leira, *Oppland* N 47 B6
Leiråmoen N 195 D5
Leiria P 154 B2
Leirvassbu N 47 A5
Leirvik, *Hordaland* N 52 A1
Leirvik, *Sogn og Fjordane* N 46 A2
Leisach A 109 C3
Leisnig D 83 A4
Leiston GB 45 A5
Leitholm GB 35 C5
Leitrim IRL 26 C2
Leitza E 144 A2
Leitzkau D 73 B4
Lejkowo PL 68 A1
Lekani GR 183 B6
Łękawa PL 86 A3
Łekawica PL 99 B3
Lekeitio E 143 A4
Lekenik HR 124 B2
Lekeryd S 62 A2
Leknes N 194 B4
Lęknica PL 84 A2
Leksand S 50 B1
Leksvik N 199 B7
Lekunberri E 144 A2
Lekvattnet S 49 B4
Lelkowo PL 69 A5
Lelów PL 86 B3
Lelystad NL 70 B2
Lem, *Ringkøbing* DK 59 B1
Lem, *Viborg Amt.* DK 58 B1
Lembach F 93 B3
Lemberg F 93 B3
Lembèye F 145 A3
Lemelerveld NL 71 B3
Lemförde D 71 B5
Lemgo D 72 B1
Lemland FIN 51 B7
Lemmer NL 70 B2
Lempdes F 116 B3
Lemvig DK 58 B1
Lemwerder D 72 A1
Lena N 48 B2
Lenart SLO 110 C2
Lenartovce SK 99 C4
Lenauheim RO 126 B2
Lencloître F 102 C2
Lend A 109 B4
Lendalfoot GB 36 A2
Lendava SLO 111 C3
Lendery RUS 3 E12
Lendinara I 121 B4
Lendorf A 109 C4
Lendum DK 58 A3
Lengefeld D 83 B5
Lengerich, *Niedersachsen* D 71 B4
Lengerich, *Nordrhein-Westfalen* D 71 B4
Lenggries D 108 B2
Lengyeltóti H 111 C4
Lenhovda S 62 B3
Lenk CH 106 C2
Lennartsfors S 54 A2
Lennestadt D 81 A4
Lennoxtown GB 35 C3
Leno I 120 B3
Lénola I 169 B3
Lens B 79 B3
Lens F 78 B2
Lens Lestang F 117 B5
Lensahn D 65 B3
Lensvik N 198 B6
Lentellais E 141 B3
Lentföhrden D 64 C2
Lenti H 111 C3
Lentini I 177 B3
Lenungshammar S 54 A3
Lenzburg CH 106 B3
Lenzen D 73 A4
Lenzerheide CH 107 C4
Leoben A 110 B2
Leogang A 109 B3
Leominster GB 39 B4
León E 142 B1
Léon F 128 C1
Leonberg D 93 C5
Léoncel F 118 C2
Leonding A 96 C2
Leonessa I 169 A2
Leonforte I 177 B3
Leonidio GR 184 B3
Leopoldsburg B 79 A5
Leopoldsdorf im Marchfeld A 111 A3
Leopoldshagen D 74 A2
Leova MD 17 B8
Lepe E 161 B2
Lepenou GR 182 E3
Lephin GB 31 B2
L'Epine F 132 A1
Lepoglava HR 124 A2
Leppäjärvi FIN 192 D7
Leppävirta FIN 8 A5
Leppin D 73 B4
Lepsény H 112 C2
Léquile I 173 B4
Lercara Friddi I 176 B2
Lerdal S 54 B2
Leré F 103 B4
Lérici I 134 A2
Lerin E 144 B2
Lerm-et-Musset F 128 B2
Lerma E 143 B3
Lermoos A 108 B1
Lérouville F 92 C1
Lerum S 60 B2
Lervik N 54 A1
Lerwick GB 33 A5
Lés E 145 B4
Les Abrets F 118 B2
Les Aix-d'Angillon F 103 B4
Les Ancizes-Comps F 116 B2
Les Andelys F 90 B1
Les Arcs, *Savoie* F 119 B3
Les Arcs, *Var* F 132 B2
Les-Aubiers F 102 C1
Les Baux-de-Provence F 131 B3
Les Bézards F 103 B4
Les Bois CH 106 B1
Les Bordes F 103 B4
Les Borges Blanques E 147 C1
Les Borges del Camp E 147 C2
Les Brunettes F 104 C2
Les Cabannes F 146 B2
Les Contamines-Montjoie F 118 B3
les Coves de Vinroma E 153 B4
Les Déserts F 118 B2
Les Deux-Alpes F 118 C3
Les Diablerets CH 119 A4
Les Echelles F 118 B2
Les Escaldes AND 146 B2
Les Essarts F 114 B2
Les Estables F 117 C4
Les Eyzies-de-Tayac F 129 B4
Les Gets F 118 A3
Les Grandes-Ventes F 89 A5
Les Haudères CH 119 A4
Les Herbiers F 114 B2
Les Hôpitaux-Neufs F 105 C5
Les Lucs-sur-Boulogne F 114 B2
Les Mages F 131 A3
Les Mazures F 91 B4
Les Mées F 132 A1
Les Mureaux F 90 C1
Les Omergues F 132 A1
Les Ormes-sur-Voulzie F 90 C3
Les Orres F 132 A2
Les Pieux F 88 A2
Les Ponts-de-Cé F 102 B1
Les Ponts-de-Martel CH 106 C1
Les Praz F 119 B3
Les Riceys F 104 B3
Les Roches F 117 B4
Les Rosaires F 101 A3
Les Rosiers F 102 B1
Les Rousses F 105 C5
Les Sables-d'Olonne F 114 B2
Les Settons F 104 B3
Les Ternes F 116 B2
Les Thilliers en-Vexin F 90 B1
Les Touches F 101 B4
Les Trois Moûtiers F 102 B2
Les Vans F 131 A3
Les Verrières CH 105 C5
Les Vignes F 130 A2
Lesaka E 144 A2
Lesbury GB 37 A5
L'Escala E 147 B4
Lescar F 145 A3
L'Escarène F 133 B3
Lesce SLO 123 A3
Lescheraines F 118 B3
Lesconil F 100 B1
Lesdins F 90 B3
Lesično SLO 123 A4
Lésina I 171 B3
Lesjaskog N 198 C5
Lesjöfors S 49 C6
Leskova Dolina SLO 123 B3
Leskovac SRB 16 D4
Leskovec CZ 98 B1
Leskovec SLO 123 B4
Leskovice CZ 97 B3
Leskovik AL 182 C2
Leslie GB 35 B4
Lesmahagow GB 36 A3
Lesmont F 91 C4
Leśna PL 84 A3
Lesneven F 100 A1
Leśnica PL 86 B2
Lešnica SRB 127 C1
Leśniów Wielkoplski PL 75 C4
Lesnoye RUS 9 C9
Lesparre-Médoc F 128 A2
l'Espérance F 91 B3
l'Esperou F 130 A2
Lesponne F 145 A4
L'Espunyola E 147 B2
Lessach A 109 B4
Lessay F 88 A2
Lessebo S 62 B3
Lessines B 79 B3
L'Estany E 147 C3
Lesterps F 115 B4
Leswalt GB 36 B1
Leszno, *Mazowieckie* PL 77 B5
Leszno, *Wielkopolskie* PL 85 A4
Leszno Górne PL 84 A3
Letchworth GB 44 B3
Letenye H 111 C3
Letino I 170 B2
Letohrad CZ 97 A4
Letovice CZ 97 B4
Letschin D 74 B3
Letterfrack IRL 28 A2
Letterkenny IRL 26 B3
Lettermacaward IRL 26 B2
Lettoch GB 32 D3
Letur E 164 A2
Letux E 153 A3
Letzlingen D 73 B4
Leucate F 146 B4
Leuchars GB 35 B5
Leuglay F 105 B3
Leuk CH 119 A4
Leukerbad CH 119 A4
Leumrabhagh GB 31 A2
Leuna D 83 A4
Leusden NL 70 B2

Lons-le-Saunier F 105 C4
Lönsboda S 63 B2
Lønset N 198 C6
Lønstrup DK 58 A2
Looe GB 42 B2
Loon op Zand NL 79 A5
Loone-Plage F 78 A2
Loosdorf A 110 A2
Lopar HR 123 C3
Lopare BIH 125 C4
Lopera E 157 C3
Lopigna F 180 A1
Loppersum NL 71 A3
Łopuszna PL 99 B4
Łopuszno PL 87 B4
Lor F 91 B4
Lora N 198 C5
Lora de Estepa E 162 A3
Lora del Río E 162 A2
Loranca del Campo E 151 B5
Lörby S 63 B2
Lorca E 164 B3
Lorch D 93 A3
Lørenfallet N 48 B3
Lørenskog N 48 C2
Loreo I 122 B1
Loreto I 136 B2
Lorgues F 132 B2
Lorica I 174 B2
Lorient F 100 B2
Lorignac F 114 C3
Lörinci H 112 B3
Loriol-sur-Drôme F 117 C4
Lormes F 104 B2
Loro Ciuffenna I 135 B4
Lorqui E 165 A3
Lörrach D 106 B2
Lorrez-le-Bocage F 103 A4
Lorris F 103 B4
Lorup D 71 B4
Łoś PL 77 C5
Los S 199 D12
Los Alcázares E 165 B4
Los Arcos E 144 B1
Los Barios de Luna E 141 B5
Los Barrios E 162 B2
Los Caños de Meca E 162 B1
Los Cerricos E 164 B2
Los Corrales E 162 A3
Los Corrales de Buelna E 142 A2
Los Dolores E 165 B3
Los Gallardos E 164 B3
Los Hinojosos E 158 B1
Los Isidros E 159 B2
Los Molinos E 151 B3
Los Morales E 162 A2
Los Navalmorales E 156 A3
Los Navalucillos E 156 A3
Los Nietos E 165 B4
Los Palacios y Villafranca E 162 A2
Los Pozuelos de Calatrava E 157 B3
Los Rábanos E 143 C4
Los Santos E 149 B4
Los Santos de la Humosa E 151 B4
Los Santos de Maimona E 155 C4
Los Tijos E 142 A2
Los Villares E 163 A4
Los Yébenes E 157 A4
Losacino E 149 A3
Losar de la Vera E 150 B2
Losenstein A 110 B1
Losheim, *Nordrhein-Westfalen* D 80 B2
Losheim, *Saarland* D 92 B2
Losne F 105 B4
Løsning DK 59 C2
Lossburg D 93 C4
Losse F 128 B2
Losser NL 71 B4
Lossiemouth GB 32 D3
Lössnitz D 83 B4
Loštice CZ 97 B4
Lostwithiel GB 42 B2
Løten N 48 B3
Lotorp S 56 B1
Lottefors S 50 A3
Löttorp S 62 A5
Lotyń PL 68 B1
Lotzorai I 179 C3
Louargat F 100 A2
Loudéac F 101 A3
Loudun F 102 B2
Loué F 102 B1
Loughborough GB 40 C2
Loughbrickland GB 27 B4
Loughrea IRL 28 A3
Louhans F 105 C4
Louisburgh IRL 28 A2
Loukhi RUS 3 C13
Loulay F 114 B3
Loulé P 160 B1
Louny CZ 84 B1
Lourdes F 145 A3
Lourenzá E 141 A3
Loures P 154 C1
Loures-Barousse F 145 A4
Louriçal P 154 A2
Lourinhã P 154 B1
Lourmarin F 131 B4
Loury F 103 B4
Lousa, *Bragança* P 149 A2
Lousa, *Castelo Branco* P 155 B3
Lousã, *Coimbra* P 148 B1
Lousa, *Lisboa* P 154 C1
Lousada E 140 B3
Lousada P 148 A1
Louth GB 41 B3
Loutra Edipsou GR 183 E5
Loutraki GR 184 B3
Loutropoli Thermis GR 186 C1
Louverné F 102 A1
Louvie-Juzon F 145 A3
Louviers F 89 A5
Louvigné-du-Désert F 88 B2
Louvois F 91 B4
Lova I 121 B5
Lovasberény H 112 B2
Lövåsen S 49 C5
Lovászpatona H 111 B4
Lövberga S 200 C1
Lovech BG 17 D6
Lövenich D 80 A2
Lóvere I 120 B3
Lövestad S 61 D3
Loviisa FIN 8 B5
Lovikka S 196 B5
Lovinobaňa SK 99 C3
Loviste HR 138 B3
Lovke HR 123 B3
Lovnäs S 49 A5
Lövö H 111 B3
Lovosice CZ 84 B2
Lovozero RUS 3 C14
Lovran HR 123 B3
Lovreć HR 138 B2
Lovrenc na Pohorju SLO 110 C2
Lovrin RO 126 B2
Lövstabruk S 51 B4
Löwenberg D 74 B2
Löwenstein D 94 B1
Lowestoft GB 41 C5
Lowick GB 37 A5
Łowicz PL 77 B4
Loxstedt D 72 A1
Loyew BY 13 C9
Lož SLO 123 B3
Loza CZ 96 B1
Łozina PL 85 A5
Loznica SRB 127 C1
Lozničko Polje SRB 127 C1
Lozorno SK 111 A4
Lozovik SRB 127 C3
Lozoya E 151 B4
Lozoyuela E 151 B4
Lozzo di Cadore I 109 C3
Luanco E 141 A5
Luarca E 141 A4
Lubaczów PL 13 C5
Lubań PL 84 A3
Lubanie PL 76 B3
Lubanów PL 86 A3
Lubars D 73 B5
Lubasz PL 75 B5
Lubawa PL 69 B4
Lubawka PL 85 B4
Lübbecke D 72 B1
Lübben D 74 C2
Lübbenau D 84 A1
Lubczyna PL 74 A3
Lübeck D 65 C3
Lubenec CZ 83 B5
Lubersac F 115 C5
Lübesse D 73 A4
Lubia E 152 A1
Lubian E 141 B4
Lubiatowo PL 75 A4
Lubichowo PL 69 B3
Lubicz Dolny PL 76 A3
Lubień PL 99 B3
Lubień Kujawski PL 77 B4
Lubienia PL 87 A5
Lubieszewo PL 75 A4
Lubin, *Dolnośląskie* PL 85 A4
Lubin, *Zachodnio-Pomorskie* PL 67 C3
Lublin PL 12 C5
Lubliniec PL 86 B2
Lubmin D 66 B2
Lubniewice PL 75 B4
Lubochnia PL 87 A4
Lubomierz, *Dolnośląskie* PL 84 A3
Lubomierz, *Małopolskie* PL 99 B4
Lubomino PL 69 A5
Luboń PL 76 B1
L'ubotín SK 99 B4
Lubowidz PL 77 A4
Łubowo, *Wielkopolskie* PL 76 B2
Łubowo, *Zachodnio-Pomorskie* PL 68 B1
Lubraniec PL 76 B3
Lubrin E 164 B2
Lubrza PL 85 B5
Lubsko PL 84 A2
Lübtheen D 73 A4
Lubuczewo PL 68 A2
Luby CZ 83 B4
Lübz D 73 A5
Luc F 117 C3
Luc-en-Diois F 118 C2
Luc-sur-Mer F 89 A3
Lucainena de las Torres E 164 B2
Lucan IRL 30 A2
Lučani SRB 127 D2
Lúcar E 164 B2
Luçay-le-Mâle F 103 B3
Lucca I 134 B3
Lucciana F 180 A2
Lucé F 90 C1
Luče SLO 123 A3
Lucena, *Córdoba* E 163 A3
Lucena, *Huelva* E 161 B3
Lucenay-les-Aix F 104 C2
Lucenay-l'Evéque F 104 B3
Lučenec SK 99 C3
Luceni E 144 C2
Lucens CH 106 C1
Lucera I 171 B3
Luceram F 133 B3
Lüchow D 73 B4
Luciana E 157 B3
Lucignano I 135 B4
Lucija SLO 122 B2
Lucka D 83 A4
Luckau D 84 A1
Luckenwalde D 74 B2
Lückstedt D 73 B4
Luco dei Marsi I 169 B3
Luçon F 114 B2
Ludanice SK 98 C2
Ludbreg HR 124 A2
Lüdenscheid D 81 A3
Lüderitz D 73 B4
Lüdersdorf D 65 C3
Ludgershall GB 44 B2
Ludgo S 56 B3
Lüdinghausen D 80 A3
Ludlow GB 39 B4
Ludomy PL 75 B5
Ludvika S 50 B2
Ludweiler Warndt D 92 B2
Ludwigsburg D 94 C1
Ludwigsfelde D 74 B2
Ludwigshafen D 93 B4
Ludwigslust D 73 A4
Ludwigsstadt D 82 B3
Ludza LV 8 D5
Luesia E 144 B2
Luftkurort Arendsee D 73 B4
Lug BIH 139 C4
Lug HR 125 B4
Luga RUS 9 C6
Lugagnano Val d'Arda I 120 C2
Lugano CH 120 A1
Lugau D 83 B4
Lugnas S 55 B4
Lúgnola I 168 A2
Lugny F 105 C3
Lugo E 140 A3
Lugo I 135 A4
Lugoj RO 16 C4
Lugones E 141 A5
Lugros E 163 A4
Luhačovice CZ 98 B1
Luhe D 95 B4
Luino I 120 B1
Luintra E 140 B3
Lújar E 163 B4
Luka nad Jihlavou CZ 97 B3
Lukavac BIH 125 C4
Lukavika BIH 125 C4
Lŭki BG 183 B6
Lukovë AL 182 D1
Lukovica SLO 123 A3
Lukovit BG 17 D6
Lukovo HR 123 C3
Lukovo Šugorje HR 137 A4
Łuków PL 12 C5
Łukowice Brzeskie PL 85 B5
Luksefjell N 53 A5
Łukta PL 69 B5
Lula I 178 B3
Luleå S 196 D5
Lüleburgaz TR 186 A2
Lumbarda HR 138 C3
Lumbier E 144 B2
Lumbrales E 149 B3
Lumbreras E 143 B4
Lumbres F 78 B2
Lummelunda S 57 C4
Lummen B 79 B5
Lumparland FIN 51 B7
Lumpiaque E 152 A2
Lumsås DK 61 D1
Lumsden GB 33 D4
Lumsheden S 50 B3
Lun HR 123 C3
Luna E 144 B3
Lunamatrona I 179 C2
Lunano I 136 B1
Lunas F 130 B2
Lund N 199 A8
Lund, *Skåne* S 61 D3
Lund, *Västra Götaland* S 54 A3
Lundamo N 199 B7
Lunde DK 59 C1
Lunde, *Sogn og Fjordane* N 46 A3
Lunde, *Sogn og Fjordane* N 46 A3
Lunde, *Telemark* N 53 A5
Lunde S 200 D3
Lundebyvollen N 49 B4
Lunden D 64 B2
Lunderseter N 49 B4
Lunderskov DK 59 C2
Lundsberg S 55 A5
Lüneburg D 72 A3
Lunel F 131 B3
Lünen D 81 A3
Lunéville F 92 C2
Lungern CH 106 C3
Lungro I 174 B2
Luninyets BY 13 B7
Lünne D 71 B4
Lunner N 48 B2
Lunteren NL 70 B2
Lunz am See A 110 B2
Luogosanto I 178 A3
Łupawa PL 68 A2
Lupión E 157 B4
Lupoglav HR 123 B3
Luppa D 83 A4
Luque E 163 A3
Lurago d'Erba I 120 B2
Lúras I 178 B3
Lurcy-Lévis F 104 C1
Lure F 105 B5
Lurgan GB 27 B4
Luri F 180 A2
Lury-sur-Arnon F 103 B4
Lušci Palanka BIH 124 C2
Lusévera I 122 A2
Lushnjë AL 182 C1
Lusignan F 115 B4
Lusigny-sur-Barse F 104 A3
Lusnić BIH 138 B2
Luso P 148 B1
Lusówko PL 75 B5
Luspebryggan S 196 B2
Luss GB 34 B3
Lussac F 128 B2
Lussac-les-Châteaux F 115 B4
Lussac-les-Eglises F 115 B5
Lussan F 131 A3
Lüssow D 65 C5
Lustenau A 107 B4
Luštěnice CZ 84 B2
Luster N 47 A4
Lutago I 108 C2
Lutherstadt Wittenberg D 83 A4
Lütjenburg D 65 B3
Lutnes N 49 A4
Lutocin PL 77 B4
Lutomiersk PL 86 A3
Luton GB 44 B3
Lutry CH 106 C1
Lutsk UA 13 C6
Lutter am Barenberge D 72 C3
Lutterworth GB 40 C2
Lututów PL 86 A2
Lützen D 83 A4
Lutzow D 73 A4
Luusua FIN 197 C10
Luvos S 196 C1
Luxembourg L 92 B2
Luxeuil-les-Bains F 105 B5
Luxey F 128 B2
Luz, *Évora* P 155 C3
Luz, *Faro* P 160 B1
Luz, *Faro* P 160 B2
Luz-St. Sauveur F 145 B3
Luzarches F 90 B2
Luže CZ 97 B4
Luzech F 129 B4
Luzern CH 106 B3
Luzino PL 68 A3
Luzy F 104 C2
Luzzi I 174 B2
L'viv UA 13 D6
Lwówek PL 75 B5
Lwówek Śląski PL 84 A3
Lyakhavichy BY 13 B7
Lybster GB 32 C3
Lychen D 74 A2
Lychkova RUS 9 D8
Lyckeby S 63 B3
Lycksele S 200 B4
Lydd GB 45 C4
Lydford GB 42 B2
Lydney GB 39 C4
Lyepyel BY 13 A8
Lygna N 48 B2
Lykkja N 47 B5
Lykling N 52 A1
Lyme Regis GB 43 B4
Lymington GB 44 C2
Lympne GB 45 B5
Lyndhurst GB 44 C2
Lyneham GB 43 A5
Lyness GB 33 C3
Lyngdal, *Buskerud* N 47 C6
Lyngdal, *Vest-Agder* N 52 B3
Lyngør N 53 B5
Lyngsa DK 58 A3
Lyngseidet N 192 C4
Lyngsnes N 199 A8
Lynmouth GB 42 A3
Lynton GB 42 A3
Lyntupy BY 13 A7
Lyon F 117 B4
Lyons-la-Forêt F 90 B1
Lyozna BY 13 A9
Lyrestad S 55 B5
Lysá nad Labem CZ 84 B2
Lysá pod Makytou SK 98 B2
Lysebotn N 52 A2
Lysekil S 54 B2
Lysice CZ 97 B4
Lysomice PL 76 A3
Lysøysund N 198 B6
Lyss CH 106 B2
Lystrup DK 59 B3
Lysvik S 49 B5
Łyszkowice PL 77 C4
Lytham St. Anne's GB 38 A3
Lyuban RUS 9 C7
Lyubertsy RUS 9 E10
Lyubimets BG 183 B8
Lyuboml' UA 13 C6
Lyubytino RUS 9 C8

M

Maaninkavaara FIN 197 C11
Maarheeze NL 80 A1
Maaseik B 80 A1
Maastricht NL 80 B1
Mablethorpe GB 41 B4
Mably F 117 A4
Macael E 164 B2
Maçanet de Cabrenys E 146 B3
Mação P 154 B2
Macau F 128 A2
Maccagno-Agra I 120 A1
Maccarese I 168 B2
Macchiagódena I 170 B2
Macclesfield GB 40 B1
Macduff GB 33 D4
Maceda E 140 B3
Macedo de Cavaleiros P 149 A3
Maceira, *Guarda* P 148 B2
Maceira, *Leiria* P 154 B2
Macelj HR 124 A1
Macerata I 136 B2
Macerata Féltria I 136 B1
Machault F 91 B4
Machecoul F 114 B2
Machrihanish GB 34 C2
Machynlleth GB 39 B3
Macieira P 148 A1
Maciejowice PL 87 A5
Macinaggio F 180 A2
Mackenrode D 82 A2
Mačkovci SLO 111 C3
Macomer I 178 B2
Macon B 91 A4
Mâcon F 117 A4
Macotera E 150 B2
Macroom IRL 29 C3
Macugnaga I 119 B4
Madan BG 183 B6
Madängsholm S 55 B4
Madaras H 126 A1
Maddaloni I 170 B2
Made NL 79 A4
Madeley GB 38 B4
Maderuelo E 151 A4
Madetkoski FIN 197 B9
Madley GB 39 B4
Madocsa H 112 C2
Madona LV 8 D5
Madonna di Campiglio I 121 A3
Madrid E 151 B4
Madridejos E 157 A4
Madrigal de la Vera E 150 B2
Madrigal de las Altas Torres E 150 A2
Madrigalejo E 156 A2
Madrigalejo de Monte E 143 B3
Madriguera E 151 A4
Madrigueras E 158 B2
Madroñera E 156 A2
Maël-Carhaix F 100 A2
Maella E 153 A4
Maello E 150 B3
Maesteg GB 39 C3
Mafra P 154 C1
Magacela E 156 B2
Magallon E 144 C2
Magaluf E 166 B2
Magán E 151 C4
Magaña E 144 C1
Magasa I 121 B3
Magaz E 142 C2
Magdeburg D 73 B4
Magenta I 120 B1
Magescq F 128 C1
Maghera GB 27 B4
Magherafelt GB 27 B4
Maghull GB 38 A4
Magione I 135 B5
Maglaj BIH 125 C4
Maglehem S 63 C2
Magliano de'Marsi I 169 A3
Magliano in Toscana I 168 A1
Magliano Sabina I 168 A2
Maglić SRB 126 B1
Máglie I 173 B4
Maglód H 112 B3
Magnac-Bourg F 115 C5
Magnac-Laval F 115 B5
Magnieres F 92 C2
Magnor N 49 C4
Magnuszew PL 87 A5
Magny-Cours F 104 C2
Magny-en-Vexin F 90 B1
Mágocs H 125 A4
Magoute P 154 C1
Maguilla E 156 B2
Maguiresbridge GB 27 B3
Magyarbóly H 125 B4
Magyarkeszi H 112 C2
Magyarszék H 125 A4
Mahide E 141 C4
Mahilyow BY 13 B9
Mahmudiye TR 187 C5
Mahora E 158 B2
Mahovo HR 124 B2
Mähring D 95 B4
Maia E 144 A2
Maia P 148 A1
Maiaelrayo E 151 A4
Maials E 153 A4
Maîche F 106 B1
Máida I 175 C2
Maiden Bradley GB 43 A4
Maiden Newton GB 43 B4
Maidenhead GB 44 B3
Maidstone GB 45 B4
Maienfeld CH 107 B4
Maignelay Montigny F 90 B2
Maijanen FIN 197 B8
Maillezais F 114 B3
Mailly-le-Camp F 91 C4
Mailly-le-Château F 104 B2
Mainar E 152 A2
Mainbernheim D 94 B2
Mainburg D 95 C3
Mainhardt D 94 B1
Maintal D 81 B4
Maintenon F 90 C1
Mainvilliers F 90 C1
Mainz D 93 A4
Maiorca P 148 B1
Mairena de Aljarafe E 162 A1
Mairena del Alcor E 162 A2
Maisach D 108 A2
Maishofen A 109 B3
Maison-Rouge F 90 C3
Maissau A 97 C3
Maisse F 90 C2
Maizières-lès-Vic F 92 C2
Maja HR 124 B2
Majadahonda E 151 B4
Majadas E 150 C2
Majavatn N 195 E4
Majs H 125 B4
Majšperk SLO 123 A4
Makarska HR 138 B3
Makkum NL 70 A2
Maklár H 113 B4
Makó H 126 A2
Makoszyce PL 85 B5
Makov SK 98 B2
Maków Mazowiecki PL 77 B6
Maków Podhalański PL 99 B3
Mąkowarsko PL 76 A2
Makrakomi GR 182 E4
Maksniemi FIN 196 D7
Malå S 195 E9
Mala Bosna SRB 126 A1
Mala Kladuša BIH 124 B1
Mala Krsna SRB 127 C3
Malá Lehota SK 98 C2
Mala Pijace SRB 126 A1
Mala Subotica HR 124 A2
Malacky SK 97 C5
Maladzyechna BY 13 A7
Málaga E 163 B3
Malagón E 157 A4
Malaguilla E 151 B4
Malahide IRL 30 A2
Malalbergo I 121 C4
Malanów PL 76 C3
Malaucène F 131 A4
Malaunay F 89 A5
Malaya Vishera RUS 9 C8
Malborghetto I 109 C4
Malbork PL 69 A4
Malborn D 92 B2
Malbuisson F 105 C5
Malcésine I 121 B3
Malchin D 74 A1
Malching D 96 C1
Malchow D 73 A5
Malcocinado E 156 B2

Malczyce PL 85 A4
Maldegem B 79 A3
Maldon GB 45 B4
Małdyty PL 69 B4
Malè I 121 A3
Malemort F 129 A4
Malente D 65 B3
Mâleras S 62 B3
Males GR 185 D6
Malesherbes F 90 C2
Malesina GR 183 E5
Malestroit F 101 B3
Maletto I 177 B3
Malexander S 56 B1
Malgrat de Mar E 147 C3
Malhadas P 149 A3
Mali Lošinj HR 137 A3
Malia CY 181 B1
Malia GR 185 D6
Malicorne-sur-Sarthe F 102 B1
Malijai F 132 A2
Malildjoš SRB 126 B1
Målilla S 62 A3
Malin IRL 27 A3
Målinec SK 99 C3
Malingsbo S 50 C2
Malinec PL 76 B3
Malinska HR 123 B3
Maliq AL 182 C2
Maljevac HR 123 B4
Malkara TR 186 B1
Małki PL 69 B4
Malko Tŭrnovo BG 17 D7
Mallaig GB 34 A2
Mallaranny IRL 28 A2
Mallemort F 131 B4
Mallén E 144 C2
Malléon F 146 A2
Mallersdorf-Pfaffenberg D 95 C4
Málles Venosta I 108 C1
Malling DK 59 B3
Mallnitz A 109 C4
Mallow IRL 29 B3
Mallwyd GB 38 B3
Malm N 199 A8
Malmbäck S 62 A2
Malmberget S 196 B3
Malmby S 56 A3
Malmédy B 80 B2
Malmesbury GB 43 A4
Malmköping S 56 A2
Malmö S 61 D3
Malmon S 54 B2
Malmslätt S 56 B1
Malnate I 120 B1
Malo I 121 B4
Małogoszcz PL 87 B4
Maloja CH 120 A2
Małomice PL 84 A3
Måløy N 198 D2
Malpartida E 155 B4
Malpartida de la Serena E 156 B2
Malpartida de Plasencia E 150 C1
Malpas E 145 B4
Malpas GB 38 A4
Malpica E 155 B3
Malpica de Bergantiños E 140 A2
Malpica de Tajo E 150 C3
Malsch D 93 C4
Malšice CZ 96 B2
Malta A 109 C4
Maltat F 104 C2
Maltby GB 40 B2
Malung S 49 B5
Malungsfors S 49 B5
Maluszów PL 75 B4
Maluszyn PL 87 B3
Malva E 142 C1
Malvaglia CH 120 A1
Malveira P 154 C1
Malvik N 199 B8
Malyn UA 13 C8
Mamarrosa P 148 B1
Mamer L 92 B2
Mamers F 89 B4
Mamirolle F 105 B5
Mammendorf D 108 A2
Mámmola I 175 C2
Mamoiada I 178 B3
Mamonovo RUS 69 A4
Mamuras AL 182 B1
Maña SK 112 A2
Manacor E 167 B3
Manavgat TR 189 C6
Mancera de Abajo E 150 B2
Mancha Real E 163 A4
Manchester GB 40 B1
Manching D 95 C3
Manchita E 156 B1
Manciano I 168 A1
Manciet F 128 C3
Mandal N 52 B3
Mandanici I 177 A4
Mándas I 179 C3
Mandatoriccio I 174 B2
Mandayona E 151 B5
Mandelieu-la-Napoule F 132 B2
Mandello del Lário I 120 B2
Mandelsloh D 72 B2

Manderfeld B 80 B2
Manderscheid D 80 B2
Mandino Selo BIH 138 B3
Mandoudi GR 183 E5
Mandra GR 185 A4
Mandraki GR 188 C2
Mandúria I 173 B3
Mane, Alpes-de-Haute-Provence F 132 B1
Mane, Haute-Garonne F 145 A4
Manérbio I 120 B3
Mañeru E 144 B2
Manetin CZ 96 B1
Manfredónia I 171 B3
Mangalia RO 17 D8
Manganeses de la Lampreana E 149 A4
Manganeses de la Polvorosa E 141 B5
Mangen N 48 C3
Manger N 46 B2
Mangiennes F 92 B1
Mangotsfield GB 43 A4
Mångsbodarna S 49 A5
Manguelde P 148 B2
Maniago I 122 A1
Manilva E 162 B2
Manisa TR 186 D2
Manises E 159 B3
Mank A 110 A2
Månkarbo S 51 B4
Manlleu E 147 C3
Manna DK 58 A2
Männedorf CH 107 B3
Mannersdorf am Leithagebirge A 111 B3
Mannheim D 93 B4
Manningtree GB 45 B5
Manoppello I 169 A4
Manorbier GB 39 C2
Manorhamilton IRL 26 B2
Manosque F 132 B1
Manowo PL 67 B5
Manresa E 147 C2
Månsarp S 62 A2
Månsåsen S 199 B11
Manschnow D 74 B3
Mansfeld D 82 A3
Mansfield GB 40 B2
Mansilla de Burgos E 143 B3
Mansilla de las Mulas E 142 B1
Manskog S 55 A3
Mansle F 115 C4
Manso F 180 A1
Mantamados GR 186 C1
Manteigas P 148 B2
Mantes-la-Jolie F 90 C1
Mantes-la-Ville F 90 C1
Manthelan F 102 B2
Mantorp S 56 B1
Mántova I 121 B3
Mänttä FIN 8 A4
Mänttyjärvi FIN 197 C10
Manuel E 159 B3
Manyas TR 186 B2
Manzanal de Arriba E 141 B4
Manzanares E 157 A4
Manzanares el Real E 151 B4
Manzaneda, León E 141 B4
Manzaneda, Orense E 141 B3
Manzaneque E 157 A4
Manzanera E 153 B3
Manzanilla E 161 B3
Manzat F 116 B2
Manziana I 168 A2
Manziat F 117 A4
Maó E 167 B4
Maoča BIH 125 C4
Maqueda E 150 B3
Mara E 152 A2
Maramaereğlisi TR 186 B2
Maraña E 142 A1
Maranchón E 152 A1
Maranello I 135 A3
Marano I 170 C2
Marano Lagunare I 122 B2
Marans F 114 B2
Maratea I 174 B1
Marateca P 154 C2
Marathokambos GR 188 B1
Marathonas GR 185 A4
Marathóvouno CY 181 A2
Marazion GB 42 B1
Marbach, Baden-Württemberg D 94 C1
Marbach, Hessen D 82 B1
Mårbacka S 55 A4
Marbella E 162 B3
Marboz F 118 A2
Marburg D 81 B4
Marcali H 111 C4
Marčana HR 122 C2

Marcaria I 121 B3
Marcelová SK 112 B2
Marcenat F 116 B2
March GB 41 C4
Marchamalo E 151 B4
Marchaux F 105 B5
Marche-en-Famenne B 79 B5
Marchegg A 111 A3
Marchena E 162 A2
Marchenoir F 103 B3
Marcheprime F 128 B2
Marciac F 128 C3
Marciana Marina I 134 C3
Marcianise I 170 B2
Marcigny F 117 A4
Marcilla E 144 B2
Marcillac-la-Croisille F 116 B2
Marcillac-Vallon F 130 A1
Marcillat-en-Combraille F 116 A2
Marcille-sur-Seine F 91 C3
Marcilloles F 118 B2
Marcilly-le-Hayer F 91 C3
Marcinkowice PL 75 A5
Marciszów PL 85 B4
Marck F 78 B1
Marckolsheim F 106 A2
Marco de Canevezes P 148 A1
Mårdsele S 200 B5
Mårdsjö S 200 C1
Mareham le Fen GB 41 B3
Marek BG 182 A4
Marennes F 114 C2
Maresquel F 78 B1
Mareuil F 115 C4
Mareuil-en-Brie F 91 C3
Mareuil-sur-Arnon F 103 C4
Mareuil-sur-Lay F 114 B2
Mareuil-sur-Ourcq F 90 B3
Margam GB 39 C3
Margariti GR 182 D2
Margate GB 45 B5
Margaux F 128 A2
Margerie-Hancourt F 91 C4
Margès F 117 B5
Margherita di Savóia I 171 B4
Margita SRB 126 B3
Margone I 119 B4
Margonin PL 76 B2
Marguerittes F 131 B3
Margut F 91 B5
Maria Neustift A 110 B1
Maria Saal A 110 C1
Mariager DK 58 B2
Mariana E 152 B1
Marianelund S 62 A3
Mariáneopl I 176 B2
Mariánské Lázně CZ 95 A4
Mariapfarr A 109 B4
Mariazell A 110 B2
Maribo DK 65 B4
Maribor SLO 110 C2
Marieberg S 56 A1
Mariefred S 56 A3
Mariehamn FIN 51 B6
Marieholm S 61 D3
Marienbaum D 80 A2
Marienberg D 83 B5
Marienheide D 81 A3
Mariental D 73 B3
Mariestad S 55 B4
Marieux F 90 A2
Marigliano I 170 C2
Marignane F 131 B4
Marigny, Jura F 105 C4
Marigny, Manche F 88 A2
Marigny-le-Châtel F 91 C3
Marija Bistrica HR 124 A2
Marijampolė LT 13 A5
Marín E 140 B2
Marina HR 138 B2
Marina di Acquappesa I 174 B1
Marina di Alberese I 168 A1
Marina di Amendolara I 174 B2
Marina di Árbus I 179 C2
Marina di Campo I 134 C3
Marina di Carrara I 134 A3
Marina di Castagneto-Donorático I 134 B3
Marina di Cécina I 134 B3
Marina di Gáiro I 179 C3
Marina di Ginosa I 173 B2
Marina di Gioiosa lónica I 175 C2
Marina di Grosseto I 135 C3
Marina di Léuca I 173 C4

Marina di Massa I 134 A3
Marina di Nováglie I 173 C4
Marina di Pisa I 134 B3
Marina di Ragusa I 177 C3
Marina di Ravenna I 135 A5
Marina di Torre Grande I 179 C2
Marina Romea I 135 A5
Marinaleda E 162 A3
Marine de Sisco F 180 A2
Marinella I 176 B1
Marinella di Sarzana I 134 A3
Marineo I 176 B2
Marines F 90 B1
Maringues F 116 B3
Marinha das Ondas P 154 A2
Marinha Grande P 154 B2
Marinhas P 148 A1
Marino I 168 B2
Marjaliza E 157 A4
Markabygd N 199 B8
Markaryd S 61 C3
Markdorf D 107 B4
Markelo NL 71 B3
Market Deeping GB 40 C3
Market Drayton GB 38 B4
Market Harborough GB 40 C3
Market Rasen GB 40 B3
Market Warsop GB 40 B2
Market Weighton GB 40 B3
Markethill GB 27 B4
Markgröningen D 93 C5
Markhausen D 71 B4
Markina-Xemein E 143 A4
Markinch GB 35 B4
Märkische Buchholz D 74 B3
Markitta S 196 B4
Markkleeberg D 83 A4
Marklohe D 72 B2
Marknesse NL 70 B2
Markneukirchen D 83 B4
Markopoulo GR 185 B4
Markovac, Srbija SRB 127 C3
Markovac, Vojvodina SRB 126 B3
Markowice PL 86 B2
Markranstädt D 83 A4
Marksuhl D 82 B2
Markt Allhau A 111 B3
Markt Bibart D 94 B2
Markt Erlbach D 94 B2
Markt-heidenfeld D 94 B1
Markt Indersdorf D 95 C3
Markt Rettenbach D 108 B1
Markt Schwaben D 108 A2
Markt-Übelbach A 110 B2
Marktbreit D 94 B2
Marktl D 95 C4
Marktleuthen D 83 B3
Marktoberdorf D 108 B1
Marktredwitz D 95 A4
Markušica HR 125 B4
Markušovce SK 99 C4
Marl D 80 A3
Marlborough, Devon GB 42 B3
Marlborough, Wiltshire GB 44 B2
Marle F 91 B3
Marlieux F 117 A5
Marlow D 65 B5
Marlow GB 44 B3
Marma S 51 B4
Marmagne F 104 C3
Marmande F 128 B3
Marmara TR 186 B2
Marmaris TR 188 C3
Marmelete P 160 B1
Marmolejo E 157 B3
Marmoutier F 93 C3
Marnac F 129 B4
Marnay F 105 B4
Marnheim D 93 B4
Marnitz D 73 A4
Maroldsweisach D 82 B2
Marolles-les-Braults F 89 B4
Maromme F 89 A5
Marone I 120 B3
Maronia GR 183 C7
Maroslele H 126 A2
Marostica I 121 B4
Marpisa GR 185 B6
Marquion F 78 B3
Marquise F 78 B1
Marradi I 135 A4
Marrasjärvi FIN 197 C8
Marraskoski FIN 197 C8
Marratxi E 166 B2
Marrúbiu I 179 C2
Marrum NL 70 A2
Marrupe E 150 B3
Mars-la-Tour F 92 B1
Marsac F 129 C5
Marsac-en-Livradois F 117 B3
Marságlia I 120 C2

Marsala I 176 B1
Marsberg D 81 A4
Marsciano I 135 C5
Marseillan F 130 B2
Marseille = Marseilles F 131 B4
Marseille en Beauvaisis F 90 B1
Marseilles = Marseille F 131 B4
Mársico Nuovo I 172 B1
Marske-by-the-Sea GB 37 B5
Marslev DK 59 C3
Marson F 91 C4
Märsta S 57 A3
Marstal DK 65 B3
Marstrand S 60 B1
Marta I 168 A1
Martano I 173 B4
Martel F 129 B4
Martelange B 92 B1
Martfeld D 72 B2
Martfű H 113 B4
Martham GB 41 C5
Marthon F 115 C4
Martiago E 149 B3
Martigné-Briand F 102 B1
Martigné-Ferchaud F 101 B4
Martigné-sur-Mayenne F 102 A1
Martigny CH 119 A4
Martigny-les-Bains F 105 A4
Martigues F 131 B4
Martim-Longo P 160 B2
Martin SK 98 B2
Martin de la Jara E 162 A3
Martín Muñoz de las Posadas E 150 A3
Martina CH 108 C1
Martina Franca I 173 B3
Martinamor E 150 B2
Martinengo I 120 B2
Martiniścica HR 123 C3
Martinshöhe D 93 B3
Martinsicuro I 136 C2
Martinszell D 107 B5
Martis I 178 B2
Martofte DK 59 C3
Martonvásár H 112 B2
Martorell E 147 C2
Martos E 163 A4
Martres Tolosane F 146 A1
Martti FIN 197 B11
Marugán E 150 B3
Marum NL 71 A3
Marvão P 155 B3
Marvejols F 130 A2
Marville F 92 B1
Marwałd PL 77 A4
Marykirk GB 35 B5
Marypark GB 32 D3
Maryport GB 36 B3
Marytavy GB 42 B2
Marzabotto I 135 A4
Marzahna D 74 B1
Marzamemi I 177 C4
Marzocca I 136 B2
Mas-Cabardès F 146 A3
Mas de Barberáns E 153 B4
Mas de las Matas E 153 B3
Masa E 143 B3
Mascali I 177 B4
Mascaraque E 157 A4
Mascarenhas P 149 A2
Mascioni I 169 A3
Mas-d'Azil F 146 A2
Masegoso E 158 C1
Masegoso de Tajuña E 151 B5
Masevaux F 106 B1
Masfjorden N 46 B2
Masham GB 37 B5
Masi N 192 C7
Maside E 140 B2
Maslacq F 144 A3
Maslinica HR 138 B2
Maşloc RO 126 B3
Maslovare BIH 138 A3
Masone I 133 A4
Massa Fiscáglia I 121 C5
Massa Lombarda I 135 A4
Massa Lubrense I 170 C2
Massa Maríttima I 135 B3
Massa Martana I 136 C1
Massafra I 173 B3
Massamagrell E 159 B3
Massanassa E 159 B3
Massarosa I 134 B3
Massat F 146 B2
Massay F 103 B4
Massbach D 82 B2
Masseret F 116 B1
Masseube F 145 A4
Massiac F 116 B3
Massignac F 115 C4
Massing D 95 C4
Massmechelen B 80 B1

Masterud N 49 B4
Mästocka S 61 C3
Masty BY 13 B6
Masúa I 179 C2
Masueco E 149 A3
Masugnsbyn S 196 B5
Mašun SLO 123 B3
Maszewo, Lubuskie PL 75 B3
Maszewo, Zachodnio-Pomorskie PL 75 A4
Mata de Alcántara E 155 B4
Matala GR 185 E5
Matalebreras E 144 C1
Matallana de Torio E 142 B1
Mataporquera E 142 B2
Matapozuelos E 150 A3
Mataró E 147 C3
Matarocco I 176 B1
Matélica I 136 B2
Matera I 172 B2
Mátészalka H 16 B5
Matet E 159 B3
Mathay F 106 B1
Mathi I 119 B4
Mathopen N 46 B2
Matignon F 101 A3
Matino I 173 B4
Matlock GB 40 B2
Matosinhos P 148 A1
Matour F 117 A4
Mátrafüred H 113 B3
Mátraterenye H 113 A3
Matre, Hordaland N 46 B2
Matre, Hordaland N 52 A1
Matrei am Brenner A 108 B2
Matrei in Osttirol A 109 B3
Matrice I 170 B2
Matsdal S 195 E6
Mattarello I 121 A4
Mattersburg A 111 B3
Mattighofen A 109 A4
Mattinata I 171 B4
Mattsee A 109 B4
Mattsmyra S 50 A2
Måttsund S 196 D5
Matulji HR 123 B3
Maubert-Fontaine F 91 B4
Maubeuge F 79 B3
Maubourguet F 145 A4
Mauchline GB 36 A2
Maud GB 33 D4
Mauer-kirchen A 109 A4
Mauern D 95 C3
Maughold GB 36 B2
Mauguio F 131 B3
Maulbronn D 93 C4
Maulde F 79 B3
Mauléon F 114 B3
Mauléon-Barousse F 145 B4
Mauléon-Licharre F 144 A3
Maulévrier F 114 A3
Maum IRL 28 A2
Maura N 48 B2
Maurach A 108 B2
Maure-de-Bretagne F 101 B3
Maureilhan F 130 B2
Mauren FL 107 B4
Mauron F 101 A3
Maurs F 116 C2
Maury F 146 B3
Maussane-les-Alpilles F 131 B3
Mautern A 110 A2
Mautern im Steiermark A 110 B1
Mauterndorf A 109 B4
Mauthaus D 82 B3
Mauthen A 109 C3
Mauvezin F 129 C3
Mauzé-sur-le-Mignon F 114 B3
Maxent F 101 B3
Maxey-sur-Vaise F 92 C1
Maxial P 154 B1
Maxieira P 154 B2
Maxwellheugh GB 35 C5
Mayalde E 149 A4
Maybole GB 36 A2
Mayen D 80 B3
Mayenne F 88 B3
Mayet F 102 B2
Mayorga E 142 B1
Mayres F 117 C4
Mayrhofen A 108 B2
Mazagón E 161 B3
Mazaleón E 153 A4
Mazamet F 130 B1
Mazan F 131 A4
Mazara del Vallo I 176 B1
Mazarete E 152 B1
Mazarrón E 165 B3

Name		Page	Ref
Mažeikiai	LT	8	D3
Mazères	F	146	A2
Mazères-sur-Salat	F	145	A4
Mazières-en-Gâtine	F	115	B3
Mazin	HR	138	A1
Mazuelo	E	143	B3
Mazyr	BY	13	B8
Mazzarino	I	177	B3
Mazzarrà Sant'Andrea	I	177	A4
Mazzo di Valtellina	I	120	A3
Mchowo	PL	77	A5
Mdzewo	PL	77	B5
Mealabost	GB	31	A2
Mealhada	P	148	B1
Méan	B	79	B5
Meana Sardo	I	179	C3
Meaulne	F	103	C4
Meaux	F	90	C2
Mebonden	N	199	B8
Mecerreyes	E	143	B3
Mechelen	B	79	A4
Mechernich	D	80	B2
Mechnica	PL	86	B2
Mechowo	PL	67	C4
Mechterstädt	D	82	B2
Mecidiye	TR	186	B1
Mecikal	PL	68	B2
Mecina-Bombarón	E	164	C1
Mecitözü	TR	23	A8
Meckenbeuren	D	107	B4
Meckenheim, Rheinland-Pfalz	D	80	B3
Meckenheim, Rheinland-Pfalz	D	93	B4
Meckesheim	D	93	B4
Mecseknádasd	H	125	A4
Meda	I	120	B2
Meda	P	149	B2
Medak	HR	137	A4
Mede	I	120	B1
Medebach	D	81	A4
Medelim	P	155	A3
Medemblik	NL	70	B2
Medena Selista	BIH	138	A2
Medesano	I	120	C3
Medevi	S	55	B5
Medgidia	RO	17	C8
Medgyesháza	H	113	C5
Medhamn	S	55	A4
Mediaş	RO	17	B6
Medicina	I	135	A4
Medina de las Torres	E	155	C4
Medina de Pomar	E	143	B3
Medina de Rioseco	E	142	C1
Medina del Campo	E	150	A3
Medina Sidonia	E	162	B2
Medinaceli	E	152	A1
Medinilla	E	150	B2
Medja	SRB	126	B2
Medjedja	BIH	139	B5
Medulin	HR	122	C2
Meduno	I	122	A1
Medveda	RUS	125	C3
Medvedov	SK	111	B4
Medvezhyegorsk	RUS	9	B9
Medvide	HR	137	A4
Medvode	SLO	123	A3
Medzev	SK	99	C4
Medžitlija	MK	182	C3
Meerane	D	83	B4
Meerle	B	79	A4
Meersburg	D	107	B4
Meeuwen	B	79	A5
Megalo Horio	GR	188	C2
Megalopoli	GR	184	B3
Megara	GR	185	A4
Megève	F	118	B3
Meggenhofen	A	109	A4
Megra	RUS	9	B10
Megyaszó	H	113	A5
Mehamn	N	193	A11
Mehedeby	S	51	B4
Méhkerék	H	113	C5
Mehun-sur-Yèvre	F	103	B4
Meigle	GB	35	B4
Meijel	NL	80	A1
Meilen	CH	107	B3
Meilhan	F	128	C2
Meimôa	P	149	B2
Meina	I	119	B5
Meine	D	73	B3
Meinersen	D	72	B3
Meinerzhagen	D	81	A3
Meiningen	D	82	B2
Meira	E	141	A3
Meisenheim	D	93	B3
Meissen	D	83	A5
Meitingen	D	94	C2
Meix-devant-Virton	B	92	B1
Męka	PL	86	A2
Meka Gruda	BIH	139	B4
Mel	I	121	A5
Melbu	N	194	B5
Melč	CZ	98	B1
Meldal	N	198	B6
Méldola	I	135	A5
Meldorf	D	64	B2
Melegnano	I	120	B2
Melenci	SRB	126	B2
Melendugno	I	173	B4
Melfi	I	172	B1
Melfjordbotn	N	195	D4
Melgaço	I	140	B2
Melgar de Arriba	E	142	B1
Melgar de Fernamental	E	142	B2
Melgar de Yuso	E	142	B2
Melhus	N	199	B7
Meliana	E	159	B3
Melide	CH	120	B1
Melide	E	140	B2
Melides	P	160	A1
Meligales	GR	184	B2
Melilli	I	177	B4
Melinovac	HR	124	C1
Melisenda	I	179	C3
Melisey	F	105	B5
Mélito di Porto Salvo	I	175	D1
Melk	A	110	A2
Melksham	GB	43	A4
Mellakoski	FIN	196	C7
Mellanström	S	195	E9
Mellbystrand	S	61	C2
Melle	B	79	A3
Melle	D	71	B5
Melle	F	115	B3
Mellendorf	D	72	B2
Mellerud	S	54	B3
Mellieħa	M	175	C3
Mellösa	S	56	A2
Mellrichstadt	D	82	B2
Mělnické Vtelno	CZ	84	B2
Mělník	CZ	84	B2
Melón	E	140	B2
Melrose	GB	35	C5
Mels	CH	107	B4
Melsungen	D	82	A1
Meltaus	FIN	197	C8
Meltham	GB	40	B2
Melton Mowbray	GB	40	C3
Meltosjärvi	FIN	196	C7
Melun	F	90	C2
Melvaig	GB	31	B3
Melvich	GB	32	C3
Mélykút	H	126	A1
Melzo	I	120	B2
Memaliaj	AL	182	C1
Membrilla	E	157	B4
Membrío	E	155	B3
Memer	F	129	B4
Memmelsdorf	D	94	B2
Memmingen	D	107	B5
Memória	P	154	B2
Menággio	I	120	A2
Menai Bridge	GB	38	A2
Menasalbas	E	157	A3
Menat	F	116	A2
Mendavia	E	144	B1
Mendaza	E	144	B1
Menden	D	81	A3
Menderes	TR	188	A2
Mendig	D	80	B3
Mendiga	P	154	B2
Mendrisio	CH	120	B1
Ménéac	F	101	A3
Menemen	TR	188	A2
Menen	B	78	B3
Menesjärvi	FIN	193	D10
Menetou-Salon	F	103	B4
Menfi	I	176	B1
Ménföcsanak	H	111	B4
Mengamuñoz	E	150	B3
Mengen	D	107	A4
Mengen	TR	187	B7
Mengeš	SLO	123	A3
Mengíbar	E	157	B4
Mengkofen	D	95	C4
Menou	F	104	B2
Mens	F	118	C2
Menslage	D	71	B4
Menstränsk	S	200	A5
Mentana	I	168	A2
Menton	F	133	B3
Méntrida	E	151	B3
Méobecq	F	115	B5
Méounes-les-Montrieux	F	132	B1
Meppel	NL	70	B3
Meppen	D	71	B4
Mequinenza	E	153	A4
Mer	F	103	B3
Mera, Coruña	E	140	A2
Mera, Coruña	E	140	A3
Meråker	N	199	B8
Merano	I	108	C2
Merate	I	120	B2
Mercadal	E	167	B4
Mercatale	I	135	B4
Mercatino Conca	I	136	B1
Mercato San Severino	I	170	C2
Mercato Saraceno	I	135	B5
Merching	D	108	A1
Merchtem	B	79	B4
Merdrignac	F	101	A3
Merdžanići	BIH	139	B4
Meré	E	142	A2
Mere	GB	43	A4
Meréville	F	90	C2
Merfeld	D	80	A3
Méribel	F	118	B3
Meribel Motraret	F	118	B3
Meriç	TR	186	A1
Mérida	E	155	C4
Mérignac	F	128	B2
Měřín	CZ	97	B3
Mering	D	94	C2
Merkendorf	D	94	B2
Merklin	CZ	96	B1
Merksplas	B	79	A4
Merlânna	S	56	A2
Merlimont Plage	F	78	B1
Mern	DK	65	A5
Mernye	H	111	C4
Mers-les-Bains	F	90	A1
Mersch	L	92	B2
Merseburg	D	83	A3
Merthyr Tydfil	GB	39	C3
Mertingen	D	94	C2
Mértola	P	160	B2
Méru	F	90	B2
Merufe	P	140	B2
Mervans	F	105	C4
Merville	F	78	B2
Méry-sur-Seine	F	91	C3
Merzen	D	71	B4
Merzifon	TR	23	A8
Merzig	D	92	B2
Mesagne	I	173	B3
Mesão Frio	P	148	A2
Mesas de Ibor	E	156	A2
Meschede	D	81	A4
Meschers-sur-Gironde	F	114	C3
Meslay-du-Maine	F	102	B1
Mesna	N	48	A2
Mesnalien	N	48	A2
Mesocco	CH	120	A2
Mésola	I	122	C1
Mesologi	GR	184	A2
Mesopotamo	GR	182	D2
Mesoraca	I	175	B2
Messac	F	101	B4
Messancy	B	92	B1
Messdorf	D	73	B4
Messei	F	88	B3
Messejana	P	160	B1
Messelt	N	48	A3
Messina	I	177	A4
Messingen	D	71	B4
Messini	GR	184	B3
Messkirch	D	107	B4
Messlingen	S	199	C9
Messtetten	D	107	A3
Mestanza	E	157	B3
Městec Králové	CZ	84	B3
Mestlin	D	73	A4
Město Albrechtice	CZ	85	B5
Město Libavá	CZ	98	B1
Město Touškov	CZ	96	B1
Mestre	I	122	B1
Mesvres	F	104	C3
Mesztegnyő	H	111	C4
Meta	I	170	C2
Metajna	HR	137	A4
Metelen	D	71	B4
Methana	GR	185	B4
Methlick	GB	33	D4
Methven	GB	35	B4
Methwold	GB	41	C4
Metković	HR	139	B3
Metlika	SLO	123	B4
Metnitz	A	109	C4
Metsäkylä	FIN	197	D11
Metslawier	NL	70	A3
Metsovo	GR	182	D3
Metten	D	95	C4
Mettendorf	D	92	B2
Mettet	B	79	B4
Mettingen	D	71	B4
Mettlach	D	92	B2
Mettlen	CH	106	B2
Mettmann	D	80	A2
Metz	F	92	B2
Metzervisse	F	92	B2
Metzingen	D	94	C1
Meulan	F	90	B1
Meung-sur-Loire	F	103	B3
Meuselwitz	D	83	A4
Meuzac	F	115	C5
Mevagissey	GB	42	B2
Mexborough	GB	40	B2
Mey	GB	32	C3
Meyenburg	D	73	A5
Meyerhöfen	D	71	B5
Meymac	F	116	B2
Meyrargues	F	132	B1
Meyrueis	F	130	A2
Meyssac	F	129	A4
Meysse	F	117	C4
Meyzieu	F	117	B4
Mèze	F	130	B2
Mézériat	F	117	A4
Mežica	SLO	110	C1
Mézidon-Canon	F	89	A3
Mézières-en-Brenne	F	115	B5
Mézières-sur-Issoire	F	115	B4
Mézilhac	F	117	C4
Mézilles	F	104	B2
Mézin	F	128	B3
Mezőberény	H	113	C5
Mezőcsát	H	113	B4
Mezőfalva	H	112	C2
Mezőhegyes	H	126	A2
Mezőkeresztes	H	113	B4
Mezőkomárom	H	112	C2
Mezőkövácsháza	H	113	C4
Mezőkövesd	H	113	B4
Mezőörs	H	111	B4
Mézos	F	128	B1
Mezőszilas	H	112	C2
Mezőtúr	H	113	B4
Mezquita de Jarque	E	153	B3
Mezzano, Emilia Romagna	I	135	A5
Mezzano, Trentino Alto Adige	I	121	A4
Mezzojuso	I	176	B2
Mezzoldo	I	120	A2
Mezzolombardo	I	121	A4
Mgarr	M	175	C3
Miajadas	E	156	A2
Miały	PL	75	B5
Mianowice	PL	68	A2
Miasteczko Krajeńskie	PL	76	A2
Miasteczko Śl.	PL	86	B2
Miastko	PL	68	A1
Michalovce	SK	12	D4
Michałów	PL	87	B4
Michałowice	PL	87	B3
Micheldorf	A	110	B1
Michelhausen	A	110	A2
Michelsneukirchen	D	95	B4
Michelstadt	D	93	B5
Michendorf	D	74	B2
Michurin	BG	17	D7
Micheldever	GB	44	B2
Mid Yell	GB	33	A5
Midbea	GB	33	B4
Middelburg	NL	79	A3
Middelfart	DK	59	C2
Middelharnis	NL	79	A4
Middelkerke	B	78	A2
Middelstum	NL	71	A3
Middleham	GB	37	B5
Middleton Cheney	GB	44	A2
Middleton-in-Teesdale	GB	37	B4
Middletown	GB	27	B4
Middlewich	GB	38	A4
Middlezoy	GB	43	A4
Midhurst	GB	44	C3
Midleton	IRL	29	C3
Midlum	D	64	C1
Midsomer Norton	GB	43	A4
Midtgulen	N	198	D2
Midtskogberget	N	49	A4
Midwolda	NL	71	A4
Miechów	PL	87	B4
Miedes de Aragón	E	152	A2
Miedes de Atienza	E	151	A4
Międzybodzie Bielskie	PL	99	B3
Międzybórz	PL	85	A5
Międzychód	PL	75	B4
Międzylesie	PL	85	B4
Międzyrzec Podlaski	PL	12	C5
Międzyrzecz	PL	75	B4
Międzywodzie	PL	67	B3
Międzyzdroje	PL	66	B3
Miejska Górka	PL	85	A5
Miélan	F	145	A4
Mielec	PL	87	B5
Mielęcin	PL	75	A4
Mielno, Warmińsko-Mazurskie	PL	77	A5
Mielno, Zachodnio-Pomorskie	PL	67	B5
Miengo	E	143	A3
Mieraslompolo	FIN	193	C11
Miercurea Ciuc	RO	17	B6
Mieres, Asturias	E	141	A5
Mieres, Girona	E	147	B3
Mierczany	PL	75	B3
Mieroszów	PL	85	B4
Mierzyn	PL	86	A2
Miesau	D	93	B3
Miesbach	D	108	B2
Mieścisko	PL	76	B2
Mieste	D	73	B4
Miesterhorst	D	73	B4
Mieszków	PL	76	B2
Mieszkowice	PL	74	B3
Mietków	PL	85	A4
Migennes	F	104	B2
Miggiano	I	173	C4
Migliánico	I	169	A4
Migliarino	I	121	C4
Migliónico	I	172	B2
Mignano Monte Lungo	I	169	B3
Migné	F	115	B5
Miguel Esteban	E	157	A4
Miguelturra	E	157	B4
Mihajlovac	SRB	127	C2
Mihald	H	111	C4
Mihalgazi	TR	187	B5
Mihaliççik	TR	187	C6
Mihályi	H	111	B4
Mihla	D	82	A2
Mihohnić	HR	123	B3
Miholjsko	HR	123	B4
Mihovljan	HR	124	A1
Mijares	E	150	B3
Mijas	E	163	B3
Mike	H	124	A3
Mikines	GR	184	B3
Mikkeli	FIN	8	B5
Mikkelvik	N	192	B3
Mikleuš	HR	125	B3
Mikołajki	PL	69	B4
Mikołów	PL	86	B2
Mikorzyn	PL	86	A2
Mikro Derio	GR	183	B8
Mikstat	PL	86	A1
Mikulášovice	CZ	84	B2
Mikulov	CZ	97	C4
Mikulovice	CZ	85	B5
Milagro	E	144	B2
Miłakowo	PL	69	A5
Milan = Milano	I	120	B2
Miland	N	47	C5
Milano = Milan	I	120	B2
Milano Marittima	I	135	A5
Milas	TR	188	B2
Milazzo	I	177	A4
Mildenhall	GB	45	A4
Milejewo	PL	69	A4
Milelín	CZ	85	B3
Miletić	SRB	125	B5
Miletićevo	SRB	126	B3
Mileto	I	175	C2
Milevsko	CZ	96	B2
Milford	IRL	26	A3
Milford Haven	GB	39	C1
Milford on Sea	GB	44	C2
Milhão	P	149	A3
Milići	BIH	139	A5
Miličín	CZ	96	B2
Milicz	PL	85	A5
Militello in Val di Catánia	I	177	B3
Miljevina	BIH	139	B4
Milkowice	PL	85	A4
Millançay	F	103	B3
Millares	E	159	B3
Millas	F	146	B3
Millau	F	130	A2
Millesimo	I	133	A4
Millevaches	F	116	B2
Millom	GB	36	B3
Millport	GB	34	C3
Millstatt	A	109	C4
Millstreet, Cork	IRL	29	B2
Millstreet, Waterford	IRL	29	B4
Milltown, Galway	IRL	28	A2
Milltown, Kerry	IRL	29	B2
Milltown Malbay	IRL	28	B2
Milly-la-Forêt	F	90	C2
Milmarcos	E	152	A2
Milmersdorf	D	74	A2
Milna	HR	138	B2
Milnthorpe	GB	37	B4
Milogórze	PL	69	A5
Miłomłyn	PL	69	B4
Milos	GR	185	C5
Miłosław	PL	76	B2
Milot	AL	182	B1
Miłowka	PL	99	B3
Miltach	D	95	B4
Miltenberg	D	94	B1
Milton Keynes	GB	44	A3
Miltzow	D	66	B2
Milverton	GB	43	A3
Milzyn	PL	76	B3
Mimice	HR	138	B2
Mimizan	F	128	B1
Mimizan-Plage	F	128	B1
Mimoň	CZ	84	B2
Mina de São Domingos	P	160	B2
Mina de Juliana	P	160	B1
Minas de Riotinto	E	161	B3
Minateda	E	158	C2
Minaya	E	158	B1
Minde	P	154	B2
Minden	D	72	B1
Mindelheim	D	108	A1
Mindelstetten	D	95	C3
Mindszent	H	113	C4
Minehead	GB	43	A3
Mineo	I	177	B3
Minerbe	I	121	B4
Minérbio	I	121	C4
Minervino Murge	I	171	B4
Minglanilla	E	158	B2
Mingorría	E	150	B3
Minnesund	N	48	B3
Miño	E	140	A2
Miño de San Esteban	E	151	A4
Minsen	D	71	A4
Minsk	BY	13	B7
Minsk Mazowiecki	PL	12	B4
Minsterley	GB	39	B4
Mintlaw	GB	33	D4
Minturno	I	169	B3
Mionica	BIH	125	C4
Mionica	SRB	127	C2
Mios	F	128	B2
Mira	E	158	B2
Mira	I	121	B5
Mira	P	148	B1
Mirabel	F	155	B4
Mirabel-aux-Baronnies	F	131	A4
Mirabella Eclano	I	170	B3
Mirabella Imbáccari	I	177	B3
Mirabello	I	121	C4
Miradoux	F	129	B3
Miraflores de la Sierra	E	151	B4
Miralrio	E	151	B5
Miramar	P	148	A1
Miramare	I	136	A1
Miramas	F	131	B3
Mirambeau	F	114	C3
Miramont-de-Guyenne	F	129	B3
Miranda de Arga	E	144	B2
Miranda de Ebro	E	143	B4
Miranda do Corvo	P	148	B1
Miranda do Douro	P	149	A3
Mirande	F	129	C3
Mirandela	P	149	A2
Mirandilla	E	155	C4
Mirándola	I	121	C4
Miranje	HR	137	A4
Mirano	I	121	B5
Miras	AL	182	C2
Miravet	E	153	A4
Miré	F	102	B1
Mirebeau	F	102	C2
Mirebeau-sur-Bèze	F	105	B4
Mirecourt	F	105	A5
Mirepoix	F	146	A2
Mires	GR	185	D5
Mirina	GR	183	D7
Mirna	SLO	123	B4
Miroslav	CZ	97	C4
Mirosławiec	PL	75	A5
Mirošov	CZ	96	B1
Mirotice	CZ	96	B2
Mirovice	CZ	96	B2
Mirow	D	74	A1
Mirsk	PL	84	B3
Mirzec	PL	87	A5
Misi	FIN	197	C9
Mišinci	BIH	125	B4
Miske	H	112	C3
Miskolc	H	113	A4
Mislinja	SLO	110	C2
Missanello	I	174	A2
Missillac	F	101	B3
Mistelbach	A	97	C4
Mistelgau	D	95	B3
Mišten	N	194	C5
Misterbianco	I	177	B4
Misterhult	S	62	A4
Mistretta	I	177	B3
Misurina	I	109	C3
Mitchelstown	IRL	29	B3
Mithimna	GR	186	C1
Mitilini	GR	186	C1
Mittådalen	S	199	C10
Mittelberg, Tirol	A	108	C1
Mittelberg, Vorarlberg	A	107	B5
Mittenwald	D	108	B2
Mittenwalde	D	74	B2
Mitter-Kleinarl	A	109	B4
Mitterback	A	110	B2
Mitterdorf im Mürztal	A	110	B2
Mittersheim	F	92	C3
Mittersill	A	109	B3
Mitterskirchen	D	95	C4
Mitterteich	D	95	B4
Mittweida	D	83	B4
Mitwitz	D	82	B3
Mizhhir'ya	UA	13	D5
Mjällby	S	63	B2
Mjåvatn	N	53	B4
Mjöbäck	S	60	B2
Mjölby	S	56	B1
Mjømna	N	46	B1
Mo, Hedmark	N	48	B3
Mo, Hordaland	N	46	B2
Mo, Møre og Romsdal	N	198	C3
Mo, Nord-Trøndelag	N	199	A8
Mo, Telemark	N	53	A3
Mo, Telemark	N	53	A4
Mo i Rana	N	195	D5
Moaña	E	140	B2
Moate	IRL	28	A4
Mocejón	E	151	C4
Močenok	SK	98	C1
Mochales	E	152	A1
Mochowo	PL	77	B4
Mochy	PL	75	B5
Mockern	D	73	B4
Mockfjärd	S	50	B1
Möckmühl	D	94	B1
Mockrehna	D	83	A4
Moclín	E	163	A4
Mocsa	H	112	B2
Möðrudalur	IS	191	B10
Möðruvellir	IS	191	B7
Moëlan-sur-Mer	F	100	B2
Moelfre	GB	38	A2
Moelv	N	48	B2
Moen	N	194	A9
Moena	I	121	A4
Moerbeke	B	79	A3
Moers	D	80	A2
Móesgard	DK	59	B3
Moffat	GB	36	A3
Mogadouro	P	149	A3
Mogata	S	56	B2
Móglia	I	121	C3
Mogliano	I	136	B2
Mogliano Véneto	I	122	B1
Mögglingen	D	94	C1
Mogón	E	164	A1
Mógoro	I	179	C2
Moguer	E	161	B3
Mohács	H	125	B4
Moheda	S	62	A2
Mohedas	E	149	B3
Mohedas de la Jara	E	156	A3
Mohelnice	CZ	97	B4
Mohelno	CZ	97	B4
Mohill	IRL	26	C3
Möhlin	CH	106	B2
Moholm	S	55	B5
Mohorn	D	83	A5
Mohyliv-Podil's'kyy	UA	13	D7
Moi	N	52	B2
Moià	E	147	C3

Moravče SLO 123 A3
Moravec CZ 97 B4
Moraviţa RO 126 B3
Morávka CZ 98 B2
Moravská Třebová CZ 97 B4
Moravské Budějovice CZ 97 B3
Moravské Lieskové SK 98 C1
Moravske Toplice SLO 111 C3
Moravský-Beroun CZ 98 B1
Moravský Krumlov CZ 97 B4
Moravský Svätý Ján SK 98 C1
Morawica PL 87 B4
Morawin PL 86 A2
Morbach D 92 B3
Morbegno I 120 A2
Morbier F 105 C5
Mörbisch am See A 111 B3
Mörbylånga S 63 B4
Morcenx F 128 B2
Morciano di Romagna I 136 B1
Morcone I 170 B2
Morcuera E 151 A4
Mordelles F 101 A4
Mordoğan TR 188 A1
Moréac F 100 B3
Morebattle GB 35 C5
Morecambe GB 36 B4
Moreda, *Granada* E 163 A4
Moreda, *Oviedo* E 142 A1
Morée F 103 B3
Moreles de Rey E 141 B5
Morella E 153 B3
Moreruela de los Infanzones E 149 A4
Morés E 152 A2
Móres I 178 B2
Morestel F 118 B2
Moret-sur-Loing F 90 C2
Moreton-in-Marsh GB 44 B2
Moretonhampstead GB 43 B3
Moretta I 119 C4
Moreuil F 90 B2
Morez F 105 C5
Mörfelden D 93 B4
Morgat F 100 A1
Morges CH 105 C5
Morgex I 119 B4
Morgongåva S 51 C3
Morhange F 92 C2
Morhet B 92 B1
Mori I 121 B3
Morialmé B 79 B4
Morianes P 160 B2
Moriani Plage F 180 A2
Mórichida H 111 B4
Moriles E 163 A3
Morille E 150 B2
Moringen D 82 A1
Morjärv S 196 C5
Morkarla S 51 B4
Mørke DK 59 B3
Mørkøv DK 61 D1
Morkovice-Slížany CZ 98 B1
Morlaàs F 145 A3
Morlaix F 100 A2
Morley F 91 C5
Mörlunda S 62 A3
Mormanno I 174 B1
Mormant F 90 C2
Mornant F 117 B4
Mornay-Berry F 103 B4
Morón de Almazán E 152 A1
Morón de la Frontera E 162 A2
Morović SRB 125 B5
Morozzo I 133 A3
Morpeth GB 37 A5
Morphou CY 181 A1
Mörrum S 63 B2
Morsbach D 81 B3
Mörsch D 93 C4
Mörsil S 199 B10
Morsum D 64 B1
Mørsvikbotn N 194 C6
Mortagne-au-Perche F 89 B4
Mortagne-sur-Gironde F 114 C3
Mortagne-sur-Sèvre F 114 B3
Mortágua P 148 B1
Mortain F 88 B3
Mortara I 120 B1
Morteau F 105 B5
Mortegliano I 122 B2
Mortelle I 177 A4
Mortemart F 115 B4
Mortimer's Cross GB 39 B4
Mortrée F 89 B4
Mörtschach A 109 C3
Mortsel B 79 A4
Morud DK 59 C3
Morwenstow GB 42 B2
Moryń PL 74 B3
Morzeszczyn PL 69 B3
Morzewo PL 69 B4
Morzine F 118 A3
Mosbach D 93 B5
Mosbjerg DK 58 A3
Mosby N 53 B3
Mosca P 149 A3
Moscavide P 154 C1
Moščenica HR 124 B2
Mošćenice HR 123 B3
Moščenicka Draga HR 123 B3
Mosciano Sant'Ángelo I 136 C2
Mościsko PL 85 B4
Moscow = Moskva RUS 9 E10
Mosina PL 75 B5
Mosjøen N 195 E4
Moskog N 46 A3
Moskorzew PL 87 B3
Moskosel S 196 D2
Moskuvarra FIN 197 B9
Moskva = Moscow RUS 9 E10
Moslavina Podravska HR 125 B3
Moşniţa Nouă RO 126 B3
Moso in Passíria I 108 C2
Mosonmagyaróvár H 111 B4
Mošorin SRB 126 B2
Mošovce SK 98 C2
Mosqueruela E 153 B3
Moss N 54 A1
Mossfellsbær IS 190 C4
Mössingen D 93 C5
Møsstrand N 47 C5
Most CZ 83 B5
Most na Soči SLO 122 A2
Mosta M 175 C3
Mostar BIH 139 B3
Mosterhamn N 52 A1
Mostki PL 75 B4
Móstoles E 151 B4
Mostová SK 111 A4
Mostowo PL 68 A1
Mostuéjouls F 130 A2
Mosty PL 75 A3
Mostys'ka UA 13 D5
Mosvik N 199 B7
Mota del Cuervo E 158 B1
Mota del Marqués E 150 A2
Motala S 55 B6
Motherwell GB 35 C4
Möthlow D 74 B1
Motilla del Palancar E 158 B2
Motnik SLO 123 A3
Motovun HR 122 B2
Motril E 163 B4
Motta I 121 B4
Motta di Livenza I 122 B1
Motta Montecorvino I 170 B3
Motta Visconti I 120 B1
Mottisfont GB 44 B2
Móttola I 173 B3
Mou DK 58 B3
Mouchard F 105 C4
Moudon CH 106 C1
Moudros GR 183 D7
Mougins F 132 B2
Mouilleron en-Pareds F 114 B3
Mouliherne F 102 B2
Moulinet F 133 B3
Moulins F 104 C2
Moulins-Engilbert F 104 C2
Moulins-la-Marche F 89 B4
Moulismes F 115 B4
Moult F 89 A3
Mount Bellew Bridge IRL 28 A3
Mountain Ash GB 39 C3
Mountfield GB 27 B3
Mountmellick IRL 30 A1
Mountrath IRL 30 A1
Mountsorrel GB 40 C2
Moura P 160 A2
Mourão P 155 C3
Mourenx F 145 A3
Mouriés F 131 B3
Mourmelon-le-Grand F 91 B4
Mouronho P 148 B1
Mourujärvi FIN 197 C11
Mouscron B 78 B3
Mousehole GB 42 B1
Moussac F 131 B3
Moussey F 92 C2
Mousteru F 100 A2
Moustey F 128 B2
Moustiers-Ste. Marie F 132 B2
Mouthe F 105 C5
Mouthier-Haute-Pierre F 105 B5
Mouthoumet F 146 B3
Moutier CH 106 B2
Moûtiers F 118 B3
Moutiers-les-Mauxfaits F 114 B2
Mouy F 90 B2
Mouzaki GR 182 D3
Mouzon F 91 B5
Møvik N 46 B2
Moville IRL 27 A3
Moy, *Highland* GB 32 D2
Moy, *Tyrone* GB 27 B4
Moycullen IRL 28 A2
Moyenmoutier F 92 C2
Moyenvic F 92 C2
Mózar E 141 C5
Mozhaysk RUS 9 E10
Mozirje SLO 123 A3
Mözs H 112 C2
Mozzanica I 120 B2
Mramorak SRB 127 C2
Mrčajevci SRB 127 D2
Mrkonjić Grad BIH 138 A3
Mrkopalj HR 123 B3
Mrocza PL 76 A2
Mroczeń PL 86 A1
Mroczno PL 69 B4
Mrzezyno PL 67 B4
Mšec CZ 84 B1
Mšeno CZ 84 B2
Mstów PL 86 B3
Mstsislaw BY 13 A9
Mszana Dolna PL 99 B4
Mszczonów PL 77 C5
Muć HR 138 B2
Múccia I 136 B2
Much D 80 B3
Much Marcle GB 39 C4
Much Wenlock GB 39 B4
Mücheln D 83 A3
Muchów PL 85 A4
Mucientes E 142 C2
Muckross IRL 29 B2
Mucur TR 23 B8
Muda P 160 B1
Mudanya TR 186 B3
Mudau D 93 B5
Müden D 72 B3
Mudersbach D 81 B3
Mudurnu TR 187 B6
Muel E 152 A2
Muelas del Pan E 149 A4
Muess D 73 A4
Muff IRL 27 A3
Mugardos E 140 A2
Muge P 154 B2
Mügeln, *Sachsen-Anhalt* D 83 A5
Mügeln, *Sachsen* D 83 A5
Müggia I 122 B2
Muğla TR 188 B3
Mugnano I 135 B5
Mugron F 128 C2
Mugueimes E 140 C3
Muhi H 113 B4
Mühlacker D 93 C4
Mühlbach am Hochkönig A 109 B4
Mühlberg, *Brandenburg* D 83 A5
Mühlberg, *Thüringen* D 82 B2
Mühldorf A 109 C4
Mühldorf D 95 C4
Muhleberg CH 106 C2
Mühleim D 107 A3
Muhlen-Eichsen D 65 C4
Mühlhausen, *Bayern* D 94 B2
Mühlhausen, *Thüringen* D 82 A2
Mühltroff D 83 B3
Muhos FIN 3 D10
Muhr A 109 B4
Muine Bheag IRL 30 B2
Muir of Ord GB 32 D2
Muirkirk GB 36 A2
Muirteira P 154 B1
Mukacheve UA 12 D5
Muker GB 37 B4
Mula E 165 A3
Mulben GB 32 D3
Mulegns CH 107 C4
Mules I 108 C2
Mülheim D 80 A2
Mulhouse F 106 B2
Muljava SLO 123 B3
Mullanys Cross IRL 26 B2
Müllheim D 106 B2
Mullhyttan S 55 A5
Mullinavat IRL 30 B1
Mullingar IRL 30 A1
Mullion GB 42 B1
Müllrose D 74 B3
Mullsjö S 60 B3
Mulseryd S 60 B3
Munaðarnes IS 190 A4
Munana E 150 B2
Muñás E 141 A4
Münchberg D 83 B3
Müncheberg D 74 B3
München = Munich D 108 A2
Munchen-Gladbach = Mönchengladbach D 80 A2
Münchhausen D 81 B4
Mundaka E 143 A4
Münden D 82 A1
Munderfing A 109 A4
Munderkingen D 107 A4
Mundesley GB 41 C5
Munera E 158 B1
Mungia E 143 A4
Munich = München D 108 A2
Muñico E 150 B2
Muniesa E 153 A3
Munka-Ljungby S 61 C2
Munkebo DK 59 C3
Munkedal S 54 B2
Munkflohögen S 199 B11
Munkfors S 49 C5
Munktorp S 56 A2
Münnerstadt D 82 B2
Muñopepe E 150 B3
Muñotello E 150 B2
Münsingen CH 106 C2
Münsingen D 94 C1
Munsö S 57 A3
Münster CH 106 C3
Münster, *Hessen* D 93 B4
Munster, *Niedersachsen* D 72 B3
Münster, *Nordrhein-Westfalen* D 71 C4
Munster F 106 A2
Muntibar E 143 A4
Münzkirchen A 96 C1
Muodoslompolo S 196 B6
Muonio FIN 196 B6
Muotathal CH 107 C3
Mur-de-Barrez F 116 C2
Mur-de-Bretagne F 100 A2
Mur-de-Sologne F 103 B3
Muradiye TR 186 D2
Murakeresztúr H 124 A2
Murán SK 99 C4
Murano I 122 B1
Muras E 140 A3
Murat F 116 B2
Murat-sur-Vèbre F 130 B1
Muratlı TR 186 A2
Murato F 180 A2
Murau A 109 B5
Muravera I 179 C3
Murazzano I 133 A4
Murça P 148 A2
Murchante E 144 B2
Murchin D 66 C2
Murcia E 165 B3
Murczyn PL 76 B2
Mureck A 110 C2
Mürefte TR 186 B2
Muret F 146 A2
Murg CH 107 B4
Murguia E 143 B4
Muri CH 106 B3
Murias de Paredes E 141 B4
Muriedas E 143 A3
Muriel Viejo E 143 C4
Murillo de Rio Leza E 143 B4
Murillo el Fruto E 144 B2
Murjek S 196 C3
Murlaggan GB 34 B2
Murmansk RUS 3 B13
Murmashi RUS 3 B13
Murnau D 108 B2
Muro E 167 B3
Muro F 180 A1
Muro de Alcoy E 159 C3
Muro Lucano I 172 B1
Murol F 116 B2
Muron F 114 B3
Muros E 140 B1
Muros de Nalón E 141 A4
Murowana Goślina PL 76 B2
Mürren CH 106 C2
Murrhardt D 94 C1
Murska Sobota SLO 111 C3
Mursko Središce HR 111 C3
Murtas E 164 C1
Murten CH 106 C2
Murter HR 137 B4
Murtiçi TR 189 C6
Murtosa P 148 B1
Murtovaara FIN 197 D12
Murvica HR 137 A4
Murviel-lès-Béziers F 130 B2
Mürzsteg A 110 B2
Murzynowo PL 75 B4
Mürzzuschlag A 110 B2
Musculdy F 144 A3
Muskö S 57 A4
Mušov CZ 97 C4
Musselburgh GB 35 C4
Musselkanaal NL 71 B4
Mussidan F 129 A3
Mussomeli I 176 B2
Musson B 92 B1
Mussy-sur-Seine F 104 B3
Mustafakemalpaşa TR 186 B3
Muszaki PL 77 A5
Muszyna PL 99 B4
Mut TR 23 C7
Muta SLO 110 C2
Muthill GB 35 B4
Mutné SK 99 B3
Mutriku E 143 A4
Muttalip TR 187 C5
Mutterbergalm A 108 B2
Muurola FIN 197 C8
Muxía E 140 A1
Muxilka-Ugarte E 143 A4
Muzillac F 101 B3
Mužla SK 112 B2
Muzzano del Turgnano I 122 B2
Mybster GB 32 C3
Myckelgensjö S 200 C3
Myennes F 104 B1
Myjava SK 98 C1
Myking N 46 B2
Mykland N 53 B4
Myra N 53 B5
Myrdal N 46 B4
Myre, *Nordland* N 194 A6
Myre, *Nordland* N 194 B6
Myresjö S 62 A2
Mýri IS 191 B8
Myrtou CY 181 A2
Mysen N 54 A2
Mysłakowice PL 85 B3
Myślenice PL 99 B3
Myślibórz PL 75 B3
Mysłowice PL 86 B3
Myszków PL 86 B3
Mytishchi RUS 9 E10
Mýtna SK 99 C3
Mýtne Ludany SK 112 A2
Mýto CZ 96 B1

N

N Unnaryd S 60 B3
Nå N 46 B3
Naaldwijk NL 79 A4
Naantali FIN 8 B2
Naas IRL 30 A2
Nabais P 148 B2
Nabbelund S 62 A5
Nabburg D 95 B4
Načeradec CZ 96 B2
Náchod CZ 85 B4
Nacław PL 68 A1
Nadarzyce PL 75 A3
Nadarzyn PL 77 B5
Nádasd H 111 C3
Nădlac RO 126 A2
Nádudvar H 113 B5
Nadvirna UA 13 D6
Nærbø N 52 B1
Næsbjerg DK 59 C1
Næstved DK 65 A4
Näfels CH 107 B4
Nafpaktos GR 184 A2
Nafplio GR 184 B3
Nagel D 95 B3
Nagele NL 70 B2
Naggen S 200 D2
Nagłowice PL 87 B4
Nagold D 93 C4
Nagore E 144 B2
Nagyatád H 124 A3
Nagybajom H 124 A3
Nagybaracska H 125 A4
Nagybátony H 113 B3
Nagyberény H 112 C2
Nagybörzsöny H 112 B2
Nagycenk H 111 B3
Nagycserkesz H 113 B5
Nagydorog H 112 C2
Nagyfüged H 113 B4
Nagyhersány H 125 B4
Nagyigmánd H 112 B2
Nagyiván H 113 B4
Nagykanizsa H 111 C3
Nagykáta H 113 B3
Nagykonyi H 112 C2
Nagykőrös H 113 B3
Nagykörü H 113 B4
Nagylóc H 112 A3
Nagymágocs H 113 C4
Nagymányok H 125 A4
Nagymaros H 112 B2
Nagyoroszi H 112 A3
Nagyrábé H 113 B5
Nagyréde H 113 B3
Nagyszékely H 112 C2
Nagyszénás H 113 C4
Nagyszokoly H 112 C2
Nagytöke H 113 C4
Nagyvázsony H 111 C4
Nagyvenyim H 112 C2
Naharros E 152 B1
Nahe D 64 C3
Naila D 83 B3
Nailloux F 146 A2
Nailsworth GB 43 A4
Naintré F 115 B4
Nairn GB 32 D3
Najac F 129 B4
Nájera E 143 B4
Nak H 112 C2
Nakksjø N 53 A5
Nakło nad Notecią PL 76 A2
Nakskov DK 65 B4
Nalda E 143 B4
Nälden S 199 B11
Nálepkovo SK 99 C4
Nallıhan TR 187 B6
Nalliers F 114 B2
Nalzen F 146 B2
Nalžouské Hory CZ 96 B1
Namdalseid N 199 A8
Náměšť nad Oslavou CZ 97 B4
Námestovo SK 99 B3
Namnå N 49 B4
Namsos N 199 A8
Namsskogan N 199 A10
Namur B 79 B4
Namysłów PL 86 A1
Nançay F 103 B4
Nanclares de la Oca E 143 B4
Nancy F 92 C2
Nangis F 90 C3
Nannestad N 48 B3
Nant F 130 A2
Nanterre F 90 C2
Nantes F 101 B4
Nanteuil-le-Haudouin F 90 B2
Nantiat F 115 B5
Nantua F 118 A2
Nantwich GB 38 A4
Naoussa, *Imathia* GR 182 C4
Naoussa, *Cyclades* GR 185 B6
Napajedla CZ 98 B1
Napiwoda PL 77 A5
Naples = Nápoli I 170 C2
Nápoli = Naples I 170 C2
Nar S 57 C4
Nara N 46 A1
Naraval E 141 A4
Narberth GB 39 C2
Narbonne F 130 B1
Narbonne-Plage F 130 B2
Narbuvollen N 199 C8
Narcao I 179 C2
Nardò I 173 B4
Narkaus FIN 197 C9
Narken S 196 C5
Narmo N 48 B3
Narni I 168 A2
Naro I 176 B2
Naro Fominsk RUS 9 E10
Narón E 140 A2
Narros del Castillo E 150 B2
Narta HR 124 B2
Naruszewo PL 77 B5
Narva EST 8 C6
Narvik N 194 B8
Narzole I 133 A3
Näs FIN 51 B7
Näs, *Dalarnas* S 50 B1
Näs, *Gotland* S 57 C4
Näsåker S 200 C2
Năsăud RO 17 B6
Nasavrky CZ 97 B3
Nasbinals F 116 C3
Näshull S 62 A3
Našice HR 125 B4
Nasielsk PL 77 B5
Naso I 177 A3
Nassau D 81 B3
Nassenfels D 95 C3
Nassenheide D 74 B2
Nassereith A 108 B1
Nässjö S 62 A2
Nastätten D 81 B3
Näsum S 63 B2
Näsviken S 199 B12
Natalinci SRB 127 C2
Nater-Stetten D 108 A2
Naters CH 119 A5
Nattavaara S 196 C3
Natters A 108 B2
Nattheim D 94 C2
Nättraby S 63 B3
Naturno I 108 C1
Naucelle F 130 A1
Nauders A 108 C1
Nauen D 74 B1
Naul IRL 30 A2
Naumburg D 83 A3
Naundorf D 83 B5
Naunhof D 83 A4
Naustdal N 46 A2
Nautijaur S 196 C2
Nautsi RUS 193 D13
Nava E 142 A1
Nava de Arévalo E 150 B3
Nava de la Asunción E 150 A3
Nava del Rey E 150 A2
Navacerrada E 151 B3
Navaconcejo E 149 B4
Navafriá E 151 A4
Navahermosa E 157 A3
Navahrudak BY 13 B6
Naval E 145 B4
Navalacruz E 150 B3
Navalcán E 150 B2
Navalcarnero E 151 B3
Navaleno E 143 C3
Navalmanzano E 151 A3
Navalmoral E 150 B3
Navalmoral de la Mata E 150 C2
Navalón E 159 C3
Navalonguilla E 150 B2
Navalperal de Pinares E 150 B3
Navalpino E 157 A3

Navaltalgordo E 150 B3
Navaltoril E 156 A3
Navaluenga E 150 B3
Navalvillar de Pela E 156 A2
Navan IRL 30 A2
Navaperal de Tormes E 150 B2
Navapolatsk BY 13 A8
Navarclés E 147 C2
Navarredonda de Gredos E 150 B2
Navarrenx F 144 A3
Navarrés E 159 B3
Navarrete E 143 B4
Navarrevisca E 150 B3
Navás E 147 C2
Navas de Oro E 150 A3
Navas de San Juan E 157 B4
Navas del Madroño E 155 B4
Navas del Rey E 151 B3
Navas del Sepillar E 163 A3
Navascués E 144 B2
Navasfrías E 149 B3
Nave I 120 B3
Nave de Haver P 149 B3
Nävekvarn S 56 B2
Navelli I 169 A3
Navenby GB 40 B3
Näverkärret S 56 A1
Naverstad S 54 B2
Navés E 147 C2
Navezuelas E 156 A2
Navia E 141 A4
Navia de Suarna E 141 B4
Navilly F 105 C4
Năvodari RO 17 C8
Naxos GR 185 B6
Nay F 145 A3
Nazaré P 154 B1
Nazarje SLO 123 A3
Nazilli TR 188 B3
Nazza D 82 A2
Nea Anchialos GR 182 D4
Nea Epidavros GR 184 B4
Nea Flippias GR 182 D2
Nea Kalikratia GR 183 C5
Nea Makri GR 185 A4
Nea Moudania GR 183 C5
Nea Peramos GR 183 C6
Nea Stira GR 185 A5
Nea Visa GR 186 A1
Nea Zichni GR 183 B5
Neap GB 33 A5
Neapoli, *Kozani* GR 182 C3
Neapoli, *Kriti* GR 185 D6
Neapoli, *Lakonia* GR 184 C4
Neath GB 39 C3
Nebljusi HR 124 C1
Neblo SLO 122 A2
Nebolchy RUS 9 C8
Nebra D 82 A3
Nebreda E 143 C3
Nechanice CZ 84 B3
Neckargemünd D 93 B4
Neckarsulm D 94 B1
Neda E 140 A2
Neded SK 112 A1
Nedelišće HR 124 A2
Nederweert NL 80 A1
Nedre Gärdsjö S 50 B2
Nedre Soppero S 196 A4
Nedreberg N 48 B3
Nedstrand N 52 A1
Nedvědice CZ 97 B4
Nędza PL 86 B2
Neede NL 71 B3
Needham Market GB 45 A5
Needingworth GB 44 A3
Neermoor D 71 A4
Neeroeteren B 80 A1
Neerpelt B 79 A5
Neesen D 72 B1
Neetze D 73 A3
Nefyn GB 38 B2
Negotin SRB 16 C5
Negotino MK 182 B4
Negrar I 121 B3
Negredo E 151 A5
Negreira E 140 B2
Nègrepelisse F 129 B4
Negru Vodă RO 17 D8
Negueira de Muñiz E 141 A4
Neheim D 81 A3
Neila E 143 B4
Néive I 119 C5
Nejdek CZ 83 B4
Nekla PL 76 B2
Neksø DK 67 A4
Nelas P 148 B2
Nelaug N 53 B4
Nelidovo RUS 9 D8
Nelim FIN 193 D12
Nellingen D 94 C1
Nelson GB 40 B1
Neman RUS 12 A5
Nemea GR 184 B3
Nemesgörzsöny H 111 B4
Nemeskér H 111 B3
Nemesnádudvar H 125 A5
Nemesszalók H 111 B4
Németkér H 112 C2
Nemours F 103 A4
Nemška Loka SLO 123 B4
Nemšová SK 98 C2
Nenagh IRL 28 B3
Nenince SK 112 A3
Nenita GR 185 A7
Nenzing A 107 B4
Neo Chori GR 184 A2
Neochori GR 182 D3
Neon Petritsi GR 183 B5
Nepi I 168 A2
Nepomuk CZ 96 B1
Nérac F 129 B3
Neratovice CZ 84 B2
Nerchau D 83 A4
Néré F 115 C3
Neresheim D 94 C2
Nereto I 136 C2
Nerezine HR 123 C3
Nerežišća HR 138 B2
Neringa LT 12 A4
Néris-les Bains F 116 A2
Nerito I 169 A3
Nerja E 163 B4
Néronde F 117 B4
Nérondes F 103 C4
Nerpio E 164 A2
Nersingen D 94 C2
Nerva E 161 B3
Nervesa della Battáglia I 121 B5
Nervi I 134 A2
Nes, *Buskerud* N 48 B1
Nes, *Hedmark* N 48 B2
Nes, *Sogn og Fjordane* N 46 A3
Nes, *Sør-Trøndelag* N 198 B6
Nes NL 70 A2
Nesbyen N 47 B6
Neset N 199 D7
Nesflaten N 52 A2
Nesjahverfi IS 191 C10
Neskaupstaður IS 191 B12
Nesland N 53 A3
Neslandsvatn N 53 B5
Nesle F 90 B2
Nesna N 195 D4
Nesoddtangen N 48 C2
Nesovice CZ 98 B1
Nesselwang D 108 B1
Nesslau CH 107 B4
Nessmersiel D 71 A4
Nesso I 120 B2
Nesterov UA 13 C5
Nestorio GR 182 C3
Nesttun N 46 B2
Nesvady SK 112 B2
Nesvatnstemmen N 53 B4
Nether Stowey GB 43 A3
Netland N 52 B2
Netolice CZ 96 B2
Netphen D 81 B4
Netstal CH 107 B4
Nettancourt F 91 C4
Nettetal D 80 A2
Nettlingen D 72 B3
Nettuno I 168 B2
Neu Darchau D 73 A3
Neu-Isenburg D 93 A4
Neu Kaliss D 73 A4
Neu Lübbenau D 74 B2
Neu-markt am Wallersee A 109 B4
Neu-petershain D 84 A2
Neu-Ravensburg D 107 B4
Neu-Ulm D 94 C2
Neualbenreuth D 95 B4
Neubeckum D 81 A4
Neubrandenburg D 74 A2
Neubruch-hausen D 72 B1
Neubukow D 65 B4
Neuburg D 94 C3
Neuchâtel CH 106 C1
Neudau A 111 B3
Neudietendorf D 82 B2
Neudorf D 93 B4
Neuenbürg, *Baden-Württemberg* D 93 C4
Neuenburg, *Niedersachsen* D 71 A4
Neuendorf D 66 B2
Neuenhagen D 74 B2
Neuenhaus D 71 B3
Neuenkirchen, *Niedersachsen* D 71 B5
Neuenkirchen, *Niedersachsen* D 72 A2
Neuenkirchen, *Nordrhein-Westfalen* D 71 B4
Neuenkirchen, *Nordrhein-Westfalen* D 81 B3
Neuenrade D 81 A3
Neuenwalde D 64 C1
Neuerburg D 92 A2
Neuf-Brisach F 106 A2
Neufahrn, *Bayern* D 95 C3
Neufahrn, *Bayern* D 95 C4
Neufchâteau B 92 B1
Neufchâteau F 92 C1
Neufchâtel-en-Bray F 90 B1
Neufchâtel-sur-Aisne F 91 B4
Neuflize F 91 B4
Neugersdorf D 84 B2
Neuhardenberg D 74 B3
Neuharlingersiel D 71 A4
Neuhaus, *Bayern* D 95 B3
Neuhaus, *Bayern* D 96 C1
Neuhaus, *Niedersachsen* D 64 C2
Neuhaus, *Niedersachsen* D 73 A3
Neuhaus, *Niedersachsen* D 81 A5
Neuhaus a Rennweg D 82 B3
Neuhausen CH 107 B3
Neuhausen ob Eck D 107 B3
Neuhof, *Bayern* D 94 B2
Neuhof, *Hessen* D 82 B1
Neuhofen an der Krems A 110 A1
Neuillé-Pont-Pierre F 102 B2
Neuilly-en-Thelle F 90 B2
Neuilly-le-Réal F 104 C2
Neuilly-l'Évêque F 105 B4
Neuilly-St. Front F 90 B3
Neukalen D 66 C1
Neukirch D 84 A2
Neukirchen A 109 A4
Neukirchen, *Hessen* D 81 B5
Neukirchen, *Schleswig-Holstein* D 64 B1
Neukirchen am Grossvenediger A 109 B3
Neukirchen bei Heiligen Blut D 95 B4
Neukloster D 65 C4
Neulengbach A 110 A2
Neulise F 117 B4
Neum BIH 139 C3
Neumagen D 92 B2
Neumarkt D 95 B3
Neumarkt im Hausruckkreis A 109 A4
Neumarkt im Mühlkreis A 96 C2
Neumarkt im Steiermark A 110 B1
Neumarkt Sankt Veit D 95 C4
Neumünster D 64 B2
Neunburg vorm Wald D 95 B4
Neung-sur-Beuvron F 103 B3
Neunkirch, *Luzern* CH 106 B3
Neunkirch, *Schaffhausen* CH 107 B3
Neunkirchen A 111 B3
Neunkirchen, *Nordrhein-Westfalen* D 80 B3
Neunkirchen, *Saarland* D 92 B3
Neunkirchen am Brand D 94 B3
Neuötting D 95 C4
Neureut D 93 B4
Neuruppin D 74 B1
Neusäss D 94 C2
Neusiedl A 111 B3
Neuss D 80 A2
Neussargues-Moissac F 116 B2
Neustadt, *Bayern* D 94 B2
Neustadt, *Bayern* D 95 B4
Neustadt, *Bayern* D 95 C3
Neustadt, *Brandenburg* D 73 B5
Neustadt, *Hessen* D 81 B5
Neustadt, *Niedersachsen* D 72 B2
Neustadt, *Rheinland-Pfalz* D 93 B4
Neustadt, *Sachsen* D 84 A2
Neustadt, *Schleswig-Holstein* D 65 B3
Neustadt, *Thüringen* D 82 B3
Neustadt, *Thüringen* D 83 B3
Neustadt-Glewe D 73 A4
Neustift im Stubaital A 108 B2
Neustrelitz D 74 A2
Neutal A 111 B3
Neutrebbin D 74 B3
Neuves-Maisons F 92 C2
Neuvic, *Corrèze* F 116 B2
Neuvic, *Dordogne* F 129 A3
Neuville-aux-Bois F 103 A4
Neuville-de-Poitou F 115 B4
Neuville-les-Dames F 117 A5
Neuville-sur-Saône F 117 B4
Neuvy-le-Roi F 102 B2
Neuvy-St. Sépulchre F 103 C3
Neuvy-Santour F 104 A2
Neuvy-sur-Barangeon F 103 B4
Neuwied D 80 B3
Neuzelle D 74 B3
Névache F 118 B3
Neveklov CZ 96 B2
Nevel RUS 9 D6
Neverfjord N 192 B7
Nevers F 104 C2
Nevesinje BIH 139 B4
Névez F 100 B2
Nevlunghavn N 53 B5
Nevşehir TR 23 B8
New Abbey GB 36 B3
New Aberdour GB 33 D4
New Alresford GB 44 B2
New Costessey GB 41 C5
New Cumnock GB 36 A2
New Galloway GB 36 A2
New Mills GB 40 B2
New Milton GB 44 C2
New Pitsligo GB 33 D4
New Quay GB 39 B2
New Radnor GB 39 B3
New Romney GB 45 C4
New Ross IRL 30 B2
New Scone GB 35 B4
Newark-on-Trent GB 40 B3
Newbiggin-by-the-Sea GB 37 A5
Newbliss IRL 27 B3
Newborough GB 38 A2
Newbridge IRL 30 A2
Newbridge on Wye GB 39 B3
Newburgh, *Aberdeenshire* GB 33 D4
Newburgh, *Fife* GB 35 B4
Newbury GB 44 B2
Newby Bridge GB 36 B4
Newcastle GB 27 B5
Newcastle Emlyn GB 39 B2
Newcastle-under-Lyme GB 40 B1
Newcastle-Upon-Tyne GB 37 B5
Newcastle West IRL 29 B2
Newcastleton GB 37 A4
Newchurch GB 39 B3
Newent GB 39 C4
Newham GB 45 B4
Newhaven GB 45 C4
Newington GB 45 B5
Newinn IRL 29 B4
Newlyn GB 42 B1
Newmachar GB 33 D4
Newmarket, *Suffolk* GB 45 A4
Newmarket, *Western Isles* GB 31 A2
Newmarket IRL 29 B3
Newmarket-on-Fergus IRL 28 B3
Newport, *Isle of Wight* GB 44 C2
Newport, *Newport* GB 39 C4
Newport, *Pembrokeshire* GB 39 B2
Newport, *Telford & Wrekin* GB 38 B4
Newport, *Mayo* IRL 28 A2
Newport, *Tipperary* IRL 29 B3
Newport-on-Tay GB 35 B5
Newport Pagnell GB 44 A3
Newquay GB 42 B1
Newry GB 27 B4
Newton Abbot GB 43 B3
Newton Arlosh GB 36 B3
Newton Aycliffe GB 37 B5
Newton Ferrers GB 42 B2
Newton Stewart GB 36 B2
Newtonhill GB 33 D4
Newtonmore GB 32 D2
Newtown, *Herefordshire* GB 39 B4
Newtown, *Powys* GB 39 B3
Newtown Cunningham IRL 27 B3
Newtown Hamilton GB 27 B4
Newtown St. Boswells GB 35 C5
Newtown Sands IRL 29 B2
Newtownabbey GB 27 B5
Newtownards GB 27 B5
Newtownbutler GB 27 B3
Newtownmountkennedy IRL 30 A2
Newtownstewart GB 27 B3
Nexon F 115 C5
Neyland GB 39 C2
Nibbiano I 120 C2
Nibe DK 58 B2
Nicastro I 175 C2
Niccone I 135 B5
Nice F 133 B3
Nickelsdorf A 111 B4
Nicolosi I 177 B4
Nicosia CY 181 A2
Nicosia I 177 B3
Nicótera I 175 C1
Nidda D 81 B5
Nidzica PL 77 A5
Niebla E 161 B3
Nieborów PL 77 B5
Niebüll D 64 B1
Niechanowo PL 76 B2
Niechorze PL 67 B4
Niedalino PL 67 B5
Nieder-Olm D 93 B4
Niederaula D 82 B1
Niederbipp CH 106 B2
Niederbronn-les-Bains F 93 C3
Niederfischbach D 81 B3
Niedergörsdorf D 74 C1
Niederkrüchten D 80 A2
Niederndorf A 108 B3
Niedersachs-werfen D 82 A2
Niederstetten D 94 B1
Niederurnen CH 107 B4
Niederwölz A 110 B1
Niedoradz PL 85 A3
Niedzica PL 99 B4
Niegosławice PL 85 A3
Nieheim D 81 A5
Niemcza PL 85 B4
Niemegk D 74 B1
Niemisel S 196 C5
Niemodlin PL 85 B5
Nienburg, *Niedersachsen* D 72 B2
Nienburg, *Sachsen-Anhalt* D 83 A3
Niepołomice PL 99 A4
Nierstein D 93 B4
Niesky D 84 A2
Niestronno PL 76 B2
Nieświń PL 87 A4
Nieszawa PL 76 B3
Nieul-le-Dolent F 114 B2
Nieul-sur-Mer F 114 B2
Nieuw-Amsterdam NL 71 B3
Nieuw-Buinen NL 71 B3
Nieuw-Weerdinge NL 71 B3
Nieuwe Niedorp NL 70 B1
Nieuwe-Pekela NL 71 A3
Nieuwe-schans NL 71 A4
Nieuwegein NL 70 B2
Nieuwerkerken B 79 B5
Nieuwolda NL 71 A3
Nieuwpoort B 78 A2
Niğde TR 23 C8
Nigrita GR 183 C5
Nigüelas E 163 B4
Níjar E 164 C2
Nijemci HR 125 B5
Nijkerk NL 70 B2
Nijlen B 79 A4
Nijmegen NL 80 A1
Nijverdal NL 71 B3
Nikel RUS 193 C14
Nikinci SRB 127 C1
Nikiti GR 183 C5
Nikitsch A 111 B3
Nikkaluokta S 196 B2
Nikla H 111 C4
Niklasdorf A 110 B2
Nikšić CG 139 C4
Nilivaara S 196 B4
Nîmes F 131 B3
Nimis I 122 A2
Nimtofte DK 58 B3
Nin HR 137 A4
Nindorf D 64 B2
Ninemilehouse IRL 30 B1
Ninove B 79 B4
Niort F 114 B3
Niš SRB 16 D4
Nisa P 155 B3
Niscemi I 177 B3
Niskala FIN 197 D10
Nissafors S 60 B3
Nissan-lez-Ensérune F 130 B2
Nissedal N 53 A4
Nissumby DK 58 B1
Nisterud N 53 A5
Niton GB 44 C2
Nitra SK 98 C2
Nitrianske-Pravno SK 98 C2
Nitrianske Rudno SK 98 C2
Nitry F 104 B2
Nittedal N 48 B2
Nittenau D 95 B4
Nittendorf D 95 B3
Nivala FIN 3 E9
Nivelles B 79 B4
Nivnice CZ 98 C1
Nižná SK 99 B3
Nižná Boca SK 99 C3
Nižne Repaše SK 99 B4
Nizza Monferrato I 119 C5
Njarðvík IS 190 D3
Njegůsevo SRB 126 B1
Njivice HR 123 B3
Njurundabommen S 200 D3
Njutånger S 200 E3
Noailles F 90 B2
Noain E 144 B2
Noale I 121 B5
Noalejo E 163 A4
Noblejas E 151 C4
Noceda E 141 B4
Nocera Inferiore I 170 C2
Nocera Terinese I 175 B2
Nocera Umbra I 136 B1
Noceto I 120 C3
Noci I 173 B3
Nociglia I 173 B4
Nodeland N 53 B3
Nödinge S 60 B2
Nods F 105 B5
Noé F 146 A2
Noépoli I 174 A2
Noeux-les-Mines F 78 B2
Noez E 157 A3
Nogales E 155 C4
Nogara I 121 B4
Nogarejas E 141 B4
Nogaro F 128 C2
Nogent F 105 A4
Nogent l'Artaud F 90 C3
Nogent-le-Roi F 90 C1
Nogent-le-Rotrou F 89 B4
Nogent-sur-Seine F 91 C3
Nogent-sur-Vernisson F 103 B4
Nogersund S 63 B2
Noguera E 152 B2
Noguerones E 163 A3
Nohfelden D 92 B3
Nohn D 80 B2
Noia E 140 B2
Noicáttaro I 173 A2
Noirétable F 117 B3
Noirmoutier-en-l'Île F 114 A1
Noja E 143 A3
Nojewo PL 75 B5
Nokia FIN 8 B3
Nol S 60 B2
Nola I 170 C2
Nolay F 104 C3
Noli I 133 A4
Nolnyra S 51 B4
Nombela E 150 B3
Nomeny F 92 C2
Nomexy F 92 C2
Nonancourt F 89 B5
Nonant-le-Pin F 89 B4
Nonántola I 121 C4
Nonaspe E 153 A4
None I 119 C4
Nontron F 115 C4
Nonza F 180 A2
Noordhorn NL 71 A3
Noordwijk NL 70 B1
Noordwijkerhout NL 70 B1
Noordwolde NL 70 B3
Noppikoski S 50 A1
Nora S 55 A6
Nørager DK 58 B2
Norberg S 50 B2
Norboda S 51 B5
Nórcia I 136 C2
Nord-Odal N 48 B3
Nordagutu N 53 A5
Nordanås S 200 B4
Nordausques F 78 B2
Nordborg DK 64 A2
Nordby, *Aarhus Amt.* DK 59 C3
Nordby, *Ribe Amt.* DK 59 C1
Norddeich D 71 A4
Norddorf D 64 B1
Norden D 71 A4
Nordenham D 72 A1
Norderhov N 48 B2
Norderney D 71 A4
Norderstapel D 64 B2
Norderstedt D 64 C3
Nordfjord N 193 B14
Nordfjordeid N 198 D3
Nordfold N 194 C6
Nordhalben D 82 B3
Nordhausen D 82 A2
Nordheim vor der Rhön D 82 B2
Nordholz D 64 C1
Nordhorn D 71 B4
Nordingrå S 200 D4
Nordkjosbotn N 192 C3
Nordli N 199 A10
Nördlingen D 94 C2
Nordmaling S 200 C5
Nordmark S 49 C6
Nordmela N 194 A6
Nordre Osen N 48 A3
Nordsinni N 48 B1
Nørdstedalsseter N 198 D4
Nordstemmen D 72 B2
Nordvågen N 193 B10
Nordwalde D 71 B4
Noreña E 142 A1

Noresund N 48 B1
Norg NL 71 A3
Norheimsund N 46 B3
Norie S 63 B2
Norma I 169 B2
Nornäs S 49 A5
Norra Vi S 62 A3
Norrahammar S 62 A2
Norråker S 200 B1
Norrala S 51 A3
Nørre Åby DK 59 C2
Nørre Alslev DK 65 B4
Nørre Lyndelse DK 59 C3
Nørre Nebel DK 59 C1
Nørre Snede DK 59 C2
Nørre Vorupør DK 58 B1
Norrent-Fontes F 78 B2
Nørresundby DK 58 A2
Norrfjärden S 196 D4
Norrhed S 196 C3
Norrhult Klavreström S 62 A3
Norrköping S 56 B2
Norrskedika S 51 B5
Norrsundet S 51 B4
Norrtälje S 57 A4
Nors DK 58 A1
Norsbron S 55 A4
Norsholm S 56 B1
Norsjö S 200 B5
Nort-sur-Erdre F 101 B4
Nörten-Hardenberg D 82 A1
North Berwick GB 35 B5
North Charlton GB 37 A5
North Frodingham GB 40 B3
North Kessock GB 32 D2
North Molton GB 42 A3
North Petherton GB 43 A3
North Somercotes GB 41 B4
North Tawton GB 42 B3
North Thoresby GB 41 B3
North Walsham GB 41 C5
Northallerton GB 37 B5
Northampton GB 44 A3
Northeim D 82 A2
Northfleet GB 45 B4
Northleach GB 44 B2
Northpunds GB 33 B5
Northwich GB 38 A4
Norton GB 40 A3
Nortorf D 64 B2
Nörvenich D 80 B2
Norwich GB 41 C5
Norwick GB 33 A6
Nøsen N 47 B5
Nossa Senhora do Cabo P 154 C1
Nossebro S 55 B3
Nössemark S 54 A2
Nossen D 83 A5
Notaresco I 169 A3
Noto I 177 C4
Notodden N 53 A5
Nottingham GB 40 C2
Nottuln D 71 C4
Nouan-le-Fuzelier F 103 B4
Nouans-les-Fontaines F 103 B3
Nougaroulet F 129 C3
Nouvion F 78 B1
Nouzonville F 91 B4
Nova H 111 C3
Nová Baňa SK 98 C2
Nová Bystrica SK 99 B3
Nová Bystřice CZ 97 B3
Nova Crnja SRB 126 B2
Nova Gorica SLO 122 B2
Nova Gradiška HR 124 B3
Nova Levante I 108 C2
Nová Paka CZ 84 B3
Nova Pazova SRB 127 C2
Nová Pec CZ 96 C1
Nova Siri I 174 A2
Nova Topola BIH 124 B3
Nova Zagora BG 17 D6
Novaféltria I 135 B5
Nováky SK 98 C2
Novalaise F 118 B2
Novales E 145 B3
Novalja HR 137 A3
Novara I 120 B1
Novara di Sicília I 177 A4
Novate Mezzola I 120 A2
Novaya Ladoga RUS 9 B8
Nové Hrady CZ 96 C2
Nové Město SK 98 C1
Nové Město na Moravě CZ 97 B4
Nové Město nad Metují CZ 85 B4
Nové Město pod Smrkem CZ 84 B3
Nové Mitrovice CZ 96 B1
Nové Sady SK 98 C1
Nové Strašeci CZ 84 B1
Nové Zámky SK 112 B2
Novelda E 165 A4
Novellara I 121 C3
Noventa di Piave I 122 B1
Noventa Vicentina I 121 B4
Novés E 151 B3
Noves F 131 B3
Novés de Segre E 147 B2
Novgorod RUS 9 C7
Novi Bečej SRB 126 B2
Novi di Módena I 121 C3
Novi Kneževac SRB 126 A2
Novi Lígure I 120 C1
Novi Marof HR 124 A2
Novi Pazar BG 17 D7
Novi Pazar SRB 16 D4
Novi Sad SRB 126 B1
Novi Slankamen SRB 126 B2
Novi Travnik BIH 139 A3
Novi Vinodolski HR 123 B3
Novigrad, *Istarska* HR 122 B2
Novigrad, *Zadarsko-Kninska* HR 137 A4
Novigrad Podravski HR 124 A2
Noville B 92 A1
Novion-Porcien F 91 B4
Novo Mesto SLO 123 B4
Novo Miloševo SRB 126 B2
Novo Selo BIH 125 B3
Novohrad-Volynskyy UA 13 C7
Novorzhev RUS 9 D6
Novoselytsya UA 17 A7
Novosokolniki RUS 9 D6
Novoveská Huta SK 99 C4
Novovolynsk UA 13 C6
Novska HR 124 B2
Nový Bor CZ 84 B2
Nový Bydžov CZ 84 B3
Novy-Chevrières F 91 B4
Novy Dwór Mazowiecki PL 77 B5
Nový-Hrozenkov CZ 98 B2
Nový Jičín CZ 98 B2
Nový Knín CZ 96 B2
Nowa Cerekwia PL 86 B1
Nowa Dęba PL 87 B5
Nowa Karczma PL 68 A3
Nowa Kościoł PL 85 A3
Nowa Ruda PL 85 B4
Nowa Słupia PL 87 B5
Nowa Sól PL 85 A3
Nowa Wieś PL 69 B4
Nowa-Wieś Wielka PL 76 B3
Nowe PL 69 B3
Nowe Brzesko PL 87 B4
Nowe Grudze PL 77 B4
Nowe Kiejkuty PL 77 A6
Nowe Miasteczko PL 85 A3
Nowe Miasto, *Mazowieckie* PL 77 B5
Nowe Miasto, *Mazowieckie* PL 87 A4
Nowe Miasto Lubawskie PL 69 B4
Nowe Miasto nad Wartą PL 76 B2
Nowe Skalmierzyce PL 86 A2
Nowe Warpno PL 74 A3
Nowica PL 69 A4
Nowogard PL 75 A4
Nowogród Bobrzanski PL 84 A3
Nowogrodziec PL 84 A3
Nowosolna PL 86 A3
Nowy Dwór Gdański PL 69 A4
Nowy Korczyn PL 87 B4
Nowy Sącz PL 99 B4
Nowy Staw PL 69 A4
Nowy Targ PL 99 B4
Nowy Tomyśl PL 75 B5
Nowy Wiśnicz PL 99 B4
Noyal-Pontivy F 100 A3
Noyalo F 101 B3
Noyant F 102 B2
Noyelles-sur-Mer F 78 B1
Noyen-sur-Sarthe F 102 B1
Noyers F 104 B2
Noyers-sur-Cher F 103 B3
Noyers-sur-Jabron F 132 A1
Noyon F 90 B2
Nozay F 101 B4
Nuaillé F 102 B1
Nuaillé-d'Aunis F 114 B3
Nuars F 104 B2
Nubledo E 141 A5
Nuéno E 145 B3
Nuestra Señora Sa Verge des Pilar E 166 C1
Nueva E 142 A2
Nueva Carteya E 163 A3
Nuevalos E 152 A2
Nuits F 104 B3
Nuits-St. Georges F 105 B3
Nule I 178 B3
Nules E 159 B3
Nulvi I 178 B2
Numana I 136 B2
Numansdorp NL 79 A4
Nümbrecht D 81 B3
Nunchritz D 83 A5
Nuneaton GB 40 C2
Nunnanen FIN 196 A7
Nuñomoral E 149 B3
Nunspeet NL 70 B2
Nuorgam FIN 193 B11
Núoro I 178 B3
Nurallao I 179 C3
Nuremberg = Nürnberg D 94 B3
Nurmes FIN 3 E11
Nürnberg = Nuremberg D 94 B3
Nurri I 179 C3
Nürtingen D 94 C1
Nus I 119 B4
Nusnäs S 50 B1
Nusplingen D 107 A3
Nuštar HR 125 B4
Nuupas FIN 197 C9
Nyåker S 200 C5
Nyáregyháza H 112 B3
Nyarlörinc H 113 C3
Nyasvizh BY 13 B7
Nybble S 55 A5
Nybergsund N 49 A4
Nybøl DK 64 B2
Nyborg DK 59 C3
Nyborg S 196 D6
Nybro S 62 B3
Nybster GB 32 C3
Nyby DK 65 B5
Nye S 62 A3
Nyékládháza H 113 B4
Nyergesujfalu H 112 B2
Nyhammar S 50 B1
Nyhyttan S 55 A5
Nyirád H 111 B4
Nyirbátor H 16 B5
Nyíregyháza H 16 B4
Nyker DK 67 A3
Nykil S 56 B1
Nykirke N 48 B2
Nykøbing, *Falster* DK 65 B4
Nykøbing, *Vestsjællands Amt.* DK 61 D1
Nykøbing M DK 58 B1
Nyköping S 56 B3
Nykroppa S 55 A5
Nykvarn S 56 A3
Nykyrke S 55 B5
Nyland S 200 C3
Nylars DK 67 A3
Nymburk CZ 84 B3
Nynäshamn S 57 B3
Nyon CH 118 A3
Nyons F 131 A4
Nýřany CZ 96 B1
Nýrsko CZ 95 B5
Nyrud N 193 C13
Nysa PL 85 B5
Nysäter S 55 A3
Nyseter N 198 C5
Nyskoga S 49 B4
Nysted DK 65 B4
Nystrand N 53 A5
Nyúl H 111 B4
Nyvoll N 192 B7

O

O Barco E 141 B4
O Bolo E 141 B3
O Carballiño E 140 B2
O Corgo E 141 B3
Ö Lagnö S 57 A4
O Näsberg S 49 B5
O Páramo E 140 B3
O Pedrouzo E 140 B2
O Pino E 140 B2
O Porriño E 140 B2
O Rosal E 140 C2
Oadby GB 40 C2
Oakengates GB 38 B4
Oakham GB 40 C3
Oanes N 52 B2
Obalj BIH 139 B4
Oban GB 34 B2
Obbola S 200 C6
Obdach A 110 B1
Obejo E 156 B3
Ober Grafendorf A 110 A2
Ober-Morlen D 81 B4
Oberammergau D 108 B2
Oberasbach D 94 B2
Oberau D 108 B2
Oberaudorf D 108 B3
Oberbruck F 106 B1
Oberdiessbach CH 106 C2
Oberdorf CH 106 B2
Oberdrauburg A 109 C3
Obere Stanz A 110 B2
Oberelsbach D 82 B2
Obergünzburg D 108 B1
Obergurgl A 108 C2
Oberhausen D 80 A2
Oberhof D 82 B2
Oberkirch D 93 C4
Oberkirchen D 81 A4
Oberkochen D 94 C2
Obermassfeld-Grimmenthal D 82 B2
Obermünchen D 95 C3
Obernai F 93 C3
Obernberg A 96 C1
Obernburg D 93 B5
Oberndorf D 93 C4
Oberndorf bei Salzburg A 109 B3
Obernkirchen D 72 B2
Oberort A 110 B2
Oberpullendorf A 111 B3
Oberriet CH 107 B4
Oberröblingen D 82 A3
Oberrot D 94 B1
Oberstaufen D 107 B5
Oberstdorf D 107 B5
Obertauern A 109 B4
Obertilliach A 109 C3
Obertraubling D 95 C4
Obertraun A 109 B4
Obertrubach D 95 B3
Obertrum A 109 B4
Oberursel D 81 B4
Obervellach A 109 C4
Oberviechtach D 95 B4
Oberwart A 111 B3
Oberwesel D 93 A3
Oberwinter D 80 B3
Oberwölzstadt A 110 B1
Oberzell D 96 C1
Obice PL 87 B4
Óbidos P 154 B1
Obing D 109 B3
Objat F 129 A4
Objazda PL 68 A2
Öblarn A 109 B5
Obninsk RUS 9 E10
Oborniki PL 75 B5
Oborniki Śląskie PL 85 A4
Obornjača SRB 126 B1
Obrenovac SRB 127 C2
Obrež SRB 127 C1
Obrigheim D 93 B5
Obrov SLO 123 B3
Obrovac HR 137 A4
Obrovac SRB 126 B1
Obrovac Sinjski HR 138 B2
Obruk TR 23 B7
Obrzycko PL 75 B5
Obudovac BIH 125 C4
Ocaña E 151 C4
Occhiobello I 121 C4
Occimiano I 119 B5
Očevlja BIH 139 A4
Ochagavía E 144 B2
Ochiltree GB 36 A2
Ochla PL 84 A3
Ochotnica-Dolna PL 99 B4
Ochotnica-Górna PL 99 B4
Ochsenfurt D 94 B2
Ochsenhausen D 107 A4
Ochtendung D 80 B3
Ochtrup D 71 B4
Ocieka PL 87 B5
Ockelbo S 50 B3
Öckerö S 60 B1
Ocniţa MD 17 A7
Očová SK 99 C3
Ócsa H 112 B3
Öcseny H 125 A4
Öcsöd H 113 C4
Octeville F 88 A2
Ocypel PL 69 B3
Ödåkra S 61 C2
Odby DK 58 B1
Odda N 46 B3
Odder DK 59 C3
Ödeborg S 54 B2
Odeceixe P 160 B1
Odechów PL 87 A5
Odeleite P 160 B2
Odemira P 160 B1
Ödemiş TR 188 A2
Ödensbacken S 56 A1
Odense DK 59 C3
Odensjö, *Jönköping* S 62 A2
Odensjö, *Kronoberg* S 60 C3
Oderberg D 74 B3
Oderzo I 122 B1
Odesa = Odessa UA 17 B9
Ödeshög S 55 B5
Odessa = Odesa UA 17 B9
Odiáxere P 160 B1
Odie GB 33 B4
Odiham GB 44 B3
Odintsovo RUS 9 E10
Odivelas P 160 A1
Odolanów PL 85 A5
Odón E 152 B2
Odorheiu Secuiesc RO 17 B6
Odrowaz PL 87 A4
Odry CZ 98 B1
Odrzywół PL 87 A4
Ødsted DK 59 C2
Odžaci SRB 126 B1
Odžak BIH 125 B4
Oebisfelde D 73 B3
Oederan D 83 B5
Oeding D 71 C3
Oegstgeest NL 70 B1
Oelde D 81 A4
Oelsnitz D 83 B4
Oer-Erkenschwick D 80 A3
Oerlinghausen D 72 C1
Oettingen D 94 C2
Oetz A 108 B1
Oeventrop D 81 A4
Offanengo I 120 B2
Offenbach D 81 B4
Offenburg D 93 C3
Offida I 136 C2
Offingen D 94 C2
Offranville F 89 A5
Ofir P 148 A1
Ofte N 53 A4
Ofterschwang D 107 B5
Oggiono I 120 B2
Ogihares E 163 A4
Ogliastro Cilento I 170 C3
Ogliastro Marina I 170 C2
Ogmore-by-Sea GB 39 C3
Ogna N 52 B1
Ogre LV 8 D4
Ogrodzieniec PL 86 B3
Ogulin HR 123 B4
Ögur IS 190 A3
Ohanes E 164 B2
Ohey B 79 B5
Ohlstadt D 108 B2
Ohrdorf D 73 B3
Ohrdruf D 82 B2
Ohrid MK 182 B2
Öhringen D 94 B1
Oia E 140 B2
Oiã P 148 B1
Oiartzun E 144 A2
Oijärvi FIN 197 D8
Oilgate IRL 30 B2
Oimbra E 148 A2
Oiselay-et-Grachoux F 105 B4
Oisemont F 90 B1
Oisterwijk NL 79 A5
Öja S 57 C4
Öje S 49 B5
Ojén E 162 B3
Ojrzeń PL 77 B5
Ojuelos Altos E 156 B2
Okalewo PL 77 A4
Okány H 113 C5
Okehampton GB 42 B2
Oklaj HR 138 B2
Økneshamn N 194 B6
Okoč SK 111 B4
Okoličné SK 99 B3
Okonek PL 68 B1
Okonin PL 69 B3
Okřisky CZ 97 B3
Oksa PL 87 B4
Oksbøl DK 59 C1
Oksby DK 59 C1
Øksfjord N 192 B6
Øksna N 48 B3
Okučani HR 124 B3
Okulovka RUS 9 C8
Ólafsfjörður IS 191 A7
Ólafsvík IS 190 C2
Olagüe E 144 B2
Oland N 53 B4
Olargues F 130 B1
Oława PL 85 B5
Olazagutia E 144 B1
Olbernhau D 83 B5
Ólbia I 178 B3
Olching D 108 A2
Old Deer GB 33 D4
Oldbury GB 43 A4
Oldcastle IRL 27 C3
Oldeberkoop NL 70 B3
Oldeboorn NL 70 A2
Olden N 198 D3
Oldenbrok D 71 A5
Oldenburg, *Niedersachsen* D 71 A5
Oldenburg, *Schleswig-Holstein* D 65 B3
Oldenzaal NL 71 B3
Olderdalen N 192 C4
Olderfjord N 193 B9
Oldersum D 71 A4
Oldervik N 192 C2
Oldham GB 40 B1
Oldisleben D 82 A3
Oldmeldrum GB 33 D4
Olea E 142 B2
Oleby S 49 B5
Olechów PL 87 A5
Oledo P 155 B3
Oléggio I 120 B1
Oleiros, *Coruña* E 140 A2
Oleiros, *Coruña* E 140 B1
Oleiros P 154 B3
Oleksandriya UA 13 C7
Olen B 79 A4
Ølen N 52 A1
Olenegorsk RUS 3 B13
Olenino RUS 9 D8
Olesa de Montserrat E 147 C2
Oleśnica PL 85 A5
Olešnice CZ 97 B4
Olesno PL 86 B2
Oletta F 180 A2
Olette F 146 B3
Olevsk UA 13 C7
Olfen D 80 A3
Olgiate Comasco I 120 B1
Olginate I 120 B2
Ølgod DK 59 C1
Olgrinmore GB 32 C3
Olhão P 160 B2
Olhava FIN 197 D8
Olhavo P 154 B1
Oliana E 147 B2
Olias del Rey E 151 C4
Oliena I 178 B3
Oliete E 153 B3
Olimbos GR 188 D2
Olite E 144 B2
Oliva E 159 C3
Oliva de la Frontera E 155 C4
Oliva de Mérida E 156 B1
Oliva de Plasencia E 149 B3
Olivadi I 175 C2
Olival P 154 B2
Olivar E 163 B4
Olivares E 161 B3
Olivares de Duero E 142 C2
Olivares de Júcar E 158 B1
Oliveira de Azeméis P 148 B1
Oliveira de Frades P 148 B1
Oliveira do Conde P 148 B2
Oliveira do Douro P 148 A1
Oliveira do Hospital P 148 B2
Olivenza E 155 C3
Olivet F 103 B3
Olivone CH 107 C3
Öljehult S 63 B3
Olkusz PL 86 B3
Ollerton GB 40 B2
Ollerup DK 65 A3
Olliergues F 117 B3
Ölmbrotorp S 56 A1
Ölme S 55 A4
Olmedilla de Alarcón E 158 B1
Olmedillo de Roa E 143 C3
Olmedo E 150 A3
Olmedo I 178 B2
Olmeto F 180 B1
Olmillos de Castro E 149 A3
Olmos de Ojeda E 142 B2
Olney GB 44 A3
Ołobok PL 86 A2
Olocau del Rey E 153 B3
Olofström S 63 B2
Olomouc CZ 98 B1
Olonets RUS 9 B8
Olonne-sur-Mer F 114 B2
Olonzac F 130 B1
Oloron-Ste. Marie F 145 A3
Olost E 147 C3
Olot E 147 B3
Olovo BIH 139 A4
Olpe D 81 A3
Olsberg D 81 A4
Olsene B 79 B3
Olserud S 55 A4
Olshammar S 55 B5
Olshanka UA 13 D9
Olszanica PL 85 A3
Olsztyn, *Śląskie* PL 86 B3
Olsztyn, *Warmińsko-Mazurskie* PL 69 B5
Olsztynek PL 77 A5
Olszyna PL 84 A3
Olszyny PL 77 A6
Oltedal N 52 B2
Olten CH 106 B2
Olteniţa RO 17 C7
Olula del Rio E 164 B2
Ølve N 46 B2
Olvega E 144 C2
Olvera E 162 B2
Olympia GR 184 B2
Olzai I 178 B3
Omagh GB 27 B3
Omalos GR 185 D4
Omegna I 119 B5
Omiš HR 138 B2
Omišalj HR 123 B3
Ommen NL 71 B3
Omodhos CY 181 B1
Omoljica SRB 127 C2
On B 79 B5
Oña E 143 B3
Onano I 168 A1
Oñati E 143 A4
Onda E 159 B3
Ondara E 159 C4
Ondarroa E 143 A4
Onesse-et-Laharie F 128 B1
Oneşti RO 17 B7
Onhaye B 79 B4
Onich GB 34 B2
Onil E 159 C3
Onis E 142 A2
Önnestad S 61 C4
Onsala S 60 B2
Ontinyent E 159 C3
Ontur E 158 C2

Onzain F 103 B3
Onzonilla E 142 B1
Oost-Vlieland NL 70 A2
Oostburg NL 79 A3
Oostende B 78 A2
Ooster-hout NL 79 A4
Oosterend NL 70 A2
Oosterwolde NL 71 B3
Oosterzele B 79 B3
Oosthuizen NL 70 B2
Oostkamp B 78 A3
Oostmalle B 79 A4
Oostvoorne NL 79 A4
Ootmarsum NL 71 B3
Opalenica PL 75 B5
Opařany CZ 96 B2
Opatija HR 123 B3
Opatów, *Śląskie* PL 86 B2
Opatów, *Świętokrzyskie* PL 87 B5
Opatów, *Wielkopolskie* PL 86 A2
Opatówek PL 86 A2
Opatowiec PL 87 B4
Opava CZ 98 B1
Opeinde NL 70 A3
Oper Thalkirchdorf D 107 B5
Opglabbeerk B 80 A1
Opicina I 122 B2
Oplotnica SLO 123 A4
Opmeer NL 70 B1
Opochka RUS 9 D6
Opočno CZ 85 B4
Opoczno PL 87 A4
Opole PL 86 B1
Oporów PL 77 B4
Opovo SRB 127 B2
Oppach D 84 A2
Oppdal N 198 C6
Oppeby, *Östergötland* S 56 B1
Oppeby, *Södermanland* S 56 B2
Oppedal N 46 A2
Oppegård N 54 A1
Oppenau D 93 C4
Oppenberg A 110 B1
Oppenheim D 93 B4
Óppido Lucano I 172 B1
Óppido Mamertina I 175 C1
Opponitz A 110 B1
Oppstad N 48 B3
Oprtalj HR 122 B2
Opsaheden S 49 B5
Ópusztaszer H 113 C4
Opuzen HR 138 B3
Ora CY 181 B2
Ora I 121 A4
Orada P 155 C3
Oradea RO 16 B4
Oradour-sur-Glane F 115 C5
Oradour-sur-Vayres F 115 C4
Oragonja SLO 122 B2
Orah BIH 139 C4
Orahova BIH 138 A3
Orahovica HR 125 B3
Orahovo BIH 124 B3
Oraison F 132 B1
Orajärvi FIN 196 C7
Orange F 131 A3
Orani I 178 B3
Oranienbaum D 83 A4
Oranienburg D 74 B2
Oranmore IRL 28 A3
Orašac SRB 127 C2
Orašje BIH 125 B4
Oravská Lesná SK 99 B3
Oravská Polhora SK 99 B3
Oravské Veselé SK 99 B3
Oravsky-Podzámok SK 99 B3
Orba E 159 C3
Orbacém P 148 A1
Ørbæk DK 59 C3
Orbais F 91 C3
Orbassano I 119 B4
Orbe CH 105 C5
Orbec F 89 A4
Orbetello I 168 A1
Orbetello Scalo I 168 A1
Orbigny F 103 B3
Ørby DK 59 B3
Örbyhus S 51 B4
Orce E 164 B2
Orcera E 164 A2
Orchamps-Vennes F 105 B5
Orches F 102 C2
Orchete E 159 C3
Orchies F 78 B3
Orchowo PL 76 B3
Orcières F 118 C3
Ordes E 140 A2
Ordhead GB 33 D4
Ordino AND 146 B2
Ordizia E 144 A1
Orduña E 143 B4
Ore S 50 A2
Orea E 152 B2
Orebić HR 138 C3
Örebro S 56 A1
Öregcsertö H 112 C3
Öregrund S 51 B5
Orehoved DK 65 B4
Orellana E 156 A2
Orellana de la Sierra E 156 A2
Ören TR 188 B2
Örencik TR 187 C4
Orestiada GR 186 A1
Organyà E 147 B2
Orgaz E 157 A4
Orgelet F 105 C4
Ørgenvika N 48 B1
Orgères-en-Beauce F 103 A3
Orgibet F 145 B4
Orgnac-l'Aven F 131 A3
Orgon F 131 B4
Orgósolo I 178 B3
Orhaneli TR 186 C3
Orhangazi TR 187 B4
Orhei MD 17 B8
Orhomenos GR 184 A3
Oria E 164 B2
Ória I 173 B3
Origny-Ste Benoite F 91 B3
Orihuela E 165 A4
Orihuela del Tremedal E 152 B2
Orikum AL 182 C1
Oriola P 154 C3
Oriolo I 174 A2
Oriovac HR 125 B3
Orissaare EST 8 C3
Oristano I 179 C2
Öriszentpéter H 111 C3
Ørje N 54 A2
Orjiva E 163 B4
Orkanger N 198 B6
Örkelljunga S 61 C3
Örkény H 112 B3
Orlamünde D 82 B3
Orléans F 103 B3
Orlová CZ 98 B2
Orlovat SRB 126 B2
Ormea I 133 A3
Ormelet N 54 A1
Ormemyr N 53 A5
Ormilia GR 183 C5
Ormos GR 185 B5
Ormož SLO 124 A2
Ormskirk GB 38 A4
Ornans F 105 B5
Ornäs S 50 B2
Ørnes N 195 D4
Orneta PL 69 A5
Ørnhøj DK 59 B1
Ornö S 57 A4
Örnsköldsvik S 200 C4
Orolik HR 125 B4
Orom SRB 126 B1
Oron-la-Ville CH 106 C1
Oronsko PL 87 A4
Oropa I 119 B4
Oropesa, *Castellón de la Plana* E 153 B4
Oropesa, *Toledo* E 150 C2
Orosei I 178 B3
Orosháza H 113 C4
Oroslavje HR 124 B1
Oroszlány H 112 B2
Oroszlo H 125 A4
Orotelli I 178 B3
Orozko E 143 A4
Orphir GB 33 C3
Orpington GB 45 B4
Orreaga-Roncesvalles E 144 A2
Orrefors S 62 B3
Orrviken S 199 B11
Orsa S 50 A1
Orsara di Púglia I 171 B3
Orsay F 90 C2
Orscholz D 92 B2
Orsennes F 103 C3
Orserum S 55 B5
Orsha BY 13 A9
Orsières CH 119 A4
Örsjö S 63 B3
Ørslev DK 65 A4
Örslösa S 55 B3
Orsogna I 169 A4
Orsomarso I 174 B1
Orşova RO 16 C5
Ørsta N 198 C3
Ørsted DK 58 B3
Örsundsbro S 56 A3
Orta Nova I 171 B3
Ortaca TR 188 C3
Ortakent TR 188 B2
Ortaklar TR 188 B2
Ortaköy TR 23 B8
Orte I 168 A2
Ortenburg D 96 C1
Orth A 111 A3
Orthez F 128 C2
Ortigueira E 140 A3
Ortilla E 145 B3
Ortisei I 108 C2
Orţişoara RO 126 B3
Ortnevik N 46 A3
Orton GB 37 B4
Ortona I 169 A4
Ortrand D 84 A1
Orubica HR 124 B3
Ørum DK 58 B2
Orune I 178 B3
Orusco E 151 B4
Orvalho P 155 A3
Orvault F 101 B4
Ørvella N 53 A5
Orvieto I 168 A2
Orvínio I 169 A2
Oryakhovo BG 17 D5
Orzesze PL 86 B2
Orzinuovi I 120 B2
Orzivécchi I 120 B2
Orzyny PL 77 A6
Os, *Hedmark* N 199 C8
Os, *Hedmark* N 48 B3
Os Peares E 140 B3
Osann-Monzelo D 92 B2
Osbruk S 62 A2
Øsby DK 59 C2
Osby S 61 C3
Oščadnica SK 98 B2
Oschatz D 83 A5
Oschersleben D 73 B4
Óschiri I 178 B3
Osciłowo PL 77 B5
Osdorf D 64 B3
Osečina SRB 127 C1
Osečná CZ 84 B2
Oseja de Sajambre E 142 A1
Osek CZ 84 B1
Osen N 199 A7
Osera de Ebro E 153 A3
Osidda I 178 B3
Osie PL 69 B3
Osieczna, *Pomorskie* PL 68 B3
Osieczna, *Wielkopolskie* PL 75 C5
Osieczno PL 75 A4
Osiek, *Kujawsko-Pomorskie* PL 76 B3
Osiek, *Kujawsko-Pomorskie* PL 77 A4
Osiek, *Pomorskie* PL 69 B3
Osiek, *Świętokrzyskie* PL 87 B5
Osiek nad Notecią PL 76 A2
Osielsko PL 76 A3
Osijek HR 125 B4
Osilnica SLO 123 B3
Ósilo I 178 B2
Ósimo I 136 B2
Osinja BIH 125 C3
Osintorf BY 13 A9
Osipaonica SRB 127 C3
Osjaków PL 86 A2
Oskamull GB 34 B1
Oskarshamn S 62 A4
Oskarström S 60 C2
Oslany SK 98 C2
Oslavany CZ 97 B4
Ošlje HR 139 C3
Oslo N 48 C2
Øsløs DK 58 A1
Osmancık TR 23 A8
Osmaneli TR 187 B4
Ösmo S 57 B3
Osmolin PL 77 B4
Osnabrück D 71 B5
Ośno Lubuskie PL 75 B3
Osoblaha CZ 85 B5
Osor HR 123 C3
Osorno E 142 B2
Øsoyra N 46 A2
Osøyro N 46 B2
Óspakseyri IS 190 B4
Ospedaletti I 133 B3
Ospitaletto I 120 B3
Oss NL 80 A1
Ossa de Montiel E 158 C1
Ossi I 178 B2
Ossjøen N 47 B5
Ossun F 145 A3
Ostanå S 61 C4
Ostanvik S 50 A2
Ostashkov RUS 9 D8
Östavall S 200 D1
Ostbevern D 71 B4
Østborg N 199 A10
Østby N 49 A4
Osted DK 61 D1
Ostenfeld D 64 B2
Oster UA 13 C9
Øster Assels DK 58 B1
Øster Hornum DK 58 B2
Øster Hurup DK 58 B3
Øster Jølby DK 58 B1
Øster-marie DK 67 A4
Øster Tørslev DK 58 B3
Øster Vrå DK 58 A3
Osterburg D 73 B4
Osterburken D 94 B1
Österbybruk S 51 B4
Østerbyhavn DK 58 A4
Österbymo S 62 A3
Ostercappeln D 71 B5
Österfärnebo S 51 B3
Osterfeld D 83 A3
Österforse S 200 C3
Osterhever D 64 B1
Osterhofen D 95 C5
Osterholz-Scharmbeck D 72 A1
Østerild DK 58 A1
Österlövsta S 51 B4
Ostermiething A 109 A3
Osterode am Harz D 82 A2
Ostersiel D 64 B1
Östersund S 199 B11
Östervåla S 51 B4
Östervallskog S 54 A2
Osterwieck D 73 C3
Osterzell D 108 B1
Ostffyasszonyfa H 111 B4
Östfora S 51 C4
Östhammar S 51 B5
Ostheim F 106 A2
Ostheim vor der Rhön D 82 B2
Osthofen D 93 B4
Ostiano I 120 B3
Ostíglia I 121 B4
Ostiz E 144 B2
Östmark S 49 B4
Östnor S 50 A1
Ostojićevo SRB 126 B2
Ostra I 136 B2
Östra Amtervik S 55 A4
Östra Husby S 56 B2
Östra Ljungby S 61 C3
Östra Ryd S 56 B2
Ostraby S 61 D3
Ostrach D 107 B4
Ostrau D 83 A5
Ostrava CZ 98 B2
Østre Halsen N 53 A6
Ostrhauderfehn D 71 A4
Ostritz D 84 A2
Ostróda PL 69 B4
Ostroh UA 13 C7
Ostrołęka PL 12 B4
Ostropole PL 68 B1
Ostroróg PL 75 B5
Ostrošovac BIH 124 C1
Ostrov CZ 83 B4
Ostrov RUS 8 D6
Ostrov nad Oslavou CZ 97 B3
Ostrów Mazowiecka PL 12 B4
Ostrów Wielkopolski PL 86 A1
Ostrówek PL 86 A2
Ostrowiec PL 68 A1
Ostrowiec-Świętokrzyski PL 87 B5
Ostrowite PL 77 A4
Ostrowo PL 76 B3
Ostrožac BIH 139 B3
Ostrzeszów PL 86 A1
Ostseebad Kühlungsborn D 65 B4
Ostuni I 173 B3
Osuna E 162 A2
Osvětimany CZ 98 B1
Oswestry GB 38 B3
Oświęcim PL 86 B3
Osztopán H 111 C4
Oteiza E 144 B2
Otelec RO 126 B2
Oteo E 143 A3
Oterbekk N 54 A1
Otero de Herreros E 151 B3
Otero de O Bodas E 141 C4
Othem S 57 C4
Otley GB 40 B2
Otmuchów PL 85 B5
Otočac HR 123 C4
Otok, *Splitsko-Dalmatinska* HR 138 B2
Otok, *Vukovarsko-Srijemska* HR 125 B4
Otoka BIH 124 C2
Otranto I 173 B4
Otrić HR 138 A2
Otrícoli I 168 A2
Otrokovice CZ 98 B1
Otta N 198 D6
Ottana I 178 B3
Ottaviano I 170 C2
Ottenby S 63 B4
Ottendorf-Okrilla D 84 A1
Ottenhöfen D 93 C4
Ottenschlag A 97 C3
Ottensheim A 96 C2
Otter Ferry GB 34 B2
Otterbach D 93 B3
Otterbäcken S 55 B5
Otterberg D 93 B3
Otterburn GB 37 A4
Otterndorf D 64 C1
Ottersburg D 72 A2
Ottersweier D 93 C4
Otterup DK 59 C3
Ottery St. Mary GB 43 B3
Ottignies B 79 B4
Ottmarsheim F 106 B2
Ottobeuren D 107 B5
Öttömös H 126 A1
Ottone I 120 C2
Ottsjö S 199 B10
Ottweiler D 92 B3
Otveşti RO 126 B3
Ötvöskónyi H 124 A3
Otwock PL 12 B4
Ouanne F 104 B2
Ouarville F 90 C1
Oucques F 103 B3
Oud-Beijerland NL 79 A4
Oud Gastel NL 79 A4
Ouddorp NL 79 A3
Oude-Pekela NL 71 A4
Oude-Tonge NL 79 A4
Oudemirdum NL 70 B2
Oudenaarde B 79 B3
Oudenbosch NL 79 A4
Oudenburg B 78 A3
Oudewater NL 70 B1
Oudon F 101 B4
Oughterard IRL 28 A2
Ouguela P 155 B3
Ouistreham F 89 A3
Oulainen FIN 3 D9
Oulchy-le-Château F 91 B3
Oullins F 117 B4
Oulmes F 114 B3
Oulton GB 41 C5
Oulton Broad GB 41 C5
Oulu FIN 3 D9
Oulx I 119 B3
Oundle GB 40 C3
Ouranopoli GR 183 C6
Ourense E 140 B3
Ourique P 160 B1
Ourol E 140 A3
Ouroux-en-Morvan F 104 B2
Ousdale GB 32 C3
Oust F 146 B2
Outakoski FIN 193 C10
Outeiro P 148 B1
Outeiro de Rei E 140 A3
Outes E 140 B2
Outokumpu FIN 9 A6
Outreau F 78 B1
Outwell GB 41 C4
Ouzouer-le-Marché F 103 B3
Ouzouer-sur-Loire F 103 B4
Ovada I 133 A4
Ovar P 148 B1
Ove DK 58 B2
Ovelgönne D 72 A1
Over-jerstal DK 59 C2
Overath D 80 B3
Overbister GB 33 B4
Øverbygd N 192 D3
Overdinkel NL 71 B4
Överenhörna S 56 A3
Overhalla N 199 A8
Overijse B 79 B4
Overlade DK 58 B2
Överlida S 60 B2
Överö FIN 51 B7
Overpelt B 79 A5
Overton GB 38 B4
Övertorneå S 196 C6
Överum S 62 A4
Ovidiopol UA 17 B9
Oviedo E 141 A5
Oviglio I 119 C5
Ovíndoli I 169 A3
Ovodda I 178 B3
Øvre Årdal N 47 A4
Øvre Rendal N 199 D8
Øvre Sirdal N 52 B2
Övre Soppero S 196 A4
Övre Ullerud S 55 A4
Øvrebygd N 52 B2
Ovruch UA 13 C8
Ovtrup DK 59 C1
Owińska PL 76 B1
Oxaback S 60 B2
Oxberg S 49 A6
Oxelösund S 56 B3
Oxenholme GB 37 B4
Oxford GB 44 B2
Oxie S 61 D3
Oxilithos GR 185 A5
Oxted GB 45 B4
Oyaca TR 187 C7
Øye N 47 A5
Øyenkilen N 54 A1
Øyer N 48 A2
Øyeren N 49 B4
Oyfiell N 53 A4
Øygärdslia N 53 B4
Oykel Bridge GB 32 D2
Øymark N 54 A2
Oyonnax F 118 A2
Øyslebø N 52 B3
Øystese N 46 B3
Oyten D 72 A2
Øyuvsbu N 52 A3
Ozaeta E 143 B4
Ozalj HR 123 B4
Ożarów PL 87 B5
Ożarów Maz PL 77 B5
Ožbalt SLO 110 C2
Ózd H 113 A4
Ožd'any SK 99 C3
Ozieri I 178 B3
Ozimek PL 86 B2
Ozimica BIH 139 A4
Ozora H 112 C2
Ozorków PL 77 C4
Ozzano Monferrato I 119 B5

P

Paakkola FIN 196 D7
Paal B 79 A5
Pabianice PL 86 A3
Pacanów PL 87 B5
Paceco I 176 B1
Pachino I 177 C4
Pačir SRB 126 B1
Pack A 110 B2
Paços de Ferreira P 148 A1
Pacov CZ 96 B3
Pacsa H 111 C4
Pacy-sur-Eure F 89 A5
Paczków PL 85 B5
Padany RUS 3 E13
Padborg DK 64 B2
Padej SRB 126 B2
Padene HR 138 A2
Paderborn D 81 A4
Paderne P 160 B1
Padiham GB 40 B1
Padina SRB 126 B2
Padinska Skela SRB 127 C2
Padornelo P 148 A1
Pádova I 121 B4
Padragkút H 111 B4
Padria I 178 B2
Padrón E 140 B2
Padru I 178 B3
Padstow GB 42 B2
Padul E 163 A4
Padula I 172 B1
Paduli I 170 B2
Paesana I 119 C4
Paese I 121 B5
Pag HR 137 A4
Pagani I 170 C2
Pagánica I 169 A3
Pagánico I 135 C4
Paglieta I 169 A4
Pagny-sur-Moselle F 92 C2
Páhi H 112 C3
Pahkakumpu FIN 197 C11
Pahl D 108 B2
Paide EST 8 C4
Paignton GB 43 B3
Pailhès F 146 A2
Paimboeuf F 101 B3
Paimpol F 100 A2
Paimpont F 101 A3
Painswick GB 43 A4
Painten D 95 C3
Paisley GB 34 C3
Pajala S 196 B6
Pajares E 141 A5
Pajares de los Oteros E 142 B1
Pajęczno PL 86 A2
Páka H 111 C3
Pakość PL 76 B3
Pakosławice PL 85 B5
Pakoštane HR 137 B4
Pakrac HR 124 B3
Paks H 112 C2
Palacios de la Sierra E 143 C3
Palaciòs de la Valduerna E 141 B5
Palacios de Sanabria E 141 B4
Palacios del Sil E 141 B4
Palaciosrubios E 150 A2
Palafrugell E 147 C4
Palagiano I 173 B3
Palagonía I 177 B3
Paláia I 135 B3
Palaiokastritsa GR 182 D1
Palaiseau F 90 C2
Palamas GR 182 D4
Palamós E 147 C4
Påläng S 196 D5
Palanga LT 8 E2
Palanzano I 134 A3
Palárikovo SK 112 A2
Palas de Rei E 140 B3
Palata I 170 B2
Palau I 178 A3
Palavas-les-Flots F 131 B2
Palazuelos de la Sierra E 143 B3
Palazzo Adriano I 176 B2
Palazzo del Pero I 135 B4
Palazzo San Gervásio I 172 B1
Palazzolo Acréide I 177 B3
Palazzolo sull Oglio I 120 B2
Palazzuolo sul Senio I 135 A4
Paldiski EST 8 C4
Pale BIH 139 B4
Palekastro GR 185 D7
Palena I 169 B4
Palencia E 142 B2
Palenciana E 163 A3
Paleochora GR 185 D4
Paleometokho CY 181 A2
Palermo I 176 A2
Paleros GR 182 E2
Palestrina I 169 B2
Pálfa H 112 C2
Palfau A 110 B1

Poros, *Kefalonia* GR 184 A1
Poroszló H 113 B4
Porozina HR 123 B3
Porquerolles F 132 C2
Porrentruy CH 106 B2
Porreres E 167 B3
Porretta Terme I 135 A3
Porsgrunn N 53 A5
Porspoder F 100 A1
Port-a-Binson F 91 B3
Port Askaig GB 34 C1
Port Bannatyne GB 34 C2
Port-Barcarès F 146 B4
Port-Camargue F 131 B3
Port Charlotte GB 34 C1
Port d'Andratx E 166 B2
Port-de-Bouc F 131 B3
Port-de-Lanne F 128 C1
Port de Pollença E 167 B3
Port de Sóller E 166 B2
Port-des-Barques F 114 C2
Port Ellen GB 34 C1
Port-en-Bessin F 88 A3
Port Erin GB 36 B2
Port Eynon GB 39 C2
Port Glasgow GB 34 C3
Port Henderson GB 31 B3
Port Isaac GB 42 B2
Port-Joinville F 114 B1
Port-la-Nouvelle F 130 B2
Port Logan GB 36 B2
Port Louis F 100 B2
Port Manech F 100 B2
Port Nan Giuran GB 31 A2
Port-Navalo F 100 B3
Port Nis GB 31 A2
Port-St.-Louis-du-Rhône F 131 B3
Port St. Mary GB 36 B2
Port-Ste. Marie F 129 B3
Port-sur-Saône F 105 B5
Port Talbot GB 39 C3
Port-Vendres F 146 B4
Port William GB 36 B2
Portacloy IRL 26 B1
Portadown GB 27 B4
Portaferry GB 27 B5
Portaje E 155 B4
Portalegre P 155 B3
Portarlington IRL 30 A1
Portavadie GB 34 C2
Portavogie GB 27 B5
Portbail F 88 A2
Portbou E 146 B4
Portegrandi I 122 B1
Portel P 155 C3
Portela P 148 B1
Portelo P 141 C4
Portemouro E 140 B2
Port'Ercole I 168 A1
Portes-lès-Valence F 117 C4
Portets F 128 B2
Portezuelo E 155 B4
Portglenone GB 27 B4
Porthcawl GB 39 C3
Porthleven GB 42 B1
Porthmadog GB 38 B2
Porticcio F 180 B1
Portici I 170 C2
Portico di Romagna I 135 A4
Portilla de la Reina E 142 A2
Portillo E 150 A3
Portimao P 160 B1
Portinatx E 166 B1
Portinho da Arrabida P 154 C1
Portishead GB 43 A4
Portknockie GB 33 D4
Portlaoise IRL 30 A1
Portlethen GB 33 D4
Portmagne IRL 29 C1
Portmahomack GB 32 D3
Portman E 165 B4
Portnacroish GB 34 B2
Portnahaven GB 34 C1
Porto F 180 A1
Porto P 148 A1
Porto-Alto P 154 C2
Porto Azzurro I 134 C3
Porto Cerésio I 120 B1
Porto Cervo I 178 A3
Porto Cesáreo I 173 B3
Porto Colom E 167 B3
Porto Covo P 160 B1
Porto Cristo E 167 B3
Porto d'Ascoli I 136 C2
Porto de Lagos P 160 B1
Porto de Mos P 154 B2
Porto de Rei P 154 C2
Porto do Son E 140 B2
Porto Empédocle I 176 B2
Porto Garibaldi I 122 C1
Porto Petro E 167 B3
Porto Pino I 179 D2
Porto Potenza Picena I 136 B2
Porto Recanati I 136 B2
Porto San Giórgio I 136 B2
Porto Sant'Elpídio I 136 B2
Porto Santo Stéfano I 168 A1
Porto Tolle I 122 C1
Porto Tórres I 178 B2
Porto-Vecchio F 180 B2
Portocannone I 170 B3
Portoferráio I 134 C3
Portofino I 134 A2
Portogruaro I 122 B1
Portokhelion GR 184 B4
Portomaggiore I 121 C4
Portomarin E 140 B3
Porton GB 44 B2
Portonovo E 140 B2
Portopalo di Capo Passero I 177 C4
Portør N 53 B5
Portoscuso I 179 C2
Portovénere I 134 A2
Portpatrick GB 36 B1
Portreath GB 42 B1
Portree GB 31 B2
Portroe IRL 28 B3
Portrush GB 27 A4
Portsall F 100 A1
Portsmouth GB 44 C2
Portsoy GB 33 D4
Portstewart GB 27 A4
Portugalete E 143 A4
Portumna IRL 28 A3
Porvoo FIN 8 B4
Porzuna E 157 A3
Posada, *Oviedo* E 141 A5
Posada, *Oviedo* E 142 A2
Posada I 178 B3
Posada de Valdeón E 142 A2
Posadas E 162 A2
Poschiavo CH 120 A3
Posedarje HR 137 A4
Posio FIN 197 C11
Positano I 170 C2
Possagno I 121 B4
Posseck D 83 B4
Possesse F 91 C4
Pössneck D 83 B3
Posta I 169 A3
Posta Piana I 172 A1
Postal I 108 C2
Postbauer-Heng D 95 B3
Posterholt NL 80 A2
Postioma I 121 B5
Postira HR 138 B2
Postojna SLO 123 B3
Postoloprty CZ 84 B1
Postomino PL 68 A1
Posušje BIH 138 B3
Potamos, *Attiki* GR 184 D4
Potamós, *Attiki* GR 184 C3
Potegowo PL 68 A2
Potenza I 172 B1
Potenza Picena I 136 B2
Potes E 142 A2
Potigny F 89 B3
Potočari BIH 127 C1
Potoci BIH 138 A2
Potoci BIH 139 B3
Potony H 125 B3
Potries E 159 C3
Potsdam D 74 B2
Potštát CZ 98 B1
Pottenbrunn A 110 A2
Pottendorf A 111 B3
Pottenstein A 111 B3
Pottenstein D 95 B3
Potters Bar GB 44 B3
Pöttmes D 94 C3
Pöttsching A 111 B3
Potworów PL 87 A4
Pouancé F 101 B4
Pougues-les-Eaux F 104 B2
Pouilly-en-Auxois F 104 B3
Pouilly-sous Charlieu F 117 A4
Pouilly-sur-Loire F 104 B1
Poujol-sur-Orb F 130 B2
Poullaouen F 100 A2
Poulton-le-Fylde GB 38 A4
Poundstock GB 42 B2
Pourcy F 91 B3
Pourrain F 104 B2
Poussu FIN 197 D12
Pouy-de-Touges F 146 A2
Pouyastruc F 145 A4
Pouzauges F 114 B3
Pova de Santa Iria P 154 C1
Považská Bystrica SK 98 B2
Povedilla E 158 C1
Povenets RUS 9 A9
Povlja HR 138 B2
Povljana HR 137 A4
Póvoa, *Beja* P 161 A2
Póvoa, *Santarém* P 154 B2
Póvoa de Lanhosa P 148 A1
Póvoa de Varzim P 148 A1
Póvoa e Meadas P 155 B3
Powidz PL 76 B2
Poyales del Hoyo E 150 B2
Poynton GB 40 B1
Poyntz Pass GB 27 B4
Poysdorf A 97 C4
Poza de la Sal E 143 B3
Pozaldez E 150 A3
Pozán de Vero E 145 B4
Pozanti TR 23 C8
Požarevac SRB 127 C3
Požega HR 125 B3
Požega SRB 127 D2
Poznań PL 76 B1
Pozo Alcón E 164 B2
Pozo Cañada E 158 C2
Pozo de Guadalajara E 151 B4
Pozo de la Serna E 157 B4
Pozoantiguo E 150 A2
Pozoblanco E 156 B3
Pozohondo E 158 C2
Pozondón E 152 B2
Poźrzadło Wielkie PL 75 A4
Pozuel del Campo E 152 B2
Pozuelo de Alarcón E 151 B4
Pozuelo de Calatrava E 157 B4
Pozuelo de Zarzón E 149 B3
Pozuelo del Páramo E 142 B1
Pozzallo I 177 C3
Pozzo San Nicola I 178 B2
Pozzomaggiore I 178 B2
Pozzuoli I 170 C2
Pozzuolo I 135 B4
Prabuty PL 69 B4
Prača BIH 139 B4
Prachatice CZ 96 B1
Prada E 141 B3
Pradelle F 118 C2
Pradelles F 117 C3
Prades E 147 C1
Prades F 146 B3
Pradła PL 86 B3
Prado E 142 A1
Prado P 148 A1
Prado del Rey E 162 B2
Pradoluengo E 143 B3
Præstø DK 65 A5
Pragelato I 119 B3
Pragersko SLO 123 A4
Prägraten A 109 B3
Prague = Praha CZ 84 B2
Praha = Prague CZ 84 B2
Prahecq F 115 B3
Praia P 154 B1
Práia a Mare I 174 B1
Praia da Rocha P 160 B1
Praia da Viera P 154 B2
Praia de Mira P 148 B1
Praiano I 170 C2
Pralboino I 120 B3
Pralognan-la-Vanoise F 118 B3
Pramanda GR 182 D3
Pranjani SRB 127 C2
Prapatnica HR 138 B2
Praszka PL 86 A2
Prat F 146 A1
Prat de Compte E 153 B4
Prata I 135 B3
Prata di Pordenone I 122 B1
Pratau D 83 A4
Pratdip E 147 C1
Pratella I 170 B2
Prato I 135 B4
Prátola Peligna I 169 A3
Pratola Serra I 170 C2
Prats-de-Mollo-la-Preste F 146 B3
Prauthoy F 105 B4
Pravia E 141 A4
Praxmar A 108 B2
Prayssac F 129 B4
Prazzo I 132 A3
Pré-en-Pail F 89 B3
Prebold SLO 123 A4
Préchac F 128 B2
Précy-sur-Thil F 104 B3
Predáppio I 135 A4
Predazzo I 121 A4
Předin CZ 97 B3
Preding A 110 C2
Predjame SLO 123 B3
Predlitz A 109 B4
Predmeja SLO 122 B2
Predoi I 108 B3
Prees GB 38 B4
Preetz D 64 B3
Préfailles F 101 B3
Pregarten A 96 C2
Pregrada HR 123 A4
Preignan F 129 C3
Preiļi LV 8 D5
Preitenegg A 110 C1
Prekaja BIH 138 A2
Preko HR 137 A4
Preljina SRB 127 D2
Prelog HR 124 A2
Prelošćica HR 124 B2
Přelouč CZ 97 A3
Prem SLO 123 B3
Premantura HR 122 C2
Prémery F 104 B2
Prémia I 119 A5
Premià de Mar E 147 C3
Premnitz D 73 B5
Prémont F 91 A3
Prenzlau D 74 A2
Preodac BIH 138 A2
Přerov CZ 98 B1
Prerow D 66 B1
Presencio E 143 B3
Presicce I 173 C4
Presly F 103 B4
Prešov SK 12 D4
Pressac F 115 B4
Pressath D 95 B3
Pressbaum A 111 A3
Prestatyn GB 38 A3
Prestebakke N 54 B2
Presteigne GB 39 B3
Přeštice CZ 96 B1
Preston, *Lancashire* GB 38 A4
Preston, *Scottish Borders* GB 35 C5
Prestonpans GB 35 C5
Prestwick GB 36 A2
Prettin D 83 A4
Preturo I 169 A3
Pretzchendorf D 83 B5
Pretzier D 73 B4
Pretzsch D 83 A4
Preuilly-sur-Claise F 115 B4
Prevalje SLO 110 C1
Prevenchères F 131 A2
Préveranges F 116 A2
Preveza GR 182 E2
Prevršac HR 124 B2
Prezid HR 123 B3
Priaranza del Bierzo E 141 B4
Priay F 118 A2
Pribeta SK 112 B2
Priboj BIH 125 C4
Priboj SRB 16 D3
Přibor CZ 98 B2
Příbram CZ 96 B2
Pribylina SK 99 B3
Přibyslav CZ 97 B3
Pričević SRB 127 C1
Pridjel BIH 125 C4
Priego E 152 B1
Priego de Córdoba E 163 A3
Priekule LV 8 D2
Prien D 109 B3
Prienai LT 13 A5
Prievidza SK 98 C2
Prigradica HR 138 C2
Prigrevica SRB 125 B5
Prijeboj HR 123 C4
Prijedor BIH 124 C2
Prijepolje SRB 16 D3
Prilep MK 182 B3
Priluka BIH 138 B2
Primda CZ 95 B4
Primel-Trégastel F 100 A2
Primišje HR 123 B4
Primorsk, *Kaliningrad* RUS 69 A5
Primorsk, *Severo-Zapadnyy* RUS 9 B6
Primošten HR 138 B1
Primstal D 92 B2
Princes Risborough GB 44 B3
Princetown GB 42 B2
Principina a Mare I 135 C4
Priolo Gargallo I 177 B4
Prioro E 142 B2
Priozersk RUS 9 B7
Prirechnyy RUS 193 C14
Prisoje BIH 138 B3
Priština SRB 16 D4
Pritzerbe D 73 B5
Pritzier D 73 A4
Pritzwalk D 73 A5
Privas F 117 C4
Priverno I 169 B3
Privlaka, *Vukovarsko-Srijemska* HR 125 B4
Privlaka, *Zadarska* HR 137 A4
Prizna HR 123 C3
Prizren SRB 16 D4
Prizzi I 176 B2
Prnjavor BIH 125 C3
Prnjavor HR 124 B1
Prnjavor SRB 127 C1
Proaza E 141 A4
Probstzella D 82 B3
Probus GB 42 B2
Prócchio I 134 C3
Prochowice PL 85 A4
Prócida I 170 C2
Prodhromos CY 181 B1
Prodo I 135 C5
Proença-a-Nova P 154 B3
Proença-a-Velha P 155 A3
Profondeville B 79 B4
Prokuplje SRB 16 D4
Propriano F 180 B1
Prosec CZ 97 B4
Prösen D 83 A5
Prosenjakovci SLO 111 C3
Prosotsani GR 183 B5
Prostějov CZ 98 B1
Prószków PL 86 B1
Proszowice PL 87 B4
Protić BIH 138 A2
Protivanov CZ 97 B4
Protivín CZ 96 B2
Prötzel D 74 B2
Provins F 90 C3
Prozor BIH 139 B3
Prrenjas AL 182 B2
Prudhoe GB 37 B5
Prudnik PL 85 B5
Pruggern A 109 B4
Prügy H 113 A5
Prüm D 80 B2
Pruna E 162 B2
Prunelli-di-Fiumorbo F 180 A2
Prunetta I 135 A3
Pruniers F 103 C4
Prusice PL 85 A4
Pruské SK 98 B2
Pruszce PL 76 A3
Pruszcz Gdański PL 69 A3
Pruszków PL 77 B5
Prutz A 108 B1
Prüzen D 65 C5
Pruzhany BY 13 B6
Pružina SK 98 B2
Pryzlęg PL 75 B4
Przasnysz PL 77 A5
Przechlewo PL 68 B2
Przecław PL 87 B5
Przedbórz PL 87 A3
Przedecz PL 76 B3
Przejęslav PL 84 A3
Przemków PL 85 A3
Przemocze PL 75 A3
Przemyśl PL 12 D5
Przerąb PL 87 A3
Przewodnik PL 69 B3
Przewodowo Parcele PL 77 B5
Przewóz PL 84 A2
Przezmark PL 69 B4
Przodkowo PL 68 A3
Przybiernów PL 75 A3
Przyborowice PL 77 B5
Przybyszew PL 87 A4
Przybyszów PL 86 A3
Przylęg PL 75 B4
Przysucha PL 87 A4
Przytóczna PL 75 B4
Przytyk PL 87 A4
Przywidz PL 68 A3
Psachna GR 185 A4
Psara GR 185 A6
Psary PL 76 C3
Pskov RUS 8 D6
Pszczew PL 75 B4
Pszczółki PL 69 A3
Pszczyna PL 98 B2
Pszów PL 86 B2
Pteleos GR 182 D4
Ptolemaida GR 182 C3
Ptuj SLO 124 A1
Ptusza PL 68 B1
Puch A 109 B4
Puchberg am Schneeberg A 110 B2
Puchevillers F 90 A2
Puchheim D 108 A2
Púchov SK 98 B2
Pučišća HR 138 B2
Puck PL 69 A3
Puçol E 159 B3
Puconci SLO 111 C3
Pudasjärvi FIN 197 D10
Puderbach D 81 B3
Pudozh RUS 9 B10
Puebla de Albortón E 153 A3
Puebla de Alcocer E 156 B2
Puebla de Beleña E 151 B4
Puebla de Don Fadrique E 164 B2
Puebla de Don Rodrigo E 156 A3
Puebla de Guzmán E 161 B2
Puebla de la Calzada E 155 C4
Puebla de la Reina E 156 B1
Puebla de Lillo E 142 A1
Puebla de Obando E 155 B4
Puebla de Sanabria E 141 B4
Puebla de Sancho Pérez E 155 C4
Puebla del Maestre E 161 A3
Puebla del Principe E 158 C1
Puente Almuhey E 142 B2
Puente de Domingo Flórez E 141 B4
Puente de Génave E 164 A2
Puente de Montañana E 145 B4
Puente del Congosto E 150 B2
Puente Duero E 150 A3
Puente-Genil E 162 A3
Puente la Reina E 144 B2
Puente la Reina de Jaca E 144 B3
Puente Mayorga E 162 B2
Puente Viesgo E 143 A3
Puentelarra E 143 B3
Puertas, *Asturias* E 142 A2
Puertas, *Salamanca* E 149 A3
Puerto de Mazarrón E 165 B3
Puerto de San Vicente E 156 A2
Puerto de Santa Cruz E 156 A2
Puerto-Lápice E 157 A4
Puerto Lumbreras E 164 B3
Puerto Moral E 161 B3
Puerto Real E 162 B1
Puerto Rey E 156 A2
Puerto Seguro E 149 B3
Puerto Serrano E 162 B2
Puertollano E 157 B3
Puget-Sur-Argens F 132 B2
Puget-Théniers F 132 B2
Puget-ville F 132 B2
Pugnochiuso I 171 B4
Puig Reig E 147 C2
Puigcerdà E 146 B2
Puigpunyent E 166 B2
Puillon F 128 C2
Puimichel F 132 B2
Puimoisson F 132 B2
Puiseaux F 103 A4
Puisieux F 90 A2
Puisserguier F 130 B2
Puivert F 146 B3
Pujols F 128 B2
Pukanec SK 98 C2
Pukavik S 63 B2
Pukë AL 182 A1
Pula HR 122 C2
Pula I 179 C2
Puławy PL 12 C4
Pulborough GB 44 C3
Pulfero I 122 A2
Pulgar E 157 A3
Pulheim D 80 A2
Pulkau A 97 C3
Pulpi E 164 B3
Pulsano I 173 B3
Pulsnitz D 84 A2
Pułtusk PL 77 B6
Pumpsaint GB 39 B3
Punat HR 123 B3
Punta Marina I 135 A5
Punta Prima E 167 B4
Punta Sabbioni I 122 B1
Punta Umbria E 161 B3
Puntas de Calnegre E 165 B3
Puolanka FIN 3 D10
Puoltikasvaara S 196 B4
Puoltsa S 196 B2
Puračić BIH 125 C4
Purbach am Neusiedler See A 111 B3
Purchena E 164 B2
Purfleet GB 45 B4
Purgstall A 110 A2
Purkersdorf A 111 A3
Purmerend NL 70 B1
Purullena E 164 B1
Pŭrvomay BG 183 A7
Pushkin RUS 9 C7
Pushkino RUS 9 D10
Püspökladány H 113 B5
Pusté Ulany SK 111 A4
Pustoshka RUS 9 D6
Puszcza Mariańska PL 77 C5
Puszczykowo PL 76 B1
Pusztamagyaród H 111 C3
Pusztamonostor H 113 B3
Pusztaszabolcs H 112 B2
Pusztavám H 112 B2
Putanges-Pont-Ecrepin F 89 B3
Putbus D 66 B2
Putignano I 173 B3
Putlitz D 73 A5
Putnok H 99 C4
Putte B 79 A4
Puttelange-aux-Lacs F 92 B2
Putten NL 70 B2
Puttgarden D 65 B4
Püttlingen D 92 B2
Putzu Idu I 179 B2
Puy-Guillaume F 117 B3
Puy-l'Évêque F 129 B4
Puylaroque F 129 B4
Puylaurens F 146 A3
Puymirol F 129 B3
Puyôo F 128 C2
Puyrolland F 114 B3
Pwllheli GB 38 B2
Pyetrikaw BY 13 B8
Pyhäjärvi FIN 3 E9
Pyhäkylä FIN 197 D11

Riba-Roja de Turia E 159 B3
Riba-roja d'Ebre E 153 A4
Ribadavia E 140 B2
Ribadeo E 141 A3
Ribadesella E 142 A1
Ribaflecha E 143 B4
Ribaforada E 144 C2
Ribare SRB 127 C3
Ribe DK 59 C1
Ribeauvillé F 106 A2
Ribécourt-Dreslincourt F 90 B2
Ribeira da Pena P 148 A2
Ribeira de Piquín E 141 A3
Ribemont F 91 B3
Ribera I 176 B2
Ribera de Cardós E 146 B2
Ribera del Fresno E 156 B1
Ribérac F 129 A3
Ribes de Freser E 147 B3
Ribesalbes E 159 A3
Ribiers F 132 A1
Ribnica BIH 139 A4
Ribnica SLO 123 B3
Ribnica na Potorju SLO 110 C2
Ribnik HR 123 B4
Rîbniţa MD 17 B8
Ribnitz-Damgarten D 66 B1
Ribolla I 135 C4
Říčany, *Jihomoravský* CZ 97 B4
Říčany, *Středočeský* CZ 96 B2
Riccia I 170 B2
Riccione I 136 A1
Ricco Del Golfo I 134 A2
Richebourg F 105 A4
Richelieu F 102 B2
Richisau CH 107 B3
Richmond, *Greater London* GB 44 B3
Richmond, *North Yorkshire* GB 37 B5
Richtenberg D 66 B1
Richterswil CH 107 B3
Rickling D 64 B3
Rickmansworth GB 44 B3
Ricla E 152 A2
Riddarhyttan S 50 C2
Ridderkerk NL 79 A4
Riddes CH 119 A4
Ridjica SRB 125 B5
Riec-sur-Bélon F 100 B2
Ried A 109 A4
Ried im Oberinntal A 108 B1
Riedenburg D 95 C3
Riedlingen D 107 A4
Riedstadt D 93 B4
Riegersburg A 110 C2
Riego de la Vega E 141 B5
Riego del Camino E 149 A4
Riello E 141 B5
Riemst B 80 B1
Rienne B 91 B4
Riénsena E 142 A2
Riesa D 83 A5
Riese Pio X I 121 B4
Riesi I 177 B3
Riestedt D 82 A3
Rietberg D 81 A4
Rieti I 169 A2
Rietschen D 84 A2
Rieumes F 146 A2
Rieupeyroux F 130 A1
Rieux F 146 A2
Riez F 132 B2
Rīga LV 8 D4
Riggisberg CH 106 C2
Rignac F 130 A1
Rignano Gargánico I 171 B3
Rigolato I 109 C3
Rigside GB 36 A3
Rigutino I 135 B4
Riihimäki FIN 8 B4
Rijeka HR 123 B3
Rijen NL 79 A4
Rijkevorsel B 79 A4
Rijssen NL 71 B3
Rila BG 183 A5
Rilić BIH 138 B3
Rilievo I 176 B1
Rillé F 102 B2
Rillo de Gallo E 152 B2
Rimavská Baňa SK 99 C3
Rimavská Seč SK 99 C4
Rimavská Sobota SK 99 C4
Rimbo S 57 A4
Rimforsa S 56 B1
Rímini I 136 A1
Rîmnicu Sărat RO 17 C7
Rimogne F 91 B4
Rimpar D 94 B1
Rimske Toplice SLO 123 A4
Rincón de la Victoria E 163 B3
Rincón de Soto E 144 B2
Rindal N 198 B6
Rinde N 46 A3
Ringarum S 56 B2
Ringaskiddy IRL 29 C3
Ringe DK 59 C3
Ringebu N 48 A2
Ringkøbing DK 59 B1
Ringsaker N 48 B2
Ringsted DK 61 D1
Ringwood GB 44 C2
Rinkaby S 63 C2
Rinkabyholm S 63 B4
Rinlo E 141 A3
Rinn A 108 B2
Rinteln D 72 B2
Rio E 140 B3
Rio do Coures P 154 B2
Rio Douro P 148 A2
Rio Frio P 154 C2
Rio frio de Riaza E 151 A4
Rio Maior P 154 B2
Rio Marina I 134 C3
Rio Tinto P 148 A1
Riobo E 140 B2
Riodeva E 152 B2
Riofrio E 150 B3
Riofrio de Aliste E 149 A3
Riogordo E 163 B3
Rioja E 164 C2
Riola I 135 A4
Riola Sardo I 179 C2
Riolobos E 155 B4
Riom F 116 B3
Riom-ès-Montagnes F 116 B2
Riomaggiore I 134 A2
Rion-des-Landes F 128 C2
Rionegro del Puente E 141 B4
Rionero in Vúlture I 172 B1
Riopar E 158 C1
Riós E 141 C3
Rioseco E 142 A1
Rioseco de Tapia E 141 B5
Riotord F 117 B4
Riotorto E 141 A3
Rioz F 105 B5
Ripač BIH 124 C1
Ripacándida I 172 B1
Ripanj SRB 127 C2
Ripatransone I 136 C2
Ripley GB 40 B2
Ripoll E 147 B3
Ripon GB 40 A2
Riposto I 177 B4
Ripsa S 56 B2
Risan CG 16 D3
Risbäck S 200 B1
Risca GB 39 C3
Rischenau D 81 A5
Riscle F 128 C2
Risebo S 56 B2
Risnes N 46 A2
Rišňovce SK 98 C1
Risør N 53 B5
Risøyhamn N 194 B6
Rissna S 199 B12
Ritsem S 194 C8
Ritterhude D 72 A1
Riutula FIN 193 D10
Riva del Garda I 121 B3
Riva Lígure I 133 B3
Rivanazzano I 120 C2
Rivarolo Canavese I 119 B4
Rivarolo Mantovano I 121 B3
Rive-de-Gier F 117 B4
Rivedoux-Plage F 114 B2
Rivello I 174 A1
Rivergaro I 120 C2
Rives F 118 B2
Rivesaltes F 146 B3
Rivignano I 122 B2
Rivne UA 13 C7
Rívoli I 119 B4
Rivolta d'Adda I 120 B2
Rixheim F 106 B2
Rixo S 54 B2
Riza GR 183 C5
Rizokarpaso CY 181 A3
Rjukan N 47 C5
Rø DK 67 A3
Rö S 57 A4
Roa E 143 C3
Roa N 48 B2
Roade GB 44 A3
Roager DK 59 C1
Roaldkvam N 52 A2
Roanne F 117 A4
Röbäck S 200 C6
Robakowo PL 69 B3
Róbbio I 120 B1
Röbel D 73 A5
Roberton GB 35 C5
Robertsfors S 200 B6
Robertville B 80 B2
Robin Hood's Bay GB 37 B6
Robleda E 149 B3
Robledillo de Trujillo E 156 A2
Robledo, *Albacete* E 158 C1
Robledo, *Orense* E 141 B4
Robledo de Chavela E 151 B3
Robledo del Buey E 156 A3
Robledo del Mazo E 156 A3
Robledollano E 156 A2
Robles de la Valcueva E 142 B1
Robliza de Cojos E 149 B4
Robres E 145 C3
Robres del Castillo E 144 B1
Rocafort de Queralt E 147 C2
Rocamadour F 129 B4
Rocca di Mezzo I 169 A3
Rocca di Papa I 168 B2
Rocca Imperiale I 174 A2
Rocca Priora I 136 B2
Rocca San Casciano I 135 A4
Rocca Sinibalda I 169 A2
Roccabernarda I 175 B2
Roccabianca I 120 B3
Roccadáspide I 172 B1
Roccagorga I 169 B3
Roccalbegna I 135 C4
Roccalumera I 177 B4
Roccamena I 176 B2
Roccamonfina I 170 B1
Roccanova I 174 A2
Roccapalumba I 176 B2
Roccapassa I 169 A3
Roccaraso I 169 B4
Roccasecca I 169 B3
Roccastrada I 135 B4
Roccatederighi I 135 B4
Roccella Iónica I 175 C2
Rocchetta Sant'António I 172 A1
Rocester GB 40 C2
Rochdale GB 40 B1
Roche-lez-Beaupré F 105 B5
Rochechouart F 115 C4
Rochefort B 79 B5
Rochefort F 114 C3
Rochefort-en-Terre F 101 B3
Rochefort-Montagne F 116 B2
Rochefort-sur-Nenon F 105 B4
Rochemaure F 131 A3
Rocheservière F 114 B2
Rochester, *Medway* GB 45 B4
Rochester, *Northumberland* GB 37 A4
Rochlitz D 83 A4
Rociana del Condado E 161 B3
Rockenhausen D 93 B3
Rockhammar S 56 A1
Rockneby S 62 B4
Ročko Polje HR 123 B3
Ročov CZ 84 B1
Rocroi F 91 B4
Roda de Bara E 147 C2
Roda de Ter E 147 C3
Rodach D 82 B2
Rodalben D 93 B3
Rødberg N 47 B5
Rødby DK 65 B4
Rødbyhavn DK 65 B4
Rødding, *Sonderjyllands Amt.* DK 59 C2
Rødding, *Viborg Amt.* DK 58 B1
Rödeby S 63 B3
Rodeiro E 140 B3
Rødekro DK 64 A2
Roden NL 71 A3
Ródenas E 152 B2
Rodenkirchen D 72 A1
Rödental D 82 B3
Rödermark D 93 B4
Rodewisch D 83 B4
Rodez F 130 A1
Rodi Gargánico I 171 B3
Roding D 95 B4
Rödjebro S 51 B4
Rødkærsbro DK 59 B2
Rodolivas GR 183 C5
Rodoñá E 147 C2
Rødvig DK 65 A5
Roermond NL 80 A1
Roesbrugge B 78 B2
Roeschwoog F 93 C4
Roeselare B 78 B3
Roetgen D 80 B2
Roffiac F 116 B3
Röfors S 55 B5
Rofrano I 172 B1
Rogač HR 138 B2
Rogačica SRB 127 C1
Rogalinek PL 76 B1
Rogaška Slatina SLO 123 A4
Rogatec SLO 123 A4
Rogatica BIH 139 B5
Rogatyn UA 13 D6
Rogätz D 73 B4
Roggendorf D 65 C4
Roggiano Gravina I 174 B2
Roghadal GB 31 B2
Rogliano F 180 A2
Rogliano I 175 B2
Rognan N 195 C6
Rogne N 47 A6
Rognes F 131 B4
Rogny-les-7-Ecluses F 103 B4
Rogowo PL 76 B2
Rogoznica HR 138 B1
Rogoźnica PL 85 A4
Rogoźno PL 76 B1
Rohan F 101 A3
Röhlingen D 94 C2
Rohožnik SK 98 C1
Rohr D 82 B2
Rohr im Gebirge A 110 B2
Rohrbach A 96 C1
Rohrbach-lès-Bitche F 92 B3
Rohrberg D 73 B4
Röhrnbach D 96 C1
Roisel F 90 B3
Roja LV 8 D3
Rojales E 165 A4
Röjeråsen S 50 B1
Rojewo PL 76 B3
Rokiciny PL 87 A3
Rokietnica PL 75 B5
Rokiškis LT 8 E4
Rokitki PL 85 A3
Rokycany CZ 96 B1
Rolampont F 105 B4
Rold DK 58 B2
Røldal N 52 A2
Rolde NL 71 B3
Rolfs S 196 D6
Rollag N 47 B6
Rollán E 149 B4
Rolle CH 105 C5
Roma S 57 C4
Roma = Rome I 168 B2
Romagnano Sésia I 119 B5
Romagné F 88 B2
Romakloster S 57 C4
Roman RO 17 B7
Romana I 178 B2
Romanèche-Thorins F 117 A4
Romano di Lombardia I 120 B2
Romans-sur-Isère F 118 B2
Romanshorn CH 107 B4
Rombas F 92 B2
Rome = Roma I 168 B2
Romeán E 141 B3
Romenay F 105 C4
Romeral E 157 A4
Römerstein D 94 C1
Rometta I 177 A4
Romford GB 45 B4
Romhány H 112 B3
Römhild D 82 B2
Romilly-sur-Seine F 91 C3
Romont CH 106 C1
Romorantin-Lanthenay F 103 B3
Romrod D 81 B5
Romsey GB 44 C2
Rømskog N 54 A2
Rønbjerg DK 58 B1
Roncal E 144 B3
Ronce-les-Bains F 114 C2
Ronchamp F 106 B1
Ronchi dei Legionari I 122 B2
Ronciglione I 168 A2
Ronco Canavese I 119 B4
Ronco Scrivia I 120 C1
Ronda E 162 B2
Rønde DK 59 B3
Rone S 57 C4
Ronehamn S 57 C4
Rong N 46 B1
Rönnäng S 60 B1
Rønne DK 67 A3
Ronneburg D 83 B4
Ronneby S 63 B3
Rönneshytta S 55 B6
Rönninge S 57 A3
Rönnöfors S 199 B10
Rönö S 56 B2
Ronov nad Doubravou CZ 97 B3
Ronse B 79 B3
Roosendaal NL 79 A4
Roosky IRL 26 C3
Ropczyce PL 87 B5
Ropeid N 52 A2
Ropinsalmi FIN 192 D5
Ropuerelos del Páramo E 141 B5
Roquebilière F 133 A3
Roquebrun F 130 B2
Roquecourbe F 130 B1
Roquefort F 128 B2
Roquemaure F 131 A3
Roquesteron F 132 B3
Roquetas de Mar E 164 C2
Roquetes E 153 B4
Roquevaire F 132 B1
Røra N 199 B8
Rörbäcksnäs S 49 A4
Rørbæk DK 58 B2
Rore BIH 138 A2
Röro S 60 B1
Røros N 199 C8
Rorschach CH 107 B4
Rørvig DK 61 D1
Rørvik N 199 A8
Rörvik S 62 A2
Rosà I 121 B4
Rosa Marina I 173 B3
Rosal de la Frontera E 161 B2
Rosalina Mare I 122 B1
Rosans F 132 A1
Rosário P 160 B1
Rosarno I 175 C1
Rosbach D 81 B3
Rosche D 73 B3
Rościszewo PL 77 B4
Roscoff F 100 A2
Roscommon IRL 28 A3
Roscrea IRL 28 B4
Rosdorf D 82 A1
Rose I 174 B2
Rosegg A 109 C5
Rosehall GB 32 D2
Rosehearty GB 33 D4
Rosel GB 88 A1
Rosell E 153 B4
Roselló E 153 A4
Rosendal N 46 C3
Rosenfeld D 93 C4
Rosenfors S 62 A3
Rosenheim D 108 B3
Rosenow D 74 A2
Rosenthal D 81 A4
Rosersberg S 57 A3
Roses E 147 B4
Roseto degli Abruzzi I 169 A4
Roseto Valfortore I 170 B3
Rosheim F 93 C3
Rosia I 135 B4
Rosice CZ 97 B4
Rosières-en-Santerre F 90 B2
Rosignano Maríttimo I 134 B3
Rosignano Solvay I 134 B3
Roşiori-de-Vede RO 17 C6
Roskhill GB 31 B2
Roskilde DK 61 D2
Roskovec AL 182 C1
Röslau D 83 B3
Roslev DK 58 B1
Rosmaninhal P 155 B3
Rosnowo PL 67 B5
Rosolini I 177 C3
Rosova CG 139 B5
Rosoy F 104 A2
Rosporden F 100 B2
Rosquete P 154 B2
Rosrath D 80 B3
Ross-on-Wye GB 39 C4
Rossa CH 120 A2
Rossano I 174 B2
Rossas, *Aveiro* P 148 B1
Rossas, *Braga* P 148 A1
Rossdorf D 82 B2
Rossett GB 38 A4
Rosshaupten D 108 B1
Rossiglione I 133 A4
Rossignol B 92 B1
Rossla D 82 A3
Rosslare IRL 30 B2
Rosslare Harbour IRL 30 B2
Rosslau D 83 A4
Rosslea GB 27 B3
Rossleben D 82 A3
Rossön S 200 C2
Rossoszyca PL 86 A2
Rosswein D 83 A5
Röstånga S 61 C3
Roštár SK 99 C4
Rostock D 65 B5
Rostrenen F 100 A2
Røsvik N 194 C6
Rosvik S 196 D4
Rosyth GB 35 B4
Röszke H 126 A2
Rot S 49 A6
Rot am See D 94 B2
Rota E 161 C3
Rota Greca I 174 B2
Rotberget N 49 B4
Rotella I 136 C2
Rotenburg, *Hessen* D 82 B1
Rotenburg, *Niedersachsen* D 72 A2
Roth, *Bayern* D 94 B3
Roth, *Rheinland-Pfalz* D 81 B3
Rothbury GB 37 A5
Rothemühl D 74 A2
Rothenkempenow D 74 A3
Röthenbach D 95 B3
Rothenburg D 84 A2
Rothenburg ob der Tauber D 94 B2
Rothéneuf F 88 B2
Rothenstein D 94 C3
Rotherham GB 40 B2
Rothes GB 32 D3
Rothesay GB 34 C2
Rothwell GB 44 A3
Rotnes N 48 B2
Rotonda I 174 B2
Rotondella I 174 A2
Rotova E 159 C3
Rott, *Bayern* D 108 B1
Rott, *Bayern* D 108 B3
Rottach-Egern D 108 B2
Röttenbach D 94 B3
Rottenbuch D 108 B1
Rottenburg, *Baden-Württemberg* D 93 C4
Rottenburg, *Bayern* D 95 C4
Rottenmann A 110 B1
Rotterdam NL 79 A4
Rotthalmünster D 96 C1
Rottingdean GB 44 C3
Röttingen D 94 B1
Rottleberode D 82 A2
Rottne S 62 A2
Rottneros S 55 A4
Rottofreno I 120 B2
Rottweil D 107 A3
Rötz D 95 B4
Roubaix F 78 B3
Roudnice nad Labem CZ 84 B2
Roudouallec F 100 A2
Rouen F 89 A5
Rouffach F 106 B2
Rougé F 101 B4
Rougemont F 105 B5
Rougemont le-Château F 106 B1
Rouillac F 115 C3
Rouillé F 115 B4
Roujan F 130 B2
Roulans F 105 B5
Roundwood IRL 30 A2
Rousínov CZ 97 B4
Roussac F 115 B5
Roussennac F 130 A1
Rousses F 130 A2
Roussillon F 117 B4
Rouvroy-sur-Audry F 91 B4
Rouy F 104 B2
Rovanieman maalaiskunta FIN 197 C8
Rovaniemi FIN 197 C8
Rovato I 120 B2
Rovensko pod Troskami CZ 84 B3
Roverbella I 121 B3
Rovereto I 121 B4
Rövershagen D 65 B5
Roverud N 49 B4
Rovigo I 121 B4
Rovinj HR 122 B2
Rovišce HR 124 B2
Rów PL 74 B3
Rowy PL 68 A2
Royal Leamington Spa GB 44 A2
Royal Tunbridge Wells GB 45 B4
Royan F 114 C2
Royat F 116 B3
Roybon F 118 B2
Roybridge GB 34 B3
Roye F 90 B2
Royère-de-Vassivière F 116 B1
Røykenvik N 48 B2
Royos E 164 B2
Røyrvik N 199 A10
Royston GB 44 A3
Rozadas E 141 A4
Rozalén del Monte E 151 C5
Różańsko PL 75 B3
Rozay-en-Brie F 90 C2
Roždalovice CZ 84 B3
Rozdilna UA 17 B9
Rozental PL 69 B4
Rozhyshche UA 13 C6
Rožmitál pod Třemšínem CZ 96 B1
Rožňava SK 99 C4
Rožnov pod Radhoštěm CZ 98 B2
Rozoy-sur-Serre F 91 B4
Rozprza PL 86 A3
Roztoky CZ 84 B2
Rozvadov CZ 95 B4
Rozzano I 120 B2
Rrëshen AL 182 B1
Rrogozhine AL 182 B1
Ruanes E 156 A2
Rubbestadneset N 46 C2
Rubi E 147 C3
Rubiá E 141 B4
Rubiacedo de Abajo E 143 B3
Rubielos Bajos E 158 B1
Rubielos de Mora E 153 B3
Rubiera I 121 C3
Rubik AL 182 B1

St. Julien-l'Ars F **115** B4
St. Julien-Mont-Denis F **118** B3
St. Julien-sur-Reyssouze F **118** A2
St. Junien F **115** C4
St. Just F **131** A3
St. Just GB **42** B1
St. Just-en-Chaussée F **90** B2
St. Just-en-Chevalet F **117** B3
St. Just-St. Rambert F **117** B4
St. Justin F **128** C2
St. Keverne GB **42** B1
St. Lary-Soulan F **145** B4
St. Laurent-d'Aigouze F **131** B3
St. Laurent-de-Chamousset F **117** B4
St. Laurent-de-Condel F **89** A3
St. Laurent-de-la-Cabrerisse F **146** A3
St. Laurent-de-la-Salanque F **146** B3
St. Laurent-des-Autels F **101** B4
St. Laurent-du-Pont F **118** B2
St. Laurent-en-Caux F **89** A4
St. Laurent-en-Grandvaux F **105** C4
St. Laurent-Médoc F **128** A2
St. Laurent-sur-Gorre F **115** C4
St. Laurent-sur-Mer F **88** A3
St. Laurent-sur-Sèvre F **114** B3
St. Leger B **92** B1
St. Léger-de-Vignes F **104** C2
St. Léger-sous-Beuvray F **104** C3
St. Léger-sur-Dheune F **104** C3
St. Léonard-de-Noblat F **116** B1
St. Leonards GB **45** C4
St. Lô F **88** A2
St. Lon-les-Mines F **128** C1
St. Louis F **106** B2
St. Loup F **117** A3
St. Loup-de-la-Salle F **105** C3
St. Loup-sur-Semouse F **105** B5
St. Lunaire F **101** A3
St. Lupicin F **118** A2
St. Lyphard F **101** B3
St. Lys F **146** A2
St. Macaire F **128** B2
St. Maclou F **89** A4
St. Maixent-l'École F **115** B3
St. Malo F **88** B1
St. Mamet-la-Salvetat F **116** C2
St. Mandrier-sur-Mer F **132** B1
St. Marcel, *Drôme* F **117** C4
St. Marcel, *Saône-et-Loire* F **105** C3
St. Marcellin F **118** B2
St. Marcellin sur Loire F **117** B4
St. Marcet F **145** A4
St. Mards-en-Othe F **104** A2
St. Margaret's-at-Cliffe GB **45** B5
St. Margaret's Hope GB **33** C4
St. Mars-la-Jaille F **101** B4
St. Martin-d'Ablois F **91** C3
St. Martin-d'Auxigny F **103** B4
St. Martin-de-Belleville F **118** B3
St. Martin-de-Bossenay F **91** C3
St. Martin-de-Crau F **131** B3
St. Martin-de-Londres F **130** B2
St. Martin-de-Queyrières F **118** C3
St. Martin-de-Ré F **114** B2
St. Martin-de-Valamas F **117** C4
St. Martin-d'Entraunes F **132** A2
St. Martin des Besaces F **88** A3
St. Martin-d'Estreaux F **117** A3
St. Martin-d'Hères F **118** B2
St. Martin-du-Frêne F **118** A2
St. Martin-en-Bresse F **105** C4
St. Martin-en-Haut F **117** B4
St. Martin-la-Méanne F **116** B1
St. Martin-sur-Ouanne F **104** B2
St. Martin-Valmeroux F **116** B2
St. Martin-Vésubie F **133** A3
St. Martory F **145** A4
St. Mary's GB **33** C4
St. Mathieu F **115** C4
St. Mathieu-de-Tréviers F **131** B2
St. Maurice CH **119** A3
St. Maurice-Navacelles F **130** B2
St. Maurice-sur-Moselle F **106** B1
St. Mawes GB **42** B1
St. Maximin-la-Ste. Baume F **132** B1
St. Méard-de-Gurçon F **128** B3
St. Médard-de-Guizières F **128** A2
St. Médard-en-Jalles F **128** B2
St. Méen-le-Grand F **101** A3
St. Menges F **91** B4
St. Město CZ **85** B4
St. M'Hervé F **101** A4
St. Michel, *Aisne* F **91** B4
St. Michel, *Gers* F **145** A4
St. Michel-Chef-Chef F **101** B3
St. Michel-de-Maurienne F **118** B3
St. Michel-en-Grève F **100** A2
St. Michel-en-l'Herm F **114** B2
St. Michel-Mont-Mercure F **114** B3
St. Mihiel F **92** C1
St. Monance GB **35** B5
St. Montant F **131** A3
St. Moritz CH **107** C4
St. Nazaire F **101** B3
St. Nazaire-en-Royans F **118** B2
St. Nazaire-le-Désert F **131** A4
St. Nectaire F **116** B2
St. Neots GB **44** A3
St. Nicolas-de-Port F **92** C2
St. Nicolas-de-Redon F **101** B3
St. Nicolas-du-Pélem F **100** A2
St. Niklaas B **79** A4
St. Omer F **78** B2
St. Pair-sur-Mer F **88** B2
Saint-Palais F **144** A2
St. Palais-sur-Mer F **114** C2
St. Pardoux-la-Rivière F **115** C4
St. Paul-Cap-de-Joux F **129** C4
St. Paul-de-Fenouillet F **146** B3
St. Paul-de-Varax F **118** A2
St. Paul-le-Jeune F **131** A3
St. Paul-lès-Dax F **128** C1
St. Paul-Trois-Châteaux F **131** A3
St. Paulien F **117** B3
St. Pé-de-Bigorre F **145** A3
St. Pée-sur-Nivelle F **144** A2
St. Péravy-la-Colombe F **103** B3
St. Péray F **117** C4
St. Père-en-Retz F **101** B3
St. Peter Port GB **88** A1
St. Petersburg = Sankt-Peterburg RUS **9** C7
St. Philbert-de-Grand-Lieu F **114** A2
St. Pierre F **130** B1
St. Pierre-d'Albigny F **118** B3
St. Pierre-d'Allevard F **118** B3
St. Pierre-de-Chartreuse F **118** B2
St. Pierre-de-Chignac F **129** A3
St. Pierre-de-la-Fage F **130** B2
St. Pierre-d'Entremont F **118** B2
St. Pierre-d'Oléron F **114** C2
St. Pierre-Eglise F **88** A2
St. Pierre-en-Port F **89** A4
St. Pierre-le-Moûtier F **104** C2
St. Pierre Montlimart F **101** B4
St. Pierre-Quiberon F **100** B2
St. Pierre-sur-Dives F **89** A3
St. Pierreville F **117** C4
St. Pieters-Leeuw B **79** B4
St. Plancard F **145** A4
St. Poix F **101** B4
St. Pol-de-Léon F **100** A2
St. Pol-sur-Ternoise F **78** B2
St. Polgues F **117** B3
St. Pons-de-Thomières F **130** B1
St. Porchaire F **114** C3
St. Pourçain-sur-Sioule F **116** A3
St. Priest F **117** B4
St. Privat F **116** B2
St. Quay-Portrieux F **100** A3
St. Quentin F **90** B3
St. Quentin-la-Poterie F **131** A3
St. Quentin-les-Anges F **102** B1
St. Rambert-d'Albon F **117** B4
St. Rambert-en-Bugey F **118** B2
St. Raphaël F **132** B2
St. Rémy-de-Provence F **131** B3
St. Rémy-du-Val F **89** B4
St. Remy-en-Bouzemont F **91** C4
St. Renan F **100** A1
St. Révérien F **104** B2
St. Riquier F **90** A1
St. Romain-de-Colbosc F **89** A4
St. Rome-de-Cernon F **130** A1
St. Rome-de-Tarn F **130** A1
St. Sadurní d'Anoia E **147** C2
St. Saëns F **89** A5
St. Sampson GB **88** A1
St. Samson-la-Poterie F **90** B1
St. Saturnin-de-Lenne F **130** A2
St. Saturnin-lès-Apt F **131** B4
St. Sauflieu F **90** B2
St. Saulge F **104** B2
St. Sauveur, *Finistère* F **100** A2
St. Sauveur, *Haute-Saône* F **105** B5
St. Sauveur-de-Montagut F **117** C4
St. Sauveur-en-Puisaye F **104** B2
St. Sauveur-en-Rue F **117** B4
St. Sauveur-le-Vicomte F **88** A2
St. Sauveur-Lendelin F **88** A2
St. Sauveur-sur-Tinée F **132** A3
St. Savin, *Gironde* F **128** A2
St. Savin, *Vienne* F **115** B4
St. Savinien F **114** C3
St. Savournin F **131** B4
St. Seine-l'Abbaye F **105** B3
St. Sernin-sur-Rance F **130** B1
St. Sevan-sur-Mer F **88** B1
St. Sever F **128** C2
St. Sever-Calvados F **88** B2
St. Sorlin-d'Arves F **118** B3
St. Soupplets F **90** B2
St. Sulpice F **129** C4
St. Sulpice-Laurière F **116** A1
St. Sulpice-les-Feuilles F **115** B5
St. Symphorien F **128** B2
St. Symphorien-de-Lay F **117** B4
St. Symphorien d'Ozon F **117** B4
St. Symphorien-sur-Coise F **117** B4
St. Teath GB **42** B2
St. Thégonnec F **100** A2
St. Thiébault F **105** A4
St. Trivier-de-Courtes F **118** A2
St. Trivier sur-Moignans F **117** A4
St. Trojan-les-Bains F **114** C2
St. Tropez F **132** B2
St. Truiden B **79** B5
St. Vaast-la-Hougue F **88** A2
St. Valérien F **104** A2
St. Valery-en-Caux F **89** A4
St. Valéry-sur-Somme F **78** B1
St. Vallier, *Drôme* F **117** B4
St. Vallier, *Saône-et-Loire* F **104** C3
St. Vallier-de-Thiey F **132** B2
St. Varent F **102** C1
St. Vaury F **116** A1
St. Venant F **78** B2
St. Véran F **119** C3
Saint Vincent I **119** B4
St. Vincent-de-Tyrosse F **128** C1
St. Vit F **105** B4
St. Vith B **80** B2
St. Vivien-de-Médoc F **114** C2
St. Yan F **117** A4
St. Ybars F **146** A2
St. Yorre F **117** A3
St. Yrieix-la-Perche F **115** C5
Ste. Adresse F **89** A4
Ste. Anne F **89** B4
Ste. Anne-d'Auray F **100** B3
Ste. Croix CH **105** C5
Ste. Croix-Volvestre F **146** A2
Ste. Engrâce F **144** A3
Ste. Enimie F **130** A2
Ste. Foy-de-Peyrolières F **146** A2
Ste. Foy-la-Grande F **128** B3
Ste. Foy l'Argentiere F **117** B4
Ste. Gauburge-Ste. Colombe F **89** B4
Ste. Gemme la Plaine F **114** B2
Ste. Geneviève F **90** B2
Ste. Hélène F **128** B2
Ste. Hélène-sur-Isère F **118** B3
Ste. Hermine F **114** B2
Ste. Jalle F **131** A4
Ste. Livrade-sur-Lot F **129** B3
Ste. Marie-aux-Mines F **106** A2
Ste. Marie-du-Mont F **88** A2
Ste. Maure-de-Touraine F **102** B2
Ste. Maxime F **132** B2
Ste. Ménéhould F **91** B4
Ste. Mère-Église F **88** A2
Ste. Ode B **92** A1
Ste. Savine F **91** C4
Ste. Sévère-sur-Indre F **103** C4
Ste. Sigolène F **117** B4
Ste. Suzanne F **102** A1
Ste. Tulle F **132** B1
Sainteny F **88** A2
Saintes F **114** C3
Saintfield GB **27** B5
Saissac F **146** A3
Saja E **142** A2
Sajan SRB **126** B2
Šajkaš SRB **126** B2
Sajókaza H **99** C4
Sajószentpéter H **113** A4
Sajóvámos H **113** A4
Sakarya TR **187** B5
Šakiai LT **13** A5
Sakskøbing DK **65** B4
Sakule SRB **126** B2
Sala S **50** C3
Šal'a SK **111** A4
Sala Baganza I **120** C3
Sala Consilina I **172** B1
Salakovac SRB **127** C3
Salamanca E **150** B2
Salamina GR **185** B4
Salandra I **172** B2
Salaparuta I **176** B1
Salar E **163** A3
Salardú E **145** B4
Salas E **141** A4
Salas de los Infantes E **143** B3
Salau F **146** B2
Salavaux CH **106** C2
Salbertrand I **119** B3
Salbohed S **50** C3
Salbris F **103** B4
Salbu N **46** A2
Salce E **141** B4
Salching D **95** C4
Salcombe GB **43** B3
Saldaña E **142** B2
Saldus LV **8** D3
Sale I **120** C1
Saleby S **55** B4
Salem D **107** B4
Salemi I **176** B1
Salen, *Highland* GB **34** B2
Salen, *Highland* GB **34** B2
Salen N **199** A8
Sälen S **49** A5
Salernes F **132** B2
Salerno I **170** C2
Salers F **116** B2
Salford GB **40** B1
Salgótarján H **113** A3
Salgueiro P **155** B3
Salhus N **46** B2
Sali HR **137** B4
Sálice Salentino I **173** B3
Salientes E **141** B4
Salies-de-Béarn F **144** A3
Salies-du-Salat F **145** A4
Salignac-Eyvigues F **129** B4
Saligney-sur-Roudon F **104** C2
Salihli TR **188** A3
Salihorsk BY **13** B7
Salinas, *Alicante* E **159** C3
Salinas, *Huesca* E **145** B4
Salinas de Medinaceli E **152** A1
Salinas de Pisuerga E **142** B2
Salindres F **131** A3
Saline di Volterra I **135** B3
Salins-les-Bains F **105** C4
Salir P **160** B1
Salisbury GB **44** B2
Salla A **110** B1
Salla FIN **197** C11
Sallachy GB **32** C2
Sallanches F **118** B3
Sallent E **147** C2
Sallent de Gállego E **145** B3
Salles F **128** B2
Salles-Curan F **130** A1
Salles-sur-l'Hers F **146** A2
Sallins IRL **30** A2
Sällsjö S **199** B10
Salmerón E **152** B1
Salmiech F **130** A1
Salmivaara FIN **197** C11
Salmoral E **150** B2
Salo FIN **8** B3
Salò I **121** B3
Salobreña E **163** B4
Salon-de-Provence F **131** B4
Salonica = Thessaloniki GR **182** C4
Salonta RO **16** B4
Salorino E **155** B3
Salornay-sur-Guye F **104** C3
Salorno I **121** A4
Salou E **147** C2
Šalovci SLO **111** C3
Salsbruket N **199** A8
Salses-le-Chateau F **146** B3
Salsomaggiore Terme I **120** C2
Salt E **147** C3
Saltaire GB **40** B2
Saltara I **136** B1
Saltash GB **42** B2
Saltburn-by-the-Sea GB **37** B6
Saltcoats GB **34** C3
Saltfleet GB **41** B4
Salto P **148** A2
Saltrød N **53** B4
Saltsjöbaden S **57** A4
Saltvik FIN **51** B7
Saltvik S **62** A4
Saludécio I **136** B1
Salussola I **119** B5
Saluzzo I **119** C4
Salvacañete E **152** B2
Salvada P **160** B2
Salvagnac F **129** C4
Salvaleon E **155** C4
Salvaterra de Magos P **154** B2
Salvaterra do Extremo P **155** B4
Salvatierra, *Avila* E **143** B4
Salvatierra, *Badajoz* E **155** C4
Salvatierra de Santiago E **156** A1
Salviac F **129** B4
Salz-hemmendorf D **72** B2
Salzburg A **109** B4
Salzgitter D **72** B3
Salzgitter Bad D **72** B3
Salzhausen D **72** A3
Salzkotten D **81** A4
Salzmünde D **83** A3
Salzwedel D **73** B4
Samadet F **128** C2
Samandıra TR **186** B4
Samassi I **179** C2
Samatan F **146** A1
Sambiase I **175** C2
Sambir UA **13** D5
Samborowo PL **69** B4
Sambuca di Sicilia I **176** B2
Samedan CH **107** C4
Samer F **78** B1
Sami GR **184** A1
Şamlı TR **186** C2
Sammichele di Bari I **173** B2
Samnaun CH **107** C5
Samobor HR **123** B4
Samoëns F **118** A3
Samogneux F **92** B1
Samokov BG **17** D5
Samora Correia P **154** C2
Šamorín SK **111** A4
Samos E **141** B3
Samos GR **188** B1
Samoš SRB **126** B2
Samothraki GR **183** C7
Samper de Calanda E **153** A3
Sampéyre I **133** A3
Sampieri I **177** C3
Sampigny F **92** C1
Samplawa PL **69** B4
Samproniano I **168** A1
Samtens D **66** B2
Samugheo I **179** C2
San Adrián E **144** B2
San Agustín E **164** C2
San Agustin de Guadalix E **151** B4
San Alberto I **135** A5
San Amaro E **140** B2
San Andrês del Rabanedo E **142** B1
San Antanio di Santadi I **179** C2
San Antolín de Ibias E **141** A4
San Arcángelo I **174** A2
San Asensio E **143** B4
San Bartolomé de la Torre E **161** B2
San Bartolomé de las Abiertas E **150** C3
San Bartolomé de Pinares E **150** B3
San Bartolomeo in Galdo I **170** B3
San Benedetto del Tronto I **136** C2
San Benedetto in Alpe I **135** B4
San Benedetto Po I **121** B3
San Benito E **156** B3
San Benito de la Contienda E **155** C3
San Biágio Plátani I **176** B2
San Biágio Saracinisco I **169** B3
San Bonifacio I **121** B4
San Calixto E **156** C2
San Cándido I **109** C3
San Carlo CH **119** A5
San Carlo I **176** B2
San Carlos del Valle E **157** B4
San Casciano dei Bagni I **135** C4
San Casciano in Val di Pesa I **135** B4
San Cataldo, *Puglia* I **173** B4
San Cataldo, *Sicilia* I **176** B2
San Cebrián de Castro E **149** A4
San Cesário di Lecce I **173** B4
San Chírico Raparo I **174** A2
San Cibrao das Viñas E **140** B3
San Cipirello I **176** B2
San Ciprián E **141** A3
San Clemente E **158** B1
San Clodio E **141** B3
San Colombano al Lambro I **120** B2
San Costanzo I **136** B2
San Crisóbal de Entreviñas E **142** B1
San Cristóbal de la Polantera E **141** B5
San Cristóbal de la Vega E **150** A3
San Cristovo E **141** C3
San Damiano d'Asti I **119** C5
San Damiano Macra I **133** A3
San Daniele del Friuli I **122** A2
San Demétrio Corone I **174** B2
San Demétrio né Vestini I **169** A3
San Donà di Piave I **122** B1
San Dónaci I **173** B3
San Donato Val di Comino I **169** B3
San Emiliano E **141** B5
San Enrique E **162** B2

Santa Margarida do Sado P 160 A1
Santa Margaridao de Montbui E 147 C2
Santa Margherita I 179 D2
Santa Margherita di Belice I 176 B2
Santa Margherita Ligure I 134 A2
Santa Maria CH 108 C1
Santa Maria E 144 B3
Santa Maria al Bagno I 173 B3
Santa Maria Cápua Vétere I 170 B2
Santa Maria da Feira P 148 B1
Santa Maria de Cayón E 143 A3
Santa Maria de Corco E 147 B3
Santa Maria de Huerta E 152 A1
Santa Maria de la Alameda E 151 B3
Santa Maria de las Hoyas E 143 C3
Santa Maria de Mercadillo E 143 C3
Santa Maria de Nieva E 164 B3
Santa Maria de Trassierra E 156 C3
Santa Maria del Camí E 167 B2
Santa Maria del Campo E 143 B3
Santa Maria del Campo Rus E 158 B1
Santa Maria del Páramo E 142 B1
Santa Maria del Taro I 134 A2
Santa Maria della Versa I 120 C2
Santa Maria di Licodia I 177 B3
Santa Maria-di-Rispéscia I 168 A1
Santa Maria la Palma I 178 B2
Santa María la Real de Nieva E 150 A3
Santa Maria Maggiore I 119 A5
Santa Maria Ribarredonda E 143 B3
Santa Marina del Rey E 141 B5
Santa Marinella I 168 A1
Santa Marta, *Albacete* E 158 B1
Santa Marta, *Badajoz* E 155 C4
Santa Marta de Magasca E 156 A1
Santa Marta de Penaguião P 148 A2
Santa Marta de Tormes E 150 B2
Santa Ninfa I 176 B1
Santa Olalla, *Huelva* E 161 B3
Santa Olalla, *Toledo* E 150 B3
Santa Pau E 147 B3
Santa Pola E 165 A4
Santa Ponça E 166 B2
Santa Severa F 180 A2
Santa Severa I 168 A1
Santa Severina I 175 B2
Santa Sofia I 135 B4
Santa Suzana, *Évora* P 155 C3
Santa Suzana, *Setúbal* P 154 C2
Santa Teresa di Riva I 177 B4
Santa Teresa Gallura I 178 A3
Santa Uxía E 140 B2
Santa Valburga I 108 C1
Santa Vittória in Matenano I 136 B2
Santacara E 144 B2
Santadi I 179 C2
Santaella E 162 A3
Sant'Ágata dei Goti I 170 B2
Sant'Ágata di Ésaro I 174 B1
Sant'Ágata di Puglia I 171 B3
Sant'Agata Feltria I 135 B5
Sant'Ágata Militello I 177 A3
Santana, *Évora* P 154 C2
Santana, *Setúbal* P 154 C1
Sântana RO 126 A3
Santana da Serra P 160 B1
Sant'Ana de Cambas P 160 B2
Santana do Mato P 154 C2
Sant'Anastasia I 170 C2
Santander E 143 A3
Sant'Andrea Frius I 179 C3
Sant'Ángelo dei Lombardi I 172 B1
Sant'Angelo in Vado I 136 B1
Sant'Angelo Lodigiano I 120 B2
Sant'Antíoco I 179 C2
Sant'Antonio-di-Gallura I 178 B3
Santanyí E 167 B3
Santarcángelo di Romagna I 136 A1
Santarém P 154 B2
Santas Martas E 142 B1
Sant'Caterina I 135 C4
Santed E 152 A2
Sant'Egídio alla Vibrata I 136 C2
Sant'Elia a Pianisi I 170 B2
Sant'Elia Fiumerapido I 169 B3
Santelices E 143 A3
Sant'Elpídio a Mare I 136 B2
Santéramo in Colle I 171 C4
Santervas de la Vega E 142 B2
Santhià I 119 B5
Santiago de Alcántara E 155 B3
Santiago de Calatrava E 163 A3
Santiago de Compostela E 140 B2
Santiago de la Espade E 164 A2
Santiago de la Puebla E 150 B2
Santiago de la Ribera E 165 B4
Santiago de Litem P 154 B2
Santiago del Campo E 155 B4
Santiago do Cacém P 160 B1
Santiago do Escoural P 154 C2
Santiago Maior P 155 C3
Santibáñez de Béjar E 150 B2
Santibáñez de la Peña E 142 B2
Santibáñez de Murias E 142 A1
Santibáñez de Vidriales E 141 B4
Santibáñez el Alto E 149 B3
Santibáñez el Bajo E 149 B3
Santillana E 142 A2
Santiponce E 162 A1
Santisteban del Puerto E 157 B4
Santiuste de San Juan Bautiste E 150 A3
Santiz E 149 A4
Sant'Ilario d'Enza I 121 C3
Santo Aleixo P 161 A2
Santo Amado P 161 A2
Santo Amaro P 155 C3
Santo André P 160 A1
Santo Domingo E 155 C3
Santo Domingo de la Calzada E 143 B4
Santo Domingo de Silos E 143 C3
Santo Estêvão, *Faro* P 160 B2
Santo Estêvão, *Santarém* P 154 C2
Santo-Pietro-di Tenda F 180 A2
Santo Spirito I 171 B4
Santo Stefano d'Aveto I 134 A2
Santo Stéfano di Camastra I 177 A3
Santo Stefano di Magra I 134 A2
Santo Stéfano Quisquina I 176 B2
Santo Tirso P 148 A1
Santo Tomé E 164 A1
Santok PL 75 B4
Santomera E 165 A3
Santoña E 143 A3
Sant'Oreste I 168 A2
Santotis E 142 A2
Santovenia, *Burgos* E 143 B3
Santovenia, *Zamora* E 142 C1
Santpedor E 147 C2
Santu Lussurgiu I 178 B2
Santutzi E 143 A3
Sanxenxo E 140 B2
Sanza I 172 B1
São Aleixo P 155 C3
São Barnabé P 160 B1
São Bartolomé da Serra P 160 A1
São Bartolomeu de Messines P 160 B1
São Bento P 140 C2
São Brás P 160 B2
São Brás de Alportel P 160 B2
São Braz do Reguedoura P 154 C2
São Cristóvão P 154 C2
São Domingos P 160 B1
São Geraldo P 154 C2
São Jacinto P 148 B1
São João da Madeira P 148 B1
São João da Pesqueira P 148 A2
São João da Ribeira P 154 B2
São João da Serra P 148 B1
São João da Venda P 160 B2
São João dos Caldeireiros P 160 B2
São Julião P 155 B3
São Leonardo P 155 C3
São Luis P 160 B1
São Manços P 155 C3
São Marcos da Ataboeira P 160 B2
Saõ Marcos da Serra P 160 B1
São Marcos de Campo P 155 C3
São Martinho da Cortiça P 148 B1
São Martinho das Amoreiras P 160 B1
São Martinho do Porto P 154 B1
São Matias, *Beja* P 160 A2
São Matias, *Évora* P 154 C2
São Miguel d'Acha P 155 A3
São Miguel de Machede P 155 C3
São Pedro da Torre P 140 C2
São Pedro de Muel P 154 B1
São Pedro de Solis P 160 B2
São Pedro do Sul P 148 B1
São Romão P 154 C2
São Sebastião dos Carros P 160 B2
São Teotónio P 160 B1
São Torcato P 148 A1
Saorge F 133 B3
Sapataria P 154 C1
Sapes GR 183 B7
Sapiãos P 148 A2
Sappada I 109 C3
Sappen N 192 C5
Sapri I 174 A1
Sarajärvi FIN 197 D10
Sarajevo BIH 139 B4
Saramon F 129 C3
Sarandë AL 182 D2
Saranovo SRB 127 C2
Saranyönü TR 189 A7
Saraorci SRB 127 C3
Saray TR 186 A2
Saraycık TR 187 C4
Sarayköy TR 188 B3
Saraylar TR 186 B2
Sarbia PL 75 B5
Sarbinowo, *Zachodnio-Pomorskie* PL 67 B4
Sarbinowo, *Zachodnio-Pomorskie* PL 74 B3
Sárbogárd H 112 C2
Sarcelles F 90 B2
Sarche I 121 A3
Sardara I 179 C2
Sardoal P 154 B2
Sardón de Duero E 150 A3
Sare F 144 A2
S'Arenal E 166 B2
Šarengrad HR 125 B5
Sarentino I 108 C2
Sarezzo I 120 B3
Sargans CH 107 B4
Sári H 112 B3
Sarıbeyler TR 186 C2
Sarıcakaya TR 187 B5
Sari-d'Orcino F 180 A1
Sarıgöl TR 188 A3
Sarıkaya TR 23 B8
Sarıköy TR 186 B2
Sarıoba TR 187 C7
Sarilhos Grandes P 154 C2
Sariñena E 145 C3
Sárisáp H 112 B2
Sariyer TR 186 A4
Sarkad H 113 C5
Sárkeresztes H 112 B2
Sárkeresztúr H 112 B2
Särkijärvi FIN 196 B6
Şarkikaraağaç TR 189 A6
Şarköy TR 186 B2
Sarlat-la-Canéda F 129 B4
Sarliac-sur-l'Isle F 129 A3
Sármellék H 111 C4
Särna S 199 D10
Sarnadas P 155 B3
Sarnano I 136 B2
Sarnen CH 106 C3
Sarnesfield GB 39 B4
Sárnico I 120 B2
Sarno I 170 C2
Sarnonico I 121 A4
Sarnow D 74 A2
Sarny UA 13 C7
Särö S 60 B1
Saronno I 120 B2
Sárosd H 112 B2
Šarovce SK 112 A2
Sarpoil F 117 B3
Sarpsborg N 54 A2
Sarracín E 143 B3
Sarral E 147 C2
Sarralbe F 92 B3
Sarrancolin F 145 B4
Sarras F 117 B4
Sarre I 119 B4
Sarre-Union F 92 C3
Sarreaus E 140 B3
Sarrebourg F 92 C3
Sarreguemines F 92 B3
Sárrétudvari H 113 B5
Sarria E 141 B3
Sarrià de Ter E 147 B3
Sarrión E 153 B3
Sarroca de Lleida E 153 A4
Sarroch I 179 C3
Sarron F 128 C2
Sársina I 135 B5
Sarstedt D 72 B2
Sárszentlőrinc H 112 C2
Sárszentmihaly H 112 B2
Sárszentmiklós H 112 C2
Sarteano I 135 C4
Sartène F 180 B1
Sartilly F 88 B2
Sartirana Lomellina I 120 B1
Saruhanlı TR 186 D2
Sárvár H 111 B3
Sarvisvaara S 196 C4
Sarzana I 134 A2
Sarzeau F 101 B3
Sarzedas P 155 B3
Sas van Gent NL 79 A3
Sasalli TR 188 A1
Sasamón E 142 B2
Sásd H 125 A4
Sasino PL 68 A2
Sássari I 178 B2
Sassello I 133 A4
Sassenberg D 71 C5
Sassetta I 134 B3
Sassnitz D 66 B2
Sasso d'Ombrone I 135 C4
Sasso Marconi I 135 A4
Sassocorvaro I 136 B1
Sassoferrato I 136 B1
Sassoleone I 135 A4
Sassuolo I 135 A3
Sástago E 153 A3
Šaštinske Stráže SK 98 C1
Såtåhaugen N 199 C7
Satão P 148 B2
Såtenäs S 55 B3
Säter S 50 B2
Sätila S 60 B2
Satillieu F 117 B4
Satnica Đakovačka HR 125 B4
Sátoraljaújhely H 16 A4
Satow D 65 C4
Sätra-brunn S 50 C3
Satrup D 64 B2
Satteins A 107 B4
Satu Mare RO 17 B5
Saturnia I 168 A1
Saucats F 128 B2
Saucelle E 149 A3
Sauda N 52 A2
Saudasjøen N 52 A2
Sauðarkrókur IS 190 B6
Sauerlach D 108 B2
Saugues F 117 C3
Sauherad N 53 A5
Saujon F 114 C3
Sauland N 53 A4
Saulces Monclin F 91 B4
Saulgau D 107 A4
Saulgrub D 108 B2
Saulieu F 104 B3
Saulnot F 106 B1
Sault F 131 A4
Sault-Brénaz F 118 B2
Sault-de-Navailles F 128 C2
Saulx F 105 B5
Saulxures-sur-Moselotte F 106 B1
Saulzais-le-Potier F 103 C4
Saumos F 128 B1
Saumur F 102 B1
Saunavaara FIN 197 B10
Saundersfoot GB 39 C2
Saurat F 146 B2
Saurbær, *Borgarfjarðarsýsla* IS 190 C4
Saurbær, *Dalasýsla* IS 190 B4
Saurbær, *Eyjafjarðarsýsla* IS 191 B7
Sáuris I 109 C3
Sausset-les-Pins F 131 B4
Sauteyrargues F 131 B2
Sauvagnat F 116 B2
Sauve F 131 B2
Sauveterre-de-Béarn F 144 A3
Sauveterre-de-Guyenne F 128 B2
Sauviat-sur-Vige F 116 B1
Sauxillanges F 117 B3
Sauzé-Vaussais F 115 B4
Sauzet, *Drôme* F 117 C4
Sauzet, *Lot* F 129 B4
Sauzon F 100 B2
Sava I 173 B3
Sävar S 200 C6
Savarsin RO 16 B5
Säväst S 196 D4
Savaştepe TR 186 C2
Savci SLO 111 C3
Säve S 60 B1
Savelletri I 173 B3
Savelli I 174 B2
Savenay F 101 B4
Saverdun F 146 A2
Saverne F 93 C3
Savières F 91 C3
Savigliano I 119 C4
Savignac-les-Eglises F 129 A3
Savignano Irpino I 171 B3
Savignano sul Rubicone I 136 A1
Savigny-sur-Braye F 102 B2
Saviñán E 152 A2
Savines-le-lac F 132 A2
Savino Selo SRB 126 B1
Savio I 135 A5
Sävja S 51 C4
Šavnik CG 139 C5
Savognin CH 107 C4
Savona I 133 A4
Savonlinna FIN 9 B6
Savournon F 132 A1
Sävsjö S 62 A2
Savsjön S 50 C1
Sävsjöström S 62 A3
Savudrija HR 122 B2
Savukoski FIN 197 B11
Sawbridgeworth GB 45 B4
Sawtry GB 44 A3
Sax E 159 C3
Saxdalen S 50 B1
Saxilby GB 40 B3
Saxmundham GB 45 A5
Saxnäs S 195 F6
Saxthorpe GB 41 C5
Sayalonga E 163 B3
Sayatón E 151 B5
Sayda D 83 B5
Säytsjärvi FIN 193 C11
Šazava, *Jihomoravský* CZ 97 B3
Sázava, *Středočeský* CZ 96 B2
Scaër F 100 A2
Scafa I 169 A4
Scalasaig GB 34 B1
Scalby GB 40 A3
Scalea I 174 B1
Scaletta Zanclea I 177 A4
Scalloway GB 33 A5
Scamblesby GB 41 B3
Scandale I 175 B2
Scandiano I 121 C3
Scandicci I 135 B4
Scandolara Ravara I 120 B3
Scanno I 169 B3
Scansano I 168 A1
Scanzano Jónico I 174 A2
Scarborough GB 40 A3
Scardovari I 122 C1
Scardoy GB 32 D2
Scarperia I 135 B4
Scarriff IRL 28 B3
Scey-sur-Saône et St. Albin F 105 B4
Sch-en-feld D 95 B4
Schachendorf A 111 B3
Schaffhausen CH 107 B3
Schafstädt D 83 A3
Schafstedt D 64 B2
Schäftlarn D 108 B2
Schagen NL 70 B1
Schalkau D 82 B3
Schangnau CH 106 C2
Schapbach D 93 C4
Scharbeutz D 65 B3
Schärding A 96 C1
Scharnitz A 108 B2
Scharrel D 71 A4
Schattendorf A 111 B3
Scheemda NL 71 A3
Scheessel D 72 A2
Schéggia I 136 B1
Scheibbs A 110 A2
Scheibenberg D 83 B4
Scheidegg D 107 B4
Scheifling A 110 B1
Scheinfeld D 94 B2
Schelklingen D 94 C1
Schenefeld, *Schleswig-Holstein* D 64 B2
Schenefeld, *Schleswig-Holstein* D 72 A2
Schenklengsfeld D 82 B1
Scherfede D 81 A5
Schermbeck D 80 A2
Scherpenzeel NL 70 B2
Schesslitz D 94 B3
Scheveningen NL 70 B1
Schiedam NL 79 A4
Schieder-Schwalenberg D 72 C2
Schierling D 95 C4
Schiers CH 107 C4
Schildau D 83 A4
Schillingen D 92 B2
Schillingsfürst D 94 B2
Schilpário I 120 A3
Schiltach D 93 C4
Schiltigheim F 93 C3
Schio I 121 B4
Schirmeck F 92 C3
Schirnding D 83 B4
Schkeuditz D 83 A4
Schkölen D 83 A3
Schlabendorf D 84 A1
Schladen D 73 B3
Schladming A 109 B4
Schlangen D 81 A4
Schleiden D 80 B2
Schleiz D 83 B3
Schleswig D 64 B2
Schleusingen D 82 B2
Schlieben D 83 A5
Schliengen D 106 B2
Schliersee D 108 B2
Schlitz D 81 B5
Schloss Neuhans D 81 A4
Schlossvippach D 82 A3
Schlotheim D 82 A2
Schluchsee D 106 B3
Schlüchtern D 81 B5
Schmallenberg D 81 A4
Schmelz D 92 B2
Schmidmühlen D 95 B3
Schmiedeberg D 84 B1
Schmiedefeld D 82 B2
Schmirn A 108 B2
Schmölln, *Brandenburg* D 74 A3
Schmölln, *Sachsen* D 83 B4
Schnaittach D 95 B3
Schneeberg D 83 B4
Schneizlreuth D 109 B3
Schneverdingen D 72 A2
Schöder A 109 B5
Schoenburg B 80 B2
Schollene D 73 B5
Schöllkrippen D 81 B5
Schomberg D 107 A3
Schönach D 95 C4
Schönau, *Baden-Württemberg* D 106 B2
Schönau, *Bayern* D 95 C4
Schönbeck D 74 A2
Schönberg, *Bayern* D 96 C1
Schönberg, *Mecklenburg-Vorpommern* D 65 C3
Schönberg, *Schleswig-Holstein* D 65 B3
Schönebeck D 73 B4
Schöneck D 83 B4
Schönecken- D 80 B2
Schönermark D 74 A2
Schönewalde D 83 A5
Schongau D 108 B1
Schöngrabern A 97 C4
Schönhagen D 81 A5
Schönhausen D 73 B5
Schöningen D 73 B3
Schönkirchen D 64 B3
Schönsee D 95 B4
Schöntal D 94 B1
Schönthal D 95 B4
Schonungen D 94 A2
Schönwalde D 65 B3
Schoondijke NL 79 A3
Schoonebeek NL 71 B3
Schoonhoven NL 79 A4
Schopfheim D 106 B2
Schöppenstedt D 73 B3
Schörfling A 109 B4
Schorndorf D 94 C1
Schortens D 71 A4
Schotten D 81 B5
Schramberg D 106 A3
Schraplau D 83 A3

Siorac-en-Périgord F 129 B3
Šipanska Luka HR 139 C3
Šipovo BIH 138 A3
Sira N 52 B2
Siracusa I 177 B4
Siret RO 17 B7
Sirevåg N 52 B1
Sirig SRB 126 B1
Sirkka FIN 196 B7
Sirmione I 121 B3
Sirniö FIN 197 D11
Sirok H 113 B4
Široké SK 99 C4
Široki Brijeg BIH 139 B3
Sirolo I 136 B2
Siruela E 156 B2
Sisak HR 124 B2
Sisante E 158 B1
Šišljavić HR 123 B4
Sissach CH 106 B2
Sissonne F 91 B3
Sistelo P 140 C2
Sisteron F 132 A1
Sistiana I 122 B2
Sistranda N 198 B5
Sitasjaurestugorna S 194 C8
Sitges E 147 C2
Sitia GR 185 D7
Sittard NL 80 A1
Sittensen D 72 A2
Sittingbourne GB 45 B4
Sitzenroda D 83 A4
Sivac SRB 126 B1
Sivaslı TR 189 A4
Siverić HR 138 B2
Sivrihisar TR 187 C6
Sixt-Fer-á-Cheval F 119 A3
Siziano I 120 B2
Sizun F 100 A1
Sjenica SRB 16 D3
Sjoa N 198 D6
Sjøåsen N 199 A8
Sjöbo S 61 D3
Sjøenden, *Hedmark* N 48 A3
Sjøenden, *Hedmark* N 48 B3
Sjøholt N 198 C3
Sjøli N 48 A3
Sjølstad N 199 A9
Sjölunda S 56 A1
Sjømarken S 60 B2
Sjørring DK 58 B1
Sjötofta S 60 B3
Sjötorp S 55 B4
Sjoutnäset S 199 A11
Sjøvegan N 194 B8
Sjuntorp S 54 B3
Skåbu N 47 A6
Skælskør DK 65 A4
Skærbæk DK 64 A1
Skafså N 53 A4
Skaftafell IS 191 D9
Skagaströnd IS 190 B5
Skagen DK 58 A3
Skagersvik S 55 B5
Skaiå N 53 B3
Skaidi N 193 B8
Skala GR 184 A1
Skała PL 87 B3
Skala Oropou GR 185 A4
Skala-Podilska UA 13 D7
Skaland N 194 A8
Skalat UA 13 D6
Skalbmierz PL 87 B4
Skålevik N 53 B4
Skalica SK 98 C1
Skalité SK 98 B2
Skällinge S 60 B2
Skalná CZ 83 B4
Skals DK 58 B2
Skalstugan S 199 B9
Skanderborg DK 59 B2
Skåne-Tranås S 61 D3
Skånes-Fagerhult S 61 C3
Skånevik N 52 A1
Skänninge S 55 B6
Skanör med Falsterbo S 66 A1
Skåpafors S 54 A3
Skąpe PL 75 B4
Skara S 55 B4
Skärberget N 194 B7
Skärblacka S 56 B1
Skarda S 200 B4
Skarð IS 190 B3
Skare N 46 C3
Skåre S 55 A4
Skärhamn S 60 B1
Skarnes N 48 B3
Skarp Salling DK 58 B2
Skärplinge S 51 B4
Skarpnatö FIN 51 B6
Skarrild DK 59 C1
Skarstad N 194 B7
Skärstad S 62 A2
Skarsvåg N 193 A9
Skarszewy PL 69 A3
Skårup DK 65 A3
Skärvången S 199 B11
Skarvsjöby S 195 F8
Skaryszew PL 87 A5
Skarżysko-Kamienna PL 87 A4
Skarzysko Ksiazece PL 87 A4
Skatøy N 53 B5
Skattkärr S 55 A4
Skattungbyn S 50 A1
Skatval N 199 B7
Skaulo S 196 B4
Skave DK 59 B1
Skawina PL 99 B3
Skebobruk S 51 C5
Skebokvarn S 56 A2
Skedala S 61 C2
Skedevi S 56 B1
Skedsmokorset N 48 B3
Skee S 54 B2
Skegness GB 41 B4
Skei N 46 A3
Skela SRB 127 C2
Skelani BIH 127 D1
Skellefteå S 2 D7
Skelleftehamn S 2 D7
Skelmersdale GB 38 A4
Skelmorlie GB 34 C3
Skelund DK 58 B3
Skender Vakuf BIH 138 A3
Skene S 60 B2
Skępe PL 77 B4
Skepplanda S 60 B2
Skeppshult S 60 B3
Skerries IRL 30 A2
Ski N 54 A1
Skiathos GR 183 D5
Skibbereen IRL 29 C2
Skibotn N 192 C4
Skidra GR 182 C4
Skien N 53 A5
Skierniewice PL 77 C5
Skillingaryd S 60 B4
Skillinge S 63 C2
Skillingmark S 49 C4
Skiloura CY 181 A2
Skinnardai S 57 A4
Skinnskatteberg S 50 C2
Skipmannvik N 195 C6
Skipness GB 34 C2
Skipsea GB 41 B3
Skipton GB 40 B1
Skiptvet N 54 A2
Skiros GR 183 E6
Skivarp S 66 A2
Skive DK 58 B2
Skjærhalden N 54 A2
Skjånes N 193 B12
Skjeberg N 54 A2
Skjeggedal N 46 B3
Skjeljanger N 46 B1
Skjeljavik N 46 C2
Skjern DK 59 C1
Skjervøy N 192 B4
Skjold, *Rogaland* N 52 A1
Skjold, *Troms* N 192 C3
Skjoldastraumen N 52 A1
Skjolden N 47 A4
Skjønhaug N 54 A2
Skjøtningsberg N 193 A11
Škocjan SLO 123 B4
Skoczów PL 98 B2
Skodborg DK 59 C2
Škofja Loka SLO 123 A3
Škofljica SLO 123 B3
Skog S 51 A3
Skoganvarre N 193 C9
Skogen S 54 A3
Skogfoss N 193 C13
Skoghall S 55 A4
Skogly N 193 C13
Skogn N 199 B8
Skognes N 192 C3
Skogstorp, *Halland* S 60 C2
Skogstorp, *Södermanland* S 56 A2
Skoki PL 76 B2
Skokloster S 57 A3
Sköldinge S 56 A2
Skole UA 13 D5
Skollenborg N 53 A5
Sköllersta S 56 A1
Skomlin PL 86 A2
Skonseng N 195 D5
Skopelos GR 183 D5
Skopje MK 182 A3
Skoppum N 54 A1
Skórcz PL 69 B3
Skorogoszcz PL 86 B1
Skoroszów PL 85 A5
Skorovatn N 199 A10
Skorped S 200 C3
Skørping DK 58 B2
Skotfoss N 53 A5
Skotniki PL 87 A3
Skotselv N 48 C1
Skotterud N 49 C4
Skottorp S 61 C2
Skovby DK 64 B2
Skövde S 55 B4
Skovsgård DK 58 A2
Skrad HR 123 B3
Skradin HR 138 B1
Skradnik HR 123 B4
Skråmestø N 46 B1
Škrdlovice CZ 97 B3
Skrea S 60 C2
Skreia N 48 B2
Skrolsvik N 194 A7
Skruv S 63 B3
Skrwilno PL 77 A4
Skrydstrup DK 59 C2
Skucani BIH 138 B2
Skudeneshavn N 52 A1
Skui N 48 C2
Skulsk PL 76 B3
Skultorp S 55 B4
Skultuna S 56 A2
Skuodas LT 8 D2
Skurup S 66 A2
Skute N 48 B2
Skuteč CZ 97 B3
Skutskär S 51 B4
Skutvik N 194 B6
Skvyra UA 13 D8
Skwierzyna PL 75 B4
Skýcov SK 98 C2
Skyllberg S 55 B5
Skyttmon S 200 C1
Skyttorp S 51 B4
Sládkovičovo SK 111 A4
Slagelse DK 61 D1
Slagharen NL 71 B3
Slagnäs S 195 E9
Slaidburn GB 40 B1
Slane IRL 30 A2
Slangerup DK 61 D2
Slano HR 139 C3
Slantsy RUS 8 C6
Slaný CZ 84 B2
Slap SLO 122 A2
Šlapanice CZ 97 B4
Slåstad N 48 B3
Slatina BIH 139 B3
Slatina HR 125 B3
Slatina RO 17 C6
Slatiňany CZ 97 B3
Slatinice CZ 98 B1
Slättberg S 50 A1
Slattum N 48 C2
Slavičin CZ 98 B1
Slavkov CZ 98 C1
Slavkov u Brna CZ 97 B4
Slavkovica SRB 127 C2
Slavonice CZ 97 C3
Slavonski Brod HR 125 B4
Slavonski Kobas HR 125 B3
Slavõsovce SK 99 C4
Slavskoye RUS 69 A5
Slavuta UA 13 C7
Sława, *Lubuskie* PL 85 A4
Sława, *Zachodnio-Pomorskie* PL 67 C4
Slawharad BY 13 B9
Sławków PL 86 B3
Sławno, *Wielkopolskie* PL 76 B2
Sławno, *Zachodnio-Pomorskie* PL 68 A1
Sławoborze PL 67 C4
Sl'ažany SK 98 C2
Sleaford GB 40 C3
Sleðbrjótur IS 191 B11
Sledmere GB 40 A3
Sleights GB 37 B6
Slemmestad N 54 A1
Ślesin PL 76 B3
Sliač SK 99 C3
Sliema M 175 C3
Sligo IRL 26 B2
Slite S 57 C4
Slitu N 54 A2
Sliven BG 17 D7
Śliwice PL 68 B3
Slobozia RO 17 C7
Slochteren NL 71 A3
Slöinge S 60 C2
Słomniki PL 87 B4
Slonim BY 13 B6
Słońsk PL 75 B3
Slootdorp NL 70 B1
Slottsbron S 55 A4
Slough GB 44 B3
Slövag N 46 B2
Slovenj Gradec SLO 110 C2
Slovenska Bistrica SLO 123 A4
Slovenská L'upča SK 99 C3
Slovenská-Ves SK 99 B4
Slovenské Darmoty SK 112 A3
Slovenske Konjice SLO 123 A4
Słubice PL 74 B3
Sluderno I 108 C1
Sluis NL 78 A3
Šluknov CZ 84 A2
Slunj HR 123 B4
Słupca PL 76 B2
Słupia PL 87 A3
Słupiec PL 85 B4
Słupsk PL 68 A2
Slutsk BY 13 B7
Smålandsstenar S 60 B3
Smalåsen N 195 E4
Smardzewo PL 75 B4
Smarhon BY 13 A7
Smarje SLO 123 A4
Šmarjeta SLO 123 B4
Šmartno SLO 123 A3
Smečno CZ 84 B2
Smedby S 63 B4
Smědec CZ 96 C2
Smederevo SRB 127 C2
Smederevska Palanka SRB 127 C2
Smedjebacken S 50 B2
Smęgorzów PL 87 B5
Smeland N 53 B4
Smidary CZ 84 B3
Śmigiel PL 75 B5
Smilde NL 71 B3
Smiřice CZ 85 B3
Smithfield GB 36 B4
Śmitowo PL 75 A5
Smögen S 54 B2
Smogulec PL 76 A2
Smołdzino PL 68 A2
Smolenice SK 98 C1
Smolensk RUS 13 A10
Smolník SK 99 C4
Smolyan BG 183 B6
Smuka SLO 123 B3
Smygehamn S 66 A2
Smykow PL 87 A4
Snainton GB 40 A3
Snaith GB 40 B2
Snaptun DK 59 C3
Snarby N 192 C3
Snarum N 48 B1
Snåsa N 199 A9
Snedsted DK 58 B1
Sneek NL 70 A2
Sneem IRL 29 C2
Snejbjerg DK 59 B1
Snillfjord N 198 B6
Šnjegotina BIH 125 C3
Snøde DK 65 A3
Snøfjord N 193 B8
Snogebaek DK 67 A4
Snyatyn UA 13 D6
Soave I 121 B4
Sober E 140 B3
Sobernheim D 93 B3
Soběslav CZ 96 B2
Sobota, *Dolnośląskie* PL 85 A3
Sobota, *Łódzkie* PL 77 B4
Sobotište SK 98 C1
Sobotka CZ 84 B3
Sobótka, *Dolnośląskie* PL 85 B4
Sobótka, *Wielkopolskie* PL 86 A1
Sobra HR 139 C3
Sobrado, *Coruña* E 140 A2
Sobrado, *Lugo* E 141 B3
Sobral da Adica P 161 A2
Sobral de Monte Argraço P 154 C1
Sobreira Formosa P 154 B3
Søby DK 64 B3
Soca SLO 122 A2
Sochaczew PL 77 B5
Sochos GR 183 C5
Socodor RO 113 C5
Socol RO 127 C3
Socovos E 164 A3
Socuéllamos E 158 B1
Sodankylä FIN 197 B9
Soderåkra S 63 B4
Söderala S 51 A3
Söderås S 50 B2
Söderbärke S 50 B2
Söderby-Karl S 51 C5
Söderfors S 51 B4
Söderhamn S 51 A4
Söderköping S 56 B2
Söderö S 56 B1
Södertälje S 57 A3
Södingberg A 110 B2
Södra Finnö S 56 B2
Södra Ny S 55 A4
Södra Råda S 55 A5
Södra Sandby S 61 D3
Södra Vi S 62 A3
Sodražica SLO 123 B3
Sodupe E 143 A3
Soengas P 148 A1
Soest D 81 A4
Soest NL 70 B2
Sofades GR 182 D4
Sofia = Sofiya BG 17 D5
Sofikon GR 184 B4
Sofiya = Sofia BG 17 D5
Şofronea RO 126 A3
Sögel D 71 B4
Sogliano al Rubicone I 135 A5
Sogndalsfjøra N 46 A4
Søgne N 53 B3
Söğüt, *Bilecik* TR 187 B5
Söğüt, *Burdur* TR 189 B4
Söğütköy TR 188 C3
Söğütlu TR 187 B5
Soham GB 45 A4
Sohland D 84 A2
Sohren D 93 B3
Soignies B 79 B4
Soissons F 90 B3
Söjtör H 111 C3
Sokal' UA 13 C6
Söke TR 188 B2
Sokna N 48 B1
Sokndal N 52 B2
Soknedal N 199 C7
Soko BIH 125 C4
Sokolac BIH 139 B4
Sokółka PL 13 B5
Sokolov CZ 83 B4
Sokołów Podlaski PL 12 B5
Sokołowo PL 76 B3
Sola N 52 B1
Solana de los Barros E 155 C4
Solana del Pino E 157 B3
Solánas I 179 C3
Solares E 143 A3
Solarino I 177 B4
Solarussa I 179 C2
Solas GB 31 B1
Solber-gelva N 53 A6
Solberg S 200 C3
Solberga S 62 A2
Solbjørg N 46 B2
Solčany SK 98 C2
Solčava SLO 123 A3
Solda I 108 C1
Sölden A 108 C2
Solec Kujawski PL 76 A3
Soleils F 132 B2
Solenzara F 180 B2
Solera E 163 A4
Solesmes F 79 B3
Soleto I 173 B4
Solgne F 92 C2
Solheim N 46 B2
Solheimsvik N 52 A2
Solignac F 115 C5
Solihull GB 44 A2
Solin HR 138 B2
Solingen D 80 A3
Solivella E 147 C2
Solkan SLO 122 B2
Söll A 108 B3
Sollana E 159 B3
Sollebrunn S 54 B3
Sollefteå S 200 C3
Sollen-tuna S 57 A3
Sollenau A 111 B3
Sóller E 166 B2
Sollerön S 50 B1
Søllested DK 65 B4
Solliès-Pont F 132 B2
Sollihøgda N 48 C2
Solnechnogorsk RUS 9 D10
Solnice CZ 85 B4
Solofra I 170 C2
Solomiac F 129 C3
Solopaca I 170 B2
Solórzano E 143 A3
Solothurn CH 106 B2
Solre-le-Château F 79 B4
Solsona E 147 C2
Solsvik N 46 B1
Solt H 112 C3
Soltau D 72 B2
Soltsy RUS 9 C7
Soltszentimre H 112 C3
Soltvadkert H 112 C3
Solumsmoen N 48 C1
Solund N 46 A1
Solva GB 39 C1
Sölvesborg S 63 B2
Solymár H 112 B2
Soma TR 186 C2
Somain F 78 B3
Somberek H 125 A4
Sombernon F 104 B3
Sombor SRB 125 B5
Sombreffe B 79 B4
Someren NL 80 A1
Somero FIN 8 B3
Somersham GB 44 A3
Somerton GB 43 A4
Sominy PL 68 A2
Somma Lombardo I 120 B1
Sommariva del Bosco I 119 C4
Sommarøy N 192 C2
Sommarset N 194 C6
Sommatino I 176 B2
Somme-Tourbe F 91 B4
Sommeilles F 91 C4
Sommen S 55 B5
Sommepy-Tahure F 91 B4
Sömmerda D 82 A3
Sommerfeld D 74 B2
Sommersted DK 59 C2
Sommesous F 91 C4
Sommières F 131 B3
Sommières-du-Clain F 115 B4
Somo E 143 A3
Somogyfajsz H 111 C4
Somogyjád H 111 C4
Somogysámson H 111 C4
Somogysárd H 125 A3
Somogyszil H 112 C2
Somogyszob H 124 A3
Somogyvár H 111 C4
Somontin E 164 B2
Somosiero E 151 A4
Somosköújfalu H 113 A3
Sompolno PL 76 B3
Sompuis F 91 C4
Son N 54 A1
Son Bou E 167 B4
Son en Breugel NL 80 A1
Son Servera E 167 B3
Sonceboz CH 106 B2
Soncillo E 143 B3
Soncino I 120 B2
Sóndalo I 120 A3
Søndeled N 53 B5
Sønder Bjert DK 59 C2
Sønder Felding DK 59 C1
Sønder Hygum DK 59 C1
Sønder Omme DK 59 C1
Sønderborg DK 64 B2
Sønderby DK 64 B2
Sønderho DK 59 C1
Sondershausen D 82 A2
Søndersø DK 59 C3
Søndervig DK 59 B1
Søndre Enningdal Kappel N 54 B2
Sóndrio I 120 A2
Soneja E 159 B3
Songe N 53 B5
Songeons F 90 B1
Sonkamuotka FIN 196 A6
Sonkovo RUS 9 D10
Sönnarslöv S 61 D4
Sonneberg D 82 B3
Sonnefeld D 82 B3
Sonnewalde D 84 A1
Sonnino I 169 B3
Sonogno CH 120 A1
Sonsbeck D 80 A2
Sonseca E 157 A4
Sønsterud N 49 B4
Sonstorp S 56 B1
Sonta SRB 125 B5
Sontheim D 94 C2
Sonthofen D 107 B5
Sontra D 82 A1
Sopelana E 143 A4
Sopje HR 125 B3
Šoporňa SK 111 A4
Sopot PL 69 A3
Sopot SRB 127 C2
Sopotnica MK 182 B3
Sopron H 111 B3
Šor SRB 127 C1
Sora I 169 B3
Soragna I 120 C3
Söråker S 200 D3
Sorano I 168 A1
Sorbara I 121 C4
Sorbas E 164 B2
Sórbolo I 121 C3
Sörbygden S 200 D2
Sordal N 52 B3
Sordale GB 32 C3
Sore F 128 B2
Sörenberg CH 106 C3
Soresina I 120 B2
Sorèze F 146 A3
Sörforsa S 200 E3
Sorges F 115 C4
Sórgono I 179 B3
Sorgues F 131 A3
Sorgun TR 23 B8
Soria E 143 C4
Soriano Cálabro I 175 C2
Soriano nel Cimino I 168 A2
Sorihuela del Guadalimar E 164 A1
Sorisdale GB 34 B1
Sørkjosen N 192 C4
Sørli N 199 A10
Sormás H 111 C3
Sörmjöle S 200 C6
Sørmo N 194 B9
Sornac F 116 B2
Sorø DK 61 D1
Soroca MD 17 A8
Sørreisa N 194 A9
Sorrento I 170 C2
Sorsele S 195 E8
Sörsjön S 49 A5
Sorso I 178 B2
Sort E 146 B2
Sortavala RUS 9 B7
Sortino I 177 B4
Sortland N 194 B6
Sørum N 48 B2
Sørumsand N 48 C3
Sorunda S 57 A3
Sörup D 64 B2
Sørvær N 192 B6
Sørvågen N 194 C3
Sorvik S 50 B2
Sørvika N 199 C8
Sos F 128 B3
Sos del Rey Católico E 144 B2
Sösdala S 61 C3
Sošice HR 123 B4
Sośnica PL 75 A5
Sośnicowice PL 86 B2
Sośno PL 76 A2
Sosnovyy Bor RUS 9 C6
Sosnowiec PL 86 B3
Sospel F 133 B3
Šoštanj SLO 123 A4
Sotaseter N 198 D4
Sotillo de Adrada E 150 B3
Sotillo de la Ribera E 143 C3
Sotin HR 125 B5
Sotkamo FIN 3 D11
Soto de la Marina E 143 A3
Soto de los Infantes E 141 A4

Soto de Real E 151 B4
Soto de Ribera E 141 A5
Soto del Barco E 141 A4
Soto y Amío E 141 B5
Sotobañado y Priorato E 142 B2
Sotoserrano E 149 B3
Sotresgudo E 142 B2
Sotrondio E 142 A1
Sotta F 180 B2
Sottomarina I 122 B1
Sottrum D 72 A2
Sottunga FIN 51 B7
Sotuelamos E 158 B1
Souain F 91 B4
Soual F 146 A3
Soucy F 104 A2
Souda GR 185 D5
Soudron F 91 C4
Souesmes F 103 B4
Soufflenheim F 93 C3
Soufli GR 186 A1
Souillac F 129 B4
Souilly F 91 B5
Soulac-sur-Mer F 114 C2
Soulaines-Dhuys F 91 C4
Soulatgé F 146 B3
Soultz-Haut-Rhin F 106 B2
Soultz-sous-Forêts F 93 C3
Soumagne B 80 B1
Soumoulou F 145 A3
Souppes-sur-Loing F 103 A4
Souprosse F 128 C2
Sourdeval F 88 B3
Soure P 154 A2
Sournia F 146 B3
Souro Pires P 149 B2
Sourpi GR 182 D4
Sours F 90 C1
Sousceyrac F 116 C2
Sousel P 155 C3
Soustons F 128 C1
Soutelo de Montes E 140 B2
South Brent GB 42 B3
South Cave GB 40 B3
South Hayling GB 44 C3
South Molton GB 42 A3
South Ockendon GB 45 B4
South Petherton GB 43 B4
South Shields GB 37 B5
South Tawton GB 42 B3
South Woodham Ferrers GB 45 B4
Southam GB 44 A2
Southampton GB 44 C2
Southborough GB 45 B4
Southend GB 34 C2
Southend-on-Sea GB 45 B4
Southport GB 38 A3
Southwell GB 40 B3
Southwold GB 45 A5
Souto P 148 B2
Souto da Carpalhosa P 154 B2
Soutochao E 141 C3
Souvigny F 104 C2
Souzay-Champigny F 102 B1
Soverato I 175 C2
Soveria Mannelli I 175 B2
Sövestad S 66 A2
Sovetsk RUS 12 A4
Sovići BIH 138 B3
Sovicille I 135 B4
Søvik N 198 C3
Sowerby GB 37 B5
Soyaux F 115 C4
Søyland N 52 B1
Spa B 80 B1
Spadafora I 177 A4
Spaichingen D 107 A3
Spakenburg NL 70 B2
Spalding GB 41 C3
Spálené Poříčí CZ 96 B1
Spalt D 94 B2
Spangenberg D 82 A1
Spangereid N 52 B3
Spantekow D 74 A2
Sparanise I 170 B2
Sparbu N 199 B8
Sparkær DK 58 B2
Sparkford GB 43 A4
Sparreholm S 56 A2
Spartà I 177 A4
Sparta = Sparti GR 184 B3
Sparti = Sparta GR 184 B3
Spean Bridge GB 34 B3
Speicher D 92 B2
Speichersdorf D 95 B3
Speke GB 38 A4
Spello I 136 C1
Spenge D 72 B1
Spennymoor GB 37 B5
Spentrup DK 58 B3
Sperenberg D 74 B2
Sperlinga I 177 B3
Sperlonga I 169 B3
Spetalen N 54 A1
Spetses GR 184 B4
Speyer D 93 B4
Spézet F 100 A2
Spezzano Albanese I 174 B2
Spezzano della Sila I 174 B2
Spiddle IRL 28 A2
Spiegelau D 96 C1
Spiekeroog D 71 A4
Spiez CH 106 C2
Spigno Monferrato I 133 A4
Spijk NL 71 A3
Spijkenisse NL 79 A4
Spilamberto I 135 A4
Spili GR 185 D5
Spilimbergo I 122 A1
Spilsby GB 41 B4
Spinazzola I 172 B2
Spincourt F 92 B1
Spind N 52 B2
Spindleruv-Mlyn CZ 84 B3
Spinoso I 174 A1
Špišić Bukovica HR 124 B3
Spišská Belá SK 99 B4
Spišská Nová Ves SK 99 C4
Spisská Stará Ves SK 99 B4
Spišské-Hanušovce SK 99 B4
Spišské Podhradie SK 99 C4
Spišské Vlachy SK 99 C4
Spišský-Štvrtok SK 99 C4
Spital A 110 B1
Spital am Semmering A 110 B2
Spittal an der Drau A 109 C4
Spittle of Glenshee GB 35 B4
Spitz A 97 C3
Spjærøy N 54 A1
Spjald DK 59 B1
Spjelkavik N 198 C3
Spjutsbygd S 63 B3
Split HR 138 B2
Splügen CH 107 C4
Spodsbjerg DK 65 B3
Spofforth GB 40 B2
Spohle D 71 A5
Spoleto I 136 C1
Spoltore I 169 A4
Spondigna I 108 C1
Sponvika N 54 A2
Spornitz D 73 A4
Spotorno I 133 A4
Spraitbach D 94 C1
Sprakensehl D 72 B3
Spręcowo PL 69 B5
Spremberg D 84 A2
Spresiano I 122 B1
Sprimont B 80 B1
Springe D 72 B2
Sproatley GB 41 B3
Spydeberg N 54 A2
Spytkowice PL 99 B3
Squillace I 175 C2
Squinzano I 173 B4
Sračinec HR 124 A2
Srbac BIH 124 B3
Srbobran SRB 126 B1
Srebrenica BIH 127 C1
Srebrenik BIH 125 C4
Središče SLO 124 A2
Śrem PL 76 B2
Sremska Mitrovica SRB 127 C1
Sremski Karlovci SRB 126 B1
Srní CZ 96 B1
Srnice Gornje BIH 125 C4
Srock PL 86 A3
Środa Śląska PL 85 A4
Środa Wielkopolski PL 76 B2
Srpska Crnja SRB 126 B2
Srpski Itebej SRB 126 B2
Srpski Miletić SRB 125 B5
St Merløse DK 61 D1
St Michel-de-Castelnau F 128 B2
Staatz A 97 C4
Stabbursnes N 193 B8
Staberdorf D 65 B4
Stabroek B 79 A4
Stachy CZ 96 B1
Stade D 72 A2
Staden B 78 B3
Staðarfell IS 190 B3
Stadl an der Mur A 109 B4
Stadskanaal NL 71 B3
Stadtallendorf D 81 B5
Stadthagen D 72 B2
Stadtilm D 82 B3
Stadtkyll D 80 B2
Stadtlauringen D 82 B2
Stadtlengsfeld D 82 B2
Stadtlohn D 71 C3
Stadtoldendorf D 82 A1
Stadtroda D 83 B3
Stadtsteinach D 82 B3
Stäfa CH 107 B3
Staffanstorp S 61 D3
Staffelstein D 82 B2
Staffin GB 31 B2
Stafford GB 40 C1
Stainach A 110 B1
Staindrop GB 37 B5
Staines GB 44 B3
Stainville F 91 C5
Stainz A 110 C2
Staithes GB 37 B6
Staíti I 175 D2
Stäket S 57 A3
Stakroge DK 59 C1
Štalcerji SLO 123 B3
Stalden CH 119 A4
Stalham GB 41 C5
Stalheim N 46 B3
Stallarholmen S 56 A3
Ställberg S 50 C1
Ställdalen S 50 C1
Stallhofen A 110 B2
Stalon S 195 F6
Stalowa Wola PL 12 C5
Stamford GB 40 C3
Stamford Bridge GB 40 B3
Stamnes N 46 B2
Stams A 108 B1
Stamsried D 95 B4
Stamsund N 194 B4
Stanford le Hope GB 45 B4
Stånga S 57 C4
Stange N 48 B3
Stanghella I 121 B4
Stanhope GB 37 B4
Stanišić SRB 125 B5
Staňkov CZ 95 B5
Stankovci HR 137 B4
Stanley GB 37 B5
Stans CH 106 C3
Stansted Mountfitchet GB 45 B4
Stanzach A 108 B1
Stapar SRB 125 B5
Staphorst NL 70 B3
Staplehurst GB 45 B4
Stąporków PL 87 A4
Stara Baška HR 123 C3
Stara Fužina SLO 122 A2
Stara Kamienica PL 84 B3
Stara Kiszewa PL 68 B3
Stará L'ubovňa SK 99 B4
Stara Moravica SRB 126 B1
Stara Novalja HR 137 A3
Stara Pazova SRB 127 C2
Stará Turá SK 98 C1
Stara Zagora BG 17 D6
Starachowice PL 87 A5
Staraya Russa RUS 9 D7
Stärbsnäs S 51 C6
Starčevo SRB 127 C2
Stare Dłutowo PL 77 A4
Staré Hamry CZ 98 B2
Stare Jablonki PL 69 B5
Staré Město CZ 98 B1
Stare Pole PL 69 A4
Stare Sedlo CZ 96 B2
Stare Strącze PL 85 A4
Stargard Szczeciński PL 75 A4
Stårheim N 198 D2
Stari Banovci SRB 127 C2
Stari Gradac HR 124 B3
Stari Jankovci HR 125 B4
Stari Majdan BIH 124 C2
Stari-Mikanovci HR 125 B4
Starigrad, *Ličko-Senjska* HR 123 C3
Starigrad, *Splitsko-Dalmatinska* HR 138 B2
Starigrad-Paklenica HR 137 A4
Staritsa RUS 9 D9
Starkenbach A 108 B1
Starnberg D 108 B2
Staro Petrovo Selo HR 124 B3
Staro Selo HR 124 B1
Staro Selo SRB 127 C3
Starogard PL 75 A4
Starogard Gdański PL 69 B3
Starokonstyantyniv UA 13 D7
Stary Brzozów PL 77 B5
Stary Dzierzgoń PL 69 B4
Starý Hrozenkov CZ 98 C1
Stary Jaroslaw PL 68 A1
Stary Plzenec CZ 96 B1
Stary Sącz PL 99 B4
Starý Smokovec SK 99 B4
Staryy Chartoriysk UA 13 C6
Staškov SK 98 B2
Stassfurt D 82 A3
Staszów PL 87 B5
Stathelle N 53 A5
Staufen D 106 B2
Staunton GB 39 C4
Stavang N 46 A2
Stavanger N 52 B1
Stavåsnäs S 49 B4
Stavby S 51 B5
Staveley GB 40 B2
Stavelot B 80 B1
Stavenisse NL 79 A4
Stavern N 53 B6
Stavnäs S 55 A3
Stavoren NL 70 B2
Stavros CY 181 A1
Stavros GR 183 C5
Stavroupoli GR 183 B6
Stavseng N 47 A6
Stavsiø N 48 B2
Stavsnäs S 57 A4
Stawiszyn PL 76 C3
Steane N 53 A4
Steblevë AL 182 B2
Stechelberg CH 106 C2
Štěchovice CZ 96 B2
Stechow D 73 B5
Steckborn CH 107 B3
Stede Broek NL 70 B2
Steeg A 107 B5
Steenbergen NL 79 A4
Steenvoorde F 78 B2
Steenwijk NL 70 B3
Štefanje HR 124 B2
Steffisburg CH 106 C2
Stegaurach D 94 B2
Stege DK 65 B5
Stegelitz D 74 A2
Stegersbach A 111 B3
Stegna PL 69 A4
Steimbke D 72 B2
Stein GB 31 B2
Stein an Rhein CH 107 B3
Steinach A 108 B2
Steinach, *Baden-Württemberg* D 106 A3
Steinach, *Bayern* D 82 B2
Steinach, *Thüringen* D 82 B3
Steinau, *Bayern* D 81 B5
Steinau, *Niedersachsen* D 64 C1
Steinbeck D 74 B2
Steinberg am Rofan A 108 B2
Steindorf A 109 C5
Steine N 46 B2
Steinen D 106 B2
Steinfeld A 109 C4
Steinfeld D 71 B5
Steinfurt D 71 B4
Steingaden D 108 B1
Steinhagen D 72 B1
Steinheid D 82 B3
Steinheim, *Bayern* D 107 A5
Steinheim, *Nordrhein-Westfalen* D 81 A5
Steinhöfel D 74 B3
Steinhorst D 72 B3
Steinigtwolmsdorf D 84 A2
Steinkjer N 199 A8
Steinsholt N 53 A5
Stekene B 79 A4
Stelle D 72 A3
Stellendam NL 79 A4
Stenåsa S 63 B4
Stenay F 91 B5
Stenberga S 62 A3
Stendal D 73 B4
Stenhammar S 55 B4
Stenhamra S 57 A3
Stenhousemuir GB 35 B4
Stenlose DK 61 D2
Stensätra S 50 B3
Stensele S 195 E8
Stenstorp S 55 B4
Stenstrup DK 65 A3
Stenudden S 195 D8
Stenungsund S 54 B2
Štěpánov CZ 98 B1
Stephanskirchen D 108 B3
Stepnica PL 74 A3
Stepojevac SRB 127 C2
Stepping DK 59 C2
Sterbfritz D 82 B1
Sternberg D 65 C4
Šternberk CZ 98 B1
Sterup D 64 B2
Stes Maries-de-la-Mer F 131 B3
Stęszew PL 75 B5
Štěti CZ 84 B2
Stevenage GB 44 B3
Stewarton GB 36 A2
Steyerburg D 72 B2
Steyning GB 44 C3
Steyr A 110 A1
Stężyca PL 68 A2
Stezzano I 120 B2
Stia I 135 B4
Stibb Cross GB 42 B2
Sticciano Scalo I 135 C4
Stidsvig S 61 C3
Stiens NL 70 A2
Stige DK 59 C3
Stigen S 54 B3
Stigliano I 174 A2
Stigtomta S 56 B2
Stilida GR 182 E4
Stilla N 192 C7
Stillington GB 40 A2
Stilo I 175 C2
Stintino I 178 B2
Stio I 172 B1
Štip MK 182 B4
Stira GR 185 A5
Stirling GB 35 B4
Štítnik SK 99 C4
Štíty CZ 97 B4
Stjärnhov S 56 A3
Stjärnsund S 50 B3
Stjørdalshalsen N 199 B7
Stobnica PL 87 A3
Stobno PL 75 A5
Stobreč HR 138 B2
Stochov CZ 84 B1
Stockach D 107 B4
Stöckalp CH 106 C3
Stockaryd S 62 A2
Stockbridge GB 44 B2
Stockerau A 97 C4
Stockheim D 82 B3
Stockholm S 57 A4
Stockport GB 40 B1
Stocksbridge GB 40 B2
Stockton-on-Tees GB 37 B5
Stod CZ 96 B1
Stöde S 200 D2
Stöðvarfjörður IS 191 C12
Stødi N 195 D6
Stoer GB 32 C1
Stoholm DK 58 B2
Stoke Ferry GB 41 C4
Stoke Fleming GB 43 B3
Stoke Mandeville GB 44 B3
Stoke-on-Trent GB 40 B1
Stokesley GB 37 B5
Stokke N 54 A1
Stokkemarke DK 65 B4
Stokken N 53 B4
Stokkseyri IS 190 D4
Stokkvågen N 195 D4
Stokmarknes N 194 B5
Štoky CZ 97 B3
Stolac BIH 139 B3
Stølaholmen N 46 A3
Stolberg D 80 B2
Stolin BY 13 C7
Stollberg D 83 B4
Stöllet S 49 B5
Stollhamm D 71 A5
Stolno PL 76 A3
Stolpen D 84 A2
Stolzenau D 72 B2
Stompetoren NL 70 B1
Ston HR 139 C3
Stonařov CZ 97 B3
Stone GB 40 C1
Stonehaven GB 33 E4
Stonehouse GB 36 A3
Stongfjorden N 46 A2
Stonndalen N 47 B4
Stony Stratford GB 44 A3
Stopnica PL 87 B4
Storå S 56 A1
Storås N 198 B6
Storby FIN 51 B6
Stordal, *Møre og Romsdal* N 198 C4
Stordal, *Nord-Trøndelag* N 199 B8
Store GB 33 B4
Store Damme DK 65 B5
Store Heddinge DK 65 A5
Store Herrestad S 66 A2
Store Levene S 55 B3
Store Molvik N 193 B12
Store Skedvi S 50 B2
Store Vika S 57 B3
Storebø N 46 B2
Storebro S 62 A3
Storelv N 192 B6
Støren N 199 B7
Storfjellseter N 199 D7
Storfjord N 192 C3
Storfjorden N 198 C3
Storfors S 55 A5
Storforshei N 195 D5
Storhøliseter N 47 A6
Storjord N 195 D6
Storkow, *Brandenburg* D 74 B2
Storkow, *Mecklenburg-Vorpommern* D 74 A3
Storli N 198 C6
Storlien S 199 B9
Stornara I 171 B3
Stornoway GB 31 A2
Storo I 121 B3
Storozhynets UA 17 A6
Storrington GB 44 C3
Storseleby S 200 B2
Storsjön S 50 A3
Storslett N 192 C5
Storsteinnes N 192 C3
Storsund S 196 D3
Storuman S 195 E8
Störvattnet S 199 C9
Storvik N 195 D4
Storvik S 50 B3
Storvreta S 51 C4
Štos SK 99 C4
Stössen D 83 A3
Stotel D 72 A1
Stötten D 108 B1
Stotternheim D 82 A3
Stouby DK 59 C2
Stourbridge GB 40 C1
Stourport-on-Severn GB 39 B4
Støvring DK 58 B2
Stow GB 35 C5
Stow-on-the-Wold GB 44 B2
Stowbtsy BY 13 B7
Stowmarket GB 45 A5
Straach D 73 C5
Strabane GB 27 B3
Strachan GB 33 D4
Strachur GB 34 B2
Stracin MK 182 A4
Strackholt D 71 A4
Stradbally IRL 29 B1
Stradella I 120 B2
Straelen D 80 A2
Stragari SRB 127 C2
Strakonice CZ 96 B1
Strålsnäs S 55 B6
Stralsund D 66 B2
Strand N 48 A3
Stranda N 198 C3
Strandby DK 58 A3
Strandebarm N 46 B3
Strandhill IRL 26 B2
Strandlykkja N 48 B3
Strandvik N 46 B2
Strangford GB 27 B5
Strängnäs S 56 A3
Strångsjö S 56 B2
Stráni CZ 98 C1
Stranice SLO 123 A4
Stranorlar IRL 26 B3
Stranraer GB 36 B1
Strasatti I 176 B1
Strasbourg F 93 C3
Strasburg D 74 A2
Strašice CZ 96 B1
Strass im Steiermark A 110 C2
Stråssa S 56 A1
Strassburg A 110 C1
Strasskirchen D 95 C4
Strasswalchen A 109 B4
Stratford-upon-Avon GB 44 A2
Strathaven GB 36 A2
Strathdon GB 32 D3
Strathkanaird GB 32 D1
Strathpeffer GB 32 D2
Strathy GB 32 C3
Strathyre GB 34 B3
Stratinska BIH 124 C2
Stratton GB 42 B2
Straubing D 95 C4
Straulas I 178 B3
Straume N 53 A5
Straumen, *Nord-Trøndelag* N 199 B8
Straumen, *Nordland* N 194 C6
Straumsjøen N 194 B5
Straumsnes N 194 C6
Straupitz D 74 C3
Strausberg D 74 B2
Straussfurt D 82 A3
Strawczyn PL 87 B4
Straž nad Nezárkou CZ 96 B2
Stráž Pod Ralskem CZ 84 B2
Straža SLO 123 B4
Straža SRB 127 C3
Strážnice CZ 98 C1
Strážný CZ 96 C1
Štrbské Pleso SK 99 B4
Strečno SK 98 B2
Street GB 43 A4
Strehla D 83 A5
Strekov SK 112 B2
Strem A 111 B3
Stremska-Rača SRB 127 C1
Strengberg A 110 A1
Strengelvåg N 194 B6
Stresa I 119 B5
Streufdord D 82 B2
Strib DK 59 C2
Striberg S 55 A5
Střibro CZ 95 B4
Strichen GB 33 D4
Strigno I 121 A4
Štrigova HR 111 C3
Strijen NL 79 A4
Strizivojna HR 125 B4
Strmica HR 138 A2
Strmilov CZ 97 B3
Ströhen D 72 B1
Strokestown IRL 28 A3
Stromberg, *Nordrhein-Westfalen* D 81 A4
Stromberg, *Rheinland-Pfalz* D 93 B3
Stromeferry GB 31 B3
Strömnäs S 200 B2
Stromness GB 33 C3
Strömsberg S 51 B4
Strömsbruk S 200 E3
Strömsfors S 56 B2
Strömsnäsbruk S 61 C3
Strömstad S 54 B2
Strömsund, *Jämtland* S 199 B12
Strömsund, *Västerbotten* S 195 E7
Stronachlachar GB 34 B3
Stróngoli I 174 B3
Stronie Śląskie PL 85 B4
Strontian GB 34 B2
Stroppiana I 119 B5
Stroud GB 43 A4
Stroumbi CY 181 B1
Stróża PL 99 B3
Strücklingen D 71 A4

Vauvert F 131 B3
Vauvillers F 105 B5
Vaux-sur-Sure B 92 B1
Vawkavysk BY 13 B6
Vaxholm S 57 A4
Växjö S 62 B2
Våxtorp S 61 C3
Vayrac F 129 B4
Važec SK 99 B3
Veberöd S 61 D3
Vechelde D 72 B3
Vechta D 71 B5
Vecinos E 149 B4
Vecsés H 112 B3
Vedavågen N 52 A1
Veddige S 60 B2
Vedersø DK 59 B1
Vedeseta I 120 B2
Vedevåg S 56 A1
Vedra E 140 B2
Vedum S 55 B3
Veendam NL 71 A3
Veenendaal NL 70 B2
Vega, *Asturias* E 142 A1
Vega, *Asturias* E 142 A1
Vega de Espinareda E 141 B4
Vega de Infanzones E 142 B1
Vega de Pas E 143 A3
Vega de Valcarce E 141 B4
Vega de Valdetronco E 150 A2
Vegadeo E 141 A3
Vegårshei N 53 B4
Vegas de Coria E 149 B3
Vegas del Condado E 142 B1
Vegby S 60 B3
Vegger DK 58 B2
Veggli N 47 B6
Veghel NL 80 A1
Veglast D 66 B1
Véglie I 173 B3
Veguillas E 151 B4
Vegusdal N 53 B4
Veidholmen N 198 B4
Veidnes N 193 B10
Veikåker N 48 B1
Veinge S 61 C3
Vejbystrand S 61 C2
Vejen DK 59 C2
Vejer de la Frontera E 162 B2
Vejle DK 59 C2
Vejprty CZ 83 B5
Vela Luka HR 138 C2
Velada E 150 B3
Velayos E 150 B3
Velbert D 80 A3
Velburg D 95 B3
Velde N 199 A8
Velden, *Bayern* D 95 B3
Velden, *Bayern* D 95 C4
Velden am Worther See A 109 C5
Velefique E 164 B2
Velen D 80 A2
Velenje SLO 123 A4
Veles MK 182 B3
Velesevec HR 124 B2
Velešin CZ 96 C2
Velestino GR 182 D4
Velez Blanco E 164 B2
Vélez de Benaudalla E 163 B4
Vélez-Málaga E 163 B3
Vélez Rubio E 164 B2
Veli Lošinj HR 137 A3
Veliiki Radinci SRB 127 B1
Velika HR 125 B3
Velika Gorica HR 124 B2
Velika Grdevac HR 124 B3
Velika Greda SRB 126 B3
Velika Ilova BIH 125 C3
Velika Kladuša BIH 124 B1
Velika Kopanica HR 125 B4
Velika Krsna SRB 127 C2
Velika Obarska BIH 125 C5
Velika Pisanica HR 124 B3
Velika Plana SRB 127 C3
Velika Zdenci HR 124 B3
Velike Lašče SLO 123 B3
Velike Središte SRB 126 B3
Veliki Gaj SRB 126 B3
Veliki Popović SRB 127 C3
Velikiye Luki RUS 9 D7
Veliko Gradište SRB 127 C3
Veliko Orašje SRB 127 C3
Veliko Selo SRB 127 C3
Veliko Tŭrnovo BG 17 D6
Velilla de San Antonio E 151 B4
Velilla del Río Carrió E 142 B2
Velingrad BG 183 A5
Velizh RUS 9 E7
Veljun HR 123 B4
Velká Bíteš CZ 97 B4
Velka Hled'scbe CZ 95 B4
Velka Lomnica SK 99 B4
Velká nad Veličkou CZ 98 C1
Velké Bystřice CZ 98 B1
Velké Heraltice CZ 98 B1
Velké Karlovice CZ 98 B2
Vel'ké Leváre SK 97 C5
Velké Losiny CZ 98 A1
Velké Meziříčí CZ 97 B4
Velké Pavlovice CZ 97 C4
Vel'ké Rovné SK 98 B2
Vel'ké Uherce SK 98 C2
Vel'ké Zálužie SK 98 C1
Vel'ke'Kostol'any SK 98 C1
Vel'ký Blahovo SK 99 C4
Velky Bor CZ 96 B1
Vel'ký Cetin SK 112 A2
Vel'ký Krtíš SK 112 A3
Vel'ký Meder SK 111 B4
Velky Ujezd CZ 98 B1
Vellahn D 73 A3
Vellberg D 94 B1
Velles F 103 C3
Velletri I 168 B2
Vellinge S 66 A2
Vellisca E 151 B5
Velliza E 150 A3
Vellmar D 81 A5
Velp NL 70 B2
Velten D 74 B2
Velvary CZ 84 B2
Velvendos GR 182 C4
Vemb DK 59 B1
Vemdalen S 199 C10
Veme N 48 B2
Véménd H 125 A4
Vemmedrup DK 61 D2
Vena S 62 A3
Venaco F 180 A2
Venafro I 169 B4
Venarey-les-Laumes F 104 B3
Venaría I 119 B4
Venasca I 133 A3
Venčane SRB 127 C2
Vence F 132 B3
Venda Nova, *Coimbra* P 154 A2
Venda Nova, *Leiria* P 154 B2
Vendas Novas P 154 C2
Vendays-Montalivet F 114 C2
Vendel S 51 B4
Vendelso S 57 A4
Vendeuil F 91 B3
Vendeuvre-sur-Barse F 104 A3
Vendœuvres F 115 B5
Vendôme F 103 B3
Venelles F 131 B4
Veness GB 33 B4
Venézia = Venice I 122 B1
Venialbo E 150 A2
Venice = Venézia I 122 B1
Vénissieux F 117 B4
Venjan S 49 B5
Venlo NL 80 A2
Venn Green GB 42 B2
Vennesla N 53 B3
Vennesund N 195 E3
Vennezey F 92 C2
Venosa I 172 B1
Venray NL 80 A1
Vent A 108 C1
Venta de Baños E 142 C2
Venta de los Santos E 157 B4
Venta del Moro E 158 B2
Venta las Ranas E 142 A1
Ventanueva E 141 A4
Ventas de Huelma E 163 A4
Ventas de Zafarraya E 163 B3
Ventavon F 132 A1
Ventimíglia I 133 B3
Ventnor GB 44 C2
Ventosa de la Sierra E 143 C4
Ventosilla E 143 C4
Ventspils LV 8 D2
Venturina I 134 B3
Venzolasca F 180 A2
Venzone I 122 A2
Vép H 111 B3
Vera E 164 B3
Vera N 199 B9
Vera Cruz P 160 A2
Vera de Bidasoa E 144 A2
Vera de Moncayo E 144 C2
Verbánia I 119 B5
Verberie F 90 B2
Verbicaro I 174 B1
Verbier CH 119 A4
Vercel-Villedieu-le-Camp F 105 B5
Vercelli I 119 B5
Verchen D 66 C1
Vercheny F 118 C2
Verclause F 131 A4
Verdalsøra N 199 B8
Verden D 72 B2
Verdens Ende N 54 A1
Verdikoussa GR 182 D3
Verdille F 115 C3
Verdú E 147 C2
Verdun F 92 B1
Verdun-sur-Garonne F 129 C4
Verdun-sur-le-Doubs F 105 C4
Veresegyház H 112 B3
Verfeil F 129 C4
Vergato I 135 A4
Vergel E 159 C4
Vergeletto CH 120 A1
Verges E 147 B4
Vergiate I 120 B1
Vergt F 129 A3
Veria GR 182 C4
Verín E 141 C3
Veringenstadt D 107 A4
Verl D 81 A4
Verma N 198 C5
Vermand F 90 B3
Vermelha P 154 B1
Vermenton F 104 B2
Vern-d'Anjou F 102 B1
Vernago I 108 C1
Vernante I 133 A3
Vernantes F 102 B2
Vernár SK 99 C4
Vernasca I 120 C2
Vernayaz CH 119 A4
Vernazza I 134 A2
Verneřice CZ 84 B2
Vernet F 146 A2
Vernet-les-Bains F 146 B3
Verneuil F 91 B3
Verneuil-sur-Avre F 89 B4
Vernier CH 118 A3
Vérnio I 135 A4
Vérnole I 173 B4
Vernon F 90 B1
Vernoux-en-Vivarais F 117 C4
Veróce H 112 B3
Verolanuova I 120 B3
Véroli I 169 B3
Verona I 121 B4
Verpelét H 113 B4
Verrabotn N 199 B7
Verrès I 119 B4
Verrey-sous-Salmaise F 104 B3
Verrières F 115 B4
Versailles F 90 C2
Versam CH 107 C4
Verseg H 112 B3
Versmold D 71 B5
Versoix CH 118 A3
Verteillac F 115 C4
Vértesacsa H 112 B2
Vertou F 101 B4
Vertus F 91 C3
Verviers B 80 B1
Vervins F 91 B3
Verwood GB 43 B5
Veryan GB 42 B2
Veržej SLO 111 C3
Verzuolo I 133 A3
Verzy F 91 B4
Vescovato F 180 A2
Vése H 124 A3
Veselí nad Lužnicí CZ 96 B2
Veselí nad Moravou CZ 98 C1
Veseliy BG 17 D7
Vésime I 119 C5
Veskoniemi FIN 193 D11
Vesoul F 105 B5
Vespolate I 120 B1
Vessigebro S 60 C2
Vestbygd N 52 B2
Vestenanova I 121 B4
Vester Husby S 56 B2
Vester Nebel DK 59 C2
Vester Torup DK 58 A2
Vester Vedsted DK 59 C1
Vesterøhavn DK 58 A3
Vestervig DK 58 B1
Vestfossen N 53 A5
Vestmannaeyjar IS 190 D5
Vestmarka N 48 C3
Vestnes N 198 C4
Vestone I 120 B3
Vestre Gausdal N 48 A2
Vestre Jakobselv N 193 B13
Vestre Slidre N 47 A5
Vesyegonsk RUS 9 C10
Veszprém H 112 B1
Veszprémvarsány H 112 B1
Vésztő H 113 C5
Vetlanda S 62 A3
Vetovo HR 125 B3
Vetralla I 168 A2
Větrný Jeníkov CZ 97 B3
Vétroz CH 119 A4
Vetschau D 84 A2
Vettasjärvi S 196 B4
Vetto I 134 A3
Vetulónia I 135 C3
Veules-les-Roses F 89 A4
Veulettes-sur-Mer F 89 A4
Veum N 53 A4
Veurne B 78 A2
Veverská Bítýška CZ 97 B4
Vevey CH 106 C1
Vevi GR 182 C3
Vevring N 46 A2
Vex CH 119 A4
Veynes F 132 A1
Veyre-Monton F 116 B3
Veyrier F 118 B3
Vézelay F 104 B2
Vézelise F 92 C2
Vézenobres F 131 A3
Vezins F 102 B1
Vézins-de-Lévézou F 130 A1
Vezirhan TR 187 B5
Vezirköprü TR 23 A8
Vezza di Óglio I 120 A3
Vezzani F 180 A2
Vezzano I 121 A4
Vezzano sul Cróstolo I 121 C3
Vi S 200 D3
Via Gloria P 160 B2
Viadana I 121 C3
Viana E 143 B4
Viana do Alentejo P 154 C2
Viana do Bolo E 141 B3
Viana do Castelo P 148 A1
Vianden L 92 B2
Viannos GR 185 D6
Viaréggio I 134 B3
Viator E 164 C2
Vibble S 57 C4
Vibo Valéntia I 175 C2
Viborg DK 58 B2
Vibraye F 102 A2
Vic E 147 C3
Vic-en-Bigorre F 145 A4
Vic-Fézensac F 129 C3
Vic-le-Comte F 116 B3
Vic-sur-Aisne F 90 B3
Vic-sur-Cère F 116 C2
Vícar E 164 C2
Vicarello I 134 B3
Vicari I 176 B2
Vicchio I 135 B4
Vicdesses F 146 B2
Vicenza I 121 B4
Vichy F 117 A3
Vickan S 60 B2
Vickerstown GB 36 B3
Vico F 180 A1
Vico del Gargano I 171 B3
Vico Equense I 170 C2
Vicopisano I 134 B3
Vicosoprano CH 120 A2
Vicovaro I 169 A2
Victoria = Rabat, *Gozo* M 175 C3
Vidago P 148 A2
Vidauban F 132 B2
Vide P 148 B2
Videbæk DK 59 B1
Videm SLO 123 B3
Videseter N 198 D4
Vidigueira P 160 A2
Vidin BG 16 D5
Vidlin GB 33 A5
Vidsel S 196 D3
Vidzy BY 13 A7
Viechtach D 95 B4
Vieille-Brioude F 117 B3
Vieira P 154 B2
Vieira do Minho P 148 A1
Vieiros P 155 C3
Vielha E 145 B4
Vielle-Aure F 145 B4
Viellespesse F 116 B3
Viellevigne F 114 B2
Vielmur-sur-Agout F 130 B1
Viels Maison F 91 C3
Vielsalm B 80 B1
Vienenburg D 73 C3
Vienna = Wien A 111 A3
Vienne F 117 B4
Vieritz D 73 B5
Viernheim D 93 B4
Vierraden D 74 A3
Viersen D 80 A2
Vierville-sur-Mer F 88 A3
Vierzon F 103 B4
Vieselbach D 82 B3
Vieste I 171 B4
Vietas S 194 C9
Vieteren B 78 B2
Vietri di Potenza I 172 B1
Vietri sul Mare I 170 C2
Vieux-Boucau-les-Bains F 128 C1
Vif F 118 B2
Vig DK 61 D1
Vigásio I 121 B3
Vigaun A 109 B4
Vigeland N 52 B3
Vigeois F 116 B1
Vigévano I 120 B1
Viggianello I 174 B2
Viggiano I 174 A1
Vigliano I 169 A3
Vigmostad N 52 B3
Vignale I 119 B5
Vignanello I 168 A2
Vigneulles-lès-Hattonchâtel F 92 C1
Vignevieille F 146 B3
Vignola I 135 A4
Vignory F 105 A4
Vignoux-sur Barangeon F 103 B4
Vigo E 140 B2
Vigo di Fassa I 121 A4
Vigone I 119 C4
Vigrestad N 52 B1
Vihiers F 102 B1
Viitasaari FIN 8 A4
Vík IS 190 D6
Vik, *Nordland* N 195 E3
Vik, *Rogaland* N 52 B1
Vik, *Sogn og Fjordane* N 46 A3
Vik S 63 C2
Vika S 50 B2
Vikajärvi FIN 197 C9
Vikane N 54 A1
Vikarbyn S 50 B2
Vike N 46 B2
Vikedal N 52 A1
Vikeland N 53 B3
Viken, *Jämtland* S 199 A10
Viken, *Skåne* S 61 C2
Viker N 48 B2
Vikersund N 48 C1
Vikeså N 52 B2
Vikevåg N 52 A1
Vikingstad S 56 B1
Vikmanshyttan S 50 B2
Vikna N 199 A7
Vikøy N 46 B3
Vikran, *Troms* N 192 C2
Vikran, *Troms* N 194 B7
Viksjö S 200 D3
Viksøyri N 46 A3
Viksta S 51 B4
Vila Boim P 155 C3
Vila Chã de Ourique P 154 B2
Vila de Cruces E 140 B2
Vila de Rei P 154 B2
Vila do Bispo P 160 B1
Vila do Conde P 148 A1
Vila Flor P 149 A2
Vila Franca das Navas P 149 B2
Vila Franca de Xira P 154 C1
Vila Fresca P 154 C1
Vila Nogueira P 154 C1
Vila Nova da Baronia P 154 C2
Vila Nova de Cerveira P 140 C2
Vila Nova de Famalicão P 148 A1
Vila Nova de Foz Côa P 149 A2
Vila Nova de Gaia P 148 A1
Vila Nova de Milfontes P 160 B1
Vila Nova de Ourém P 154 B2
Vila Nova de Paiva P 148 B2
Vila Nova de São Bento P 161 B2
Vila Pouca de Aguiar P 148 A2
Vila Praja de Ancora P 148 A1
Vila Real P 148 A2
Vila-real de los Infantes E 159 B3
Vila Real de Santo António P 160 B2
Vila-Rodona E 147 C2
Vila Ruiva P 160 A2
Vila Seca P 148 B1
Vila Velha de Ródão P 155 B3
Vila Verde, *Braga* P 148 A1
Vila Verde, *Lisboa* P 154 B1
Vila Verde de Filcalho P 161 B2
Vila Viçosa P 155 C3
Viladamat E 147 B4
Viladrau E 147 C3
Vilafranca del Maestrat E 153 B3
Vilafranca del Penedès E 147 C2
Vilagarcía de Arousa E 140 B2
Vilajuiga E 147 B4
Vilamarin E 140 B3
Vilamartín de Valdeorras E 141 B3
Vilanova de Castelló E 159 B3
Vilanova de Sau E 147 C3
Vilanova i la Geltrú E 147 C2
Vilapedre E 140 A3
Vilar de Santos E 140 B3
Vilar Formosa P 149 B3
Vilarandelo P 148 A2
Vilardevós E 141 C3
Vilasantar E 140 A2
Vilaseca E 147 C2
Vilassar de Mar E 147 C3
Vilasund S 195 D5
Vilches E 157 B4
Vildbjerg DK 59 B1
Vilémov CZ 97 B3
Vileyka BY 13 A7
Vilhelmina S 200 B2
Vilia GR 184 A4
Viljandi EST 8 C4
Villa Castelli I 173 B3
Villa Cova de Lixa P 148 A1
Villa de Peralonso E 149 A3
Villa del Prado E 150 B3
Villa del Rio E 157 C3
Villa di Chiavenna I 120 A2
Villa Minozzo I 134 A3
Villa San Giovanni I 175 C1
Villa Santa Maria I 169 B4
Villa Santina I 122 A1
Villabáñez E 150 A3
Villablanca E 161 B2
Villablino E 141 B4
Villabona E 144 A1
Villabragima E 142 C1
Villabuena del Puente E 150 A2
Villacadima E 151 A4
Villacañas E 157 A4
Villacarriedo E 143 A3
Villacarrillo E 164 A1
Villacastín E 150 B3
Villach A 109 C4
Villacidro I 179 C2
Villaconejos E 151 B4
Villaconejos de Trabaque E 152 B1
Villada E 142 B2
Villadangos del Páramo E 141 B5
Villadecanes E 141 B4
Villadepera E 149 A3
Villadiego E 142 B2
Villadompardo E 163 A3
Villadóssola I 119 A5
Villaeles de Valdavia E 142 B2
Villaescusa de Haro E 158 B1
Villafáfila E 142 C1
Villafeliche E 152 A2
Villaflores E 150 A2
Villafrades de Campos E 142 B2
Villafranca, *Avila* E 150 B2
Villafranca, *Navarra* E 144 B2
Villafranca de Córdoba E 157 C3
Villafranca de los Barros E 155 C4
Villafranca de los Caballeros E 157 A4
Villafranca del Bierzo E 141 B4
Villafranca di Verona I 121 B3
Villafranca in Lunigiana I 134 A2
Villafranca-Montes de Oca E 143 B3
Villafranca Tirrena I 177 A4
Villafranco del Campo E 152 B2
Villafranco del Guadalquivir E 161 B3
Villafrati I 176 B2
Villafrechós E 142 C1
Villafruela E 143 C3
Villagarcia de las Torres E 156 B1
Villaggio Mancuso I 175 B2
Villagonzalo E 156 B1
Villagotón E 141 B4
Villagrains F 128 B2
Villaharta E 156 B3
Villahermosa E 158 C1
Villaherreros E 142 B2
Villahoz E 143 B3
Villaines-la-Juhel F 89 B3
Villajoyosa E 159 C3
Villalago I 169 B3
Villalba E 140 A3
Villalba I 176 B2
Villalba de Calatrava E 157 B4
Villalba de Guardo E 142 B2
Villalba de la Sierra E 152 B1
Villalba de los Alcores E 142 C2
Villalba de los Barros E 155 C4
Villalba del Alcor E 161 B3
Villalba del Rey E 151 B5
Villalcampo E 149 A3
Villalcázar de Sirga E 142 B2
Villalengua E 152 A2
Villalgordo del Júcar E 158 B1
Villalgordo del Marquesado E 158 B1
Villalmóndar E 143 B3
Villalón de Campos E 142 B1
Villalonga E 159 C3
Villalonso E 150 A2
Villalpando E 142 C1
Villaluenga E 151 B4

Notes

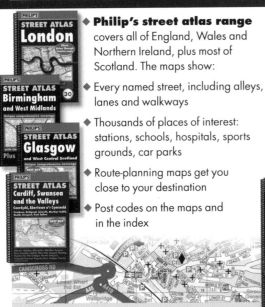

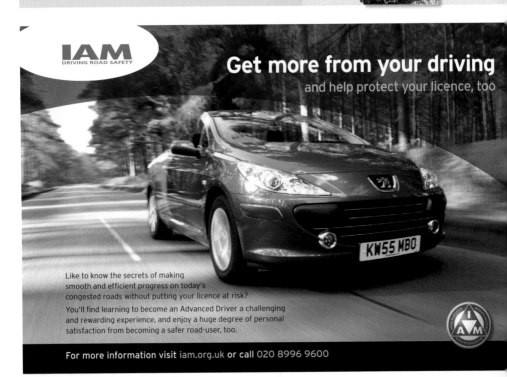